New Venture Experience

REVISED EDITION

Karl H. Vesper
University of Washington

Seattle, Washington 98105

New Venture Experience

Published by Vector Books, 4505 University Way, N.E., Suite 1, Seattle, WA 98105. Telephone (206) 522 5905, Fax (206) 545 7207.

Cases in this book have been made possible by entrepreneurs, businesses and other organizations which may wish to remain anonymous by having names, quantities and other identifying details disguised. Basic relationships within the cases, however, are maintained. Cases are prepared as a basis for class discussion rather than to illustrate either effective or ineffective handling of business situations.

Typesetting: Kathleen Dufour, LaserWorks
Cover Design: Robert O. Hutchins
Printed in the United States of America
by RR Donnelley & Sons Company

Library of Congress Cataloging-in-Publication Data

Library of Congress Catalog Card Number: 95-060014

ISBN 1-884021-25-5

To

W. Ed McMullan,
*a most creative and supportive
scholar and
entrepreneur*

Preface

This book represents over a decade and a half of work in developing, testing and refining text, cases and exercises to aid learning about entrepreneurship. It is in some ways novel, and a few minutes spent in scanning some special features may make it easier and more effective to use.

This preface begins with suggestions especially for students, followed by comments for instructors and others.

Comment to the Student

Please take a few minutes to scan through the book and notice its design. Some special features to notice include the following:

1. Three main parts comprise the book: (1) text with exercises, (2) cases, and (3) appendices. The text is presented in 10 chapters. Each of these is followed by cases that are linked primarily to that chapter. Following these chapters and cases at the back of the book are three appendices pertaining to venture plans. The first offers illustrative excerpts from several plans. The other two present rating sheets used by judges in two international venture plan contests.

2. Each of the 10 text chapters is subdivided into two or three subchapters. This allows the instructor to link topics and arrange the reading schedule with greater flexibility by assigning various combinations of chapters and/or subchapters, possibly coupled with outside readings. Questions for the cases appear at the end of each chapter, not at the ends of subchapters.

3. The table of contents lists chapters of the text and also notes the location of case questions at the end of each chapter. The instructor may or may not follow the same chapter sequence as the book and may or may not choose to assign cases with the particular chapters that they immediately follow. A given case may link equally well to any of several chapters. A case index at the end of the book lists the cases alphabetically and briefly notes the type of product or service each concerns.

4. Several types of questions and assignment statements appear in the book. At the end of each subchapter are: (1) exercise questions, (2) venture history questions, and (3) questions for developing a business plan. Which ones are appropriate

depends upon what cases and what projects have been assigned. There should be no presumption that the questions are either comprehensive or in the best order for any particular assignment. It all depends. Part of the student's job is to figure out what questions should be asked, perhaps using those in the book if they are helpful as prompts, but not mechanically attempting to plow through them from beginning to end. None of these questions is intended to substitute for thought.

5. Unique to this book are "Application" questions embedded in the body of the text itself, as opposed to those that might appear at the ends of chapters or cases. These crop out in fine italics print in the left hand margin of the page and cut into the text at points where it may be helpful to stop and think about how the text section just read may apply to either an assigned case or a venture project. Please take a brief look at them now. Examples appear on pages 4 and 29. The instructor may choose to assign particular application questions by noting the pages on which they appear, or simply may ask the class to decide which questions should be considered and why for a particular case or project.

6. Venture plan examples appear in part or in whole at various points in the book. You may find it helpful early in the term to flip quickly through the text and cases spotting these examples for ideas about how to design a venture plan. Appendix 1 at the back of the book presents a collection of excerpts from various venture plans which illustrate the variety of elements a plan may include. These excerpts, however, are not offered as models. Every business plan calls for its own fresh design. Many of the excerpts can be criticized and improved upon. They are intended to stimulate ideas, not imitation. The same is true of venture plans that appear in the cases. An introduction at the front of Appendix 1 suggests further ways of considering the business plan excerpts.

7. The text is designed to stand alone or to be complemented by companion texts or lectures. It is comprehensive in coverage but limited in depth of detail. Any number of companion books or articles may be chosen as suitable complements. Two books in particular that fit as complements are *New Venture Strategies* and *New Venture Mechanics* by the author. The pertinent complementary chapters of these two are noted as supplementary readings at the end of each chapter in this book.

The overall theme of this book in treating the subject of entrepreneurship is **application**. Both the text and cases are intended to help the reader learn information that applies usefully to the task of creating or acquiring a business. The text gives information that applies to cases, field projects and actual ventures. The cases give illustrations of application of text information and also give information that elaborates the text. As you read the book, your emphasis should be on using the information, not just learning it, to become more resourceful in following a business career, whether as an independent venturer or as part of a team developing an enterprise.

The instructor may indicate what to read first: assigned text, non-assigned text, assigned or non-assigned cases, or case questions. Or that may be left for each student to decide individually. The rule should be to do whatever works best. This book is not a mathematical treatise or a novel that should be read from front to back. A better reading strategy may be to jump around among topics, taking whatever is useful for getting the assignment done.

Comment to the Instructor

It can help greatly to have students read the above and examine the design of the book in class, as soon as they have copies. Several text features should be noted.

The text is comprised of chapters containing subchapters, rather than simply a large number of chapters. Intended advantages of this new arrangement include flexibility and convenience for the instructor. Having subchapters allows a total of 23 separate subchapters for assignment. Grouping them into chapters, however, clusters the number down to 10. From the learner's point of view this leaves only 10 main chapters to remember, which is much easier than 23. Yet the subchapters are clustered by related topics so the learner may remember all 23, as well.

An instructor may assign a given chapter, which carries with it all the subchapters on that topic automatically. Alternatively partial chapters can be assigned through selection of subchapters. Assigning one chapter per week fits a quarter term nicely. To fit a semester, subchapters can be selected to increase the number of assignments.

Another feature of the book is the embedding of "Application" questions in the body of the text. These are intended to help students stop and think about the meaning of the text by relating it to its application. From the instructor's point of view, the presence of these questions within the text makes assignments easier to focus and specify. They link the text to cases and projects as the instructor or the student chooses. Students should know, after the brief introduction suggested here, what an instructor means by assigning "the Application question on page 4" or "the second Application question on page 29." It will be helpful for clarity to describe during the first or second class meeting such an example in class.

It is not essential to follow the topics of this book in the same sequence as the table of contents. All subchapters end with exercise questions that could be used as starting points. Regardless of the sequence it should be possible, as the term progresses, to explore issues of earlier cases again in later cases, so that as the term proceeds, readers can continually practice and reinforce skills and knowledge learned earlier. Among those skills should be virtuosity in foreseeing problems that lie ahead during venture development, identifying alternative ways of dealing with venture problems and capability to treat them quickly. This should help on a later "real" venture by leaving free more time and processing capacity to treat idiosyncrasies of real ventures that cannot be foreseen in school.

There are some things school can give to a person interested in pursuing entrepreneurship, and other things it cannot very effectively give. This book offers readers an acquaintance with the kinds of adventures entrepreneurs encounter in quest of independent business, the kinds of problems they face and some ways of grappling with those problems. It can't tell an individual what specific venture opportunities lie ahead for him or her, and it can't give specialized skills and knowledge that a particular venture as distinguished from all other ventures will require. Those generally must come from field investigation or life beyond school. Cases illustrate only a tiny fraction of the variety.

All cases and characters in the book are real and no attempt has been made to distort them, except for the disguising of names and locations in some of the cases. The cases were not selected to glamorize entrepreneurship or convey any particular image other than what it is. They were, however, selected to cover different stages and different types of problems, and some attempt was made to focus upon entrepreneurs who were either in or not far beyond their university experience so students could more readily identify with their circumstances.

Acknowledgments

I would like to thank many who have been helpful in the process of developing this book. Those who permitted cases to be written on their ventures contributed not only information but more importantly time—usually when pressing demands of the enterprises made that difficult for them to spare.

Several people also helped writing the cases. They include Joe Crosswhite, who not only skillfully wrote, but also drew illustrations for some of the cases, Bill Gartner, who helped develop the John Morse case, Bob Mighell, who wrote the case on himself, and Nancy Tieken, who helped in finding leads for many of the cases as well as in writing several of them. Innumerable students at several institutions contributed by participating in the testing and refining as well as adding ideas and examples.

Institutional support for much of the case writing was provided by Babson College under the leadership of President Ralph Sorenson during my year there, 1980 to 1981, in the Babson Professorship. Some of the cases begun at Babson were later developed further by the Harvard Business School with the understanding that freedom to adapt and use them would be shared by both schools. The Foster and Shane cases were handled in this way.

Several reviewers added helpful suggestions for the first edition of this book. These included Ray Bagby, Alan Carsrud, Bartlett Finney, Bill Gartner, Charles Hofer, Don Huffmire, Ed McMullan, Tom Monroy, Dennis Ray, Bill Rice, Jim Schrager, Harriet Stevenson, Sherman Timmins and Warren Weber. In addition, there were several others whose reviews were given to me anonymously. My hope is that they will identify themselves so they can be recognized with thanks in a future edition.

Crucial help in editing and formatting was provided by several people. Copy editing was done by Ratna Anagol, Philippa Brunsman, Patricia Pasantino and Karen Vesper. Robert Hutchins helped greatly with the cover design and graphics in some of the cases. Kathleen Dufour of Seattle's LaserWorks worked heroically, patiently and most constructively on the formatting. Joan Vesper contributed to all parts, writing, editing, designing and making sure things were as right as we could make them.

Vital encouragement to pull this collection together and make it available was provided by all of the above and by the New Venture Development group at the University of Calgary.

Finally, helpful suggestions for this revised edition were provided by early users, including the following:

Jim Ashman	Ray Bagby	MacRae Banks	Gene Baten
Adam Berman	John Boos	Bill Bullard	John Butler
Gary Cadenhead	Radha Chaganti	Alex DeNoble	Richard Dorf
Karl Egge	Tony Fattal	James Fiet	Bartlett Finney
Beth Freeman	John Freeman	Barbara Fuller	Connie Marie Gaglio

Bill Gartner	Arthur Gerstenfeld	Newell Gough	Jim Halloran
Steven Hanks	Gerald Hills	Kjell Knudson	Paul Lapides
Lawrence Lapin	Ken Loucks	Ed McMullan	Stewart Malone
Ralph Miller	Ron Mitchell	Lamar Nichols	Newman Peery
Donald Porter	Rebecca Reuber	Joeseph Singer	Richard Singson
Clifton Smith	William Soukup	Jeff Shuman	Harriet Stevenson
Jeff Susbauer	Erwin von Allmen	Ervin Williams	Srinamal Withane
David Wilemon	Gerrit Wolf		

Although not all of the suggestions from these helpful individuals were implemented, and undoubtedly more should have been, further ideas and advice about how to improve the book are always welcome. There is certainly room for further substantial improvement, and efforts to accomplish that will continue.

Karl H. Vesper
Seattle, Washington

Contents in Brief

Contents

3   Screening   133

❏ Subchapter 3A **Physical Feasibility and Market Fit**   133

Evaluation Questions. Seek Out Weak Spots for Priority. Test Physical Practicability: *Modeling. Prototypes.* Check Market Fit.

❏ Subchapter 3B **Financial and Founder Fit**   145

Compute Financial Attractiveness. Assess Founder(s)' Fit. Forecast Competitors' Moves. Cross-check Competitive Advantages. Accept, Refine, Table or Reject.

Case Questions   156

4   Formal Plans   229

❏ Subchapter 4A **Plan Elements**   229

Purposes for Plans. Matters of Priority: *Important General Qualities. What to Present First. Organization of the Rest.* Some Elements to Include: *Opening. Description of Product or Service. Market Analysis. Operations. Spending Plans. Pricing Considerations. Financial Analysis.*

❏ Subchapter 4B **Evaluation of Venture Plans**   241

What Bankers Look For. What Investors Look For. What Venture Capitalists Look For. What Competition Judges Look For. Evaluation Help from Other People. Review Help From Software. Style. Some Things to Avoid. Oral Presentation. Final Test.

Case Questions   253

Venture Plan Appendices

Chapter 1

Introduction

❑ SUBCHAPTER 1A - The Entrepreneur's Job

The path to entrepreneurship, self-employment, owning and managing a business, can begin at any time by happenstance or by design.

> An artist has developed an improved surface for drawing and painting. He has found that some art supply stores are interested in carrying it. After producing some in his garage he has become frustrated with that activity and with the interruption of his art work. How best can he benefit from his invention?

> ❖ ❖ ❖

> Two women, one a lawyer and the other a beautician, have designed what they believe to be a better backpack for a mother to carry her baby. Both have some acquaintance with business, but neither has previously been involved in manufacturing and selling a product. How should they start?

No situation is a "typical" jumping off place for becoming an entrepreneur. As these two examples illustrate, many starting points are possible. Both are described further in cases that appear later in this book. Examples throughout the book will illustrate even more variety.

What does it take to become a successful entrepreneur? It is hard to think of a single statement in reply that is not either complex or incomplete.

Is the answer "a million dollars to capitalize a new business?" With that amount, a would-be entrepreneur could hire a lawyer to form a corporation, rent an office, take out an advertisement in the Yellow Pages, and put up a sign saying "inventions wanted, capital available." Meanwhile, most of the money could be invested to earn interest which would finance the office until a "hit product" came in. Then the capital could be invested to produce and sell the invention. If such an invention did not turn up, then the money could simply be left invested, the profits would continue, and the venture could be called a success, all thanks to one key ingredient, capital.

The catch, of course, is that the return on investment is not likely to be great enough to justify putting up the money. If part of the return is drained off to operate the office, then the remaining income would be less than the investor could gain by simply investing all the money and not letting part be used for the office. The hope that a sufficiently promising invention will come in to justify the cash drain of the office is hard to support, although advertisements are certain to attract some inventions.

An office was set up with $1 million from the National Science Foundation to provide only services, not including capital, for inventors. It operated at the University of Oregon for five years and succeeded in drawing as many as 3,000 invention submissions per year. But out of that huge number none proved profitable enough even to replenish the office expenses, let alone provide a capital gain.

Venture capitalists, those who operate firms whose business is simply to invest in start-ups and small firms, have better success. But they start with much more than $1 million in capital, they don't try to be entrepreneurs, and they don't invest in inventions. They invest most often in businesses that are already ongoing and much less frequently at the inception stage of ventures that entrepreneurs want to start.

Historically, the returns derived by venture capitalists have ranged widely, both over time and among firms as well as among investments. Less successful venture capitalists have tended to be those with smaller funding who pursue investment activity only part time. With a smaller volume of money to work with, they aren't as well known, and don't attract as many deals of higher quality and larger size. Thus, they are less able to justify hiring complementary expert help or to spend as much time on making deals and assisting with problems and opportunities of the venture as it develops. Even less well set up to make venture investments are individual investors. Yet, both individual investors and small venture capital firms are sometimes very successful, though their results are usually a private matter.[1]

Some of the larger venture capital firms, such as Heizer Corporation, have become public companies and have gained excellent returns on the capital they invested. Examples of ventures that have paid off well for some of them have included Apple, Compaq, Conner, Digital Equipment, Intel, and Microsoft. Most of the big successes have been in high technology fields such as microelectronics and biotechnology. But some have been in more prosaic activities such as broadcasting and discount retailing. Average rates of return for the more successful venture capital firms have ranged upwards from 26 percent per year.[2]

So another answer to the question of what it takes to become a successful entrepreneur might be "whatever those start-ups have that major venture capitalists would invest in." But this answer too has its inadequacies. One is that not all companies venture capitalists invest in are successful. About 20 percent fail entirely. Roughly another 60 percent become investments the capitalists are sorry they made, either because although the ventures in which the money was invested survive, their profits are too low, or because although profitable the ventures cannot be sold and the capitalists are stuck with their capital tied up. For the remaining 20 percent of their investments to make up for shortcomings of the less satisfactory 80 percent, the few real winners must generate very large profits indeed. It is at that top 20 percent of winners that the venture capitalists must aim.

To do so, venture capitalists impose criteria such as favorable reviews by other investor colleagues of a written business plan that includes convincing information about market potential, financial forecasts, and action steps to start the venture. These financial forecasts must indicate a high probability that the company will allow the venture capitalists to earn returns of 30 percent or more per year on a minimum investment of about $1 million with the prospect that they will be able to cash out within about five years. Other criteria that venture capitalists impose are verification of technical feasibility by expert consultants, and demonstration that the venture is headed by a team possessing both proven track records in relevant activity and balance among the different functional areas of the business.

The odds of satisfying such criteria are slim. Consequently, very few venture proposals submitted are funded by venture capitalists (around 1 percent or less on average). Out of one-half million or so businesses per year started in the U.S. only a microscopically small fraction receive such support. Almost no ventures, whether successful or not, meet the venture capitalists' standards. Venture capital criteria may be fine, but they are not the only measure of what a venture requires to be successful.

So what is required to succeed with a venture that is less ambitious than venture capitalists aim for but still worthwhile? As a starting point, how about simply having a good idea for a business? A good idea might be one that defines a product or service that prospective customers can be expected to desire.

But, of course, that alone is not enough. The customers must also be able to pay for that product or service, and they must want it more than something else they could buy with the same money. The price they are willing to pay must be high enough to pay the entrepreneur for producing and delivering it with something left over for profit. Moreover, there must be enough customers in total so that their payments not only cover costs and give profit to the venture, but do so over a long enough period of time to produce a return on the venture investment.

Thus, inevitably, the requirements that must be satisfied to create a successful venture become complex. Furthermore, the (1) good idea and (2) customers must be coupled with (3) production capability on the entrepreneur's part. If he or she does not possess that capability personally, then others must be recruited or hired to help with the task. Setting up operations and recruiting such needed help often requires financing, both to set up the venture and to live on while it is getting started. The financing will not likely come from venture capitalists, since they finance only an extremely small percentage of the venture population. But it has to come from somewhere, probably personal and family savings of the entrepreneur and any cofounders.

The idea has to be implemented, and beyond that the venture that carries it out must be able to withstand competitors who come up with the same business idea, possibly as a result of seeing the venture or possibly by independent discovery of their own. If the idea can be patented or protected in some way it may be possible to exclude competitors. But usually before much time elapses substitutes are introduced, and competition grows stronger.

Application: What will it take for the venture ideas in the assigned case to be carried to success?

Game Theory and Entrepreneurship

Analyzing the complex set of requirements noted above can make creation of a new venture seem almost impossible. But it is not. Every year hundreds of thousands of new firms are started in the U.S. and a large fraction of them manage to keep going, albeit at a small size and relatively low level of profit.

What simplifies the task of the entrepreneur is cooperation from other people who have something to gain by his or her success. The purpose of an entrepreneur is to create a new real-life business game in which all the players can win. Those players may include employees, who get new jobs, suppliers, who get a new customer, investors, who share the profits, lenders, who draw interest from the venture, and various levels of government that extract taxes from it. Because they, like the entrepreneur, believe they have something to win from the game, they agree to participate in transactions with the entrepreneur that help set up the game in which the venture forms a core.

Games in general can be divided into two types, zero-sum and non-zero-sum. It is crucial to recognize that what an entrepreneur must set up is the second type. Game theorists use the term "core" to describe that part of a game, within the rules of a game, that allows all the players to win. One player may win more than another one, and the activity of the game is what determines what the split will be. But no player only loses. It is in the interest of the entrepreneur to recognize just what kind of core is being created. When the entrepreneur attempts to set up a new game in the form of a venture he or she must arrange an option to be in the core for all the needed players, such as customers, suppliers, financers, and governmental agencies. Beyond that, the entrepreneur must enable those desired players to recognize that the core is there so that they will choose to join it.*

---

*One way of viewing the economy is as consisting of two parts, free and forced. In the free economy individuals choose for themselves how to spend their time and money (which can be viewed as saved time). In the forced economy people's time and/or money is confiscated through taxes or other measures and spent by others, usually governmental agencies. It is usually not within an entrepreneur's capability to harness the power to manipulate the forced economy. Hence, he or she can only operate in the free economy where players have the option of playing the game or not as they choose.

Application: *Whose cooperation will be most needed to enable the entrepreneur and/or venture in the assigned case to succeed? What should that person get out of it?*

Characteristics of Entrepreneurs

People new to the subject of entrepreneurship sometimes ask what characteristics determine who will be an entrepreneur. One person may take advantage of an opportunity that arises while another does not. Is there something different in those two people's makeup that decides who will do what? Or does each of them operate from a different vantage point that somehow directs their decisions for them?

Decades ago scholars began looking for personal determinants of entrepreneurial proclivity. Their studies gave some indications, albeit of arguable strength. Entrepreneurs seem to score slightly higher on tests of achievement motivation, striving for goals that require challenge but that are achievable. Entrepreneurs seem to believe that they, not their environment or their treatment, determine what becomes of them. Entrepreneurs seem to place especially high value on personal independence, choosing their own hours, and doing what they choose rather than what they are told.

There are two problems with these studies. One is that the measurements are made *after* the subjects become entrepreneurs, so that their experiences may skew the test results. The other is that the results deal with group averages which may have no meaning for an individual.

The judgment of one consultant who had started several companies and also worked with many other entrepreneurs, Dr. Joseph Mancuso, was that "If nothing else, my experience has taught me that it is nearly impossible to predict what makes a 'successful' entrepreneur."[3] He then posited an "Entrepreneur's Quiz" for someone to "see if you've got what it takes to be an entrepreneur" based on observations some have made that an entrepreneur tends, among other things, to be

1. the first-born in a family
2. the child of self-employed parents
3. married
4. between 30 and 40 years old
5. a moderate risk taker
6. uncomfortable working for others

A longer list of similar questions was proposed by Dr. Phil Shragge,[4] a successful Canadian entrepreneur. Some personal qualities he suggested as favorable for entrepreneurship included having

7. worked in a small business or in close contact with the chief of a small division

8. ventured as a child

9. lived in three or more cities

10. been fired

11. worked in several functional areas of business

12. had improvement ideas rejected

13. a preference for doing, rather than planning, things

14. a tendency to set long-term goals and stick to them

15. an inclination to accept workable solutions even if they aren't perfect

16. a preference for games of skill rather than luck

17. a liking for solving problems, including seeking help from others

18. a tendency to view failures as learning opportunities

19. a tendency to seek situations where personal initiative is possible

Still other qualifications were drawn from an examination of the histories of especially successful entrepreneurs conducted by Mitton.[5] Such entrepreneurs, he found, possessed the following:

20. a big-picture perspective

21. an ability to spot unique business opportunities

22. a tendency to commit totally to a cause

23. a need for complete control

24. a utilitarian view of what is right

25. an appetite for uncertainty

26. a tendency to use contacts and connections

27. an attitude that embraces high competence

28. special know-how

Another characterization of successful entrepreneurs, made by Robert Kunze, an outstandingly successful venture capitalist, was that "Almost to a person they are daring, single-minded, egocentric, disenchanted with the status quo, impatient, and obsessive. Many are also brilliant, innovative, charismatic workaholics. Some are jealous, greedy, angry, grandiose, messianic, hateful and sociopathic. The single quality every successful entrepreneur shares is the ability to endure an all-or-nothing world."[6]

One of the first questions Kunze said he asked those who came to him for money was why they wanted the life of an entrepreneur. Few, he observed, gave the obvious answer, to become rich and famous. "When I prompt them with that answer," he said, "they nod, grin and blush a bit. A few entrepreneurs actually tell me they aren't in it for the money. I always assume that means money is all they want."

Another famously successful venture capitalist, Arthur Rock, had a somewhat different answer: "I'm looking for entrepreneurs who ask, 'How can I make this business a success?'–not 'How do I make a fortune?'"[7]

These venture capitalists specialized in high-technology ventures based on innovative products developed by highly trained and experienced engineers and scientists to achieve multimillion-dollar sales within a very few years. Of seven ventures described by Kunze, one failed, two earned a million dollars or less for their shareholders, one earned $85 million, and the average produced around $30 million for an average shareholder investment of around $10 million, all within seven years or less.

Only one of his ventures was still headed by its founding entrepreneur, and that one had become part of another company that bought it. All six other founders had been fired, although those whose ventures succeeded profited handsomely. Contrasting a founder of one venture (Steve Quade) with the manager (John Diekman) who replaced him in running it, Kunze commented:

> *It would be wrong to conclude that Quade sounds like someone to be avoided. He's a genius. I would back him in a minute in any reasonable new idea and would build a company around him. He would probably still be the same tyrannical pigheaded person he was at Salutar. I'd also probably make 14 times on my investors' money. It's important to remember that there are hundreds of people like John Diekman who can run a company. The Steve Quays come along but once in a decade.[8]*

In other, less technological and/or less capital-demanding start-ups, all sorts of different entrepreneurial personalities may be found. Games like Trivial Pursuit, Pictionary, and Myst, a best-selling CD-ROM game, came from avocational interests, not hard-driving industrial research. One of the Miller brothers who developed Myst was on welfare, and they needed outside financial help. Paula Bock, a writer, described their quest for it as follows:[9]

> What tipped off the investors that the Millers were motivated by ideas more than money was that when the time came to negotiate contracts and license agreements, the brothers pulled out hand-drawn maps. Blueprints of weird contraptions. Pine trees. Some sort of strange ship. A planetarium. The investors looked at the sketches, watched the brothers' exuberant faces. The older brother recalls, "We were this nothing little company that doesn't even have an office, and we're telling them we're going to build a world." The businessmen could not fathom the Millers' presentations, but they understood the brothers' excitement. It was, Mr. Kawai says, "as if boys told us their dreams."
>
> "It will be a best game?" Mr. Furukawa asked.
>
> "Yes! Yes! It will be good!" the Millers promised.
>
> And so the three investors trusted the brothers and advanced them $300,000. Two years and several hundred thousand dollars later, the Millers

created Myst. When the game became successful, the Millers donated some of their profits to support Christian missionaries and some of their time to delivering brown-bag lunches to the poor.

It's hard to be categorical about entrepreneurs. No studies of whether different types of ventures seem to go with different types of personalities have been reported. Ventures come in many forms, and the experiences of creating them are varied as well. Entrepreneurs themselves are unique and often unusual individuals, so that how they feel about their experiences in venturing is bound to span a wide spectrum.

Motivations

Ventures sometimes start part time and shift to full time, and sometimes develop the other way around. *Inc.* reported in 1990 that one out of eight people held a secret desire to start a business. Among executive and professional women 19 percent were planning to go into business for themselves and another 19 percent were considering doing so.[10]

Some people start ventures from necessity such as unemployment and others as a result of requests for help or even offers of financing. Many ventures arise from frustration with another job, sometimes because the entrepreneur's "better idea" is rejected by higher management. Some undertake ventures out of preference for the independence that self employment offers. Many accept a financial sacrifice for the sake of liberty, independence or opportunity to implement an idea rejected at work.

Economic benefits to the entrepreneur from venturing can be vastly higher than those from a job on an established company's payroll, but on average they are probably lower. Success stories in the press and television tend to play up the most exceptionally successful entrepreneurs such as Michael Dell, Bill Gates, Steve Jobs, and Scott McNealy who have become worth many millions at early ages by starting enterprises that prospered and grew rapidly. Most new enterprises, however, never grow beyond four or five employees. They exact very long hours of hard work, particularly from their owners, pay below average salaries and wages, provide less actual vacation, pay for less in the way of life and health insurance, and offer fewer other fringe benefits such as training programs, gym facilities and recreational activities. Company-paid travel for business purposes is non-taxable in both large and small companies, but the Internal Revenue Service is more likely to quarrel with it if done by the owner of a small company than by an employee of a big company.

Steve Mariotti, who left a large company to start his own venture and later won numerous awards for teaching disadvantaged youths in the Bronx to become legitimate entrepreneurs, described his path to venturing as follows:

> *After I graduated from the University of Michigan's business school in 1977,*
> *I got an offer from Ford Motor Company to be a financial analyst. I walked into*

the best conceivable job a young MBA can get—incredible responsibility and I got to see how a big company was run. But after two and a half years I lost the job in an internal power struggle, so I moved to New York City and started an import-export business.

When I came out of Ford, I was very bruised and real bitter. I had been in this hierarchy and I was on the bottom of it: I was a grade 7 and Henry Ford was a grade 27. I felt constant anxiety. I would go into work and they could pretty much do whatever they wanted with me. There'd be this guy down the hall in this big office, and he'd be a grade 17. He'd have control of my life: if he was going to send me to Australia, I was going to go.

But the minute I went into business for myself—and I really didn't know that much about it—I felt equal to Henry Ford psychologically. I felt like, well, I'm president of this company, and he's president of a company. I just don't have as much capital as he does, and I don't really care. But the effect it had on my own psyche was enormous, marked and immediate.[11]

Not reported in this example was the level of pay this entrepreneur received before he took to venturing, and how that pay compared with his prospects either at his place of employment or at the venture. However, a study reported by Amit, Muller, and Cockburn found that in a sample of 352 Canadian entrepreneurs, after correcting for demographic factors such as age, sex, experience, and so on, those who left jobs to go venturing had been receiving on average 12 percent lower pay than their job counterparts who did not go venturing. Apparently financial opportunity costs help determine who chooses to venture. Interestingly, though, when Birley and Westhead searched for a correlation between reasons for venturing and start-up success among 405 enterprises in the United Kingdom, they found none.

The Experience

There have been relatively few systematic investigations of what it feels like to be involved in setting up or in playing a new venture game. One study of 2,994 independent start-ups by Cooper et al.[12] reported that although 39 percent of the responding founders said they would make major changes in the way they went about forming their businesses, 82 percent would still do it even given current knowledge. The largest fraction (43 percent) said their level of satisfaction in business was about as expected, while 21 percent said it was higher and 32 percent said it was lower. These responses, it should be noted, came from those entrepreneurs in the sample whose businesses were still in operation one to three years after start-up. No study has reported on how entrepreneurs whose ventures did not survive felt about what they had done. Anecdotally, they rarely seem to report that they regret having ventured, even if the venture failed.

Those who are employed in their own ventures, even struggling ones, often say they would never again work for a company owned by others if they could help it. Along the course of getting started entrepreneurs tell anecdotally of being:

- terrified by problems of maintaining positive cash flow
- thrilled by profit generating events
- frustrated by government paperwork
- angered by feeling cheated in working with landlords, employees or suppliers
- infuriated by legal machinations, and the expense of legal help
- anxious in dealing with lenders and investors
- gratified by winning over customers
- satisfied by making their own decisions about what to sell, how to price, which equipment to buy, when to take vacations, where to set up new operations, how to arrange the shop, whom to hire, and how to answer the question "what kind of work do you do?"

The price of such a privilege can be high. If the venture fails, the entrepreneur may lose everything. Even if the firm survives, the pay may not be very high. In the Cooper et al. study only 2.9 percent of the entrepreneurs responding three years after start-up reported taking over $75,000 per year out of their businesses, while 27.8 percent reported taking out less than $10,000.[13]

They also reported that the hours were long. Table 1-1 following shows a comparison of CEO work hours reported by the Cooper study, which includes mostly very small firms, with those of very high growth firms of the *Inc.* 500, all of which were five or more years old.[14] In both cases the largest fraction appeared to require between 60 and 70 hours per week on the business. Over a third of entrepreneurs in the Cooper study reported that in addition to their own time other family members gave 10 or more hours to the business per week for no pay.[15]

Table 1-1 Entrepreneurs' Work Weeks (Hours)

| | Percent of Entrepreneurs in | |
Number of Hours per Week	NFIB firms	*Inc.* 500 firms
Under 50 hours	23%	15%
50 - 59	23	26
60 - 69	28	32
70 - 79	13	13
Over 80	12	3
N/A	1	11
Total	100%	100%

Application: *What work hours and income level would you predict the entrepreneur in the assigned case will have to live with to get this venture going, and how will those estimates change over the first 36 months of start-up?*

Failure

Failure rates for new ventures average around 10 percent per year following inception—not as high as has been commonly supposed. A popular estimate for years was that 80 percent of new firms fail in the first five years. More recent studies indicate that only around 50 percent do so, and the rate depends greatly on line of business.[16] In fields such as high technology manufacturing, for instance, some researchers have found all but about 20 percent still in business after five years. Moreover, even the 20 percent they could not find still in business may not necessarily have failed. They may have been sold, had their names changed or simply have been closed down without failure by owners choosing to pursue other ventures instead. The odds of losing a job in self employment are probably not much higher than losing one in an established firm.

It is relatively easy to imagine why the failure rate should be higher in a start-up than in an established firm. For one thing, the established firm has many things going for it: certainty that there is a market for its products, established habit patterns of customers, and suppliers. The new venture, in contrast, must be built out of a chain of fresh decisions, each of which has some probability of being wrong, and all of which together rapidly increase the odds that the venture will sink. Singer illustrates this quantitatively by pointing out that if a venture faces 10 hurdles and the probability of surviving each one is 0.9, the probability of surviving them all is $(0.9)^{10}$, or only 35 percent.[17] He notes that attempts to explain failure fully have generally been frustrated by the complexity of possible explanations and the limitations of data, but postulates several directions of causality, including the following:

- There tend to be many hurdles for new ventures, which adversely affect the odds of success (as above).

- Rapid growth tends to propagate structural errors, so that they become worse.

- Because of limited resources, new ventures can be killed off by relatively few bad decisions or small setbacks.

- A new venture requires a lot of learning about how to succeed, and this is expensive.

- Hurdles in early days are especially critical, and occur when there has been little time to learn about how to succeed.

- New ventures may bring with them "improper inheritance of business strategies and tactics from successful firms."

- New firms, limited by their small number of participants, lack the "multiple antennae" that larger competitors have for picking up cues about how to redirect themselves.

Survival

Notwithstanding these reasons for pessimism, a large percentage of start-ups do succeed. The long-touted estimate that 80 percent of new ventures fail within five years is clearly wrong. As mentioned above, more recent and more carefully done studies have found that ventures fail at a rate of roughly 10 percent per year, so that after five years, depending on line of business, around half are still going. Mitigating the reasons for start-ups' possible failure are the following considerations:

- While new ventures may face many hurdles, established firms often have to deal with changes in their markets, personnel, and suppliers. Sometimes they respond incorrectly; sometimes they fail to respond at all.

- Ways of working and politicking in an established business may evolve in dysfunctional directions, because of rivalries and changes in personal ambitions. Takeover campaigns by corporations, for instance, have generally been found not to pay off. Yet managements continue to bet against the odds by pursuing them, presumably for economically irrational reasons such as empire building.

- Having more resources can cause established companies simply to waste them, rather than using them effectively as a defense against lesser entrepreneurial entrants.

- New ventures may compensate for their lack of experience and limited "antennae" by recruiting helpers as members of the internal team, external team, or shareholders. Stakeholders in a venture such as bankers who lend to them, suppliers who sell to them, partners who invest, or employees who depend on them for jobs may get help from their own networks of friends.

- Statistical probabilities of passing or flunking hurdles may be an over-simplistic way of looking at them. Through smart persistence, entrepreneurs can learn from their failures and become more effective; by keeping their gambles small they can convert their losses as limited "tuition" payments. Moreover, stakeholders may pitch in and help more aggressively when a venture stumbles. For instance, developers often use huge financial leverage to build skyscrapers and shopping centers whose solvency depends on occupancy rates. If those rates are not met, the lenders could foreclose. But instead they often reduce their payment requirements so they can be met by lowered rents to raise occupancy. That way the developers fail to make money as fast as they had hoped, but the lenders let them avoid losing everything and their projects remain viable.

Success

Although most new firms never grow large, some do and some achieve very high profitability. The supreme example may be Microsoft, which in less than 20 years achieved a total valuation rivaling that of General Motors, made millionaires out of nearly a thousand of its employees and multibillionaires out of its two founders, Bill Gates and Paul Allen. In mid-1995 the *Seattle Times* reported that Gates had become the richest man in the world, with a net worth of $12.9 billion.[18]

High profits are possible when a venture enjoys a monopoly position on some product, service, location, talent, name brand or the like that makes it difficult for others to compete against it on price. The monopoly in Microsoft's case was its ownership of the DOS operating system used on roughly three-fourths of all microcomputers. This ownership constituted a barrier to entry and price cutting by any competitors. The list of possible barriers that inhibit competitors from encroaching includes the following:

- **"First mover" advantages** by being original or possibly even by being quick to copy in a new territory.

- **Patents or secrets** on products and/or processes. Some patents and secrets protect more powerfully than others and allow correspondingly higher profits.

- **Special know-how** possessed by the entrepreneur or loyal employees of the venture.

- **Licenses** with the state which exclude competitors. Physicians, lawyers, and veterinarians are protected by licensing requirements that cost great amounts of preparation to satisfy. Barbers and real estate agents are also protected, but by less demanding licensing requirements and hence their margins are lowered.

- **Capitalization** Banks must meet minimum capitalization levels by law to do business. In manufacturing, capital may be needed to pay for expensive tooling. To gain economies of large scale in manufacturing, capital may be needed for long production runs. To take advantage of a fad, or to gain market share ahead of competitors, cash may be needed in advance to pay for advertising.

- **Staying power** One major hurdle for many new firms is simply lasting long enough to build sales momentum in the market. Advertising usually has to be repeated several times to take effect. New stores and services usually take time to build a clientele and/or traffic. A radio station needs time to let listeners know what it offers, listeners need time to acquire habits of tuning in to it, and so forth.

- **Special status and relationships with customers** Obtaining certification as a supplier of parts for airplanes, railroads or even home furnaces can be an expensive and difficult process. But having attained such certification, a venture may enjoy margin protection that preserves healthy profits and at the same time reduces the effort needed to obtain repeat sales from the certifying customer. Of course, the owner still needs to make sure production is up to specification, delivery times are adhered to and prices do not become so high as to provoke customers to take the trouble to seek out and certify other sources.

- **Special relationships with suppliers** Leases on prime locations, exclusive distribution agreements and personal connections with key suppliers can help to varying degrees and for varying lengths of time. Such relationships may or may not be backed up with formal written agreements.

Application: How would you expect the odds of success for the venture/entrepreneur in the assigned case will compare to the average and why? What can the entrepreneur most effectively do to raise his or her odds?

But most ventures aren't launched with heavy shielding to protect their margins from competitive attack. Instead they offer services such as eat-out dining, printing and maintenance help for homes and autos where it is relatively easy for competitors to enter the field. Some people enter ventures out of inability to obtain other employment.

Why Study Entrepreneurship?

The proposition that studying about entrepreneurship might help make someone more likely to succeed as an entrepreneur is often challenged with "can entrepreneurship really be learned?" Evidence that such study can be helpful is to date mostly anecdotal. Those who have taught the subject occasionally hear former students say, "That entrepreneurship course certainly helped me in starting my business." But who can say whether they are representative or only exceptional?

A survey of 600 business major alumni of Babson College who had graduated six to 10 years earlier found that participation in entrepreneurship courses tended to correlate with later owning a business. Half had taken one or more entrepreneurship courses in college and the other half had not. In the half that had not, the survey found that 17 percent had a business, which illustrates the unsurprising fact that study of entrepreneurship is certainly not prerequisite for becoming a successful entrepreneur.

However, the other half of the sample displayed some contrasts. Among those who had taken an undergraduate entrepreneurship course, 27 percent were found to be owning a business six to 10 years following graduation. Among those who had taken an entrepreneurship course at MBA level, 34 percent now owned a business. Thirty in the sample had taken both an undergraduate and a graduate entrepreneurship course, and over 50 percent of this group was found to be owning a business. That certainly does not prove that courses caused alumni to become self-employed. Perhaps those who as students were already oriented toward starting businesses were simply more likely to choose entrepreneurship courses. But at least the courses didn't dissuade them.

Study of entrepreneurship may or may not be significantly helpful for those bent upon venture start-up. Others who may want to learn about the subject include:

- Some who might work with entrepreneurs in other capacities such as bankers, consultants, suppliers, partners or employees.

- Some who would like to consider entrepreneurship as a career path and might find that knowledge about the subject helpful in deciding whether to pursue it or not.

- Some who were planning on another career initially but would like to understand more about entrepreneurship as a possible alternative for later career change.

- Some who regard it as an interesting aspect of business and want to expand their knowledge for the satisfaction of learning.

Ventures sometimes start part time and shift to full time, and sometimes develop the other way around. It is rare for a substantial enterprise to emerge directly from an entrepreneurship course or to be started by a graduate immediately following school, but occasionally that too happens, as will be seen in some of the cases in this book.

The role of formal study is ambiguous in entrepreneurship as well as in other business fields. Some people learn to be journalists without going to journalism school and artists without going to art school, others learn business without going to business school. Bing Crosby and Carmen Miranda became skilled musicians without learning formalities of music, Abraham Lincoln became highly literate without class instruction. William Lear was a prolific inventor and entrepreneur without college training. Most business people, regardless of their success levels, haven't attended business schools. Countries like Japan and Germany became industrially successful without business schools, though more recently they have been adding them. And most entrepreneurs start companies without having taken courses in entrepreneurship.

Application: *What knowledge would most help the entrepreneur in the assigned case and how could it best be obtained?*

Supplementary Reading

New Venture Strategies Chapter 1. (Vesper, K.H., Prentice-Hall, 1990)

Exercises

1. **Self Assessment** For how many of the questions under the section entitled "Entrepreneurs" would you estimate your personal fit to be better than someone you consider typical

   a. at this time?
   b within 15 years?
   c. if you became involved in starting a venture?

2. **Entrepreneurial "Truths"** List a few generalizations you think could be made about entrepreneurship (e.g., entrepreneurs are born, not made, ventures are usually high risk, etc.). Be prepared to comment on your list in class. Occasionally during the term, reconsider your reactions to this list.

Longer Term Exercises

3. **Personal Log** During the term, begin, maintain and regularly date a log of your venture idea search and whatever follows it in terms of plan development and venture start-up.

4. **Venture Idea Search** Take 10 minutes to list on a sheet of paper as many ideas for new ventures as possible. Then each week for eight weeks add to the list the best additional venture idea you can think of. Turn these sheets in weekly to the instructor so copies can be shared and discussed with other members of the class. (If an idea is simply too good to share, then share the next best one.)

5. **Contact Development** Each week contact at least five people you have not talked to before and seek from each some information that might be helpful to you in developing a venture. Turn in to the instructor each week a list of their names, addresses and phone numbers.

6. **Venture History Report** Develop a written history of the creation of a company begun five or fewer years ago through interviews with its founders and initial backers. Begin by making a list of questions to ask. Then, if you wish, look at the list of suggested questions at the end of each chapter in this book to extend your list. It is not expected that all these questions should be answered in the history or that there are not others which might be more appropriate. It is impor-

tant to choose for development those aspects that are most important and instructive. The way to do it best is through a series of short visits spread over time as the term progresses, not all at once, and to interview more than one person involved in the start-up. It will likely help the process if on each visit the entrepreneur or other participant receives a summary of what has been developed thus far on the history.

7. **Venture Development Portfolio** Compile specimens of your (individual or team) creative efforts in pursuing venture ideas. Include a table of contents with page numbers. Include as chapters whichever of the following you did during the term:

   a. Venture ideas generated
   b. Checkout screening work done on venture ideas
   c. Venture plan developed
   d. Feedback received, and by whom, on venture plan submitted for review
   e. Business results obtained if the venture was actually attempted
   f. Tasks to be performed for further improvement of venture or venture plan

Team Venture Options

As a team of not more than five members choose one of the following options for developing a written venture plan to be turned in at the end of the term.

Venture Project Option I

Plan a very high profit potential start-up, such as one that aims at achieving $5 million or more in sales by year five and/or an ROI of 30 percent or more on an investment of $300,000 or more. If this option is chosen, the report should include:

a. A one to three page (maximum) executive summary.
b. A detailed plan for the venture, including financial forecasts and explanation of the assumptions and details behind them.
c. A description of reactions to the plan obtained from some person(s) who would be key to proceeding with the venture. They could be a venture capitalist, banker, technical expert, customer, supplier, etc.

Venture Project Option II

Start and operate a small venture with the aim of producing a profit during the term plus prepare a plan for taking it to a higher level of operation in the future. If this option is chosen, the report should include:

a. A venture history of the enterprise in detail, including a copy of the preliminary plan, a breakdown of time spent on it and the result.
b. An analysis of the economics of how the venture turned out based upon its financial statements.
c. A projection of strategic alternatives illustrating what further could be done to build upon the venture in the future, backed up by evidence from the initial experimental operation.

Venture Project Option III

If the team fails to find a venture that will work for one of the above two assignments, then it is to turn in a venture search report which includes:

a. A log of the search process, including person-hours spent, broken down into sufficient detail such that no single entry accounts for more than two person-hours. The dates of these activities should also be specified. This should be the sort of breakdown that you would want a consulting firm to give you if you hired it with your own money to seek a viable venture idea and paid it hourly for the work.

b. A list of all the venture ideas considered in a table that includes the date each occurred, the date it was abandoned and a brief statement as to why.

c. Partial written plans for the ideas that were pursued farthest before being abandoned. These partial plans should indicate which venture plan questions were answered, which were not and why.

Venture Project Option IV

Assist a local entrepreneur off campus who wants help in starting a business. Prepare a consulting report of your activities and results. There should be at least two copies of the report, one for the instructor and one given to the entrepreneur. It should concern creation of a new, for-profit independent venture that is not yet operating. The report should include as appendices:

a. A written statement of work to be performed signed by the consulting student(s) and read by the entrepreneur turned in by no later than the third week of class and appended to the final report.

b. A history of the entrepreneur(s) and venture up to the point where you entered.

c. An analysis of what the venture could become and how.

d. A tabulation of time costs of your effort and results produced. The detail on this breakdown should be of the type you would use if it were a bill to be given the client charging on an hourly basis (such as you might want to see if you were paying for the time).

Venture Project Option V

Prepare a written deal for purchase of an ongoing local business. This report should include:

a. A full description of what is to be bought and for what price and terms. This could take the form of a purchase contract which buyer and seller would sign.

b. An analysis of the business explaining the rationale behind the price and terms.

c. A plan for the future of the business following takeover, including appropriate financial projections and the reasoning behind them.

d. An analysis of the search and negotiation experience including a breakdown of the hours spent and on what, as well as a description of how you would do an acquisition search and negotiation differently if you were to do it again in the future.

Some teams may wish to begin development of more than one alternative project as a basis for deciding which has most promise. Turning in partial development of several projects which were terminated after finding their feasibility was not high enough to warrant full follow-through is acceptable. Whatever is turned in will count toward credit for effort.

Venture Planning Guide

1. As a way of anticipating what should go into a venture plan, imagine yourself in the position of someone with savings who is being asked by an entrepreneur to invest in a start-up.

   a. What information would you want to see in a plan to assess it for investment?
   b. Where would you expect the entrepreneur might be able to obtain such information?

Notes

[1] Arthur Lipper III , *Venture's Guide to Investing in Private Companies* (New York: Dow Jones-Irwin, 1984).

[2] William Bygrave and others, "Rates of Return of Venture Capital Investing: A Study of 131 Funds," in *Frontiers of Entrepreneurship Research, 1988*, eds. Bruce A. Kirchhoff and others (Wellesley, Mass.: Babson Center for Entrepreneurial Studies, 1988), p. 275.

[3] Joseph R. Mancuso, *How to Start, Finance and Manage Your Own Business* (Englewood Cliffs: Prentice-Hall, 1978), p. 9.

[4] Phil Shragge, *Be Your Own Boss* (Edmonton: Northern Alberta Institute of Technology, 1985), p. 9.

[5] Daryl G. Mitton, "The Compleat Entrepreneur,"*ET&P*, 13, no. 3, Spring 1989, p. 9.

[6] Robert J. Kunze, *Nothing Ventured* (New York: Harper, 1990), p. 44.

[7] Arthur Rock, "Strategy vs. Tactics From a Venture Capitalist," *Harvard Business Review*, November-December 1987, p. 63.

[8] Robert J. Kunze, *Nothing Ventured* (New York: Harper, 1990), p. 200.

[9] Paula Bock, "Into the Myst," *The Seattle Times*, July 23, 1995, p.10.

[10] "Notebook," *Inc.*, July 1990, p. 20.

[11] "Steve Mariotti," *Inc.*, April 1989, p. 66.

[12] Arnold C. Cooper and others, *New Business In America* (Washington, D.C.: The NFIB Foundation, 1990), p. 62.

[13] Ibid.

[14] "Notebook," *Inc.*, September 1990, p. 27.

[15] Cooper and others, *New Business In America*, p. 16.

[16] Karl H. Vesper, *New Venture Strategies* (Englewood Cliffs: Prentice-Hall, 1990), p. 32.

[17] Barry Singer, "Countours of Development," *Journal of Business Venturing*, 5, no. 4, July 1995, p. 303.

[18] *Seattle Times*, July 9, 1995, p. 1.

❏ SUBCHAPTER 1B - Thinking Through Ventures

Certainly some kinds of knowledge are crucial to venturing, and that knowledge must either be learned by the entrepreneur or be provided by others who help create the venture. It can be divided into four types: (1) general business knowledge, (2) general entrepreneurship knowledge, (3) opportunity-specific knowledge and (4) venture-specific knowledge. Each of these is worth examining more closely to see why it is needed and how it can be obtained.

Four Types of Knowledge for Venturing

The following four types of knowledge can all be helpful in venturing. Some are natural for teaching in school. Others are not.

1. General Business Knowledge

Conventional business functional area courses convey knowledge that is applicable to businesses in general, whether start-ups or ongoing firms. It includes the familiar categories of marketing, finance, operations, "people" topics, business law, accounting, and the like. It may also include management of research and development, engineering and other subjects that work on product and service improvement frontiers.

Each of these subjects, although typically taught with an orientation toward established businesses, applies also to start-ups. An entrepreneur with prior knowledge of methods used in market research for established firms may be better equipped to check out the likelihood of customer acceptance for a new product or service to be offered by a venture. One with knowledge of accounting should be better able to prepare records and financial statements that a banker or investor will find reassuring in making a decision to advance money to the start-up, and so forth.

Problems in each of the business functional areas are bound to arise as the company gets started. The entrepreneur's responses will presumably be based on common sense, prior work experience, possibly formal study of business and counsel from others. How effective the "answers" must be to make the venture succeed will depend upon how strong the venture's profit margin and strategic position are relative to competitors. A high margin enjoyed by a monopoly product or service, such as one protected by patents or licenses, can compensate for substantial mismanagement. Without such protection, however, managerial error can easily lead to failure. Moreover, even with such protection it is likely that the degree of success will be higher if the business side of the venture is more competently performed. Learning the facts and methods of business may help raise the level of competence with which the business side of the venture is performed.

This learning can be undertaken at two different times: either before the venture is begun or after. Most entrepreneurs become involved in a start-up through some sequence of unanticipated events, find a need for certain know-how, sometimes through calamity, and then seek it, often through trial and more error than they would like.

The "catch" in this learn-only-when-needed approach is that (1) to a person without such knowledge the need for it may not be apparent, and (2) when the knowledge becomes acutely needed there may not be enough time available to seek it out. Countless other tasks and decisions may simultaneously be clamoring for attention. Developing the product or service, working out deals with customers and suppliers, arranging facilities and production, obtaining permissions from government agencies, setting up records for taxes and many other chores also require acquisition of special knowledge. If at least some of the necessary knowledge can be acquired in advance the bustle of start-up activities may go more smoothly.

Application: *How much general business knowledge of what type(s) will the entrepreneur in the assigned case most need, and how might it best be obtained?*

2. General Entrepreneurship Knowledge

More specialized information within each of the functional business areas that is applicable to start-ups in general more than to ongoing firms can be considered general entrepreneurship knowledge. For instance, in the area of finance the entrepreneur can learn about various sources of capital used for funding ventures by reading about them in Chapter 5 of this book or in many other books and articles on the subject. They treat such subjects as what sources exist, what types of ventures use them, what kinds of terms are struck in making deals, how well venture funds perform, how venture capitalists participate beyond putting up money, how the procedures of banks differ from those of investors and many other topics associated with raising start-up capital.

Alternatively, an entrepreneur can wait until there is need for capital, and then go looking for it, usually by asking people and proceeding from one referral to another until he or she either gets the capital or gives up. Acquisition of entrepreneurial know-how on an "as needed" basis can and often does work, although the acquisition process will take time, and also may consume mental processing capacity that could be used for other tasks of getting the business started: setting up shop, arranging for supplies, making advertising decisions, seeking out needed employees, and so forth.

Entrepreneurship knowledge can include simply awareness of what venturing is like. Most entrepreneurs learn this by doing, but study in advance can add insight. David Birch, an MIT professor who started his own consulting company, commented as follows:

> *I was starting in 1983, and I'd studied histories of 12 million companies. I knew it would take me 8 or 10 years to build the kind of business I wanted to build. I knew it wouldn't happen fast, that I wasn't going to get rich in a couple of years. I also knew that I wouldn't be able to grow in a straight line. I knew there'd be plateaus, dips, and bobs—that it would be erratic—and I was prepared for it. I knew I'd have to work 12 to 14 hours a day. I'd talked to a whole bunch of people and I knew what they went through.*
>
> *Profitability is not really a problem—cash is always the problem. They're very different. In my kind of company, profitability goes all over the place and is really quite manipulatable. If you want to grow, you expense every dollar you've got and keep it working in the company. Cash flow is a constant issue if you don't go for large outside financing, which we've chosen not to do. You've got a fixed payroll. Everything on the expense side is fixed, and everything on the revenue side is variable. Somebody gets sick and doesn't pay up on his receivable, or a salesperson gets lazy and doesn't sell for a couple months. All of a sudden your cash flow goes to hell. You find yourself constantly managing cash flow. It's a major issue.[1]*

That this type of knowledge is of great importance seems evident in the findings of Stuart and Abetti[2], who, in a study of 52 technical ventures, reported that the number of previous ventures and the management roles played in them had by far the strongest relationship to performance of start-ups in their sample. They indicated that general management experience was not particularly important, which seems to suggest that knowledge about venturing is what counts. How important experience in the same line of business as the venture was could not be ascertained from the reported results, although many other studies have found a strong connection between line of business in the start-up and prior work in the same field.

Application: *What will likely be the importance of general entrepreneurship knowledge to the entrepreneur in the assigned case and why?*

3. Opportunity-Specific Knowledge

The third type, opportunity specific knowledge, is that which is possessed by a person who knows about the existence of a specific opportunity but does not necessarily know how to take advantage of it. Inventors often consider themselves to be in this situation. Sometimes they are right. For example, Chester Carlson was repeatedly stymied when he sought to commercialize his process which later became known as Xerography. Sometimes inventors are wrong, thinking they have winning innovations when they really don't. But Carlson clearly was right. If anything, the opportunity was in his case vastly greater than he or anyone else anticipated.

An important aspect of opportunity specific knowledge is that it is unlikely to be found in business curricula. It usually involves insightful awareness of a market and possibly also of an available resource or technological frontier. This sort of knowledge most often comes from work or hobby experience.

Application: *What opportunity-specific knowledge has the entrepreneur in the assigned case possessed, where did it come from and how important is it to get more?*

4. Venture-Specific Knowledge

The fourth category, venture-specific knowledge, includes further information that those who have opportunity-specific knowledge require in order to capitalize on their ideas. To illustrate, if the entrepreneur believes there is a potentially viable market for a new radio station and wants to start one to exploit that opportunity, he or she will need information about how to obtain an FCC license. Some of that information can be read in books and government literature. But much of the essential venture-specific information is too specialized for publication. For instance:

- What frequencies are available in a particular transmitting site?

- What real estate is available to use for a station location? How much does it cost? Who owns it? What do they want?

- Who are the potential listeners and what might they be interested in hearing?

- What do competing stations of the area offer and what do they leave out?

- What should the shows be for this particular circumstance, how will they be acquired, from whom, and at what cost?

- Where can equipment be obtained? What will it cost? Who can operate it and how can their services be obtained?

- What is the best month to begin operations, and what hours are best to be on the air?

- How much financing will be needed, when and where will it come from, and on what terms?

- What will be the operating expenses of this station, at this site, and with this particular format?

- Who will buy air time for advertising, what type and at what prices?

Three ways to obtain knowledge helpful in answering questions like these are (1) to take a job in such a business and learn it as an insider, (2) to undertake a start-up of the venture and learn what is required step by step, or (3) to develop a business plan for the venture through study and investigation. Each of these three approaches has its strengths and shortcomings.

Working in someone else's venture will impart unforgettable memories of what the start-up process is like, and may even lead to riches. Every day, it is said, a thousand millionaires go to their jobs at Microsoft, people who joined the company early and gained some ownership interest in it. Since each start-up is unique, working for one may give only venture general knowledge pertinent to a student's later venturing, not venture specific knowledge for it. An advantage is that the learner in someone else's venture is likely to be paid for the experience without having to risk a financial investment. Problems with this first approach are that it will delay venturing by the learner and it may risk a conflict of interest with the employer.

Learning through personally starting a business imposes a greater financial risk, but will impart venture specific knowledge. A study by Gartner and others,[3] indicated that the extent to which an entrepreneur learns through developing a venture is a powerful influence on the extent to which the venture succeeds. While learning in all functional areas is important, the authors found that especially powerful was learning "street smarts," which they defined as "practical and real-world knowledge of how industry really works and how to survive as a new business in this industry."

Something that can be done using the classroom as a base is to develop a plan for a venture, seeking the necessary information outside school and using the classroom as a sounding board and feedback mechanism. Often best suited to school is this third approach, developing a venture plan, and possibly even starting up a very small venture or beginning the start of a more major one. Here the learning is direct and usually the motivation is high. A problem may be that school tends to be away from markets and so a hard place to find good market opportunities. Also, the venture effort may consume so much time that it becomes a conflict with other courses if it is pursued with strong dedication.

Any of these three approaches should add both general business knowledge and general entrepreneurship knowledge, as well as venture-specific knowledge needed by the entrepreneur. Probably the higher the level of such knowledge, the greater the odds of success. Almost certainly the most important knowledge will be that which is opportunity-specific and/or venture-specific. Unfortunately, however, these two are usually by far the least teachable in school and usually little described in books or periodicals. Possibly they can be learned in advance of the venture through work experience or deliberate investigation. But often it is not clear in advance what all must be learned. The need for these types of knowledge is idiosyncratic to the individual person, time and circumstance.

Application: *What venture-specific knowledge will the entrepreneur in the assigned case most need and why? How can it best be obtained?*

Learning Through Venture Planning

A would-be entrepreneur may wonder, "Once you have an idea for a venture, where do you start?" A good first step may be to sketch out a venture plan on paper. This can begin with (1) a brief description of what the product or service is, (2) what it will do for the customer, (3) what it will cost to produce, (4) why customers might be expected to buy it and (5) how much they will probably be willing to pay. These notes may only represent guesses. Much more work may be needed to treat these and other topics of importance, as will be discussed later in chapters on idea screening and venture plans. But brief notes can form a suitable beginning.

Eventually, the venture will have to demonstrate that it can make money, so another early step is to guess whether that is possible by making some rough calculations. What is the break-even sales volume (fixed costs per month divided by the difference between sales price per unit and variable cost per unit)? Does that rate of selling seem reasonably possible? How much capital will be needed to get started? What level of return on investment or how short a payback period will the venture likely produce? If the venture idea seems to hold up under such tests, then more investigation and possibly action will be appropriate. If not, it's time to modify or drop the idea to seek a better one.

Perspectives from which to view the idea include those of (1) resource provider and (2) operator as well as (3) owner. Even if all three are embodied in one person it will be a good idea to consider them separately. Will this business adequately pay back any investor? Who will be capable of performing the venture and will they want to? Will this business be worth the time, cost and trouble if it succeeds? Is the risk that it will fail worth taking?

Writing a business plan may not answer these questions as surely as might be wished, but it is usually a low-cost, low-risk starting point. Both in and after graduation from school, preparing and critiquing business plans can be an effective learning exercise. For a real venture, although most start without formal written plans, the plan can serve as a helpful guide as well as a device for persuading people to advance capital.

Most business plans cover the same general topics, but there is no standard format, as can be seen by comparing plans of different ventures. For a starting point, however, here is one possible outline:

Table of Contents List page numbers of important sections, including appendices.

Executive Summary In one or two pages hit the main points of the plan with specific figures and facts. This summary should not be vague just because it is short, and it should include the main "punch lines" of the plan.

Company Description The description should tell what the venture will make and sell. (Sketches and diagrams may be helpful.) It should state what benefits customers will receive and how, as well as what the distinctive competence and hoped for sustainable competitive advantage(s) of the company will be.

Sales Tell who will buy from this venture and why, how many will do so, how much they will pay and why, how the selling will be done, by whom and on what timetable. If possible present specific evidence that people will buy, such as market research data or letters of intent.

Competition Describe other choices customers currently have for obtaining such a product or service and how those choices can be expected to change. What companies offer such choices, what their competitive advantages are now and how those will likely change in the future should be stated.

Technology Tell how well-proven the venture's product or service and the venture's ability to produce it are. What else will be done to keep its performance up with or ahead of the times? What sorts of legal protection, such as patents, will be available and when?

Operations Say who will produce the output of the venture and how the venture's production capability will compare to that of competitors. What, if any, special location and facilities will be required, and at what cost and timing? (Flow and Gantt charts may help.)

Financial Aspects Include pro forma income statements, along with balance sheets and a cash flow forecast which breaks down figures monthly for two years and annually for three with footnotes explaining assumptions and important details behind the figures. The plan should indicate how and when any lenders or investors recover their cash.

Team Provide data on founders' capabilities that will be critical to success of the venture, what their task-relevant training and experiences are, and what their stakes in the venture will be.

Appendices Present details behind the body sections in order to keep the body down to about 20 pages of main facts and exhibits plus the summary and table of contents. Financial statements, resumes, market research details, copies of patents, letters of intent and such can appear here.

Application: *What should the outline of a written plan for the venture in the assigned case be, down to first and second level headings?*

Although venture plans can be written and helpful at any time, most are prepared part way along in a venture when some kind of a start has been made and more money is needed. The entrepreneur and any partners will have used personal savings to make a prototype, open a shop or otherwise get the venture partly going. They will see the cash supply running out and seek more, either from a bank or other investors. Financers will welcome any accomplishments of the venture to date that indicate it has been moving toward success. The entrepreneur(s) will prepare a cash flow forecast to show in dollars and cents how that will happen. Those dollars and cents imply occurrence of other events which also must be described to show there is a basis for believing the figures. Hence other supporting information such as market data, resumes showing prior accomplishments of the venture's founders, diagrams showing how the venture's product or service will work and will compare to competitors, and whatever else is important to the venture's success should be included in the plan.

For prospective partners or key employees the written plan can clarify parts they should play to bring about profits. For the entrepreneur and any others who participate in preparing the plan, that activity itself should help in anticipating problems, working out in advance ways of heading them off as well as discovering ways to improve and refine the venture sooner rather than later. As the venture moves along, the plan can serve as a basis for coordinating activities and checking progress.

The test of a plan ultimately will be how well it serves the venture. It is not possible to assess that in advance. But adopting the viewpoint of those who might read the plan for alternative purposes, such as the parties mentioned above, and asking how well it is likely to serve each purpose can provide an assessment. That assessment can be used for revising and improving the plan. Is more information needed? Are priorities clear? Have the points of greatest potential vulnerability been given thorough treatment? Have facts supporting them been included? Is the plan logical? Does it read well? Is it made easy to read by inclusion of an introductory paragraph explaining organization of the presentation, and by keeping the text compact through relegating details to appendices?

Three overall questions in evaluating a plan are (1) how viable is the venture concept itself, (2) how well suited are the founders for carrying out that concept against prospective competitors, and (3) how effective is the plan for its main purposes? The best way to cross-check answers to these questions, short of starting the venture and seeing what happens, is to ask other knowledgeable people to read and comment on it. Experienced business people are usually the best reviewers.

Application: *What elements in a plan for this venture will be the most (1) critical, (2) troublesome, and (3) "grunt work" to develop?*

Four Thought Modes

Enhancement of business plans can be accomplished through deliberate application of several different modes of thought, each of which at certain times may be most important and all of which should work together. Four such modes are (1) Absorptive, (2) Analytic, (3) Divergent, and (4) Projective.

1. Knowledge-Absorption Mode

The absorptive mode of thought involves acquisition of the four types of knowledge described earlier. General entrepreneurship knowledge includes both facts (e.g. patents are good for 17 years, at least until the law changes) and routine skills (e.g. how to develop a cash flow spreadsheet) as well as beliefs, rules of thumb, lore and myths about entrepreneuring (e.g. some entrepreneurs seem to be born, others made). Levels of venture-specific knowledge include information about the firm, the economic environment it operates in, how such a business performs its functions, and details of particular people, technologies, and so forth. These facts may have to be sought out through information gathering.

An important part of the absorptive process is perception and discernment. When one potential entrepreneur spots an opportunity there are usually other people who also could do so but for some reason fail to. Practice in looking consciously for venture ideas may help develop this capability. For absorption of routine skills, such as mentally going through a checklist in order to evaluate venture alternatives or developing cash flow projections, practice can improve performance.

Study of written cases and business plans developed by others can provide practice in some kinds of routine skills, such as thinking through a venture proposition from the perspectives of different players. A strength of studying cases is that many can be examined in a fairly short period, since they are ready at hand and self contained. Their weakness is that they don't allow interrogation or practice in searching for needed information. Seeking out references and making "cold calls" to get information can add both facts and valuable skills. Much of entreprenurship is new information gathering, not just application of knowledge already possessed. To push the application and acquisition of knowledge beyond what comes naturally in considering a particular case the following questions may be helpful.

- What are the most important facts in this case for dealing with the situation it presents? How certain are they?

- What knowledge of skills and facts from other courses apply to this situation?

- What knowledge of skills and facts acquired in this course apply to this situation?

- What additional opportunity-specific or venture-specific knowledge is most important in this case, what more of it would be most valuable, how could it be obtained, and would it be worth that?

- (Optionally) What facts and/or lessons from this case might most helpfully apply to other situations?

Application: *What is the difference between the factual knowledge possessed by the entrepreneur in the assigned case and that which would be needed to succeed with the venture? By what different combinations of actions by the entrepreneur could/should the gap be filled?*

2. Analytic Mode

The analytic mode is used for exploring and explaining how different aspects of the venture and its plan work. It can take several forms, including assessment of information, discovery of relationships between causes and effects, diagnosis of problems, quantification of important variables, prediction of the effects that changes in some variables will have on changes in others and critical scrutiny of the logic in supposed relationships or arguments.

At any stage in the process of venture creation, from advance preparation and savings accumulation, to opportunity recognition, planning, resource application, start-up, operation and eventually disposition of the enterprise, there are threats, problems and opportunities to be identified and dealt with. Often these can be brought to the surface by asking the following diagnostic questions:

- What, if anything, can we learn from crunching the numbers in this case?

- How good seem to be the important data in this case?

- What are the main problems (differences between the way things are and the way they should be) faced by the entrepreneur(s) in this case?

- What seem to be important issues (matters of potential dispute) in this case?

- What should be their order of priority?

- What is at the base of these issues? What forces cause them? What is the evidence? How do those forces work?

- What assumptions are being made? How strong are they?

- What are pros and cons of the most important choices in this case situation?

- What impact would reasonable changes in important facts or assumptions have on these pros and cons?

Application: *Which of the above questions are most important to answer in this case, and how can they best be answered?*

Areas of issue in venturing include: gaining cooperation from customers, suppliers and financers, trading off benefits versus costs, striking compromises among conflicting preferences, choosing among alternative sequences and allocating time among conflicting demands for it. Some questions that raise issues in start-ups are: (1) Is the apparent start-up opportunity attractive? (2) What strategy should be followed to exploit it? (3) How much money will be needed? (4) How should the entrepreneur(s) raise it? (5) Would debt or equity be better? (6) If equity, how should it be split? (7) What other terms of the relationship should partners work out? (8) When should other employment alternatives to pursuing this venture be dropped?

In the analytic mode, application of valid information from the absorptive mode will be crucial, and part of the analytic task is to assess the validity of that information. Sometimes the information will already be available, as when the assignment is to review another's business plan or examine a case. Other times, as in real-life venturing, new decision making information must be sought out from publications, interviews and/or experiments. Subtleties and underlying implications need to be surfaced. Deciding what questions to ask is an important part of this phase, along with valid logic.

For each issue there will be alternative potential solutions, and for each of those solutions there will be pros and cons. Sometimes the pros and cons can only be weighed logically and other times they can be quantified with such tools as break-even, discounted cash flow, present value and probabilistic expected value analysis. These standard mathematical routines are essential for measuring the extent or degree of critically important quantities such as amount of cash needed, cash available at specific times and rate of return on investment.

Graphical depiction of quantities and relationships is a powerful tool for both analysis and communication. It is typically underutilized in venture plans. Graphs, histograms and pie charts all can help in thinking through a venture and so should be used. Other graphical tools not limited to quantities, such as decision trees, flow charts, schematics, perspectives, machine drawings, freehand sketches, models and photographs also should be brought into the analysis wherever they can help clarify thinking. Simply writing out in words the logic of analysis and description can often be a powerful way to check for completeness and correctness.

Risks in the analytic thought mode include overlooking issues, misdiagnosing causes and effects, making incorrect applications of systematic techniques or jumping to conclusions without applying such techniques at all. Such "impulse management" may be appropriate if the decision is inconsequential or if there is insufficient time for analysis. It may also be useful as a "first cut." A sense of priority should be brought to bear here. Where the consequences are great, the best analytical tools available should be carefully applied. Skill in applying them comes with practice.

Application: *What alternative computations could be performed with the numbers and/or possible estimates in the assigned case, and what do they show both quantitatively and graphically?*

3. *Divergent Mode*

The analytic mode above aims mainly at drawing correct conclusions from among choices already identified. The divergent mode, in contrast, seeks out additional possible choices. The earliest stage for applying it may be in searching out a venture idea or, perhaps earlier, more ways for looking for one. Most entrepreneurs turn out to have been lucky enough to have the venture idea come upon them without having to search for it. But leaving opportunity discovery completely to chance probably reduces the odds of accomplishing successful entrepreneurship. Some questions that should trigger divergent thinking are the following:

- What are other possible alternatives or branches for a decision tree of the situation in this case?

- What are other possible answers to earlier trigger questions?

Whereas a main risk in applying the other modes of thought is that the wrong choice will be made among identified alternatives, the main risk in divergent thinking is that of failing to discover a better possible choice. A way to escape overlooking important possibilities is always to ask whether there are other possibilities that might be considered and then to examine them. The divergent mode should enhance the absorption mode by seeking better ways of finding useful information. In the analytic mode examining an issue ever more closely should reveal more and more ways of treating it. Thus the divergent mode can work in conjunction with other modes.

There is no presumed order. A way in which the analytic mode can produce divergent thinking is to compute limits of important quantities such as what the maximum reasonable upside potential of a venture is.

Other prompting questions to help avoid overlooking important possibilities include:

- How could this be done better?

- What are the opportunity implications of possible future scenarios?

- What other possibilities exist for solving problems?

In divergent thinking, the more answers the better. The more practical the answers, the better yet.

Application: *What issue in the assigned case most urgently calls for divergent thinking, and what are 10 (or 20) possible answers for it?*

4. *Projective Mode*

A thought mode that deals in projecting future business scenarios is probably required more in entrepreneurship than in other business activities.

Whether viewed as visioning, envisaging, forecasting, generating scenarios or projecting chains of events and consequences, the essence of venture planning is to foresee sequences of actions, results and their implications into the future. These scenarios can be grouped into two categories: (1) speculative visions of the future, and (2) prescriptive descriptions of what should be done.

Speculative application of the projective mode explores such questions as:

- If a particular set of actions is taken, what results will likely follow?

- And then what?

- And then what?

- And then what?

- What might be an appropriate mission statement at some future point in time for this venture?

- How might a future portrait of success for this venture best be described?

- How might that pattern be different at alternative future points in time?

- What scenario could lead to that portrait? By accomplishing what set of milestones?

- What might go wrong, what could be done if it did, and what action might forestall it?

Repeating these questions, particularly if coupled with divergent thinking, could cause a decision tree to explode in possibilities. Hence, both these modes must be coupled with analytic thinking to keep the possibilities within bounds—but not too far within bounds.

Application: How should the above projective thinking questions be answered for the assigned case?

Prescriptive application of the projective thought mode should work through the details of implementing decisions made through analysis based on the other modes. Relevant questions include.

- What plan of action is recommended?

- Who, what, how, when ... ?

- What might a Gantt chart look like?

- What might the recommended budget look like?

- What milestones will indicate successful accomplishment, when should they occur and how should that occurrence be evident?

- What should the contingency plan(s) be?

When thinking prescriptively, the entrepreneur sets targets and specifies individual assignments. Prescription can take such forms as written description, a list of steps with statements of who, how, when and at what cost, possibly depicted in graphics. Some of the prescribed action will be contingent upon other events in the venture plan coming true, such as capital becoming available or customers responding favorably to the product or service concept. But the action will be definite.

Application: How should the above projective thinking questions be answered for the assigned case?

Presentation

Preparing business plans is a logical way to develop skill in these thought modes. Working them will likely not be a straightforward process. But communicating the reasoning to others and implementing its conclusions is likely to work better if the reasoning is crystallized and presented in a way that is clear and coherent. Some questions that may help in checking accomplishment of this goal include:

- What is the logic behind this venture?

- How have the pros and cons of alternatives been weighed to reach the main conclusions?

- Are priorities in the reasoning evident?

- Is there a clear picture of where the action should lead, such as a future portrait of success?

- Can a mission statement in some form be discerned?

- Is there a phrase or slogan that captures the essence of what this venture aims for? (like Xerox's "office of the future" concept that led to discovery of the microcomputer)

- Is it easy to see what will produce break-even and, beyond that, what the ROI (return on investment) should be? Can the reason why this venture may get away with earning a profit against competitors for customers' money be quickly and easily discerned?

- Can effective application of all thought modes in the plan be seen?

- Do the pieces produced by different modes of thinking fit together coherently?

- Are there any visual pictures of how the pieces fit included that could go with the verbal descriptions, mottoes, or depictive catch phrases?

How to organize the reasoning for review by others depends on the situation. Three alternative very general patterns are as follows:

1. Diagnosis, identification of issues, alternatives for responding to the issues, pros and cons of the alternatives, conclusions.

2. Future portrait of success, rationale behind that portrait, what it will take to get there, recommendations for doing so.

3. Two or three alternative scenarios for development of the venture over time, comparison of those scenarios against criteria for success, choice of a particular scenario and steps for implementing it.

In venture planning, how well these modes are applied and also how effectively the result is presented are both important. Vastly more important, however, is effective action, regardless of the venture plan.

Application: *Depict on a transparency three alternative schemes describing how the main pieces will go together in the venture's strategic future.*

Standard Questions for Cases

When considering potential ventures it is always possible to identify reasons for rejecting them. The objective, however, is to find ways to make the most of opportunities, not just dismiss them, although often dismissal is in fact the best choice. Some questions to consider in connection with any new venture case, insofar as possible, include those below. Unfortunately, there is no science for predicting "the" right answers. Inevitably, guessing and approximation are required.

1. **Basic Profitability and Estimated Financial Attractiveness**

   - How much sales will be needed to cover fixed costs in this venture? (Break-even)

   - How much profit can the venture make if things go as well as they reasonably can? (Upside potential)

   - How much could the venture be sold for? (Cash-out option)

   - How much must be invested to give the venture a try, and what is the ratio of most likely profits to that investment? (ROI)

   - How much can it lose of the cash put in? (Downside risk)

2. **Odds Assessment**

   - What main assumptions underlie the profitability analysis?

   - How sensitive to them are the profitability results?

- How good is the information on which they are based?

- What is most likely to happen, and how can it be influenced?

3. **Fit with the Entrepreneur**

    What could this particular entrepreneur gain by proceeding with the venture, and how might that compare with what some other person might gain from it?

4. **Action**

    What, based upon analysis of these and any other appropriate questions for this case, should the entrepreneur(s) do in this situation and why?

Application: How should the above questions be answered for the chosen case?

Supplementary Reading

New Venture Strategies Chapter 3. (Vesper, K.H., Prentice-Hall, 1990)
New Venture Mechanics Chapter 10. (Vesper, K. H., Prentice-Hall, 1993)

Exercises

1. **Thought Mode Assessment**   List the thought modes in rank order as to how you think you compare to most other people (starting with the one on which you are strongest relative to other people. Come to class prepared to discuss how someone might seek out others to build a team that would collectively be as well-balanced as possible on thought mode strengths.

2. **Thought Mode Consequences**   For each of the thought modes list one or more mistakes that failure of that mode might lead to in a venture, and one or more competitive business successes that might result if that mode were particularly well exercised. Be prepared to comment on your conclusions, and also on the relative premium you would place on performing each mode well in starting a venture. Also be prepared to comment on how a career might change each of the modes in relative strength and what a person could do to strengthen them.

Venture History

The following are some questions that may help in ferreting out the history of the venture you are studying. For any particular venture, however, different questions may at times be more appropriate.

1. What was the background and "prior mental programming" or "task-relevant experience" of the entrepreneur in the venture whose history you are investigating?

2. How much prior knowledge, of the four types mentioned in this chapter, did the entrepreneur have and what else was most necessary to learn for accomplishing the venture?

Venture Planning Guide

1. Sketch a "hindsight plan" (what the start-up sequence must have been) for an existing business similar to one you might be interested in starting. Estimate the role of venture-specific knowledge required and how it might be obtained (Absorptive/Analytic thought mode). What events in the company's creation would a plan most likely have anticipated best and which ones least well? What impacts might such planning have had on development of the venture itself?

Notes

[1] "Coming of Age," *Inc.*, April 1989, p. 38.
[2] Robert W. Stuart and Pier A. Abetti, "Impact of Entrepreneurial and Management Experience on Early Performance," *Journal of Business Venturing*, 5, no. 3, May 1990, p. 151.
[3] William B. Gartner, Jennifer A. Starr, and Jon P. Goodman, "The Value of Content Analysis for Developing Venture Screening Skills", paper presented at the 1994 Babson Entrepreneurship Research Conference.

Case Questions

General Case Questions

1. What, in order of priority, are the issues in the assigned case? What are the main alternatives for dealing with those of top priority? What are pros and cons of the alternatives?

2. What kind of enterprise could be created in the situation of this case?

3. What would be required to make it that?

4. How well suited to the task are the entrepreneurs?

5. What should the entrepreneurs do and why?

Case 1 - Charles and Barbara Ewing p. 38

1. What do you think the Ewings should do, based on the information in the case?

2. How would you estimate a break-even volume for Charles and Barbara Ewing's Clayboard production?

3. If your assignment for this class were to carry out a project to help Charles and Barbara Ewing, what would be:

    a. A statement of the work to be performed.
    b. The end product of your effort for them.
    c. A timetable of tasks for accomplishing this result.

Case 2 - Janet Luhrs and Rene Williams p. 43

1. What else needs to be done to make this venture a success?

2. What changes in the business plan should do most to make this venture appealing to a potential investor?

3. How have the capabilities of the entrepreneurs in this venture to succeed with it changed over time, and what events caused those changes?

4. If your assignment for this class were to carry out a project to help Janet and Rene, what would be:

   a. A statement of the work to be performed.
   b. The end product of your effort for them.
   c. A timetable of tasks for accomplishing this result.

Charles and Barbara Ewing

Turning an Invention Into a Business

In mid 1992 Charles and Barbara Ewing were contemplating whether they could create a profitable and substantial business around a product Charles had developed and named "Clayboard." Its purpose was similar to that of a canvas used by artists, but instead of being cloth stretched across a frame it was a thin rigid board covered with a hard, smooth, absorbent coating of white clay on one side for drawing and painting.

He had recently sold a few Clayboard panels of various sizes to individual artists. In 1991 a local Colorado art supply distributor had encouraged Charles and Barbara to put the art panel into distribution for the art supply retail trade. Their first major move towards a relationship with this distributor began with a commitment the Ewings had made to introduce the panel in a major art supply trade show. The two were producing it in the garage of their home in southern Colorado, but they were having problems with both the quality and quantity of production. As they prepared for the show, Barbara asked:

> But if a lot of people decide to buy the panel, how can we make enough to meet demand? We can't keep up with the orders we already have.

Charles, covered with dust in the summer heat from sanding clay surfaces replied:

> And we aren't really making much on it either, at least if you put any value on our time.

The Product

Clayboard consisted of a mineral coating that was applied to a hard, rigid sheet of one-eighth-inch thick Masonite to produce a superior painting panel. Charles Ewing, an artist living in Colorado, had developed it for his personal use. When he showed it to other artists and local art classes, he found that they liked it too. He sent out samples to other artists. Written responses had included a number of complimentary comments. A few art stores in Colorado had bought the product from him. Barbara had designed packaging for the product, which read "Clayboard, real neat stuff."

Charles had been exploring the possibility of obtaining patents on the composition and process, but had not actually filed. Essentially, the coating involved a complex mixing and ingredient process. The coating, which cost under $0.50 per square foot, was applied to Masonite, which came in 4x8 foot sheets costing around $15 each that were cut into standard-size rectangles ranging from 8"x10" to 18"x24". After applying the coating and allowing it to dry, the surface had to be sanded smooth, something Charles accomplished with a hand-held electric orbital sander bought from a local hardware store for around $100. The process was slow and tedious, limiting the number he could produce to less that 300 Clayboards per week at most.

Clayboard was better than paper for drawing and painting on for several reasons. One was that it could be used directly without the need for some other backing such as a drawing board. Unlike artist papers, it did not bend or warp under repeated applications of water. The mineral surface of the panel allowed multiple erasures without affecting the surface texture. Erasure was accomplished by rubbing with steel wool to remove applied colors. However, when sealed with a clear acrylic fixative coat an artwork on Clayboard could be framed to last without need for glass covering.

Painting on panels went back at least as far as the Renaissance. Many artists, including Michelangelo, painted on wooden panels that had been coated with chalk gessoes.* While Charles Ewing's product was not an entirely new concept, he had developed a coated panel with a level of smoothness he explained was not easily attainable by modern-day artists. Many artists would spend days preparing wooden panels for painting. The coating Charles had developed also allowed an artist to manipulate the surface extensively. His art panel accepted all types of paints, including ink, pencil, watercolors, oils and acrylics. It would not age or yellow, and could be erased. Pictures on Clayboard could be framed easily without other backing.

The other art surface on the market with a coating similar to Clayboard was "scratchboard". This paper-based panel was clay coated with a top layer of ink that could be scratched away to develop etching-type drawings, commonly known as "scratchboard" art work. Other competition consisted of papers and canvas panels for painting. Estimated typical prices at retail for these alternative surfaces compared approximately as shown in Figure 1 below.

Figure 1 - Costs of Alternative Art Surfaces

Material	Typical Size	Cost**
Quality Watercolor Paper	22"x30"	$14.65
Gessoed (Primered) Masonite	18"x24"	8.13
Scratchboard	19"x24"	15.55
Pre-Stretched Canvas	18"x24"	10.00

Background

Charles Ewing had studied wood technology at Colorado State university. In the early 1970s he had taken a Peace Corps assignment at a University in Chile. His father had been a commercial illustrator who did fine art as a hobby. He did not encourage Charles to take up art; but when he died, Charles inherited his art tools and took them with him to Chile. There he began taking art lessons at night on the side, using his father's tools.

When Chile was swept by the turmoil of a new political regime, Charles lost his position at the university there and transferred to another Peace Corps group that was preparing a book on Chilean mammals. With his newly-learned art skills, he became their illustrator. Eventually, that project ended, and after some other travels, he returned to the southwestern U.S. and opened an art gallery in Cimarron, New Mexico. It burned down. Broke, he returned to a cabin owned by his family in the thinly-populated southern area of Colorado.

To earn a living, he began producing art and selling it through galleries. The typical arrangement, he said, was for the

---

* Webster defines gesso as "plaster of Paris prepared for use in sculpture or bas-reliefs, or as a surface for painting."
** Charles explained that prices ranged fairly widely with quality. Art paper and canvas, for instance, might sell well below the cost of Clayboard or well above it, depending upon grade.

artist to set the price, then display it on consignment in the gallery. If and when it sold, the gallery would keep 25 to 60 percent, depending upon the prominence of the gallery.

During summers Charles worked for a local outfitter leading hunting parties. When the outfitter decided to retire, Charles recruited a partner and the two took over the business. He recalled:

I was still painting. That went on for about five years, and then I got out of the outfitting business. I could get by on painting alone, and the outfitting took too much time away from it. Being a painter is something like being a musician. Unless you keep practicing, your skill drops off.

Like most artists, I tried different things, watercolors, oils, sculpting, pen and ink. Typically an artist will find that one particular thing sells better than others, and for me that turned out to be drawing on scratchboard. I enjoyed the technique, but not its lack of permanency. It had to be mounted on a backing board with glue and framed under glass, which was tedious. But what was worse was that sometimes it bubbled up in the middle where the glue came loose. I had some work come back to me with that problem from unhappy customers.

So I went to the hardware store and bought some Masonite and glue. Then I went to a pottery store and bought some white clay. I mixed it with the glue, painted it on the board with a brush, let it dry and then sanded it smooth, so I could paint on it. That seemed to work fine, so I began doing my artwork on it from then on.

This, as best he could recall, took place in the late 1970s, and Charles kept using his product. He was essentially the only one who did anything like it for the next fifteen years. He would make just two or three sheets at a time, a process that was very laborious but produced a surface he liked to use and that did not give him problems later due to lack of durability.

Occasionally, someone else would use his board. For instance, he sometimes taught local art classes. When students saw him use the Clayboard, some took an interest in it and wanted some. He would then sell some, but the volume of sales was minuscule from invention of the board through the 1980s.

Producing for the Art Supplies Market

In early 1991, Charles was told by the owner of an art supply store in Alamosa, Colorado that there was an art supplies distributor who might be interested in selling Charles' Clayboard product. The distributor had been having a hard time finding good sources for scratchboard, most of which was imported from England. The store owner had told him about Clayboard. He told Charles: "If you can make it, he can sell it."

Taking down the distributor's phone number in Denver, Charles gave him a call. The man expressed interest and, after seeing samples, offered to buy it for resale. The two worked out an arrangement. Charles gave a retail price of $9 per square foot, with 25 percent to 50 percent off for the distributor.

As a result, the distributor began buying Charles' product, starting with all the inventory Charles had available. He resold it to stores. He also let Charles share his booth to demonstrate Clayboard at the NAMTA (National Art Materials Trade Association) show in Denver during July of 1991. This too produced orders, and some letters came from other artists complimenting Charles on his product. Charles and Barbara started thinking in terms of creating a business around it. She quit her job as a health care professional to help. He began experimenting with more efficient production methods.

Charles' formula for making the boards was in part secret. A reason for his hesitation to file for a patent was that he understood issuance of a patent would make public the details of his process. Also, he had been told that legal fees in the application process would probably be in the range of $3,000 to $10,000.

Increasing the volume of production produced problems. Setting the boards out to dry took much more room than he had needed before. Sanding the boards was very laborious, even with electrically-powered, hand-held sanders. The process produced a great amount of dust which made working conditions difficult. And the time needed for all this work kept him busy about 60 hours per week, even though Barbara helped about 40 hours per week, and in addition they hired a laborer at $4 per hour who put in another 40 hours per week. Having to hire someone, Charles said, added annoying paperwork:

> I never had any idea how much red tape and expense would be involved in hiring someone—unemployment insurance, workmen's compensation insurance, tax deductions—not to mention all the taxes and forms I have to file on account of buying materials and selling the boards.

The most they could produce, Charles and Barbara found, was around 1,000 square feet of finished board per month in sizes typically around two to three square feet each. Even the packaging, he found, was much more work than he had anticipated. Each board was wrapped in a sheet of spongy plastic to protect the surface, then taped and labeled. This wasn't really hard work, just time consuming and monotonous. It was taking Charles' time away from painting, and he didn't like that.

Seeking Sales

Getting sales also took more work for less results than expected. There was demand and complimentary letters from users, but no great flood of orders as they had hoped. Charles found he had to demonstrate the product and found himself traveling to other cities to do so. Even then, many artists would pass it up. He commented:

> Some artists are just very conservative and stick to traditional materials like oil on canvas. Some pick up a particular medium because that is what their mentor used, and they stay with that. Others may experiment, but mostly when they are just getting started. Then when they find something that works for them they hang onto it.
>
> Every material requires practice for becoming proficient with it. It is obvious to me that you can do many things with my board, pen and ink, watercolors, oils, all sorts of things work with it. But for someone who hasn't seen it before, it can take time to figure these things out. If I demonstrate it for them they catch on faster, but even then a lot of them just watch, say it looks nice, and go back to what they were using before.
>
> The cost should not be a big deal for them. The board only costs around $10 for a painting they might sell for $200. They buy other materials that cost that much. With mine, they can sand down the surface and start over if they don't like the way a picture is turning out. They can't do that with the other materials, although they may be able to paint over with more layers if they are using oils. But the fact that cost should not be a problem doesn't mean it isn't. The best people for me to sell to might be students, since they are less likely to be set in their ways. Unfortunately, they tend to care about cost of materials because they don't have much money, and they

rarely get good prices for their work at that stage.

The dream we have is that if we can just get established in the market, then people will stick with our product, and we can have a good business. I'd like to have some people do the selling, someone else be the foreman and get out the product, and get myself back to producing art before I get rusty at that.

But right now I find myself doing all these other things. On top of that, I have been struggling with how to get little bubbles out of the clay that always seem to form. They have never been a problem for me personally, but my impression is that stores like to sell a product that looks perfect. Otherwise people take off the wrapper, decide there is something wrong with the product and the store has to give their money back. Then what should the store do with the board, send it back to me? And what should I do with it?

Janet Luhrs and Renee Williams

In October 1988 Janet Luhrs and Renee Williams were moving forward with a product idea Renee had developed called "Babypak," a fabric sling for a parent to use in carrying a baby. Traditionally, American mothers had carried babies in front and Japanese mothers in back by means of such slings. After trying both methods, Renee had preferred the Japanese arrangement and had consequently developed a Japanese-style sling with what she regarded as improvements in configuration and strength over the Japanese product.

After considerable work on improvement of the product, unsuccessful attempts to sell through mail order, design and development of a box-type package and exploration for suitable manufacturers in the Orient, the two had visited the headquarters of Toys 'R Us and received an order for 15,000 units, to begin with a first shipment of 5,000. This put them, Janet observed, "in the process of trying to figure out the best way to set up our business so it will be a successful one."

Renee Williams

Renee Williams had attended art school and beautician school following graduation from high school, and then gone to work as a beautician. She commented:

> One of my classmates who had dropped out before graduating from high school had also become a beautician, and by the time I was ready to go to work she already had her own beauty salon. So I went to work for her.

After working a while in other shops, Renee decided in 1977 to open her own. She recalled her reasoning at the time.

> I figured, that if my friend could set up her own business without even graduating from high school, then I ought to be able to do it, too. Besides, the shop I was working for at the time didn't seem to me to be treating people very well. I wanted to leave, and it turned out some of the other beauticians did too. So when I opened my own salon several of them came to work for me.

A problem, she said, was that running a salon and managing other people was very demanding work, which provided meager returns. Beauticians who worked for her, she found, often made more money than she did after she paid for wages, rent, health insurance and other costs of doing business. The salon was always profitable, but revenues in the best year were only $150,000, leaving income after expenses for her and her husband, who worked as receptionist, of around $30,000. When the difficulty of operating it was compounded by arrival of her first baby in 1982, she sold the salon and opened a small solo salon in her home, to which some of her clients followed her.

Occasionally she came up with other product ideas.

> I've always been inventive. Even back in school I used to think I would like to invent something and patent it. The trouble was that at the time I

couldn't think of any products worth patenting.

While operating the salon she had tried commercializing some ideas with a friend she had met in art school, Janet Luhrs, about whom she said:

> *Janet is also inventive, and we had fun working together even though our ideas didn't pan out.*

They had tried making some products they called "Terrific Toilets," which were toilet covers, and packaged "Schmores" for microwaves. A combination of peanut butter, cookies, chocolate and sugar in plastic bags, the schmores were supposed to be a product that could be quickly heated to a sweet, gooey consistency in microwave ovens. Renee recalled the result:

> *The trouble was that the sugar crystallized into a hard substance that made the schmores hard to eat.*

Renee and Janet had also tried working up a video program for high school students. After paying a small fee the students would progress through a series of videotaped lessons presented by well-known personalities. After watching these, the students would prepare and present their own fashion show. Renee recalled:

> *We showed it to schools and they liked it. The problem was they didn't have any money to pay for it, so they just took the lesson plans we had developed and used them on their own without the tapes and without paying us anything.*

Baby Pak

Then had come the Baby Pak idea. When Renee's first baby arrived in 1982, a Japanese lady had given her a sling from Japan, which Renee had used with pleasure and then passed along to another mother when her baby outgrew it. Arrival of Renee's second baby in late 1986 had prompted Renee to wish for another such sling and consequently to design a copy for herself which a friend who was skilled as a seamstress helped her make. Working through a series of a half dozen prototypes, Renee added improvements to the design which fitted it better to the baby and made it stronger. A flyer depicting applications of the Baby Pak appears in Exhibit 1.

Having created what she considered to be a superior product, she decided to try selling it. She had noticed advertisements for baby products offered by other individuals in a diaper service newspaper and decided to telephone some of them to learn how selling through the paper worked. Running the advertisements cost, she found, around $60 per month. After enlisting her mother-in-law's help as a seamstress to make the products, she ran advertisements in that paper and in *Mothering* magazine, but found that the volume of sales did not cover the costs of advertising.

She concluded that she needed to find a source of greater sales volume and it occurred to her that a store like K-Mart or Toys R Us might afford such an opportunity. For help in writing letters to them, she decided to ask her friend, Janet Luhrs. "If there's one thing I can't do it's write anything," Renee observed, "and Janet is a good writer."

Janet Luhrs

Janet picked up the conversation from there.

> *Writing and art are two strong points with me, so when Renee asked me in April to help her out with these letters, I was glad to.*

Following high school Janet had gone to art school, where she met Renee. Janet recalled her own career.

In high school I had been the best in art. But in art school everyone else had been the best, too. It was really competitive, and I just didn't feel like buckling down on it at that point. So I needed to move on to something else and went on to the University of Washington where I got a bachelor's degree in journalism.

After journalism school I worked for a while in the newspaper business and then did my own freelance writing. Then I went to law school. I had met my husband, and he had gone to law school. A woman I had worked with in the writing business had also gone to law school. So why hadn't I gone to law school? One morning I woke up and said 'I think I'll go to law school.' I had been getting tired of the writing anyway, and thought maybe going to law school would lend another dimension to my writing and my research.

Law really wasn't for me, although I enjoyed parts of it, like working for the public defender up in Alaska and conducting trials. A lot of it is just too dry. I'm good at writing and artistic work. But in law you just gobble up what some judge said and spit it back out in a nice way.

Then when I had a baby I found I couldn't flip my brain on and off to do law. That work is intense and I found I could not do it all day and then go home and say goo goo. And besides I just didn't want to work full-time any more. It was just too much.

Also, I had continued to do freelance writing all through law school, and in fact, I have one account, a newsletter, that I still do work for. Then I got pregnant again, and when I'm that way, I'm just a wreck and can't do anything.

But about three months after I had

the second baby, I started to get "antsy" again and think about what else to do. I thought maybe I'd start writing again, and then Renee approached me with this baby pack design and asked if I wanted to go into business with her. It was perfect, so I said sure.

First Steps

The two women asked advice of anyone whom they thought could help. Renee told her hairdressing clients what she and her partner were trying to do and through one of them met a successful inventor in Bellingham, Washington who gave them suggestions and leads on packaging the product. Janet asked her husband, a maritime lawyer, for leads and through them located a man who specialized in making arrangements for manufacturing in the Far East. Through inquiries with manufacturers' representatives they learned about sales markups and "hidden" costs. For instance, there might be a requirement that 98 percent of the products be perfect or else the buyer could cancel the deal. And to obtain a UPC bar code for the box they found they would have to pay $300 to a company which monopolized the standard code.

A manufacturer's representative told them that the best way to follow up on the encouraging mail response they had received from Toys R Us would be to make a personal appointment and both fly to New Jersey to meet with the buyer. Renee recalled:

It was hard for me to accept the idea of such a big expense. But we did it, and everything worked out perfectly.

Janet added:

Others told us either we wouldn't get in to see the buyer at all, or if we did, he'd only give us five minutes. But he was very friendly, we had no trouble getting in, and he spent two hours looking over the product and giving us helpful advice.

One of the things a sales representative told us was that we had to ask for an order to get one. If he had not told us that, I would have just waited for the buyer to tell us he would place an order. And he probably never would have. But in the interview we did ask for the order, and we got one for 15,000 units, the first delivery to be for 5,000. He didn't even try to beat us down on price, but took what we offered, $15 a unit.

Renee concluded:

I couldn't believe we would be able to get an order without a successful test marketing program first. But we did.

The partners had also explored possible manufacturing arrangements. Currently, it appeared that a local firm would be able to have them made in the Orient and deliver them to the partners for $7 per unit, including customs. It also appeared that there would be no problem with import restrictions that applied to clothing.

The supplier wanted guarantee of payment on delivery, however. This would require more cash than either partner could provide and consequently they had started to prepare a business plan, excerpts of which are attached in Exhibits 2 and 3, and

approached banks for possible loans. Rainier bank had said it could probably provide a letter of credit guaranteeing payment if the two women could produce enough cash to back up the letter. Renee figured she could raise part of the money from her house but not enough.

Next Concerns

A question on the mind of both women was how to turn these beginnings into a longer term business with high profitability. A schedule of activities Janet saw as necessary to start the company appears as Exhibit 2. She had also prepared a financial forecast which appears as Exhibit 3. Both had young children and wanted to be able to stay home with them. Neither had much capital. Janet observed that she hated borrowing money and did not want to be in debt personally. Renee said she had thought of selling stock, but did not want more partners and was not anxious to have the profits diluted by other owners.

I read in a magazine about two women who were making a lot of money selling designer bottles, and we heard about a couple of women back east with another product. The first pair seem to be making a lot of money and the other two are just squeaking by. We want to know what will determine which we will be like and figure out a way to be like the ones who are really successful.

EXHIBIT 1   Baby Pak Advertising Flyer

Baby Pak
The Best Baby Carrier!

P.O. Box 25332
Seattle, Wa.
98125
(206) 633-4514

1 - Although Baby Pak is best used as a back pak:

2 - You can also use Baby Pak as a front pak for smaller babies.

3 - Or as an emergency high chair. (Directions: Sit baby in contoured seat of Pak. Insert legs through leg holes. Criss-cross shoulder straps across baby's chest, and around chair back, criss-cross and thru D-rings and tie straps.)

4 - Or a safety seat for shopping carts. (Use directions from #3 above.)

5 - Or a safety seat for high chairs. (Use directions from #3 above.)

If baby falls asleep while on your back, use receiving blanket folded into a triangle to hold baby's head close to your body. Tuck corners of blanket under shoulder straps, or simply use a shawl around baby and yourself.

EXHIBIT 2 List of Activities (copied from handwritten notes)

Sept '88
> Letter of credit - #1 for $53,000
> Manufacturing Order - # 1 Thaw, 5,300paks
> Miscellaneous - Incorporate

Oct. '88
> Loan on A/R, Bank Pays - #1 Box co. $3,500 for 5,000, R. Mann $1,000
> Box Orders - #1, 5,300 boxes
> Miscellaneous - Work with R. Mann on box design

Nov. '88
> Make Sales - 2,400 pks to Kids R Us, Target
> Miscellaneous - Source RSVP better price on pak mfg.

Dec. '88
> Box Orders - Receive Box #1
> Payments to others - Box co $1,590 #1

Jan. '89
> Letter of credit - LOC for run #2
> Loan on A/R, Bank Pays - Loan on A/R - Pays Thaw $53,000
> Manufacturing Order - Order Thaw 5,000 pks #2
> Deliver to Stores - 5,000 pks to Toys R Us #1, 100 pks to REI, run #1

Feb. '89
> Receive payment from stores - REI $1,500, apply to box co #2
> Box Orders - Order box #2
> Payments to others - Box co, $1,500 #2

Apr. '89
> Letter of credit - LOC for run #3
> Payment to Bank - $60,000 #1
> Receive payment from stores - Toys R Us $75,000 less 3,000 hold back
> Manufacturing Order - 5,000 paks #3 Thaw
> Box Orders - Receive boxes #2
> Payments to others - Box co $1,500 #2

May '89
> Loan on A/R, Bank Pays - Loan on A/R #2
> Box Orders - Order boxes #3
> Deliver to Stores - 2,600 pks Toys R Us, 560 Kids R Us, 100 REI, 1,755 Target, run #2
> Payments to others - Box co $1,500 #3

Jun '89
> Make Sales - Large sales push for run #5 K Mart

Jul '89
> Letter of credit - LOC's for run #4
> Manufacturing Order - Thaw for 5,000 pks #4
> Box Orders - Receive box #3
> Make Sales - Dallas trade show
> Payments to others - Box co $15,00 #3
> Miscellaneous -

Aug. '89
> Loan on A/R, Bank - Loan on A/R #3
> Payment to Bank - Pay $50,150 on loan #2
> Receive payment from stores - $75,000
> Deliver to Stores - 2,600 pks to Toys R Us, 560 Kids R Us, 100 REI, 1,755 Target, run #3

EXHIBIT 2 **(continued)**

Payments to others - Box co $1500   #4

Oct. '89

Letter of credit - For run #5
Manufacturing Order - Thaw run #5, 13265 pks
Box Orders - Receive boxes #4
Payments to others - Box co $1,500 $4

Nov. '89

Loan on A/R, Bank - Loan on A/R #4
Payment to Bank - $50,150 From Thaw #3
Box Orders - Order box #5, 0.47/box, 13,265 pks
Deliver to Stores - 2,600 toys R Us, 560 Kids R Us, 100 REI, 1,755 Target, run #4

Jan. '90

Letter of credit - LOC #6
Manufacturing Order - 13,265 pks, Thaw, #6
Box Orders - Receive box #5 for 13265 pks, $3,117, 0.47/box
Payments to others - Box co $3,117

Feb. '90

Loan on A/R, Bank - $132,650 on #5
Payment to Bank - pay on #4
Receive payment from stores - Receive #4, $75,000
Box Orders - #6 for 13,265 pks, $3,117
Deliver to Stores - #6, 5,015 Service PX, 8,250 K-Mart
Payments to others - Box c $3,117

Apr. '90

Letter of credit - #7
Manufacturing Order - 13,265 pks, Thaw #7
Box Orders - Receive #6 for 13,265 pks, $3,117
Payments to others - Box co, $3,117

May '90

Loan on A/R, Bank pays Thaw- $132,650 onA/R #6
Payment to Bank - #5
Receive payment from stores - Receive #5 for $198,975
Box Orders - Order box #7 for 13,265 pks, $3,117
Deliver to Stores - #6 to first yr accts 5,015 and to K-Mart 8,250
Payments to others - Box co, $3,117

Jul. '90

Letter of credit - #8
Manufacturing Order - Thaw #8 for 13,265 pks
Box Orders - #7 for 13,265 pks, $3,117
Make Sales - Dallas show
Payments to others - Box co. $3,117

Aug. '90

Loan on A/R, Bank Pays Thaw - $132,650 on #7
Payment to Bank - Pay #6
Receive payment from stores - #6 for $195,975
Box Orders - #8 for 13,265 pks $3,117
Deliver to Stores - ## to first yr accts 5,015, to K-Mart 8,250

EXHIBIT 2   (concluded)

      Payments to others - Box co, $3,117

Oct. '90

      Letter of credit - #9
      Manufacturing Order - Thaw #9
      Box Orders - Receive #8 for 13,265 pks $3,117
      Deliver to Stores - #8 to first yr accts 5,015, to K-Mart 8,250
      Payments to others - Box co $3,117

Nov. '90

      Loan on A/R, Bank Pays Thaw - $132,650 on A/R #8
      Payment to Bank - Pay #7
      Receive payment from stores - #7 for $198,975

Feb. '91

      Payment to Bank - #8
      Receive payment from stores - #8 for $198,975

      Deliver to Stores - #9

EXHIBIT 3a   Financial Forecast Sept. '88 - Aug. '89   (copied from handwritten notes)

	Sep'88	Oct'88	Nov'88	Dec'88	Jan'89	Feb'89	Mar'89	Apr'89	May'89	Jun'89	Jul'89	Aug'89	Totals
Revenue													
Toys R Us								72,000			37,440		109,440
4% Hold Back						1,500					1,500		3,000
REI													
40 Sm. Specialty											3,000		3,000
Kids R Us											3,375		3,375
Toys R Us Canada											1,125		1,125
Toys R Us Intnl											900		900
Target													
K-Mart											26,325		26,325
Total Revenue						1,500		72,000			73,665		147,165
Cost of Sales													
Thaw					53,000				50,150			50,150	153,300
Eagle Box		5,300		1,590		1,500		1,500	1,500		1,500		12,890
Richard Marin		1,000											1,000
Total Cost of Sales		6,300	—	1,590	53,000	1,500	—	1,500	51,650	—	1,500	50,150	167,190
Gross Profit		(6,300)		(1,590)	(53,000)	—		70,500	(51,650)		72,165	(50,150)	(20,025)
Expenses													
Salaries $1K Each								2,000	2,000	2,000	2,000	2,000	10,000
Payroll													
Outside Services													
Supplies													
Repairs and Maint													
Advertising													
Deliv and Travel													
Acctg and Legal			1,500							1,500	1,500		4,500
Rent		50	50	50	50	50	50	50	50	50	50	50	550
Telephone		20	24	24	24	24	24	24	24	24	24	24	260
Utilities													
Insurance			200	98	98	98	98	98	98	98	98	98	1,082
Other Expenses													
Total Expenses		70	1,774	172	172	172	172	2,172	2,172	3,672	3,672	2,172	16,392
Net													(36,417)

EXHIBIT 3b Financial Forecast, Sept. '89–Aug. '90 (copied from handwritten notes)

	Sep'89	Oct'89	Nov'89	Dec'89	Jan'90	Feb'90	Mar'90	Apr'90	May'90	Jun'90	Jul'90	Aug'90	Totals
Revenue													
Toys R Us			37,440			37,440			37,440			37,440	149,760
4% Hold Back		3,000				1,560			1,560			1,560	7,680
REI			1,500			1,500			1,500			1,500	6,000
40 Sm. Specialty			3,000			3,000			3,000			3,000	12,000
Kids R Us			3,375			3,375			3,375			3,375	13,500
Toys R Us Canada			1,125			1,125			1,125			1,125	4,500
Toys R Us Intnl			900			900			900			900	3,600
Target			26,325			26,325			26,325			26,325	105,300
K-Mart									123,750			123,750	247,500
Total Revenue		3,000	73,665			75,225			198,975			198,975	549,840
Cost of Sales													
Thaw			50,150			132,650			132,650			132,650	448,100
Eagle Box		1,500	3,117		3,117	3,117		3,117	3,117		3,117	3,117	23,319
Total		1,500	53,267		3,117	135,767		3,117	135,767		3,117	135,767	471,419
Gross Profit													
Expenses													
Salaries $1K ea.	2,000	2,000	2,000	2,000	2,000	2,000	2,000	2,000	2,000	2,000	2,000	2,000	24,000
Payroll													
Outside Services													
Supplies													
Repairs and Maint													
Advertising											1,500		1,500
Deliv and Travel													
Acctg and Legal	50	50	50	50	50	50	50	50	50	50	50	50	600
Rent													
Telephone	24	24	24	24	24	24	24	24	24	24	24	24	288
Utilities													
Insurance	98	200	98	98	98	98	98	98	98	98	98	98	1,278
Other Expenses													
Total Expenses	2,172	2,274	2,172	2,172	2,172	2,172	2,172	2,172	2,172	2,172	3,672	2,172	27,666
Net													

EXHIBIT 3c Financial Forecast, Sept. '90- Aug. '91 (copied from handwritten notes)

	Sep'90	Oct'90	Nov'90	Dec'90	Jan'91	Feb'91	Mar'91	Apr'91	May'91	Jun'91	Jul'91	Aug'91	Totals
Revenue													
Toys R Us			37,440			37,440							
4% Hold Back			1,560			1,560		1,560		1,560		1,560	
REI			1,500			1,500							
40 Sm. Specialty			3,000			3,000							
Kids R Us			3,375			3,375							
Toys R Us Canada			1,125			1,125							
Toys R Us Intnl			900			900							
Target			26,325			26,325							
K-Mart			123,750			123,750							
Total Revenue			198,975			198,975		0		0		0	
Cost of Sales													
Thaw			132,650			198,975							
Eagle Box		3,117											
Total		3,117	132,650			198,975							
Gross Profit		(3,117)	17,425					1,560		1,560		1,560	266,863
Expenses													
Salaries $1K ea	2,000	2,000	2,000	2,000									
Payroll													
Outside Services													
Supplies													
Repairs and Maint													
Advertising													
Deliv. and Travel													
Acctg and Legal	50	50	50	50									
Rent													
Telephone	24	24	24	24									
Utilities													
Insurance	200	98	98	98									
Other Expenses													
Total Expenses	2,274	2,172	2,172	2,172									

Chapter 2

Ideas

❏ SUBCHAPTER 2A - Searching Methods

"How can I find a good new venture idea?" Usually, effective answers to this question either come easily or not at all. For most entrepreneurs the ideas, in hindsight, apparently came by themselves, unanticipated, often somewhat by surprise. They arose seemingly unbidden—from work, hobbies, acquaintances and everyday observations—as the result of unforeseen events.

Trying to force the process by *deliberately* looking for ideas is a much harder way to find good ones. But if simply waiting and hoping for coincidence is not enough, there may be no choice except to search. Some methods for doing that will be described in this chapter, following a look at historical experience.

From hindsight, it seems that there have been many new business opportunities which could have been found earlier if only someone had searched for them. Federal Express could have been done earlier. Collecting and selling replacement parts for antique houses, which turned out to be the basis of a successful mail order enterprise, could also have been done earlier. The shipping container industry and discount securities brokerage came from still other ideas that waited for someone to discover them.

How could other people have made those discoveries by deliberate searching? What knowledge would they have needed? What searching strategy would have done most to increase their odds of discovering opportunities? Could those same strategies be useful for discovering other opportunities that are as yet undiscovered, lying in wait now to be found and exploited? What could an individual adopt as a search procedure to find a venture idea? This chapter will explore those questions.

How Entrepreneurs Find Ideas

Considering the importance of business ideas in new ventures, it seems surprising that where original venture concepts come from has not been given much systematic study. From informal review of case histories on start-ups written by students at the University of Washington, it appears that the most common source is prior employment (e.g., the employer fails to follow through on a business opportunity and an employee leaves to pursue it independently), followed by hobbies, and then other sources such as social encounters, in that order. When systematic venture searching turns up in the histories, it is usually linked to acquisition as a mode of entry, rather than start-up of a new firm.

A 1988 study by Koller[1] of 82 entrepreneurs randomly selected from the Yellow Pages found that most entrepreneurs:

- Recognized, rather than sought out, business opportunities.

- Learned of opportunities from someone else (business associates, relatives and social contacts, in that order)

- And found them in fields where they had work experience. (Especially frequent was the response that they were attracted to the opportunity because it offered a chance to apply their prior training.)

Koller also found that 33 percent had entered via takeover rather than start-up. His study did not discuss how their opportunity discovery patterns differed, if at all, from those of new company founders.

A very different sample is that of the *Inc.* 500 fastest growing companies. A 1989 survey by the magazine asked the founders of those companies where they first got their venture ideas. Most (43 percent) said their ideas came from work. As can be seen in Table 2-1 below, the other categories of idea sources could overlap, either with this category (e.g., "saw an unfilled niche") or with others, such as hobbies, which was credited with only 3 percent of the ideas.

Table 2-1   Where *Inc.* 500 Founders Got Venture Ideas

Source	Percent
Got idea while working in same industry	43%
Saw someone else try, figured I could do better	15
Saw unfilled niche in consumer marketplace	11
Did systematic search for business opportunities	7
Can't really explain it	5
Got idea from hobby or avocational interest	3
Other	16
Total	100%

Summarizing the results of this *Inc.* study, the author, John Case, observed:

> *More common than the out of the blue inspirations were the explicable ones, the ideas that caught their creators by surprise, but in retrospect seem pretty logical…. The mythology of entrepreneurship celebrates such serendipity, propagating an image of the lone company-inventor suddenly flashing on the idea of a lifetime—and sometimes it happens that way.*

> *Typically, though, the idea for a fast-growing business appears in much more pedestrian fashion. The structure of a marketplace shifts, maybe ever so slightly. A new niche opens up. And all at once people… who may never have expected to become entrepreneurs, are out on their own and amazed by their own success.*[2]

Finally, in another quite different sampling of members of the National Federation of Independent Businesses, a survey by Cooper et al. asked owners of 2,994 firms the question: "Where did you get the idea to go into this kind of business?" Again, the most frequent answer was "prior job," which accounted for 43 percent. Second most frequent, accounting for 18 percent, was a hobby or personal interest. Next came chance events (10 percent) and suggestions by others (8 percent). Interestingly enough, this was closely followed by "education/courses." Also interesting was the fact that those firms which did not survive the first year drew upon the same sources with about the same frequency, as seen in Table 2-2, which was derived from the study.[3]

Table 2-2 Where NFIB Founders Got Venture Ideas

Idea Sources	For percent of Firms Found to Be			
	Discontinued	Sold	Surviving	Total Sample
Prior Job	42%	38%	43%	43%
Hobby/Personal Interest	18	16	18	18
Chance Event	10	13	10	10
Someone Suggested It	9	12	7	8
Education/Courses	6	3	6	6
Family Business	5	5	6	6
Activities of Friends/Relatives	6	6	5	5
Other	4	7	5	5
Total	100%	100%	100%	100%

How an entrepreneur's behavior may influence favorable chance events or new business opportunities has been studied very little. An exception is an investigation by Kaish and Gilad[4] that compared behaviors presumed to constitute opportunity search of entrepreneurs versus managers and of entrepreneurs after success versus entrepreneurs before venture success. These authors distinguished (1) *sources* of information from which opportunities might be discovered, such as reading and personal contacts, (2) *alertness* to information that might reveal venture opportunities, and (3) *cues* in the information that suggest the presence of venture opportunity.

They also found that entrepreneurs appeared to engage more than managers do in solitary pursuit of ideas through reading and introspection, and to get ideas from such sources as patent filings and strangers. Managers tended to draw more on subordinates, professional acquaintances, customers, and consultants. Managers paid more attention to issues of profit and market, while entrepreneurs focused more on "implementing factors" such as deal participants, government, and capital needed. After succeeding, entrepreneurs appeared to become averse to seeking business ideas through conversations. The authors suggested that success may reduce feelings of need for new business opportunities. Another possibility is that opportunities may more readily present themselves to successful entrepreneurs without the need for search through a *sidestreet effect*—starting a venture is like entering an avenue down whose sidestreets opportunities previously invisible start to appear as progress occurs.

An investigation by Teach, Schwartz and Tarpley[5] of relationships between idea sources and subsequent venture performance in software firms found some indication that firms founded on "accidentally" discovered venture ideas which had not been subjected to formal screening or planning tended to break even faster and double their break-even sales faster than firms whose founders used more formal techniques of search and planning. Apparently, the founders of "non-formal" firms were also more able to manage with their own funds as opposed to using others' money. This may indicate that it is better to win by luck than effort. However, later it appeared that total sales levels for the different groups were essentially the same.

Application: *How much does it matter where the entrepreneur in the assigned case discovered the idea for the venture?*

Limitations of the statistics in studies to date include: (1) they don't say much about connections between idea sources and just how the ideas come about, and (2) there is no indication of how they may apply in any individual case. To learn more about these questions, a closer look at the following examples may help.

Prior Job

When Louis Krouse suggested to his employer, the NYNEX telephone company, that it consider the idea of arranging for lower income utility customers without checking accounts to pay their bills someplace besides utility offices, which are scarce, and banks, which lose money on such transactions, NYNEX told him to investigate further. An experimental project in Albany worked, but NYNEX decided not to carry it further and instead suggested that Krouse pursue it himself.

Quitting his job, Krouse formed National Payments Network, Inc. (NPN) to collect for companies such as NYNEX for 50 cents per payment (less than banks charge.) He then persuaded retail stores, such as Seven-Eleven, for about 10 cents per payment to allow customers to pay through them. From the stores' standpoint this helps draw customers. In each store a point of sale terminal transmits payment to a central computer, which in turn arranges electronic funds transfer from the stores to the utilities. Founded in 1986, NPN was processing over $2 billion by 1988.[6]

Recreation

In 1989 Scott Griffiths formed a baseball team at his advertising agency, named it the Rhino Chasers, and had the name emblazoned on T-shirts and hats. He also made up labels with the name and pasted them on bottles of beer for post-game parties. People began asking where they could obtain that brand of beer. Griffiths sought out a local micro brewery to manufacture the product and within a year was shipping 800 cases per month.[7]

Chance Event

Tom Stemberg had worked 12 years in the supermarket industry, starting as a management trainee with Star Market and rising to head of sales and merchandising. He then became division president of another supermarket chain, Edwards-Finast, where he developed a warehouse food business, but then had a falling out with higher management and was fired.

With a year's severance pay he was looking for a job and potential start-up ideas when he visited a discount warehouse in Langhorne, Pennsylvania, for an employment interview. In the store he noticed that the office supplies section was a shambles: empty boxes, torn packages and goods spilled on the floor. He concluded that "this merchandise was moving very fast." Checking with industry analysts, he found that only 100 items in office supply sections accounted for up to 7 percent of the volume in such stores.

He now envisaged a chain of discount stores selling just office supplies. Instead of buying from the half dozen major wholesalers who sold such supplies to retail stores, he would buy from manufacturers and sell direct as did Toys 'R Us. Rather than continuing his job search, he next wrote a business plan and took it to potential venture capital sources. The result was that "dozens of offers poured in." One venture capitalist commented that Stemberg "wasn't proposing just a chain of stores, but an entirely new retailing category. That really catches your attention. It slaps you in the face with the idea that this could be big." The deal chosen included $4 million in the first round and $31 million in three later rounds.

The first Staples store opened on the outskirts of Boston in 1986. Not until 1989 did the company report a profit. But then it was $858,000 on $24.8 million in sales. In April of that year the company raised another $62 million through public offering.[8]

These three examples illustrate only part of the wide range of ways new venture opportunities and ideas are discovered. In each, the role of past experience and unforeseen events can be seen. Also, in each case the opportunity was available for discovery by others. Only in the third example does it appear that the entrepreneur was actively searching, but even there the discovery came by surprise.

Application: *How many other people should have been in as good a position to discover the idea for this venture as the entrepreneur in the assigned case? Where might they be found?*

Discovery Questions

Although would-be entrepreneurs usually don't discover ideas by a deliberate searching strategy (except when pursuing acquisitions of ongoing firms), it is nevertheless possible to impute to their discoveries some implicit searching patterns. These are illustrated by the following questions.

Search

Venture ideas may be prompted by search questions which put the mind into a mode where it might be presumed to try different combinations and to seek answers which may turn out to be product and service ideas. This searching process may well operate subconsciously. Evidence that it happened might be presumed to appear when the mind pushes an idea forward to a conscious level. Search questions might include:

1. ___ What is bothering me? a.___ What might relieve that bother?

2. ___ What else might I like to have?

3. ___What is a.___a situation where something is missing, or b.___ what else might anyone else like to have? (that I might be able to provide)

4. ___What is a.___ missing in a certain situation or b.___ bothering anyone else? c.___ What might satisfy that need?

5. ___ How could this be made or be done differently than it is now?

6. ___ How could this be made or be done better than it is now?

7. ___ What could I make or do with this a.___ resource or b.___ situation that I might want?

8. ___ What could I make or do with this? (that anyone else might want)

9. ___ What do I have the capability to make or provide for a.___ this situation or b.___ others, that might satisfy the want?

10. ___ How can I follow the family tradition?

11. ___ How can I do what I like doing?

Encounter

Idea prompting may occur from encounter with (1) someone else's idea, (2) a customer request or (3) some other event. Questions by which this process might produce a business idea include:

12. ___ Somebody has asked me to provide them with something. a.___Is it something I could provide?

13. ___ Has this a.__ event, b.__ development or c.__ circumstance change, created an opportunity I could seize?

14. ___ That seems to be done badly a.___ Could there be a way to do it better? (Or b.___ could I do it better?)

15. ___ People went for this same thing elsewhere. a.___ Could I play some role in providing it to a broader market?

16. ___ People went for something like (though not exactly the same as) this elsewhere. a.___ Could I play some role in providing it to a broader market?

17. ___ This seems like a straightforward advance on what is working now. a.___ Could I play a role in providing it to a broader market?

18. ___ I like this thing I encountered by accident. a.___ Could I play a role in providing it to a broader market?

Evaluation

Evaluative reactions to a prompted idea might be:

19. ___ Could I do this job I have on my own instead of as an employee?

20. ___ I wonder if other people might like this idea. a.___ If I were they, would I like it?

21. ___ I like the idea. I'll make one for me. If I like it, maybe others will too. a.___ I wonder if others might like this.

22. ___ Somebody has asked me to provide them with something. a.___If this person whom I have encountered wants it, might others too?

23. ___ People went for this elsewhere. a.___ Might they here too?

24. ___ People went for something like this elsewhere. a.___ Might they here too?

25. ___ Should I take over this enterprise a.___ found through search, or b.___as a result of encountering a seller's initiative.

26. ___ Will doing this give me greater satisfaction than what I'm doing now?

Action Decisions

Decisions to take action might take such forms as:

27. ___ I think people will want this. a.___ So I'll offer it, b.___ and see if they go for it, or c.___and I'm sure it will succeed.

28. ___ I like this, so I suppose others will. I'll offer it.

29. ___ This seems like a straightforward advance on what works now. So I will carry it out a.___ because I believe it will work, or b.___ to see how it will work.

Application: *Which idea discovery questions might do most to help reveal possible improvements in the entrepreneur's most promising venture idea so far? How could those be pursued?*

Innovation Inevitability

Each new venture is an innovation. It, like a person, is individual. Though perhaps very similar in some ways to some other enterprises, it will always have differences. Even if the venture is a franchise that follows all the formats and procedures of the parent firm, the address and immediate surroundings, phone number, employee(s) and combinations of customers will still be different. If the venture is independent rather than a franchise, then its product or service, ways of doing things, logo, decor, hours and prices will be individualized. The success of the venture may be determined by such differences.

Mental Blocks to Departure

Departure can be regarded as having two components: divergence and direction. Hence, generation of an innovative idea as a mental goal can be divided into two tasks. One is to depart from the beaten path. The other is to direct that departure in an effective way. Each of these two tasks has its own set of obstacles to be overcome. And for each of these obstacles there are techniques that might be applied as part of a deliberate search strategy in a divergent mode of thinking.

Obstacles to the first task, that of departing from what is customary, include the following "blocks":[9]

1. **Perceptual Blocks**

    a. Failing to notice clues to opportunity at all.
    b. Difficulty viewing it from different perspectives.
    c. Delimiting the opportunity too closely or too conventionally.
    d. Seeing only what you expect to see or think others expect you to see.
    e. Saturation: perceptual numbness.
    f. Failing to use all sensory inputs available.

2. **Emotional Blocks**

    a. Lack of challenge or interest in a new opportunity.
    b. Excess zeal, tunnel vision, insufficient patience to see ways of exploiting it.
    c. Fear of failure and/or risk.
    d. Intolerance of ambiguity; obsession with security, order.
    e. Preference for judging rather than seeking ideas.
    f. Inability to relax, incubate after strong effort on idea search.

3. **Cultural Blocks**

   a. Disdain for fantasy, reflection, idea playfulness, humor.

   b. Belief that reason, logic, numbers is superior to feeling, intuition, pleasure.

   c. Thinking that tradition is preferable to change.

   d. Feeling that analytic thinking is the truly correct way to contemplate business.

   e. Accepting that taboos are taboo.

4. **Imagination Blocks**

   a. Fear of subconscious thinking.

   b. Inhibition about some areas of imagination.

   c. Compulsions such as worry, order, activity.

   d. Confusion between reality and fantasy.

5. **Environmental Blocks**

   a. Distrust of others who might help.

   b. Distractions.

   c. Unavailability of supporting elements.

   d. Discouraging responses of other people to ideas (devil's advocates).

   e. Too much else to do and disinclination to rearrange priorities.

6. **Intellectual Blocks**

   a. Lack of information or incorrect information.

   b. Ineffective application of formal idea-generating techniques.

   c. Misperception of the situation.

   d. Intimidating or distracting weakness of formal skills such as break-even or cash flow analysis.

7. **Expressive Blocks**

   a. Lack of facility in writing, speaking, drawing, or constructing prototypes.

Working from a list such as this, a creatively inclined reader should readily be able to generate a companion list of antidotes for coping with each of the blocks.

Application: *If the entrepreneur in the assigned case fails to find a most promising way to improve on the venture idea(s) presently in view, which mental block will most likely be the reason, and what might be done about it?*

Findings about Creativity

Those who have studied processes for seeking good ideas have found, through controlled experimentation, the following:

1. There is no correlation between IQ and creativity in the normal range. IQ generally correlates with school ability.[10] But it is possible to be low in IQ and very successful in business or high in IQ and unsuccessful as an entrepreneur.

2. Deliberate practice in idea generation can raise idea generation rates of individuals.[11]

3. Effects of such practice do persist with time, although they also decay if not maintained.[12]

4. Suspending judgment and deliberately withholding criticism (no matter how weird the idea seems) increases idea output.[13]

5. Quantity of ideas tends to beget quality.[14]

6. Seeking cleverness in ideas tends to beget fewer, but more clever ideas.[15]

7. Better ideas tend to come later in idea-generating sessions. Best ideas may come days, weeks or longer after deliberate idea generating efforts.[16]

8. Many heads produce more good ideas than one person alone. But sometimes the best ideas come from individuals operating alone.

Clearly, there are contradictions in some of these patterns, and individuals must impose judgments to strike compromises between such things as freedom versus focus and search versus evaluation. However, there do seem to be similarities in mental sequences through which outstanding ideas have been discovered in a variety of fields, including entrepreneurship. Identifiable phases in the creative process seem to be:[17]

1. **Preparation** in which the searcher acquires knowledge and skills, most often through work or hobbies, related to the venture opportunity to be discovered.

2. **Searching**, which may involve periods when the individual wants to find new directions of activity and reflects about the possibilities for doing so. Looking back later, a person who discovered a successful venture idea

may recollect, "I always wanted to have my own business, but I needed...."

3. **Frustration** arises when the opportunity or better idea does not crop up when desired. Consequently, the searcher stops reflecting and moves on to other things.

4. **Incubation** takes place subconsciously while the individual is engaged in mundane activities (such as showering or commuting) quite unrelated to searching.

5. **Discovery** occurs quite unexpectedly, perhaps as the result of an external event or change in circumstances, or possibly from revelation inside the seeker's mind.

Tactics for Departure

To help in idea generation, those who have studied and practiced creative proficiency have generated many suggestions, including the following:

1. Try different ways of looking and thinking about venture opportunities.

2. Work at being prolific in ideas about both what the opportunities are and how they might be exploited.

3. Seek leads from other people, not necessarily opportunities per se, but clues such as problems or unmet needs that might lead to them. Potential sources of leads include business and personal contacts, trade shows, government and private technology licensing offices. Making new contacts and asking for help lead to other contacts.

4. Don't be discouraged by others' negative views. Devil's advocates are plentiful. Experts in the past have predicted impossibility for gas turbines, atomic power, FM radios, and powered flight.

5. Avoid stating negative views until you have generated possible solutions for obstacles. Then offer the solutions rather than problems. (This alone will make you much rarer than devil's advocates and hence higher in market value.)

6. Set quotas and deadlines for identifying potential opportunities, but be open to opportunities that may come later from incubation.

7. When going to bed command your mind either to dream about possible needs or to find solutions to them.

8. Resist the temptation to accept ideas that come early or ideas that meet primarily your own needs. Reach for solutions that might be useful to others able to pay for them.

9. Use idea-generating tricks such as:

    • Brainstorming with formal rules, such as not criticizing, piggybacking ideas and seeking quantity

    • Elaborating on ideas that emerge

    • Considering multiple consequences of possible future events or changes

    • Rearranging, reversing, expanding, shrinking combining or altering ideas

    • Fantasizing, developing scenarios

    • Listing attributes, criteria and possible characteristics of alternative approaches in parallel columns, then randomly connecting items from column to column

    • Identifying with a situation or object and imagine what that would be like or what might make it better

    • Developing analogies between different circumstances, times or aspects of nature

10. Reach beyond the ordinary in seeking opportunities or ways of exploiting them. If you don't reach as far as ideas that make you laugh, you are being too conservative.

11. Discuss with others what you would like to find in the way of business opportunities. Learn what their aspirations are and whether you could work together.

12. Critique an existing product or service. List ways of improving on it that you might be able to sell.

Application: *In rank order, which five departure tactics would most likely lead to improvement on the venture idea(s) presently seen by the entrepreneur(s) in the assigned case? Should those tactics be applied?*

Supplementary Reading

New Venture Strategies Chapter 5. (Vesper, K.H., Prentice-Hall, 1990)
New Venture Mechanics Chapter 1. (Vesper, K. H., Prentice-Hall, 1993)

In-Class Exercises

1. In five minutes, list as many possible uses as you can for a brick. First work individually, then join with a group and add to the list. Consider the differences in the productivity of ideas (1) between individuals, (2) depending upon the approach taken, and (3) of individuals versus groups.

2. On a sheet of paper, draw nine dots in a rectangular arrangement, three rows of three, each equally spaced with a half-inch between them. See if you can con-

nect them by drawing four straight lines without lifting your pen or pencil from the paper.

3. How can you enlarge a square window that is two feet high and two feet wide while keeping it square without making it any higher than two feet or any wider than two feet?

4. How can you plant ten trees, four trees to a row in five straight rows?

Homework Exercises

1. Venture Idea Search: Please refer to description in Exercise 4, Subchapter 1A, page 16.

2. Interview one or more entrepreneurs and inquire about how they came upon their venture ideas. Carry out question #1 under Venture History below. Compare the patterns and comment on the similarities and differences.

3. Set up an idea notebook for collecting potential business ideas. On the first page make a list of approaches to try. On the second page (more if needed) make a timetable for exploring those ideas. On succeeding pages keep a diary of approaches tried. At the end, list what seem to be the best ideas in rank order and briefly describe steps for pursuing each of the top three. Make an assessment of how well the schedule fit the task, how much time per idea each of the approaches cost, which approach was most effective and why. Describe what would be the best approach to follow if the task were to be taken further.

4. Which of the tricks for generating ideas noted in the section of this chapter on Tactics for Departure do you think would be most effective for generating ideas in a one-hour period? Try two and compare results. Alternatively, try one, first alone, and then with one or more other people.

5. Read the example of Tom Stemberg again. Did this opportunity discovery have to be a chance event? Test your answer by visiting one or more stores and looking for potential opportunities by studying the store, the customers and what goes on. Perhaps in a brief effort no truly viable opportunity will appear. But which can you identify that is closest to viable? What would be the product or service? What, from your observation and possibly an interview or two, would be the makeup of a typical target customer?

6. Study three stores or other lines of business you can readily observe in action. Determine which you could come closest to competing with by analyzing how effectively they do their work and how their performance could be improved.

7. Interview two entrepreneurs and ascertain as well as you can what sequence each used in terms of the venture idea Discovery Questions of this chapter. Discuss the similarities and differences, and the degree to which there was any possible choice of sequence open to the individuals involved.

Venture History

1. Investigate the chain of thoughts through which the entrepreneur discovered the idea for his or her business. Using the list in the "Discovery Questions" section

above, and adding any other questions if needed, number in sequence the implicit series of mental questions that the entrepreneur seems to have gone through in discovering the venture idea(s).

2. Insofar as possible, list and/or describe the ideas that were passed up or rejected in favor of the one which the entrepreneur chose to pursue. Did anyone else pursue those ideas and demonstrate their level of viability?

3. Who else could have pursued the idea the entrepreneur chose? How did their positions for doing so compare?

Venture Planning Guide

1. Apply tactics for departure described in this chapter to expand your search for a viable business idea or to develop improvements for a chosen idea.

2. Keep a log of your search and occasionally note which approaches seem to be more effective for you and why.

Notes

[1] Roland H. Koller, "On the Source of Entrepreneurial Ideas," in *Frontiers of Entrepreneurship Research, 1988*, eds. Bruce A. Kirchhoff and others (Wellesley, Mass.: Babson Center for Entrepreneurial Studies, 1988), p. 194.

[2] John Case, "The Origins of Entrepreneurship," *Inc.*, June 1989, p. 54.

[3] Arnold C. Cooper and others, *New Business In America* (Washington, D.C.: The NFIB Foundation, 1990).

[4] Stanley Kaish and Benjamin Gilad, "Characteristics of Opportunities Search of Entrepreneurs Versus Executives," *Journal of Business Venturing*, 6, no. 1, January 1991, p. 45.

[5] Richard D. Teach, Robert G. Schwartz, and Fred A. Tarpley, "The Recognition and Exploitation of Opportunity in the Software Industry," in *Frontiers of Entrepreneurship Research 1989*, eds. Robert H. Brockhaus, Sr. and others (Wellesley, Mass.: Babson Center for Entrepreneurial Studies, 1989), p. 383.

[6] "The Emerging Entrepreneur," *Inc.*, January 1990, p. 59.

[7] "Where Packaging Is Job One," *Inc.*, June 1990, p. 30.

[8] Stephen D. Solomon, "Born To Be Big," *Inc.*, June 1989, p. 94.

[9] Developed based upon James L. Adams, "Individual and Small Group Creativity," *Engineering Education*, 63, November 1972.

[10] John P. Guilford, *The Nature of Human Intelligence* (New York, N.Y.: McGraw-Hill, 1967), p. 170.

[11] Sidney J. Parnes and H. F. Harding, *A Source Book For Creative Thinking* (New York: Charles Scribner's Sons, 1962), p.357.

[12] Ibid. p. 360.

[13] Guilford, *Human Intelligence*, p. 330.

[14] Parnes, *Creative Thinking*, p. 190.

[15] Guilford, *Human Intelligence*, p. 330.

[16] Parnes, *Creative Thinking*, p. 190.

[17] Calvin Taylor and Frank Birron, Scientific Creativity (New York: Wiley, 1963), p. 355.

❑ *SUBCHAPTER 2B - Imposing Direction*

The main emphasis in the techniques described above is to break free of present practices and enter new mental territory. That by itself leaves out the all-important need to discover not just a new idea, but one that usefully exploits a profitable opportunity. Ideas, per se, are limitless in number, and almost all those "off the beaten path" are useless. It is the rare ones with value that must be found, and this imposes a need for direction on the search.

Role of Information

To pay off, mental departure in quest of opportunity must be guided by knowledge of some sort. That knowledge may come from work or hobbies, as indicated earlier. Or it may come from school. Engineers are taught, for example, that nobody has ever found a way to make a perpetual motion machine, and also what the physical laws are that make this so. Hence, they don't waste time on ideas that violate those laws. Information about a new technology that does work can also be a helpful guide. With it, a would-be entrepreneur can go searching for the market that wants something that technology can do. Thus, one type of information helpful for guidance in searching is knowledge about what is not technologically possible as well as what is.

A second helpful type of information concerns what a market is likely to want. With a potential market desire in mind a would-be entrepreneur can go searching for a profitable way to satisfy it. Obtaining useful entrepreneurial information of either type and recognizing the value of that information are both necessary tasks. Either task may or may not come easily, depending on circumstance and mental programming. Information about what markets want can come through observing what goes on naturally, asking questions of other people, or conducting formal market research. In the following example recognition of the magnitude of an opportunity did not occur until after the venture had begun.

> Once he had put so much work into rebuilding the Altair, though, Millard thought he might just as well try to sell his version of the small computer. He called his adaptation the IMSAI 8080, and placed a one-inch ad announcing its availability in *Popular Electronics*.
>
> What happened next? "You ought to picture this," Millard told us. "I mean, here are five people—two of whom are myself and my wife—in this little place in San Leandro. And we're just trying to survive, okay? The mailman came in with the mail sack. We got 3,500 responses to our ad—our little one-inch ad."[1]

The information that came from experiments like Millard's in turn prompted other entrepreneurs to perceive the existence of opportunity. This was illustrated by the subsequent start-up of Osborne Computer. Adam Osborne recalled that he was able to predict sales of his own company, thanks to his observation of what had been going on in the new microcomputer industry, as follows.

> *Taking into account the one-month slip, my original plan proved remarkably realistic. As anticipated, we were able to sell everything we could build. For dealers the Osborne I was a "cash cow."*[2]

Osborne's decision to build the Osborne I which led initially to success was based on knowledge he obtained as a writer about the computer industry. For technical work of the actual design, however, he needed further knowledge he did not possess, and so he hired it. In the longer term, Osborne made decisions less effective than those of competitors, and his venture went bankrupt. Those competitors who succeeded in the longer term probably possessed better information and sometimes made blind choices that turned out to be luckier than Osborne's.

Information sources actually used by owner-managers of small firms listed customers first and foremost (see Table 2-3) and suppliers next, according to a study by Fann and Smeltzer.[3] The sources most used after that depended on the type of decision making, whether operational or longer term.

Table 2-3 Rank of Information Sources for Operational Decision Making versus Long-term Planning in Owner-Managed Firms

Source	Rank	
	Operational Decision Making	Long-term Planning
Customers	1	1
Suppliers	2	2
Competitors	3	4
Trade publications	4	3
Other business people (non-competing)	5	6
Newspapers	6	10
Trade associations	7	5
Trade shows	8	8
Economic information		7
Government regulations		9

It would seem reasonable to suppose that the less familiar a field was to an entrepreneur, the more he or she would seek new information. Ironically, according to a study of 1,176 new ventures by Cooper, Folta and Woo,[4] the opposite seems to be the case. Information sources they considered included professionals such as accountants, bankers and lawyers, and less formal sources such as friends, business contacts and written materials. The authors suggest that entrepreneurs should beware of this pitfall, and note that the more entrepreneurs are confident about what they are doing, the less likely they are to inform themselves about a new project. Failure to seek adequate information for a project may be caused by overconfidence. Beguiling catch phrases such as "Bumblebees fly because they don't know that according to aerodynamics they can't," "Nothing great was ever accomplished without unwarranted optimism," and "We were successful because we were too ignorant to realize that what we did couldn't be done" may have some truth to them but may also be misleading. A helpful precaution may be to seek more counsel from others on important venture decisions whether it feels needed or not.

Application: *What facts should form the main boundaries within which "wild" alternatives for the assigned case venture should be selected?*

Individual Specifics

Awareness of precedent patterns from others' experiences may help. But the most important information for guiding an opportunity search is not about general types of opportunities, causes, strategies or idea sources. Rather, it is very specific information about particular individuals, technologies and circumstances. This information generally cannot be learned from publications but instead must come from encounters by the to-be entrepreneur with other individual people and events in the course of life.

Note in each of the following what role was played by prior information and by information that happened to be gained just prior to getting the business idea. It may be helpful to classify information according to when it was obtained relative to the date of start-up.

In 1981 Mark Swislow, a part-time MBA student, received a suggestion from a friend that he look into the possibility of producing dust covers for microcomputers to satisfy a marketing course assignment to select a market niche and research it. He and his friend rented a computer show booth and encountered enough interest in not-yet-made covers that they set up shop to make and sell them. By 1989 their company, Computer Coverup, Inc., employed 50 people.[5]

❖ ❖ ❖

Michael Dell acquired knowledge about microcomputers from hanging around computer stores as a boy. One thing that caught his attention was the large markup. "Let's say," he said, "that you buy a computer from a retail store, and you pay $4,000. The retailer sends $2,500 of that back to the manufacturer and keeps $1,500. The question I asked myself was: What was the retailer doing to earn his $1,500? Was he adding $1,500 of value to that machine for me, a knowledgeable computer buyer? The answer was no."

This inspired Dell to start selling computers. To make his product, he bought stripped-down IBM's and to them added options purchased from other suppliers. At first he sold through direct response advertisements, then through telemarketing, and finally through a sales force as well. At age 19 he entered the industry (in 1984), after competition had already squeezed many other entrants out. He not only survived this competition as a newcomer entering late, but he built a company which by 1989 had sales of over a quarter billion dollars.[6]

❖ ❖ ❖

The first clue that there might be an opportunity in "designer" toilet partitions came to actor, Greg Braendel via his cousin, Adrian Emck, who had designed them for an English company, Thrislington Sales, Ltd. Emck wanted to develop sales of the product in the U.S. and asked Braendel for help. Braendel discussed the idea with a U.S. architecture firm, then with the help of Thrislington's managing director, Brian Moore, went looking for a U.S. company to make them. After several discouraging responses in late 1989, according to *Inc.,* Braendel and Moore were sitting on the patio outside Braendel's Hollywood home. "Brian," said Braendel, "why don't I just manufacture the damn things myself?" "Bloody 'ell," he remembered Moore saying, "why not?" Braendel consequently formed a company, negotiated for rights from Thrislington, which already had all the manufacturing business it could handle abroad, and began organizing a team to enter business.[7]

❖ ❖ ❖

For Ken Girouard the information leading to a start-up began to flow after he made something on impulse. He recalled, "I had to make a birthday gift for a friend of mine, so I took a pair of sandals and sewed a big plastic banana and lemon on top of them. I really don't know why. Somebody saw them and asked me to make her five pairs for gifts. Then a stylist saw those, and she asked for three pairs and put them on an extra in a new James Bond movie. Then someone told me I should take them to this boutique the next time I was in New York City. I did, and they encouraged me to add big grapes and plastic flowers. They advised me to go to a trade show, which I did. Even though I didn't have a booth, I came back with 3,000 orders. I upgraded them to higher-quality sandals in neon colors, and I started packaging them in green mesh bags. I called them Fruit Flops. The detail can't be automated. I tried paying the local Girl Scouts to make them for me. What a nightmare. They had no concentration. 'This is stupid,' they kept saying. But in the first six months I have sold $18,000 worth of these - everywhere from St. Martin to Saudi Arabia to Chicago. I now have 14 reps. I had no idea there would be any demand for this, and I think it's hysterical."[8]

❖ ❖ ❖

The first information leading directly to Steve Bedowitz's business idea came from study of a market he undertook as partner in an advertising agency that was hired by a home siding wholesaler. From market data he observed that "siding was a $3 billion-a-year industry, and the biggest company I could find did $8 million. I said to myself, 'wait a minute.'" He and a partner invested $3,000 in 1979 to form Amre, Inc. and worked to avoid weaknesses of the existing small firms in the industry. They opened a storefront to avoid a "fly-by-night" image, obtained a Sears franchise to establish credibility, bought the best materials, followed a "tell the truth" policy and utilized computers to maximize efficiency. By 1989 they became the biggest company in the industry, with sales of over $250 million.[9]

In each of these examples it is clear that discovery of the venture idea and shaping it for implementation were influenced by both of the following two kinds of knowledge: first, knowledge that the entrepreneur had acquired along the way starting long before the idea discovery; second, knowledge that the entrepreneur came upon directly before the discovery which both facilitated and triggered the discovery. Sometimes the entrepreneurs took initiatives that gained them the information. Other information came to them apparently unbidden. Greater appreciation of how possession and acquisition of information help in idea discovery may be developed by applying the following questions to examples like those above.

1. What role did information play in these ideas coming to these people?

2. What did these people do to bring about their having effective information?

3. What could they or anyone else have done to influence the likelihood of receiving that information?

4. How else could the same idea have been found by the same person, or someone else, without the same information?

5. Who else probably had the information but did not benefit from using it to discover the idea?

6. Who else could have done the start-up better?

Application: *What would answers to the above questions be for this particular case entrepreneur's main venture idea?*

Something these examples illustrate is that discovery of venture ideas is not a matter of randomly looking around. Each venture is highly specific, as is each individual entrepreneur, and the information needed for idea discovery is similarly special. General looking may build habits that increase the odds of an individual picking up on ideas others might overlook. But the discovery probably will not occur immediately upon application of a search. More likely, persistence over time will be needed until fortunate coincidence adds the needed final element(s) of discovery.

3. Subdivide, for that segment, in another way. Considering the above segment, another way to subdivide, for example, might be into workdays versus holidays, or vacation days. For instance, choose workdays of adults aged 35-45.

4. Subdivide again; for instance, into parts of the day.

5. Eliminate, with care lest something good be lost, sectors of the last subdivision that do not fit at all, but keep the rest in view.

6. For those remaining sectors, brainstorm to identify possible problems to which solutions might be sought. Some of the example problems White suggests for the end-of-workday sector include (1) when work ends, I am tired, (2) traffic is frustrating on the way home from work, and (3) my feet are tired and hot. His list included 14 items beyond these three.

7. Narrow the above list (White's 14 items) to a smaller number (White picked four) by eliminating those whose fit with the criteria of step one are weakest.

8. List the remaining problem areas from step seven along one side of a worksheet and the criteria from step one across the top. Draw lines to make a matrix.

9. On the right side of the sheet list possible solutions to each of the problem areas. For traffic frustrations, White suggested possibly intelligent street signs that would reroute traffic to reduce congestion. For tired and hot feet he suggested slippers containing vibrators.

10. Assess the solution ideas against each of the criteria listed across the page-top and proceed with further testing on them.

White claims both entrepreneurs and established companies have found dozens of viable new product and service opportunities with this approach. He recommends group meetings for higher productivity. He also notes it is possible to perform a "reverse" market gap analysis by seeking out in already-served markets, suppliers that for one reason or another are not performing well and creating a venture to outperform them.

Alternative Venture Strategies

Another set of patterns to assimilate that may help later in recognizing opportunity includes the different alternative strategies new ventures can follow. One set of strategic patterns proposed in *New Venture Strategies*[11] includes the following:

- **New Product or Service** A study of 8,000 innovations revealed that small companies produced more of them than did large firms (55 percent vs. 45 percent), but often the start-ups with innovations were performed by people who gained their know-how from big firms. [12]

- **Parallel Competition** The most common strategic approach among new ventures is to do what others do, but a bit better, without being radically different.

- **Buying a Franchise** This strategy requires no ingenuity. It does call for care in selecting the franchisor, and it takes money to buy the franchise. Profits are usually reduced by royalty requirements, and freedom is restricted by the franchise contract.

- **Geographic Transfer** When a new business idea catches on in one locale it usually appears before long in others as well. Looking for new businesses that seem suitable for such transfer and then copying them in new regions is a feasible approach.

- **Exploiting Supply Shortage** Discovery that something is in short supply may come unbidden or it may be pursued by asking people, such as purchasing agents, what they are having trouble getting. Then the entrepreneurial task is to find a way to supply it.

- **Exploiting Unused Resources** These too may be discovered by accident. Mineral prospectors go looking for them, but they know just what they want to find and geologically where they are most likely to occur. Analogies in business are not easy to find.

- **Parent Company Sponsorship** This too requires credibility, usually borne of a track record plus a history of working with the parent company.

- **Government Sponsorship** The Federal Government's 400 laboratories are under mandate to work at transferring technology to small firms. What kinds of help the government gives, either as a customer or as a financing source for start-ups, shifts with time and political pressures. [13]

- **Acquiring a Going Concern** Of all the strategies for entering business, this one lends itself most readily to systematic searching. To find a good buy, however, can be difficult, and establishing credibility with the seller can be also.

Application: *Which of the above strategies apply to the entrepreneur in the assigned case's main venture idea and to what extent?*

Other elements of strategic choice in formulating a venture direction are numerous. They include such dimensions as:

Industry and competitors
Product/package/service differentiation and uniqueness
R&D and degree and rate of innovation
Product line breadth
Market segment focus and geographical breadth
Channels chosen for distribution
Quality targets
Price point
Advertising level and type
Promotion level and type
Type and clarity of image sought
Production, make or buy, and degree of vertical integration

In the search for a winning venture idea, it would be useful to know which combinations of such elements have a higher probability of success. But studies on winning combinations inevitably come up with mixed messages or, at best, general tendencies that apply in some cases but not in others. A study of 192 small manufacturing firms by Chaganti, et al.[14] for instance, reported that when competing firms placed a strong emphasis on promotion, those that stressed a quality image tended to fare better than average. When price competition was emphasized, firms with lower manufacturing costs tended to do better. In other environments, companies with broader product lines did better. However, this was on the average. What will win for a particular venture idea cannot be foreseen, only guessed at.

Guidance from Others

An uncommon but sometimes highly effective way to focus a business idea search is to pick a field of technology, recruit partners who are expert in it, and let them narrow the choices. In the mid-1950s, for instance, a number of successful start-ups were created by engineers and scientists such as Ramo and Wooldridge (co-founders of what eventually became TRW, a New York Stock Exchange listed company), who, having worked for defense contractors, formed expert teams to seek defense contracts on their own. Eventually, they expanded from defense contracts into commercial markets, usually either by acquiring other companies or being acquired by other companies.

More recently, the creation of Calgene, a genetic engineering company, illustrates this pattern of imposing direction on the venture idea through recruitment of people with special know-how.

Norman Goldfarb, an electrical engineer whose technical experience had been limited to semiconductors, read about how Robert Swanson had telephoned Herbert Boyer, a world-renowned gene-splicing expert at Stanford University, and persuaded Boyer to join him in founding Genentech in 1976. By 1981 that venture had become the world's leading company in pharmaceutical biotechnology and made its founders rich. Despite his lack of experience in the field, Goldfarb decided to try the same pattern in plant, as opposed to human, biotechnology. He telephoned a famous plant geneticist, Daniel Cohen, at the University of California at Davis and persuaded him to collaborate in founding Calgene, a company that would specialize in the genetic engineering of plants to create better agricultural products. Goldfarb wrote a business plan, invested $500,000 from his family's trust, and recruited still other plant geneticists and outside venture capital.

Some products created by the geneticists failed: corn plants modified to fix nitrogen did so, but failed to produce corn. But other products succeeded: a tomato containing a third less water consequently cost less to ship. Enough developments showed high promise to multiply the company's total equity investment of $9 million up to a cash-out for investors of $85 million in six years.[15]

Not Over-narrowing

The quest for a special competitive edge in a new venture need not rule out existing technologies. It can concentrate on areas where existing companies find it hard to be flexible in applying existing know-how. Thus, as Cooper, Willard, and Woo pointed out,[16]

- MCI entered ATT's long-distance phone markets with rates ATT was restricted from matching.

- Amdahl got started with a computer that IBM did not want to make lest it undermine its existing product lines.

- IBP cut into markets of existing meat packers by choosing cheaper locations and introducing production methods that let it use cheaper labor.

- Nucor entered steel production by selectively picking off certain aspects of the business that let it use cheaper plants and lower-cost labor than the established companies, which, because of bigger "full-line" plant costs and union rules, could not quickly respond.

- People Express and other airlines took advantage of changes in government regulations to pick off routes from established airlines, underpricing them with the lower costs of non-union crews.

Even the rule that new firms should avoid entry into mature or over-crowded industries has been successfully violated by new entrants. Thus Dell

Computer entered the microcomputer industry after it had already been "shaken out" with the elimination of excessive original entrants. Moreover, it did so using an already phased-out distribution method—mail order—that had been used by the first microcomputer company, MITS, and then had been superseded by selling through stores. Customers had originally left mail order for store buying to gain the benefits of sales points that could help them set up and use the products and could stand behind products whose reliability was spotty at best. Later, when the products became user-friendly and reliable, the time for mail order came again.

Connor Peripherals entered the microcomputer disk-drive market when too many companies had entered it,[17] but it prevailed with a better product as great numbers of the earlier entrants died off. Thus the "don't enter after the window of opportunity" rule was flouted again by one more entrant with a better way of doing something.

How are those better ways found? Probably through exploring with search questions like those suggested in the preceding subchapter. That searching usually produces the best answers for people with the relevant industrial experience. Often the answers take forms that are fairly subtle and complex, even though the "tricks" such as those noted in the examples above may make focusing appear simple in hindsight.

Managing the Search

In summary, it appears that there are some controllable factors which can be influential, albeit not rigidly governing, in an idea-searching process.

- **Attitudes** that rate opportunity discovery as important and that affirm the searcher's capacity to be creative can be cultivated.

- **Knowledge** about the nature of new business opportunities and ways of exploiting them can be acquired, and relevant skills can be practiced.

- **Circumstances** such as choice of associates, contacts, employment, and geographical region where start-up happens more often can be sought.

- **Methods** of generating venture ideas, such as formal creativity exercises, can be applied at will.

- **Persistent effort** is a strengthening ingredient that can be deliberately brought to bear and — at least in some cases, such as Staples, Inc. — seems to make an important difference. Downstream from start-up it may be even more important in the fine tuning needed to prevail against competitors.

Application: *Which of the above five elements appears to be most appropriate to the entrepreneur in the assigned case for finding and shaping an effective venture idea?*

The discovery of a promising venture idea, whether through techniques such as these or through unsought serendipity, is only a starting point for further exploration. The idea may be good, but not good enough. Or it may be good enough, but only for someone other than the person who discovered it, someone in a better position to exploit it. Consequently, beyond the goal of the activities described here, which is to produce promising ideas for ventures, lies the next goal, which is to check those ideas out for commercial viability and for fit with the particular entrepreneur(s). How to perform this checkout will be taken up in the next chapter and continue through others that follow.

Supplementary Reading

New Venture Strategies Chapters 7 and 8. (Vesper, K.H., Prentice-Hall, 1990)

Exercises

1.   How would you set up your idea searching boundaries to seek ways of exploiting the kinds of situations described in Chapter 1A under Survival and Success?

2.   In 200 words or less, describe how someone can find a good venture idea, other than by luck?"

3.   How can opportunity causes and alternative strategies be used to generate ideas for new ventures? Illustrate with some examples of your own.

4.   Apply the questions about information in the section on Individual Specifics to examples described in that section and/or other examples.

5.   Introduce yourself to one or more people who might have either (1) needs that are unmet which a new venture might serve, or (2) technical capability to create a new product or service as the basis for a venture. Describe briefly in writing the opportunity(s) you discovered by this process and what would be required for exploitation.

Venture History

1.   What developments gave rise to the opportunity that the entrepreneur exploited?

2.   To what extent would those developments have permitted someone to exploit that opportunity either sooner or later than the entrepreneur did?

3.   What elements of the situation helped to center the entrepreneur on an appropriate direction relative to the status quo and not diverge too widely?

Venture Planning Guide

1. Describe briefly the extent of departure from the competition that your venture idea represents.

2. Describe alterations that could be made to extend or reduce that departure.

Notes

[1] Robert Levering, Michael Katz, and Milton Moskowitz, *The Computer Entrepreneurs* (New York: New American Library, 1984), p. 351.

[2] Adam Osborne and John Dvorak, *Hypergrowth* (New York: Avon, 1985), p. 33.

[3] Gail L Fann and Larry R. Smeltzer, "The Use of Information From and About Competitors in Small Business Management," *ET&P*, 13, no. 3, Spring 1989, p. 21.

[4] Arnold C. Cooper, Timothy B. Folta and Carolyn Woo, "Entrepreneurial Information Search," *Journal of Business Venturing*, 10, no. 2, March 1995, p. 107.

[5] Martha E. Mangelsdorf, "Making the Grade," *Inc.*, January 1989, p. 20.

[6] Tom Richman, "The Entrepreneur of the Year," *Inc.*, January 1990, p. 43. Also, Joel Kotkin, "The Innovation Upstarts," *Inc*, January 1989, p. 70.

[7] John Case, "With A Little Help From His Friends," *Inc.*, April 1989, p. 132.

[8] "The Year in Start-Ups," *Inc.*, November 1989, p. 75.

[9] Edward O. Welles, "Tin Men," *Inc.*, October 1990, p. 66.

[10] White, *The Entrepreneur's Manual*, (Radnor, PA: Chilton Publishing, 1971), p. 52.

[11] Karl H. Vesper, *New Venture Strategies*, revised edition (Englewood Cliffs, N.J.: Prentice-Hall, 1990), p. 193.

[12] John Case, "Sources of Innovation," *Inc.*, June 1989, p. 29.

[13] *Inc.*, October 1990, p. 26.

[14] Radha Chaganti, Rajeswararao Chaganti and Vijay Mahajan, "Profitable Small Business Strategies Under Different Types of Competition," *ET&P*, 13, no. 4, Summer 1989, p. 35.

[15] Robert J. Kunze, *Nothing Ventured*, (New York: Harper Business, 1990), p. 201.

[16] Arnold C. Cooper, Gary E. Willard and Carolyn Y. Woo, "Strategies of High-Performing New and Small Firms: A Reexamination of the Niche Concept," *Journal of Business Venturing*, 1, no. 3, Fall 1986, p. 247.

[17] William A. Sahlman and Howard H. Stevenson, "Capital Market Myopia," *Journal of Business Venturing*, 1, no. 1, Winter 1985, p. 7.

Case Questions

General Questions

1. Discuss the extent to which one or more venture opportunities appear to exist in the assigned case, why, and what sort of venture might best exploit them.

2. What companies or individuals should be best positioned to take advantage of those opportunities and how?

3. What is your assessment of the idea discovery method(s) used thus far by the entrepreneur(s) in the assigned case?

4. What criteria would you propose that the entrepreneur(s) in the assigned case should use for selecting which business idea(s) to pursue from among possible ideas discovered?

5. What business ideas can you think of that the entrepreneur(s) in the assigned case did not think of but might do well to consider?

Case 3 - John Morse p. 84

1. In the John Morse case we find someone attempting to discover good business ideas through systematic searching procedures. Before reading about his procedures think about how to go about such a search. Then read through Morse's experience and evaluate his approach.

    • Was there a better way for him to proceed at any point, and if so, how?

    • Where should he go at the end of the case?

    • Has he come up with too many ideas or too few?

    • Rank order the viability of ideas discovered so far.

    • Which of his ideas are best and why?

    • Did they seem to come earlier in the search, or later?

    • What should John Morse have learned from this process?

    • How might the "right" approach for someone else be the same or different?

    • To what extent does the nature or quality of ideas discovered so far in the case seem to be dependent on the timing of their discovery?

Case 4 - Chem Synthesis Inc. (A) p. 106

1. What does the experience of CSI illustrate about how to find new product ideas?

2. How could CSI increase the volume of new ideas it is finding? The quality? Which does it most need more of, volume, or quality of new ideas, and how could it get that?

3. What guidelines for seeking new product ideas should CSI give to its employees?

4. How should Jim's questions at the end of the case be answered?

Case 5 - Michael Shane (A) p. 121

1. Without applying hindsight, insofar as possible, prepare at least one page of a questionnaire for Michael Shane's market survey. On it include what you would consider to be the most crucial questions, selected from a presumably larger list of questions, to be answered.

2. Postulate hypothetical answer patterns to the above key questions. Explain the action implications for Michael if in fact those patterns did emerge from the survey.

3. The Shane case in fact took place many years ago. How would the prospect and the task of starting a company such as Michael was contemplating be similar and how would it be different today? Could it be done now? If so, who could do it best?

John Morse

Midway through a two-year MBA program at the University of Washington, John Morse had begun a venture search with the objective of achieving self-employment upon graduation. Now graduation was just two weeks away and, although he had generated many possible venture ideas, John had not yet found one he was sure he wanted to pursue. He felt it was time to review the steps taken in his search to date and decide whether to continue it or to adopt a different approach.

Background

As the ninth of 12 children, John spent the first 18 years of his life (1952-1970) growing up in a suburb north of Chicago, going right from high school to college. He spent one year at Boston College, his sophomore year abroad in Rome, and finished up the last two years at Northwestern University in 1974 with a B.S. in Sociology. During the next four years, until starting his MBA program in 1978, he held the following jobs: waiter, bartender, phlebotomist, law clerk, factory worker in a sausage plant, hospital purchasing agent, and purchasing agent for a printing plant. John said his experiences working with other individuals as his supervisors and "carrot danglers" were not very rewarding or fulfilling.

I seem to be intimidated and uninspired in that environment. I suspect it would be a frustrating life for me as an employee, and it would probably be riddled with continual disappointment. My nature is especially attracted to the independence associated with being one's own boss. I am far more secure with the uncertainties this entails. Three or four years ago, in 1976, I realized what I wanted out of a career in business was to run one, ideally my own. My plan was to get a master's degree in Business Administration, spend three to five years as an employee gaining experience and capital, and then launch a business.

For part of his MBA program, John spent a year as an exchange student in England. While there, he took a course in entrepreneurship which triggered the thought that it might be possible for him to start a business of his own following graduation, if he could line up a suitable venture idea. Upon returning to Seattle in June 1979, he approached one of his professors at the University of Washington about doing a feasibility study of a new venture idea as an MBA research project. Since John did not have a specific venture idea in mind, the professor suggested that he come back before fall quarter (three months hence) with a study proposal.

During the next three months, once or twice a week John would go into a vacant classroom for a couple of hours at a time with a notebook. He would try to force himself to think of business innovations. He relied largely on his imagination and inspiration. He would try to picture in his mind where business trends were headed. Some ideas that came out of those sessions were:

1. Develop a product for a fast grow-

ing market segment—senior citizens.

2. Start a service to capitalize on the increase in foreigners visiting Seattle (for example, day care or tour bus guide service).

3. Develop a marketing device (for example, a nondefaceable billboard to put up on stall walls) to take advantage of the captive market in public toilets.

4. Set up camps for adults.

5. Begin a service to alleviate some of the difficulties facing the growing number of women executives traveling alone to Seattle on business.

6. Organize an information network with subscribers hooked up via computer terminals.

About three weeks before he was scheduled to get back to his professor with his proposal for a topic, John came across an article in *Newsweek* on "Snob Ice Creams" that he said "came the closest to eureka" since he began searching for a business idea. He now wanted to investigate the feasibility of manufacturing locally a top-quality ice cream to compete with brands currently imported from the Midwest. During the next week-and-a-half he tried to get a feel for what he was considering. He went to the library and pulled some books on ice cream manufacturing. He called all the local ice cream manufacturers to find out what they manufactured in the way of high-quality ice cream. He contacted, either by phone or in person, a number of retail ice cream stores to find out whose ice cream they were distributing and what sort of demand it was generating.

This informal research left John less than convinced that his ice cream manufacturing idea was bound to be a sure-fire success. His professor also expressed

doubts, noting that the gourmet brand uppermost in John's mind was imported not only to Seattle but also to Los Angeles from the Midwest. If the Los Angeles area with its many millions of people did not represent a large enough market to justify setting up a local manufacturing plant, the professor asked, how could the Seattle area, which was only a fraction that size and even closer to the Midwest, justify doing so? Instead of plunging ahead with the "hot flash" idea of manufacturing gourmet ice cream, he suggested that John might undertake, under his sponsorship, a methodical search for a business venture as a research project. The professor pointed to three donated boxes of IEA (International Entrepreneur Association) manuals as a possible source of ideas but left the door open to any other sources John might want to mine.

John took a sample of an IEA manual home and discovered it to be a report on a business venture that might appeal to an aspiring entrepreneur. It outlined, step-by-step, what an individual might do to pursue the profiled venture. Some of the items covered were market research, a suggested list of readings, sources for equipment and supplies, and typical cost figures. At the end of each manual was a section devoted to business, legal and governmental considerations in establishing a new venture. A list of manuals available to him in the school library appears in Exhibit 1.

Unsure how he was going to approach the search, but with the desire to do it, John arranged with his professor to begin the MBA research project in fall quarter, two weeks away.

Anticipating a Market

Weeks 1 and 2

In discussion with his professor, John decided to attempt a systematic search for a business venture by reviewing the various manuals in the light of his desires and

Seattle's business makeup. But he began the search far from convinced that this method would lead to anything tangible or practical. He chose to combine his search through manuals with a review of the Puget Sound area. It seemed to him that it should be possible to view the marketplace as a "case study," and analyze the Puget Sound area for its demographics, economic factors, market profile and any apparent trends. From some such combination of information, he figured, it would be only a matter of deduction to recognize where opportunities existed for a successful start-up.

Week 3

John began his search with a visit to the Seattle office of the Washington State Department of Commerce. He asked for any information that they had on local and state demographics, market studies, consumer profiles, trade figures, growth projections, economic forecasts and anything else they thought relevant.

> *What stumped both them and me was the question: relevant to what? Since I wasn't really sure what information I was seeking, I couldn't be specific. They gave me all the publications they had that might have any connection, even remotely, to the somewhat broad boundaries of my request.*

They included a 1978 *Pocket Data Book of the State of Washington* (a reference volume of population, economic, government, education, and human resource statistics and trends), a "Community Level Target Industry Identification Program" report, the "Washington State Economy Review of 1978, Outlook for 1979," "Washington State Exporter's Guide," and the "International Trade Directory." He also spent an hour speaking with the Small Business counselor in that office about general trends in the state, as he perceived them,

and what he felt were the areas for opportunity. Energy and transportation were cited as the industries providing the greatest opportunities.

Later that same day John visited the Seattle Chamber of Commerce with the same request for information. They too indicated that his request was very broad and gave him a number of publications, including a 1978 Economic Review of the Seattle-Everett area, a booklet entitled "Corporate Headquarters: Central Puget Sound Region," a sample of "Business Profiles," a "Business Migration Study: An Analysis of Out-Migration Patterns in Seattle Firms," and a listing of other publications available through the Chamber of Commerce. Both the state and city Commerce Departments recommended a visit to the Seattle City Library's business department.

Week 4

Skeptical about where his search was going, John next visited the city library with the same request used at the Commerce Departments. The librarian in the business section presented him with a large volume of statistics profiling metropolitan Seattle consumers. "It could conceivably have been a great marketing aid, but since I didn't know yet what I was trying to market, I had a hard time extracting any value out of that book," he recalled.

The librarian also pointed out a file cabinet of resource documents which contained a drawer devoted to the Small Business Administration. John perused that file and while finding it of general interest, came away with no concrete information.

> *At this point I had accumulated a small library of information and the more I looked through it, the more confused I became as to what I was trying to learn. From all this data I discovered that trying to absorb all the information available on the Puget Sound area and then translate it into some business*

opportunity(s) was far too broad, difficult and abstract for my purposes and abilities. I also discovered that the approach I was taking could offer no more direction than that which I was already bringing to it. The flip side of that, however, was the realization that there is a wealth of information and assistance available to the individual who knows exactly what information he is seeking.

Four weeks into the project John was still devoting most of his mental energy searching for a business idea that would anticipate a market, either a new product or service that would capitalize on a currently unmet need or else a business that would take advantage of a growing market demand. He began to think that perhaps the best way to enter a market would be to let an innovative or quality product or service lead him into the market rather than entering a market first and then searching for an idea.

Week 5

I remember once reading an article which stated that even when you are not looking for a job, it is prudent to keep an eye on the "Help Wanted" classified ads so that you can get a feel for which employers are having a hard time finding and/or keeping employees, which professions are (not) in great demand, pay scales for various positions, and so forth. Using that same line of thinking I started to read the `Business Opportunities' section in the classifieds to learn what I could about the business climate as evidenced by what types of businesses were up for sale, where, and at what price.

So far, John was still avoiding analysis of the IEA manuals, feeling they were "somebody else's song," which he did not want to imitate. He was trying to be highly methodical, keeping and analyzing a log of his time and the degree of output different approaches were producing for him. The log was something he had agreed with his professor to do as part of the research paper he was supposed to produce for course credit. However, he found the chronicling difficult and was acutely aware that the sixth week of the search was at hand and, so far, no satisfactory venture idea had turned up. He intensified his efforts at becoming more systematic.

Establishing a List of Possible Ventures

Week 6

John observed:

My single most difficult step in undertaking a methodical and rational search for a business (and it really didn't begin until this point) was overcoming the gut feeling that it is inspiration and innovation that lead the entrepreneur to the marketplace, not scientific inquiry. The prospect of starting or buying a business before having an outstanding idea or product seemed like the proverbial cart before the horse. At the same time, there was fear that by forcing entry into one market, I could be preempting the discovery or recognition of a successful enterprise in another field. Fortunately, I came to see that line of thought as counterproductive. The way I was able to bridge the gap between my desire to be creative and methodically arriving at a list of possible ventures was the belief that the latter does not have to preclude the former.

Next he began to write down what it was he was looking for versus what he was trying to avoid in various types of businesses, as shown in Exhibit 2. As he did this, he also noticed that the venture search project was becoming the main focus of his school interest, notwithstanding three other courses he was taking.

Weeks 7 through 12

A help, John found, was Kenneth Albert's *How to Pick the Right Small Business Opportunity*. One of its features was a capability assessment guide, which he used to take an inventory of his strengths and weaknesses. He continued:

> *The Alberts book revealed to me that it was easy when looking at existing entrepreneurs and executives to be impressed with what I don't know without counterbalancing it with how much I do know, which is also important.*
>
> *A hard part of trying to be systematic was figuring out what step to take next. As with any exercise, if you know where you're going to end up, the direction of your steps is fairly obvious. But otherwise, it's confusing.*
>
> *One thing I discovered, though, in thinking of potential business ideas, was that step-by-step progression had to take place in their development, and that I should avoid sitting back and viewing the 'go-no-go' decision as a quantum leap.*

Other outside reading John did at this stage was Sandman and Goldenson's, *How to Succeed in Business Before Graduating,** plus the record of another student's venture search and an article in the *Harvard Business Review* on the origin of venture ideas.** The Sandman book seemed to him limited to ventures of only short-term viability. The other student's study did not seem to have found much pay dirt. The article suggested that most venture ideas come from jobs and hobbies rather than from any systematic study such as John was pursuing.

Also in the seventh week of the project, John xeroxed a 13-page index of major groups in the Standard Industrial Classification. His intent was to go through this index and circle any industry or product that he could conceivably get involved with in some capacity. In weeks eight and nine, he went through this list two more times on different days to check and recheck his choices. He applied the same procedure to a Seattle Yellow Pages index. By the end of the fourteenth week, he had consolidated the products and services list as shown in Exhibit 3. A couple of hours scanning the *Thomas Register* and the *National Directory of Associations* revealed to him no additional ideas or categories that weren't already covered in the consolidated list.

Week 13

During spring break John began reading through some of the IEA manuals in an attempt to identify positive and negative features of each of the profiled ventures (Exhibit 4). He commented:

> *Some of the available manuals (e.g., Christmas tree lot) I didn't even glance at, either because they were too small-time or they didn't even have a minimal attraction. The ideas most worth serious consideration in the manuals I read seemed to be a cookie shop, a secretarial service and a mobile restaurant. The mobile restaurant (vending truck) seemed potentially viable as a business to take downtown during the lunch hour rush. After thinking about it, however, I decided that I didn't want to get involved with retail food service. That clouded the cookie shop idea as well.*
>
> *The secretarial service had the appeal*

---

* Sandman, Peter, and Dan Goldenson, *How to Succeed in Business Before Graduating*, New York, Collier Books, 1968.
** Vesper, Karl H., "Finding New Venture Ideas, Don't Overlook the Experience Factor," *Harvard Business Review*.

of low capital required and seemed like maybe it could be a good interim step and experience-builder in case I didn't get something else going. But those advantages still left me feeling unmotivated, so I decided not to follow through with it.

It began to seem to John that the more effort he spent defining what he was looking for, the less time he would have to spend searching for it, but with the trade-off for defining versus searching not being one-for-one. This impression persisted. John sketched what he meant on a time-line as follows:

how I would assign 30 points or allocate $30 among the criteria to indicate its importance to me," he recalled. Then, although his knowledge of what these businesses entailed in terms of financial, technical and personal resources was sketchy, he computed two scores for each line of business: one by counting the number of plusses and the other by multiplying the number of plusses by their respective criteria priority weightings and adding up those totals.

With these numerical values computed for each of the business categories, he selected eight products and five services that were both high-rated numerically and

```
/Defining----------------------------------->/Search------------->time

                          versus

/Defining------------->/Search----------------------------------->time
```

The first of these two patterns, he believed, was more difficult but more efficient. It also occurred to John at this time that his search process might be helpful in clarifying what he was seeking in a job, even if it did not yield a business.

Week 14

By the fourteenth week of the project, John felt ready to narrow his search further. He began by listing 11 criteria he considered important in the evaluation of a business. Then he took a list of product and service areas he had consolidated earlier and went through each business category, rating it against his criteria (see Exhibit 5). He assigned plusses and minuses subjectively based on how he felt about it. He also assigned priorities to the criteria (indicated by the number next to each criterion in Exhibit 5). "I asked myself

comfortable to his "gut feeling." They were:

PRODUCTS	SERVICES
Frozen Desserts	Circulation Library
Ice Cream	Day Care
Sporting Goods, Wholesale	Freight Forwarding
Cookies and Crackers	Lodging, hotel, motel, hostel
Cider, Fruit and Vegetable Juices	Delivery Service
Woolen Goods	
Salad Dressings	

Next, he began pruning this list, beginning with day care. He commented:

A friend who is a good friend of a woman who runs a day care business told me about all the headaches she encounters trying to run a business that deals with people's most precious concern, their children. That conversation and subsequent reflection made day care an easy deletion. Owning a lodge struck me as beyond my immediate skills, experience, finances and interests so I dropped it from the list. The circulating library is really a take-off on the information services that I was trying to structure in my thoughts before I began this project. I realized that unless I had something concrete, this business idea would have to wait. Since six of the remaining eight products were food-related, I decided to concentrate my interviews with the food industry and the remaining two services on my pared-down list, freight forwarding and a delivery service.

Interviews

Weeks 15 and 16

Now began what John regarded as the most enjoyable and rewarding phase of the project, interviews with business owners and executives. The interview process, visiting firms, talking with people about getting into businesses like theirs, and getting around to see and hear what was happening, gave John what he described as the most tangible feelings of accomplishment and progress.

Throughout this project I felt my status as a student was a real asset and could probably make information and individuals far more accessible than they may be otherwise. It seemed a natural and logical move then to contact business owners and executives and see if I could draw on their experiences and knowledge to aid in my search.

He prepared a questionnaire (Exhibit 6) to guide his interviews, then visited nine people, all of whom were in the food business, either manufacturing or wholesaling. Which questions on his list were appropriate varied among interviews. Sometimes items would come up in the interview that led to new questions.

To find interviewees John used two references, the *King County Manufacturer's Directory* and *Contacts Influential*. He chose these sources for three main reasons: (1) they listed companies by their S.I.C. (Standard Industrial Classification) numbers, which made it easy to locate prospects; (2) they gave valuable information about these companies such as when they were established, their sales volume, number of employees and whether the office is a branch or headquarters, and (3) they listed names of company presidents or owners.

He was hesitant to let interviewees know that his reason for pursuing this project was to consider entering their lines of work as a potential competitor. He suspected they would be reluctant to answer the questions. John's professor argued to the contrary and, as it turned out, John's fears were unjustified. In fact, he found all whom he interviewed were helpful and encouraging. Two of them spoke with him over lunch, and one invited him to sit in on his annual marketing meeting.

In reviewing the notes taken during the interviews, John said the following points appeared to represent a consensus of the interviewees' remarks:

An individual must have money and related experience to get started in the food business. Also mentioned on more than one occasion as necessary were traits of courage, desire, ambitiousness, and determination.

The most instrumental factors in determining a company's success seemed to be good business management (awareness of costs and cost efficiencies, working capital management, and common sense), good product, and integrity in that order of frequency among the interviewees.

Respondents were about evenly divided on the relative advantages and disadvantages of a small business in the food industry. On the plus side for small firms were quick response time, simplicity and close supervision, while heavy investments, distribution channels, and governmental requirements favored large companies.

The trend in the food industry is toward more convenience foods and prepared high quality frozen foods.

Good business sense, obviously, is important. Also frequently mentioned were the ability to get along with and motivate people and the ability to be a jack-of-all-trades.

In order, the three biggest problems facing the businesses seemed to be (1) government (local and federal) interference; (2) finding and keeping good employees; and (3) financial management, maintaining good cash flow and finding money to expand the business.

To date, John had not looked for possible acquisitions, and none had presented themselves. But he recognized that buying a business was another possibility worth considering.

A product-oriented business, especially manufacturing, seemed to call for buy-out rather than starting from scratch. Product development could take too much time; equipment and setting up would cost too much capital. In contrast, an established business, if its owner were willing to sell it for a small down payment borrowed at the bank, and take payments over time, could be a way around those problems.

Services seemed less difficult capital-wise, but they presented other problems. Among delivery service firms, for instance, John called five individuals before one agreed to speak with him. The owner described a heavy role of government licensing and regulating in his business, as well as in freight forwarding. John decided that line of work was not for him.

Week 17

By the seventeenth week of the project and halfway through his planned interviewing, John said he was disappointed with his progress and frustrated by the shortage of time left before he would be done with school and have to move on.

Up to this point, I hadn't really considered what I would do if the right opportunity didn't turn up. But a glance at the calendar and a pinch of foresight was telling me that, ready or not, school was almost over. Thinking it would help me clarify my thoughts, I took out a piece of paper, titled it "Going For It" as immediate entrepreneurship, and then listed the pros and cons of pursuing a venture tenaciously right away (Exhibit 7). Even though I didn't really make a conscious decision, judging from the subsequent six weeks, I chose to continue trying to arrange something.

Having already established a set of business criteria and attached relative weightings to them (Exhibit 5), John slowly began to conclude during the interviewing process that a good share of the criteria would be met only if the business he attempted were successful.

Selecting a Business

Week 18

In the eighteenth week of the project, and with graduation only a few weeks away, John saw two major concerns in deciding on a business venture. First, he was approaching this decision as though he had a gun with only one bullet, so the aim had to be excellent. Second, it seemed to him that undertaking risk was directly related to conviction. Starting and/or running a business seemed likely to require heavy investments in time, energy and probably money, at least relative to his meager resources. Without a solid commitment and the necessary determination, that investment could be wasted.

As he reflected on his situation, several options were on his mind. One was to continue searching. In that line, he felt he should consider not only the degree of effectiveness his procedure had demonstrated so far, but also how it could be done better. He had collected a log of activities and time spent, as shown in Exhibit 8, which he thought might be useful in refining his process. There was also the question of whether one or more of the ideas generated so far should be carried further.

Overall, there seemed to be four broad choices: (1) continue searching for more ideas, (2) investigate several present ideas further, (3) select one idea and put all efforts into going ahead, and (4) look for employment in someone else's organization.

EXHIBIT 1   International Entrepreneur Association (IEA) Manuals

1.	Dive-For-A-Pearl-Shop	28.	Tool & Equipment Rental Service
2.	Plant Shop	29.	Ghost Dog Making
3.	Balloon Vending	30.	Contest Promotions
4.	Tennis & Racquetball Club	31.	Parking Lot Striping
5.	Athletic Shoe Store	32.	Maintenance Service
6.	Pizzeria	33.	Antique Store
7.	Pet Shop	34.	Pet Hotel & Grooming Service
8.	Handwriting Analysis by Computer	35.	Janitorial Service
9.	Tune-Up Shop	36.	Do-It-Yourself Auto Repair Shop
10.	Flower Vending	37.	Old-Fashioned Ice Cream Bar Stand
11.	Furniture Store	38.	Dry-Cleaning Shop
12.	Window-Washing Service	39.	Copy Shop
13.	Instant Print Shop	40.	Stuffed Toy Animal Vending
14.	Adult Bookstore	41.	Adults-Only Motel
15.	Mail Order	42.	Robot Lawn Mower
16.	Hamburger Stand	43.	Mini-Warehouse
17.	Quit-Smoking Clinic	44.	T-Shirt Shop
18.	Consignment Used Car Lot	45.	Muffler Shop
19.	Cheese & Gourmet Food Shop	46.	Worm-Farming (expose)
20.	Swap Meet Promoting	47.	Psychic-Training Seminars
21.	Art Show Promoting	48.	Trade School
22.	Bicycle Shop	49.	Auto-Parking Service
23.	Rental List Publishing	50.	Rent-A-Plant
24.	Liquor Store	51.	Auto-Painting Shop
25.	Popcorn Vending	52.	Employment Agency
26.	"Who's Who" Publishing	53.	Furniture-Stripping Service
27.	Antique Photo Shop	54.	Carpet-Cleaning Service
		55.	Ten-Minute Oil Change Shop
		56.	Fried Chicken Takeout-Restaurant

EXHIBIT 1 (continued)

57.	Mobile Restaurant		100.	Gift Shop
58.	Bonsai Collecting		101.	Women's Apparel Shop
59.	Day-Care Center		102.	Used Car Rental Agency
60.	Coffee Shop		103.	Windsurfing School
61.	Earring Shop		104.	Free Classified Newspaper Publishing
62.	Stained Glass Window Manufacturing		105.	Promotional Gimmicks
63.	Low-Cal Bakery		106.	Candid Key Chain Photos
64.	Lie Detection by Voice Analysis		107.	Used Bookstore
65.	Bust-Developing Product		108.	Handicrafts Co-Op
66.	Sunglass Shop		109.	Salad Bar Restaurant
67.	Custom Rug Making		110.	Sculptured Candle Making
68.	Newsletter Publishing		111.	Coin-Op TV
69.	Self-Service Gas Station		112.	Plastics-Recycling Center
70.	Flea Market-Finding Products		113.	No-Alcohol Bar
71.	Homemade Candy Stand		114.	Health Food Store
72.	Seminar Promoting		115.	Donut Shop
73.	Mattress Shop		116.	Shrimp Peddling
74.	Hot Dog Stand		117.	Soup Kitchen
75.	Hot Tub Manufacturing		118.	Pipe Shop
76.	Car Wash		119.	Roommate-Finding Service
77.	Vinyl-Repairing Service		120.	Backpacking Shop
78.	Yogurt Bar		121.	Hobby Shop
79.	Weight Control Clinic		122.	Discount Fabric Shop
80.	Skateboard Park		123.	Paint & Wall Covering Store
81.	Cookie Shop		124.	Do-It-Yourself Cosmetic Shop
82.	Computer Store		125.	Secretarial Service
83.	SBA Financing-New Businesses		126.	Furniture Rental Store
84.	SBA Financing-Existing Businesses		127.	Pet Cemetery
85.	Hidden Franchise Laws		128.	Seasonal Christmas Tree And Ornament Business
86.	Roller Skate Rental Shop			
87.	Free University		129.	Tropical Fish Store
88.	Roller Skating Rink		130.	Gourmet Cookware Shop
89.	Burglar Alarm Manufacturing		131.	Flower Shop
90.	Import & Export		132.	Do-It-Yourself Framing Shop
91.	Burlwood Tables Manufacturing and Retail Store		133.	Insulation Contracting
			134.	Automobile Detailing
92.	Homemade Cake Shop		135.	Private Post Office
93.	Digital Watch Repairing Service		136.	Telephone Answering Service
94.	Sculptures by Computer		137.	Sailboat Leasing
95.	Video Cassette Recorder		138.	Exterior Surface Cleaning
96.	Liquidated Goods Broker		139.	Consulting Service
97.	Selling Your Business		140.	Intimate Apparel Shop
98.	Pinball Arcade		141.	Flat-Fee Real Estate Agency
99.	Kitchen-Remodeling Service		142.	Travel Agency

EXHIBIT 1 (concluded)

143. Chimney Sweep Service	164. Women Getting Into Business
144. Sandwich Shop	165. Businesses You Can Start for Under
145. Cross-Country Trucking	$1,000
146. Specialty Bread Shop	166. Mail-Order Business
147. Security Patrol Service	167. How To Franchise Your Business
148. Maid Service	168. Franchise Pros & Cons
149. Children's Apparel Shop	169. Selling Ideas
150. Coin Laundry	170. How to Develop a Successful Plan
151. Shell Shop	171. Businesses You Can Run and Keep Your
152. Churro Snack Shop	Present Job
153. Jojoba Plantation	172. How to Make Quick Profits in
154. Video Store	Real Estate
155. Financial Broker	173. Tax-Saving Angles for Small Businesses
156. Vitamin Store	174. Advertising Techniques for
157. Raising Money	Small Businesses
158. Hottest New Businesses and	175. Recession-Proof Businesses
Future Trends	176. Preventing Bad Checks, Pilfering
159. How to Get Free Publicity	& Embezzlement
& Promote Your Business	177. Four Millionaires Tell How They
160. Manufacturing & Distributing	Did It
Products	178. Negotiating Techniques
161. Legal Ins & Outs of Small Business	179. How to Protect Your Ideas
162. How to Intelligently Buy a Business	180. How to Test Market Your Products
163. Getting Into Import & Export	& Ideas
	181. Millionaire's Secrets to Success

EXHIBIT 2 Thoughts about Preferences

LOOKING FOR
Something that I can be proud of; a product or service that is a contribution; allows for quality input/differential.

A business that I can sell.

Stability - a business that I can sink my feet into without concern that its market/usefulness will quickly vanish.
A business that I am interested in, will make it easy to spend the extra hours to make it fly.

A business that will utilize my talents, staple, no gimmicks.

Challenge - competitive.

Ideally a product rather than a service.

A business that can be flexible in its location, allow for the best of two worlds.

Opportunity for eventual absentee ownership.

Very profitable business, both financially and spiritually. One that will give me and the company the power (freedom) to enact some positive contributions.

Flexible work hours; both in days and hours.

Slow, healthy growth in a growth industry.

Independence.

A business of ideas, innovation in substance, not style.

A business centered around communications, communication skills important.

Success criteria that match my abilities.

A market that I can relate to, get excited about and enjoy dealing with. Not necessarily high labor intensive; will allow for small, sole beginning.

AVOIDING
Franchise; a business that appears to be a commodity.

Faddish business, more a fashion.

High technology/capital requirements.

Being a middleman, a conduit.

Fast buck business.

Fabricated need, product oriented.

Business/industry in tail-end of product life cycle.

High capital requirement.

Art, cultural, design business.

EXHIBIT 3   Products and Services from S.I.C. List and Yellow Pages

Products	Services
Bakery	Amusement Park
Cocoa and Chocolate Products	Bridge Teacher
Coffee	Camps
Dairy Products	Chauffeur Service
Fruits and Vegetables, Wholesale	Circulating Library
Frozen Desserts	Cold Storage Lockers
Frozen Fruits	Day Care
Games	Messenger Service
General Merchandise Store	Food Lockers
Wholesale Groceries	Freight Forwarding
Retail groceries	Gymnasium
Hardware; Wholesale and Retail	Motel, Hotel, Hostel
Ice Cream	Laundry
Knit Mills	Linen Supply Delivery Service
Wood Products Dealer	Picnic Grounds
Musical Instruments	Resort
Records and Tapes	Trucking, Local Cartage
Slippers	Air Port Terminal Services
Sporting Goods; Wholesale & Retail	Accounting & Bookkeeping Services
Book Store	News Dealers
Hobby, Toy and Game Store; Whole-	Floor Laying
sale and Retail	Library and Information Center
Wooden Goods	Rental Business
Vaults and Safes	Taxicabs
Children's Vehicles	Local - Suburban Transit
Wines; Wholesale and Retail	Transportation, Chartered, on Land,
Cookies and Crackers	Rivers, Air, Etc.
Salad Dressings	Transportation Broker
Stereo, Video Cassette Equipment, Retail	Food Broker
Pies	
Bicycle Rentals	
Camping Equipment	
Carpet and Rug Dealer	
Cider	
Vending Machines	
School Supplies	
Dehydrated Foods	
Fruits and Vegetables	
Nuts	
Soda Fountain	
Swings	
Vending Trucks	

EXHIBIT 4   Survey of IEA Businesses

FREE CLASSIFIED NEWSPAPER PUBLISHING

+ high return
+ could lead to many more opportunities
        in related fields
+ little know-how necessary
- mechanical
- not very exciting, largely a money
        machine

GIFT SHOP

- retail
- high risk
- out of my league

DONUT SHOP

+ food
- restaurant business, retail headaches

BACKPACKING SHOP

+ product line
+ growth industry in good area of
        country
+ personality of market
- high investment, risk
- barriers to entry
- retail

PIPE SHOP

+ clientele
+ specialty
+ stable
- boring
- retail

GOURMET COOKWARE SHOP

+ specialty shop
- cannot relate to the market
- retail
- risk

TROPICAL FISH STORE

+ product
- small time
- risk

HEALTH FOOD BAR

+ could be an idea whose time has come
- a tavern, or a restaurant; either one
        is unacceptable

SCULPTURED CANDLE MAKING

+ product
+ has low investment, easy startup
- small time
- art and art shows, flea markets

PAINT AND WALL COVERING STORE

+ stable
+ reasonable profit
- not a comfortable industry
- heavy investment

SECRETARIAL SERVICE

+ good employee relations
+ reasonable investment
+ tap marketing skills
+ reasonably stable
+ easy growth/management
- lack of familiarity
- competition, mature market

EXHIBIT 4   (continued)

HOMEMADE CANDY SHOP

+ easy start up
+ quality output
+ business atmosphere (customers)
+ growth and expansion potential
+ stable
- product
- roadside scenario

SEMINAR PROMOTING

+ an idea that has its financial merits
+ down the road it certainly offers a
    source of revenue
- not exactly what I am looking for

STAINED GLASS WINDOWS

although it is a product, it does
not offer anything other than a
short term attraction

CAR WASH

- doesn't grab me
- high risks
- high investment
- out of my ball park

FURNITURE RENTAL STORE

+ stable, over established
+ profitable, easy absenteeism
- doesn't excite me
- high investment
- little outlet for quality, creativity

INSULATION CONTRACTING BUSINESS

+ timing
+ seasonal
- not my style
- this is where the pack is
- heavy investment in money & time to
    get going

FURNITURE STRIPPING

+ appears to involve minimum startup
+ craft
- reasonably stable
- tough to break away from "Mom & Pop"
- small ROI

SCULPTURE BY COMPUTER

- not me

MOBILE RESTAURANT

+ dealing with food
+ relatively low start up
+ opportunity for creative application
+ reasonably simple
- difficult quality input
- questionable future in terms of growth
    and potential

EXHIBIT 4 (concluded)

SUN GLASS SHOP

+ stable market
+ low investment
+ easy absentee
- too narrow
- not exciting enough

NEWSLETTER PUBLISHING

- lack of interest/expertise

YOGURT BAR

+ product, different
- market seems saturated
- somewhat faddish

KITCHEN REMODELING

- do not have the skills to do the job
- high investment in time and money

DIGITAL WATCH REPAIRING

+ low start up
+ work and location flexibility
+ good growth potential
- an area I do not feel comfortable with
- seems high risk

DAY CARE CENTER

+ good future
+ good product-opportunity for contribution
+ good customer base
+ room for quality differential
+ could be fun
+ survives on its own momentum
- dependent on high volume
        high start up costs
- governmental influence
- competition can be fierce, money

EXHIBIT 5   Comparisons

BUSINESS PRODUCTS	Favorable Content	Business Flexibility	Product	People Contact	Independence	Quality Differential	Artistic Contribution	Fun	Stability	Status	Income	Total "+"s	Total Points
Weights	2	3	3	2	3	3	1	2	5	3	3		
Cookies and Crackers	+	+	+	-	+	+	-	+	+	+	+	9	27
Bicycle Rentals	+	-	-	+	-	-	+	+	-	-	-	4	7
Camping Equipment	+	+	+	-	+	+	-	+	+	+	+	9	27
Carpet and Rug Dealer	+	-	-	+	-	+	-	-	+	-	+	5	15
Cider	+	+	+	-	+	+	-	+	+	+	+	9	27
Vending Machines	+	-	-	-	-	-	+	-	+	-	+	4	11
School Supplies	+	-	-	+	-	-	-	+	+	-	-	4	11
Foods (Dehydrated)	+	+	+	-	+	+	+	+	-	+	+	9	23
Fruit and Vegetable Juice	+	+	+	-	+	+	-	+	+	+	+	9	27
Nuts	+	+	-	-	+	-	-	+	+	+	+	7	21
Soda Fountain	+	-	+	+	-	-	-	+	+	-	-	5	14
Swings	+	+	+	-	+	+	-	+	+	+	+	9	27
Vending Trucks	+	-	-	+	-	-	+	+	-	-	-	4	7
Woolen goods	+	+	+	-	+	+	-	+	+	+	+	9	27
SERVICES													
Amusement Park	+	-	-	+	+	+	+	+	-	+	+	8	19
Bridge Instructor	+	-	-	+	+	-	-	+	-	+	-	5	12
Camps	+	+	-	+	+	+	+	+	-	+	+	9	22
Chauffeur Service	-	-	-	+	-	-	-	-	+	+	-	3	10
Circulating Library	+	-	-	+	+	+	+	+	+	+	+	9	24
Cold & Food Storage Lockers	+	-	-	-	+	-	-	-	+	-	+	4	13
Day Care	+	-	-	+	+	+	+	+	+	-	+	8	21
Messenger Service	+	-	-	+	-	+	+	+	+	-	-	6	15
Freight Forwarding	+	-	-	+	-	+	-	+	+	+	+	7	20
Gymnasium	+	-	-	+	-	+	+	+	-	+	-	6	13

EXHIBIT 6 **Interview Questions**

COMPANY_____INTERVIEWEE_____

1. What does an individual need to get started in your business?
2. What factors are most instrumental in a company's success in your business? (e.g., service, location, contacts, product).
3. How much is product and how much of it is service?
4. Do you feel that a small company is at a distinct disadvantage in your business?
5. How important are economies of scale?
6. What trends do you see developing in your industry? Why?
7. Do you see a market that is currently not being satisfactorily served?
8. Do you see any opportunities in the _____ industry? Why do you think this is?
9. Would you characterize your industry as extremely competitive?
10. What are the competitive pressures?
11. What skills or attributes do you consider most essential in successfully running a _____?
12. How are they different from running, say, a cardboard box plant?
13. How much people-contact do you have? What type?
14. What do you consider to be the biggest problems you are faced with in running your business?
15. How large a market is there for top-of-the-line _____?
16. Are you currently trying to serve it? Why? Why not?
17. What sort of work week does your _____ have (# of days, shifts)?
18. What sort of work week do you have?
19. Could you, if you wanted, have a non-conventional work week?
20. Could you locate anywhere in the greater Seattle metropolitan area without serious consequences?
21. Can you think of anything particular to your industry that would influence a decision to buy a going concern vs. starting from scratch?
22. What background did you bring to your business?
23. What experience do you consider most helpful in running your business?
24. What attracted you to the _____ business?
25. Were your expectations and hopes realistic?
26. If you knew then what you know now, what would you do differently?
27. Would you start up your business today? Why(not)?
28. If you were to start your business from scratch today, what do you think would be the biggest difficulty?
29. If you were to start your business today, how much technical and product know-how would you need?
30. Dealing with such a stable and established product, do you sometimes find this too staid, too conventional?
31. Are there opportunities for creativity?
32. What do you feel are the greatest rewards from your position?
33. What do you find exciting about your work?
34. What do you consider to be the biggest challenges in running a _____?

EXHIBIT 7 Going For It

PROS	CONS
Little to lose, in a position to take a risk, short-term needs are mounting.	Precarious financial situation; short.
The earlier I dedicate the time, the easier it should be.	Lack of experience/exposure.
Personal financial needs are slight.	Am I prepared to handle the setbacks?
It's what I want to do.	Will I choose a business only for the sake of choosing?
It would be exciting.	Want vs. need (is the timing right)?
I owe it to myself/personal tranquillity.	Is the opportunity really there? Am I forcing it?
Pass?	
If not now, when?	Do I need the pressure this search is causing?
Overcome a fear.	
Start up something and sell it in a few years if it's not what I'm looking for.	
I'll be disappointed.	
Quit delaying; sink or swim.	

EXHIBIT 8   Time Log

CALENDAR	ACTIVITY	TIME EXPENDED
Weeks 1&2	Trying to figure out what I was going to do and how I was going to do it.	?????
Week 3	Visited State Dept. of Commerce (and spoke with Maurice Alexander)	two hours
Week 4	Went to downtown branch of the city library (business section)	four hours
	Read booklets and pamphlets gathered thus far.	six hours
Week 5	Started reading "Business Opportunities" section in Times and P-I classifieds	one hour
Week 6	Started log; started writing down what I'm looking for and avoiding in a business.	three & 1/2 hours
Week 7	Xeroxed S.I.C. index; started circling interesting categories	two hours
	Read "Business Opportunities"	one hour
Week 8	Read Sandman's book " Albert's book " Business Opportunities"	two hours one & 1/2 hours one hour
	Screened S.I.C. index twice	three hours
Week 9	Skimmed *Thomas Register,* *National Directory of Assoc.*	one hour one hour
	Read "Business Opportunities"	one hour
Week 10	Drew up "Capability Assessment Guide" Began screening index to Yellow Pages	two hours five hours
	Read "Business Opportunities"	one hour
Week 11	Continued screening Yellow Pages index	four hours

EXHIBIT 8 (continued)

CALENDAR	ACTIVITY	TIME EXPENDED
	Read "Business Opportunities" Read Alberts book	one hour one hour
Week 12	Read "Business Opportunities"	one hour
Week 13	Read or skimmed twenty IEA manuals	eight hours
	Read Albert's book Read "Business Opportunities"	one hour one hour
Week 14	Read or skimmed twenty IEA manuals	eight hours
	Consolidated the Yellow Page and S.I.C. indices and narrowed the list via the criteria checklist.	six hours
	Read "Business Opportunities"	one hour
Week 15	Devised a questionnaire for interviews	two hours
	Used Manufacturers' Directory and Contacts Influential to locate prospects for interviews	three hours
	Read "Business Opportunities"	one hour
Week 16	Called to arrange interviews	1/2 hour
	Interviews with: Bill Mynar Howard Stanford Eugene Holland Bob Lindsay	one & 1/2 hours one hour one & 1/4 hours two hours
	Used *Contacts Influential* to locate prospects in freight forwarding and delivery service	one hour
	Read "Business Opportunities"	one hour
Week 17	Called to arrange interviews	1/2 hour

EXHIBIT 8   (concluded)

Wrote down pros and cons of "Going For It"	one hour
Interviews with:	
Jim Reynolds	one hour
Henry Gai	one & 1/2 hours
Paul Baertch	one & 1/2 hours
Cecil Neilsen	one & 1/2 hours
Dave McDonald (including sitting in on marketing meeting)	six and 1/2 hours
Read "Business Opportunities"	one hour

Note: The time expenditures listed above are rough estimates. They represent time spent only on listed activity and do not include travel time, waiting time, time spent locating information, etc.

Case 4

Chem Synthesis, Inc. (A)*
Creating New Products in a Start-Up

In January 1995 Jim Tolivre was worrying about the developmental strategy of the venture he headed, Chem Synthesis, Inc. The company's line had expanded over the past five years into a broad variety of products for a wide range of commercial customers. The number of potential industries and countries to which CSI had attempted to sell had also expanded. He could see that it might be preferable to concentrate on a few large customers nearby. But the sales opportunities that CSI discovered turned out to be scattered widely. At one time or another the new company was working on sales leads on every continent of the world. It took time to distinguish those who would really buy from those who just might.

Jim was concerned about his lack of industry expertise and whether it had handicapped CSI. The venture had just sustained its fifth straight year of losses since being initiated. Despite record sales in 1994, losses were almost double those of the prior year. Comparative financial statements for the venture since its inception appear in Exhibits 1 and 2.**

Inception

Jim Tolivre, a professor of entrepreneurship at the University of Niagara Falls, had wanted to try a start-up, partly because he studied and taught about entre-

preneurship and partly as an escape from frustrations in trying to persuade his business school to move faster in developing an entrepreneurial program. He had explored a number of business possibilities. One fell apart when the scientist left the start-up team to take a job in another city. In another, Jim shortly concluded that nobody in the venture had a sufficiently high level of technical expertise in that line of business, to be successful. He wanted to team with a real expert. With another contact who happened to be in the roofing business he raised the idea of teaming up to start some sort of enterprise. The roofer suggested that Jim seek out a product with potential.

Ted Ulrich was a business student of Jim's who had immigrated from Europe where he had earned a Ph.D. in chemistry and won a major prize for the technical excellence of his research. He was also seeking a new venture opportunity because of discontent with his present employment in a partnership. A prior immigrant to Canada from Ted's home country and Ted had formed a partnership in which Ted was doing product development. Ted had also put up the money. The other partner was supposed to seek sales. With only 49 percent interest, Ted felt he was being excluded from decision making and was being unfairly exploited because of his

---

* Written in collaboration with Drs. W. Ed McMullan and James Chrisman of the University of Calgary as a basis for class discussion. Names have been disguised.

** All dollar amounts in this case are expressed in Canadian currency.

immigrant status. He had told Jim about how promises made by his partner were not coming true. He also mentioned an acrylic waterproofing substance he had become familiar with in Europe that might be useful in North America.

Ted told Jim, who in turn called his friend in the roofing business. The friend told a partner and the four met during the fall of 1989 to talk about venture possibilities. By the first of December 1989, they had worked out an initial four-way split of shares for creating a company that would develop, produce, sell, and if necessary, apply new and better roof-covering materials. Ted set about the tasks of developing products and Jim went to work on obtaining capital. The other two partners were to be responsible for sales and marketing; however, both decided that there wasn't much they could do until a product was fully developed.

The four attended the National Roofing Contractors Association trade show in San Diego in early 1990, where Ted began to extend and elaborate ideas he had for a liquid-applied, polymer-based material for flat roofs that the two roofing people said looked promising. In mid-1991 Jim and Ted found a potential customer for an adaptation of his new system. They forged a marketing alliance through the president of this customer, a locally-based Canadian subsidiary of a mid-sized North American roofing products manufacturer. Ted now worked on two roofing systems, one based upon the waterproofing substance he had seen in Europe and a second aimed at specific needs of the roofing manufacturer.

The manufacturer, Highdry, installed "inverted roof systems." In this system the roof insulation, rather than being the bottom of two or more layers, was an upper layer with a liquid-applied asphalt membrane beneath it. It was more expensive than more conventional systems where the insulation was below the membrane ($6 to $7 per square foot compared to

around $2 per square foot). The higher cost system was justified in circumstances where complete reliability was especially important. This was the case, for instance, in many high-rise buildings where the roof protected valuable furniture and other objects and where any leaks could damage several floors at once. It would not likely be used on a one-floor warehouse.

Ted undertook the task of creating a material that could be applied on top of an inverted roof covering. Highdry saw this as a way of adding reroofing work to the new construction they already did. This prospect was of particular interest to Highdry because it installed only new roofs, while approximately 70 percent of all commercial building roofing work was reroofing rather than new roofing. At that time building construction was currently in a down cycle and Highdry's sales were impacted accordingly. Since Highdry had 50 agents in Canada and another 150 in the U.S., Jim Tolivre anticipated substantial benefits from the alliance.

Ted soon figured out how to create a new two-coat system to protect Highdry's asphalt membrane. His new system involved four layers. First was the customary asphalt. Second was a layer of fabric to provide tensile strength. Third was a liquid-applied barrier coat to keep the asphalt from leeching upward. Fourth was a top layer of acrylic coating such as CSI used in its own roofing system. Unlike most liquid-applied acrylics, Ted's new formulation would hold up under standing water for long time periods. This was important because in the flat roofing business contractors sometimes observed wryly that drains always got placed at the highest point on the roof.

The CSI product was also cheaper. Jim explained that most producers of roofing materials were small companies that simply blended chemicals that they bought from a large chemical company. The chemical company provided both the chemicals and a recipe for mixing them together to get desired properties. The recipe would even tell what type of impeller blades should be used on machines that would do the mixing.

Blending was simple, whereas formulating the chemicals to be mixed and coming up with the blending formulas was much more sophisticated work. The chemical companies, Tolivre said, in effect charged for the sophisticated part of the work by giving recipes that required use of chemicals with high profit margins. By doing not only the blending but also the formulation, CSI was able to "end run" these higher priced components and produce its roofing materials at costs that were much lower; he estimated on the order of 15 percent to 20 percent less than it cost the blending-only producers. Jim Tolivre commented:

> *Our concept was to offer better products for less money, based on this cost advantage, but the roofing business is actually more complicated than that, especially when trying to decide what is better. Different roofing systems have different advantages, and they vary in quality greatly according to how well they are applied. The roofers who apply them typically have very strong opinions about what is best but disagree a lot among themselves. In our market segment, acrylic roofing competes not only with other acrylics but also with other types of roofing. The biggest market segment is for tar and gravel roofs, which have been around since the Phoenicians and are very good if well applied. It's not easy for a person inexperienced in roofing technology to discern the quality differences.*

Seeking Sales

Meanwhile, as Ted Ulrich was developing, testing, and debugging the new roofing systems, Jim was struggling to raise capital to keep the company going. He had expected that the two roofing co-founders would be conducting market research, developing marketing strategies, and preparing sales materials. But they weren't. He became increasingly frustrated and angry, which created a confrontational atmosphere among the four co-founders. Negotiations for a separation agreement concluded in December 1991. By then additional financing was required not only to cover operating deficits, but also to buy out the other two. Jim set about raising more money.

In January of 1992 Jim searched for marketing replacements by contacting business acquaintances and telling them he needed sales help for the company's new products. One acquaintance told him about someone he knew, Ron Standal, who had over 20 years of sales experience and had helped build a $5 million sales distribution company before selling his interest in it to his business partners. Jim said:

> *I called him and suggested we meet. He agreed, and we set a date for breakfast. He said he would pick me up, and I told him where I lived. He said he could find it all right. It turned out that he lived directly across the street from me, so he just walked over. Within a week of our meeting, I hired him—really feeling lucky to get someone with such impressive credentials. It seemed to me that now we had once again managed to cover the three major legs of an R&D based manufacturing business: R&D/production, finance/administration and sales/marketing.*

Standal and Ulrich now worked on demonstrating to Highdry's sales force the marketability of the new hybrid Highdry system while at the same time continuing tests to make sure it was fully debugged. Each of its

Focusing

Understanding what kinds of forces give rise to opportunity may help guide idea search by giving the mind awareness of patterns that work. So when, in the course of life, such patterns happen to be encountered the would-be entrepreneur will be more likely to recognize them.

Discussions of the future are not hard to find in books and magazines. It is well known that the population is aging, tastes change, technology introduces new capabilities, resources are under increasing demands, pollution is a mounting problem, new markets and sources of supply are opening in former communist countries and third-world countries. The supply of information has been growing at an increasing rate and thereby introducing needs for better ways of handling and communicating it. Advances in telecommunications and computers are helping make that possible, and in the process of doing so they are creating new markets for services, software and hardware.

It is not easy to find start-up ideas that were discovered by a general awareness of these trends. Entrepreneurs don't report, for instance, that they noticed the rising cost of health care and suddenly realized what kind of company to start based on that general information alone, or even based on that information plus brainstorming or use of focus groups. But at the same time, those who have taken advantage of such trends were usually aware of them as at least part of the knowledge base from which they discovered opportunity. Awareness of what is going on certainly can be useful in the idea search process.

Application: *What caused the main opportunity that the entrepreneur in the assigned case aims to exploit to come into existence and when?*

Gap Analysis

One way of formulating boundaries for a venture idea search has been suggested by White.[10] His "Market Gap Analysis" involves a ten-step process for finding viable unserved market opportunities. Prior to White's ten steps is an implicit preliminary step, which is to choose an industry, such as his example, the leisure industry. Briefly, here are the ensuing ten steps:

1. List criteria for the product or service. Typical target criteria might include market size, rate of return, capital intensity, markup level, degree of newness of the product or service and of the market, level of technology, outsourceability, and likely attractiveness to potential investors.

2. Segment the potential market population of the industry. Examples would be by age, income, or education. Pick one of these; for instance adults between ages 35-45.

layers had to contribute different purposes, such as shielding from sun rays, waterproofing, adhesion to the substrate, providing tensile strength, and so forth.

The arrangement that CSI worked out with Highdry provided that Highdry would become the exclusive representative for the new roof system. Highdry insisted on a staged introduction over three years—first regionally, then nationwide in Canada, and then in the U.S. As the new system was brought onto the market, the local Highdry agent was able to double his total sales. But this turned out not to be typical, and by summer most of the Canadian sales program had collapsed.

One reason, Jim explained, was that Highdry's salespeople had been accustomed to selling only new roofs. This they did simply by responding to requests for roofing bids put out by builders. To sell reroofing jobs, he said, required going out and knocking on doors to find out how old the existing roofs were, whether there were any present or predictable leakage problems that the owners should be concerned about, and so forth. Moreover, Highdry interposed another markup which made the end price less competitive. Jim observed:

> So although top management at Highdry was enthused about selling the new reroofing system, their agents were not. Also there was a more personal problem. The man responsible for Canadian operations turned out to have cancer, which flared up out of remission. He started flying to Europe to buy treatments that were not available in Canada. I'm not sure how much his absence affected the sales-collapse problem.

Sales in the U.S. part of the program also failed to materialize for other reasons. U.S. applications, because of regulatory differences, required a different formulation, which took several months to prepare. The CSI team expected that the U.S. roll-out of the new system during the fall of 1992 starting in California and Nevada through Highdry's established network of 150 U.S. agents should generate enough sales to make CSI profitable in year four. Jim said that the failure of the Canadian sales effort probably explained why the U.S. program never got off the ground.

Standal also initiated a telephone, fax, and mail-based, direct-sales campaign into the U.S. in the fall of 1992 aimed at southern states from California to Florida to sell CSI's acrylic roof membrane as a substitute for similar products. The campaign, including the salary of the person hired by Standal to implement it, cost about $40,000 and aimed to provide a better "me too" (imitative) product at a lower price. Jim said:

> We expected Ron Standal's campaign to succeed because he claimed to have run 14 or so such direct sales programs before, all successfully. He really seemed to know what he was doing. But after nine months of essentially no results, we decided to cancel the program.
>
> People are slow to change commercial roofing systems. There are high risks associated with leaking, because rainwater can cause serious damage to all sorts of machinery and merchandise that it might fall on. This produces quite a few lawsuits from roofing jobs. In order to be sure that there won't be leaks when you change from one roofing system to another, you almost have to be a scientist, because the mechanical and chemical components of the systems behave in subtle ways that can be hard to understand. It is hard to convince people to change on the basis of logic. The science is too complex. Experienced business people who are not scientists act on their own opinions.

We were trying to sell roofing materials in the U.S. all through telephone and mail with no face-to-face encounters, and on a small budget, which is tough. It is made worse by the fact that there are a lot of different market segments in terms of roofing contractors, types of buildings, climates, and prior roofing used by the customers. Finally, there are a lot of fly-by-night firms in the roofing business and lots of shoddy products that they stick people with. It's hard to distinguish yourself from them, especially when you are a new company.

Meanwhile, yet another new potential roof coating customer had been found. One of Jim's students, who was from Czechoslovakia, put him in touch with his father, who lived in Canada and had started an import-export company with contacts in the Czech Republic. CSI agreed to sell exclusively through his firm in the Czech Republic, and at prices that would allow him to compete with existing domestic products there. He in turn agreed to seek sales actively for it there. Jim said:

To help their sales effort, we extended credit for around $100,000 because we were desperate for sales. We probably went overboard to help more than we would now. But the result of this effort was that we soon had more sales in the Czech Republic than we did in Canada.

The hoped-for level of break-even, however, did not materialize. As with earlier applications, CSI found that the Czech market called for some special adjustments to its product applications. Moreover, the pricing formula for that country left CSI with a reduced margin of 28 percent in contrast to its customary 30 percent minimum target.

A tabulation illustrating the variety of customers and locations to which CSI sold appears in Exhibit 3.

The Coating and Adhesives Industry

CSI viewed itself as a member of the coatings and adhesives industry. Attributes of this industry by which companies and products could be differentiated included the following:

- **Size of company.** At the big end were giants like Imperial Chemicals, DuPont and 3M. At the small end were innumerable firms, including one-person enterprises that mixed and sold product out of their back yards and garages. CSI saw itself as small but innovative.

- **Type of application.** CSI began with roof coatings but then had gone into binders for floor tile, waterproofing for grain bins and fire-retardant paints. The list of other products in each of these categories and numerous others made by thousands of companies was virtually endless.

- **Type of customer.** In contrast to familiar brand names, like Super Glue and Dutch Boy, found in retail stores, CSI's products were sold directly to other companies. These included applicators, distributors at several levels, and end users, including building owners and farmers.

- **Types of base polymers used in formulation.** Acrylics and epoxies were different types of base polymers. Companies sometimes specialized in one or the other. CSI worked with a variety, including acrylics, epoxies, waxes, asphalt, polyurethanes and others. "We tend to go wherever Ted has expertise and do what he can do. That guy is really good at his work," Jim observed.

- **Level of process integration.** Many smaller firms simply mixed and blended their raw materials following simple recipes. CSI formulations included producing chemical reactions to produce different substances that were then mixed with others in vertically-integrated reactive processes. CSI operated at different levels in the chemical process depending upon the materials. In epoxies, for instance, CSI produced hardeners, which were more fundamental compounds typically produced by chemical companies. CSI did not as yet produce the polymers which were the basis of its other products, so in some product areas it was less a chemical company and more of a formulator and blender.

- **Participation in R&D.** Most major chemical companies had large laboratories wherein numerous scientists and engineers developed new formulations. Smaller companies most often sold products that had been developed by others. Many simply bought commodity chemicals in bulk and resold them in smaller quantities, either by delivery or through repackaging. As Tolivre saw it, creation of new products through research and experimentation was a strength of CSI, for which it possessed the scientific sophistication, but not the overhead, of a much larger specialty chemical company.

Jim Tolivre said that the organization of CSI was exceptionally strong technically for its size. Three of its employees held Ph.D.'s, one a Master's, and two, Bachelor's degrees. At least four he characterized as also extraordinarily creative "rare talent." The company philosophy, he said, was to treat all employees as professionals. He also noted that most CSI employees were in effect accepting pay cuts in the range of 5 percent to as much as 50 percent, depending upon the individual, to work at CSI.

CSI Products

The number of CSI products had grown substantially over the past five years. Tolivre believed that CSI had significant competitive advantages in: (1) the two liquid-applied acrylic roof coating systems along with support products such as fabric, (2) two different price and quality epoxy binders for stone floors, (3) a repulpable paper coating and adhesive, (4) an epoxy paint and flooring product containing no solvents and consequently no smell or air pollution, and (5) most importantly, a coating system for sealing the bases of grain bins. In addition, CSI had other products he characterized as high in quality but low in price which gave CSI at least a regional advantage—good quality "me-too" products, essentially comparable to those of other companies, that filled gaps in the specialty product lines or met the specific needs of existing customers. Jim said he was really not sure how to define either the exact industry that CSI was in, the customer segments it served or the number of products it had.

Did different package sizes or different labels on the same substance constitute different products? The epoxy binder for flooring contractors was also sold in much smaller packages to jewelers for gluing gems in settings. Did that make it two different products? Or how about changes in chemical composition to improve an existing product, after which the company might be selling both versions? Ted and his technician, George, sometimes had to reformulate products when different components became more scarce or relatively more expensive than other components which, Jim said, was quite often:

The technical experts have to keep formulating and reformulating. The job is never done. Whereas production might save 1 or 2 percent of total product cost by clever reorganization, R&D could save 4 to 8 percent with the same amount of work. Then you never know what new things they might come up with. They also helped manage accounts. After all, this is a technical game.

In 1994 CSI entered the agricultural market with a grain bin sealing system developed by Chuck Matchet, a mechanical engineer with many years of experience in the agricultural products industry. Matchet became a serious investor in 1993 and was asked to join the company in the spring of 1994. Jim Tolivre referred to the circumstances surrounding the grain bin system:

It looks like a company-maker, and it is only eight months old. Agricultural markets! We didn't even give them a consideration until Chuck and Les Banner, another investor, joined us early in the year, both to help with the Czech production build up. When they saw that the Czech orders were going to be way down, they got to work thinking about alternatives. Chuck has a Master's in Engineering and 20 years' experience in agricultural research. Les is an old farm boy. They saw the problem, and with the help of our R&D guys, concocted a solution.

Ron told them they were wasting their time, since he had already looked at the agricultural markets. I think his ego couldn't stand having things going on outside his control. I supported them despite Ron's protest. There was no love lost between Ron and them. Chuck designed the system, and then Les used his net of contacts to generate interest, starting with one farmer or retailer at a time. It wasn't planned from the top. It just happened because two guys had a better idea. They are also both major investors. Perhaps that helped.

Most recently, Jim continued, the company had come up with yet another product, an epoxy hardener or curing agent that Jim said was of particularly high quality:

Anybody sophisticated in buying curing agents should be able to recognize its quality attributes and, we think, might buy after sampling it through the mail, as often happens in the industry. If it works, then we expect they will begin to ask us about prices for various quantities. So we are going to run a $10 advertisement in a magazine that deals with commodity products for the whole chemical industry. It will be interesting to see what results we get on that. Ted, of course, is working on a line of such curing agents to enhance overall marketability.

Product Development

Jim said that CSI sometimes operated as a custom formulator for customers who requested particular products and sometimes as a developer of its own product ideas. When customers wanted new products developed, CSI attempted to be sure that the customers would represent big enough markets to justify the development. In the case of the grain bin coating product, which had been suggested by one of the company's own sales people, CSI had done considerable analysis of secondary data on the market to ascertain that it was big enough.

At other times, a new product might come as a natural companion to something CSI was already working with. For instance, the company was drawn by customer interest into developing an epoxy binder for stone floors. From this it was able to respond quickly when another potential customer asked about epoxy coating for the inside of metal containers, indicating it would buy about $300,000 worth per year. This in turn led to an epoxy paint for concrete floors.

Four stages, Jim said, were typically required to create a new product: formulation, lab testing, production scale-up and site testing. The first stage, formulation, involved careful consideration of the end use, alternative compounds and ways of preparing them. Ted Ulrich especially liked doing this phase. Jim observed:

> *Ted attends a lot of trade shows where he sees things about the market and gets ideas about new products and he has good instincts of his own about ones we should undertake. He studies literature in the library for new developments, phones suppliers, orders chemicals, and they discuss ideas together. The suppliers send him free samples of a lot of things. You can really build up a collection of ingredients and then try out other product possibilities.*

Jim explained that the next phase, lab testing, involved creating large numbers of new formulations and then subjecting them to in-house tests to determine their resultant properties. A new roof coating material might be painted on a small sample of surface material and then immersed for weeks in a bucket of water to see whether its adhesion to the surface would endure. It would be stretched to see what its maximum elongation before snapping was or how great its strength was after being subjected to intense ultraviolet light in a weathering chamber. The tests were typically those recommended by the American Standards for Testing Materials (ASTM), and sometimes tested by independent testing companies or provincial government laboratories. CSI had used one testing company in Arizona, another locally, plus a government laboratory in the province.

In the third phase, production scale-up, the formulation was created in bigger batches. Laboratory-test batches usually were tried first in Styrofoam coffee cups. Next might come batches in buckets that could be tried on larger surfaces, then 20 gallon drums. Finally, it might be scaled up to batch plant quantities of two to ten tons.

In site testing, the fourth phase, the new material was applied in a situation of actual use. Jim explained that the first roofing material was applied to the roof of a local restaurant that had been persuaded to try it, partly through the incentive of an exceptionally low price:

> *The material worked all right. But we ran into other problems, like getting some of it on the suit of a passing pedestrian and some of it onto a parked car.*

This whole process of development from creation through site application, he continued, might take three months to two years, depending on the process. The R&D team would be looking for some features in the material during laboratory blending, others one week after application, others after another season, and so forth. There might be well over a dozen different physical properties in the material whose changes would have to be monitored, some in the laboratory phase and others in the site testing.

Because of its formulation capabilities CSI continually encountered opportunities to develop other new compounds. After the first roofing product the company began work for a large public company on a repulpable paper coating and adhesive for wrapping paper that was used to protect large rolls of newsprint. Jim commented:

People will hear about what we can do and tell us about some formulation they would like to have and that they could sell a lot of if they had it. For instance, the packaging company that wanted a particular type of paper coating that did not as yet exist was talking to some researchers in the provincial government about where it might get help finding such a product. The researchers knew about Ted because we have received government grants on some of our work, and they put the company in touch with him.

Another new product lead came out of a trade fair, where the user of an adhesive for stone floors was asking where he might find an alternative source of supply. He was going to sue the supplier of his present adhesive because it was yellowing excessively. He approached a sales representative in our booth, who said we could probably formulate something to meet his needs. That led to our producing a new epoxy binder. In another case, a man knew me and contacted me because he thought he had a market if we could produce a low-cost fire-retarding paint for him.

Sometimes Ted will get a product idea on his own and suggest a formula to George, who then figures out just how much of each ingredient to put in. George's part does not really require training in chemistry, just high intelligence. You need a scientist for the design role, plus a technician who need not be a scientist. George is an electrical engineering genius with talent for solving complex problems. There are an infinite number of possible combinations, and George judges which proportions to try. Meanwhile, Ted gets interrupted a lot by people wanting to talk to him. George tends to stay away from the interruptions and concentrate on following through in the laboratory.

Facilities for this development were relatively small and spare. The laboratory occupied a room approximately 10 by 12 feet in which were tables with many Styrofoam cups containing samples of different formulations. The first piece of equipment needed was an accurate scale for weighing ingredients. Beyond that the company had acquired only what it needed and it actively sought bargains in buying equipment. Recently, they had found a local company that was getting rid of its laboratory and were able to buy an estimated $10,000 worth of laboratory glassware for around a tenth of that amount. Another time they bought at government auction a weathering machine consisting of a refrigerator-like metal cabinet with a glass door in which temperature and humidity could be regulated. New, the machine would have cost around $20,000. CSI paid $600 for it. Jim recalled:

The only problem with it was that it had previously been used for processing by a taxidermist, and it reeked of formaldehyde. We had to clean it again and again until we got rid of the stench. But since then it has worked fine.

Jim believed CSI's R&D capabilities and reputation were steadily getting stronger. Policies for managing product development were also changing. He continued:

We test more thoroughly before going to market now than we did at the start. As we get farther along, we have more at risk and so have to be more conservative. Also, we're getting more selective. We used to say yes to almost anyone who wanted us to try a new product idea, but now we are more careful about doing it.

Other entrepreneurs come to us with ideas, and you never can know in advance which of them might really turn out to be good. Our policy has generally been that if someone is interested in having it and can convince us that they can sell it, we will make it. The key judge in the process, though, is Ted. If it is within our competence and he wants to do it, we go ahead."

A tabulation illustrating the variety of CSI's products and how they arose appears in Exhibit 4.

Jim noted that availability of tax credits and the fact that CSI had been able to get government grants for some of its R&D work had been advantageous. According to the accountants, who had capitalized the non-governmental portion of R&D spending, CSI had spent around $600,000 on R&D up to February 1995. Approximately $135,000 of this had been paid by government grants, and 35 percent of the rest had, he said, come back in the form of tax credits.

Organization

CSI's sales and marketing was now reorganized around Don Jensen, who became CSI's new president in January 1995 and was, Jim said, in transition to become chief executive officer. Jensen held a Ph.D. in Chemistry and a recent MBA, plus he had acquired five years experience with a high-technology company in a variety of functions. Les Banner, a landscape contractor and a major investor, was asked to help with the production before switching to a sales capacity when sales fizzled in the late spring of 1994. Jim Tolivre had relinquished his position as president at the beginning of 1995 to become Chairman of the Board and chief financial officer. Ron Standal had been let go in late 1994. Jim reasoned these changes as follows:

I had hired Don with the idea of his becoming president in about a year.

With Ron gone our need was to shore up sales and marketing. I could have put Don in as VP of Sales and Marketing. He was certainly showing potential there. Don was productive in sales and marketing from the outset. His Ph.D. in Chemistry was also useful in binding the company together. In reality his being president provided credibility for managing major accounts.

As for me, I think I can do what I'm good at from the chairman role. I only had part time to be president, given my continuing university responsibilities. I want to spend more time on university projects as well. I guess I'm tired after five years of struggle. I haven't managed sales particularly well. Taking so long to become profitable has been blowing my credibility. As a new president, Don may acquire some additional time to try new things out. He can still focus on sales and marketing. There are many factors.

On the question of what had gone wrong on sales and marketing Jim Tolivre had a number of observations:

I didn't know much about sales and marketing technical products. It was all I could do to raise capital, one and a half million from investors and another half million from various government sources, pull together the talent, and be a university professor. I had to count on others. I bet on a number of people through time: first, my two co-founders; second, Ron; third, Don and Les. (Les has really stirred up a lot of action over the last six months.) One thing I learned about sales and marketing is that it requires a differentiated set of skills and knowledge bases. Few people have a full set, and a full set is what a new company with new products for new markets requires. My co-founders couldn't do market research or provide a market focus. We ended up with a first product that was best suited to the southern states and here we are way up north in Canada.

Ron couldn't seem to do market research, provide a market focus or develop a market strategy, and he would not or could not do prospecting. However, he was good at sales and at client management, had good product knowledge and was good at providing sales support material. Don and Les I'm getting to know. Les is certainly good at prospecting. Don is strong on market research and market strategy. Between the two of them we are beginning to fill in the gaps. I'll probably only discover their limitations through time as I did with Ron.

For the organization as a whole Jim saw challenges associated with trying to reach a critical mass:

Even to sell a small amount of a product you need to have all of the functions, R&D, production, accounting, marketing, quality control, customer service, and so forth. You have to have product-description flyers for it and application instructions, package labels and price lists. The problem, it seems to me, is lack of enough sales volume to cover all those things and still make a profit. The question is, should we be doing anything differently to make that happen?

One thing I believe from my experience to date is that it is not simply a matter of throwing more money at sales and marketing. It's too easy to give responsibility for spending to people in those areas and see cash instantly vanish without producing significant results. They are so persuasive about the budget needed and what it will accomplish. But how can you know in advance whether they're right? With product development people, you can look at what they have done before and rely on that as a fairly good gauge of what they will be able to create. But that doesn't seem to work so well with sales people. I'm not sure why or what to do about it.

EXHIBIT 1 - CSI Comparative Financial Statements (Years Ending December 31)

	1990	1991	1992	1993	1994
Assets					
Current Assets					
Cash	30,186	0	18,289	72,235	113,710
Accounts receivable		84,588	12,655	174,957	108,333
Grants receivable	3,666	6,900	2,205	10,532	10,033
Investment tax credits receivable	13,357	15,386	24,746	26,923	53,341
Inventory	4,396	24,637	43,266	67,115	163,316
Prepaid expenses		1,850	2,910	1,850	29,649
Recoverable contract costs					101,362
Total Current Assets	51,605	133,361	104,071	353,612	579,744
Capital assets		12,794	25,234	63,736	303,835
Deferred development costs	32,844	63,599	91,990	118,857	159,718
Total Assets	84,449	209,754	221,295	536,205	1,043,297
Liabilities					
Current Liabilities					
Bank Indebtedness		33,843			
Accounts payable	3,646	129,515	67,557	94,609	238,749
Current portion of long-term debt*			2,913	117,800	36,222
Total Current Liabilities	3,646	163,358	70,470	212,409	274,971
Long term debt*			194,571	184,542	253,322
Due to shareholders	75,000	146,683	136,683	136,683	136,683
Share Capital and Deficits					
Share capital	30,080	96,225	187,386	580,111	1,250,414
Contributed surplus			36,495	10,214	11,532
Deficit	-24,277	-196,512	-404,310	-587,754	-883,625
Total Liabilities and Equity	84,449	209,754	221,295	536,205	1,043,297
# Shares outstanding (thousands)**	18,665	19,930	14,672	15,642	18,932

* In 1992 and 1993 the company acquired a $250,000 interest-free negotiable (and renegotiable) term debt from a government agency.
** The company was both selling shares to new investors and buying shares back to buy out other investors at different share values over time.

EXHIBIT 2 - CSI Comparative Income Statements (Year ending December 31)

	1990	1991	1992	1993	1994
Sales		306,289	382,724	467,723	700,862
Cost of Sales					
Wages and subcontract		189,655	217,773	36,239	29,576
Materials		119,474	96,406	326,285	501,032
Depreciation		3,261	3,716	8,492	20,525
Total		312,390	317,895	371,016	551,133
Gross Margin		-6,101	64,829	96,707	149,729
Interest Income					20,940
Total		-6,101	64,829	96,707	170,669
Expenses					
Business taxes and licenses			1,823	1,683	13,123
Bad debts					63,185
Insurance	332	6,869	3,081	3,219	25,044
Interest and bank charges	107	2,094	5,006	3,794	3,898
Interest on long-term debt			1,423	1,845	1,167
Marketing	987	3,237	13,898	14,242	23,296
Market research		1,500	4,930	3,820	0
Office	1,302	7,169	15,790	11,554	18,179
Professional fees	4,644	12,057	17,705	17,473	26,509
Rent	100	15,193	23,787	24,581	70,556
Repair and maintenance					4,024
Salaries and consulting fees	12,472	121,688	113,678	144,211	141,734
Telephone	46	7,175	8,184	13,583	19,126
Travel	5,091	1,103	5,950	8,392	11,475
Vehicle	347	2,602	4,256	1,332	1,814
Warehouse supplies				3,931	5,199
Amortization of development costs		4,542	32,051	22,841	29,694
Depreciation		344	2,779	3,650	8,517
Total Expenses	25,428	185,573	254,341	280,151	466,540
Net Income Before Interest	-25,428	-191,674	-189,512	-183,444	-295,871
Interest Income	1,151	597			
Net Income	-24,277	-191,077	-189,512	-183,444	-295,871

EXHIBIT 3 - CSI Customers Over Time

DATE	PRODUCT	CUSTOMER COUNTRY	MET VIA	DISPOSITION
Sumr 91	Roofing	Canada (local)	Jim while selling shares.	Ted envisaged system to fit company's need. Ron managed. Failed to grow materially.
Sprg 92	Roofing	Czech Republic	Jim's student was partner in export firm with father.	Ron managed. Became a credit problem but still purchases product.
Sprg 93	Flooring	Canada (local)	Salesperson with company for a few months met customer at local trade show.	Ted developed a system to meet their needs. Little growth but a steady customer.
Wint 94	Flooring	Kuwait	Local flooring customer (above) introduced his Kuwaiti client to CSI as alternate source of supply.	Ron managed the account. Failed to grow to date.
Sprg 93	Paper Coating	Canada (local)	CSI scientist introduced to customer by provincial government scientists.	Potentially sizable customer but a long period required to develop both products and relationships. Managed by Ted.
Wint 94	Roofing	U.S.	U.S. trade show.	Managed by internal salesperson. Slow to mature. Appears to have moderate potential.
Wint 94	Roofing	Thailand	Agent for Japan found the company on the Internet.	Visit has been made to Canada. Bids are in place in Thailand. Visit to Thailand planned for June 1995.
Fall 94	Agricultural System	Canada (regional)	Les' contacts.	Ordered a significant amount of product and promises to be a significant customer. $500 million company with 33 sales outlets.
Wint 95	Roofing & Agricultural	Canada	Don Jensen's contact.	Bidding underway.
Wint 95	Agricultural System	Canada (regional)	Les' direct sales effort.	Potentially sizable client $2 billion firm with 26 potential outlets for product.
Wint 95	Epoxy Paint	Canada (regional)	Les' direct sales effort.	Ted developed a system to fit their requirements.
Wint 95	Agricultural System	Canada (regional)	Les' direct sales effort.	Potentially sizable firm. $2 billion annual revenues. Between 50 and 150 potential outlets for product.

EXHIBIT 4 - CSI Products Over Time

PRODUCT Category	PRODUCT TYPE	DATE BEGUN	MARKET INTRO	SOURCE OF IDEA	RATIONALE OF CHOICE	RESULTS THAT OCCURRED	ESTIMATED PROFITABILITY
Roofing	Liquid-Applied Acrylic - Final Coat	Sumr 89	Sprg 91	Scientist	Thought to be a better product for the future	Product has been the financial mainstay of the firm from 1992 through 1994.	Margins originally tight but becoming larger both through reformulation and better purchasing.
	Concrete Primer	Fall 91	Sprg 92	Customer application requirement	Needed for over concrete roofs in Korea in order to properly adhere final coat.		
	Asphalt Barrier	Fall 91	Sprg 92	Customer application requirement	Needed for use with new system for Highdry.		
Flooring	Epoxy Binder for stone floors	Sumr 92	Sprg 93	Customer request	Customer dissatisfied with existing supplier.	Generated $100,000 to $200,000 sales from 1992-1994.	Contributed to overhead. No expenditures undertaken to promote product.
Paper Coating	Repulpable Paper Coating	Sprg 92	Sumr 94	Customer request	Customer would use large volume if formulated to spec.	Took two years to develop and a sizable proportion of lab time during the period.	Only an expense to date. Product trials only.
Specialty Paint	Fire-Retardant Paint Primer	Fall 92	Sumr 94	Entrepreneur's request	Entrepreneur felt that he could sell a substantial volume if formulated to specs.	Took a sizable amount of time to develop.	Only an expense to date.
Roofing	Single Coat Acrylic Roofing for over asphaltic surfaces	Sumr 92	Sprg 94	Sales Department Request	Wanted an easier-to-use one-coat system.	Replacing older product for some customers.	Contributing to overhead while adding little to sales or marketing expense.
Textured Coating	Parging Material (outer texture for concrete walls)	Sprg 94	Wint 95	Customer request	Needed a new type of material to adhere to a Styrofoam form.	A moderate development cost.	No sales to date.
Agricultural Coating	Used Firstly as Coating for Bases of Grain Bins	Sumr 94	Fall 94	Salesperson and applications engineer	Two people in company saw need for system.	Moderate development costs.	Becoming firm's most important system from a financial point of view.
Paper Adhesive	Adhesive for Adhering Paper to Paper	Fall 94	Sprg 95	Customer request	U.S. supplier closed Canadian plant and moved south.	Relatively low development cost.	Trial sales to begin.
Specialty Paint	Epoxy Paint	Fall 94	Sprg 95	Customer request	U.S. supplier closed Canadian plant and consolidated in U.S.	Moderate development costs.	Product trial sales to begin.

Michael Shane (A)

The first time you try to start a business is the easiest. Everyone expects you to fail. It's the second or third time around that can shake your confidence. People expect you to do better than the time before; and if you don't, they think that something is wrong. Not only that—you're going into another unknown area, just when you've gotten comfortable with what you've been working on so hard before.

Michael Shane, was reflecting on his "third time around" for starting a business. His latest idea for a venture was to get involved with the growing computer industry—perhaps as a distributor for retail computer stores. Two months earlier, in December of 1979, he had assembled a core of five people to find out if a "super distributor" was needed. In addition to himself, Michael's brother, Tom Shane, and sister, Sandy Fromm, were helping in planning and learning about the industry through calls to computer stores and going through trade magazines. His administrative assistant, Elaine Cresto, had worked for Michael in his previous business for the past five years and agreed to help with this possible venture. To survey stores, Michael had just hired Dick Sanders, the only one of the five who would admit to knowing "a little bit about computers."

Now, in February of 1980, the five were working out of Michael's recently purchased condominium in suburban Boston. Each had a telephone line for making calls to stores and manufacturers throughout the United States to learn about trends and needs in the industry. Michael explained

that if there was need for a "super distributor," their next step would be to develop a strategy for the venture. If not, perhaps they might be able to discover through market inquiry another niche relating to computers that would afford them a business opportunity. The trick, Michael emphasized, would be to interpret the information they got correctly. Otherwise, the past months of preparation and nearly $20,000 already invested in the unnamed venture could turn out to be a complete loss.

Wig Flair

Michael Shane was 17 years old in 1967 when he started his first business. Using $235 in savings he began selling wigs, which he bought from New York wholesalers for $35 and sold for $35 out of the trunk of his car. His mother had owned several beauty salons and most of the wigs she carried cost from $38 up. He reasoned that by starting at a low price and building volume he would be able to buy in larger quantities at lower costs to net a profit. Emphasis on service and fast delivery paid off. Soon his cost dropped to $30 per wig, then dropped further as his sales rose to $100,000 per month by the end of the first year.

He rented 2,500 square feet of warehouse space in Canton, Massachusetts, and quit Babson College as a sophomore to become a wig distributor. He chose the name "Wig Flair" for the business and began selling to retail stores. With profits he began to buy larger volumes and varieties of wigs and go to more exclusive boutiques and retail chains. Timing decisions, he said, came from an intuitive sense, based on casual observation of fashion trends, that the market was ripe for wider distribution of wigs. Enlisting his younger brother, Tom, to help in the stock room after school, Michael developed contacts for buying wigs directly from a Hong Kong-based manufacturer instead of going through New York suppliers.

To support further growth he took in as 50-percent partner a customer who ran a wig salon at night and worked as a meat salesman during the day. By 1969, their joint company had developed a nationwide network of sales representatives who called on beauty supply houses. It also employed a telephone sales force, which sold to wig wholesalers. All Wig Flair sales were C.O.D. Volume continued growing, and in 1970 Wig Flair bought its own Hong Kong manufacturing plant.

Later that year, with sales at $12 million, the two sold out for 150,000 shares of U.S. Industries, then traded on the NYSE at $12 per share. They also received employment contracts of $60,000 per year each, plus dividends of $100,000 per year each. In addition, they received incentive options, which could earn them up to another $5.5 million over the next five years, if performance met projections. The projections were, in fact not met, as the market for wigs declined in profitability. But Michael was able to sell his U.S. Industries shares at $27.

His partner stayed on, but Michael left Wig Flair a year after selling out. He explained.

> It wasn't like we were building toward anything, and I hated it. I realized that my partner was only interested in the money. I was interested in money, but also in creating something. Just sitting there and drawing money on my five-year employment contract and not making waves was of no interest to me.

> When I left the company, I didn't know what I was going to do. I was 21 years old and I had good instincts and some money. I wanted to be independent. I figured I'd dabble in some things for a while.

Michael started investing, mostly in real estate. One deal his accountant introduced him to was a retail blue jeans business needing capital. He invested $25,000 in what became a five-store operation. He also arranged with the Wig Flair plant in Hong Kong to make jeans with its spare sewing capacity. The first $300,000 order, however, was patterned on Hong Kong styles unacceptable to Americans. Michael wrote off his investment and gave his interest to a store manager.

Faded Glory

Subsequently, however, the manager had a dispute with his partner that threatened to break up the jeans business. The Hong Kong plant manager called Michael in a panic to say that he was going to lose the jeans business. Michael had been thinking that there was still opportunity in jeans. His brother, Tom, commented on Michael's vision:

> He told me in 1973 that he thought the next thing in fashion would be blue jeans that went beyond the traditional concept of dungarees. He turned out to be right.

Michael purchased $10,000 in denim, and set up the factory to begin production of private label fashion jeans. His own vision of the situation was as follows:

> In those days, there was no fashion denim like we know fashion denim today. Hard blue denim, like Levi's, that's all there was. They weren't even washing them out. But you had to be stupid

not to see everybody bleeding their blue jeans out in the bathtub. So we took them, washed them out, and put studs on them or dragons or pansies, or whatever, and that was fashion. We were fashion, and the first year we had $12 million in sales.

This new business, Faded Glory, was a family affair. Michael allowed some of his brothers and sisters to obtain ownership on favorable terms, but retained voting control himself. His brother, Jim, managed internal administration, while Michael took care of marketing and other "outside" functions. Tom continued to work in the back room, filling orders and taking inventory in his spare time from undergraduate work at Boston University. Sandy joined the two in early 1974 to set up a sales force and telephone system to keep in touch with retail customers. She recalled:

My job was to build a sales group that would rely on telephones as the main way to get orders and service accounts. I started by myself, sitting with one phone in a big empty room. Five years later, there were over 40 people working the phones and a field sales force of 100, calling on thousands of stores we had as customers.

Although Faded Glory had a head start in fashion jeans, competitors quickly appeared, not only with other designs but also aggressive prices and service. Telephone salespeople called individual stores periodically to inform retailers of lines and promotions available. The calls also obtained information about retailer problems, such as late delivery, with suppliers' services.

In addition, a field sales force called on stores to get orders. Eventually, phone salespeople collaborated to coordinate for better service. For very large accounts, a VIP "hot line" was set up to provide still better service. Mass mailings were also used to provide stores with posters, product announcements and promotional literature.

Tom Shane continued his description of how Faded Glory developed and grew:

Initially, we were selling to specialty retail stores—boutiques—which were relatively small. I was responsible for seeing that the orders were filled, and Jim made sure that the volume of the jeans we needed came from overseas at the right times. In the early days, you would get the requisition from the salesperson, grab a basket, and walk around the back room filling the order. We added data processing capabilities as our sales increased, and we finally had to move out of our original warehouse to larger facilities.

Faded Glory's distribution system provided retail stores with much better service than they had previously received. We had a competitive edge because we could make large volume purchases, promise shipments to be ready at the start of the five or six fashion seasons each year, and maintain service credibility with individual stores.

Refining Distribution Capabilities

While Wig Flair relied on relatively few accounts, keying on large retail department stores for sales, Tom recalled that Faded Glory had developed a more extensive distribution system:

In the case of Faded Glory, we were selling to specialty retail stores, which were relatively small. I was responsible for seeing that the orders were filled and the volumes of the jeans we needed came at the right times. At first, it was pretty simple. You would get the requisition from the salesperson, grab a basket, and walk around the back room filling the order. As our sales increased, we added data processing capabilities and finally had to move from the Canton warehouse to larger facilities.

In the company phone bank, Sandy had directed employees who called stores periodically to inform retailers of the different lines of jeans currently carried and any special promotions being conducted, and to learn of any problems stores might have in terms of delivery or other parts of the relationship. A field sales force also called on stores to obtain initial orders and solicit reorders. Sandy recalled that over time they merged the two functions so that the person on the phone handled both sales and service of a particular account:

We divided the workload by geographic region so a person might be handling all the stores in North and South Carolina, for instance. The field sales force still recruited new accounts and helped with promotion and displays. As for any national chains, they typically bought from one central area, such as New York, so the person who had New York would handle that particular chain.

Sandy added that much of a typical phone salesperson's time was spent on responding to incoming calls and taking orders for a particular design of jean. A "VIP hot line" was set up to provide quick service to the company's largest customers. Mass mailings provided stores with posters, product announcements on accessory outerwear, and other promotional literature. These efforts, according to Tom, provided retail stores much better distributor service than they had previously received. Making large-volume purchases, having shipments ready at the start of each of the five or six fashion seasons per year, and maintaining service contact with indi-

vidual stores was a competitive edge he cited as central to the firm's success. He commented:

A lot of things we did were strictly by seat of the pants. But it didn't take long to find out which jeans were the dogs and which ones were the stars. You simply tried to order less dogs and more stars and make sure that the retail outlet got the kind of attention that you knew you would like to have if you were in their shoes.

Faded Glory's sales grew to $40 million in its second year, as it focused on the high-end fashion business. Pretax profit was about $6 million. Gross margin reached 45 percent and Michael guessed it might reach 60 percent. Instead, however, it started dropping, down to 32 percent as sales reached $50 million. The company booked $175 million in orders its third year, but delivered only $55 million because the Hong Kong supplier refused to expand capacity.

Michael went looking for suppliers elsewhere and soon took over a Nicaraguan plant that had been foreclosed by its bank. Progress there, however, was shortly terminated by a revolution. One of the plant managers was shot. The factory was closed and a $700,000 write-off was taken by Faded Glory.

The search for yet another supplier in Guatemala was interrupted by a disagreement between Michael and Jim over how Jim managed. The company now had 600 employees, including eight of Michael's relatives. In 1978, Michael asked to be bought out. He recalled:

I wasn't interested in keeping the company at the $50 million level. Also, I was getting up every morning and saying, "There's got to be more to life than the garment business and making money." I wanted to do other things. I was a little interested in politics among other things, so in early 1979, I sold out to my partner and my brother.

His brother, Jim, and sister remained with Faded Glory, as did his administrative assistant, Elaine. Tom had graduated from Boston University in 1977 and was now entering his second year of law school at Suffolk University.

Considering a Computer Venture

Michael spent the end of 1978 and first half of 1979 working with one of the major political parties in its Washington, D.C. office. He developed a friendship with the director of an East Coast educational institute and recalled that whenever he visited or traveled with this friend, the man would be carrying around a portable computer. He showed Michael how the machine worked and the capabilities microcomputers have for problem solving. Michael said his friend's fascination with computers further piqued his own interest in the machines. A subsequent trade show he attended inspired him to serious discussions with his brother about the prospect of entering the computer industry. He observed:

> I was attending a blue jeans trade show at the Coliseum in New York. Half of the floor was being used for jeans while the other half had a trade show for personal computers going on. I wandered over and started talking with some of the sales manufacturers representatives and manufacturers and found out that they regarded themselves as the kingpins of the future. I realized that computers could be a good bet if I started another business.
>
> I met with several guys who owned retail stores. I was willing to match the capital they had in the business for a 50 percent interest, but I was perfectly happy to let them run it. I'd have been

delighted to have been a passive investor, just talking to them once a week or so, and offering them my expertise where it was needed. What I was looking for was someone I saw eye-to-eye with in business philosophy and who had the ability to run a big company. But I never found the situation I was looking for.

Elaine Cresto had joined Faded Glory in 1974 as a result of seeking part-time work through an employment agency, which in turn, referred her as a two-week replacement for a secretary on vacation. She recalled fearing that if she insisted upon a permanent part-time referral, the employment agency might never call her back. But now, six years later, she was still working for Michael. Her duties gradually increased, as she kept telling Michael, "I don't have enough work to do." One aspect of her work, she remembered, was occasionally clipping an article on computers from a magazine at Michael's request, and filing it for future reference. She said the articles ranged from impacts computers were expected to have on society to information about major manufacturers and their product lines. When Michael asked her to help think about a new venture that would be involved with the computer industry, Elaine said it came as no surprise to her.

By autumn of 1979, Michael, Tom and Sandy were contemplating ways to begin dealing in small computers and peripheral equipment. Their consensus was to explore whatever gaps might exist in distribution channels between manufacturers and retailers. Michael stated that start-up capital would be provided from his personal savings and that the apartment complex where he lived could serve as an office initially. It had recently been converted to condominiums and he decided to make a down payment on both his unit and the one immediately above it.

Michael requested another three phone lines for the condo, in addition to the two already present, and ordered subscriptions to magazines carrying computer advertisements and information. Sandy and Elaine scanned the magazines to find names of computer stores and products that they most often sold, as well as information about their typical customers. Tom spent much of his time talking with the stores by telephone, calling manufacturers to inquire about their products, and discussing overall strategy with Michael.

The common advice to get a good lawyer and accountant to start a business was true, Michael said. "But first and foremost," he emphasized, "you need a good market researcher." He placed an advertisement in the *Boston Globe* in late November for someone to conduct studies for the prospective venture. Elaine screened the respondents by phone, commenting that she was looking for persons who had experience in the computer industry and who seemed to come across well over the phone. One person whom she advised Michael to interview was Dick Sanders, who recalled his reaction when he first read the ad and later met Michael:

> *I told myself this must be a waste of time; it was a real small ad. On the other hand, I was out of work because the company I was with had just gone bankrupt. My job prospects were pretty dim except for a major local mainframe manufacturer, and I had the feeling that I would just get lost in their type of environment. So I went in to interview and was immediately impressed to find out that Michael had an entrepreneurial spirit. I quit interviewing elsewhere and was hired in three days. Most managers look for the big, glossy position announcements and tend to value a job by the size of ad in the classified section. I'm glad that this time I didn't.*

Dick had spent most of his professional career with a Boston-based market research firm which specialized in the computer industry. In his words: "I've been doing market surveys all my life." He said his task now was to design a survey to send computer stores that would determine:

1. Whether need for a distributor existed.

2. How such a venture should be set up.

3. What type of services should be provided to both manufacturers and retailers.

4. How to position the business to take advantage of growth trends and set it apart from other competitors.

He explained that the "hunch" they were all basing the venture on presumed that computer retailers were not getting good service, nor low enough prices to encourage wider sales of microcomputers and related peripheral equipment. At the other end, he said, manufacturers were burdened with selling small lot quantities to individual stores. This required maintaining nationwide sales forces and inventory systems, which drained manufacturer's resources away from their primary strengths in product development.

By December, the five had each "mapped out" their own work responsibilities to learn more about the computer industry and plan the venture. Dick was focused on putting together his mail survey. Michael was calling on manufacturers to learn about products and discuss terms that could be established for a distributor relationship. Elaine was still compiling information on manufacturers and distributors by going through magazines and reading about them. She also reviewed advertisements sent in by a hired clipping service. The service had been instructed to send any ads by computer stores that appeared in major newspapers around the country. Dick said they soon found that the information was of little value to them:

> *You get charged 50 cents an article and they started pulling every Radio Shack ad in the country. Needless to say, we didn't rely on them too much after that. We've ended up doing most of the clipping ourselves.*

Sandy and Tom were responsible for planning operations of the potential venture. Tom said he expected inventory control and shipping to require methods similar to those used in the jeans business. Sandy added that they would likely use a phone bank as a sales and service link with retail stores:

> *I've found out that when you set up a telephone system like we used with Faded Glory, you don't need a telephone for every person. If you have nine outgoing lines for every 12 or 15 people, that should be enough. Part of their time is spent recording information on each store in a loose leaf notebook, which all of the sales people use. They also might be reviewing literature on a particular product that we're trying to sell. The question of whether you can get by with nine lines or 12 is based to a large degree on how many incoming phone calls you expect to receive.*

She explained that the Faded Glory sales force had attempted to call each retail store at least once every two weeks. This allowed each retailer to keep abreast of any promotional activities and also stay in touch with the distributor. It was, she said, a means of showing that service was being stressed.

Besides dealing with likely operational issues, both Tom and Sandy were also contacting computer stores by phone and through personal visits to outlets in the New England area. Tom estimated that everyone was averaging at least 50 hours per week on the potential venture, and Sandy guessed she was putting in up to 80 hours a week if her week-end visits to computer stores were included. Having a telephone for each person was a logical step in Tom's view:

> *I probably spend 40 percent of my time on the phone. Michael's probably on the phone 70 percent of the time. Sandy's on the phone about 30 percent and Elaine 20 percent—the phones are not going unused.*

Often, Dick said, the owners appeared to be people who were simply opportunistic and/or interested in computers but had little, if any, business knowledge or financing capacity. The flow of newcomers into this industry was pointed up, he noted, by a recent *Datamation* article, which predicted that, by 1983, there would be over 2,000 computer stores in the United States.

Working on a Market Survey

Dick said he usually followed a number of rules when putting together a market survey. First, the mailing list should include precisely those people or firms whom the survey was trying to reach. Second, the questions should be written out. Then they should be reviewed by several people to make sure that they wouldn't be misinterpreted by respondents. "Finally, and probably most important," Dick added, "is to ask yourself, just what is it that you want to find out."

He said that reviewing the questions for clarity wasn't much of a problem, since he had been doing surveys for so long. He recalled that a questionnaire typically took him about two hours to write and proof. Dick related his methods in composing a survey:

You want to stay away from essay-type answers; have questions they can check answers to. You want to keep the appearance light. Otherwise, they'll look at it and say, "I'm not going to take the time to finish this." Make sure that they receive a copy of the results and assure them that the survey won't be published without their permission. And finally, offer a little reward up front—it doubles the response rate. On our last survey we estimated that by offering a drawing for a camera we roughly doubled our response rate.

The four prepared their own lists of retail computer stores from names out of magazines. The only other alternative, Dick said, was to purchase a list from one of the subscription houses or magazine publishers.

Current Distribution Patterns of the Microcomputer Industry

While considered an "infant" when compared to established industries such as autos, steel and chemicals, data processing equipment was widely hailed in media articles as "the greatest growth and glamour industry since World War II." Technological advances had made it possible for computing power to be packaged in ever smaller equipment that was easier to use in a variety of applications and by people with little, if any, technical background in electronics or computer science.

Current terminology divided computer products into three major classifications: mainframes, minicomputers, and microcomputers. Each was designed to address a particular customer application and evolved as advances were made in data storage.

Mainframes came from the industry giants such as IBM, Control Data, Honeywell, and Cray Research. The machines were designed for very complex

and exacting scientific and analytical needs and could cost well over a million dollars, including software and peripheral equipment. Distribution in this segment was by one of two routes: the manufacturer sold directly to the end user, thus using a strategy called OEM (original equipment manufacturer), or sold to an intermediary systems house. The systems house would then add peripheral equipment made by other manufacturers and custom design software for more specific applications. The final product was then sold as a "turnkey" package, where the buyer would simply have to turn on switches and the system would be operational.

Minicomputers were generally less expensive units with substantial computing power, memory and speed, although less than that of mainframes. Recent products called "super minis" had somewhat blurred the distinction between minis and mainframes. Distribution channels for minis were similar to mainframes, with salespersons typically making four or five calls to a prospect before a purchase was made. Principal manufacturers included Hewlett-Packard, Digital Equipment, Data General, Prime computer and Tandem. Customers were considered to be medium and large businesses or government agencies, with lengthy lease or purchase periods and service agreements with the manufacturer or the systems house.

Microcomputers represented a radical departure from other computer products in several respects. Microprocessor chips as a form of central processing unit or "brain" for the computer instead of massive cabinets full of electronic circuits and magnetic tape drives had been in existence only since the mid-1970s. These chips made microcomputers unique in size. For the first time, computers could be small enough to be placed on top of a desk. Previously, computers had to be housed in special rooms with temperature and humidity controls. Now, not only did they not need such rooms, but they also cost tens of thousands of dollars less, under $10,000 for the first time. Programming also became vastly simpler and for the first time software was becoming standardized, as well as much cheaper, easier to use and widely available.

Users for the first time included small businesses, home hobbyists who would use the machines for recreation or developing applications for personal use, schools, and larger businesses. An increasing number of companies had started manufacturing peripheral equipment specifically for microcomputers, including printers, memory storage units, special-purpose plug-in circuit boards and plotters. The largest manufacturers were Apple Computer, Tandy's Radio Shack division and Commodore. An assortment of companies followed, from IBM to small ventures, some of which had already failed, including two of the earliest, MITS and IMSAI. It was widely expected that there would be many more entries and many more failures among the makers of microcomputers before the industry stabilized.

Since the value added per unit with microcomputers was much less than that for minis and mainframes, the use of direct sales people calling on individual accounts didn't make economic sense. Apple, for example, had used mail order as a strategy to build sales and gain a leadership position in the industry but was currently selling mainly through regional distributors to retail computer stores. Distributors were mostly regional, serving at most two or three states.

Radio Shack added its TRS-80 microcomputer to its existing line of stereo equipment and sold the machine in the retail outlets it had developed throughout the United States and overseas. Other manufacturers used a combination of mail order and retail sales through locations such as the estimated 700-1,000 computer stores in the U.S. For mini and mainframe builders, as well as peripheral equipment manufacturers, the addition of a microcomputer to their product line could be touted to existing customer accounts as an added product from their sales forces.

The fact was, Michael pointed out, that no clear distribution pattern yet existed for microcomputers. He said the trend toward selling microcomputers in retail computer stores appeared to be the most likely avenue to persist. Whether the stores would remain largely independent, be comprised of chains such as Radio Shack or Computerland, or be a retail outlet of a computer manufacturer, such as Digital Equipment's computer stores, he hoped he could divine from the market survey.

Sandy commented that the inquiries they had made to date had already provided some clues as to what they could expect from Dick's more formal survey:

> *We've found that the retail outlets are used to waiting five or six weeks for delivery on an order and when it comes, the manufacturer often requires them to pay C.O.D. In part, the payment terms are due to the fact that most of the retail stores are fairly new. Another factor is that these store owners come from a technical background, and they have no concept of what retailing is all about. So they often fail. If you look at a list more than six months old, many of the store numbers have been disconnected, and people have gone out of business. About one out of every six stores we tried to contact had gone out of business in the last six months. But for every one that closed, two more are opening up. At that rate, we figure there will be about 1,500 independents by the end of 1982.*

She added that the people running the retail stores were much more willing than the jeans store operators to talk on the phone about their products. They gave their thoughts on where the industry was headed, even though she gave them only her name and simply said she was interested in learning more about computers. In many ways she thought retail personal computer stores were similar to stereo outlets in the 1960s, when hobbyists were the major "promoters." The general public was just becoming aware of the products offered and what the terminology meant in terms of performance or application.

Michael continued his commentary concerning difficulties that computer retail stores seemed to be up against:

> Retailers aren't getting the newest products as fast as they want, nor can they reorder quickly. The underlying issue here is that entrepreneurs in any new business always have limited capital. To compete in the long run with the big manufacturer's stores like Radio Shack and Xerox, the independent computer retailer needs fast delivery of the best products available. This way he ties up and risks less capital. There is need for someone who will do the market research and take the risk of stocking new products, so stores can concentrate on what they do best, which is making sales. What is needed is, in a sense, a buying service.

A Printer Possibility

Michael had sent requests for product information to every manufacturer in the microcomputer business he could locate. The response of one company, LRC, was to send a salesman to call on him. Michael recalled:

> The LRC salesman said his company is coming out with this new 40-column printer and they want us to carry it. He had no sales figures because there are no 40-column printers on the market, as yet. Everyone is selling 80-column printers, but the salesman said it is logical that hobbyists using a small com-

> puter will want a small printer. His argument makes sense to me.
>
> When we asked about terms, he said if we take 55 printers COD, LRC would give us a $5,000 credit limit. We figure the gross margin would be about 14 percent. We don't like the terms, but I know we're not in a good negotiating position. Here he is calling on us in our condominium where we have nothing at all to show him.

Other Start-up Issues

As Dick faced the task of designing a survey, the other four were concerned about other issues. Education about the products and the industry was a must, according to Michael, since none of them had a technical background in computers or electronics. Dick was acquainted with computers from the perspective of following the industry and market trends, although he admitted that he still had trouble trying to figure out how to simply turn on a machine:

> We'll have manufacturers come in to talk about their product and they'll start in on some heavy technical presentation. They don't realize that Michael and I are thinking about goats when they're talking about ROMS and RAMS. So, we've got some catching up to do in learning about the jargon and products.

If the venture were attempted, Michael thought they should try to develop a sales force dedicated to maintaining close contact with the stores and keeping up with product developments. Sandy pointed out that this might be hard, since experienced technical sales people were in short supply and were prone to switching companies for higher salaries or improved benefits. "Company loyalty doesn't seem to extend very far down the ladder in the computer industry," she lamented.

Dick remarked that people they had talked to with computer experience "want the moon for a salary." The five were hoping to start people at $12,000 per year and increase the amount as they developed experience. With Faded Glory, the sales staff had worked on a straight salary basis. Whether any commission incentive should be included in this venture idea wasn't yet known. Dick added that they would probably settle for people who simply had general sales experience, figuring that someone who had sold Tupperware was better than someone with no sales experience at all.

Another concern was finding a more suitable office and warehouse facility to work from. The Canton Massachusetts warehouse, which had been used in previous businesses, was currently under lease. The tenant indicated he might vacate it when the lease expired in April, but Tom and Sandy continued to spend part of their time searching for other space in the Boston area.

Another question was what their initial product line should include. Michael suggested distributing first some relatively non-technical product with potential for high volume to offset the low margins he expected they would be able to command. He wanted 20- or 30-percent-margin product lines but believed that realistically, they would have to settle for 10 to 15 percent to attract manufacturers to an unknown business like theirs.

One possible initial product to distribute would be floppy disks and diskettes. A manufacturer they had investigated seemed to have a good reputation for such products, yet held a mere 3 percent market share in sales. Michael and Dick reasoned that if they told the manufacturer they could boost market share to over 10 percent, they might be able to get advantageous distribution rights. Their strategy would then be to build on that success by adding microcomputer peripherals to their line. Another emphasis, they stated, would be to concentrate on products compatible with the leading computers such as those of Apple, Radio Shack, and Commodore— which together currently comprised 60 percent of the total installed base of personal computers.

Industry standards for negotiating margins followed the assumptions that retail stores required 30 percent off list price for every item sold. Michael and Dick estimated they would need between 20 and 30 percent to act as a full service distributor, even though some distributors in the industry were taking as little as 6 percent on products. Dick pointed out that these companies simply purchased products from manufacturers and resold them to retailers with no attempt to provide service or assistance beyond product delivery.

The two figured they could attempt to purchase from manufacturers at 50 percent off the suggested retail price. They would keep 40 percent of the discount and pass the remaining 60 percent along to the retailers. To be successful, manufacturers would have to agree to forego 10 to 20 percent of the list price which they were now keeping for themselves.

Another element of strategy Michael believed would be extremely important was advertising. He commented that since the venture would be starting from scratch, a disproportionate amount would be needed for promotion. He said that they would probably spend 10 percent of annual sales on advertising for the first year or two until the venture became recognized as a leading distributor of computer products.

Dick said conversations with retailers and manufacturers indicated that a gap did exist in terms of distribution. Most of the retail emphasis was being put on carrying only the leading printer, CRT, or other peripherals for each particular product line. One result was that periodic price cutting, rather than product variety, was the major competitive tactic being used, and lesser known manufacturers were having difficulty selling their products. Another result was that retailers became dependent on a small number of suppliers. At the mercy of those suppliers, the retailers found that fast delivery was the exception. Maintenance and repairs often required shipping machines back to a manufacturers and could take weeks to accomplish. Shortages of user-oriented software impeded selling new microcomputer systems to the general public.

Possible Implications of a Formal Market Survey

As March 1980 approached, Dick considered it important to find out what a formal survey could tell him about market potential for the prospective venture. He, Michael and Tom believed that, if they decided to move ahead, conclusions from the survey should form the basis for structuring the venture. If the type of service, markets, pricing and related issues were handled appropriately, the business could succeed. If not, Michael's third attempt in starting a business might result in failure.

Dick reviewed a number of questions that he hoped the survey results would help answer:

We want to find out what the stores think of the manufacturers and their products. Which one are the best?

Worst? Where are the retailers getting their sales people? How are they hiring them? Who are the stores selling products to? What needs could a distributor fulfill?

We want to know what kind of money it takes to start a store. Who are the store's competitors? What about problems with software and maintenance? How much do they spend on advertising? Should they put out a catalog featuring the store's product line? Does the store use mail order?

What does the future hold for retail computer stores? Where would they invest capital if they had more of it to spend: inventory or another store? What are their sales revenues? What about in three years?

The answers to these questions will tell us if there is a place for us as a distributor. And it will tell us how to structure our business, in terms of what products to go after and what services to offer. Also, we'll be able to develop some expectations about growth and competition down the road.

At the same time, we can't forget the importance of getting our name out to people in the business. That's very important. Right now, we have manufacturers come to the condominium with their product, they look at the five of us, look around the room in disbelief, and say, "Hey! What's going on here? You call yourself a business?"

Chapter 3

Screening

❏ *SUBCHAPTER 3A - Physical Feasibility and Market Fit*

Any idea generating process, whether a systematic search or simply reaction to chance encounters, should produce far more ideas than can be explored in detail. Giving some direction to the discovery process, as discussed in the last chapter, can help winnow the possibilities. Cursory reflection will be the most attention that can be paid to nearly all the ideas. It may eliminate them all, leaving the search to continue in quest of more. Or it may highlight a few that deserve more serious attention. For those, more intensive and methodical examination, which can help with both selection and refinement of ideas worth significant time, effort and possibly dollar investment, is appropriate. This chapter will describe methods for that more detailed examination, concentrating on four aspects. The first subchapter will consider tests for feasibility and market fit. The second subchapter will treat financial advisability and fit between the venture idea and the individual(s) who might found a venture to exploit it.

Evaluation Questions

Checklists for evaluating venture ideas can readily be generated. In detail they must depend on the particular venture, but some general questions include the following:

- What kind of business can this venture become in the short run and the long run?

- Why does the opportunity for this venture exist? Are the causes of the opportunity likely to last long enough for the venture to become profitable?

- Who will be the first customer and why can that person be expected to buy? How many more people will buy and why?

- What will make it possible for this company to withstand competition if it comes?

- Who else seems to be in as good or a better position to accomplish this venture, what are they likely to do, and what can be done about it?

- What, in rank order, are the three most critical assumptions upon which success of this venture is projected? What can be done to test those assumptions, and what can be done to make sure they come true?

- What is the upside profit potential of the business if things go as well as can reasonably be hoped? How does that compare to the prospects if things only go fairly well?

- What is the likely downside loss if things go unfavorably?

- What has to happen for break-even to occur? For cash flow to become positive?

- How sensitive are these projections to variations in key assumptions underlying them?

Application: *What would be the answers to the most important of these questions above for this particular case?*

Answers to these questions should be developed in sufficient detail that the same set would not fit another business. They should be true, not simply made up to support a prejudged conclusion either to go ahead with the business or to brush it aside. Likely the answers will be mixed, some favoring termination and others favoring acceptance of the venture idea. So judgment must be made about which route to follow.

Maintaining balance in this analytical process can be difficult. Some analysis may be important, but over analysis is wasteful, and success is produced only by action. More important than making the best decisions is to follow through on them effectively. Part of the evaluation should address how to make the decisions work out even if assumptions underlying them prove invalid, or they turn out to be not the best decisions that could have been made. To keep balance between over- versus under-analysis it can be helpful to consult with other knowledgeable people.

Evaluation of ideas can be viewed as a spiraling process. A possibility is glimpsed, either because of happenstance or search. The impression is tested, either against prior knowledge or through acquisition of additional knowledge. Checkout reveals new facets of the possibility which may be problems or opportunities or both. Possible ways of responding to these are sought and assessed. Thus the search continues until either it no longer appears worthwhile or an action plan for the venture emerges.

All this may happen in the mind, either over time or through a flash of inspiration. Some evaluation may be conscious, but much is bound to be subconscious. If the start-up steps are low cost, the easiest way to test a business idea may be simply to go ahead and implement it. Usually, however, there is justification for some systematic screening first.

Seek Out Weak Spots for Priority

Ideas are easy to come up with. To economize time in screening, attack first those questions most crucial to success of an idea, even if they are harder to answer or face. Almost all product or service ideas are no good, particularly as originally perceived. To find one that is viable requires passing up those that are not and probably reshaping one that is partially all right. A learning process is required both to refine the idea and to test it.

Allocation of time in this process must repeatedly be adjusted between such tasks as:

1. Looking for strong points of a venture idea to build on and ways to do the building.

2. Looking for weak points and either finding ways to fix them or dropping the venture idea.

3. Searching out and gathering information to help with the above tasks.

4. Searching for a better venture idea.

5. Turning to some other task and leaving the current one temporarily to the subconscious.

Application: *In what order should the entrepreneur in the assigned case proceed through the above five actions after the end of the assigned case?*

One way to economize time in evaluating an idea is first to seek out the most worrisome aspects and work on those. Which aspects are most likely to be weak will vary from one venture idea to another. Here are some possibilities:

1. Though the product or service of the prospective venture might be valuable, it is not physically feasible, and/or development would cost too much.

2. Some people might like to have what the venture would produce, but either there would not be enough of them, or they would be too hard to find and sell to, or they would not be willing to pay enough to yield a profit for the venture.

3. The venture would likely make some profit, but not enough to justify the investment required.

4. The return on investment would probably be attractive initially, but competitors in more advantageous positions would likely enter and shrink it prematurely.

5. Such a venture could prosper adequately, but it doesn't fit this particular entrepreneur well enough.

Application: *How would the above five possibilities rank in likelihood for the venture in the assigned case?*

Generating alternative future scenarios both of the company and of the competitive arena in which it will operate will give a basis for this assessment. Each scenario should characterize what the company might be like in one, two or five years including such aspects as:

- What it sells and to whom
- For how much individually and in total
- Using what appeals
- Against what competitors
- With what market share
- Providing it how
- With how many employees
- Owned how
- Aiming to achieve what next
- Thanks to what competitive advantages

Two or three such future "portraits of success" which contrast fairly sharply from each other can be formulated. Then the steps necessary to bring each about can be considered as well as the risks, costs and benefits of arriving at these alternative outcomes. This can serve as a basis for deciding which strategy offers most promise initially. All this should help with the decisions of whether to proceed with the venture and if so, how best.

Application: *What would be three alternative "Portraits of Success" for the venture(s) in the assigned case(s)?*

Another approach, making successively deeper penetrations in setting priority, is to:

1. Quickly guess the answer to "what is the most vulnerable aspect of tн̲ business idea?"

2. List five general aspects, and for each list in rank order the most vulnerable points: physical practicability, marketability, financial attractiveness, entrepreneur fit and competitiveness.

3. For these five aspects in any order perform a more detailed analysis.

Application: *What would be the priority of concerns for the entrepreneur(s) in the assigned case(s)?*

For most ideas mental reflection will be enough to conclude rejection. Others that cannot be easily rejected will raise the need for more information to make a decision. The search for this information may itself uncover still better ideas.

Test Physical Practicability

Questions of physical feasibility include whether the venture is legally permissible, whether it can be made to work within reasonable development costs and whether the prospective founder can muster the capability to perform it.

Legal permission for most ventures is not a problem. As much as entrepreneurs condemn problems of dealing with the government, it generally presents little barrier to their getting started. In some fields there are legal monopolies, such as postal delivery to mailboxes and fields where licenses exclude competitors, such as medicine, barbering, law, broadcasting and so forth. In others there are controls over effluents, noise and safety. Zoning sometimes restricts location of businesses. But for the great majority of start-ups such restrictions are not important. It is after the business has started that governmental burdens of reporting, taxation, inspections and ordinances become more serious.

Modeling

Demonstration that the product or service can actually be produced and will work can often be accomplished with pencil and paper analysis. If the idea is for a product, then some sort of prototype(s) should be made. If it is a service, then sketches and possibly physical models of facilities should be made. In this more concrete form, the concept can then be tested to see how well it works and how it might be improved. If there is a possibility that the idea is truly novel, then legal protection, such as copyrighting or patenting should be considered, as will be discussed in Chapter Six.

Prototypes

Preparing a prototype in some form, a working model, a mock-up or even just drawings and sketches, can help greatly in not only testing feasibility but also improving a new product or service idea. For patenting, a prototype may be essential to demonstrate that the concept will work, and drawings that show how it will work are absolutely required.

One path of refinement, once a prototype is in hand, is to test, critique, modify, retest and thereby improve the design. Another is to let others try it, show it to prospective buyers and receive feedback as part of the testing. If there is concern that the idea might be stolen, then those to whom it is shown should be selected with careful attention to both their reputations for integrity and the incentives they may be subject to. Additionally, they may be asked to sign a non-disclosure agreement in which they promise not to divulge the idea to others or take advantage of it themselves without approval. It may be appropriate to compensate such people for agreeing thus to bind themselves and for their efforts in helping improve the idea.

Professionals accustomed to helping with prototypes include job manufacturing shops, custom plastics molders, industrial designers and testing laboratories. These can readily be located through the Yellow Pages and by asking around. To get the most help from them as economically as possible, it will probably be a good idea for the entrepreneur to attempt prototyping personally first, at least in the form of sketches, dimensions, target specifications and, if possible, physical models. Physical working prototypes can be very powerful not only for determining that a concept is truly workable and for finding ways to improve upon it, but also for persuading potential backers to put up money and even for persuading customers to buy. In the following example a customer's enthusiasm for buying the prototype itself led to a premature sale.

> In 1968 a printing press mechanic recently arrived in Seattle and set up a repair shop. He also began development of a new four-color press that would produce greatly improved clarity but cost less than existing machines. He made two prototypes at a cost of $90,000 and began showing them to potential customers. One responded with a high-priced cash offer to buy the prototype itself. The mechanic, seeing how the cash could help him advance his venture, agreed to sell it, provided he could set up and service it as well.
>
> The machine was shipped to the customer in California and installed satisfactorily. But some operating problems developed soon after, and when the mechanic went to fix them he found himself blocked in California by a union contract provision allowing only their people to work on it. Union personnel hung a sign on the machine reading "Lost Horizon." Fearing that word of the machine's failure would spread and stymie future sales, the mechanic bought it back.

Application: *Describe the steps and costs required to develop a prototype or working version for test of the product or service in the assigned case.*

Testing of physical feasibility must not only show that the product or service can be produced, but also must assure that it can be done well enough. Among *Inc.* 500 firms 88 percent of founders, according to a survey by the magazine, attributed their success to exceptional execution of an ordinary idea, while only 12 percent said they succeeded because of an unusual or extraordinary idea.[1]

In another study of 2,994 firms Cooper et al.[2] reported that odds of survival were on the average not higher among firms that claimed a "reputation for quality" as part of their strategy. However, firms which attributed more than 40 percent of their strategy to better service and those which said 40 percent or more was focused on providing previously unavailable products or services did have higher odds of survival. Emphasis on lower prices, or on serving customer groups previously poorly or not at all served, was associated with higher failure rates.

What this seems to suggest is that high quality of the product or service as perceived by customers is a main key to raising odds of success (at least, on average). Hence, in evaluating plans for the venture a most important question is not just whether the product or service physically will be able to work, but also how an extraordinarily high quality in its level of performance will physically be brought about.

Kinds of excellence in performance that seem to distinguish winners in the *Inc.* 500 are illustrated by some examples such as the following.

Tom Tjelmeland, who had worked on construction sites since age 14, entered a most prosaic line of work, roof repair, by concentrating on commercial customers and doing enough small things better than competitors so his firm would get the orders without need to give quotes. His tactics included clean white trucks and white uniformed workers in an industry notorious for the opposite. Use of computers gave him clearer awareness of costs in order to control them and facilitated reminders to customers about roof inspections. Careful sleuthing of competitors' performance in neighboring markets revealed which would be easiest to expand into. Questionnaire follow-ups of both jobs the company won and those it lost helped show why. Adding a 24-hour emergency service staffed by workers with cellular phones improved responsiveness. Numerous experiments with other ways of marketing and controlling helped identify which ones worked best. All these activities helped set the company apart from competitors and propel it to *Inc.* 500 membership.[3]

❖ ❖ ❖

James Ake built a six-employee bottle filling machine company to 100 employees in six years by emphasizing speed of delivery to customers. He guaranteed delivery in 10 days. By devising control systems for ordering, manufacturing, shipping and installing to cope with such difficulties as running with almost no backlog, by training, motivating and compensating employees for flexibility and speed, and by managing inventory to allow fast production he was able to achieve to make good on that guarantee.[4] He also offered to subtract air fare for a visit to his plant if a customer bought. "If we can convince a customer to visit our place, we'll make the sale about 90 percent of the time....When they see this company has meat on its bones and will be here to service the equipment, it means a lot."[5]

❖ ❖ ❖

In September, 1990, *Inc.* reported that Direct Tire near Boston was offering its tires for $60 to $120 each while the Goodyear store down the street was charging $50 to $100. And yet Direct Tire was also selling far more tires, despite the price differential. Willingness to provide fast service, having seven loaner cars available, making good on tires that go bad, even after 30,000 miles, seem to be part of the explanation, according to the article's author, Paul B. Brown.[6] Noting that the shop's owner, Barry Steinberg, has been in the business for 42 years, Brown observes a combination of many refinements that set his firm apart from competitors. "State-of-the-art equipment not only lets Steinberg offer better service, but it helps him attract the best technicians. For the same reason, he pays technicians 15 percent to 25 percent over the industry average.... Steinberg takes care to order the right magazines for the waiting room and to provide fresh coffee."

Part of what these examples illustrate is that the key to physical feasibility need not have anything to do with technological breakthroughs or esoteric schooling. None of these apparently success-producing actions seems particularly exotic or difficult to accomplish compared to the start-up feats of some companies that clone genes or design microchip testers. Rather, it appears that these firms are winning by doing ordinary physical things extraordinarily well. In hindsight, the ability to perform them may seem straightforward common sense, something many entrepreneurs should be able to do. And yet the competitors of these firms apparently don't learn how to reach the same level of competence. A prospective founder should consider just how well his or her venture will be able to perform ordinary functions relative to its competitors.

Successively deeper penetrations in testing physical practicability could include the following:

1. Imagine trying to implement the idea, and guess what could interfere with making the product, having it work, or operating it at a competitively superior level of performance.

2. Develop a written scenario and sketches that show how the product or service will be produced and delivered, noting any impediments, legal, physical or capability-wise for carrying it through, and how this will be done with excellence.

3. Solicit "expert" reviews of whatever seem to be the most critical items on the above list.

4. Make a physical prototype, if the venture will make a new product, and use it to see what happens. If the venture will introduce a service, try performing it, and see how well it can be done.

Application: *What tasks should be performed to check out the physical and legal feasibility of the assigned case venture?*

Check Market Fit

Anything that can be foreseen about customer reactions to the venture's product or service helps in screening and refining the venture idea. Some of this foreseeing can be done by imagination with information a would-be entrepreneur already possesses, possibly to eliminate an idea or possibly to improve upon it. If the entrepreneur previously worked in the industry and knows the customers personally, then information already known may confirm the venture idea and shape it to fit the market. Some ventures even start with customers already in line to buy their products and services. In such a case more market information may eventually be needed to capitalize on future changes in the market, but for inception of such a venture existing information may well be sufficient.

Without some sort of prior confirmation of market fit, however, there will likely be need to gather information about the hoped-for market in order both to establish its existence and to shape the venture to fit it well. Such information may be any combination of data from the following:

- **Prior studies** of the market or related markets by other companies, government agencies or entrepreneurs.

- **Polls** of population samples believed to typify customers. Mail questionnaires, advertisements incorporating feedback mechanisms such as mail-in responses, phone interviews and/or personal interviews may be used.

- **Negotiations** with prospective customers to solicit orders and determine whether they will actually buy.

In analyzing the prospective market to estimate sales and design market strategy some familiar marketing concepts such as "target customers," "segmentation," "nichemanship," "positioning," "price-performance relationships," "comparison grids," and "relative market share" can be very helpful and should be considered, perhaps examined extensively, before giving the idea a "thumbs up" on market fit. Briefly, some aspects to look at for each of these concepts are as follows:

- **Target Customers** What can be said in detail about the first person who will say "I'll buy" when the venture opens for business? What pattern of logic and emotion in that person's mind will trigger the buying decision? How much of a "close call" will that buying decision be? What can be said about the next few who will buy and about the first one who will give a repeat order? What aspects in design and operation of the venture will affect this process and how?

- **Segmentation** How many customers like those targeted are there? What are the features common to them that distinguish them from other groups of customers somewhat similar but not targeted by the company? What about the venture will enable it to sell one segment if not the other? What might be required for expansion of sales to other segments later?

- **Nichemanship** Within its targeted segment what fraction of the potential customers can the venture hope to capture and how? How is that fraction or sub-segment different from the larger group, and how will the company tune to it in particular? How will it beat out competitors who also target on that particular niche?

- **Positioning** How will the venture's product or service compare to those of competitors in terms of line breadth, quality, price, follow-up and other features customers in the market seem likely to care about? Who is qualified to make that comparison? What evidence can be used to test the extent to which customers will see it that way?

- **Price/Performance** In assessing physical feasibility there must have been assumptions about properties of the product or service that would most appeal to customers. What were they? What evidence is there that customers agree with the assumptions? How much will it cost to provide the appeals that matter most? What must be charged to provide them? Are the features worth enough to customers? Could more be added to justify a higher price or others of less importance to customers be removed to permit a lower price? To explore such relationships it may be helpful to plot curves of price versus various performance dimensions, and of expected price elasticity.

- **Comparison Grids** Like graphs, grids are another way to explore relationships between variables that can be traded off in fitting the venture's product or service to its chosen market. One straightforward grid approach is to list along one axis such things as competitors' predicted offerings and along the other axis features (such as price, appearance, convenience, durability, reliability, performance, service quality, speed of delivery, etc.) of the product or service. Articles comparing products in such magazines as *Consumer Reports* or *Infoworld* illustrate application of such grids, and also provide some alternative ways of rating the products in cells of the grids to generate an overall rating for each that allows easy comparison.

- **Relative Market Share**   It is well known that a large market share relative to competitors tends to produce higher profitability due to economies of scale. Hence an important prediction to arrive at from analysis of market fit is just what share the new venture can hope to capture relative to whomever its largest two or three competitors will be. To arrive at a prediction a starting point can be to estimate present market shares from industry interviews and observation, then forecast venture sales, and finally guess how competitors' shares may change from their present values.

Application: *Which of the above marketing concepts are most important to the assigned case venture, and how do they apply? Please create one or more transparencies illustrating how they fit.*

In summary, some successively deeper penetrations of analysis in checking market fit could include:

a.   Imagine who might want to buy the product or service of the new venture. Describe why they would buy it instead of whatever else they buy now or will be able to buy from others.

b.   Talk to some people who fit the above scenario and ask for their reactions to it.

c.   Segment the market into reasonably homogeneous groups and conduct a more formal market survey by mail, telephone or personal interview.

d.   Ask for an order.

Application: *How could market feasibility of the assigned case venture best be assessed, using methods such as those four above?*

To say there should be some "market research" to determine what people will buy, moreover, is not enough. The entrepreneur must figure out very specifically what market information to obtain, how much to spend on it, how soon to get it and how to get it. The prospective customers, whoever they happen to be, may not be able to appreciate what the venture proposes to offer. For example, Xerox, microcomputers and pocket calculators all proved to have wildly different markets than any future customer or entrepreneur foresaw.

Supplementary Reading

New Venture Strategies Chapter 2. (Vesper, K.H., Prentice-Hall, 1990)
New Venture Mechanics Chapter 2. (Vesper, K. H., Prentice-Hall, 1993)

Exercises

1. Write out a "portrait of success" or future scenario of some venture idea that seems promising. Do this on one page, and on a second page list the things that could prevent that scenario from occurring. On a third page describe what could be done to solve those problems, weigh the main pros and cons of the idea and state whether it is worth pursuing further.

2. Prepare a comparison grid for a venture idea that includes numerical ratings multiplied by weightings for each cell to produce overall comparative product scores across the bottom totalling the cells in each column.

3. Study, as best you can in the time available, three different local firms. Estimate the profitability of each and formulate a comparison grid to explain differences in their relative profitabilities. Comment on the extent to which you consider them successful.

Venture History

1. Make a comparison grid for the product or service of the venture versus its competitors.

2. Which checkout procedures, including those of this chapter and any others that may apply, were used in making decisions about proceeding with the venture?

3. How did the strengths and weaknesses of the venture compare to its competitors at two contrasting time points in its development?

Venture Planning Guide

1. Rank the questions and techniques described thus far in this chapter in their order of likely effectiveness for testing and shaping your main venture idea. In the time available to you, apply them, starting from the top of your priority list down.

2. Make a comparison grid listing features of your product or service versus its competition at two contrasting time points in the projected development of your venture.

Notes

[1] John Case, "The Origins of Entrepreneurship," *Inc.*, June 1989, p. 54.

[2] Arnold C. Cooper and others, *New Business In America* (Washington, D.C.: The NFIB Foundation, 1990), p. 8.

[3] Joshua Hyatt, "Out of the Ordinary," *Inc.*, December 1990, p. 110.

[4] John Case, "The Time Machine," *Inc.*, June 1990, p. 48.

[5] "On the Floor Sales," *Inc.*, August 1990, p. 108.

[6] Paul B. Brown, "The Real Cost of Customer Service," *Inc.*, September 1990, p. 49.

❏ SUBCHAPTER 3B - *Financial and Founder Fit*

Compute Financial Attractiveness

To test the financial attractiveness of a venture idea in terms of two critical dimensions, investment and profitability, there are at least five approaches. Investment includes money and other resources that must be put up to make the venture go, as well as unpaid effort the founders put into it. If these are small enough, then the *first* approach for testing viability of a venture idea can be simply starting it up and seeing what happens.

If a larger investment is required, then profit and elapsed time are probably worth computing. There are still shortcuts that may be worth taking to avoid bogging down in long analysis of an idea that may not work. The *second* approach is to consider profitability of comparable businesses. If that is high, then there is reason to hope that the venture's profitability will also be high.

A *third* approach is to look at the margin percentage and guess how much the venture can earn. If the venture will manufacture something, one rough rule of thumb, for instance, is that it should wholesale its product for at least twice the cost of labor plus material. (Jobs and Wozniak sold their first computers to the Byte Shop for twice the cost of parts, not including labor.) If the venture makes a product and it is to be sold at retail, then probably the margin will have to be doubled again to provide for advertising, sales and distribution.

However, such rules of thumb are very rough, often don't fit a particular industry, and are typically on the low side anyway. If the venture is a store, for instance, the critical number is not margin percentage but rather margin in total dollars per month. The question is often how adequately that margin will cover rent, utilities and help.

A *fourth* approach, and the next step beyond margin estimation, is to compute break-even sales level. This is done by adding up fixed costs of the venture, such as rent, wages, utilities, advertising and other more or less fixed costs and dividing by the number of cents per sales dollar left after paying variable costs on each unit sold. If the venture does not seem certain to exceed that roughly estimated break-even sales volume, then it probably will not succeed. It's easy to be too optimistic in such forecasts. For instance, the impact of competitor moves on sales is hard to foresee and so may be neglected while at the same time some items of cost are almost certain to be missed. Thus profits may look higher than they should.

A *fifth* approach, if the idea still seems to hold up, is to generate a financial statement forecast for specific time periods such as monthly for the first year or two and annually for another two or three years beyond that. Estimation begins with an income statement "top line" projecting sales volume over time, derived from analysis of the market fit as discussed in the preceding section. The validity of that top line can be cross checked by such steps as:

- Making global estimates of overall sales by year for the first two to five years and comparing them to those of other similar types of businesses.

- Making detailed lists of customers, market segments, geographic regions and sales channels, and estimating how much sales will flow to each.

- Setting out a spread sheet and estimating by month the actions that will be taken to produce sales, the orders that will be received in units, customers, transactions or the like, then listing for each month the amount of sales each of these will produce, and finally how much money each month will be collected from these sales.

From these sales estimates should flow consequences in terms of expenditures needed for selling, production and delivery of the venture's product or service. Easiest to generate will probably be the profit and loss statement, on which cost of sales may introduce complications by having different levels at different volumes.

Balance sheet forecasting comes next. Some items, such as fixed assets and necessary cash balance may be easy to estimate. If the venture will have inventory, accounts payable and/or accounts receivable those can be scaled in terms of "days on hand" as percentages of sales. Some possible "for instances" are:

- If receivables will on average take one month to collect, then the balance sheet figure for that will be one month's sales. (Watch out for seasonality.)

- If creditors will require payment within one month on average, and if purchased materials amount to about one-third of the venture's selling price, then payables will be about one-third of one month's sales.

- If inventory will turn on average six times per year: (in other words, two months' supply of it will be on hand), then the balance sheet figure will equal two months' cost of goods sold. If the company's gross margin is 50 percent, then the figure for inventory will be half of two months' sales revenue, which is one month's sales revenue.

Another short cut approach for estimating both balance sheet and income statement figures is to obtain statements of a comparable company and "adjust" the figures in those statements to fit expectations of the new venture. Sources of "look alike" company statements include the ratios published by Robert Morris Associates and those published by Dun and Bradstreet as well as possibly the annual reports of selected companies that might be available through publications, personal connections or trade associations.

Cash flow figures are usually most important. These may be complicated by things hard to estimate in both income statements and balance sheets: cost/volume shifts, seasonal sales variations, lags in collections, and both leads and lags in payments required. Using a microcomputer spread sheet such as Microsoft Excel or Lotus 1-2-3 can help greatly, but thought will still be needed to work out calculation formulas, and judgment will be required for estimating figures.

Once complete, the cash flow and balance sheet figures will show investments required, while the income statements will show profit levels. The profits can then be divided by investments to compute return on investment (ROI). Venture capitalists typically require rates on the order of 30 percent per year and more. Other investors may accept less, but almost surely will want a return well above 10 percent to 15 percent for a start-up venture. This return, moreover, should be generated on a scale of investment that justifies the time and worry needed to work out and live with the venture deal.

Of personal interest to the founder, of course, is the level of compensation it can provide him or her as well as what he or she must do to earn it. Is the return on a copy center, bicycle manufacturing or software company enough to live on? It depends on the individual venture. Some can pay nothing and eventually fail, while others grow and prosper thanks to powerful competitive advantages devised by their entrepreneurs.

How income and compensation will vary with changes in key assumptions must also be considered. With spreadsheet microcomputer programs it is relatively easy to vary the assumptions and see what happens to net cash flow and profits. In what month will the worst cash demand occur, and how much cash will be needed to get through it? How much worse will the need be if hoped for events, such as collections from customers are either below expectations or arrive later than anticipated? What is the downside worst case? How much will be lost if the venture fails, how much will be recoverable and how hard will it be to recover any salvage value? Such a sensitivity analysis should be prepared in the form of alternative financial scenarios to check both the downside risk as well as the upside potential of the venture.

Odds of success range fairly dramatically among industries according to a number of studies performed over the years.[1] For instance, according to a 1988 study of the statistics on 3.6 million firms by Phillips and Kirchhoff, the overall survival percentage of start-ups was 40 percent for six years. The figures ranged from 35 percent for construction and 38 percent for retail firms to 44 percent for wholesaling and 47 percent for manufacturing firms.[2] Most recently, Cooper et al. reported that 77 percent of new businesses formed in the U.S. during the mid-1980s survived three or more years, and another 4 percent were sold to new owners.

Also of interest to founders may be forms of compensation other than those that are purely financial. What will be learned from trying the venture? How much fun will it be? What are the odds that it might lead to other attractive opportunities? Starting a venture is like entering an avenue down whose sidestreets lie contacts, adventures and opportunities that cannot be discovered any other way than by proceeding. Just what constitutes success and how to gauge it is a question that each prospective founder must answer individually.

In summary, successively deeper penetrations in computing financial attractiveness for checking out venture ideas include to:

1. Estimate gross profit margin percentage and compare it to norms for the industry.

2. Estimate fixed and variable costs and compute a break even.

3. Project financial statements based on typical figures for the industry and assess whether those figures can be achieved by the venture.

4. Project financial statements for the venture based upon a buildup of sales and cost figures.

5. Add to the above financial statements a cash flow forecast.

6. Show the above financial statements and cash flow forecast to other knowledgeable people and request that they provide a critique or, better yet, an investment or loan.

Application: *Which of the above six methods for assessing financial attractiveness of the assigned case venture are most appropriate, and what does their application show?*

Assess Founder(s)' Fit

A winning opportunity for one potential founder may be not at all a winner for another. Statistically, some lines of business have clearly higher odds of start-up survival than others. The study of 2,994 start-ups by Cooper et al. reported that although most were in retailing (46 percent) or non-professional services (19 percent), those were the areas where firms were least likely to grow or even survive. Three-year survival rates were 73 percent in retail and 75 percent in non-professional services, compared to 85 percent in professional services, 83 percent in financial services and 82 percent in manufacturing. Another study of a half million start-ups between 1978 and 1982 by Birch[3] found that the start-up area with the highest average survival rate was in veterinary services. Those with the highest average rates of growth were banks.

Who can do ventures such as veterinary clinics and banks best, or even at all, is not a matter of entrepreneurial virtue, character, general business savvy or knowledge of start-up "technology." Rather, it is mainly determined by such qualifications as credentials, training, experience, contacts and reputation. A study of 100 automation start-ups by Chambers, Hart and Denison, reported that "previous start-up managerial experience of the founders is not as predominant a feature of high performing firms as previously believed."[4] Another by Hills and Welsh reported that highest incidence of success factors among 150 small business award winners were in "knowledge of product," "knowledge of market," and "knowledge of industry."[5]

Clearly that does not rule out other possibilities for a would-be entrepreneur. The findings are only on average. There are great successes in virtually all lines of work, even hamburgers, as McDonald's and many other food stores illustrate. Moreover, an entrepreneur who lacks the know-how or connections, to start a bank for instance, may be able to recruit those capabilities in partners.

But these patterns of success do highlight the fact that technical capability can be an important if not all-important factor in pursuing venture success. As noted earlier, it is not enough to be able simply to perform the work of the business. Venturing often requires that it be performed exceptionally well. If the entrepreneur possesses the technical capability, there will still be question as to whether it is good enough. Or if expert help is to be recruited through partners, there will remain the question of just what skills, talent and experience the recruiting entrepreneur brings to the enterprise.

Successively deeper penetrations in assessing the fit of founder could include:

1. Contemplating the question "how well would it fit me to work on this venture idea?"

2. Making lists on paper of (a) capabilities needed to implement the venture idea and (b) personal prior experience, qualifications and resources. Compare the two lists. What complementary talents might it be wise to recruit?

3. Making a third list which includes other people who might be interested in competing with the venture. How do their qualifications compare? What might it take to recruit complementary talents to make a "bulletproof" venture team?

4. Asking one or more other suitably qualified people to comment on the comparisons made in the above lists.

Application: *Which of the above four methods for assessing founders' fit with the assigned case venture are most appropriate and what does their application show?*

The following personal dimensions of motivation and realism concerning what the venture will require of a founder were adapted from suggestions by Shragge[6] and others:

1. Willingness to make work on the venture a first priority

2. Willingness to invest life savings

3. Willingness to accept a reduction in living standard if needed by the venture

4. Willingness to work long hours at low initial pay

5. Expecting to become immersed in the venture as a way of life

6. Wanting to figure out better ways of doing things

7. Liking to work with other people

8. Valuing honest ethics and good working relationships more than a fast buck

9. Having good health and high energy

10. Willingness to deal with the impact of venture demands on family life and of the family to deal with it

11. Willingness to live with uncertainty and insecurity

12. Conviction that venturing will satisfy personal goals, even if it fails

13. Appetite for making decisions and being the boss

14. Need for independence from working for others

15. Being able to self-organize effectively

16. Conviction that the time is propitious for the particular venture

17. Knowledge of how to perform or get the technical aspects of the business performed well

18. Clarity as to the goals of the business for specific dates on the calendar ahead

19. Degree of certainty that there is a market for the venture's output

20. Level of awareness as to what competitors may do, and how to cope with their actions

21. Ability to identify specific customers and how much they will buy from the venture

22. Strength of knowledge about how much cash the venture will need, and when

23. Clarity as to how cash can be raised for the venture, especially if it needs more than expected

24. Certainty that making half as much from the venture would be preferable to wages possible from a job

25. Strength of personal credibility with others for being a reliable performer

Some of these demands may seem unappealing in the abstract. The question is what the answers will be in the actual process of starting a specific individual venture. Participating in a start-up often changes the way people feel. Usually, their excitement and enthusiasm rises greatly. So, too, may their apprehension and anxiety.

If the answers to these preliminary questions are less than encouraging, there may be ways to modify them by recruiting other partners or by acquiring needed capability through study or work experience. This will test another important issue, namely how strong is the entrepreneur's preference for that particular type of enterprise.

Forecast Competitors' Moves

The importance of competitors can be viewed in the following way. Before the new venture starts, its competitors are getting all the customer orders. If too large a fraction of those orders continue going to competitors after it starts, the venture will fail. The typical competitors of new businesses, according to a study of 2,994 start-ups by Cooper et al., are other small firms. However, a substantial minority, 25 percent, of entrepreneurs in their second year of operations said their primary competitors were more than five times larger. Beyond inception the entrepreneurs expected that the number of their competitors would grow, and two years later they continued to hold that view.[7]

A starting point for competitor analysis is to make a grid which contrasts features of the venture's product or service with those of its competitors. These can range on a spectrum from very direct in competing for customers' money to very indirect. This may explain why 23 percent of the entrepreneurs in the Cooper study were unable to name their primary competitor. The direct competitor for a new hamburger stand may be a nearby fast food franchise. The competition could also include to some degree fancier restaurants, home cooking and even diet programs. The question to consider is, where will a customer spend the same dollar if the venture does not exist or if it does not function quite well enough to win that dollar?

Future tense is also important in answering this question. Comparing what the venture plans to offer with what competitors currently offer is a good starting point. More important, however, is the comparison with what competitors will be offering in the future when the venture actually starts, and how their offerings will change after the venture becomes a factor in the marketplace.

Awareness of how competitors have responded before to new entrants or other changes in the market may give clues as to how they will adjust in the future. The entrepreneur then needs to think for competitors. What will they do if they are smart? Are they likely to be that smart and to do what they logically should?

Historical evidence suggests that on average market share is a powerful determinant of profitability. Market share in turn seems to be driven by product or service quality and by value (roughly, performance divided by price) as perceived by customers. Therefore a good starting point in analysis of competition is to write down specifically how high the quality and value of competitors' offerings are relative to each other. To that description can be added what the quality and value of the venture's offering will be. A grid or matrix display such as those of *Consumer Reports* and other product magazines will be an effective choice for this.

Other aspects of competitive position may include such things as talents, know-how, location, ideas, reputation, contacts, financial resources, special production equipment or unique elements of the venture's strategy and of the policies through which the venture will be implemented. Dedication level and the willingness to work extra hours per dollar of income can also make an important difference.

After such factors have been assessed, likely changes in competitors' and the venture's performances can be estimated, which should then provide a good basis for assessing prospects of venture success. To forecast competitors' moves probably requires looking first at where they are today, then asking what would be smart for them to do tomorrow. Should they have full lines or does it matter? Will they add offerings to match the venture? Should they cut price to match it? Should they be working on next generation designs now that will leapfrog what the venture introduces in the way of a product or service? What can or might competitors do about any legal protections the start-up might have such as contracts, leases, patents, trademarks or copyrights? Might they sue the venture on such grounds? It's easier to get into a venture than it is to get out, particularly if the venture gets into trouble, and the time to anticipate troublesome eventualities is before taking the plunge.

Successively deeper penetrations in analyzing competitors' moves could therefore include:

1. Guessing what they will do by imagining different scenarios and judging which would make most sense.

2. Writing out grids that compare them in such aspects as price, quality, features, market share, breadth of line, rate of growth, apparent ambitions and strategy, and competitive advantages now and again in the future versus the contemplated new venture.

3. Investing more time and money in gathering the above information.

4. Obtaining reactions to the above grids from one or more suitably knowledgeable people.

Application: *Which of the above four methods for analyzing competitors' moves against the assigned case venture are most appropriate, and what does their application show?*

Cross-check Competitive Advantages

Throughout the idea testing process assumptions will inevitably be made about the venture's competitive advantages and those of the particular entrepreneur(s) for creating that particular venture. At some point these assumptions should be audited explicitly. Questions to consider in this process include the following:

1. What was the entrepreneur's prior task-relevant experience?

2. What factors will govern the profit-generating potential of this venture? Which of the following can it be expected to possess which will give it an advantage over existing and potential competitors?

- License
- Patent
- Lease
- Known brand
- Known personalities
- Invisibility
- High risk activity
- Secret methods
- Resource ownership
- Capital access
- Advertising power
- Political power
- Personal connections
- Skill level
- Rare knowledge/skill
- Personal charisma
- Exceptional intellectual power
- Exceptional energy level
- Habit patterns among constituents and contacts

Presumably, the levels of each of these will start at one point, then change in the future. Similarly, their levels of importance to the venture's prosperity will also change. Part of assessing the venture idea, shaping it and reshaping it additionally in the future must depend on how these levels can be expected to change over time. Hence, they should be forecasted for different future points in time as part of the assessment and planning processes.

Application: *What does application of the above two questions for cross-checking competitive advantages of the assigned case venture idea show and how?*

Accept, Refine, Table or Reject

How much analysis is enough? Each of the above sections ends with questions which may be partially or more fully answered. Having cycled once through the facets of analysis listed above, presumably some more deeply than others based on considerations of priority, the would-be entrepreneur faces a question of whether to drop the venture idea or to continue the analysis with still deeper study of one of the facets. Possibly the first round of analysis has suggested ways to modify the venture concept calling for another round to examine viability of the changed idea. If the idea still holds up, likely the next step will be to obtain information for testing and developing it further.

Successively deeper penetrations in deciding whether to improve further or drop could include:

1. Accept this idea and move ahead to implement it.

2. Keep checking further aspects of this idea in successively greater depth to reach a verdict.

3. Table this idea for now. Work on other ideas and maybe come back to this one later.

4. Reject this one and concentrate all processing capacity on either pursuing other ideas already found or seeking out still more ideas to check.

Application: *Which of the above four alternative actions with respect to the proposed venture concept in the assigned case should be taken and why?*

Supplementary Reading

New Venture Strategies Chapter 6. (Vesper, K.H., Prentice-Hall, 1990)

Exercises

1. How high on a scale from one to five, where five is high relative to a typical person, would you rate yourself (or the case entrepreneur) on each of the 25 self-evaluation questions suggested under Founder's Fit, (a) before undertaking a venture and (b) during the early stages of undertaking a venture?

2. This chapter contains many questions to use in assessing venture ideas. For each of three ideas identify the page and line for 10 different questions that would be best to start with in performing evaluation. Indicate the rank order of priority of those questions for each idea. Be prepared to comment on how the patterns of questions selected differ for each of the three ideas. Also be prepared to comment on how it would be best to go about developing answers for those top priority questions.

3. Apply the evaluation questions of this chapter, in order of their importance to the particular venture, to one or more of your own venture ideas.

Venture History

1. Which techniques described in this chapter seemed to have been used by the entrepreneur, which were not, and why?

2. How far off were expectations of the entrepreneur from the way the venture actually developed and why?

3. What responses did competitors make to the start-up? Which were foreseen by the entrepreneur and which were not?

4. What comparison grid of the venture versus its competitors does the entrepreneur foresee downstream in time?

Venture Planning Guide

1. Prepare a five-minute report describing what has been accomplished on your venture plan to date. Begin with description of the current status and then tell about different aspects in terms of what has been accomplished.

2. Apply screening questions of this chapter to rank the 10 most promising venture ideas considered along the way in arriving at your venture plan. Indicate where you put highest priority in screening and how you controlled the depth of investigation to fit the time available for this task. Rank the ideas in some sort of systematic way, and indicate what action you think is called for next in your venture development project.

3. Copy the list of possible competitive advantages from this chapter, and rate the prospects of your venture versus those of competitors on each of them at three different future time points.

4. Make a prototype in some form of your top ranked idea.

5. Do some sort of market testing of your most promising idea by talking to at least one other person about it.

6. Make pro forma financials and a cash flow forecast monthly for the first two years of implementing your most promising venture idea so far.

Notes

[1] Karl H. Vesper, *New Venture Strategies*, revised edition (Englewood Cliffs, N.J.: Prentice-Hall, 1990), p. 32.

[2] Bruce D. Phillips and Bruce A. Kirchhoff, "An Analysis of New Firm Survival and Growth," Babson Entrepreneurship Conference, Calgary, 1988. A more recent study by Kirchhoff cited in The *Christian Science Monitor* (May 7, 1993) states that no more than 18 percent of all start-ups fail in the first eight years, while 28 percent voluntarily terminate without losses to the creditors. The remaining 54 percent survive either with their original or new owners.

[3] David L. Birch, "The Truth About Startups," *Inc.*, January 1988, p. 14.

[4] Brian R. Chambers, Stuart L. Hart, and Daniel R. Denison, "Founding Team Experiences and New Firm Performance," in *Frontiers of Entrepreneurship Research, 1988*, eds. Bruce A. Kirchhoff and others (Wellesley, Mass.: Babson Center for Entrepreneurial Studies, 1988), p. 117.

[5] Gerald E. Hills, and Harold P. Welsch, "High Growth Entrepreneurial Ventures," in *Frontiers of Entrepreneurship Research, 1988*, eds. Bruce A. Kirchhoff and others (Wellesley, Mass.: Babson Center for Entrepreneurial Studies, 1988), p. 496.

[6] Phil Shragge, *Be Your Own Boss* (Edmonton, Alberta: Northern Alberta Institute of Technology, 1985) p.11.

[7] Arnold C. Cooper and others, *New Business In America* (Washington, D.C.: The NFIB Foundation, 1990), p. 9.

Case Questions

General Questions

1. Do the elements of a potentially viable start-up opportunity exist in the situation described by the assigned case? Explain why or why not.

2. As best you can with the information provided in the assigned case, lay out at least one action plan for starting a business in this situation, estimate the upside potential and downside risk (both amount and likelihood) of loss.

3. How well suited is the entrepreneur(s) in the assigned case to compete with others who might start a similar venture?

4. How well suited to the start-up contemplated in the assigned case would be one or more entrepreneurs who were encountered in previously studied cases?

5. If a prospectus were written to invite investment in this potential venture, what factors of promise should it describe to possible investors and what factors of risk should a Securities and Exchange Commission official want to see listed for a public offering circular?

Case 6 - Fred Ingersoll p. 158

1. What would the entrepreneur in this case have to gain, potentially, by attempting it? Please include analysis of the financial aspects.

2. How much would have to be risked to get that gain? How do the expected benefits and risks compare?

Case 7 - Michael Shane (B) p. 168

1. What implications appear in results of the market survey regarding (a) whether Michael Shane should go ahead with start-up of a distributorship, and (b) what the strategy and design of the venture should be if he does go ahead with it?

2. In hindsight, how effective was the survey in pointing up future directions of opportunity in the microcomputer business? What questions, if asked by the survey, might have been more revealing to a person in Michael's position?

3. What should be the role of formal market research in creating new ventures, as you see it?

Case 8 - Prize-Winning Plan p. 190

1. What is your assessment of the venture (not the written document that constitutes the plan) that this plan proposes based upon Charles Ewing's invention? What is your assessment of its prospects for success?

2. What other strategies could the students have proposed to make the most of Charles Ewing's invention and how would those compare to the one described in the plan?

3. What value has the student team added thus far to the business opportunity associated with Charles Ewing's product? What did it take for them to do that?

4. How else could they have applied their effort to help him? Which would have been the better choice and why?

Fred Ingersoll

In December of 1989, Fred Ingersoll said he was one step away from turning his idea for a business venture into reality—to print baseball logos on high-quality T-shirts to sell in retail stores around the country. He had spent the past three months imprinting shirts slowly by hand, soliciting orders for them and trying to find a bank that would lend him $350,000, which he figured was necessary to capitalize the business properly. He had been told, to his disappointment, that to secure such a loan he would have to invest $100,000 in equity, an amount he didn't have. His list of estimated first-year costs appears in Exhibit 1.

Without the money, he said, much of the $200,000 in orders he had lined up could not be filled in time to meet spring and summer shipping dates. That, he said, could mean losing important customers and consequent demise for his Atlanta-based venture. If funding was not forthcoming by the end of the month, he expected he would have to choose between continuing limited production by hand, closing the business, or looking for another alternative to keep his enterprise going.

Getting a Business Idea

Fred Ingersoll graduated from the University of Georgia in 1979 with a B.S. in Economics. His first job after college was as a bank examiner for the Comptroller of Currency in the Southeast Region. Fred recalled that the work helped him understand "what business financing was all about." His job involved reviewing business loans made by commercial banks in the six-state region. He said that although this work was a valuable learning experience, he longed to become more closely involved with actual business operations.

In 1983, he went to work for a company selling novelty T-shirts. He switched employers three years later, although the type of work he was doing was the same. Fred described the product as poor quality T-shirts imprinted to be sold in places where people would not expect the shirts they bought to last with continued use. The sales approach relied heavily on impulse buying. He went on to explain how the T-shirts were processed for selling to retail customers:

> The fabric was purchased from a factory in the Far East. The nylon and cotton blend was out of proportion to what a high quality T-shirt would contain, and the weave was poor and thin.
>
> We'd get the T-shirts, apply lettering or pictures on the front, and sell them to vendors or small stores as novelty items. When you wash a shirt like that, it's possible that after three or four times through the machine, you'll have to throw it away. The dye will fade or run, the shirt will shrink, and any flaws in the weave will get worse—the T-shirt can literally fall apart in your hands.

As a result, Fred said, he had little faith in the products he was selling. He started considering the possibility of selling T-shirts of high-quality cotton weave that would be imprinted with a more permanent dye and would last as long as sports shirts purchased in clothing stores. He talked to his boss about the idea but was told that there was no incentive to make a costlier product that might lose out in the intense price competition prevailing in that business. His boss explained that his company operated on a very thin margin. A difference of just pennies on an order of a thousand shirts, he said, would not only hurt the company's profitability, but would force him to raise his price slightly, and this would prompt his customers go to a different manufacturer for the $20 or $30 total savings on a typical purchase order.

Fred commented on his experience in the novelty T-shirt market:

> *I'd call these independent vendors you'd see in Atlantic City or other tourist places in the summer. Some of them would set up for a week or two and peddle as many novelty items as they could. Then they would literally 'pack up shop' and move somewhere else.*
>
> *The business is really seasonal and for the guy out on the beach who decides to buy a T-shirt with something funny on it, the $2 or $3 doesn't seem like much. He knows there's no chance for him to return the shirt if it's defective. He goes to the beach maybe once or twice during the summer and it's just not worth his time to complain about such a small amount of money. The retailer knows that and consequently buys low quality to get a low price.*

Deciding to Venture

By 1989, Fred decided he couldn't continue to sell a product he didn't believe in, even though sales for cheap novelty T-shirts were growing despite their generally poor-quality reputation. He thought about other options he might have if he quit his present job. The idea of imprinting high-quality T-shirts that would last longer still appealed to him. The prospect of being his own boss was also pleasing, and he thought his experience in the field gave him a good idea of how to succeed.

First, he said, there would have to be some customer orders from major retailers to lend the product credibility and assure sufficient volume. Second, the design on the T-shirt would have to be popular with a large segment of the population, and be inoffensive for display in stores. Fred recalled seeing many people in New York wearing hats and shirts with a New York Yankees baseball logo imprinted. He reasoned that sports-related designs and logos would sell throughout the country, and could be regionalized depending on local team and fan loyalties.

Since the logos were registered trademarks, Fred called the Commissioner of Baseball's office to see what would be needed to buy rights for using the designs on T-shirts. He was referred to a department that specialized in handling royalties and promotions for the major leagues, and discovered they were interested. Their philosophy, Fred recalled, was that high-quality products with team logos helped to promote major league baseball. A percentage would typically be negotiated as a minimum royalty that would increase as the person's sales of a product increased. In Fred's opinion, the figures quoted him were an insignificant cost. He should be able to make the venture work if he could get sufficient orders and capital to purchase equipment. Encouraged by these findings, he quit his job with the T-shirt company and set out to see which stores would be willing to order his shirts for the upcoming 1990 baseball season.

He purchased a few dozen high quality T-shirts from a department store and used a homemade setup to print logos on them. With the completed samples, he called on buyers for department stores and sporting goods shops in southern and mid-Atlantic states. Several said they would be willing to take delivery on such shirts for spring and summer. By the end of 1989, he had obtained orders for approximately $200,000, including one from a nationwide department store chain, and several from regional department stores who would display the shirts either with other sporting goods equipment and clothing, or as an added line in their sportswear sections.

Planning for Operations

Fred's present production method used screen printing, which could be done either by hand or machine. The simple procedure used a fine mesh screen over a wooden frame large enough to be placed on a T-shirt. The letters or design would be blocked out on the shirt with masking tape. Ink would then be forced through the screen onto the shirt by spreading it with a squeegee. The masking tape was then peeled off and the shirt left to dry.

This, he said, was hard and tedious work that could produce blisters from using the squeegee all day. He estimated that the mesh was about eight times as fine as would be found on a screen door, so pressure had to be applied to push the ink through it. He explained that the ink needed for imprinting was a very thick solution and tended to be cohesive.

In a more sophisticated process, which he planned eventually to use, a stenciled screen would be prepared. This would eliminate the need for masking tape and would print a more accurate image. To make this screen, a logo or design would first be cut from a sheet of red acetate. This formed a "positive" image of the emblem, identical to the way the logo would look when printed on a T-shirt. Next, the positive image was placed atop a light-table, and the screen, stretched over an oblong wooden frame and saturated with a light-sensitive emulsion, was positioned on top of it, as illustrated in Exhibit 2. The light source would then be turned on for up to 10 minutes, hardening the emulsion wherever the light was not blocked by the ac-

etate stencil between it and the light. Finally, the non-hardened part was washed away with water, leaving porous a part of the screen in the exact shape of the image.

Supplies such as the acetate, screen, and emulsion could be purchased from any graphic arts supplier. A light-table, Fred said, could be built for about $600:

Essentially, you build a wooden table which has a piece of glass resting on top. Beneath the glass, you cram as many light bulbs as you possibly can to provide a high-intensity light source.

In use, a screen which had been prepared by this process was placed over a T-shirt resting on a hard back palette shaped like the shirt. The shirt could then be printed, with ink passing through the screen to the shirt only where the light had been blocked out by the acetate, which thereby kept the emulsion soft and let it be washed away.

Fred wanted to automate as much of the printing as possible, particularly by doing away with hand application of the ink and squeegee. After chasing down leads to see if such equipment could be purchased anywhere, he learned of a man who had been in the specialty T-shirt printing business, left, and then returned to concentrate now on developing designs to be used on shirts. This man owned the type of equipment Fred sought and, although he wanted to keep it, agreed to sell plans and specifications for a modest price. Fred said the next step would be to take those "specs" to a machine shop to obtain bids for building a printer and dryer. He observed:

The printer and dryer have to be compatible units. The printer applies pressure to force ink through the screen and the dryer allows the ink to be baked quickly onto the shirt. The dryer is essentially a long conveyor belt passing through a heat source. When that's finished, you can fold and pack the shirt for shipment.

Advantages of automating the printing process were to allow more production per worker, and to assure consistently high quality in affixing ink to the shirt. Fred estimated that to have the main machine made by a machine shop would cost about $60,000. Other equipment would then be purchased or made to complete the set-up for production.

Fred estimated he would need 2,000 square feet of space to house the equipment and inventory. He knew of loft space in old warehouses near downtown Atlanta that could be leased for as little as $2 per square foot per year. His main concern was that the location be properly wired for the electrical equipment. He stated that the machinery would use "quite a bit" of electricity, since the dryer had to operate at a high enough temperature to bake the ink onto the T-shirt for a permanent fix. He estimated that leasehold improvements could run as much as $10,000, and annual electricity bills around $4,000. He guessed that 60-65 percent of his cost of goods sold would be for blank T-shirts. Other major expenses would be for salary and printing supplies. Costs of office furnishings and related items would, he expected, be insignificant.

According to Fred, finding workers with both experience in screen printing and artistic skills to help prepare the designs would probably not be hard:

I've got a friend who does screen printing, and he's carrying more trained workers than he actually needs. I've talked briefly with a couple of them and they would be willing to come and work for me, assuming I get the money I need. Jobs in the printing business are pretty hard to find right now and it seems to

me we'd all come out ahead with this type of arrangement. It's not as if I'd be raiding his shop.

From his past experience in the business, Fred said that much of the work would still be manual. All the folding, packing, and storage of shirts would be done by hand, and he estimated that at least half of the production labor time would be spent performing such tasks.

Orders would be taken by the dozen, the minimum being one dozen for any single baseball team. He had called department stores to ask if there were any standards for the number of shirts by size that should be packed with an order. One person explained that most orders came with two shirts small, four each medium and large, and two shirts extra large. Fred explained that if the major stores were comfortable with this combination, he would arrange his production accordingly.

If he imprinted only baseball logos, he expected his business would be highly seasonal. People who sold similar products told him it was common for 80 percent of annual sales to be delivered in about 40 percent (or nearly five months) of the year. Thus, he could either (1) produce for a portion of the year and then shut down, (2) search out offsetting lines that peaked at different times of the year, or (3) seek custom work for slack times.

Another option, he said, might be to seek rights for major league football as well as baseball logos; however, he hadn't pursued this possibility. Instead, he had contacted wholesalers and retailers of specialty items to seek custom work for slow periods. They would provide shirts, and Fred would print the desired wording or artwork at a specified rate. This work would reduce the shirt inventory he needed. He said he might be able to build the custom part of the business to as much as 25 percent of total sales during slack months.

Developing a Marketing Strategy

Fred estimated that a selling price 70 percent above the $4 or $5 paid for a good quality T-shirt would be competitive and affordable to a wide segment of the population. Display in retail clothing and sporting goods stores might associate them with quality that could command a premium price. To his knowledge, no one else was currently providing stores with similar quality shirts carrying baseball logos. Possible competitors such as Wilson or Rawlings had stayed with sports uniforms and focused on football instead of baseball. Many buyers Fred talked with said they liked the appearance of his samples and would order " . . . as many as you can get us, if the shirts take off."

Payment terms for customers, Fred figured, would be net 30 days. He expected that once he was able to establish credit, his payables would be on a similar basis. A few stores had indicated willingness to order shirts with baseball logos and colored borders around the neck and sleeves. For these, Fred said he would buy the fabric and ship it to a mill for sewing to customers' specifications. Current orders for such shirts accounted for nearly 25 percent of total orders received to date (shown in Exhibit 3).

According to estimates Fred had heard, total sales of the entire sports clothing products market ranged between $100 million and $300 million per year. This size market meant that there would be numerous trade shows and significant amounts of money invested in advertising each year, Fred said. However, he preferred to put all of his available capital into inventory during early years of the venture. He explained that it made more sense to him to build on current accounts than to spread himself too thin by promoting a larger customer base.

He knew there were about a dozen cities with teams in each of the two main baseball leagues, American and National. He had been told that attendance was around 20 million people per year in each of them, with some teams, such as Los Angeles, drawing over two million per year while others, such as Atlanta, drew about half that. In football, he estimated that there was a roughly comparable attendance; while in hockey, the total number was about half as large.

Fred had heard estimates for football products sales ranging between four and 10 times those of baseball products. Coincidence of the football schedule with "back to school" and Christmas seasons was cited for part of its larger appeal, he added. He speculated that a related benefit that would come with rights to produce football as well as baseball logos was that the same concessionaires and stadium owners were often involved.

Seeking Capital

Fred discovered during the final months of 1989 that bankers he talked to did not share his optimism about the venture. When he pointed to over $200,000 in orders lined up for the upcoming 1990 summer season, a banker countered by stating the business existed only on paper; there were no established lines of credit, no equipment, inventory or accounts receivable to secure a loan, hence no basis for lending. Despite the orders and $5,600 Fred had invested from his total personal savings of $7,600, the responses he reported from lending officers had a common theme. He recalled:

> Since the company was a start-up, they said that there was no track record to show I'd likely be able to repay the loan. They also said there were too many steps between an order and creation of a receivable. The stores could cancel, I might not be able to produce the product in the quantity or quality desired,

and I might not be able to meet shipping deadlines. In essence, I was being told that my orders were worthless—there was no evidence that the orders would clearly become deliverable products or any other form of collateral.

During conversation with one large Atlanta bank, Fred was told that he should consider going to the Small Business Administration (SBA) for help with financing. The SBA, he was told, only considered persons who had been rejected by a commercial lending institution, a requirement Fred would have no trouble meeting. He made an appointment and met with an SBA loan officer in November 1989. Fred described how the SBA might be able to help finance his start-up:

They guarantee a bank loan. The bank is responsible for helping the business along and taking the active role. The SBA is a back-up for the bank in case the loan defaults. The limit on this program is $500,000 and the SBA will guarantee up to 90 percent of the total. The catch is, they won't touch anything that has a debt-to-equity ratio higher than three-and-one-half or four to one. For me, that means finding $100,000 in equity to get the $350,000 I need to get started.

Fred mentioned that he had an uncle who might be willing to lend the $100,000; but if the money came as a loan, it would show up on the balance sheet as debt. Stock issued to the uncle was another possibility, although Fred didn't want to lose control of the business. Also, he would have to take time out for the added administrative tasks of incorporating, preparing and issuing stock certificates, holding directors' meetings, keeping minutes and preparing corporate tax reports. Fred commented that his uncle's present portfolio "is not one you should clutter up with a

bunch of risky paper from a start-up company." He understood, moreover, that the SBA would require all shareholders of the company to accept full personal responsibility for repayment of such a guaranteed loan.

A third idea he had would be for his uncle to invest in a certificate of deposit at the bank where Fred had been discussing possible loan arrangements for SBA participation. With a $100,000 certificate at the bank pledged against his loan, the bank would have recourse. If the business failed and could not repay, the bank could take over the $100,000 certificate for coverage.

Fred said he was unaware of other leveraging possibilities. As it now stood, he thought the SBA might provide the guarantee if a bank would finance the loan. One bank said it would grant the loan if he could provide the $100,000 in the form of equity. His uncle said he would provide such equity if there were some sure method arranged for him to receive repayment over a period of time, and if Fred could assure him that he was being treated fairly.

Current interest rates were in the range of 9 percent annually. Part of the funding would consist of a seasonal line of credit, requiring a zero balance for at least 30 consecutive days sometime during the year. Compensating balances, wherein the bank required that a minimum balance be maintained by the borrower, would not be required if Fred maintained an account with the bank and honored terms of the credit line.

Fred remarked that a typical SBA guarantee commitment stretched over five years at most. Beyond that, a commercial bank should be willing to lend the amount needed for the business, with equipment and current assets secured if necessary. Since the guarantee limit was $500,000, Fred added that he would have to move from reliance on the SBA anyway, or the business would never be able to grow as large as he wished. He explained that his strategy would be to use increased sales and retained earnings to obtain a larger commitment from the bank each year. He estimated, based on a collection period of 30 days and stock turn of 4, that to obtain a loan of $500,000 secured against 80 percent of accounts receivable and 50 percent of inventory, sales would have to be in excess of $6,000,000 per year.

Fred summarized options he currently saw as follows:

1. Raise the $100,000 in equity, either through his uncle or other sources he had not yet found, to leverage the $350,000 needed to set up production for the venture.

2. Operate the business using a manual screening process, and cut back on the volume of orders received, either by eliminating certain customers or filling only a portion of each order to the retailer.

3. Arrange for trade credit through suppliers and other sources of cash, and reduce start-up needs, lessening the amount of money needed to begin operations, and secure a smaller SBA loan.

4. Search out some other yet-to-be-discovered option. One he was not at this point ready to accept was to abandon the business entirely without attempting to satisfy his obligations, and glean the most possible from what he had accomplished so far.

Deciding upon Action

The longer his venture continued without the necessary financing, the dimmer Fred said prospects became. He pointed out that peak production to meet present orders should have begun by the first of December and continued through May. He was attempting to meet orders by doing the printing by hand, but this was a much slower process. While two dozen shirts with the same logo could be printed in an hour by hand, 20 dozen could be printed with proper machinery. Time for folding and packing would remain the same either way.

To date, he had been able to obtain lines of credit from two of the five suppliers he was using, one for $10,000 and the other for $20,000. The other three required him to pay by certified check or C.O.D. He had considered approaching customers for funding, but said this would be highly unlikely. The retail stores had placed orders on the assumption that Fred would be able to meet shipping deadlines and that the shirts would sell. While Fred could start the business at a lower volume and with less funding, he thought he would lose growth potential if he started too small. Starting small and remaining small was a prospect he said he did not want, commenting:

> It's kind of a vicious circle. The bank won't touch me unless the SBA comes in. The SBA won't go in unless I have the capital to keep the debt to equity ratio at four-to-one, or less. But I've got the concept, orders, and competitive edge in designs, fabric, and printing that I would use. That's why the stores, not to mention the baseball commissioner's office, have gone along with me in the first place. It seems to me there has been a real value created there that I should be able to capitalize on somehow.

EXHIBIT 1   Financial Forecast

ESTIMATE OF START-UP COSTS
FOR FIRST YEAR OF OPERATIONS

Expense Category		Amount
Machinery (Printer and Dryer)		$60,000
T-shirts		
Standard (1455 dozen @ $4.00/shirt)	$70,000	
Special (480 dozen @ $5.00/shirt)	$29,000	
Total, Current Orders	$99,000	
Standard (725 dozen @ $4.00/shirt)	$35,000	
Special (240 dozen @ $5.00/shirt)	$14,400	
Total, Re-orders and inventory for	$49,400	
1991 (Expect to fund one-half of		
re-orders and inventory from funds		
provided by operations)		
Total, All Orders		$148,400
Salaries ($6/hour, times factor of 1.3 to		
include benefits, insurance and other		
compensation; estimated for 2 persons		
@ 40 hours/week for six months)		$16,000
Rent, Utilities, and Leasehold Improvements		$24,000
Ink and Production Supplies		$24,000
Selling, Administrative and Other Expense		
(Includes salary for principal @ $1,000		
per month for one year)		$54,000
Working Capital		$23,600
TOTAL FUNDING REQUIREMENTS		$350,000

EXHIBIT 2   Diagram of the Inking and Printing Process (manual process)

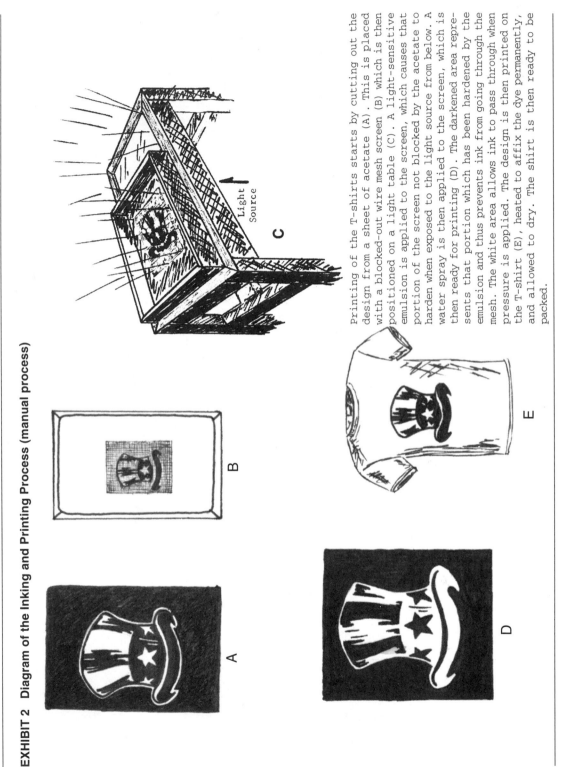

Printing of the T-shirts starts by cutting out the design from a sheet of acetate (A). This is placed with a blocked-out wire mesh screen (B) which is then positioned on a light table (C). A light-sensitive emulsion is applied to the screen, which causes that portion of the screen not blocked by the acetate to harden when exposed to the light source from below. A water spray is then applied to the screen, which is then ready for printing (D). The darkened area represents that portion which has been hardened by the emulsion and thus prevents ink from going through the mesh. The white area allows ink to pass through when pressure is applied. The design is then printed on the T-shirt (E), heated to affix the dye permanently, and allowed to dry. The shirt is then ready to be packed.

EXHIBIT 3   Orders Received as of December 31, 1989

Type of Customer	Quantity (in dozens)	Type of Shirt (std. or spl.)	Revenue (per shirt)	Total Revenue
Department Stores				
380		standard	$7.00	$ 31,920
185		special	$9.00	$ 19,980
Sub Total	565			$ 51,900
Sporting Goods Stores Nationwide Chain				
600		standard	$7.00	$50,400
200		special	$9.00	$ 21,600
Sub Total	800		—	$ 72,000
Other Sporting Goods Stores				
475		standard	$7.00	$ 39,900
95		special	$9.00	$ 10,260
Sub Total	570			$ 50,160
Total, T-shirt Orders	1935			$174,060
Custom Work	960		$2.50	$28,800
TOTAL, ALL ORDERS	2895			$202,860

Price estimates based on cost of $4.00 per standard shirt and $5.00 per special order shirt. Fred assumed that these "splits" would continue in roughly the same proportions for future volumes of business. Delivery dates range from late February through June, with some indicating a willingness to reorder if sales meet expectations.

Case 7

Michael Shane (B)

Market Research Responses

As described in the earlier case on Michael Shane (A), he decided to conduct a market survey to help him decide whether to establish a new wholesaling company in the microcomputer industry and, if so, what form it should take. Dick Sanders, who had professional experience in market research, was hired to design and conduct the survey. He prepared a questionnaire and mailing list with the help of Michael and his associates.

One day was spent getting the mailing out. Within a week, results began coming in the mail, and a week after that Dick started tallying answers on large sheets of paper. By the end of January, 45 stores had responded. A number of other replies were received but discarded. Some were discarded because their answers indicated that those respondents had not understood the questions. Also discarded were answers that came not from retail stores but rather from systems houses. These were vendors which packaged software and hardware for end users and sold microcomputer products as custom-designed turnkey systems.

Another 80 questionnaires were returned as undeliverable. Dick commented that these returns did not bother him. He said it simply indicated that one of every six stores had gone out of business in the last six months, reflecting the recent emergence of the computer store as a retail growth phenomenon. To offset the loss, Dick speculated that two stores were popping up for every one that closed. His assessment was supported, he said, by a recent *Datamation* article which predicted that by 1983 there would be over 2,000 computer stores in the United States.

Exhibit 1 is a summary of the survey results Dick prepared. The task now, he said, was to figure out just what the implications of these results were for design of Mike Shane's business.

EXHIBIT 1   Dick Sanders' Summary of Survey Results

I.   <u>Store Demographics</u>

A.   The following table analyzes the demographics of the responding stores.

Table 1
Demographics

Average number of stores per business	1.3*
Range of number of stores per business	1 to 6*
Average length of time in business	24.2 months
Ranges of length of time in business	3 to 48 months

Types of locations (% of responding
 stores)

Small Mall	42%
On a Main Street Location	19
Downtown Business Area	13
Industrial Park	10
Office Building	8
Shopping Center	6
At a University	2
Total	100%

* One return was not used in the averages in that they answered for the whole Computerland chain (107 stores), and this would have distorted the independent stores' figures.

EXHIBIT 1 (continued)

II.   Sales Ratings of Personal Computer Manufacturers   Table 2

| | | Percent of the Responding Stores Mentioning | | | |
| | | Now | Now | 1983 | 1983 |
Manufacturer	Carry the Mfr.	Mfrs. Being in their top 4 in Sales	Mfrs. Being their Top Seller	Mfrs. Being in their Top 4 in Sales	Mfrs. Being their Top Seller
Apple	67%	67%	38%	67%	23%
North Star	31	27	8	13	4
Commodore	29	25	8	18	11
Cromemco	25	21	8	11	9
T.I.	23	17	0	29	11
Ohio Scientific	21	19	8	18	4
Alpha Micro	17	17	4	16	4
Atari	17	13	0	24	0
Vector Graphics	15	13	10	11	11
Exidy	15	13	0	2	0
Dynabyte	10	8	0	2	0
Pertec	8	8	4	11	2
Compucolor	8	6	0	4	0
NEC	8	8	0	11	4
Altos	8	4	0	2	0
SWTPC	6	4	2	4	0
DEC	4	2	0	2	0
IMSAI	4	2	0	0	0
Tandy	4	0	0	0	0
Heath	4	0	0	2	0
Many (20 companies)*	2	0	0	-	-
Data General	-	-	-	4	2
H-P	-	-	-	7	0
Many (13 companies)**	-	-	-	2	-

* Others Receiving One Mention: MSI, Western Digital, Polymorphic, Digital Micro, Micromation, Computex, SD Systems, Zilog, Industrial Microsystems, Micro V, Percom, Hazeltine, Interec, Ithaca, Thinker, Elf, RCA, Interact, and Rexou.

** Others Receiving One Mention: MSI, FUSI, AMD, ISC, Micromation, Zilog, Ind. Micro., Prime, Polymorphic, Digital Micro, TEI, Rexou, and Micro V.

EXHIBIT 1 (continued)

III.   <u>Salespeople</u>

    The following tables describe what a store looks for in potential salespeople and also whether they have a formal or informal training program once hired.

Table 3A
Desired Characteristics of
Potential Salespeople

Desired Characteristics	% of Responding Stores Mentioning
Sales Experience	52%
General Sales Experience	43%
Computer Sales Experience	6
Retail Sales Experience	3
Technical/Computer Knowledge or background	46
Motivated/Hungry People	14
Good Personality	11
Ability to Analyze Customer Needs	9
College Degree	9
Programming Experience	9
Business Knowledge	9
Ability to Communicate	6
Honesty	6
Others*	3

* Others were: Appearance, Female, Non-Computer Experience, Young, Intelligent, and Anything Noteworthy.

EXHIBIT 1 (continued)

Table 3B
Type of Training Programs

	% of Responding Stores
Formal	32%
Informal Floor Training	68%
Total	100%

IV.   Sales by Product Category

Table 4
Percent Each Category Represents

The following table analyzes the percent of total sales each product category represents for the responding stores.

Product Categories	Average % for All Responding Stores	Percent of Stores Offering	Percent Breakdown Encountered the Most
CPU	37%	80%*	60%*
Peripherals	20	88 *	20
Software	11	88	10
Books	5	71	10
Turnkey Systems	27	58	0
Total	100%		100%

* The stores not offering CPUs and peripherals were stores offering only turnkey systems.

EXHIBIT 1 (continued)

V.   Sales By Market Sector

The following table describes stores' sales according to the market sector they are being made in, both now and projected for 1983.

Table 5
Sales By Market Sectors
Now vs. 1983

Market Sectors	Now			1983		
	Average % For All Responding Stores	Ranges For All Responding Stores	Breakdown Most Encountered	Average % For All Responding Stores	Ranges For All Responding Stores	Breakdown Most Encountered
Small Businesses	53%	0-100%	60%	58%	0-100%	80%
Home/Hobbyist	23	0-75%	20	18	0-85%	20
Educational	14	0-60%	10	14	0-32%	0
Scientific	6	0-50%	10	6	0-30%	0
Others	4	0-70%	0	4	0-60%	0
Totals	100%		100%			100%

VI.   Need for Distributorship Offering Better Terms, Immediacy, Low Quarterly Buys

The following table expresses how stores viewed the need for distributorships which could offer better financial terms, immediate availability, and the opportunity to purchase smaller quantities than some distributors or manufacturers might offer—at prices not much higher than they were currently paying.

Table 6A
Need for These Specialized Distributorships
by % of Responding Stores

% Seeing a Need	80%
% Not Seeing a Need	20%
Total	100%

EXHIBIT 1 (continued)

Table 6B
Reasoning Behind Responses
of Either Needing or Not Needing
These Specialized Distributorships

Reasons for Needing	% of Positively Responding Stores Mentioning	Reasons for Not Needing	% of Negatively Responding Stores Mentioning
Immediate Deliveries	86%	Can Margins be Maintained?	33%
Ability to Buy in Small Quantities	60	Not Needed	11
Better Credit Terms	40	Are an OEM	11
Ability to Get Better Systems	9	Are a Franchise	11
No Long Commitment for Blanket Orders	6	Are a Distributor Themselves	11
Better Prices (Higher Margins)	3	Question on Support Capabilities	11
Help with Floor Planning	3	Would Just Create More Problems	11
Provide Product Knowledge	3		

EXHIBIT 1 (continued)

Current and Future Sources of Distribution which Stores Use

     The following table analyzes the sources of distribution which stores are currently using to buy both their systems (CPUs) and peripherals—now and anticipated for 1983.

Table 6C
Methods of Distribution Stores Are (Will Be) Using
Now and in 1983
Average % Of All Responding Stores

Methods of Distribution	Systems		Peripherals	
	Now	1983	Now	1983
Manufacturers (Direct)	63%	58%	45%	46%
Distributors	32	39	50	51
Parent Companies or Franchise	3	1	3	1
Other	2	2	2	2
Total	100%	100%	100%	100%

VII.   Store Startup Factors

    The following tables examine two factors of store startup: Characteristics which stores perceive manufactures look for when granting the rights to sell their products; and also the stores' opinions as to the amount of capital necessary to comfortably open a store.

Table 7A
Characteristics Manufacturers Look for in Stores
When Granting Rights to Carry Their Products

Characteristics	% of Responding Stores Mentioning
Financial Stability	40%
Good Personnel	29
Nothing Needed (NONE)	27
Ability to Provide Service for the Equipment	20
Good Location	9
Commitment From the Store (Blanket Orders)	7
Ability to Provide Sales Support	7
Sales Potential	5
Good Store Image	5
Been in Business for a While	5
Formal Business Plan Done	5

EXHIBIT 1 (continued)

Table 7B
Amount of Capital Necessary to
Open a Computer Retail Store Comfortably

Categories of Necessary Capital	% of Responding Stores Mentioning
$50-75K	2%
76-100K	31
101-150K	40
151-175K	12
>175K	15
Total	100%

VIII.   Competition as Viewed by the Stores

The following table analyzes just whom stores view as their major competitors—both now and anticipated for 1983.

Table 8
Competition as Viewed by the Stores

Types of Competition	% of First Place Ranking Received		Weighted Average Ranking	
	Now	1983	Now	1983
Large Computer Chains (5 or more stores)	31%	51%	.85	1.00
Small Independent Stores (1 to 5 stores)	40	13	1.00	.81
Direct Sales by Mfr's Salesforce (IBM, DEC, DG, etc)	21	10	.75	.68
Manufacturer Owned Stores (DEC)	7	23	.42	.76
Sales thru Office Supplies Salesforces (Moore Bus. Forms sells for TI)	0	2	.12	.33
Other*	Negligible	Negligible	Negligible	Negligible

* Others were: Radio Shack, Mail Order, Sears, and Audio/Retail stores.

EXHIBIT 1   (continued)

IX.   Sources For Software

The following tables analyze computer stores' sources and methods of software acquisition.

Table 9A
Sources of Software, Current and in 1983
(Avg. % Each Source Represents for All Stores)

Sources	Average % for All Responding Stores Now	Average % for All Responding Stores 1983
Manufacturers	30%	29%
Independent S/W Houses	45	47
User Developed	12	14
Other Sources*	13	10

* Other sources were: Self-developed by the store.

Table 9B
Independent Software Houses Most Mentioned

Independent Software Houses	No. of Mentions	Independent Software Houses	No. of Mentions
Personal	8	Creative	3
Hayden	6	Microsoft	3
Serendipity	6	Micro Source	3
Peachtree	5	Independent Consultants	3
Muse	5	Retail Sciences	2
Instant	4	Programma	2
Structured Systems	4	Others* (20 companies)	1

* Others were: Quality, Softside, Daykin 5, Dr. Daileys, Basic, Bus Enhancements, Abacus, Astra, Digital Research, Program Design, Mad Hatter, Rainbow, Q Type, Indecom, AMS, International Micro, Microware, Softape, Laselle and National.

EXHIBIT 1 (continued)

Table 9C
Methods Software Distributors Use
to Contact Stores

Methods	% of Stores Mentioning
In person sales call	11%
Telephone sales call followed by in-person sales call	18
Telephone sales call only	25
Saw ad and called them*	74
Other**	20

* Publications where ads were seen: Byte (12 Mentions), Interface News (4), Creative Computing (4), Kilobaud (4), Computer Retailing (2), Computer Dealer (2), Computer Business News (1), and Computerworld (1).

** Other methods were: Direct Mail, Word of Mouth, Customer Requests Upon Seeing Ads, and Manufacturers Send Salespeople to the Stores.

Table 9D
Methods Stores Would Use to
Find Additional Software

Methods Ranked by No. of Mentions	% of Total Mentions
Through reading industry magazines	44%
Would develop software themselves	13
Go to manufacturers	9
Check out other dealers' products	9
Ask manufacturers where to go	7
Directly to industry software houses	4
Shows	4
Inquiries after seeing ads	2
Others	9
Total	100%

EXHIBIT 1   (continued)

X.   <u>Maintenance/Repair Performance and Manufacturers Mentioned as Having Main-</u>
<u>tenance Problems</u>

Table 10A analyzes how maintenance, repairs are being handled by the stores. Table 10B analyzes manufacturers mentioned as having the greatest degree of breakdowns.

Table 10A
Handling of Maintenance/Repairs

Methods	Average % of All Responding Stores	Ranges Encountered for All Stores	Breakdown Most Encountered
In House	85%	0 - 100%	90%
Sent Back to Mfrs	14%	0 - 100%	10%
3rd Party Maintenance*	1%	0 - 75%	—
Total	100%		100%

* Only one store was using.

△ Stores were able to repair 85% of their customers' equipment problems in-house, with only 14 percent of the cases being sent back to the manufacturers. This high degree of in-house repairability is of utmost importance in any area of the computer industry, as downtime is the industry's major problem. This high in-house capability is mostly due to the business of microprocessors, and the ability to replace chips and boards independently.

EXHIBIT 1 (continued)

Table 10B
Manufacturers Mentioned as Having
Equipment which Experiences
the Most Downtime

Manufacturers	% of Stores Mentioning a Mfr. as Having Downtime Problems—Based on the Number of Stores Carrying Each Manufacturer	% of Stores Mentioning a Mfr. as Having Serious Recurring Downtime Problems—Based on the Number of Stores Carrying Each Mfr.
Imsai	100%	100%
Ohio Scientific	80	30
Pertec	75	—
Compucolor	75	50
Commodore	57	7
SWTFC	50	—
Cromenco	42	—
Apple	38	12
Exidy	29	14
Vector Graphics	29	—
Dynabyte	20	20
North Star	14	—
TI	8	—
Peripherals		
Centronics	40	—
Other Peripheral		
Manufacturers	44	22
No Problems	20	—
No Serious Problems	—	65

EXHIBIT 1 (continued)

XI.   Advertising Expenditures

The following table analyzes the average amount stores are spending per month on advertising.

Table 11
Advertising Expenditures
Responding Stores

Average Per Month- All Responding Stores	Average Per Month- Stores Which Were Advertising	Range Per Month- All Responding Stores
$810	$920	$80 to $5,000

XII.   Mail Order Business

The following table expresses the degree to which stores are involved in mail order business, now and anticipated for 1983.

Table 12
Stores Selling Through Mail Order
% of Responding Stores

	% Involved in Mail Order		Average % of Sales Represented All Stores	
	Now	1983	Now	1983
% Selling Systems - Mail Order	25%	25%	6%	6%
% Selling Peripherals - Mail Order	25	21	6	6
% Selling Software - Mail Order	19	15	4	5
% of Stores Selling Anything Through Mail Order	2	25		
% of Stores With No Mail Order Business	75	75		
Total	100%	100%		

EXHIBIT 1 (continued)

XIII.   Buying Motives of Computer Retail Store Customers

The following table lists the major buying motives (related by the stores) as to why customers buy personal computers and why the customers chose their store in particular.

Table 13
Buying Motives
% of Mentions by Responding Stores

Buying Motives of Customers For Personal Computers	% of Total Mentions	Buying Motives of Customers in Selecting Particular Stores	% of Total Mentions
Business needs	29%	Application/system solution	20%
Curiosity	21	Good equipment/demo	
Low price	12	Systems	16
Child education	6	People related	
Service offered by stores	6	Knowledgeable salespeople	16
Home/hobbyist interest	6	Honesty/soft sell	3
Prestige	3	Store reputation	10
Desire to learn about		Good service	10
Computers	6	Location of store	8
Interest created by		Store atmosphere	5
advertising	4	Support	5
Gadget appeal	2	Direct mail/advertising	3
Atmosphere of the stores	2	Dollar savings	2
Total	100%	Total	100%

△ 50% of the total mentions as to why stores felt customers were interested in personal computers were a combination of business needs and curiosity. These two factors explain the interest of the major sectors in the marketplace, business and the home/hobbyist contingents.

△ Store owners said the major reasons customers chose their stores in particular were their stores' ability to provide application/system solutions to problems (20%), and the good equipment/demo systems (18%) they displayed on their store floors, which attracted customers. Knowledgeable salespeople were also mentioned as being important. This factor and the system solution factor are closely related to the primary aim of stores' being able to interpret and then supply application solutions to problems and needs of customers.

EXHIBIT 1 (continued)

XIV.   <u>Problems Faced by Computer Retail Stores</u>

The following table lists the major problems which computer retail stores feel they are faced with.

Table 14
Major Problems of Computer Retail Stores

Major Problems	Ranking According to Weighted Average of Mentions	% of Mentions as Being Primary Problem
Margins too low on equipment	1.00	22%
Cash flow, lack of strong financial backing	.87	32
Getting good employees	.81	22
Keeping abreast of technology	.64	4
Training required with each new product or new salesperson	.62	6
Servicing the equipment	.47	2
Keeping good employees	.42	6
Inventory control (balance between cost and immediate delivery needs)	.40	4
Unhappy with store location	.22	2

The problems that computer retailers characterized as greatest were: Margins too low on the equipment, cash flow (lack of strong financial backing) and getting good employees. Almost one of every three stores (32%) mentioned cash flow as their major problem. Collectively the three just-mentioned problems represented the primary one for three out of every four stores (76%).

EXHIBIT 1 (continued)

XV.   Application Usage

The following tables analyze the major applications for which end users—both small businesses and home hobbyists—buy personal computers.

Table 15A
Major Applications for which Small
Businesses Buy Personal Computers

Applications	Weighted Average Ranking Of Mentions	Number of Primary Mentions Received
General accounting	1.00	32%
Word processing	.90	21
Inventory control	.76	16
Accounts receivable	.87	16
Billing	.62	5
Mailing lists	.58	5
Accounts payable	.51	5
Total		100%

△ Other Applications mentioned were: Payroll, Process Control, Data Base-Management, and Property Management.

Table 15B
Major Applications for which Home
Hobbyists Buy Personal Computers

Applications	Weighted Average Ranking of Mentions	Number of Primary Mentions Received
Games	1.00	57%
Child Education	.81	20
Personal Accounting	.76	23
Total		100%

△ Other applications in order of number of mentions were: Adult Education, Software Development, Energy Conservation, Custom Business, Word Processing, and Mail Lists.

EXHIBIT 1 (continued)

XVI.   <u>Stores</u>

Table 16A
Year When Stores Will Reach Their Peak
or Saturation Point

<u>Years</u>	<u>% of Responses</u>
1981/2	12%
1983/4	22
1985/6	35
1987/8	5
1989/90	13
Beyond 1990/Never	<u>13</u>
Total	100%

Table 16B
What Factors Will Allow Smaller Stores (1-5 units)
to Survive versus Large Chains

<u>Factors</u>	<u>% of Total Mention</u>
Sevice	26%
Turnkey systems	18
Market niches/application solutions/market positioning	11
Support	8
Product selection	7
Product expertise	7
Price cutting	7
Personal service	5
Location	3
Good sales people	2
Word of mouth advertising	2
Higher margins	2
Acting as a service bureau	<u>2</u>
Total	100%

EXHIBIT 1 (continued)

Table 16C
What Stores Would Invest in
if They Had Additional Capital

Investments % Of Total Responses

Increase inventory	32%
New store(s)	19
Software company	17
Turnkey system Hhuse	9
Expand current store	7
Additional software	4
More/better salespeople	4
Advertising/seminars	4
Distributorship	4
Total	100%

Table 16D
Will Particular Stores be Seeking Additional
Capital in the Near Future?

% Yes	67%
% No	33
Total	100%

EXHIBIT 1 (continued)

Table 16E
Fastest Growing Manufacturers
in the Personal Computer Marketplace

Manufacturers	% of Total Fastest Growing Responses Received	% of Total New Participants Responses Received
Apple	29%	—
Alpha Micro	10	—
Commodore	8	—
Vector Graphics	8	—
North Star	7	—
TI	6	25%
Ohio Scientific	6	—
Japanese manufacturers	4	12
Cromemco	4	—
Atari	4	13
Heath	3	—
Altos	3	—
DEC	1	11
IBM	1	13
Dynabyte	1	—
Industrial Microsystems	1	—
Others	4	—
Mattel	—	7
NEC	—	7
HP	—	4
Data General	—	2
Tano	—	2
Edo	—	2
Pexou	—	2
Total	100%	100%

EXHIBIT 1 (continued)

Table 16F
Important Technological Developments
Stores Foresee in the
Personal Computer Industry

Technological Developments	% Of Total Mentions	
Memory (Disk) Related	(49%)	
Bubble memories		16%
Increased memory capacity		12
Increased memory per dollar		9
Hard disks		5
New disk technology		3
Video disk association		2
Eliminate disks for other storage medium		2
Product Improvements	(34%)	
16/32 bit processing (faster)		12
Better graphics		5
Decrease size of system		3
Laser technology		3
Voice recognition		3
Home terminals		2
Flat CRT's		2
Increased overall capabilities		2
Plasma CRT's		2
Software	(9%)	
User oriented software		3
Better software		2
Standard languages		2
Data base capability		2
Pricing	(8%)	
Decrease printer prices		5
Decrease in whole system prices		3
Total		100%

EXHIBIT 1 (concluded)

XVII.   <u>Revenue Size of Stores</u>

The following table analyzes the current and anticipated 1983 revenue sizes of responding stores.

Table 17
Revenue Size of Stores

	% Of Responding Stores	
<u>Revenue Classifications</u>	<u>Now</u>	<u>1983 (est.)</u>
Under $100K	9%	0%
$101 - 250K	36	4
$251 - 500K	22	9
$501 - 750K	7	24
$751 - 1,000K (Million)	13	18
Over $1 Million	<u>13</u>	<u>45</u>
Total	100%	100%

△ 45% of the stores expect to have grown to over $1 million in sales by year end 1983.

△ The average sales for current stores were approximately $430,000, based on the midpoints of the ranges they fell in. By 1983, these reporting stores expect to have average sales of $905,000. This represents an average growth of 110% over these 4 years, or 21% a year compounded growth.

Prize-Winning Venture Plan

The business plan following was prepared by a student team at the University of Texas at Austin both as a basis for starting a business and for entry into a series of competitions. In the first competition, which took place in professor Gary Cadenhead's entrepreneurship course in December 1992, the team won first place with this plan and received a $500 prize plus free office space in the Austin Business Incubator.

The second contest anticipated by the team would be the International Business Plan Competition at San Diego State University on April 30, 1993 where first prize would carry a $5,000 cash award. Third would be the International Moot Corp® competition at the University of Texas on May 5, 1993 which did not offer a cash prize. The plan is reproduced here with the team's permission as a basis for class discussion.

For prior information about the source of the project and the product, please refer to the case entitled Charles and Barbara Ewing.

AMPERSAND
ART SUPPLY

Graduate School of Business
The University of Texas at Austin

Management Team

CEO	Elaine Salazar
VP of Marketing	Katherine Henderson
CFO	
VP of Operations	
Faculty Advisor	Dr. Gary Cadenhead

Copy ___ of ___

Confidentiality Agreement

This business plan is the property of Ampersand Art Supply. It is to be used by the official judges of the International Moot Corp. Competition at the University of Texas at Austin May 6, 1993 for evaluation purposes only. The information contained within this plan is not to be divulged to a third party without the express written consent of the owners of Ampersand Art Supply.

TABLE OF CONTENTS

EXECUTIVE SUMMARY

1.1 The Opportunity

Ampersand Art Supply will establish itself as a provider of high quality art products with its initial product, Claybord TM. This exciting new art surface has the potential of $4.6 million in annual sales by year five. This business opportunity exists because:

- Claybord addresses a fundamental need shared by artists for a surface product that will enhance their creativity.

- A $2.4 million target market in a $2.8 billion industry demonstrates the vast potential for Claybord.

- Ampersand's aggressive marketing and manufacturing strategy, and trademark and patent protection will sustain long-term profitability.

- Ampersand's management team has the breadth of experience and skills needed to capitalize on this lucrative opportunity.

1.2 Products and Benefits

An artist's surface is his/her fundamental tool. Its versatility determines the degree of freedom and range of expression an artist will have when approaching his/her work. Claybord's rigid clay-coated surface provides artists with a level of control and flexibility unmatched by any other surface on the market. For example, without ruining the integrity of the surface an artist using Claybord can completely erase and rework his/her design multiple times until the desired effect is achieved. This flexibility is impossible with any other surface product. Additional product features provided by Claybord and demanded by professional artists include durability, freedom from smudging, pH-neutrality, consistent quality, and a wide range of sizes. Finally, Claybord's acceptance of all types of media including acrylic, oils, pen and ink, pencil, and watercolors makes it a desirable surface for all artists.

1.3 The Market

Claybord's primary market is the 2.4 million professional artists in the United States who are characterized by their need and willingness to pay for high quality surfaces. Within this market, Ampersand has targeted 1.2 million pen and ink artists as its primary segment and 1.1 million artists working in oil and acrylics as a secondary segment. In extensive test marketing, these artists found Claybord to be an exciting addition to the surfaces they currently use. By targeting both market segments Ampersand will achieve an 8.5% penetration of the professional artist market by year five, representing 1,200,000 board sales to 200,000 customers.

1.4 Competitive Strategy

Ampersand will create effective barriers to entry and achieve a sustainable competitive advantage through its marketing and manufacturing strategies and its trademark and patent protection. An aggressive marketing and distribution strategy will be employed to quickly establish the Claybord brand, create product awareness, generate customer demand, and build volume sales. Outsourcing manufacturing in strategic market locations will enable Ampersand to produce and transport Claybord to its customers at lower costs than any potential competitors.

1.5 Management

Ampersand's management team collectively has over 20 years of real world experience in the areas of entrepreneurship, corporate and small business finance, marketing and design. Elaine Salazar and Kathy Henderson have extensive backgrounds in marketing and distribution, including experience starting their own companies and working as consultants to small businesses. Kathy Henderson also has an extensive art background and an intimate knowledge of the needs of Ampersand's customer base. Ampersand also has an advisory board of talented individuals, including Charles Ewing, the inventor of Claybord, who will contribute their vast experience as business professionals, artists, and entrepreneurs.

1.6 Financial Summary and Offering

As a result of Ampersand's aggressive marketing strategy, the company will break even in fiscal year two. Revenues are projected to reach $4,500,000 by fiscal year five. The company's average gross margin is approximately 60% across the five-year projected horizon. Average operating cash flows and net margins are estimated at 20% and 25%, respectively. Ampersand is seeking $200,000 in equity capital. This will be used to fund working capital requirements during the first year of operations. In return, the investor will receive at least 25% of the pro-rata outstanding common shares of Ampersand with a projected compounded annual rate of return of 70%.

COMPANY OVERVIEW

2.1 Company Background

Claybord was invented by artist Charles Ewing to meet his own requirement for a high quality surface for his fine art. As illustrators and fine artists became familiar with Mr. Ewing's work on Claybord, many sought the product for their own use. In July Mr. Ewing approached Ampersand's CEO Elaine Salazar with the proposition of developing a partnership to manufacture and market Claybord.

2.2 Current Status

Mr. Ewing, in exchange for equity, has agreed to give Ampersand the exclusive right to manufacture Claybord. The patent application and trademark registration for the Claybord name will be completed under the direction of Winstead, Sechrest and Minick, Esq. This Texas law firm has completed the initial review of our patent search and has determined that patentability exists.

Ampersand has identified World Research Company (W.R.C.) in Tyler, TX as the first of the company's outsourcing facilities. W.R.C. will provide the flexibility and capacity needed in the initial years of operation. Since consistent quality is critical to Claybord's success, Ampersand has recruited a team of UT students involved in a Total Quality Management class to develop a quality program for Claybord.

Distribution options have been analyzed and channel members have been contacted. Claybord is currently being evaluated by selected retailers, mail order catalogs, and major distributors. Pearl Paint, one of the largest art retailers in the US, contacted Ampersand within one day of receiving a sample of Claybord. They expressed a serious interest in Claybord and are currently testing additional samples of the product.

Finally, Ampersand has occupied office space in the Austin Technology Incubator. In the next six months Ampersand's management team will continue to build the infrastructure for the company and establish contracts and financing in order to launch the business upon completion of their MBA's in 1993.

Timeline

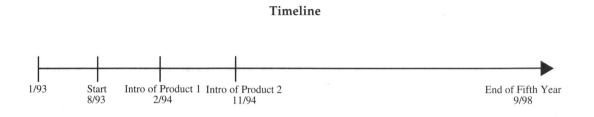

| 1/93 | Start
8/93 | Intro of Product 1
2/94 | Intro of Product 2
11/94 | End of Fifth Year
9/98 |

MARKET ANALYSIS

3.1 Market Research Conclusions

To determine the viability of Claybord in the art materials market Ampersand conducted a number of test marketing initiatives.

A random sample of 40 professional illustrators was selected from a national mailing list of science and medical illustrators. These illustrators were asked to test the product and complete a short telephone survey. Ampersand selected this group of artists as the basis for its test marketing because of the segment's familiarity with scratchboard and illustration board - products that most resemble Claybord. Following are highlights of the survey results. (Exhibits M-1 and M-2 contain a complete summary of survey results and selected comments from these artists.)

The results of the survey illustrate that (1) Claybord offers unique advantages for pen & ink applications and (2) Claybord is a superior and preferred product when compared to even the highest quality scratchboard and illustration board.

Ampersand also tested Claybord in three drawing classes at the University of Texas Department of Arts. The reactions in the classroom mirrored those of the professional artists. Students working in pen and ink found the surface exceptional. Students working in other media found the board's versatility and manipulation attractive for experimenting and developing unique styles.

Purchase Likelihood	Percentage
Definitely	81%
Probably	7%
Occasionally	6%
Seldom	0%
Never	6%

Favorite Characteristics	
Ability to Take all Media	76%
Erasability	73%
Pen & Ink Application	58%
Easy to Work With	55%
No Surface Glare	22%
Durability	22%
Feel of Surface	22%
pH-Neutral	11%
Size	11%
No Puddling Effect	11%

Average Number of Boards Purchased per Year	
5-15	30%
15-30	38%
30-50	26%
50+	6%

In order to assess the potential for Claybord's use in commercial art programs, Ampersand asked the Austin Community College to evaluate the product. Four professors who teach illustration and design evaluated Claybord for classroom use and concluded that they would prefer to use Claybord when teaching scratchboard technique. As a result, Austin Community College has committed to order Claybord for its second semester classes beginning in January.

Management also asked other professional artists working in oils, watercolor and acrylics to test Claybord. These artists all indicated that the surface's acceptance of these media rendered the Claybord an excellent medium for their work.

To test artists' response to direct mail promotions designed to encourage product sampling, 200 artists were selected from the mailing list of *Science and Medical Illustrators*. Within the first 3 weeks after mailing, 20 requests for samples were received. This appears to indicate a high level of interest given that typical responses to direct mail promotions average a 1.5% response rate.

Finally, Ampersand acquired three major studies that provided critical data for its analysis of the market and industry. The 1991 National Artists Survey, sponsored by *Artists Magazine,* provided a broad base of statistically valid data on artists, art activity, and art product purchasing. The 4th Annual Art Supply Store Survey gave Ampersand extensive information on retail channel characteristics and the *Yearbook of Who's Who in Art Materials* provided us with data on manufacturers in the industry. Both these studies were obtained from the National Art Materials Trade Association (NAMTA).

3.2 Customer Profile

According to the 1991 National Artists Survey (NAS) there are 13.2 million artists in the US. Seventy eight percent or 10.3 million of these artists do their primary art activity in pencil, acrylics, oils, pen and ink, and pastels. Approximately 24% or 2.4 million of these artists are professionals who rely partially or entirely on their art for their income. It is this segment of the art market that Ampersand Art Supply will target with our introductory product, Claybord.

This professional art segment is less price sensitive when purchasing art supplies and is more prone to experiment with a new product. A fine artist who commands $300 to $10,000 for his/her work will not hesitate to pay for a high quality surface. Moreover, professional artists by their very nature are constantly experimenting with new products and looking for ways to differentiate themselves and create their own unique style. Claybord offers these artists the opportunity to explore and expand their techniques, thereby creating a unique approach to their work.

Ampersand Art Supply has segmented the targeted 2.4 million professional artists in line with its two-phase strategy for entering the market. Ampersand's primary segment is pen and ink artists and its secondary segment is artists who work primarily in oil and acrylics. Additionally, Ampersand will target schools and programs of science and medical illustration and commercial art.

Exhibit M-3 outlines the number of boards that will be sold yearly in each of Ampersand's target segments. The volume estimates are extremely conservative given that Ampersand's test market results showed that artists use anywhere from 5 to 50 sheets of scratchboard or illustration board per year. Ampersand's volume estimates for the first three years of sales are based on 5 Claybords per professional artist per year and 2 claybords per student.

Target Segments

Pen & Ink (176,000)

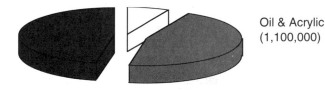

Oil & Acrylic (1,100,000)

Other (1,124,000)

3.3 Primary Target

Of the 2.4 million professional artists, 176,000 work in pen and ink as a primary activity. There are approximately another one million professional artists who work in pen and ink as a secondary activity. By targeting these pen and ink artists Ampersand expects a 1.0% penetration rate by year two. This penetration will be followed by a 2.2% and 3.7% penetration in years three and four, respectively. This penetration represents sales of 700,000 boards by year five. This number is conservative when one considers that the total number of artists who work in pen & ink, both as a primary and secondary activity totals 4.96 million.

3.4 Secondary Target

Ampersand has found through its test marketing that artists who work primarily in oil and acrylics find the surface exceptional. According to NAS there are approximately 1.1 million professional artists who work primarily in acrylic and oils. In targeting the acrylic and oil segments Ampersand is keenly aware that its competition is no longer pen and ink surfaces, but quality pre-stretched canvas and gessoed masonite. In year two, Ampersand will target these artists with a version of our Claybord product at a price comparable to that of the surfaces these artists currently use. Approximately 116,000 boards will be sold in the first year of introduction and grow to 532,000 boards in year five.

3.5 Schools

Ampersand also will target schools of science and medical illustration and commercial art programs. In discussions with these schools across the country, Ampersand found that scratchboard is taught as a technique and students are required to purchase products similar to Claybord. Many of the professors, however, expressed that students are often frustrated with the technique due to the inferior quality of the scratchboard currently available. The ease of working with Claybord makes it an ideal product for these schools.

There are 130 commercial art programs in the country and 52 schools of illustration and design, including medical and science illustration. In these programs, we have estimated, an average of 60 students per year will be required to purchase products similar to Claybord. Ampersand will contact these schools in the first year through direct mail and telemarketing. Targeting this market is key for future sales growth. The NAS showed that 36% of artists are influenced by their teachers' and peers' choice of art product brands. A 25% penetration of this segment is projected in years one and two and growing by approximately 10% yearly. Ampersand's focused marketing efforts justifies these penetration estimates.

3.6 Customer Benefits

The surface an artist chooses to use is one of the most critical decisions he or she will make when creating a work. Surfaces are often fraught with problems that artists must find ways around. Claybord solves many of these current surface problems.

Current Problems	Claybord Solutions
Limited surface size	Many available sizes
Surface glare	Soft, nonglare surface
Fragile	Durable
Limited erasures	Up to 30 cut-ins & erasures
Yellowing	pH-neutral
Limited media application	Accepts all forms of media
Smudging	No smudge surface
Inconsistent quality	Top quality manufacturing
Poor availability	Strong distribution strategy

THE INDUSTRY

4.1 Industry Overview

The $2.8 billion art supply industry is dominated by six major companies who control approximately 80% of US retail sales volume. The remaining 20% is shared among approximately 300 other manufacturers. Similar to Ampersand's strategy, the majority (81%) of the industry's manufacturers produce either a single line or limited family of products and grow by introducing line extensions. Very few surface manufacturers produce a diversified product line. A breakdown of the manufacturers in each product area is shown below:

Art Supply Manufacturing Breakdown

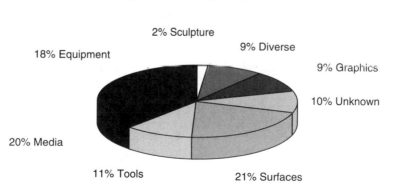

2% Sculpture
9% Diverse
18% Equipment
9% Graphics
10% Unknown
20% Media
11% Tools
21% Surfaces

4.2 Distribution

Retail stores are important players in the art materials industry. According to NAMTA, the majority or 60% of all retail stores had gross revenues of under $250,000 while 23.5% reported revenues in excess of $1 million. 17.6% of the large resellers reported revenues in excess of $10 million. Many of these resellers operate warehouses and sell out of multiple retail locations and some act as distributors for other retailers. The retail channel is powerful in the industry, commanding 65% margins from manufacturers. These margins clearly indicate that a successful manufacturer must maintain low manufacturing costs in order to achieve meaningful profits.

4.3 Competition

Claybord's attributes make this product most similar to "scratchboard" products. There are approximately six companies currently who manufacture scratchboard. Four of these companies produce low-priced, low-quality products targeted at elementary education and craft markets. Claybord's price point and product positioning places it in competition against only two existing scratchboard products—Essdee Scraperboard and Paris Scratchboard, representing the higher quality scratchboard on the market. These products are both produced in Europe and imported into the US.

Our test marketing has shown that Claybord appeals to a wider spectrum of users and therefore will be competing with other surfaces as well. The three most popular surface types are paper, canvas and film products (e.g. vellum, acetate, etc.). In the US market there are approximately 62 manufacturers who sell art surface products. These manufacturers are primarily specialists and can be aggregated by product type.

Three manufacturers, Canson Talons, Windsor Newton and Strathmore are large volume producers of art surface products, mostly paper. These manufacturers focus on volume and target the price sensitive 75% of the art supply industry. They rarely manufacture specialty products. From our discussions with these large manufacturers we found that because the manufacturing process of Claybord differs significantly from their core competency, these players do not pose a serious threat to Ampersand's market. In fact, these industry leaders often form partnerships with successful small manufacturers of specialty products.

The smaller manufacturers are Ampersand's greatest threat, since they are often able to produce and distribute specialty products at low costs. The emergence of national mail order catalogs has provided a low-cost distribution channel for these small manufacturers, making the barriers to entry low in the industry. It is clear that Ampersand must create strong barriers against these manufacturers to maintain its profitability.

4.4 Competitive Strategy

Ampersand has strategically positioned itself to be successful in light of these industry challenges. Ampersand will (1) provide a unique and high-quality product that will differentiate Ampersand from other manufacturers, (2) incorporate a strong marketing strategy to create demand which in turn will exert pull on the powerful distribution channel, (3) target the 25% of the market consisting of professional artists who are less price sensitive and currently not the primary target for industry leaders, (4) erect trademark and patent protection barriers to keep other manufacturers from copying our product, and (5) achieve a low cost structure with low fixed costs in order to deliver the necessary margins to the retail channel while maintaining a high profit margin for the company.

MARKETING STRATEGY

5.1 Overview

In order to achieve our projected sales volume of 1.2 million boards by year five, Ampersand will launch an aggressive marketing campaign to quickly establish our product and generate customer demand. According to NAMTA over 90% of all retailers, regardless of size, indicated that customer demand was the primary influencer in stocking new products. The $130,000 in marketing expenditures forecast for Year 1 will be used for direct mail promotions, print advertising, product demonstrations, trade show participation, and retail sales support. Our product introduction efforts will precede and overlap retail product release. This will ensure an active customer base for sales partners. This strategy will allow Ampersand to quickly establish the Claybord brand and trademarked name, thereby creating a marketing barrier against potential competitors.

5.2 Direct Mail

In terms of Claybord, our market research has shown product acceptance and purchase intention are enhanced when the artist has an opportunity to sample the product. To facilitate sampling, a direct mail promotion to 100,000 artists in the primary target group is planned. Mailing lists will be obtained from state-wide artist guilds and professional organizations. The mailing will consist of an informational brochure that includes a coupon enabling artists to request a sample. A small "shipping and handling fee" will be required to qualify respondents. Finally, a mailing list of samplers will be compiled and forwarded to our retailers as sales leads.

5.3 Advertising and Promotion

To support product introduction Ampersand will place 1/2 page advertisements in industry publications for three consecutive months. This campaign is to create top-of-mind awareness of the product in our target market and the retail channel.

Brochures, press releases, reproductions of articles, and product samples will be mailed to all state artists guilds. Typically these organizations produce monthly newsletters and hold monthly meetings. To increase product awareness and to facilitate product demonstrations we are developing an instructional video to be used as an integral part of the Claybord demonstration and sales support program. The video will highlight the advantages and applications of Claybord. Accompanying the video will be product samples and brochures. Product media material will include information on how guilds can request the loan of the video and free samples. Additionally, Ampersand will target national meetings of artists in our primary target market and provide live demonstrations to these groups.

Finally, we will contract with well-known illustrators/authors for articles on the features and benefits of Claybord. These articles will be published in trade journals and used in our promotional efforts. Well-known science illustrator Trudi Nicholson recently published an article about Claybord in the national newsletter of the National Science Illustrators Guild.

The response to this article has been immediate and very encouraging. Ruth Lozner, illustrator for the *Washington Post* and author of *Scratchboard for Illustration* also has offered to write articles for publication.

5.4 Trade Shows

According to the Art Supply Store survey, over 95% of all retailers attend trade shows to identify new products. The most influential trade shows for retailers are sponsored by the National Art Materials Trade Association (NAMTA) and are held three times a year in various geographic locations. According to sources at NAMTA, new products are showcased at these trade shows. A team of influential retailers present awards, and a video highlighting promising new products is produced and then distributed to NAMTA's retail members. In addition to the NAMTA shows we will attend and demonstrate Claybord at national meetings of artist guilds.

5.5 Product Distribution

A majority of artists interviewed stated that they purchase the bulk of their art materials from art supply retailers and mail order catalogs. They indicated product selection and price as the primary factors. According to NAMTA over 65% of large resellers operated warehouses and sold products out of multiple retail locations. 46.5% acted as distributors for other retailers. Also, large resellers carried on average twice the number of product lines in each general category as small retailers and had lower annual inventory turns. 98.9% of large retailers carried a variety of art surfaces and 64.5% cited surfaces as one of their most "successful" product categories.

Initially we have targeted twenty large retail outlets and national mail order catalogs as our primary distribution channels. This will allow us to focus our resources on building product awareness and demand by utilizing the most supportive and easily penetrated channel members. Once product acceptance has been achieved and a sales history established, we will expand our distribution to include small and medium sized retailers by working through national and regional distributors.

5.6 Channel Strategy

Initial contacts with the targeted retailers indicated a high level of interest in the product. Product samples are currently being evaluated by channel members who are providing sales estimates to support our sales projections. We will provide standard industry discounts and incentives for volume purchases and prompt payment. All retailers contacted reported monthly to bimonthly ordering. Stock balancing and product returns are not significant factors in this industry with the exception of damaged merchandise which is typically returned to the manufacturer for credit. To protect against damage and to enhance product visibility Claybord will be individually packaged.

To support our sales partners' efforts we will provide dealers with sales leads and sales kits to include product samples, brochures and training videos. A training video will be used to introduce sales staff to the features and benefits of Claybord and can be used as a basis for in-store workshops. Live in-store demonstrations are planned to enhance visibility, to educate sales staff, and to obtain feedback from channel members and customers.

Mail order catalogs will offer the standard Claybord product line as well as an "Introduction to Claybord" product. This product grouping will include three 8" x 10" boards, instructional brochures, and training video. It will be used to encourage product trial. According to buyers in the mail order industry this type of SKU, called a "put-up," is a popular and successful way to establish a new product. It will allow our customers to learn about and experiment with Claybord with a minimum of risk. Historically, once customers are successful with the put-up they continue to experiment with the product and will purchase "open stock."

With the introduction of our second product in Year 2 we will expand our distribution into second-tier retailers and college bookstores by working through national and regional distributors. We will follow the same pattern of product introduction, retail sales support, and discounting.

5.7 Products and Pricing

Within the first two years of operation we will introduce two different Claybord product families. The initial product, Claybord Premium, will be priced in competition with Essdee Scraperboard and Paris Scratchboard. Claybord Premium is a superior product and addresses many of the weaknesses found in competing products. Sixty two percent of Ampersand's survey respondents said that our proposed prices for Clayboard Premium were in line with what they would expect to pay for this type of quality art surface. We will offer nine different sizes of Claybord in a smooth surface.

A second product, Claybord for Oil & Acrylic, will be offered in fewer sizes and with a textured surface. It will also have a thinner coating of clay and a different hardboard backing. This product will be targeted at oil and acrylic painters and will be priced to compete with high-end surfaces currently favored by these artists. These surfaces include pre-stretched canvas and gessoed masonite board. Cannibalization of Claybord Premium with the introduction of the oil and acrylic line is not expected to be significant. Each product has unique attributes that are targeted to meet the needs of two distinct customer segments.

Ampersand Product Pricing

Size	Variable cost/unit	SRP (1)	Wholesale (2)	Gross Margin
Claybord Premium				
8" x 10"	$0.37	$2.00	$0.75	50.7%
9" x 12"	$0.50	$3.60	$1.35	63.0%
11"x14"	$0.71	$5.50	$2.06	65.5%
19"x12"	$1.06	$10.00	$3.75	71.7%
14"x18"	$1.17	$9.10	$3.41	65.7%
16"x20"	$1.48	$12.00	$4.50	67.1%
18"x24"	$2.00	$14.00	$5.25	61.9%
20"x24"	$2.22	$16.00	$6.00	63.0%
24"x30"	$3.33	$23.70	$8.89	62.5%
Claybord Oil & Acrylic				
9" x 12"	$0.37	$3.00	$1.13	67.3%
14"x18"	$0.85	$6.25	$2.34	63.7%
18"x24"	$1.46	$9.00	$3.38	56.8%

Notes: (1) Suggested retail price (2) Price received by Ampersand

Price Comparisons

Type	Size	SRP	Wholesale
Claybord Premium	18"x24"	$14.00	$5.25
Essdee Scraperboard	19"x24"	$15.55	$5.83
Paris Scratchbord	19.5"x25.5"	$13.20	$4.95
Claybord Oil & Acrylic	18"x24"	$9.00	$3.38
Gessoed Masonite	18"x24"	$8.13	$3.05
Pre-stretch canvas	18"x24"	$10.00	$3.75

MANUFACTURING

6.1 Overview

To ensure a successful and sustainable entry into the market, Ampersand must have low fixed costs to achieve high profit margins. Ampersand will therefore outsource its manufacturing to World Research Company (W.R.C.) in Tyler, TX. W.R.C. has been in operation for four years providing flexible manufacturing to the custom hardboard industry and has the facilities and capacity to meet Ampersand's current needs.

6.2 Process and Quality Partnership

Claybord is currently being manufactured by hand by the inventor in small quantities. With the precision and accuracy required in the type of artwork for which Claybord was designed, quality is a critical factor. In mass production the primary determinant will be the capabilities of the surface application process. Because the current process can achieve appropriate quality levels with hand application, we are confident that the decrease in variability resulting from automation can produce the product within the same levels and with less post-production patchwork.

Ampersand also plans to integrate a quality program to ensure the consistent integrity of the Claybord surface, and has engaged a project team from the UT MBA program to explore the issue. Ampersand's partnership with W.R.C. in building this quality initiative will ensure long-term customer satisfaction.

An additional advantage to Ampersand's partnership with W.R.C. is flexibility. As a smaller but automated manufacturer of custom hardboard products, W.R.C. not only has the ability to customize their process to meet our requirements but can also offer us one to two week lead time on production. This flexibility is critical as Ampersand begins its operation and builds its volume sales.

6.3 Packaging

Appropriate packaging will be developed in-house during the initial months of preparation. Although similar products simply "stack" on shelves in retail outlets, some form of surface protection is necessary. Innovative packaging also will promote the image of a brand new type of product.

6.4 Manufacturing Barriers to Entry

Ampersand's manufacturing strategy is designed to sustain profitability by maintaining a low cost structure. After we have finalized the process with W.R.C. and generated sufficient demand for the product, we will spread our manufacturing to similar facilities in locations closer to our distributors. By doing this we will generate cost savings both in production and in transportation. Through volume-based contractual agreements with these manufacturers and the decrease in shipping costs, we will erect a significant cost barrier in later years.

Initially, however, our barriers will be of a different nature. Not only will Ampersand have trademark protection and the protection of the patent pending label, but we will also have equity in the Claybord name generated from our expansive marketing strategy and first mover advantage.

RESEARCH AND DEVELOPMENT

7.1 Overview

Beginning in Year 3 our product development efforts will be focused on expanding our surface product line, creating Claybord accessories, and developing completely new products. The research and development costs on the financial statements are intended directly for this purpose.

7.2 Inventor Involvement

As a part owner of Ampersand, Charles Ewing will play a significant role in research and development. An inventor by nature with an intimate understanding of the needs of professional artists, Mr. Ewing already has a number of products under development, including surface product line extensions and prototypes of several erasing tools.

7.3 Surface Product Line Extensions

By altering the composition of the surface, products similar to Claybord Premium but designed to meet the specific needs of artists working in various media can be produced. Prototypes of boards designed specifically for artists working in oil and acrylics, watercolor, and pastels have already been developed and are currently being field tested. Eventually, a full line of high-quality surface products will be manufactured and marketed under Ampersand's direction.

7.4 Claybord Accessories

Because Claybord is a unique surface with unusual properties, the opportunity for adjunct products is considerable. The majority of these will involve manipulation of the surface, especially in erasing or removing pigment from the board. At this moment the recommended tool for erasing is different grades of steel wool. However, greater precision and ease of use could be obtained with an object designed specifically for that purpose. This is one area we would like to explore. Other areas for development could include: surface cutting tools, texture creators, display products, color manipulators, board cutting tools, etc.

7.5 New Products

One of the major needs that Claybord fills is something that afflicts most artists—the need for new opportunities in which to express themselves creatively. Ampersand will continue to explore new media, surfaces and applicators. Through the vigorous identification and definition of the specific needs of specific groups in the art community, Ampersand will be able to introduce products which satisfy a niche yet provide opportunity for the masses.

MANAGEMENT

8.1 Management Team

The management of Ampersand Art Supply is one of the company's greatest strengths. The members collectively have more than 20 years of real world experience in the areas of entrepreneurship, corporate and small business finance, marketing, operations management and design. The individual members of the management team and their positions are listed below.

Elaine Salazar, Chief Executive Officer - Ms. Salazar has a background in marketing and small business operation. In addition to serving as a small business consultant for the past five years, Ms. Salazar has founded and operated an FM radio station located in Southwest Colorado. She also founded the public radio industry's first national broadcast training program in her capacity as the Director of Training for National Public Radio (NPR).

Kathy Henderson, Vice President of Marketing and Distribution - Ms. Henderson has more than 10 years experience in marketing and entrepreneurship. In addition to developing the marketing and distribution strategy for two existing companies, Ms. Henderson currently serves as founder and co-owner of her own successful software publishing company. Ms. Henderson is an artist in her own right, with several years of formal art training.

8.2 Role of the Inventor

Charles Ewing, the inventor of Claybord, is a well-known southwestern artist. His work can be seen in galleries throughout the country. He is often commissioned to render major works of art for large corporations and art connoisseurs. Charles Ewing is excited about the opportunity Ampersand Art Supply and its management present to turn his invention into a lucrative endeavor.

This partnership meets the artist/inventor's goals and needs. Mr. Ewing's first and foremost priority is to focus his attention on his art work, and not the manufacture of Claybord. Building this partnership with Ampersand Art Supply enables him to accomplish this goal while creating long term value from his invention. Mr. Ewing will be a critical member on Ampersand's board of advisors and will support the company's initial marketing efforts by conducting many of the live demonstrations planned.

8.3 Board of Advisors

The Company has selected a number of individuals to serve as its Board of Advisors. A number of these advisors will assume positions on the Company's Board of Directors on the date of formal incorporation. The selected advisors were chosen because of their valuable experience in the art and small business industries.

Mr. Charles Ewing - The inventor of Claybord is a well-known southwestern artist. His work can be seen in galleries throughout the country. He is often commissioned to render major works of art for large corporations and art connoisseurs. Mr. Ewing is often asked to teach workshops on illustration and drawing techniques for professional and student artists. As an equity partner, Mr. Ewing will play a key role in the development and operation of Ampersand Art Supply.

Mr. Alex Howard - Partner, Howard Frazier Barker Elliott, Inc. - Since 1972, Mr. Howard has prepared or supervised numerous studies encompassing diverse industries for both private and public companies ranging in size from revenues of less than $1 million, to over $1 billion. These studies were performed for purposes including corporate and estate planning; estate, gift, and income tax requirements; going-private situations; mergers and acquisitions, and others.

Mr. Robert Santangelo - Mr. Santangelo is a patent attorney and operates his own private law firm in Fort Collins, CO. Mr. Santangelo has been involved in the patent search process for Claybord. He also has served as an advisor to dozens of small businesses in the Rocky Mountain area.

Ms. Ruth Lozner - Ms. Lozner is a renowned illustrator for the *Washington Post* and a fine artist. She is the author of *Scratchboard for Illustration* and is a professor of illustration at the University of Maryland.

FINANCIAL PLAN

9.1 Deal Structure

Ampersand is seeking $200,000 in equity capital. Management will contribute the remaining $100,000 required. In return, the investor will receive 25% of the outstanding common shares of Ampersand and the right to select a pro-rata share on the board of directors. The remaining 75% of the outstanding shares will be divided among Charles Ewing and management. Upon completion of the transaction Mr. Ewing will own approximately 37% of the company, with management retaining equal shares of the remaining 38%. We would note that these ownership percentages are negotiable. Therefore the transaction, as represented herein, represents one of many possible avenues available to the investor. The following table illustrates varying rates of return given different ownership levels.

% Ownership	ROI
25%	69.6%
30%	75.9%
35%	81.4%
40%	86.3%

9.2 Use of Funds

Given that Ampersand intends to fully outsource all manufacturing of the product, the primary use of funds generated from the private placement will be financing of working capital requirements. The largest component of these requirements will be advertising and marketing expenses (approximately 50% of operating expenses in fiscal year 1). As mentioned previously, management believes that an aggressive marketing and advertising campaign, coupled with sufficient patent protection, will serve to erect formidable barriers to entry.

9.3 Financial Review

The five year pro-forma summary financials for Ampersand Art Supply are included below.

	Fiscal Year 1	Fiscal Year 2	Fiscal Year 3	Fiscal Year 4	Fiscal Year 5
Revenues	$271,925	$840,378	$1,925,060	$3,009,805	$4,585,495
Cost of Product Sold	65,076	353,995	813,797	1,251,342	1,883,365
Gross Profit	206,849	486,383	1,111,263	1,758,463	2,702,130
Operating Expenses	280,864	293,812	506,975	637,736	833,219
Operating Income	-74,015	192,571	604,288	1,120,727	1,868,911
Tases (@34%)		65,474	205,458	381,047	635,430
Net Income	-74,015	127,097	398,830	739,680	1,233,481
Total Assets	194,646	396,575	1,015,913	2,136,224	3,981,141
Book Value	194,646	387,217	991,504	2,112,231	3,981,141
Cash Flow From Operations	-173,096	115,400	346,743	1,144,584	1,423,282

The illustrated financials represent the "Most Likely" case analysis. In addition to this scenario, two other scenarios were created (Best and Worst cases) which differ primarily with respect to market penetration and terminal operating cash flow (EBDIT) multiples. Exhibit F-1 illustrates the assumptions made for each case. We feel that these areas represent the most significant areas of risk to the investor. In the above illustrated case, Ampersand expects revenues from its Claybord product to grow at an annually compounded rate of approximately 103% over the analyzed five year horizon. While this growth rate may initially seem somewhat ambitious, management would note that these projections are based on extremely conservative assumptions as discussed previously. Full five year financials are included in Exhibit F-5.

9.4 Investor Return

Exhibit F-3 illustrates the calculation of the investors' return on investment (ROI) given the Most Likely Case scenario. Two possible exit strategies exist for the investor at the end of the five year projection horizon. The first option is an equity offering in which the investor could offer his/her shares to the public. The second option will involve the sale of the Company. The Most Likely Scenario yields an ROI of approximately 70%. This ROI is largely dependent upon the selection of the exit multiple. Management has determined, in consultation with venture capitalists and valuation experts, that an EBDIT multiple of approximately six times is appropriate for a firm with growth and earnings characteristics similar to those of Ampersand. The resulting return is in line with the relatively high risk level associated with the venture (i.e. start-up firm, no interim returns, etc.). Once again, we would note that these exit strategies represent platforms for negotiation. Staged exits (as well as entries) are possible given our current projection framework. Note, however, that such staging strategies (especially exit strategies) will result in lower aggregate returns.

9.5 Sensitivity Analysis

Exhibit F-8 illustrates sensitivity analyses for revenue, earnings and cash flow given management's three case scenarios (Best, Most Likely, Worst), as well as a graph illustrating the sensitivity of return on investment (ROI) to these scenarios. The primary areas of risk in the deal are associated with overall market projections and terminal valuation parameters. As the graph illustrates, returns at all levels of possible market conditions are quite favorable to the investor in terms of ROI, given the inherent riskiness of the deal.

EXHIBIT CONTENTS

Survey - Overview of Artists' Responses

Survey Respondents	# of Artists
Illustrator Only	17
Illustrator/Fine Artist	26
Fine Artist Only	12

Do you work primarily with one medium or many types?

Response	# of Artists
Mixed Media	41
Primarily One Medium	13

What is the primary surface you use?

Response	# of Artists
Scratchboard	21
Illustration board	14
Gessoed masonite	4
Canvas	4
Quality paper	4
Other	8

How many boards do you purchase yearly?

Response	# of Artists
5-15	17
15-30	21
30- 50	14
50+	3

Where do you find out about new art materials ?

Response	# of Artists
Journals	25
Word of mouth	35
Newsletters	42
Conferences	27
Catalogs	11
Trade shows	0

How did Claybord compare to your current surfaces?

	Inferior	Same	Superior
Erasability	1	8	46
Manipulation	1	11	43
Line Control	1	17	37
Detail	0	17	38
Versatility	1	4	50
pH neutral	0	7	48
Durability	0	0	55
Surface (smooth)	1	24	30

Will you purchase Claybord?

Response	# of Artists
Definitely	45
Probably	4
Occasionally	3
Seldom	0
Never	3

Where do you currently buy your art materials ?

Response	# of Artists
Local retail stores	35
Mail order catalog	28
Direct from manufacturer	5
Other	8

What did you like best about Claybord?

Response	# of Artists
Pen & Ink Application	32
No Surface Glare	12
Size	6
Ability to Take all Media	42
Manipulation of Surface	40
Durability	12
pH Neutral	7
Easy to Work With	30
No Puddling Effect	6
Feel of Surface	12

Note: Theses results are based on a survey of 55 artists. Forty of these artists were selected using a random sampling of science & medical illustrators. Another 15 artists who work in other media were asked to test Claybord.

Exhibit M-1

Selected Comments from Artists*

Margy O'Brien, Albuquerque, NM, fine Artist

Surface quality is critical for me. I need to have a surface that is absolutely smooth to do my silver point drawing. Besides being smooth I have to make sure that the surface will accept silver point. I loved the Claybord! It was so smooth and tactile. The soft feel of the surface made it so inviting to work on.

Craig Gosling, Indianapolis, IN, Medical Illustrator

I run a medical illustration department of four people. I had each of my illustrators try the board and they all loved the way it accepted pen and ink. It didn't smudge and the ability to erase the ink was remarkable. I personally see the Claybord as a replacement for scratchboard because it is far superior. I also think it's perfect for rendering beautiful originals. I'm planning to do my next set of wildlife illustrations on Claybord.

Jan Bishop, Denver, CO, Fine Artist/Illustrator

I happened upon Claybord when I mentioned to a colleague of mine that I was having a hard time finding a surface that would take egg tempera well. He told me that I might want to try Claybord so I called Charles and asked him to send me a few boards. I was amazed the way the surface took the tempera-- it was perfect! I also tried my pen and ink techniques that I use on scratchboard and again, found Claybord to be superior. The surface was so smooth and did not create the puddling that you sometimes get with scratchboard and illustration boards. I love the way the surface sucks the paint in.

Ed Heck, New York, NY, Illustrator for the American Museum of National History

I liked the idea of a more stable surface and really liked the tone of the board. Claybord was much easier to work with than any other board I've used. I do a lot of wildlife illustration so creating fine detail is important. On the Claybord I could achieve the detail I wanted much easier than with Essdee scratchboard, for example. Also, the medium was so forgiving -- this was great! I'm really excited to try water media on the board to see how it takes it.

Lynette Cook, San Francisco, CA, Fine Artist/Science Illustrator

Claybord is certainly a superior substitute for scratchboard but I think it's so much more. The fact that I can now apply guaches, inks, watercolors and oils to one single medium is amazing. This is going to give me as an artist an entire new set of tools for expression.

Lloyd Logan, Osawatomie, KS, Fine Artist/Science Illustrator

This is by far the most durable surface available. I was able to have so much more control of the pigment I was laying down and I was able to experiment with the entire range value on a color so easily.

June Mullins, Blacksburg VA, Science Illustrator

Claybord is so much better than scratchboard. You can build up an image so much easier and you can achieve different levels of color gradation so easily it really is amazing. The board (Claybord) allows for so much more correction.

* From telephone conversations with the artists.
Exhibit M-2

Boards Sold in Each Target Segment

	Year 1	Year 2	Year 3	Year 4	Year 5
Claybord Premium (Prof. Artists)	2,400,000	2,400,000	2,400,000	2,400,000	2,400,000
Penetration	0.48%	0.98%	2.20%	3.67%	3.67%
Number	11,400	23,626	53,039	88,479	88,479
Boards/Artist	5	5	5	5	8
Boards Sold	57,000	118,130	265,195	442,395	707,828
Claybord Oil & Acrylic (Prof. Artists)	2,400,000	2,400,000	2,400,000	2,400,000	2,400,000
Penetration	0.00%	0.93%	2.33%	3.26%	4.66%
Number	0	23,157	58,017	81,174	116,034
Boards/Artist	0	5	5	5	5
Boards Sold	0	115,785	290,085	405,870	580,170
Total Prof. Penetration	0.5%	1.9%	4.6%	7.1%	8.5%
Claybord Premium Schools (182)	10,860	10,860	10,860	10,860	10,860
Penetration	15.50%	25.00%	35.00%	50.00%	60.00%
Number	1,687	2,715	3,801	5,430	6,516
Boards/Artist	2	2	2	2	2
Boards Sold	3,374	5,430	7,602	10,860	13,032
Watermedia Board					
Claybord Oil & Acrylic Schools (1,500)	90,000	90,000	90,000	90,000	90,000
Penetration	0.00%	10.00%	15.00%	20.00%	20.00%
Number	0	9,000	13,500	18,000	18,000
Boards/Artist	2	2	2	2	2
Boards Sold	0	18,000	27,000	36,000	36,000

Exhibit M-3

Overall Assumptions

Revenue Assumptions

Most Likely Case	50% of original Projections
Best Case	Most Likely Case x 1.5
Worst Case	Most Likely Case x 0.75

Expense Assumptions

Administrative Expense   Increases at rate of inflation between years 2-5

Payroll Expense

    Salaries   24,000 per officer, Increasing by 10% per year

    Payroll Taxes   13% of salaries

Warehouse Rental   5,000 square feet x \$0.32/ sq. ft./year, Increases by inflation in years 2-5

Research and Development   10% of revenues beginning in year 3

Advertising   See Exhibit F-2

Inflation   5%

Tax rate   34%

Accounts Receivable Terms

    Sales received in month of sale   10%

    Sales received one month after sale   30%

    Sales received two months after sale   60%

Accounts payable terms - raw materials   Cash terms first year, Net 30 thereafter*

Accounts payable terms - production   Cash terms

*Note: All inventories that appear on the balance sheet are raw materials <u>only</u>. We plan to utilize a just-in-time inventory control system with respect to our finished goods inventory. This is possible because our customers allow a 4-6 week lead time while our manufacturer has a 1-2 week lead time. Thus, calculated inventory turns of 20-26x are overstated because CGS includes production costs which are paid in cash.

Exhibit F-1

Marketing Expenditures - Year 1

Conversion Fees $3,000
    Costs involved in contact with retail channel. Includes product sampling,
    postage, telephone, etc.

Print Promotions $600
    Press release creation and mailing.

Print Advertising $20,000
    Ad production and media fees for three consecutive half-page ads in
    Artist magazine and *American Artist*. Combined circulation 410,000.
    Average C/M $20.51.

Direct Mail $55,000
    Targeted mailing 100,000. Includes design, production, printing,
    mailing list, postage, mail house fee and product sampling costs.
    Print quantity 150,000

Trade Shows $12,250
    Includes trade show booth design, registration fees and transportation
    costs. Seven scheduled shows including three sponsored by NAMTA.

Retail support $13,700
    Production and packaging of video training systems and "how to" brochure.

Telemarketing $4,176
    Follow up on direct mail to educational institutions.

Live Demonstrations $11,667
    Site visits to retailer locations. Includes transportation and materials.

Dealer Sales Kits $10,000
    To include video training and sales support materials. Estimate 100 training kits.

Exhibit F-2

Ampersand Art Supply
Return on Investment Calculation

(a) Invested Value	$200,000
(b) Percent of corporation	25.0%
(c) Exit Value Multiple (EDBIT) (Note 1)	6.0
(d) EDBIT at Year 5 (See Exhibit F-4)	$1,868,910
(e) Terminal Value at Year 5 - (d) x (c)	$11,213,462
(f) Share of terminal value at Year 5 - (e) x(b)	$2,803,365

Cash Flows

Year 1	-$200,000
Year 2	
Year 3	
Year 4	
Year 5	$2,803,365
ROI (Note 2)	69.6%

Notes:

(1)This figure is representative of transaction multiples for firms with earnings and growth characteristics similar to that of Ampersand's. (According to valuation experts at Howard, Frazier, Barker, Elliot, Inc.)

(2) Compounded annual rate of return.

Exhibit F-3

Ampersand Art Supply
Pro-Forma Summary Financials
Most Likely Case

	Fiscal* Year 1	% of Total	Fiscal Year 2	% of Total	Fiscal Year 3	% of Total	Fiscal Year 4	% of Total	Fiscal Year 5	% of Total
Revenues	$271,925	100%	$840,378	100%	$1,925,060	100%	$3,009,805	100%	$4,585,495	100%
Cost of product Sold	65,076	23.9%	353,995	42.1%	813,797	42.3%	1,251,342	41.6%	1,883,365	41.1%
Gross profit	206,849	76.1%	486,383	57.9%	1,111,263	57.7%	1,758,463	58.4%	2,702,129	58.9%
Operating expenses	280,864	103.3%	293,812	35.0%	506,975	26.3%	637,736	21.2%	833,219	18.2%
Operating income	-74,015	-27.2%	192,571	22.9%	604,288	31.4%	1,120,727	37.2%	1,868,910	40.8%
Taxes (@34%)			65,474	7.8%	205,458	10.7%	381,047	12.7%	635,430	13.9%
Net income	$-74,015	-27.2%	$127,097	15.1%	$398,830	20.7%	$739,680	24.6%	$1,233,481	26.9%
Total assets	194,646		397,092		1,014,704		2,137,556		3,981,141	
Book value	194,646		387,217		991,504		2,112,231		3,981,141	
Cash flow from operations	-173,008		113,902		365,519		1,102,943		1,376,143	

Exhibit F-4

INCOME STATEMENT — Year 1

	Sept	Oct	Nov	Dec	Jan	Feb	Mar	Apr	May	June	July	Aug	Total	%
Revenue						$37,696	$38,073	$38,454	$38,839	$39,227	$39,619	$40,016	$271,925	100.0
Cost of Goods sold						13,505	13,640	13,776	13,914	14,053	14,193	14,335	65,076	23.9
Gross Margin						24,192	24,434	24,678	24,925	25,174	25,426	25,680	206,849	76.1
Operating Expenses														
Administrative														
Office rent	500	500	500	500	500	500	500	500	500	500	500	500	6,000	2.2
Office supplies	100	100	100	100	100	100	100	100	100	100	100	100	1,200	0.4
Telephone	300	300	300	300	300	300	300	300	300	300	300	300	3,600	1.3
Postage	1,000	1,000	1,000	1,000	1,000	1,000	1,000	1,000	1,000	1,000	1,000	1,000	12,000	4.4
Total Admin. Expense	1,900	1,900	1,900	1,900	1,900	1,900	1,900	1,900	1,900	1,900	1,900	1,900	22,800	8.4
Payroll Expense														
Salary	8,000	8,000	8,000	8,000	8,000	8,000	8,000	8,000	8,000	8,000	8,000	8,000	96,000	35.3
Payroll Taxes	1,040	1,040	1,040	1,040	1,040	1,040	1,040	1,040	1,040	1,040	1,040	1,040	12,480	4.6
Total Payroll Expense	9,040	9,040	9,040	9,040	9,040	9,040	9,040	9,040	9,040	9,040	9,040	9,040	108,480	39.9
Equipment														
Warehouse rent	1,600	1,600	1,600	1,600	1,600	1,600	1,600	1,600	1,600	1,600	1,600	1,600	19,200	7.1
Total Equipt. Expense	1,600	1,600	1,600	1,600	1,600	1,600	1,600	1,600	1,600	1,600	1,600	1,600	19,200	7.1
R & D														
Advertising														
Distributors	500	500	500	500	500	500							3,000	1.1
Print promotion/PR			300	300									600	0.2
Print advertising		6,667	6,667	6,667									20,001	7.4
Direct mail campaign		10,000	45,000										55,000	20.2
Trade shows	2,042		2,042		2,042		2,042		2,042		2,042		12,250	4.5
Retail support			13,700										13,700	5.0
Telemarketing					833	833	833	833	833				4,167	1.5
Live demos						1,667	1,667	1,667	1,667	1,667	1,667	1,667	11,667	4.3
Dealer sales kit				10,000									10,000	3.7
Total advertising	2,542	17,167	68,209	17,467	3,375	3,000	4,542	2,500	4,542	1,667	3,708	1,667	130,384	47.9
Total Operating Exp.	15,082	29,707	80,749	30,007	15,915	15,540	17,082	15,040	17,082	14,207	16,248	14,207	280,864	103.3
Operating Income	-15,082	-29,707	-80,749	-30,007	-15,915	8,652	7,352	9,638	7,843	10,968	9,178	11,474	-74,015	-27.2
Income before tax	-15,082	-29,707	-80,749	-30,007	-15,915	8,652	7,352	9,638	7,843	10,968	9,178	11,474	-106,354	-39.1
Income taxes														
Net Income	-15,082	-29,707	-80,749	-30,007	-15,915	8,652	7,352	9,638	7,843	10,968	9,178	11,474	-106,354	-39.1

Exhibit F-5.1

INCOME STATEMENT ($)	Year 2 Q1	Q2	Q3	FY 2	%	Year 3 Q1	Q2	Q3	FY 3	%	Year 4 FY 4	%	Year 5 FY	%
Revenue	146,831	209,403	230,347	840,378	100.0	310,534	403,577	525,483	1,925,060	100.0	3,009,805	100.0	4,585,495	100.0
Cost of Goods sold	57,163	88,847	98,530	353,995	42.1	133,372	171,815	221,777	813,797	42.3	1,251,342	41.6	1,883,365	41.1
Gross Margin	89,668	120,555	131,816	486,383	57.9	177,162	231,763	303,706	1,111,263	57.7	1,758,463	58.4	2,702,129	58.9
Operating Expenses														
Administrative														
Office rent	1,575	1,575	1,575	6,300	0.7	1,654	1,654	1,654	6,615	0.3	6,946	0.2	7,293	0.2
Office supplies	315	315	315	1,260	0.1	331	331	331	1,323	0.1	1,389	0.0	1,459	0.0
Telephone	945	945	945	3,780	0.4	992	992	992	3,969	0.2	4,167	0.1	4,376	0.1
Postage	3,150	3,150	3,150	12,600	1.5	3,308	3,308	3,308	13,230	0.7	13,892	0.5	14,586	0.3
Total Admin. Expense	5,985	5,985	5,985	23,940	2.8	6,284	6,284	6,284	25,137	1.3	26,394	0.9	41,570	0.9
Payroll Expense														
Salary	26,400	26,400	26,400	105,600	12.6	29,040	29,040	29,040	116,160	6.0	127,776	4.2	140,554	3.1
Payroll Taxes	3,432	3,432	3,432	13,728	1.6	3,775	3,775	3,775	15,101	0.8	16,611	0.6	18,272	0.4
Total Payroll Expense	29,832	29,832	29,832	119,328	14.2	32,815	32,815	32,815	131,261	6.8	144,387	4.8	158,826	3.5
Equipment														
Warehouse rent	5,040	5,040	5,040	20,160	2.4	5,292	5,292	5,292	21,168	1.1	22,226	0.7	23,338	0.5
Total Equipt. Expense	5,040	5,040	5,040	20,160	2.4	5,292	5,292	5,292	21,168	1.1	22,226	0.7	23,338	0.5
R & D						31,053	40,358	52,548	192,506	10.0	300,981	10.0	458,549	10.0
Advertising														
Distributors	1,500	1,500		3,000	0.4	788	788	788	3,150	0.2	3,308	0.1	3,473	0.1
Print promotion/PR	300	300		600	0.1	158	158	158	630	0.0	662	0.0	695	0.0
Print advertising	13,334	6,667		20,001	2.4	5,250	5,250	5,250	21,001	1.1	22,051	0.7	23,153	0.5
Direct mail campaign	55,000			55,000	6.5	14,438	14,438	14,438	57,750	3.0	60,638	2.0	63,669	1.4
Trade shows	4,083	2,042	4,083	12,250	1.5	3,216	3,216	3,216	12,863	0.7	13,506	0.4	14,181	0.3
Retail support	13,700			13,700	1.6	3,596	3,596	3,596	14,385	0.7	15,104	0.5	15,859	0.3
Telemarketing		1,667	2,500	4,167	0.5	1,094	1,094	1,094	4,375	0.2	4,594	0.2	4,823	0.1
Live demos		1,667	5,000	11,667	1.4	3,063	3,063	3,063	12,250	0.6	12,863	0.4	13,506	0.3
Dealer sales kit	10,000	10,000		10,000	1.2	2,625	2,625	2,625	10,500	0.5	11,025	0.4	11,576	0.3
Total advertising	87,917	23,842	11,583	130,384	15.5	34,226	34,226	34,226	136,903	7.1	143,748	4.8	150,936	3.3
Total Operating Exp.	128,774	64,699	52,440	293,812	35.0	109,671	118,975	131,166	506,975	26.3	637,736	21.2	833,219	18.2
Operating Income	-39,106	55,586	79,376	192,571	22.9	67,491	112,788	172,540	604,288	31.4	1,120,727	37.2	1,868,910	40.8
Income before tax	-39,106	55,586	79,376	192,571	22.9	67,491	112,788	172,540	604,288	31.4	1,120,727	37.2	1,868,910	40.8
Income taxes				65,474	7.8				205,458	10.7	381,047	12.7	635,430	13.9
Net Income	-39,106	55,586	79,376	127,097	15.1	67,491	112,788	172,540	398,830	20.7	739,680	24.6	1,233,481	26.9

Exhibit F-5.2

BALANCE SHEET

	Sept	Oct	Nov	Dec	Jan	Feb	Mar	Apr	May	June	July	Aug	Total	%
ASSETS														
Current assets														
Cash	285,918	256,212	175,463	142,449	123,497	98,161	82,495	91,503	98,710	109,034	117,195	127,992	127,992	65.8
Accounts Receivable														
Due in 30 days						11,309	34,040	34,380	34,724	35,071	35,422	35,776	35,776	18.4
Due in 60 days						22,618	22,844	23,073	23,303	23,536	23,772	24,009	24,009	12.3
Total Receivables						33,927	56,884	57,453	58,027	58,608	59,194	59,786	59,786	30.7
Inventory				3,007	6,044	6,105	6,166	6,227	6,290	6,353	6,783	6,868	6,868	3.5
Other current assets														
Total Current Assets	285,918	256,212	175,463	145,456	129,541	138,193	145,545	155,183	163,027	173,994	183,172	194,646	194,646	100.0
Total Assets	285,918	256,212	175,463	145,456	129,541	138,193	145,545	155,183	163,027	173,994	183,172	194,646	194,646	100.0
LIABILITIES														
Current liabilities														
Total payables														
Short term debt														
Other current liabilities														
Total current liabilities														
Shareholders' Equity														
Paid in capital	300,000	300,000	300,000	300,000	300,000	300,000	300,000	300,000	300,000	300,000	300,000	300,000	300,000	154.1
Common Stock	1,000	1,000	1,000	1,000	1,000	1,000	1,000	1,000	1,000	1,000	1,000	1,000	1,000	0.5
Retained earnings	-15,082	-44,788	-125,537	-155,544	-171,459	-162,807	-155,455	-145,817	-137,973	-127,006	-117,828	-106,354	-106,354	-54.6
Total shareholders'equity	285,918	256,212	175,463	145,456	129,541	138,193	145,545	155,183	163,027	173,994	183,172	194,646	194,646	100.0
Total liabilities & equity	285,918	256,212	175,463	145,456	129,541	138,193	145,545	155,183	163,027	173,994	183,172	194,646	194,646	100.0

Exhibit F-5.3

BALANCE SHEET ($)	Year 2 Q1	Q2	Q3	FY 2	%	Year 3 Q1	Q2	Q3	FY 3	%	Year 4 FY 4	%	Year 5 FY 5	%
ASSETS														
Current assets														
Cash	58,671	90,791	158,682	241,894	60.9	279,694	340,082	443,978	607,413	59.9	1,710,356	80.0	3,086,499	77.5
Accounts receivable														
Due in 30 days	44,308	63,468	69,828	76,951	19.4	95,739	124,448	162,068	211,447	20.8	226,832	10.6	463,569	11.6
Due in 60 days	39,322	43,208	47,554	52,424	13.2	67,586	87,888	114,503	149,447	14.7	151,328	7.1	323,074	8.1
Total receivables	83,630	106,676	117,382	129,375	32.6	163,325	213,336	276,571	360,895	35.6	378,160	17.7	786,643	19.8
Inventory	19,830	21,239	22,828	25,824	6.5	24,410	31,498	40,723	46,396	4.6	49,040	2.3	108,000	2.7
Other current assets														
Total current assets	162,131	218,706	298,893	397,092	100.0	467,429	583,916	761,272	1,014,704	100.0	2,137,556	100.0	3,981,141	100.0
Total assets	162,131	218,706	298,893	397,092	100.0	467,429	583,916	761,272	1,014,704	100.0	2,137,556	100.0	3,981,141	100.0
LIABILITIES														
Current Liabilities														
Accounts payable	6,592	7,310	8,120	9,875	2.5	12,721	16,420	21,236	23,199	2.3	25,325	1.2		
Short term debt														
Other current liabilities														
Total current	6,592	7,310	8,120	9,875	2.5	12,721	16,420	21,236	23,199	2.3	25,325	1.2		
Stockholders' Equity														
Paid in capital	300,000	300,000	300,000	300,000	75.5	300,000	300,000	300,000	300,000	29.6	300,000	14.0	300,000	7.5
Common stock	1,000	1,000	1,000	1,000	0.3	1,000	1,000	1,000	1,000	0.1	1,000	0.0	1,000	0.0
Retained Earnings	-145,460	-89,604	-10,228	86,217	21.7	153,708	266,496	439,036	690,504	68.0	1,811,231	84.7	3,680,141	92.4
Total equity	155,540	211,396	290,772	387,217	97.5	454,708	567,496	740,036	991,504	97.7	2,112,231	98.8	3,981,141	100.0
Total liabilities and equity	162,131	218,706	298,893	397,092	100.0	467,429	583,916	761,272	1,014,704	100.0	2,137,556	100.0	3,981,141	100.0

Exhibit F-5.4

CASH FLOW STATEMENT

	Sept	Oct	Nov	Dec	Jan	Feb	Mar	Apr	May	June	July	Aug	FY 1
Net Income	-15,082	-29,707	-80,749	-30,007	-15,915	8,652	7,352	9,638	7,843	10,968	9,178	11,474	-106,354
Operating Activity Adjust.													
Asset & liab. changes													
Accounts receivable				-3,007	-3,007	-33,927	-22,957	-569	-575	-580	-586	-592	-59,786
Inventories						-60	-61	-62	-62	-63	-431	-85	-6,868
Total changes				-3,007	-3,037	-33,987	-23,018	-630	-637	-643	-1,017	-677	-66,654
Cash from operations	-15,082	-29,707	-80,749	-33,014	-18,952	-25,335	-15,666	9,008	7,207	10,324	8,161	10,797	-173,008
Cash flows from investing													
Plant additions													
Other													
Cash flows from financing													
Short term debt													
Long term debt													
Long term repayments													
Sale of equity	1,000												
Capital contributions	300,000												300,000
Total	301,000												300,000
Net cash incr. (decr.)	285,918	-29,707	-80,749	-33,014	-18,952	-25,335	-15,666	9,008	7,207	10,324	8,161	10,797	126,992
Beginning cash balance		285,918	256,212	175,463	142,449	123,497	98,161	82,495	91,503	98,710	109,034	117,195	
Ending cash balance	285,918	256,212	175,463	142,449	123,497	98,161	82,495	91,503	98,710	109,034	117,195	127,992	127,992

Exhibit F-5.5

CASH FLOW ($)	Year 2					Year 3					Year 4		Year 5	
	Q1	Q2	Q3	FY 2	%	Q1	Q2	Q3	FY 3	%	FY 4	%	FY 5	%
Net Income	-39,106	55,856	79,376	192,571		67,491	112,788	172,540	604,288		1,120,727		1,868,910	
Adjust. for Operations														
Changes in op assets & liabs														
Accounts receivable	-23,844	-23,046	-10,706	-69,589		-33,950	-49,011	-64,235	-231,520		-17,265		-408,483	
Inventories	-12,962	-1,408	-1,589	-18,955		1,413	-7,087	-9,225	-20,572		-2,645		-58,960	
Other current assets														
Accounts payable	6,592	718	810	9,875		2,846	3,699	4,816	13,324		2,126		-25,325	
Other current liabilities														
Total changes	-30,215	-23,736	-11,485	-78,669		-29,691	-52,400	-68,644	-237,768		-17,784		-492,767	
Cash flow from operations	-69,321	32,120	67,891	113,902		37,801	60,388	103,896	365,519		1,102,943		1,376,943	
Cash flows from investing														
Short term borrowings														
Long term debt														
Debt repayment														
Sale of Equity														
Capital contribution														
Net Cash Increase	-69,321	32,120	67,891	113,902		37,801	60,388	103,896	365,519		1,102,943		1,376,143	
Beginning cash	127,992	58,671	90,791			241,894	279,694	340,082						
Ending cash	58,671	90,791	158,682	241,894		279,694	340,082	443,978	607,413		1,710,356		3,086,499	

Exhibit F-5.6

REVENUE DETERMINATION Year 1

Product #1

Quantity of Item	Share %	Sept	Oct	Nov	Dec	Jan	Feb	Mar	Apr	May	June	July	Aug	FY 1
8" x 10"	4						335	338	342	345	348	352	355	2,415
9" x 12"	4						335	338	342	345	348	352	355	2,415
11"x14"	4						335	338	342	345	348	352	355	2,415
19"x12"	4						335	338	342	345	348	352	355	2,415
14"x18"	20						1,674	1,691	1,708	1,725	1,742	1,759	1,777	12,075
16"x20"	20						1,674	1,691	1,708	1,725	1,742	1,759	1,777	12,075
18"x24"	20						1,674	1,691	1,708	1,725	1,742	1,759	1,777	12,075
20"x24"	20						1,674	1,691	1,708	1,725	1,742	1,759	1,777	12,075
24"x30"	4						335	338	342	345	348	352	355	2,415
							8,370	8,453	8,538	8,623	8,709	8,796	8,884	60,375

Revenue per Item	Price $	Sept	Oct	Nov	Dec	Jan	Feb	Mar	Apr	May	June	July	Aug	FY 1
8" x 10"	0.75						251	254	256	259	261	264	267	1,811
9" x 12"	1.35						452	456	461	466	470	475	480	3,260
11"x14"	2.06						690	697	704	711	718	725	732	4,975
19"x12"	3.75						1,255	1,268	1,281	1,293	1,306	1,319	1,333	9,056
14"x18"	3.41						5,708	5,765	5,823	5,881	5,940	5,999	6,059	41,175
16"x20"	4.50						7,533	7,608	7,684	7,761	7,838	7,917	7,996	54,337
18"x24"	5.25						8,788	8,876	8,965	9,054	9,145	9,236	9,329	63,393
20"x24"	6.00						10,043	10,144	10,245	10,348	10,451	10,556	10,661	72,449
24"x30"	8.89						2,976	3,006	3,036	3,066	3,097	3,128	3,159	21,469
							37,696	38,073	38,454	38,839	39,227	39,619	40,016	271,925

Product #2

Quantity of Item	Share %
9" x12"	33
14"x18"	33
18"x24"	33

Revenue per Item	Price $
9"x12"	1.13
14"x18"	2.34
18"x24"	3.38

Market Projections	Size $	Market Penetration	Number Purchasers	Board/Artist	Boards Sold	Growth Rate	Factor
Product #1	2,410,860	0.52%	12,617	4.79	60,374	1%	7.21
Product #2	2,490,000				60,374		
Case Adj. Factor							

Exhibit F-5.7

COST & INVENTORY Year 1

	Sept	Oct	Nov	Dec	Jan	Feb	Mar	Apr	May	June	July	Aug	FY 1
Total Costs													
Raw Mat'l 1						557	562	568	574	579	585	591	4,017
Raw Mat'l 2						425	429	434	438	443	447	451	3,068
Board						2,025	2,045	2,066	2,086	2,107	2,128	2,150	14,607
Raw Materials (Inventory)						3,007	3,037	3,068	3,098	3,129	3,160	3,192	21,692
Production						10,497	10,602	10,708	10,816	10,924	11,033	11,143	43,384
Cost of Finished Goods Sold						13,505	13,640	13,776	13,914	14,053	14,193	14,335	65,076

Raw Mat. Order Schedule
Raw mat'l lead time, mos (1 or 2)   1
Finished goods lead time, mos   1

	Sept	Oct	Nov	Dec	Jan	Feb	Mar	Apr	May	June	July	Aug
Raw Mat'l 1 purchased at end of mo				557	562	568	574	579	585	591	665	607
Raw Mat'l 2 purchased at end of mo				425	429	434	438	443	447	451	508	463
Board purchased at end of month				2,025	2,045	2,066	2,086	2,107	2,128	2,150	2,418	2,207

Item Costs	Sq. In.	Raw Matl 1	Raw Matl 2	Board	Raw	Prod	Total	Margin $	Margin%
8" x 10"	80	0.02	0.01	0.06	0.08	0.29	0.37	0.38	50.60
9" x 12"	108	0.02	0.02	0.08	0.11	0.39	0.50	0.85	62.95
11"x14"	154	0.03	0.02	0.11	0.16	0.55	0.71	1.35	65.38
19"x12"	228	0.04	0.03	0.16	0.24	0.82	1.06	2.69	71.84
14"x18"	252	0.05	0.04	0.18	0.26	0.91	1.17	2.24	65.77
16"x20"	320	0.06	0.05	0.22	0.33	1.15	1.48	3.02	67.07
18"x24"	432	0.08	0.06	0.30	0.45	1.56	2.00	3.25	61.89
20"x24"	480	0.09	0.07	0.33	0.50	1.73	2.22	3.78	62.95
24"x30"	720	0.14	0.11	0.50	0.74	2.59	3.33	5.56	62.49

Raw Mat'l 1 cost/sq. in.	0.0002
Raw Mat'l 2 cost/sq. in.	0.0001
Board cost/sq. in.	0.0007
Production cost/sq. in.	0.0036

Exhibit F-5.8

Pro Forma Summary Financials - Best Case ($)

Fiscal	Fiscal Year 1	% of Total	Fiscal Year 2	% of Total	Fiscal Year 3	% of Total	Fiscal Year 4	% of Total	Fiscal Year 5	% of Total
Revenues	407,887	100.0%	1,260,567	100.0%	2,887,590	100.0%	4,514,708	100.0%	6,878,242	100.0%
Cost of goods sold	97,614	23.9%	530,992	42.1%	1,220,696	42.3%	1,877,013	41.6%	2,825,048	41.1%
Gross profit	310,274	76.1%	729,575	57.9%	1,666,894	57.7%	2,637,694	58.4%	4,053,194	58.9%
Operating expenses	280,864	68.9%	293,812	23.3%	603,228	20.9%	788,226	17.5%	1,062,494	15.4%
Operating income	29,410	7.2%	435,763	34.6%	1,063,666	36.8%	1,849,468	41.0%	2,990,700	43.5%
Taxes (@34%)			148,159	11.8%	361,646	12.5%	628,819	13.9%	1,016,838	14.8%
Net Income	29,410	7.2%	287,603	22.8%	702,020	24.3%	1,220,649	27.0%	1,973,862	28.7%
Total assets	281,900		731,700		1,817,942		3,666,786		6,718,427	
Book value	281,900		717,663		1,781,329		3,630,797		6,621,497	
Cash flow from operations	-119,213		320,006		677,349		1,885,254		2,246,516	

Pro Forma Summary Financials - Worst Case

	Fiscal Year 1	% of Total	Fiscal Year 2	% of Total	Fiscal Year 3	% of Total	Fiscal Year 4	% of Total	Fiscal Year 5	% of Total
Revenues	203,944	50.0%	630,283	50.0%	1,443,795	50.0%	2,257,354	50.0%	3,439,121	50.0%
Cost of goods sold	48,807	12.0%	265,496	21.1%	610,348	21.1%	938,507	20.8%	1,412,524	20.5%
Gross profit	155,136	38.0%	364,787	28.9%	833,447	28.9%	1,318,847	29.2%	2,026,597	29.5%
Operating Expenses	280,864	68.9%	293,812	23.3%	458,849	15.9%	562,491	12.5%	718,581	10.4%
Operating Income	-125,728	-30.8%	70,975	5.6%	374,598	13.0%	756,356	16.8%	1,308,015	19.0%
Taxes (@34%)			24,132	3.8%	127,363	8.8%	257,161	11.4%	444,725	12.9%
Net Income	-125,728	-61.6%	46,844	7.4%	247,235	17.1%	499,195	22.1%	863,290	25.1%
Total assets	151,018		229,012		614,898		1,370,943		2,720,247	
Book value	151,018		221,993		596,592		1,352,948		2,660,964	
Cash flow from operations	-200,038		13,097		181,440		774,249		941,961	

Exhibit F-6

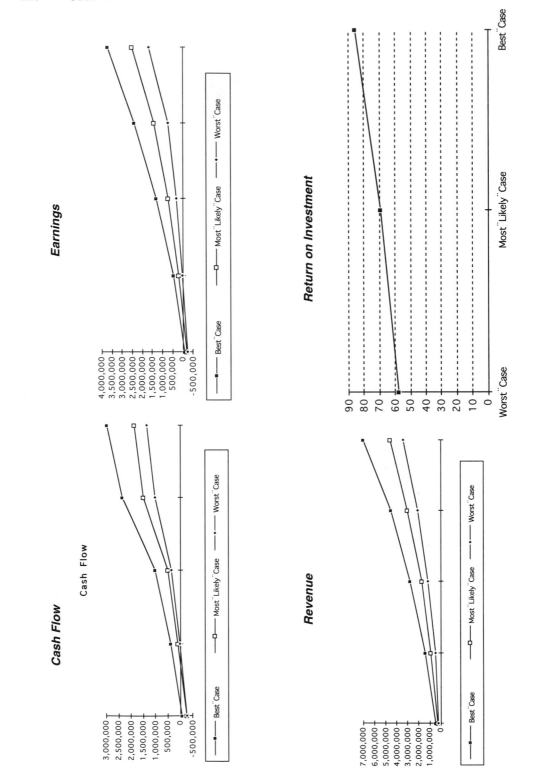

Elaine Salazar

3209 IH-35 South #2051
Austin, TX 78741
(512) 444-9706

Education	The University of Texas at Austin, Austin, TX	August 1993
	Master of Business Administration Marketing/Operations	
	The Colorado College, Colorado Springs, CO	June 1982
	BA History	

Experience

Summer 1992   **SLV Economic Development Council**, Alamosa, CO
Marketing Associate (Summer Intern)
- Consulted eight companies in marketing, operations, and financial areas.
- Designed and executed four major marketing initiatives to bring new products into the market.
- Conducted major research project to identify potential for increasing market share in the institutional market for selected food products.

11/86-8/91   **National Public Radio**, Washington, D.C.
Director of Training
- Created NPR's Department of Training. Planned and managed all staff and financial resources for the department.
- Designed the first comprehensive national broadcast training program for 400 public radio stations.
- Designed and implemented curriculum for management training programs and launched the first interactive satellite training program in the industry.

6/83-11/85   **KRZA-FM**, Alamosa, CO
General Manager
- Built and managed a public radio station to serve southern Colorado and northern New Mexico.
- Initiated and secured financing for construction, equipment, and operations.

Honors
- Consortium for Graduate Study in Management Fellowship Recipient
- The Thomas J. Watson Fellowship Recipient, 1982
- Josephine McLaughlin Fleet Award for Scholastic Achievement & Community Service, Colorado College, 1981
- Alpha Lambda Delta Honor Society, Colorado College

Activities
- National Association for Hispanic MBA's
- Mexican American Women's National Association, Vice President for Communications on national board of directors, 1989-1991
- Hispanic Graduate Business Association, UT Austin
- Graduate Business Women's Network, UT Austin
- Academic Affairs Committee, UT Austin

Personal
- Fluent in Spanish

Exhibit 0-1.1

Katherine M. Henderson

2502 Cedarview Drive • Austin, TX 78704 • (512) 326-3009

Education	**The University of Texas at Austin**	August 1993
	Master of Business Administration: Marketing / Management	

Southern Illinois University - Carbondale   May 1981
Bachelor of Science: Journalism / Advertising
University Scholar, Awarded certificate of achievement for academic merit

Experience
Summer 1992   **Apple Computer, Inc.**, *Marketing Analyst*   Cupertino, CA
- Researched alternate distribution channels for development tools and training software
- Made recommendations based on projected reach, cost effectiveness, and profitability
- Delivered white paper and presentation to key management

1990   **Blue Poppy Productions**, *Co-Founder*   San Diego, CA
- Identified a business opportunity and founded a software company that required zero start-up capital
- Developed a distribution system targeted at mail-order and direct mail channels
- Created a computer-based instructional enhancement program for secondary teachers and coordinated product development using royalty programmers
- Number 2 unit sales producer in catalog of 260 items

1985 to   **Chariot Software Group**, *Director of Marketing*   San Diego, CA
1991
- Established in-house marketing department for an Educational Software Publisher which resulted in an increase in sales to end users from 0% to 65% of total revenue
- Analyzed alternative means of product distribution and successfully recommended establishment of a mail order catalog which was profitable its first year; current circulation 80,000+, annual sales over $1,000,000
- Planned for company growth through product and market diversification

1983 to   **Over-Lowe Co.**, *Sales Promotion and Advertising Manager*   Englewood, CO
1985
- Created promotional and sales support materials; designed and coordinated press releases, direct and co-op advertising for a construction equipment manufacturer
- Managed the administration of trade shows, sales meetings and training programs
- Provided in-house sales, support, and demonstration equipment allocation

1981 to   **BHCD Engineers, Inc.**,*Marketing Coordinator*   Denver, CO
1983
- Initiated and designed promotional programs including corporate identity pro gram and project marketing materials for a large Mechanical Engineering firm

Activities   Graduate Women's Business Network, Board of Directors Liaison
Membership in various professional organizations, 1981-1991: Macintosh Software Publisher's Association, Direct Marketing Club of San Diego, Society for Marketing Professional Services, Student Advertising Association/AAF

Art Background   Nineteen hours college level art training plus numerous courses under private instruction since age 5. Exposure to all types of media. Current interests include watercolor, charcoal & pastels, and ceramics. Experience: Free-lance desktop publishing, paste-up, layout, design and process camera work.

Exhibit 0 - 1.2

Chapter 4

Formal Plans

❑ SUBCHAPTER 4A - Plan Elements

Writing a venture plan is the easiest part of creating a venture, and sometimes the least necessary. What makes a venture work is effective action by the founder(s) and others whose help they need. If planning inspires that action, it is helpful. If planning does not lead to that action, the planning process may still have been educational. But then the education must have utility or the planning will have wasted time.

Planning does not have to be done in written form to be useful. In their study of 2,994 new ventures, Cooper et al. found that 43 percent of the founders seriously contemplated business entry for a "long time" before taking action and 14 percent said they had thought someday they might do so. Undoubtedly some of these, particularly among the 43 percent, formally planned. Another 13 percent said they entered business simply because it was the best alternative available and 28 percent reported that the opportunity simply came along and they jumped into it.[1] It seems less likely that these last two groups formally planned. From this and much anecdotal evidence it appears that most businesses start without formal planning and even more without *written* formal plans.

Cooper et al. go on to point out that most firms start very small, 90 percent with less than 10 employees and over half with two or less.[2] This and other studies have also found that most firms stay small, under five employees. It might be supposed that these firms are therefore simple enough for owners to keep any planning in mind while at the same time keeping their enterprises flexible enough to respond to events quickly without much need for anticipation.

There is also evidence that planning works. Duchesnau and Gartner[3], for instance, found, in contrasting a group of 13 more successful with 13 less successful fresh-juice distribution firms, that the more successful firms on average spent more time (237 versus 85 hours) on planning. This is only one of many studies on the relationship between small firm performance and strategic planning.

Schwenk and Shrader[4] identified 26 other studies on the helpfulness of planning, some of which showed a positive relationship while others did not.

From an analysis of all those studies combined, they concluded that the evidence "clearly demonstrates a planning/performance link across studies," and that "it strengthens the case for recommending the use of strategic planning in small firms." They also noted that "since the effect sizes for most studies are small, however, it may be that the small improvement in performance is not worth the effort involved in strategic planning unless a firm is in a very competitive industry where small differences in performance may affect the firm's survival potential."

Purposes for Plans

Some very successful entrepreneurs, however, believe strongly in formal planning. For instance, Steve Bostic, who built his start-up to top performer on the 1987 *Inc.* 500 list before selling it to Eastman Kodak for a reported $45 million commented about his experience as follows:[5]

> *I'm saying it has to be planned. You have to take your vision, think it through, and turn it into a consistent strategy. And then you have to get it on paper. That's key. I maintain that if you can't put your vision on paper, you can never do it in the real world.*

When asked about the many companies that succeed without such planning, he continued:

> *You're talking about companies that are one-man shows. Yes, if you're guiding the ship out front and pulling everybody else along, you don't need to write it down. But if you want to be able to walk out of the room and have life continue in an orderly way, you'd better put your vision and your plan on paper.*

Although most businesses start without formal business plans, some do develop them before starting and many develop them if they start to grow. Some ways a plan can be used include the following:

- As an exercise for learning about entrepreneurship.
- As a test of reasoning about the venture design.
- As a scenario against which founders can test their "fit."
- As a device for obtaining counsel from others.
- As a portrait of the venture as a basis for improving its design.
- As a touchstone for guidance, should events become hectic.
- To obtain a bank loan.
- To help in thinking a start-up idea through.
- To obtain credit from a supplier.
- To obtain capital from an investor.

- To recruit needed partners.
- To recruit key employees.
- To provide guidelines to work from for founders and employees.
- To convince a wanted customer that the venture will deliver.
- To anticipate long lead times required for some action.
- To set up benchmarks for tracking performance.

Application: *How should the above purposes for a venture plan in the assigned case venture be ranked and why? How might that affect the design of the plan?*

The contents of the plan and how it is structured may vary depending on its main purpose. The majority of plans are written to help in attempting to raise money. This puts emphasis on financial projections in the plan. A banker will be particularly interested in debt coverage and support for a repayment schedule. An investor may be more interested in sales growth, profits and the backup information that supports claims about those dimensions of performance. Prospective employees, however, might be more interested in organization and staffing plans.

Matters of Priority

The place to begin a formal plan, unless another one occurs and looks better, is to brainstorm and write out answers to screening questions that were discussed in the preceding chapter. That will automatically provide key portions of a venture plan. The financial forecasts needed for screening will form a core, since much of the purpose of a plan is simply to explain in more detail just what will cause the estimates for sales and expenses to come true. Hence the writing process can start by setting forth the pro forma financial statements and then working back from them. They will help guide description of the product or service (categories of sales), who will buy how much of it (sales figures), what labor, materials and other expenditures will have to be in order to produce and deliver it (expenses), what physical items the company will need on hand to perform that work (assets) and where the financing (liabilities) will come from to obtain them.

Important General Qualities

Although venture plans can be fancy, there is no need for them to be. Some ventures have raised millions in start-up capital with very simple plans. Sophisticated investors can look past flashiness to assess whether the founders and their venture have credibility, or at least they like to believe they can. If the venture is basically flawed, the remedy should be to redesign or abandon it, not waste effort on gimmicks to make it look good. Founders should also not assume that if they simply plan well enough, they can make any venture work. Validity, realism, truthfulness and full disclosure of worrisome as well as encouraging factors are elements to reach for in creating a plan.

What To Present First

The purposes of the plan and nature of the venture should determine what it first describes. If the market is relatively apparent, as for something that will lengthen life or safety, then it may be best to start with description of the product or service, showing how the venture will be able to improve on what is now available in the marketplace. If the market is not so apparent, then the starting point may be to show readers what kind of need exists, how that was determined and what characteristics of it demonstrate that it can be profitable for the venture.

These are by no means the only two possibilities, as was suggested in the preceding chapter on screening. The objective is to start by letting readers know as directly as possible just what the venture will deliver, what the most outstanding virtue of the venture is and upon what basis that virtue rests. Maybe the basis is some unarguably unusual and powerful talent on the management team, unique property rights to an invention or a location. It could also be a lucrative contract or access to endorsement by some party whose word is likely to be strongly influential with important customers.

Organization of the Rest

In general, the organization of a venture plan should attempt to present more important aspects ahead of those less important, as a newspaper article does. If the reader needs an explanation to understand an important point, then possibly the explanation should come first. If only some readers, not all, will need the explanation, then it can be placed in an appendix at the back, with reference in the text as to where it can be found.

The list of topics to be covered is fairly predictable, although there can be striking differences in sequences, as appropriate to the individual ventures. A sample sequence of topics was presented earlier in Chapter 1. A variety of other arrangements taken from various plans appears in the first section of Appendix 1 illustrating venture plans.

Application: *Develop two contrasting venture plan outlines for the assigned case venture. Explain the pros and cons of each.*

Some Elements to Include

There are two main parts to the plan, the body and the appendices. The body should typically be no longer than about 20 to 30 pages. The purpose of appendices, which appear at the back, is to allow a reader to go through the plan without having to tackle all the details. The body might contain a summary of market research findings and simplified financial statements. But the details, such as copies of questionnaires used in the market research or more extended financial statements and footnotes explaining the figures, should be relegated to appendices. Within the body of the plan some of the main elements to include are as follows. Some are also illustrated by examples in Appendix 1.

Opening

1. **Tables of contents** vary in order of topics. A common feature they share, however, is the listing of page numbers for both sections of the plan: the body and the appendices. A deficiency which makes some plans harder to read is that their tables of contents lack any page numbers or list page numbers for the text only, not the appendices.

   Among the example tables of contents in Appendix 1, the longest happens to come from a company that proposed to make ground-effect (hovercraft, air cushion) boats. It did not get funding despite a very well written plan. The reason for rejection was that when the financing was being sought, oil prices shot up dramatically, venture capital available shrank and money became difficult or impossible for any venture to obtain.

   The briefest table of contents example in the appendix here is from a disk drive maker, Priam, which became very successful. That venture's success may not necessarily have been because of its plan, which like its table of contents was very simple and short.[6] But the founder who led the company to success was a staunch advocate of systematic planning.

2. An **executive summary** which follows the table of contents in a venture plan should be an abbreviated version of the overall plan so a reader can catch the main features of a venture in one page, if possible. Making it brief, however, does not mean it should be vague. Wherever possible, specific facts and figures, such as the internal rate of return (IRR) should be given. Introducing specifics need not add much, if any, length. This page is extremely important in approaching any prospective professional backers who are accustomed to reading many plans. If it does not hold their attention, they will not read further and the rest of the plan will be wasted.

3. Following the one page summary, the plan should open with **one summary paragraph** which briefly indicates (1) what the venture will sell, (2) what the principal competitive advantage of the venture is expected to be, (3) what the venture will need to be able to accomplish that, (4) what sequence of presentation the rest of the plan will follow and, (5) why that

sequence. A vital function this paragraph should perform is to let the reader know the line of reasoning by which the remainder of the plan is organized and how it is laid out.

Application: *Write a new Executive Summary page and an introductory paragraph of a plan for the assigned case venture.*

4. **Risk factors** may or may not be listed in a section under that title. In principle, a business plan should be designed with maximum realism, and in real life risk is a part of the picture. In contrast to a legal brief or an advertisement, whose purpose is to bias a reader by loading all the arguments only on one side, a venture plan should be balanced. An unbalanced presentation makes the reader and the writer antagonists rather than the collaborators they should be. Grouping risk factors into one section is sometimes an efficient way to introduce this balance. The facts on which those factors are based may speak adequately for themselves. Alternatively, risk factors may be pointed out at those points in the plan where important assumptions are made.

Description of Product or Service

Another task the front section of the plan must do in both the introductory or executive summary and the plan's opening paragraph is let the reader know just what the venture will offer potential customers. Usually this can be done briefly at the outset and then be further elaborated later in the body of the plan.

5. **Product (or service)** refers to what the company will sell. A section in the body of the plan should state clearly what the important features of the product or service are, what stage of development they are currently in, what will be needed to develop them further and how the venture can be expected to do that as well as or better than anyone else. For readers who may be expert in the venture's technology a few facts may suffice. For other readers there may be need for an appendix that will enable them to educate themselves about it.

    The excerpts shown in Appendix 1 of this book illustrate different modes of describing products and services. The first two use words, the first for a service and the second for a product which, as noted earlier, turned out to be highly successful.

    The other description excerpt in Appendix 1 presents an artist's rendering. It would likely benefit from some words and possibly dimensions that point out important features. If a prototype exists, then a photograph of it, possibly altered to conceal any features that may be secret, can be helpful. Even an amateur sketch, although perhaps not as elegant, can be a big help for readers of the plan. Pictures can truly be worth thousands of words and most business plans would be better if they used more graphics. Recruiting help by someone with art training may be worthwhile.

Application: *Write on one side of one page as full a description of the product or service in the assigned case as you can.*

Market Analysis

The market arena and how it works encompasses the next five sections. Illustrative excerpts appear in Appendix 1 of this book.

6. **Competitive analyses** should certainly have been part of the idea screening process, and it was suggested earlier that grids, matrices and tables can be particularly helpful in that process. Examples of such tables appear regularly in product-centered magazines such as *Consumer Reports, Infoworld, Motor Trend*, and *Motor Cyclist*.

Application: *Develop a competitive grid for the product or service of the assigned case, fill in the boxes insofar as possible and describe how information to fill the others might be sought by the entrepreneur.*

7. **Market research methodology** can take many forms, including library search, questionnaires, interviews, test marketing, and focus groups. Market claims for a venture should, wherever possible, be based on factual information from such sources. In school it may be appropriate only to design and pilot test a market research investigation in a way much more limited than would be called for by "the real thing." An appendix in the plan should show clearly how this study was performed, including sample questionnaires and protocols, if any were used.

Application: *Sketch out the design of a market research study to evaluate the selling power of the assigned case's product or service.*

8. **Market research data** should also be presented in an appendix. Excerpts in the appendix to this discussion illustrate use of both verbal description and tabular forms. The data need not be massive, particularly in a school study. Some data, however meager, are better than none, provided they are factual. The data should be accompanied by enough discussion to indicate clearly how they were analyzed.

9. **Market plan elements** may be simple or complex. Tabulating sales and where they will come from for a market plan can help the writer con-

sider alternatives more thoroughly. Writing out tends to highlight any incompleteness. Noticing empty cells is a prompt to search for options that might fill them. If none are found, cells can still be left without diminishing value of the tabulation. The blanks can stimulate searching by readers, who also may be able to suggest more alternatives to formulate a better marketing strategy.

10. **Sales projections** will probably come directly from notes made during idea checkout. The text of the venture plan should contain at least a summary, perhaps in graphical form. One in the form of a histogram and one as a table appear among the appendix excerpts here. The table goes a step farther to present three sales projections; optimistic: pessimistic and most likely. Such an array forms the basis for better financial projections which follow from the sales forecasts.

Application: *Describe two different ways that sales projections could be developed for the assigned case venture by its entrepreneur. Produce a hypothetical set of figures with each.*

Operations

11. **PERT and Gantt charts** are useful tools for planning the sequence of important actions in getting a venture started and for communicating them to others. Also helpful can be a time line with important milestones. Those milestones should include in particular any key accomplishments upon which additional outside funding might appropriately be contingent. Examples shown in Appendix 1 of this book illustrate only a small amount of the variety possible in formatting such charts.

Application: *Prepare a Gantt Chart and a PERT Chart for development of some aspect of the assigned case venture. Assess the advantages and disadvantages of each.*

12. **Organization charts**, both before and after the venture actually starts, should show clearly who will be the main leader and how other key members of the venture's workforce will be positioned in the power structure.[7] Somewhere in the plan there should also be indication of how ownership will be divided and a list of any key outside advisors. This should include, as soon as they have been chosen, names of any law and accounting firms that will be retained.

Application: *Draw two organization charts for the venture, one for a very early stage and another for later after break-even. Comment on when and how the change should be accomplished.*

13. **Resumes** are not included among the appendix examples, but appear in the Prize-Winning Plan case of this book. Their inclusion in a venture

plan should be completely straightforward. Of particular importance in them should be those aspects of prior experience that show (1) relevance to the job tasks of this particular venture and (2) evidence of accomplishment in prior challenging projects where something new had to be created under difficult circumstances.

Spending Plans

14. **Applications of funds** will be a matter of considerable interest to whomever puts up money for a venture. Presumably some applications, such as advertising or administrative costs, will be unrecoverable in the event the venture terminates. Others, such as capital equipment, inventory or development that results in patents, may continue to have value that will reduce potential losses.

15. **Cost breakdowns** must be made as part of forecasting both cash needs and profitability. The more that major elements of the costs can be subdivided and explained or backed up with references, the more convincing the forecasts become. How much effort to apply to this versus other elements of a forecast, such as sales, is a matter of judgment. One option is to give brief treatment to costs in the "first cut" of a plan but to include with it a brief discussion of how the figures would be further refined if more time were available to work on them.

Application: *List the largest purchases that the assigned case venture will have to make, and describe for each how best the amount of cash outlay required for it can be forecasted.*

Pricing Considerations

Price considerations should be given explicit attention from several perspectives in the venture plan.

16. **Pricing rationale** does not rest solely upon costs. But certainly the relationship between price and costs must be examined, including the way that costs are likely to vary with volume.

17. **Price/volume curves** can be important in formulating competitive strategy. Whichever company is able to move more quickly to lower costs, either by economies of scale or other ingenuity, can enjoy a pricing advantage. Competitors' prices, how they have changed in the past and what competitors might be able to do about them in the future should be explained.

Application: *How, in very specific terms, should the entrepreneur in the assigned case set the price initially for the product or service, and how should it change over time?*

Financial Analysis

Financial analysis includes five different aspects. Each was called for in checking out the venture idea. All that should be required for the venture plan is to copy that analysis over with refinements of the calculations and explanations so that readers will understand how they were done. The text of the plan should include key summary elements of this analysis, with details relegated to backup appendices.

18. **Break-even analysis** Two approaches are available for this analysis, numerical and graphical. The advantage of a numerical approach, dividing fixed costs by unit contribution, is speed and simplicity. The advantage of a graphical approach, which can most accurately be done by using figures from a pro forma income projection, is that it can take into account non-linearity and should be more accurate. It may also be quicker and easier for a reader to absorb. Two different dimensions desirable for the horizontal axis are (1) sales volume and (3) target date.

Application: *To the extent possible compute a new and contrasting break-even analysis for the assigned case venture.*

19. **Pro forma financial projections** are the heart of most business plans. Generating them for a new venture offers an excellent chance to apply anything learned in prior studies of finance and accounting as well as to learn more about them in the forecasting process. These projections form the heart of a venture plan and set forth what the founders will have as goals in creating the new enterprise. It is helpful to include in the plan at least three different forecasts, one optimistic, one pessimistic and one most likely. Explanations of the rationale behind each should appear in footnotes that follow the statements.

Application: *To the extent possible prepare a new and contrasting pro forma income statement and balance sheet for the assigned case venture, monthly for the first six months and quarterly thereafter up to six months beyond break-even.*

20. **Cash flow projections** Notwithstanding the importance of pro forma financial statements for setting goals, it is cash flow that the venture will have to live by. The shortcut approach in creating cash flow projections is to add back non-cash charges to changes in the balance sheet. Much more useful, since non-cash charges don't actually tell where cash is coming from or going, is to list all the actual cash inflows, outflows and their sources by month.

Application: *To the extent possible prepare a cash flow forecast for the first year of the assigned case venture monthly for the first six months and quarterly thereafter up to six months beyond break-even. Explain which of the underlying assumptions are most worrisome and why.*

21. **Footnotes to the forecasts** Numbers in the financial projections have no meaning unless a reader believes them. Explaining the causes of the num-

bers will help strengthen such belief. Factual bases and important assumptions behind the numbers should be clearly stated and distinguished from each other. In a very early "first cut" plan, such as might be prepared as part of a one-term course in school, it may not be possible to have strong substantiation for the numbers. In that case, it is still important to say how they were arrived at, even though a fair amount of imagination may have been involved. Beyond that, the plan can be strengthened by describing what specific action might be taken to increase the reliability of the numbers further, if more time were available.

22. **Return on investment (ROI) analysis**   The long run test of a venture may include many aspects. Survival and satisfaction of founders, employees, and customers are some. From a financial standpoint, the main test will probably be return on money invested in the enterprise. An important aspect of this return will be the internal rate of return that the venture earns on assets entrusted to it. If this is strong, then the investors' return is likely to be strong also. Not illustrated in the appendix sample here is just how the return on investment was calculated. Although straightforward, those calculations too should appear in an actual plan.

Application: *Compute ROI for the assigned case venture over its first five years and explain the assumptions to which that figure is most sensitive.*

Venture plan excerpts in Appendix 1 illustrate graphical and textual features worth considering. Not everything desirable in a plan is illustrated, however, and some specimens in Appendix 1 may not be important to a particular plan. Sketches of products are included, but not photos, which if available might be better, even if they were only photos of models. Also not illustrated are any number of aspects that would presumably be developed in the text of a plan and perhaps illustrated with tables or charts. How the venture's market would be segmented and how target customers in each segment would be profiled, for instance, is an aspect that should not be neglected.

Supplementary Reading

New Venture Strategies Chapter 4. (Vesper, K.H., Prentice-Hall, 1990)
New Venture Mechanics Chapter 10. (Vesper, K. H., Prentice-Hall, 1993)

Exercises

1. Write a cover letter for submission of a written plan based on one of your business ideas to a professional venture capitalist.

2. Prepare pro forma financial statements and a cash flow statement for one or more venture ideas of your own.

3. Interview three or more entrepreneurs, and describe in as much detail as you can just how planning was handled during start-up of their companies.

4. Critique the excerpted examples from venture plans in Appendix 1

   a. Which seems to be the most exceptionally well done and in what way(s)?
   b. Illustrate how some of the quantitative exhibits might be made more graphical.
   c. Which seems to fall the farthest short of its potential? Why do you suppose it is that way? What actions would be required to improve it? Illustrate, if possible.
   d. Discuss how the format of some examples might depend upon the nature of the product or service.
   e. Discuss which of the approaches illustrated would apply to your venture plan.

Venture History

1. What form did the entrepreneur's mental anticipation of future events in the venture take? What were expected to be the highest priority elements and most crucial assumptions? In hindsight which ones actually turned out to be?

2. Was there a written plan, and if so what was its nature, how was it used, and what functions did it turn out to serve?

3. If there was no written plan or if it was not much used, how were the functions suggested in this chapter for a plan accomplished?

Venture Planning Guide

1. Write the two most critical sections of a plan for your venture. Add a note that explains why they are most critical and how you would carry them further, given more time and resources.

2. List features which you could incorporate in your plan to make it unusually distinctive and interesting without compromising technical quality. Consider Appendix 1 examples in this process.

3. For a future point in time when your venture should be able to apply for a bank loan, prepare a bank loan proposal.

Notes

1 Arnold C. Cooper and others, *New Business In America* (Washington, D.C.: The NFIB Foundation, 1990), p. 18.

2 Ibid., p. 5.

3 Donald A. Duchesnau and William B. Gartner, "A Profile of Success and Failure in an Emerging Industry," *Journal of Business Venturing*, 5, no. 5, September 1990, p. 297.

4 Charles R. Schwenk and Charles B. Shrader, "Effects of Formal Strategic Planning on Financial Performance of Small Firms,"*ET&P*, 17, no. 3, Spring 1993, p.53.

5 "Thriving on Order," *Inc.*, December 1989, p. 48.

6 A copy of the full plan can be seen in Karl H. Vesper, *New Venture Mechanics* (Englewood Cliffs, N.J.: Prentice-Hall, 1993), Appendix B.

7 A two-stage organization chart example from a venture plan appears in Karl H. Vesper, *New Venture Mechanics* (Englewood Cliffs, N.J.: Prentice-Hall, 1993), pp. 338 - 339.

❏ *SUBCHAPTER 4B - Evaluation of Venture Plans*

What a venture plan reader wants to see in a plan depends on who the reader is. What audience(s) it was written for can be stated along with its purpose for that audience at the front of the plan. How such choices should affect contents of the plan will be discussed in this section.

Regardless the choice of audience, however, two aspects of the plan are important. One is what the plan can truthfully say about the venture. The second is how effectively the plan communicates that information. In "real business" the first of these is what people care about. But if the second of these is not adequately done, they may not be able to assess the first. So both aspects can matter and must be attended to. If the venture is inherently unattractive, then in the business world it is not worth planning. If it is attractive, then the plan must help it move forward or else the planning is a waste.

In school the purpose of plan writing is mainly to learn. The best way to accomplish that learning may be to aim for a viable venture with the plan. The odds are that the venture itself, particularly in the "first cut" form that time in school allows, will not be truly viable. The aim of the plan should be both to design the venture as close to viability as time and resources permit, and to make the most of what the venture allows. The plan should be done well enough that if the venture concept itself were viable and the information at hand were adequate, then the plan could be followed to create it.

That purpose, as noted above, can take different forms for different possible participants in the venture, including the following:

- Bank loan officer
- Supplier
- Prospective customer
- Prospective investor
- Potential partner
- Potential key employee
- Employees later on
- Founders later on
- Adviser to the founders

To some degree all these audiences will care about central issues such as viability, profit potential, downside risk, likely life cycle time and potential areas for dispute and for improvement. Beyond that, however, different audiences will care about different details. Two important audiences for the plans of most entrepreneurs are potential lenders, such as banks, and potential investors. Investors include mainly individuals and venture capital firms.

Of likely importance to students is yet another audience, the instructor, who is presumably neither a potential lender nor investor, but who may choose to take the perspective of either or both in addition to that of teacher.

Application: *Rank the importance of the above nine potential audiences for a plan written by the entrepreneur in the assigned case.*

What Bankers Look For

Most venture plans are written to raise money, and the source most common to businesses beyond founders' savings is bank borrowing. A banker's first concern has to be recovery of the loan. This is because banks are limited on the upside to a fixed interest rate controlled by usury laws, while on the downside they can lose everything. Moreover, most of the money banks lend is not their own. Rather, it is entrusted to them by depositers who expect to be able to withdraw it any time they choose.

Consequently, questions a banker will have in reviewing a venture plan loan proposal include:

- How reliable is this borrower? What has the person done before? What indication is there that he or she can be counted upon to repay?

- What will be done with the money? To what extent will it be put into things that can be sold versus non-recoverable expenditures? How sure is it to generate profit?

- What is the repayment schedule? How reliable are the sources from which repayment is supposed to come? Will the venture's customers be good credit risks?

- What collateral will there be to insure repayment of the loan? How much equity capital coverage is there on top of the proposed debt money? Will the venture's debt/equity ratio be conservative for its type of business? (Comparison to Dun and Bradstreet or Robert Morris Associates ratios?) Will there be salable equipment or inventory? Will there be a guarantor who can be depended upon? Should the entrepreneur personally guarantee it?

- How gratifying will it be to handle this loan? Will it be hard or easy to set up? Will the venture's control system provide timely and accurate financial reports? Will the entrepreneur be easy to get information from and keep the banker up to date, especially if problems crop up?

Beyond these questions, the banker will be interested to know what the odds are that by lending to this particular enterprise, he or she will be gaining the loyalty of a customer with a future of growing prosperity.

Application: *As a banker, what would be your answers to the above questions for the venture plan in the assigned case?*

What Investors Look For

With prospective investors the likelihood of profit growth is relatively more important than it is with bankers. The power and durability of the venture's competitive edge relative to those of future competitors is central to this. What the venture aims to become, and alternative future visions indicating the possibilities it has, will be particularly interesting parts of the plan. Indication of whatever special capabilities the venture's founders may have that will enable them to prevail over problems of getting started and surviving competitor responses will also be of high interest. Some key questions are likely to be:

- How catchy does the basic idea of this venture seem? Is it likely to be worthwhile to read this plan?

- How much time and money will it cost to check out this proposal thoroughly? Will that be worthwhile?

- What benefit will the venture offer to customers and at what cost compared to other things they might buy instead? Will the cost/benefit performance be sufficient to persuade buyers to switch to a new and unproven supplier? What assurance is there that the venture's technology will not soon be bypassed or surpassed?

- What segments of which markets will the venture seek to dominate and how? How big can they be expected to become? Upon what concrete information from which specific sources do these claims rest?

- Who will make the sales and how? What evidence is there so far to assure they will happen?

- What competitors will the venture be up against, and what will be its relative strengths and weaknesses both initially and later? According to whom or what sources and by what logic?

- What is the present stage of development of the venture's product or service? What testing has been performed, and what are the quantitative dimensions of performance? How fast can competitors catch up? Are any patents held by either the venture or its competitors?

- How will production be accomplished, and what will assure that it will match or exceed competitors in both quality and cost? What investment will be required for this? How much of that investment will be recoverable if the venture folds, and how?

- What levels of gross margin, net profit and return on investment are projected for the venture, and what is the basis for believing they can come true?

- How much money can the venture put to good use at what points in time, and what will it be spent on? What accomplishments will signal the arrival of those points?

- How financially committed are the founders personally?

- When and how should it be possible for the investors to cash in on this investment?

A convenience for investors will be inclusion of the name, address, phone and, if available, fax number of the founder to be contacted regarding any aspects of the plan. To maintain control of copies left with investors for review, it is appropriate to limit the quantity of copies prepared and number them clearly. As will be further discussed in Chapter 5, a legal risk of public offering can arise if too many copies, more than one or possibly two dozen, are released.

Application: *As a prospective investor, what would be your answers to the above questions for the venture plan in the assigned case?*

What Venture Capitalists Look For

The term "due diligence" is used by bankers for assessing the credit worthiness of loan proposals. Venture capitalists also use it for their activities in assessing ventures that seek money from them. The plan itself is only one piece of evidence among many, and usually serves them as a quick screening device to decide whether the venture is worth looking into. For almost all, the answer is no.

What Instructors Look For

School assignments to prepare business plans usually have a different primary purpose, namely learning. Giving this top priority tends to rearrange what is called for somewhat. Some possible differences are the following:

- Requirements for the venture to be able to show near-certain loan repayment and/or high profitability potential can no longer be imposed. Finding such deals is too much a "long shot" for a school requirement.

- Expectation that such tasks as prototype construction or market research be done to a professionally adequate level in the limited time available for homework is unrealistic. Such time-consuming tasks must be shortcut and compromised.

Instead, some things an instructor may look for that a banker or investor would not be particularly interested in could include the following:

- Evidence of good digging (e.g., pavement pounding). For many students it will be a new and therefore educational experience to approach strangers to obtain needed venture-specific information.

- Effective application of all thought modes described in Chapter 1 of this text. Most people have a natural bias toward using some thought modes to the exclusion of others. School should stretch the mind by pushing it to exercise underutilized capacities.

- Good writing. Other things being equal, a better written plan should be more successful in "real life" than a poorly written one. Usually in real ventures other things are not equal and the importance of those outweighs elegance in writing. In school those other things cannot be required as important, but writing well can. If a plan is written by a team, then a particularly challenging part of the writing will be to have the plan sections well coordinated. Doing this requires that enough time be reserved at term end for accomplishing the coordination. Last minute combination of plan sections is not the way to win.

Application: *If you were the instructor in a course where the assigned case plan was submitted, what grade would you give it and why?*

What Competition Judges Look For

Some business schools, such as the University of Arizona and Babson College, not only offer courses in which business plans are prepared, but also conduct local contests in which their students compete for prizes on the basis of their business plans. In addition to these local contests there are others at the Universities of Nebraska, Oregon, San Diego State, and Texas, Austin in which students from many other schools compete.

Judges in these contests include faculty members as well as venture capitalists, entrepreneurs, bankers and other business professionals. Examples of the rating sheets used for judging plans at two of these universities, Texas and San Diego State, appear at the back of this book as Appendices 2 and 3. From these it may be seen that, in addition to contents of the written plan, two factors that count heavily are the quality of an oral presentation and the viability of the venture itself as estimated by the judges. The chances of winning may be enhanced by implementing a plan as far as possible before the contest.

Evaluation Help from Other People

As a cross-check in evaluating the business plan, it can be helpful to have others read and comment. They may include friends or family members not necessarily familiar with business who can assess readability and perhaps also market feasibility, to the extent that they can empathize with the venture's potential users. For solider business reactions, the opinions of people experienced in related lines of work may help. These might include prospective employees, suppliers or sellers of what the company will offer. People affiliated with the Small Business Administration such as active and retired executives who volunteer their time may be good reviewers. Other successful entrepreneurs often like to help new start-ups and may be willing to look over their plans.

Those most qualified to review plans in general may be venture capitalists, people who make a living at reviewing others' plans in a variety of businesses. *Inc.* magazine reached this conclusion after presenting each of 27 business plans to panels of experts, then tracking the ventures over time to see how they worked out. Of the 27, the number of ventures surviving two or three years later was 17.

Inc. ranked the experts it used in terms of quality of advice as proven by hindsight, as follows: (1) venture capitalists with positions in companies comparable to the start-ups they were evaluating, (2) operators of similar businesses, (3) direct competitors, (4) customers, and (5) observers, including academics and editors of trade journals.[1] Venture capitalists were "hands down" best at foreseeing the ventures' futures, said the magazine, pointing out, however, that it was probably easier for the magazine to get counsel from them. It would be difficult for an entrepreneur in whose venture they were not actually investing to get venture capitalists to give much, if any, review effort.

Surprisingly, perhaps, future competitors may be willing to help, although obviously it can be risky to share an idea with them. How Hewlett-Packard reacted to what turned out to be a future competitor is illustrative:

William Hewlett temporarily left the company he had founded with David Packard to serve in the U.S. Army during World War II. There he met and was impressed by a young engineer, Howard Vollum, who had an idea for a new kind of oscilloscope. At Hewlett's suggestion Vollum met with David Packard, who recalled:

"During our conversation it became clear to both of us that rather than joining HP, Vollum really wanted to start his own company . . . and we helped him do just that. We lined him up with Norm Neely and many of our other sales representative firms across the United States. Thus was born Tektronix, the Oregon-based company that became the dominant oscilloscope supplier in the world.

"As time went on it became quite clear that if we were going to offer a complete line of electronic measuring instruments, we needed to fill in the line with our own oscilloscope. So in 1956 we designed an oscilloscope, the model 150, which we hoped would provide a strong challenge to Tektronix."

Packard continued, pointing out that the model 150 was unreliable, and subsequent Hewlett-Packard challenges to Tektronix' dominance were unsuccessful for a number of years until his company developed a computer-managed system which eventually prevailed.[2]

According to experts recruited by *Inc.*, venture plans should anticipate a number of pitfalls, such as the following:

- Sales will grow more slowly than expected.

- Selling costs are particularly vulnerable to underestimation on many items, from salespeople's salaries to conference attendance expenses.

- Most start-ups aim at markets that are too broad in terms of customers or geographic territories, or they introduce too many different products.

- People with experience crucial to the start-up are too often not given stock or other incentives to keep them dedicated to the venture.

- Operating costs and overhead easily and too often are allowed to rise.

- Gaining a customer does not mean that the customer will be loyal.

The *Inc.* editors also suggested some rules of their own from the way the ventures eventually turned out, including the following:

- "Nobody likes your product as much as you do." The more successful entrepreneurs put more effort into assessing the need for their products.

- "If you don't have experience, buy it." Founders with experience in their industries did better than those without it.

- "Your competitors aren't dumb." Studying how they operate and expecting them to respond to new entrants pays.

- "It isn't the sales. It's the sales cycle." Founders tend to underestimate the capital needed, particularly for coping with the length of time it will take to gain market acceptance.

- "Don't underestimate how much time simply being the boss will eat up." The only way to avoid being buried by the enormous amount of minutiae that will arise is through delegation. Each element by itself is simple—government reporting, sick leave, holidays, little things that go wrong—but together they can become overwhelming without help.

Review Help from Software

A number of microcomputer programs, such as *Ronstadt's Financials*, are available for help in planning. However, their output is limited by the quality of the planner's input. Their questions and prompts may indicate areas that need consideration. Financial forecasts can be generated either with a planning program or by using simple software. Either way, each major assumption used should be explicitly stated and keyed to the forecast with an appropriately positioned footnote, so that readers can judge the validity of the assumptions independently. Danger signals in the assumptions may include:

- Absence of footnotes to go with numbers that represent substantial fractions of total sales or total assets

- Figures that, with no explanation, stay flat or escalate in regular steps over time

- Amounts that seem unreasonable compared with industry averages such as those of Robert Morris Associates or Dun and Bradstreet, those of comparable companies, or those to which the reader reacts based on prior experience

Sometimes, of course, it is necessary in forecasting to pull numbers out of the blue, even though they cannot be well supported. In such cases, the footnotes should admit that this has been done. Readers may then offer their own improved estimates.

Besides running the obvious computer cross-checks on spreadsheet totals and spell checking on textual sections, it may be helpful to apply a project management program, such as Microsoft's *Project*. Based on examination of 20 ventures, Dean reported that project management techniques were useful in start-up planning for[3]

- examining the use of critical resources.

- coordinating control of tasks in development of the venture.

- reducing unnecessary duplication of work and increasing staff efficiency.

- enhancing adaptation to a dynamic competitive environment.

Use of project management tools requires identification of tasks to be performed during the start-up, an estimated dollar cost for each, and beginning and completion dates. Entry of these into a project management software program will result in review displays such as Gantt and Pert charts, which are useful in uncovering potential omissions and conflicts in the plan. They are also helpful in showing the plan to others who, before undertaking the venture, can help with cross-checking and with implementation during start-up.

Dean identified the following common tasks for carrying through the high-tech ventures he studied:

1. Completing concept design and formulation

2. Completing prototype development

3. Obtaining initial financing for significant production

4. Completing initial production tests

5. Performing market testing of the new product

6. Beginning large-scale production of the new product

7. Obtaining substantial sales of the new product

8. Running into the first competitive response

9. Completing the first redesign or redirection of the new product

10. Obtaining subsequent financing to achieve continual expansion

Each of these tasks, in turn, includes more sub-tasks, all of which must mesh so that one does not hold up the others unduly. Displays from the project analysis can forewarn of such dangers so they can be headed off.

Style

Some other elements to include are, as noted earlier, a one page executive summary, a table of contents with page numbers, and descriptive sections putting main points first plus appendices with supporting details.

Experts who have reviewed hundreds of venture proposals point out that plans which are too sketchy or sloppy will discourage potential investors from struggling to discern what they mean, and also reflect adversely on the competence and craftsmanship of founders who submit them. Plans that are too long, elaborate, complex or fancy may be rejected if they seem to reflect a misapplication of priority from substance to form. A balance between these extremes that is clean, clear, easy and interesting to read, should be sought. That still leaves room for creativity in written presentation, as experts Stanley Rich and David Gumpert have pointed out.

> *Of all the hundreds of business plans that have been submitted to the MIT Enterprise Forum, one stands out as so exemplary in its format that it can serve as a model plan. This plan was like other plans in that it contained text on each right-hand sheet through the book; what distinguished it from other plans was that each page was summarized on the left hand page. That is, each left-hand page—left blank in other plans—contained sets of bulleted highlight phrases, so that it was possible to read the summarized version of the entire business plan in somewhat under ten minutes!*
>
> *Those of us who reviewed the plan… all felt that we had seen the ultimate in business plans. Each of us approached it the same way: We read the summary through, from cover to cover, to gain an overview of the company's objectives and approaches to achieving them. Once our appetites were sufficiently whetted, we then read the detailed document. This business plan truly turned into a book we couldn't put down until we had read through to the last page—in one sitting![4]*

Some Things to Avoid

Some other things to avoid in plan writing, whether for school or for the real thing, are the following:

- Length for its own sake. It is easy to bulk up a plan with magazine articles about the industry and various kinds of literature or, even worse, with simple verbosity. No reader is likely to welcome that.

- Irrelevant information. If there is a shortage of information on something important to the venture there may be a temptation to make up for it by including information on something else that happens to be conveniently available even though irrelevant. Such compensation does not help.

- Duplication of references readily available elsewhere. It may be appropriate to excerpt sections selectively. However, references available in a library should simply be footnoted.

- Adulation of venture or its founders (e.g. "Our excellent product and highly talented management group..."). Such judgments as whether the founding team is competent and virtuous, whether the venture is highly likely to succeed and whether its product or service will be wonderful should be left to the reader. What will help the reader arrive at those judgments are facts the plan should include.

- Directly imitating another plan or adopting a "canned" format. Not letting the design of the plan follow from the logic of the individual venture introduces risks of mismatch in priorities, illogical reasoning, apparent imitation and shallow thinking.

- Reliance on the written document alone. For a venture plan to be accepted, there will have to be personal meetings between the writer and the reviewer.

Oral Presentation

The way to make the most of a personal presentation is to rehearse it ahead of time in front of one or more sympathetic but knowledgeable and critical audiences. If there is a time limit, then those rehearsals should be timed and practiced until they fit within the limit. The natural temptation will be to try packing too much into the available time and to do it by talking faster. That will simply lose the listener.

To keep the talk both slow and within the time limit, one device is to use some graphical displays. They should not be too complex to comprehend, but they can still compress more information into less time.

Another device is to have ready some backup presentations of subsections which present more details. These can be held in reserve and brought forth in response to questions or requests for more detail that the listener may raise.

Finally, of course, the listener can be given access to more details in a copy of the written plan either before or after the oral presentation, whichever seems most appropriate.

Application: *If you were going to make a 10-minute oral presentation of the assigned case venture plan, what highlights would you pull out to present and how would you organize the talk? What graphics would you use?*

Final Test

Implementation, if it happens, provides the final test of the plan and intelligence for its revision. Starting the venture will give the entrepreneur(s) new information that makes the plan, part by part, obsolete even as it serves its purpose and the time arrives to plan again.

Supplementary Reading

New Venture Mechanics Chapter 10 and Appendices A and B. (Vesper, K. H., Prentice-Hall, 1993)

Exercises

1. For each of the elements noted above as important to (a) bankers and (b) investors, indicate specific evidence that could most helpfully be incorporated in a business plan and how it might be obtained.

2. Bankers, investors and instructors are three potential plan readers discussed above. Name three others, describe how their interests in a venture plan might be different, and how those differences might change how a plan should be shaped to fit their particular interests.

3. Interview a banker or investor who has received business plans, and write a description of the procedure that person typically used for reviewing proposals. Describe the implications of your findings for someone who wants to write such a proposal.

Venture History

1. If the entrepreneur had a plan, what audiences was it aimed at and for what purposes? What was their reaction to it?

2. If there was no written plan, what audience does the entrepreneur think such a document might most have helped influence?

Venture Planning Guide

1. Prepare alternative graphical aids for your business plan. Develop a rating scheme to evaluate them and select the most effective ones for inclusion in your final plan.

2. Perform a dress rehearsal of a venture plan presentation, complete with visual aids. Time it with a stopwatch and stay within 10 minutes total. Role play a question and answer session with questions as tough as possible.

3. Appendix 1, Venture Plan Excerpts, presents examples of 18 different types of elements that might be included in a venture plan. How many of them will be included in your plan? Which ones will not be, and why?

4. Perform an assessment of your plan using the rating sheets of Appendix 2 or Appendix 3, both for your plan in its present form and in the form you hope to develop it into by the end of this term.

Notes

[1]Leslie Brokaw, "The Truth About Start-Ups," in *Anatomy of A Startup* (Boston: Inc. Publishing, 1991), p. 364.

[2]David Packard, *The H P.Way* (New York: Harper Business, 1995), p. 78.

[3]Burton V. Dean, "The Project-Management Approach in the 'Systematic Management' of Innovative Start-U p.Firms", *Journal of Business Venturing*, 1 no. 2, Spring 1986, p. 149.

[4]Stanley R. Rich, and David E. Gumpert, *Business Plans that Win $$$* (New York: Harper & Row, 1985), p. 41.

Case Questions

General Questions

1. Critique the business plan in the assigned case and describe actions that should be taken to improve upon it. List the presumed use(s) of the plan upon which your critique is predicated.

2. Which elements illustrated in Appendix 1 at the back of the book does the plan incorporate and which might it benefit from adding?

3. As a prospective investor, how would you value (negative numbers are allowable) the venture described in the assigned case and why? What sort of terms could you put into a deal to make it more appealing, and how should the entrepreneur react to those terms?

4. What should be done next by whom in the assigned case to move the venture forward and why?

Case 9 - Elaine Salazar and Kathy Henderson p. 255

1. What is your assessment of the Ampersand business plan (Prize-winning Plan Case) as a plan, as opposed to the venture it depicts? Why, as best you can tell without seeing the team's oral presentation, did it win a prize?

2. How well is it suited to winning the future competitions whose judging criteria appear in Appendices 2 and 3 at the back of the book?

3. Give the plan a score
   a. Using Appendix 2
   b. Using Appendix 3

4. What are the major decisions that Elaine and Kathy now face for developing the plan to bring Claybord into the market?

5. How should Elaine and Kathy allocate their efforts on this project for the school term ahead? State your assumptions concerning personhours available to them.

Case 10 - Andrew Hammoude (A) p. 260

1. What is your assessment of Andrew Hammoude's plan so far? If you were there, what might you be able to do to help him make it better?

2. Based on the work he has on plan development, what share of ownership or amount of pay from the other entrepreneurs would you say Andrew deserves as of the time of the case?

3. What should Andrew do over the next three months and why?

4. What should be the prospects for obtaining formal venture capital for ImageSystems?

5. What sort of amounts, timing and terms should a venture capital deal for this company include, assuming venture capital is the route to take?

Case 11 - Bill Foster (A) p. 275

1. What is your forecast of the numbers Bill Foster proposes to generate for his plan?

2. What is your assessment of the method Bill has been using to develop his business plan?

3. What else is needed to finish up the plan?

4. What recommendations can you suggest for the venture itself? How should they be put into effect?

Appendix 1 - Venture Plan Excerpts p. 695

1. Look over Appendix 1, Venture Plan Excerpts, at the back of the book. Select what you consider to be the four best done and the four least well done examples it includes. Be prepared to explain why.

2. For each of the four least well-done examples prepare an improved revision and be prepared to display it in class.

3. For further explanation of the Venture Plan Excerpts and more questions for analysis, please refer to the first page of Appendix 1.

Elaine Salazar and Kathy Henderson

January 1993 - Beyond a Win

In early 1993 as the resumption of school approached following New Year's vacation, Elaine Salazar and Kathy Henderson, students at the University of Texas, Austin, were considering how to allocate their energies and resources on a project they had begun the preceding term. With two other teammates, who had since withdrawn, they had developed a venture plan, which appears herein as the Prize-Winning Plan case. They had also taken a number of steps toward actually starting the business.

Before them were two goals they had earlier set for themselves. One was to continue starting the venture. The other was to win a venture plan contest being held in a few weeks at San Diego State University. First prize in the contest consisted of $5,000, an amount that they believed would help them greatly in their start-up. How best to work toward both goals at the same time was a question they considered important.

Aiming for a Venture

When, back in September 1991, they had begun their first year in the MBA program at the University of Texas, Austin, Elaine and Kathy both dreamed of some day starting their own business. Elaine recalled:

My plan in enrolling in an MBA program was to learn more about business, get a job where I could learn about

some line of business, and then use that knowledge to start one of my own. Kathy's thinking was similar.

Resumes presenting the prior education and experience of both women can be seen in the business plan of the Prize-Winning Plan case.

Toward the end of the first year of their MBA program, both signed up to take professor Gary Cadenhead's entrepreneurship course, which would start in the fall term of the next school year, beginning September 1992. The course required preparation of a plan for a new business. At the end of the term in December the class held a competition in which the plans were submitted both in writing and orally to a judging panel comprised of both faculty and business practitioners, including some venture capitalists. The oral presentations were announced publicly and held in an auditorium where anyone could attend.

In the summer of 1992 Elaine worked with the Ewings as part of a summer internship on a project by the Colorado Economic Development Council in Alamosa, Colorado. The Ewings, who had known her brother for many years, had signed up for help from the Economic Development Council's "Leading Edge" consulting program to seek a way for moving to the next step of expansion with their business. Elaine continued:

As part of my summer work in the 'Leading Edge' program, I identified some more art schools and told them about the program at the University of Texas where I might be able to recruit some students to work on developing a fuller plan for creating a business. So I asked them if they would let me bring Clayboard to U.T. and use their product as the subject for developing a business plan for the International Moot Corp[SM] project. I needed an idea to work on and they needed someone to help them conduct market research and put together a business plan. It was a win-win situation.

The Ewings had encountered some demand for Charles' painting panel invention which he referred to as "CEC," or "Charles Ewing Clayboard." Description of the product, its background and what the Ewings had done with it so far can be seen in the case entitled "Charles and Barbara Ewing." Elaine found in working on the summer consulting project with the Ewings that they had prepared the beginnings of a business plan. Sales the Ewings had made so far consisted of a small volume of Clayboard sold directly to a few artists and a couple of art stores in the Denver area. An art distributor had met them, liked the product, and said that he could sell the product if the Ewings could make it. The distributor wanted to take the Clayboard to the National Art Materials Association trade show that summer and put it on display. Barbara Ewing had expressed concern about how to meet demand if more orders came. Elaine Salazar recalled:

> The Ewings were trying to put Clayboard on the market, but they finally decided that it was too much for them. They wanted to scale back. They had decided not to show Clayboard at the National Art Materials Trade Association Show in Las Vegas the summer of 1992, fearing that they would not be

able to meet demand if the trade show went well.

Recruiting a Student Team

The day class began in the fall of 1992 Elaine showed Kathy the Clayboard and asked if she was interested in working with her on the business plan. Not only was Kathy interested in the venture idea, but she also had an art background. Elaine continued:

> I approached Robert Tavarez, but at that time he said he wanted to work on something a little more high-tech. Two other students, Drew Tingleaf and David Shackleton were also approached. David was an industrial designer and Drew had a finance background. They agreed to join the team.

The name, Ampersand, was suggested by David who stressed the importance of choosing a name that was unique and yet could easily become familiar so it would stick in customers' minds when they saw the company's product. Ampersand is the name of the "&" sign.

Now the team had 12 weeks to crystallize their business idea and develop a plan to carry it out. Their goal, however, was not just to satisfy requirements of the course, but to help Barbara and Charles create a real business plan.

Early Explorations

After the competition victory Elaine and Kathy drove to visit Clayboard's inventor, Charles Ewing and his wife, Barbara. Kathy recalled:

> I wanted to get more background on the product and how it was positioned, since I was going to look at the marketability of it. Because Elaine and I were more driven by doing the business than getting a grade we started this project

with skepticism. Even though Charles Ewing had received personal endorsements from several happy customers, we wanted to know whether there was really a profitable market for Clayboard. We picked up samples of the Clayboard and then started by calling a few retailers. They sounded interested.

Elaine continued:

We mapped out information we needed to know. Kathy explored and researched the retail channel and I worked on discovering artists' reaction to the product. We sent samples and followed up with calls to over 100 artists and others in the industry. We paid for the mail and phone bills out of our own pockets. During our research we explained to those we spoke with that we were a team of students doing a research project on the art industry for one of our classes. People were more willing with their information to students than to some prospective competitor.

One person they talked to was a professor in the University of Texas Art Department. He suggested that they contact the country's largest art supply store, Pearl Paint in New York City, which sold both direct from its premises and through its own mail order catalog. Kathy called Pearl's purchasing department and described Clayboard, which the team had now given the new name "Claybord," after their attorney had advised them to seek a name less generic as a stronger basis for trademarking. Pearl responded to the phone call with a suggestion that the team send a sample. When asked to whom in particular, they said simply the purchasing department.

In November 1992 via second day express, Kathy sent a sample of the Claybord obtained from Charles Ewing to Pearl Paint requesting their feedback on the product. Four days later they received a phone call from Pearl saying the store was very interested and would like to explore the possibility of carrying Claybord.

Kathy had looked in the library for appropriate trade associations and through one of them had obtained a list of companies that sold art materials, including wholesalers as well as individual stores. There were many questions regarding how to set up the distribution strategy. Should the venture sell to individual stores like Pearl Paint which was a chain of 10 stores or should it sell through wholesalers? What sales support materials should it provide? Should there be any kind of sales training program for anyone?

To establish a price for the boards, the team felt they should consider what Charles Ewing had been selling them for, what competitive materials such as art panels and scratchboard sold for, how attractive artists were likely to consider the product, and what they would be willing to pay, as well as the industry discount structure.

Through their contacts with the stores and manufacturers' representatives, the team had learned about discounts in the art supply channels. The typical arrangement was to give wholesalers a discount off retail price of 50 percent plus another 25 percent on the remaining 50 percent. The wholesalers then gave 50 percent off retail price to the stores. Manufacturers' representatives typically operated on a commission from 5 percent - 10 percent on whatever they sold.

A Win at the End of the Term

Meanwhile, the term was rapidly coming to a close. The team had to make assumptions and wrap up their plan for oral presentation and written submission. There were 10 teams competing. Two rounds of presentations would be held before panels of judges that included not only instructors but also venture capitalists, entrepreneurs, bankers, advertising agents and other professionals.

The presentations were to be competitive. First prize would be a stipend of $500 plus free rent and an office space at the University of Texas business incubator, a facility provided to help startup companies by offering low-cost office space complemented by ancillary services such as phone answering, fax and copy services and the companionship of other entrepreneurs. The first round of competition would eliminate half of the teams and the second would pick the overall winner. Kathy commented:

> We were not too surprised when we made it through the first round. We felt we had a promising product and a good plan, even though there were still a lot of questions to be answered.
>
> But we thought the odds would be against us on the second round. All the other teams had high tech products or ideas, and we just had a very simple-looking low-technology product. Most of the entrepreneurs and venture capitalists on the judging panel seemed to be oriented toward high technology, so we thought that would give the other teams an important advantage.
>
> When we took first prize in the second round, it just amazed us. As it turned out, our low technology may have worked in our favor, because the judges could touch and feel the product. We had market affirmation and a solid plan. I don't know if that is what worked for us, but anyway, we won!

Comments from the judges included questions about how reasonable the inventory figures were in the team's balance sheet projections and whether the team might have trouble controlling quality, since none of the team members had much experience in manufacturing. One judge expressed the view that this venture should indeed go forward. He said he would personally consider investing, probably lending the money and taking some equity in the business.

Elaine's Trip to New York

During Christmas break after the team won first place, Elaine flew to New York and visited Pearl Paint. She recalled:

> It happened that the buyer who had initially reviewed our product was no longer there. It had been turned over to a man named Victor. We met. I showed him samples and what the product could do. I explained that we were not yet ready to go nationwide with it, but we would like to run a test market to obtain more market information and before we launched a national sales campaign. Victor said, "Why don't you put together a proposal for a test market program and send it to us, and maybe we will try it."
>
> That seemed encouraging, but I wasn't sure how to take it. The store was like nothing I'd ever seen. Five floors of art supplies. Each floor was dedicated to some particular category of supplies, but it seemed so disorganized with very little merchandising. There were 10-foot high shelves with everything imaginable on them. No point-of-purchase displays, just paper brochures hanging off the shelves. I called Kathy and said, "This store is very different from what I expected. I don't know if they'll be able to move our product or really help us identify the right national campaign."

Kathy recalled:

> When Elaine said that Pearl, the biggest art store in the country, was inter-

ested in placing an order, it just about blew me away. It sounded as though Pearl might order as many as 2,000 Claybords as part of a test market experiment.

The two worked out a proposal letter to Pearl. Elaine passed along the good news to Charles and Barbara Ewing and suggested that perhaps together they could find a way to expand production in southwestern Colorado to fill the Pearl order. They realized, however, that this would require a substantial expansion of capacity from the 300 boards per week that Charles was currently able to produce only if he sacrificed his art work.

Looking Ahead

The venture now had office space in the incubator rent free plus $500 prize money they had received for winning the competition. If they could win the San Diego State University venture plan contest in April that would give them another $5,000. Was there anything else they should do to their venture plan to increase the odds of that happening? Criteria to be used by judges in the San Diego contest appear in Appendix 2 of this book. Those to be used by the judges in the International Moot CorpSM , which would be held in May, appear in Appendix 3 of this book. A copy of the team's plan appears in the Prize-Winning Plan case.

In addition, each of the team members had other classes, since all were full-time students aiming to graduate at the end of May. At the end of the first term Elaine had asked all team members to consider seriously whether they wanted to continue on the project as a real venture, since it would likely call for increasing investments of not only time but also money. After thinking about it David and Drew decided to part ways from the venture and pursue other interests.

The team members expected to interview for potential jobs at the campus career center, which would demand an appreciable amount of their time. One open time that would be available to produce Claybord for Pearl's test market, if the hoped-for order came, was a one-week spring break from school in early March. There seemed to be a variety of issues calling for resolution and then a considerable amount of action required. Meanwhile, there was the substantial demand of school work.

Andrew Hammoude (A)

We are four guys who are very competent technically. But none of us has any management experience. We have a prototype product and about $10,000 left from an original capitalization of $40,000. So where do we go from here?

Dr. Andrew Hammoude had prepared a draft business plan, which appears as Exhibit 1. As he had just said, and comments he had written in the draft of the plan itself indicated, there were still many important questions unanswered.

Background

He and his associates had developed a circuit board and accompanying software for IBM AT computers, which would enable them to perform "image processing." This product had sprung from a masters thesis project in electrical engineering by one of the founders, Alan Steiner. The project, suggested by Alan's supervising professor, was to design an imaging board. Alan finished the device and thought it could be marketed. Two colleagues, Tom Alexander and Jerry Stone, with whom he had worked in the University of Washington's Imaging Processing Lab, agreed. They believed the technology was the best available. Jerry Stone recalled:

We came into contact with a large number of different image processors with different capabilities, and so on. We had some applications to develop, such as things in pathology and radiology. So we looked at the available equipment, but it just wouldn't do the job.

Tom's board was a response to that. We set out to build a better workstation.

In January 1986 they began working in their spare time to develop "a state-of-the-art PC-based imaging system." Another colleague in electrical engineering, Andrew Hammoude, recalled becoming interested in the project and being invited to join.

I thought it over very carefully, because as the only full-time person in the company, I would be way out on a limb. When I listed the pros and cons on paper, a major factor for me was that I believed the technology was the best available.

Hammoude joined the venture in June 1988. Alan Steiner commented:

When we first started the company, there was a lot of work being done in radiology for PC-based imaging. Radiologists spend millions on imaging systems from GE and Phillips. Every time they need another console for their MRI machine, it's another $150,000. That console they're buying is just an archaic display with knobs and switches on it.

The Product

IMAGEsystems' product consisted basically of two parts, a circuit board for installation in I.B.M. personal computers and software to go with it, enabling a user to handle, display, and manipulate pictorial data, such as a chest X-ray or a Nuclear

Magnetic Resonance (NMR) image. Dr. Hammoude observed:

> We haven't yet beta tested it. We haven't given it to a potential customer and said, "Here, use it." When they do, they will find it is really something new.
>
> Many people are familiar with pictures generated on a computer screen, but these are referred to as "graphics" not "imaging," which our product makes possible. Graphics refers to synthesis, such as renderings artists make on televisions, like in the movie "Star Wars." With imaging the pictures originate in some other form external to the computer, in a camera perhaps. The computer may be fed image data from sensors, such as an X-ray machine, satellite signals, electron microscopic output, or astronomical telescope output. We do things like enhancing the display, transmitting it over phone lines, storing it, showing it on the screen in new ways, and performing processing functions to do such things as increasing the contrast. We might, for example, be able to improve poor quality in a photographic negative.
>
> Normally with such things as a chest X-ray, for instance, you expose the film and then stick it up in a light box to analyze it with the human optical system, eyes. A couple of doctors might look at it, be concerned about some features of it, and so forth. The same is true with CAT scans and nuclear magnetic imaging. They can, I believe, do some computer analysis on such things, but it probably requires a mainframe at present.
>
> What our system will let you do is apply computers to these images. Then they can be displayed on a TV screen without the actual physical records, which are often a great burden in terms of storage and retrieval. To compare the X-rays of a given patient at two periods six months apart is a lot of trouble. Sometimes the records get lost.
>
> Radiologists get their data either by a film sent to them by courier or by going down to the radiology lab directly. There is at present no way for them to pull an image up on a PC. Our system opens the possibility of storing the records in a remote archival setting and retrieving any of them over a phone line in a few seconds. The doctor need only dial up. That is a market we see.
>
> We know one physician who has said it would be ideal. But we would have to do development work to perfect the system before he could start using it. We would like to develop a user system that is simple and menu-driven. We want to get it to the point where users don't have to develop code but can simply modify an ASCII file to the way they like to use the system. But that takes a great deal of work, not only developing the software, but also writing the manuals to go with it—not to mention debugging, producing, marketing and all the rest.
>
> You may sometimes have a mix of both graphics and imaging combined. In an advertisement, for instance, there may be a photograph of a model, which is imaging, together with an artist-generated logo, which is graphics. When you have those two things together you may be able to use our product. But when the goal is graphics alone, the capabilities of our product are very limited.
>
> Apollo and Sun, which are workstation manufacturers, can't use our product. Other third-party suppliers provide units for them. Sun and Apollo have more powerful computers than the PC AT, which is the only computer that our product runs on. If our company is successful, of course, we'll bring out a Sun

line, a Macintosh line, and so forth.

The greatest advantage of our product is programmability. There are similar products available in the market, but only one is programmable. A second advantage of our system is the software. What we've written is, we think, much more advanced, sophisticated and broad-ranging than anything else available. For display capability and moving images around, it makes the system more user-friendly and appealing for people in graphic arts, publishing and printing, and medical diagnoses, for instance. Some other features of our system are a bit more arcane. We include a system for networking, to allow the software to interact in a computer network.

As regards price, I have some ideas. I know the minimum because I know what it costs to make the board. I know the maximum because I know what our competitors charge. But between those extremes I don't know where we ought to be. A major feature could be that we do things at low cost. Economies of scale could let us bring the cost of a system down to $5,000.

There are some markets where our advantages mean nothing. In machine vision, it isn't very interesting that we have a nice display capability. There are several areas, such as medical imaging, publishing and printing, graphic arts, and scientific research and development applications that constitute broad markets we might go after. But we have not defined a small segment of a market where the features of our product are dramatically important.

The total market for machine vision and remote sensing is very fragmented. Part of the reason for this is that images are so different. When you're formatting numerical data or words, numbers are numbers, text is text; even if you want to reformat the document in French or Spanish, it's about the same. But the nature of images is different. The NMR image is quite different in nature from an ultrasound image and from a 35mm slide in both resolution and color. It's different in the very data content itself.

We seem to be faced with a market where there is no typical case. Every single end user seems to be involved with something a bit different. I was speaking to somebody in metallurgy, and what he was doing was so specific as to be completely unique. What the metallurgist needs is a value-added retailer (VAR) who can take our board and our basic display software tools and add specific software to solve his particular application.

That sort of market, if I see it right, is completely immature. It's true that boards to run on the PC have existed for some time, but there has not been the great array of problems wanting VAR solutions, requiring a programmable board like ours. There is no main player in that market.

Competition

We've got about five competitors out there who are producing PC-based imaging systems comparable to ours. Four of those we can pretty much write off in the sense that their capabilities don't overlap with ours. They run at higher speed but have a lot less versatility. Ours is programmable. It has a little minicomputer on the board that can be programmed. A person can put new instructions into the board by writing a program for the board and feeding it into that minicomputer.

The other four companies' boards are not programmable. They have only "hard wired" boards. There is no programmable processor on them. That limits the range of what they can do, although it lets them do it faster. They can, for instance, add a couple of functions or carry out convolutions, which is a very common image processing function. But they can't do anything else. Maybe someone says, "we just got a smoothing algorithm that was developed at Stanford University. Some guy has written a paper on it, and we'd like to try it out." With our board they could put that function in, whereas with our competitors' boards, they could not.

Only one competitor really has similar capabilities to ours. That's a company called Truevision, started by some former AT&T people. Reportedly they have about 35 employees, but we have no knowledge at all about what they are up to. They have a product they call a "vistaboard" that's very good. Our performance is better than theirs because in addition to the main processor on our board we have a second auxiliary processor which carries out very high-speed image number crunching functions. We have offset the slowness that normally accompanies programmability by adding this processor, which runs very fast. So we can run things faster than the Truevision board. But we think our system is unlikely to sell on the basis of hardware alone. The difference between us and True Vision doesn't seem great enough.

However, we have more programs than they do. Hardware alone is no good unless you've got programs to drive it. The scope, breadth and sophistication of our software greatly exceeds that of our competitors. With some modification, our software could run on the Truevision board, and with some modification theirs could run on ours. Of course, neither theirs nor ours has any applicability to the other four competitors, nor does theirs have applicability to us.

Truevision has a family of products, including systems for Sun as well as the PC and various others, as we would plan to have also. They have only a distributor here locally. I plan to look into the company further, find out where they are located, what they consist of, and so forth to be able to look over their specs and make a comparison. But what specific information should I most seek? And how much time should I be willing to spend trying to get it? I'm not sure.

Only one competitor, Data Translation, is public. It has 126 employees and sales of $25 million. Two of the other companies, Datacube and Matrox, are listed in Dun's Million Dollar Directory. But there is no information given about them.

We have very little idea about industry sales and distribution. Three months ago I knew nothing about marketing and sales. After working at it since then I feel I now know less than nothing. For instance, the approach to a retailer who caters to medical imaging end-users would be very different than the approach to scientific end-users in university research environments. But what should we do about it?

We've been told several times that it's vital for us to define our market precisely and not speak in general terms about the huge number of applications for handling pictorial data. Instead we should pick something very specific. We've been trying to do that but finding it hard. We've been energetic in looking up references, going through databases, calling competitors, talking to whomever we can, and trying to get information out of marketing companies. But we haven't had much success.

The best way to get market data, some have told us, might be to use a market research company. Should we hire a marketing consulting company?

If so, how would we choose one and how much should we be willing to pay for what? We just have no idea.

We could also get market information through buying a report by Frost and Sullivan entitled "The U.S. Commercial Image Processing Market." We could get information by subscribing to Dataquest's market research services. But the Frost and Sullivan report costs $2,000, and Dataquest's service costs $12,500. We don't have enough money. Should we get the money for that, or are there better alternatives?

Some industrially experienced people are critical of those market research studies. But bear in mind that we know nothing. Maybe their forecast is not very good, but their information about the present market might be helpful. If they say that 16.4 percent of the imaging market is in printing and publishing, isn't that helpful information? Wouldn't it be useful for us to know how many vision systems one of our competitors is selling?

It seems to be commonly agreed upon by analysts of the low-cost imaging field that it is about to grow explosively. The underlying reason is that the handling of image data is very pervasive in our society. People deal with visual information constantly. It is very clear that with numerical and text data, computers have taken over much of the human handling of those sorts of data.

The reason it has not happened with image data is the technical difficulty and expense of designing systems to handle it. But now the costs are coming down for things like the high-density memory needed to store images and the powerful processors needed to deal with it. For the first time, we are approaching a point where it will be possible to put together a non-trivial imaging system—one that can do something meaningful and useful with images—for less than $10,000.

Everybody knows this, and many expect the field will explode soon. The Frost and Sullivan estimate of the imaging processing market for 1990, we hear, is $1.58 billion. So, undoubtedly, there are other companies looking at it. Hearsay has it that there are several heavyweights out there, like IBM and Apple, looking at it and likely to enter.

Management Concerns

Right now there is really nobody out there who is the image processing company. We would like to be that company, dominating our market segments, known and respected for producing high-quality products, personnel, documentation, and support. We'd like to be a prestigious, thriving, profitable company at the cutting edge of innovation; the company that people try to beat. We are not yet thinking in terms of number of employees and sales. We are thinking only in terms of what we want the company image to be, and what we want to do. We want to be a presence in the image processing field.

If achieving our goals means we will be a hundred million dollar company in five years, then that's what we'd like to be. If it means we should have 80 employees, then that is what we would like to have. But we have been cautioned against the line of thinking that aims for sales and employment targets. We haven't begun to think in terms of pure profit making. But we're flexible.

Dr. Hammoude said his main concern at present was how to move ahead with management of the startup. The business plan draft that he had prepared included in its text some questions he and other founders thought needed answering. (See Exhibit 1.) Hammoude observed that none of the founders was experienced in management, commenting:

Of our specific business concerns, the first one of all is marketing. We realize that this is very important, and that the success or failure of the venture depends on how skillfully we market.

We have a bunch of ideas, but no discriminatory ability. For instance, we could place an ad. We could do a direct mailing. We could recruit sales reps. We could try to find distributors. We could try to generate some kind or royalty or licensing agreement with some big-time, heavy-duty marketing outfit. But we don't know what is the smartest or the best thing to do, and we don't know how to find out.

A second thing is the financial picture. Right now, we are doing everything on a shoestring. We are four guys working out of a spare bedroom in Renton. The other three are moonlighting, and working on the company evenings and weekends. I'm the only one who's full time. We're doing everything on the cheap. I run around xeroxing things and stand in line at the post office, sending information out.

That saves us money and lets us retain all the equity in the company. But in terms of efficiency, we're just a bunch of clowns. When we send out information, I hand write the envelopes, stuff them personally and stand in line at the post office. When I stand there, I think to myself, 'I just don't see the CEO of IBM doing this.'

Is this OK? We are spending three hours a day, three of us in cars, commuting to Renton to work together. The most massive inefficiency is that three guys are moonlighting. Instead of spending 16 hours a day, which they should, working on the company, they are spending three hours a day plus the weekend.

One thought is that we might place an ad, get a couple of orders, sell a couple of systems, take the money we make from that and build a couple more. If that is going to work, fine. The orders come in. We make some money, then gradually scale things up. Then we can rent office space somewhere and hire a secretary.

The other alternative, it seems, would be to "do it right." Get a quarter million, a half million or a million bucks, from where we're not sure, give up somewhere between 25 percent and 50 percent of the company, move to offices, hire a manager, bring in a marketing consulting company, pay them $30,000 for the consultation, pay an advertising agency another $30,000 to design an ad, place the ad, design brochures, manufacture brochures. Pay for a mailing list. Mail the stuff out.

The question is, what's the best way to do it?

It seems to us that one major milestone would be getting the business plan into a condition where, with a straight face we could show it to someone and they could read it with a straight face.

A second would be to get the venture capital we need. Until then we need some sort of interim financing. It's going to take a while for these things to happen; for us to get our act together. And in the meantime we have expenses. The more the act of getting the business together is costly, the more an immediate milestone is to get some cash.

If inevitably we're just not going to make it working out of a spare bedroom in Renton this way, I want to know now. If we should go big, how do we do it? What's the best way to get venture capital? How much should we get? Those are the kind of things we'd like to know.

Beyond that, what should we do about administration, taxation, legal aspects? I've done the rough of a business plan (attached as Exhibit 1) working from a guide on business plans from the

Small Business Administration. But I don't know what it means. It would be nice to have somebody tell us what is important. What else should be in the plan and how should I get it there?

We started with about $40,000 pooled from family and friends. About $22,000 was spent to work up the design and creation of the prototype, which was done by a company in California. We could manufacture more like it without much retooling cost. And we have about $10,000 of our original capital left. None of us is taking any salary.

We know that since we lack experience, we need help in finance, sales, marketing and overall management. But which do we need the most? Or should we go out right now and hire a sales and marketing person and use that as a way to get financing? Or should we look for a financial expert first to get the money, and then hire two marketing people? Or should we be able to find one good management person who would take care of both needs?

Finally, as regards financing, we know we need money but we are a bit confused, still, about the various possible sources. We've heard there are alternatives like venture capital, or corporate partners and private investors. Somebody I spoke to on the phone recently asked, "Why don't you go public now?" Was that a joke?

EXHIBIT 1   Draft Business Plan (including some questions by Andrew Hammoude)

BUSINESS PLAN WORKING DRAFT
IMAGEsystems, Inc.
September 25, 1988

IMAGEsystems is a start-up company, and is involved in the development, manufacturing and sales of high-technology computer imaging hardware, together with appropriate support software. The following is a statement of our business plans for the next year of operation.

1. PERSONNEL

IMAGEsystems presently consists of four persons: Tom Alexander, Andrew Hammoude, Alan Steiner and Jerry Stone. The company was founded in January 1988. All four of us have advanced degrees in electrical engineering, and together represent an extraordinary concentration of skill and expertise in hardware design, software development and image processing technology.

Tom Alexander is currently working toward his Ph. D. degree in computer architecture at the University of Washington and has extensive experience in both hardware and software design.

Andrew Hammoude recently completed his Ph.D. degree at the University of Washington; his area of research was computer analysis of medical ultrasound images.

EXHIBIT 1 (continued)

Alan Steiner graduated from the University of Washington with a master's degree in electrical engineering. His research project was the design of a hardware imaging system, of which our first product is the direct descendant.

Jerry Stone also graduated from the University of Washington with a master's degree in electrical engineering. His thesis topic was the design of a machine vision system for automated inspection of printed circuit boards.

2. MANAGEMENT

None of the four principals has any management experience. We are well aware that this is a major problem, and are actively trying to deal with this lack of expertise.

To determine which management issues we should be most concerned with, and how we should deal with them, we have met with several institutions, such as the Small Business Administration, the Small Business Development Center, and the University of Washington Small Business Institute, which offer free consultations. This has led us to several other sources of management guidance. Two we think most likely to be useful to us are:

A. The M.I.T. Enterprise Forum
B. The Northwest Venture Group

Both of these offer management critique and guidance services at nominal cost; the M.I.T. Enterprise Forum through their Start-up Forums, and the Northwest Venture Group through their Venture Advisory Panels. We are planning to make use of both of these services, and hope that this will provide the sort of detailed and focused advice we need.

Some of the specific questions that we'd like to answer are: How should we deal with our lack of management know-how? Should we hire a manager? If so, how? Or would we be better off pulling in a management consulting company? How would we go about choosing a suitable consultant?

3. PRODUCT DESCRIPTION

Our first product is an image processing and display system. This consists of a single computer board, which plugs into an IBM PC/AT or any compatible, together with a complete software support system. Together, the hardware and software give the PC the ability to display, manipulate, and process images with a high degree of flexibility, thereby in effect converting the PC into a general-purpose imaging workstation. Some of the specific capabilities of the system are as follows:

Display: Display of multiply overlapping images; image zoom, pan and scroll; instant replay of stored image sequence; image annotation; superimposition of color graphics.

Visual improvement: Contrast enhancement; filtering (e.g., edge-enhancement); image averaging (e.g., for noise reduction); pseudo-coloring.

Storage and transmission: Electronic storage and transfer; image teleconferencing; image compression and decompression.

EXHIBIT 1   (continued)

Analysis: Histogram generation; statistical analysis; motion analysis; correlation, template matching, feature extraction; measurement.

Miscellaneous: Image addition, subtraction and convolution; image cropping and compositing; image warping.

A detailed description of the entire system can be found in the Product Overview, which accompanies this business plan. The following is a summary of the major distinctive features of our system.

1.   The processing hardware is <u>fully programmable</u>. It can be programmed to carry out virtually any image processing operation. This means that the user can write his own application-specific programs and is not restricted to the software library that we provide. Furthermore, our software system has been designed to allow the user to carry out this software expansion very easily.

2.   The processing hardware includes <u>two</u> programmable processors. In addition to the main system processor, there is a second, auxiliary processor, which carries out computationally intensive operations at very high speed. This second processor allows our system to operate at the substantially higher speed than comparable products from the competition.

3.   The hardware includes high-speed image transfer circuitry, which allows images to be displayed and manipulated with extreme versatility.

4.   The hardware is easily expandable; additional hardware devices (such as extra memory) can be incorporated into the system without difficulty.

5.   The hardware is constructed by means of **surface mount technology**. Surface mounted boards are easier to manufacture, allow higher operating speeds and are inherently more reliable than the more conventional through-hole assembly process.

6.   The software system allows **multiprocessing**—that is, the system can carry out several tasks simultaneously. For example, the user can initiate a lengthy series of processing operations on a particular image, and meanwhile continue to use the system for other things.

7.   Images are displayed in a fully **windowed** environment. That is, different images can be overlapped with each other on the display, allowing several different images to be viewed simultaneously. The windowing system allows extreme flexibility in the manipulation of images on the display.

8.   Extensive software support libraries are available with the system, including a complete repertoire of image display and manipulation functions.

9.   The software system allows easy expansion; it has been designed to allow the user to include additional programs without difficulty.

In summary, both hardware and software represent state-of-the-art technology. The hardware architecture incorporates several unique design features and is supported by a sophisticated software system. The result is a versatile, powerful, and interactive image processing system.

EXHIBIT 1 (continued)

Product Expansion

The above base system allows abundant opportunity for product expansion. We have already designed a digitizer board to work in conjunction with the base system and are planning several other expansion products, such as a memory expansion board, a high-speed processor board, and a second-generation, higher resolution imaging board.

4. COMPETITION

Various companies are currently producing image processing systems. Among these companies there are five with products similar to ours in terms of capability and price, which therefore represent our closest competition. These five companies, and the price of their most comparable systems, are:

Data Translation	$6690
Datacube	$9500
ITI	$6490
Matrox	$5995
Truevision	$5995

Comparisons among imaging systems can be made on the basis of many factors. However, the three most critical issues are:

- The versatility of the hardware
- The processing speed of the hardware
- The available software support

In terms of hardware versatility, IMAGEsystems and Truevision have a major advantage over the other four manufacturers. The systems from IMAGEsystems and Truevision are based on programmable processors, whereas the systems from Data Translation, Datacube, ITI and Matrox do not contain a programmable processor. The range of processing functions that these latter systems from IMAGEsystems and Truevision offer are fully programmable and can carry out virtually any image processing operation.

On the other hand, the four non-programmable systems have a clear advantage in terms of processing speed. Although their repertoire of processing operations is very limited, they can carry out these operations much faster than the two programmable systems; in fact, they can do operations in real time, which the programmable systems require several seconds to complete.

In a nutshell, IMAGEsystems and Truevision have designed for versatility, while the other manufacturers have designed for speed. Which of these two factors is the more important depends entirely on the application. The systems from IMAGEsystems and Truevision are not suitable for applications that require true real-time processing. On the other hand, the systems from Data Translation, Datacube, ITI and Matrox are almost completely useless for general-purpose image processing applications. This means that these latter systems address a market that is largely different to that addressed by IMAGEsystems and Truevision. For this reason, we consider Truevision to be our most serious rival.

EXHIBIT 1 (continued)

Since each system is fully programmable, there is little to differentiate IMAGEsystems from Truevision in terms of versatility. In terms of speed, however, IMAGEsystems has a distinct advantage; the dual processor design allows our system to operate at a substantially higher speed than the Truevision system.

In terms of software support, IMAGEsystems has a major advantage. The scope and sophistication of our software system greatly exceeds that of any of our competitors. None of the above companies has multiprocessing or windowing as part of their software system, and none allows the sort of flexibility and expandability that is possible with our system.

In summary, the versatility of our product greatly exceeds that of all our competitors, except Truevision. However, these competitors are able to carry out a limited range of processing operations at a considerably higher speed than IMAGEsystems. Our system is able to operate at significantly higher speed than Truevision, our nearest rival in terms of versatility. In terms of software, IMAGEsystems has a major lead over all competitors.

5. PRODUCTION

Manufacturing

Manufacture and assembly of the boards will be carried out by SCI Manufacturing in California; we will acquire the necessary parts and ship them to SCI for assembly. Availability of parts is, therefore, an extremely important issue for IMAGEsystems; inability to acquire parts would leave us unable to satisfy our orders. We will deal with this by maintaining adequate inventory of long-delivery items. At present, we have all the parts required for the first system already on hand. Long-delivery parts for the following 11 systems are on order, and we expect to take delivery of these well before our first production run. SCI manufacturing time is approximately three weeks per production run, so that, barring unavailability of parts, we can ship orders in a timely manner.

All software development will be carried out by IMAGEsystems. All documentation will be written in-house by IMAGEsystems.

Quality Assurance

The hardware will be tested at several stages during manufacture. Each board will first be subjected to a bare board test before any electrical components are mounted to make sure the board itself is correct. All components will then be mounted, and the complete assembled board subjected to a component test; this will ensure that each individual component is functioning correctly. These two tests will be carried out by SCI, and any errors corrected by them.

The completed boards will then be shipped to IMAGEsystems, and we will carry out a functional test by running hardware diagnostic programs to ensure that the system, as a whole, is functioning correctly. Any errors will be corrected either locally, or in-house by IMAGEsystems.

How should the software be tested?
Should we carry out beta testing? How?
Should we offer a warranty? What will be the terms?

EXHIBIT 1 (continued)

Distribution

The entire system (hardware, software, and documentation) is sufficiently small and light that packaging and shipping are not major considerations. Delivery will be by UPS or Federal Express.

6. PRICING

The direct costs to deliver a single system are as follows:

Parts	$1,200
Assembly	(1,300)
Testing	(100)
Other costs	
TOTAL	(2,650)

The price for a complete system will be $7, 995. This is distinctly higher than the prices of similar systems from our competitors. However, we believe that this is easily justifiable given the significant advantages of our system, so that even at this price, we can successfully capture a portion of the imaging market. If this should prove not to be the case, this price allows room for price cutting while still maintaining profits.

7. MARKETING

The operations our system can carry out are useful in virtually any application that involves pictorial information, so that the potential market for this device is vast. Some of the applications that involve the handling of image data are:

Medical: X-ray radiology; ultrasound imaging; CAT scanning; magnetic resonance imaging; positron emission tomography; thermography; electron microscopy; optical microscopy; dentistry; 3-D reconstruction.

Scientific: Inspection and quality assurance; tolerance verification; missing parts detection; robotic; object location and manipulation.

Graphic Arts: Computer art; image overlay and compositing; animation.

Miscellaneous: Teleconferencing; security, access control; signature verification, fingerprint analysis; anti-counterfeiting.

Among these applications there are several broad markets for our system:

1.   End-user. This refers to someone who wishes to buy the hardware board and support software alone. This implies that the person already owns a PC system, and now wants to add advanced image handling capability. Typically this would be someone in an R & D environment, either industrial or academic.

EXHIBIT 1 (continued)

2.   Turn-key system user. This refers to someone who has a specific and immediate need for image handling capability, but who does not have the time, inclination, or know-how to assemble and configure the required system piecemeal. This user wants to have a complete working system shipped, one that can be operated without requiring any particular knowledge of its inner workings.

3.   The OEM market. This refers to a company that is manufacturing a system, for example a turn-key system as described above, of which our hardware is an integral part.

In addition to these major markets, two other potential markets are worth mentioning:

4.   Standard software only. Our standard software is general and portable to other systems, so it does not necessarily require our hardware to be useful.

5.   Contract programming. In the case of any of the above markets, the user may require high-level, application-specific software in addition to the more general standard-system software.

Our initial marketing effort will be directed towards the end-user and OEM markets. The last two markets mentioned above, though potentially important in the future, are very small in comparison to the gigantic size of the first three markets. Furthermore, any attempt to address these markets would divert effort away from the continued development of our existing product, and at this stage we cannot afford this distraction.

The turn-key market would require that we be able to provide service and maintenance for the installed system. This is practical only in the Seattle area, and even there, the drain on our manpower is very undesirable at this stage in our operation. Furthermore, supplying the turn-key market would greatly complicate our inventory, packaging, freight and insurance requirements.

In the case of the end-user and OEM markets, however, we can ship the system simply and rapidly and can guarantee quality by means of a warranty. Furthermore, both of these markets can be reached by means of the same marketing strategy, which is not true of the turn-key market. Our initial marketing effort, therefore, is simplest when directed at end-user and OEM.

Marketing Plan

At present we do not have a coherent marketing plan, and this is one of the issues that we hope to get assistance with from the two previously mentioned advisory services.

However, we do have several ideas that we intend to put forward for criticism:

1.   We are planning to place an advertisement in *ESD* (*Electronic System Design*) magazine. This magazine is most closely concerned with the sorts of imaging applications for which our system has been designed. All of our competitors advertise regularly in this magazine.

2.   We are planning to attend "Electronic Imaging West '89" in San Jose, California in March. This trade show is an ideal forum for presentation of our system. All of our competitors will certainly be in attendance.

EXHIBIT 1 (continued)

3.   Should we do direct mailing? It is possible to buy mailing lists from *ESD* magazine and other sources, consisting (supposedly) of persons who are likely to be interested in our system.

4.   Should we recruit sales representatives? If so, how?

5.   We have decided that selling via distributors is not practical because of the large price mark-up they will require. Is this a reasonable conclusion?

6.   If possible, we will publish an article on our system, in *ESD* magazine or elsewhere. We published an article in *ESD* in March 1988, and this generated quite a lot of interest in our system.

7.   We plan to make a demonstration of our system on request to any seriously interested persons in the Puget Sound area. Since the entire system is easily portable, this is quite practical.

8.   Should we pursue some sort of licensing or royalty arrangement with some organization that already has a powerful marketing infrastructure? What are we talking about? How do these arrangements get set up and how do they work?

We would like to get answers to all of these questions.

Some minor marketing activity has taken place already. As previously mentioned, we published an article in *ESD* in March, and this generated approximately 95 inquiries requesting information about our system. In April we attended "Electronic Imaging West '88" in Anaheim California, and this also generated numerous requests for information. Finally, Texas Instruments wrote our system up in the summer issue of their Pixel Perspectives newsletter, and this too resulted in several inquiries. We have responded to all of these inquiries by sending out a package of information about our system.

8. SCHEDULE

10/1/88	Manufacturing prototype completely functional
12/1/88	Software version 2.0 ready for release
12/1/88	New brochure ready for mailing
12/1/88	First ad runs in *ESD* magazine
1/1/89	Documentation completed

9. FINANCIAL PLAN

To date, July 1, 1988, the following costs have already been incurred:

Parts	1,814.63
Prototype	17,114.25
Legal fees	1,249.70
Office supplies	672.42
Telephone	660.25
Trade shows	792.00
Travel	1,795.28
Advertising	978.34
Freight	355.09
Miscellaneous	123.17
TOTAL	25,555.13

EXHIBIT 1 (concluded)

Costs over next six months (7/1/88 - 12/31/88):

Prototype		4,000.00
Parts (first 5 systems)		6,000.00
Assembly (first 5 systems)		(6,500.00)
Testing (first 5 systems)		(500.00)
Long-delivery inventory		2,832.50
Advertising	Ad design	(1,000.00)
	Ad placement (ESD)	2,450.00
	Brochure design	(1,250.00)
	Brochure production	(2,000.00)
	Brochure mailing	(100.00)
Documentation		(1,000.00)
Packaging		
Telephone		650.00
Office Supplies		(500.00)
Miscellaneous		1,000.00
Total		(30,000.00)

Costs over following six months (1/1/89 - 6/30/89):

1989 Trade Show	Booth rental	1,188.00
	Booth design	1,000.00
	Travel	396.00
	Hotel, per diem	480.00
Capital equipment	Logic analyzer	4,000.00
	Oscilloscope	2,000.00
	Laser printer	1,200.00
	SMD rework station	5,000.00
	DSP Assembler	500.00
	GSP C compiler	1,000.00
	Office equipment	1,000.00
Salaries		4,800.00
Telephone		1,300.00
Office supplies		500.00
Miscellaneous		1,000.00
Total		25,284.00

Are these figures realistic? This is a "shoe-string" budget, with three of the four princi-pals moonlighting, the fourth working for nothing, and everything being done on the cheap. Is this a realistic way of going about things, or are we heading for disaster? What is the current dollar value of the AT-based image processing market? How much of this market can we expect to capture?

Bill Foster (A)

Bill Foster turned his desk calendar to February 25, 1980 and penciled in "Meeting with venture capital firms—Boston." In six weeks he would begin negotiations with two different venture capital groups in an attempt to raise up to $2,000,000 for starting a new computer firm, Alta Computing Systems. He expected it would take at least two years to prepare the first product for sale. Within the next six weeks, Bill explained, he needed to accomplish two specific tasks to be ready for the negotiations:

1. Complete the pro forma statements in the business plan; to date, financial issues had been discussed only in general terms and amounts.

2. Map a strategy with his three cofounders that would place them in the best possible bargaining position for striking a deal with the venture capital firms.

Bill's goal was to create a major computer company within five years, a company that specialized in producing an extremely reliable system for experienced data processing users, such as Fortune 1000 firms. He went on to add that without venture capital support the prospects that the business would ever get started were slim:

The venture capital market is a very close-knit group. Once a major venture capital firm turns you down, they might all turn you down.

He had spent the last six months inquiring about the venture capital market and recruiting a management team with a proven track record in developing computer hardware and software. Bill was currently living off $30,000 in savings which would be exhausted by summer. Consequently, he said, getting cash as soon as possible was essential for starting the business. Otherwise, he might be forced to put the idea aside and return to work to support his family. His three partners had either quit their jobs or announced their intention to do so. Bill said he hoped to have from 10 to 20 people working for Alta by June of 1980.

We're going to put together the pro formas, working off some basic assumptions and a general idea of how much money we'll need. Then we'll take the business plan to two groups. One will be made up of four venture capital firms in New York. The other will include a company in San Francisco, one in Connecticut and the lead firm here in Boston. The meeting on the twenty-fifth is with the second group, and I'm not sure what to expect. We've never been through this before.

There are a lot of issues to consider. For example, how much ownership should the venture capitalists versus the founders get? What should the price of the stock be? How do you work out different prices for different classes of stock? And how do we position ourselves for the possibility that we may later have to go back for more money? We're going to need several million dol-

*lars of capital before we can call our-
selves a profitable company, but we
probably won't get it all up front. Finally, what criteria should we use for
choosing the appropriate source and deal
for capital?*

Personal Background

Bill Foster grew up in California and
graduated from San Jose State in 1966 with
a bachelor's degree in math. Following
graduation, he went to work for Lockheed
in the San Francisco Bay Area. He completed a graduate degree in applied math
at Santa Clara University while working
for Lockheed and continued night school
until 1973, when he also received his MBA
from the same institution.

Bill reflected on his coursework in the
business school:

> *The last course I took was on entre-
> preneurship, and the professor told us
> that the only way we would ever use his
> course or our MBA was if we went out
> and started our own business. Looking
> back at the last six months, he's prob-
> ably right.*

In 1969, the Federal government canceled two major military projects, which
sent the aerospace industry into a tailspin.
The events prompted Bill to look for other
work and resulted in his entry into the
computer industry:

> *I used to drive right by this place
> called Hewlett-Packard on the way to
> work, and I really didn't know what it
> was. So I decided to stop in one day and
> apply for a job—and they hired me.*

Bill went to work for Hewlett-Packard
(HP) in the company's then fledgling data
products division. During the next seven
years, he rose from programmer to engineering manager of a computing systems
group. As manager, he was responsible for

Hewlett-Packard's research and development for computer system hardware and
software. About one-third of his time was
spent talking with prospective customers
to assure them that the product being considered was technically sound and able to
perform the desired tasks.

In 1976, he was recruited by a rapidly
growing New England-based minicomputer company to become the firm's vice
president for software development. Bill
recalled that the opportunity of working
for the president of a smaller but faster-
growing company appealed to him, as did
the move to the East Coast:

> *I'd always lived in the Bay Area and
> thought that going to New England
> would be a very educational experience
> for both my family and me.*

Over the next three years, Bill established a reputation within the company as
a good manager and became an officer of
the firm. He said this work was rewarding,
and the salary and stock option benefits allowed him to accumulate nearly $50,000 in
savings.

The Decision to Start a Company

Bill recalled that he first began thinking
of starting his own company in 1978. After
returning from a business trip in England
the following May, he told his wife that he
wanted to quit his job and attempt to form
a new business. This meant that he would
give up the salary and prestige that went
with being a vice-president of a Fortune
500 company. Since the firm had a restricted stock option plan, he would also
lose the right to exercise the options which
he had on about 800 shares.

The exercise price averaged $13 per
share, compared with the current price of
$70 on the open market. His annual salary
was in the $50,000 range. Rumors within
the company included speculation that he
had been fired, since "they thought no one

in their right mind would be crazy enough to walk away from the position and benefits I had." Within three weeks after returning from Europe, Bill submitted his resignation. He continued to work for another three weeks and left the firm near the end of July 1979.

Bill talked about why he decided to leave a job which he said he enjoyed very much:

I guess I'll never really know exactly why it happened the way it did. I had been thinking for over a year about starting a company. I tried to think about what I could do, but that didn't lead anywhere. I had no ideas that seemed worthwhile. Maybe I also didn't have the guts to do it. It didn't seem smart to leave the great job I had, making all that money and so forth.

But I knew a lot of other people who had gone off, started companies and become very successful. All of them were high technology-related. Most of the founders of Tandem Computer had worked for me when I was at HP. I knew many of the founders of Apple, too. I was somewhat envious of these people who had left other jobs and gotten involved with start-ups. It seemed to me that technically I was their equal. Yet my conclusion was that it just wasn't the right time for me to take the plunge; maybe never would be, and I had no ideas for what to do.

I almost feel foolish saying this, but when I went on another business trip to Europe in June of 1979, the first night I was there I woke up about three o'clock in the morning and had just decided to do it. When I got back home to Massachusetts, I was going to quit my job and try to start a company. It's almost as if I told myself I was really stupid not to have done it a year ago. I must have been thinking about it somewhere in the back of my mind, but I wasn't really

aware of it. I called my wife on the phone the next day and told her I was going to do it. She kind of said, "Oh, yeah, I've heard this before." When I got home, I talked some more about it, and then she knew I was going to do it.

I can't really explain why it was, but all of a sudden, I started thinking that the worst possible thing that could happen would be to wake up one day when I was 70 years old, look back over my life, and say to myself, "Gee, you never even tried to do it." I was 35, I was not being particularly challenged by my job, and I was envious of my friends who had gone off and done something similar. I finally realized that all of the constraints I had were basically artificial. I felt that I would be very disappointed with myself if I didn't at least attempt this...that all my options would be closed.

Once that happened, it was an easy decision. I had no qualms about it. Financially, it could have been a tough decision, but it wasn't. I had a lot of stock options that I had to leave behind. I didn't have a lot of money. It cost about $30,000 for our family of five to live on for a year. So my wife and I figured that if I treated this as an investment in myself, we could withdraw $600 a week and in a year's time, the business would either be on its way or would have flopped. I would reserve another $20,000 in savings to invest as my share of the equity. We would have to use the money we'd saved for our children's college, which was probably the biggest hang-up. But I had worked my way through school; if they had to work their way through, they could do it. That was not reason enough not to go ahead with the plan.

Starting to Look for Capital

The first step Bill took after leaving the

computer firm was to contact a friend whom he thought might be able to steer him to a venture capital firm. Bill explained that he knew nothing about that part of the financial community, but he "had a hunch" that there was a lot of money to finance a business such as the one he had in mind. The friend referred him to a Boston-based venture capital company. Bill described the experience:

> Three days after I quit my job, I went to talk to these people. I had no business plan, no partners. I didn't know if I should start the company on the East or the West Coast. I wasn't even sure what I was going to make, but I did know it would have something to do with general-purpose computer systems, since that's what I was familiar with. I was selling myself on my reputation as a technical manager.
>
> One of the venture capitalists and I spent two or three hours over lunch just basically talking about money being available, what they looked for, what they expected in terms of business planning and all the rest. I was impressed with the amount of time this partner was spending with me. He was very helpful.
>
> When I said I planned to do this in California, since that is where I was from originally, he gave me an introduction to two West Coast firms. They all owe each other favors. "You let me in this deal, and I may let you in another." They all talk to each other all the time. Besides, to do a large-scale start-up that might require as much as $10 million, they would have to collaborate with several other firms. They would not do that big a deal alone.
>
> I also found out that many venture funds normally do not do start-ups. They're not going to invest in three people and a briefcase where there's no track record. They ask, "Can this guy who's worked inside a big company do it

> on his own? Can he hire the people, can he meet his schedules? Can he do it without constant changes in direction?" Still, after I had visited three of the top venture capital firms in the business, I had the impression that if one of them would take the lead, the others might join in.

Developing the Business Concept

Bill decided to spend the next two months outlining the type of business he was going to start and developing a marketing strategy that would set his company apart from the competition. He spent the rest of July and August researching the computer market in search of a niche. In September he visited several friends in California from Hewlett-Packard. The conversation about computers came to Tandem, which focused on applications where failure could not be tolerated.

> These might be at banks for automatic tellers or funds transfers. Banks can lose literally tens of thousands of dollars in interest in the time it takes to get a failed computer back up. Other applications are in stock exchanges, airlines and medical systems. There are quite a few.
>
> Tandem has done very well, with sales of $24 million after only three years in business. They have a nice niche, but there's no competition for them, no similar product.

He began to look for ways to improve on Tandem's product (see list in Exhibit 1) and to write a business plan that would allow investors to see what he was trying to accomplish (see Exhibit 2). The type of product to be manufactured would be a commercial computer system in the "super mini" category for the end user market. Sales would be aimed at selected Fortune 1000 firms and independent system houses

(ISOs). Bill commented:

> Today, the market for commercial computer systems in the $100,000 to $500,000 class is huge. It's expected to increase over the next five years from $3.5 billion to $20 billion. So, if we can get 1 percent of that market, we're a $200 million dollar company in five years.
>
> Our problem isn't going to be in getting orders. Our problem is focusing on who we want to sell to and where geographically. The key factor in this industry is not what you're going to be making but how you carry it out.

Likely competition, according to Bill, would include Tandem Computer, Prime Computer, Digital Equipment, IBM and Hewlett Packard. A major advantage, he expected, was that he would be able to design fresh architecture while his established competitors would be held back from doing so by the investment they had in existing designs. This would put him in a better position to incorporate the latest technical advances.

Searching for Support

By October 1979 Bill Foster had developed a general business plan to use in "prospecting" for venture capital. He met with two San Francisco firms his Boston contact had suggested, and encountered much advice but no offers to invest.

> I found myself working for the venture capitalists. They would say, "Do this; do that; go find a marketing person." That wasn't my objective. My objective was to work for myself. I found that I was wasting my time, doing the wrong things. I was constantly talking to the venture groups, looking for lawyers and CPAs.
>
> One group tried to get me to join

with another entrepreneur who was also trying to start a company. He had a lot more experience and had already made a lot of money in the computer industry. They got us together and it was just like oil and water. There was no way I could see myself working <u>for</u> that guy and it would have been hard to work <u>with</u> him. Because of his experience, I was sure he expected to be my superior.

> This was really tough because I <u>knew</u> he was going to get his money. With his record, the venture capitalists were going to invest in whatever he wanted to do. I told my wife it would be really disappointing if two or three years out he would have built a really successful company while I never got off the ground. She said, "Look, what you want to do is run your own company. Don't start to lower your goals." So I called him up and said I wasn't interested. He said I was making a big mistake.
>
> Actually, my biggest mistake was to think that the venture capitalists were going to invest in me, Bill Foster. There's nobody who's going to put $2 million dollars on one individual; it's just too risky.

He attempted to contact old acquaintances at HP to see if they might be interested in joining him in the venture. Bill recalled what he found:

> I went to San Francisco with a list of 30 people whom I had been associated with and felt would be good to have involved in the company. I discovered there were only two still with HP. The others had gone on to start their own business or work for entrepreneurs. The start-up activity in California had been going strong from 1976 to 1979 while I was gone. It didn't take me too long to realize that getting a team together in California would be tough.

By November, Bill was still in California trying to assemble a team and attract interest in the financial community. He explained his frustration at the lack of progress:

> The venture firms all wanted to talk to everybody I tried to recruit. They were testing me, which I didn't realize. They wanted to see if Foster could attract those people. They'd say, "We may invest in Bill Foster. What do you think of his venture? Why would you join hirn? How would your job function?" They were really conducting job interviews! Remember, I knew nothing about raising money. It appeared that this was the way you do it. I didn't know any better.

Taking Another Tack

Bill finally decided to go back to New England and try starting his business there by lining up his management team <u>first</u> and then going to the venture capitalists. The traveling expenses to California had eaten into his weekly $600 withdrawals, and the real estate market had collapsed to the point where selling and buying a house was a difficult prospect at either end of the country. Added to that was the desire of his family to stay in New England where they had made new friends and enjoyed the change of seasons absent in San Francisco.

The major risk he saw in abandoning California as a start-up location was in breaking off discussions with the one venture firm with whom he had been meeting. Bill explained that this might destroy his credibility among such investors, since they didn't seem to like people shopping around for the best deal.

A number of calls came from friends who were curious about his progress to date. He contacted one of these friends who had started his own software firm af-

ter working with Bill at the computer company in New England. Their conversation led to an agreement where the friend would become the vice president of software development for Bill's prospective company, Alta. The friend had software developed that could be used for the venture and said he would provide it on a deferred payment basis—that is, if and when Alta became profitable, the friend would get paid for the software which was used.

Bill recalled his surprise at being able to bring the friend on as part of the management team:

> My original plan when I approached him was to buy some of his software for my product. But when he learned what I was trying to do, he said, "Wow! this really sounds neat. I've always wanted to get into a manufacturing company instead of just a service company. I'll throw in my resources with you."

Bill was able to locate another individual who had some experience in hardware and a third, who was not in California, for marketing. Three days before Christmas, he got a telephone call from his partner who would be handling hardware engineering. The person had called to tell Bill he was backing out—his present employer had offered him a financial package that was too attractive to turn down. Bill's response reflected the setback:

> That was a real blow. I had told one of the venture capital firms I was keeping in touch with that I was back to two people. I was convinced that the whole project was going to fall through. Things just weren't going well at all as we moved into 1980.

Bill contacted an individual who had an outstanding reputation in the hardware side of the industry. He admitted that there was little chance of convincing the person to come with Alta. Even so, he arranged a meeting with the man and the software vice-president. In Bill's words, "They hit it off. Both had respect for each other. What looked like disaster last month suddenly turned out to be good luck."

With a management team in place, Bill contacted a number of venture capital firms to line up meetings to discuss possible financing. Two groups expressed interest over the phone and agreed to meet with him in the near future. The Boston-led group could sit down with the founders in February and had technical expertise on board to understand the product aspects of the venture. The New York group wanted to bring in a California-based consultant to look at the business plan. Since the consultant was booked up with other commitments, the earliest that Bill could meet with this group of venture capitalists would likely be in March.

With this in mind, Bill set up a February appointment with the first group and thought about some of the advice he had received in the last six months:

> *Various people have told me that the most important thing in raising venture capital is to have a good relationship with your investors. They say that's more important than the terms worked out in the deal.*
>
> *Another bit of advice I'd heard fre quently was that venture firms are somewhat like sheep. If you get one group to follow you, the others will be right behind, looking for a piece of the action. How you translate those observations into your negotiating strategy, I'm not sure.*

Projecting Financial Requirements for the Venture

Bill's experience from previous work in product development helped him imagine how long it would take to complete the first product and what would be required in staffing and money. He listed assumptions for creating pro forma financial statements for a business plan. (See Exhibit 3). He said the key factor during the first two years would be money spent on research and development (R & D). He planned to spend a fixed amount on it until sales were high enough that 6 to 10 percent of sales would cover it, and after that keep it at the high end of this range. He expected that most R & D costs would be tied up in salary, and that purchases of computer equipment wouldn't be significant until the second or third year.

His estimated current costs for software development professionals averaged $50,000 per year and for hardware development engineers averaged $80,000 including overhead expenses such as telephone, rent, and fringe benefits. Staffing would be primarily engineers until sales commenced. Then he would develop a sales force, adding administrative staff incrementally as needed. A bank would handle payroll paperwork and pay all employees from the first day the firm was in business.

Bill had received conflicting advice on how to show the year-end balance for cash on hand. An accountant suggested that he "pay by account" by getting more money in the first round than would actually be needed. He suggested that Bill might put $400,000 as the year-end figure to show the venture capital firms that he was being "frugal" in his spending. Venture capital professionals had mentioned that they didn't like giving out any more than was actually needed for funding during a given period.

He decided to construct pro forma statements for help in obtaining sufficient cash flow for operations and product development until sales could sustain needed working capital. He expected to break even about one year from the first shipment, although he wasn't sure when the exact timing of the first shipment would occur. Although he had yet to secure office space, he estimated that he would need approximately 10,000 square feet for the development phase.

As a general guide in forecasting, Bill decided to use the financial statements of similar computer firms. This would include Tandem, Prime Computer and Data General, among others. He expected that the margins and percentage ratios for the various accounts would likely be similar, even though the dollar volumes would be less than these firms. Percentages would likely differ in the first portion of the five-year projections, since there would be little sales, if any.

Because Alta was aiming for the end-user market as an OEM (original equipment maker), Bill figured marketing expenses would be a slightly higher percentage of total costs than at other computer firms. He said this would require a higher gross margin on the products sold by Alta. The company was expected to service the equipment once installed, and such revenues would be included in later years' projections.

The cash needed for purchase and lease of capital equipment was expected to range between $100,000 and $200,000 through the development phase of the business. Other assets would principally be current, with a set-aside for finished goods to be used as replacements in case a customer's computer failed for any extended period of time.

Bill outlined the accounts he needed to complete for pro formas. These included five-year projections for an income statement, balance sheet, and sources and uses statement (see Exhibits 4 and 5). He also developed further details regarding needed assumptions to project them (Exhibit 6). He then went to a local library to get copies of financial data from the annual reports of publicly-held companies that he thought would be similar to Alta in terms of costs and margins (see Exhibits 7 and 8).

Looking at the information he had gathered and the base assumptions he had prepared, Bill outlined the work that lay ahead of him:

> We've been talking in general terms about the money that will be needed to pull this off. Now I've got to figure out how that $1.5 or $2 million gets spent the first year, and what happens after that. My MBA background really helps out here . . . otherwise there's no way I would be able to put together the pro formas. I want to make sure that my numbers are precise for a couple of reasons. First, I've been told over the last six months that venture capitalists really focus on the financial side. They've got to. They might not understand the product side, but they do understand the financial and people aspects.
>
> The other thing is that for about the first six months, you've got a honeymoon with the venture capital people. But then they are going to start looking over your shoulder to see if where you are is where your numbers said you would be. If you're way off, they can get pretty nervous.

He also saw other issues yet to be worked out: What type of employee stock option plan should be set up? When would a controller be needed for the company? Bill summed up the situation as he prepared for the first negotiation session:

> I need to work on the pro formas and get them to a level of detail that will be useful in monitoring our performance. And I want to be informed enough so that we can be in the best position for getting the terms and percentages on the deal. But at the same time, I know that without any money by summer, the terms or the pro formas won't make a dime's worth of difference.

EXHIBIT 1 Thoughts about Competition

A survey of minicomputer users is conducted for *Datamation* magazine each fall. The 1979 survey (see *Datamation*, November 1979, pp. 95-8) noted the following preferences by minicomputer users about products currently available. The proposed product described would be at the top end of the price range for minicomputer systems, referred to as superminis. Three most important features cited by users in making a purchase of a minicomputer system are:

1. Vendor Reputation
2. Price
3. Operational Software

Other findings:

1. The top reason for switching suppliers was due to dissatisfaction with software support.
2. Customers tended to be loyal to their current main supplier.
3. Two or more suppliers were considered by 77 percent of all users when making an initial purchase of a minicomputer.
4. One in five users was either switching suppliers or considering a switch during 1979.
5. Delivery dates missed by suppliers was mentioned as a source of dissatisfaction by users.
6. Tandem Computer had the highest degree of customer loyalty: none of the 18 sites surveyed having a Tandem computer was considering a switch.

Competitive Features of the Proposed Alta Product

PRODUCT

— Reliability
— Price
— Modular Design of the CPU
— Use with non-English languages
— Large memory size for applications
— Stand alone system complete with peripheral equipment
— Growth of the 32-bit market
— Philosophy of not taking orders before product completion

MANAGEMENT TEAM

— Experience in hardware, software and marketing
— Risking savings and careers for the venture

DISTRIBUTION

— Targeted Market (Fortune 1000)
— Direct Sales Force
— Single product to boost installation base
— International Sales within five years

— Awareness of transitional needs from engineering to marketing

— Contacts within the computer industry
— Proprietary software available for use in development

EXHIBIT 2   Business Plan Draft

ALTA COMPUTING SYSTEMS, INC.

Proprietary Information

I - SUMMARY

The business of Alta Computing Systems is to design, manufacture and market small computer systems focused at commercial applications. Alta computer systems will sell in the $40,000 to $500,000 range. The product will consist of central processors and all necessary peripherals (discs, displays, tape, line printers), and system software (operating system, languages, utilities, communications). There are three design features that will provide significant differentiation from competitive products:

1.   Highly reliable hardware architecture that can protect the user from almost any hardware failure.
2.   Modular system architecture that permits the performance of any system to be expanded with additional central processing units.
3.   A unique software offering including an operation system that is much easier to use than existing products.

A.   Reliability

Aita believes that one of the best possible uses of current and future technology is to substantially improve computer system reliability. While hardware costs continue to decrease, all other costs associated with computer system ownership are increasing: software, training and field service. Also, as the daily operations of businesses depend more on computers to do work that was previously done by people, the indirect costs of computer failure can become major. Unlike people, computers generally give little, if any, warning that they are about to fail. When they do fail, they are useless until repaired, and sometimes critical information is lost that is very difficult and expensive to recover. As the hardware costs drop and other costs of computer ownership rise, the percentage of the computer market that is willing to pay extra for high reliability will increase. Alta plans to take advantage of this technology trend.

B.   Expandability

One of the first questions potential computer purchasers ask is: What happens when I outgrow my system? Traditional computer manufacturers offer a family of computers based on several central processors of differing performance and cost. The user may upgrade the system with a more powerful processor, but this means that somebody is stuck with the old hardware, and the performance range form the smallest to largest model is limited.

The Alta approach is totally different. An Alta Computing System can consist of one to 10 or more identical central processing units. Thus, performance is increased by adding processors to the system. This architecture provides a very broad range of power, and gives Alta a family of computer models by replicating a single processor design, rather than designing several different processors.

EXHIBIT 2 (continued)

C.   <u>Operating System</u>

The operating systems of existing computer manufacturers are old and difficult to use. Most were designed about ten years ago when there was little understanding of the ways that small computers would be used in the '80s. Because of compatibility requirements, manufacturers have been forced to stick with their old systems and add new commands for new functionality. A significant advantage that Alta will have over all of its competitors is the ease-of-use of its operating system. The command language has the power required by application programmers but is also designed to be used by unskilled operators. It can be tailored for use by non-English speaking people so that commands and error messages have meanings in their language. The operating system also provides a transparent interface between the user and the multiprocessor architecture.

An important capability of the Alta operating system and central processor is the support of virtual memory. Alta will support applications as large as one million-plus bytes, even though physical memory will be much smaller. This means that all programmers, including Alta system software developers, are much more efficient than they would be in a limited address-space.

D.   <u>Market</u>

Alta will compete in the so-called "supermini" market, which had shipments of almost $1.5 billion in 1979 and is growing at approximately 30 percent per year (source: International Data Corporation). The large size of this market means that Alta can achieve its fifth-year revenue projections with 6 percent or less of the market. Alta will initially offer a highly reliable computer with excellent software development tools but no industry-specific applications. Hence, the Company will sell to computer-knowledgeable customers who will then add the required applications. Alta will sell primarily to *Fortune* 1000 companies, who will distribute computers within their company, and application system builders who will add application software and re-sell into specific vertical markets. The obvious customers will be those who already have specific requirements for reliability (financial, medical, manufacturing, communications), but Alta will also sell to customers with "conventional" reliability needs who recognize that the extra hardware cost may be more than offset by the "indirect" costs of down-time, particularly as hardware becomes cheaper.

Alta will sell to commercial users in the fast-growing 32-bit segment of the small computer market. According to Martin and Simpson Research Associates, Inc., this segment will grow at a compound annual rate of 56 percent through 1985 (*Electronic News*, Sept. 1979). Commercial applications are overtaking industrial, and will climb from 27 percent to 40 percent of the market by 1985.

E.   <u>Competition</u>

At this time the only general purpose computer manufacturer that has a product line focused at reliability is Tandem Computers. Tandem is a highly successful company that achieved approximately $109 million in revenues in its sixth year of operation. Alta's product will have several advantages over Tandem's, including: higher reliability, software-transparent architecture, lower price and a superior operating system.

Alta will also compete with the other established small computer manufacturers such as

EXHIBIT 2 (concluded)

Digital Equipment, Hewlett-Packard, Prime and IBM. All of these companies certainly recognize Tandem's success because they have all lost business to Tandem. However, it is difficult for any of them to make an adequate response because that would require developing a completely new product line from the ground up. This would not only be very expensive, but would create severe compatibility problems with their existing product line. Since most of their revenue comes from existing customers, compatibility is a key issue in all new product development programs. It appears that the strategy of these companies is to address the "Tandem" issue with an inferior technical solution consisting of a combination of existing products (thereby maintaining compatibility with minimum investment), and rely on their size and past reputations to win the business.

F.   Financing

   Alta anticipates equity financing of between $1.5 and $2 million by the spring of 1980. It also expects to negotiate a bank line-of-credit of $100,000 or more for the purchase of capital equipment. Alta is currently completing a lease and rental agreement for computer equipment valued at $500,000 from one of its founders. This financing will carry the company for one year, by which time a prototype system will be ready. Alta projects a need for $3.5 million for second-year funding. It is the Company's objective to grow rapidly and achieve a 20-percent pre-tax margin on sales of at least $40 million by year five.

EXHIBIT 3   Assumptions for Financial Forecasts

1. Revenues
   - All sales revenues produce a constant gross margin.
   - First customer shipments will occur no later than mid-1983.
   - Service revenues will grow at less than the industry average of 0.6 percent to 0.8 percent of installed base per month, and will account for less than 10 percent of sales through the period.
   - Reduced margins from OEM discounts will be offset by reduced marketing expense.
2. Warranty
   - Because of high system reliability, warranty expense will not be a significant factor.
3. Foreign Sales
   - Sales are expected to be made internationally by the end of the five-year period.
4. Marketing Expense
   - A higher than average industry rate will be spent on marketing.
   - The sales force will be compensated through a very aggressive commission plan.
5. Development Expense
   - The percentage of revenues spent on new product development will be at the high end of the industry average.
   - The development staff will remain at a constant level by the end of 1980, until the revenue base is supported with product shipments.
6. Taxes
   - Loss carry-forwards for both state and federal taxes will be applied during the five year period.
   - A tax rate of 45 percent is assumed, which is reasonable in light of:
     - ITC
     - Jobs Tax Credit
     - Surtax Exemption
     - Tax Planning
7. Accounts Receivable
   - Assumes initial turn cycle of 120 days, going to 90 days by the end of 1983. Representative companies, by comparison, range between 60 and 120 days.
8. Notes Payable
   - Notes payable in 1980 and 1981 will be secured by the purchase of engineering and production test equipment.
   - Notes payable in later years will be secured by receivables (not to exceed 70 percent of receivables).
9. Inventories
   - Assumes 2.7 inventory turns per year. Representative companies range between 2.5 and 2.8 turns.
10. Accounts Payable
    - Assumes $75,000 in 1980 and thereafter a 75-day turn cycle. Representative companies range between 60 and 110 days.
11. Property, Plant and Equipment
    - Early requirements will be financed through leasing. Assumes capital leases from an accounting point of view.
    - Currently anticipate the need to own two computer systems—valued at approxi-mately $400,000—for use in product development, corporate administration, and manufacturing control systems.
12. Interest
    - Interest income is 8.5 percent of cash balances, with a $20,000 reserve.
    - Interest expense is 16 percent of notes payable.

EXHIBIT 4 Spreadsheet for Five-Year Pro Forma Financial Statements ($000)

Income Statement	1980	1981	1982	1983	1984
Revenue					
Total Cost of Goods Sold					
Gross Margin					
Operating Expenses					
Development					
Marketing					
G&A					
Total Operating Expenses					
Income (Loss) From OPS					
Interest Expense					
Interest Income					
Net Interest					
Depreciation					
Income (Loss) Before Taxes					
Tax					
Net Income (Loss)					

Balance Sheet	1980	1981	1982	1983	1984
Cash & Cash Investments					
Accounts Receivable					
System Spares					
Inventories					
Prepaid Expenses					
Total Current Assets					
Production & Test Equip.					
Electronic Test Equipment					
Computer Equipment					
Leasehold Improvements					
Subtotal					
Less-Accumulated Dep.					
Net Plant & Equipment					
Total Assets					
Notes Payable					
Accounts Payable					
Taxes Payable					
Accrued Expenses					
Total Current Liabilities					
Founders' Equity					
Other Stock					
Retained Earning (deficit)					
Total Stockholder Equity					
Total Liabilities & Equity					

EXHIBIT 5   Spreadsheet for Five-Year Sources and Applications Forecast ($000)

Cash Flow

	1980	1981	1982	1983	1984
Cash Provided by (Used in) Operations:					
Net Income (Loss)					
Add: Charges Against Income Not Requiring Use of Cash:					
Depreciation					
Net Cash Provided By (Used in) Operations					
Other Sources of Cash					
Increase in Notes Payable					
Increase in Accounts Payable					
Increase in Taxes Payable					
Increase in Accrued Expenses					
Sales of Stock					
Total Sources (Uses)					
Uses of Cash					
Increase in Accounts Receivable					
Increase in System Spares					
Increase in Inventories					
Increase in Prepaid Expenses					
Additions to Property, Plant and Equipment					
Total Uses					
Increase (Decrease) in Cash					
Cash Balance Start of Period					
Cash Balance End of Period					

EXHIBIT 6   Additional Assumptions for Pro Forma Statements

I.   INCOME STATEMENT
Assumes average selling price per unit of $200,000.
Installation base by year is as follows:

	1980	1981	1982	1983	1984
Number Sold	0	13	91	183	365
Total Units Installed	0	13	104	287	652

Cost of Goods Sold scaled from Data General's as percent of revenues.
Service revenues assumed to be negligible.
Development expense at $1.5 million or 10 percent of sales, whichever is greater.
Marketing expense at 20 percent of sales; 17.5 percent of sales in 1984.
G and A expense for 1980, a plug; thereafter, 5 percent of sales.
Interest expense and income based on assumptions in case materials.
Taxes assume loss carry-forward at 45 percent rate through 1982.

II.   BALANCE SHEET
Assets
Cash at $40,000 in 1980; 7 days sales in 1981; 8 days sales in 1982; 9 days sales in 1983; 10 days sales in 1984.
Accounts Receivable at 120 days in '81; 105 days in '82; 90 days thereafter.
System Spares equivalent to unit cost at 2 percent of installed base.
Inventories assumed to be $100,000 in 1980; thereafter, 2.7 times stock turn based on annual cost of goods sold.
Prepaid expenses assumed to increase by $25,000 per year.
Computer equipment at $400,000 in 1980; 10 percent of sales in years 2–4; 15 percent of sales in 1984.
Production and Test Equipment and Electronic Test Equipment assumed to be 25 percent of amount for Computer Equipment, with relatively equal split between accounts.
Leasehold improvements of $50,000 assumed for 1980; thereafter one-fifth of annual sales through 1983 and one -sixth of annual sales for 1984.
Depreciation taken at 10 percent of total fixed assets in 1980; 14 percent thereafter.

Liabilities
Notes Payable assumed to be $150,000 in 1980; $500,000 in 1981; two-thirds of accounts receivable thereafter.
Accounts Payable assumed to be $75,000 in 1980; 75 day cycle on cost of goods sold thereafter.
Taxes payable at 45 percent after loss carry-forward applied.
Accrued expenses assumed to increase by $25,000 each year.

Equity
 From partner/employees: $60,000 in '80; $40,000 in '81; $100,000 in '82; and $125,000 in both '83 and '84.

EXHIBIT 7   Data General Corporation Comparative Financial Statements ($000)

Consolidated Balance Sheets

	1974	1973	1972
Assets			
Current Assets	2,168	384	553
Short Term Investments	846	15,255	19,639
Accounts Receivable	22,842	11,90	6,124
Inventories	29,868	8,748	1,890
Prepaid Expenses	1,795	1,625	1,559
Total Current Assets	$57,519	$37,921	$29,765
Property, Plant & Equip.	17,673	11,516	5,557
Less Accrued. Depr.	3,968	1,708	642
Net Property, et al.	13,705	9,808	4,915
TOTAL ASSETS	$71,224	$47,729	$34,680
Liabilities and Stockholders' Equity			
Current Liabilities			
Notes Payable	2,049	—	—
Accounts Payable	10,813	5,380	3,864
Accrued Payroll	1,320	550	407
Taxes Payable	8,168	4,175	2,397
Other Accrued Expenses	2,088	2,171	932
Total Current Liabilities	$24,438	$12,276	$7,600
Stockholders' Equity			
Common Stock, $.01 Par Value			
Authorized 20,000,000 shares			
Shares issued and outstanding			
8,010,000 at 9/28/74			
7,903,000 at 9/29/73			
2,603,000 at 9/30/72	80	79	26
Capital in Excess of Par	$24,482	$23,096	$21,455
Retained Earnings	22,302	12,407	5,178
Less: Treasury Stock	1	1	1
Less: Deferred Compensation, ESOP	77	128	119
TOTAL LIABILITIES AND STOCKHOLDERS' EQUITY	$71,224	$47,729	$34,139

EXHIBIT 7 (concluded)

Data General Consolidated Statements of Income

	1974	**1973**	**1972**
Net Sales	83,196	53,306	$30,324
Costs and Expenses			
Cost of Goods Sold	38,268	24,521	——
Development Expense	8,514	5,970	——
G & A Expense	4,582	2,539	——
Marketing Expense	13,509	8,423	——
	64,873	41,453	——
Income from Operations	18,323	11,853	——
Other Income	722	1,108	——
Income Before Taxes	19,045	12,961	5,562
Provision for Taxes	1,265	6,220	1,665
Net Income	$9,895	$6,741	$3,897

Related Financial Information

	1972	1971	1970
Net Sales	$30,324	$15,341	$7,035
Net Income	4,297	1,561	633
Expenditures for Plant,			
Property and Equip.	3,897	770	456
Current Assets 30,232	23,020	5,225	
Current Liabilities	7,600	2,677	1,175
Working Capital	22,632	20,343	4,050
Stockholders' Equity	27,080	21,446	4,377
Per Share Income	$.49	$.2	$.11
Cumulative Computers Installed	4,170	1,710	690
Employees at Year End	840	480	240

Note: Dollars Expressed in Thousands.

EXHIBIT 8   Financial Statement Data from Prime and Tandem Computers ($000)

Tandem Computer: Consolidated Statement of Changes in Financial Position

	1979	1978
Working Capital Provided From (Used For)		
Net Income before Extraordinary Credit	4,920	2,153
Add Back:		
Depreciation and Amortization	1,365	457
Deferred Income Taxes	737	—
Working Capital Provided From Operations	7,022	2,610
Extraordinary Credit	—	1,218
Acquisition of Property and Equipment	(5,770)	(2,387)
Net Book Value of Equipment Sold or Retired	337	84
Increase in Capital Lease Obligations	429	399
Increase in Deferred Income Taxes	304	—
Sale of Preferred Stock	—	1,000
Sale of Common Stock, Net	10,837	8,196
Tax Benefit of Stock Options	235	234
Net Increase in Working Capital	$ 13,394	$ 13,964

Prime Computer: Consolidated Statement of Stockholders' Investment

	Common Stock				Treasury Stock	
	Number of Shares	$0 Par Value	Capital in Excess of Par Value	Retained Earnings (Deficit)	Number of Shares	Cost
Balance, 12/31/71	300,000	$8,000	$23,000	($1,000)	32,000	($1,000)
Sale of common stock	1,132,000	28,000	1,506,000	—	—	—
Treasury stock changes, net	(32,000)	(1,000)	26,000	—	(30,800)	(1,000)
Net loss for the year	—	—	—	(966,000)	—	—
Balance, 12/31/72	1,400,000	$35,000	$1,555,000	($967,000)	1,200	($2,000)
Sale of common stock	325,000	8,000	1,283,000	—	—	—
Treasury stock changes, net	—	—	32,000	—	4,000	1,000
Net loss for the year	—	—	—	(1,831,000)	—	—
Balance, 12/31/73	1,725,000	$43,000	$2,870,000	($2,798,000)	5,200	($1,000)
Public offering	400,000	10,000	2,451,000	—	—	—
Treasury stock changes, net	—	—	26,000	—	56,600	(9,000)
Net loss for the year	—	—	—	(532,000)	—	—
Balance, 12/31/74	2,125,000	$53,000	$5,347,000	($3,330,000)	61,800	($10,000)
Sale of common stock	—	—	15,000	—	312	(5,000)
Treasury stock changes, net	—	—	8,000	—	—	—
Net income for the year	—	—	—	692,000	—	—
Balance, 12/31/75	2,125,000	$53,000	$5,370,000	($2,638,000)	62,112	($15,000)
Sale of common stock	(52,886)	(1,000)	18,000	—	(62,112)	15,000
Treasury stock changes, net	—	—	20,000	—	—	—
Net income for the year	—	—	—	2,429,000	—	—
Balance, 12/31/76	2,072,114	$52,000	$5,408,000	($209,000)	—	—

Chapter 5

Financing

❏ *SUBCHAPTER 5A - Inception Capital*

Overview

To an entrepreneur who wonders how to raise it, capital often appears to be the main key to moving forward with a venture. In fact, the real key is evidence that the venture can justify capital with an appropriate positive cash flow. Capital represents social permission to use the physical resources and efforts of others in the economy to produce something new. That permission may be inherited, won in a lottery, or earned through work and savings. It can also be acquired on the basis of a convincing track record, persuasive argument, business plan or combinations of such factors.

Since start-up money may not be as readily available as a would-be entrepreneur might hope when contemplating a venture, he or she should consider alternative financing scenarios. Four possibilities are: (1) the money becomes available as planned, (2) the money available is less than planned, (3) the money is not available as soon as projected, and (4) other elements of the venture plan do not occur as projected, affecting both the amount of money needed and the difficulty of obtaining it.

Some Patterns

The range of styles and methods entrepreneurs use for financing ventures includes extensive variety, and any "typical" examples are bound to fall short of full representation. Here, however, is some illustration of the spectrum.

The **True Independent** starts with savings. Nobody else's permission is needed to apply resources for starting the business. Possibly there is some use of personal credit, as by running up bills on credit cards or borrowing at the bank against personal assets. But commercial loan funds or trade credit are not usually part of the initial picture. If they become available it will probably be later, after the business is going and creditworthy in its own right.

As a **variant**, the entrepreneur may have another job or an employed spouse for support while getting started. The Cooper et al. study of 2,994 firms[1] found that 8 percent of the entrepreneurs held other full-time jobs during the first year of start-up, while 7 percent held part-time jobs and another 4 percent held irregular jobs. Thirty-five percent of the entrepreneurs had a spouse who was employed full-time outside the start-up, and another 11 percent had a spouse employed part-time outside.

About half the ventures drew upon services of unpaid family members during start-up. When they did, it was one member in half the cases, two in about a third and three or more in the remainder. In about a third of the cases the typical time given by those members was less than 10 hours per week and in another third it was 40 or more hours per week. Thus, family member "sweat equity" contributions are significant in many start-ups.

The **Enticing Deal Seller** hasn't adequate savings to start alone or as a family unit. Instead, the venture concept is so apparently attractive and/or the individual is so persuasive that other private investors put up the money. They may be family, friends or individuals met through business contacts such as stock brokers, other professionals and other entrepreneurs. Their investment may be based on hard-headed business analysis, emotion or both. An enticing deal, for instance, might be stock in the company or a royalty in exchange for the personal guarantee of a loan at the bank. This could offer an infinite rate of return to the guarantor while restricting leverage of the borrower. However, the venture does not get to keep the money, and the guarantor could lose the amount of the loan.

The **Partner** extends personal savings by joining forces with others, either Independents or Deal Sellers, to undertake the venture as a mutual effort. Family members of partners may also become involved, as with the True Independent.

The **Founding Team Creator** extends the partner concept further, ideally recruiting complementary talents to produce a balanced top management. The team may be dedicated to objectives other than ambitious profits, in which case the start-up financial resources will be limited to personal savings of the team members and those of their families and friends. The enterprise might be a capital-intensive investment, such as a plant, possibly with prospects of employing the team, or of yielding capital gains. Alternatively, the venture may be some sort of cooperative enterprise with idealistic aims.

The **Very-High-Profit-Idea Team Creator** justifies the high cost of multiple members by aiming to start a business with very high total profit potential. This potential is based upon such competitive advantages as exceptional talents on the team, powerful patent protection or other major barriers to competitive entry, combined with a market of high growth potential. The prospect of selling out within a few years may justify interest by venture capitalists who work as independents or in corporate venture divisions and make a profession of investing the pools of money they manage in high-growth smaller companies and start-up ventures. Alternatively, if the "big idea" of the venture appears to have enough economic promise and the team has sufficiently impressive credentials, the venture may even be able to obtain its starting capital from a public stock offering.

Application: *Which of the above financing "styles" could the entrepreneur(s) in the assigned case use? Which makes most sense and why?*

The very first seed capital for almost all start-up ventures begins with income from another job or personal savings of the entrepreneur and his or her partners, family, friends and possibly employees. Then, as the venture becomes more fully formed, it may be able to obtain financial help from suppliers and possibly customers and banks. Individual investors are always a possibility, as are venture capitalists. Generally, however, venture capitalists take interest only in situations where there seems to be a large upside potential, on the order of a 30 percent return on investment (ROI) on an investment large enough to make it worthwhile spending time on the deal. As investment professionals they have offices, staff and other overhead to maintain, and this overhead as well as their salaries and profits for the investors must be paid for by adequately lucrative deals. Moreover, since some of their deals lose entirely, they must seek winners big enough to cover those losses as well.

Deal Elements

When it is possible to obtain capital from others, the terms are usually formulated according to "the golden rule" (the person with the gold makes the rules). But it can be helpful for the entrepreneur (1) to know something about deal possibilities in order to help the process, (2) to know what particular kinds of ventures different capital sources prefer to invest in and what they can provide for their investees, and (3) to consider any venture proposition from the money-provider's point of view. Elements that may come into play for making deals include the following:

1. **Stock Investment** Raising money through stock sales conveys ownership to those who provide financing. Consequently, a question frequently asked by entrepreneurs who are considering this financing approach is how much ownership must be yielded by founders for a given amount of money. The answer to this question is always, "it depends." The basis will likely be what level of return on investment is generated for the investor. The academically customary way of computing return on investment (ROI) is by dividing the annual profit by the amount invested to get a return percentage. Venture capitalists, however, more often speak in terms of multiples, such as getting back three to five times the investment in three to five years, rather than return percentages. Who has how much control is sometimes an important issue to be negotiated. Terms may also be incorporated in the deal to provide that the better the com-

pany does, the smaller the ownership fraction investors will be entitled to.

2. **Borrowing Cash** When and how a loan to the venture will be repaid and what interest rate it will carry are two immediate considerations. But there are others. Terms may allow conversion of the debt into equity at the lender's discretion. They may also provide that lenders can step in and take control if certain performance levels or ratios set forth in the venture plan are not maintained. Having someone guarantee a loan can sometimes be a way of borrowing where otherwise it would be impossible to do so. One catch is that the entrepreneur will then have to pay something to the guarantor on top of the customary costs of the loan itself.

3. **Other Forms of Debt** Instead of conventional borrowing, loans may take the form of trade credit from suppliers, advance payment by customers, or temporary use of others' plant and equipment. Rental involving leasing or installment purchase can be viewed as forms of debt. It is sometimes possible to borrow equipment or people's efforts directly. The indebtedness in such cases may be formal or informal. One entrepreneur recalled such an experience.

> *This other entrepreneur had really helped me out. I told him so, and said I hoped some day I could pay him back. He told me other people had helped him when he was getting started, and said that if I wanted to return the favor he would prefer that I pass it along to someone else rather than to him.*

4. **Payment by the Entrepreneur** Compensation for the use of capital can take the form of share ownership in the company, options to buy shares, royalties based on sales or profits, interest or other cash payments including consulting fees, agreements by the entrepreneur's company to do business with or favors for those who make the capital available, or possible tax shelter advantages for them.

5. **Splitting Off Assets** An investor may put up money for real estate against a mortgage and lease that property to the venture, or may advance cash for advertising in return for a royalty on sales, or may buy stock in the venture as part of an employment package. The potential variety of deals involving "I'll give you this in exchange for that" is endless. This type of deal also carries a limitless variety of possible problems. Thinking ahead about implications and what could go wrong is a necessary part of rationally approaching such deals. Consideration of the deal by both parties from both parties' points of view is also needed.

Entrepreneurs often commandeer resources they don't have title to. In addition to borrowing, they sometimes barter and sometimes presume. Doing favors is part of entrepreneurship, both giving and receiving. Author George Gilder has pointed out that the entrepreneur begins by a charitable act, putting forth effort and resources before receiving anything back in order to make a venture happen.[2] Other times entrepreneurs receive favors from sympathizers, including other entrepreneurs who wish them well, and community supporters who appreciate what ventures add to the store of available jobs, goods and services. Effort, initiative, imagination, vision and persuasion can be important forms of currency for obtaining use of other people's effort and resources.

Application: *Which of the above financing mechanisms, in rank order, should be most appropriate for the needs of the assigned case venture in its early stages?*

Maintaining Control

The "golden rule" mentioned earlier entitles those who put money into a venture to take some rights of control in return. This may take the form of written rules the company must follow, such as not to make any investments over a certain amount without permission, not to pay more than a certain amount to executives, to submit specified financial information on a certain timetable, to maintain certain balance sheet and income statement ratios, or to employ certain people in specified capacities. Control can also take the form of continuing interaction between investors and managers of the venture.

It is natural for an entrepreneur not to want to share control. There is plenty to worry about in creating the venture without having to consider how investors feel about it. There is plenty for the entrepreneur to do without having to take time out for interacting with investors. To the entrepreneur, sharing control can mean danger of distraction, interference and wasted time.

It is also easy to see why an investor would want elements of control. Incentive to be careful with the money would be higher if it were the entrepreneur's own. To make up for this limitation the person with the money attaches strings. It is possible to structure the arrangement such that the strings take hold only if the venture is falling too far short of its forecast.

Investors and lenders more experienced in dealing with ventures really don't want control. It can lead to interference that handicaps the venture and possibly destroys the enthusiasm and motivation of its creators. It is the founders, after all, who are most expert about the venture. Lenders and investors don't know how to create it or run it as well as they do. It may be wise for them to have some strings on the venture, but they should leave them loose as much as possible, stepping in only if the venture seems to be heading disastrously off track.

The entrepreneur should seek investors based upon their prior experience and reputations. In arranging a deal both sides should consider possible future problems, what will best motivate the founders and what sorts of deviations from course should trigger investor or lender action in the best interests of both their money and the venture.

Retaining Ownership

Division of ownership raises issues similar to those of control. Taking too much away from entrepreneurs can reduce their incentives. Taking too little can limit the investor to inadequate returns considering the risk. In the end, division of ownership must be negotiated, and the investor usually has the upper hand. The entrepreneur may have some of the following choices:

- Taking a "bigger piece of a small pie or a smaller piece of a bigger one"

- Keeping ownership by assuming the risk of borrowing, or giving up some ownership in return for someone else sharing the risk

- Seeking more capital at early inception, even though that makes it more expensive. The alternative is to begin with less capital and wait until the venture grows to where it needs more. Seeking it then, however, may take time away from the many demanding tasks of building the venture, a sacrifice that may be serious or even fatal to the venture's continued development.

There are no standard formulas for choosing among such alternatives. They must be negotiated by each entrepreneur for each individual venture, with careful thought about the alternative scenarios that can follow.

Pitfalls

The ultimate evidence of error in venturing is a shortage of cash. Either too little came in, or it went out too fast or both. The general pitfall of venture financing is to run out of cash. Ways this can come about include:

- Failing to foresee needs adequately
- Lacking good financial controls
- Waiting too long to seek capital
- Underestimating effort required to raise capital
- Pursuing capital sources that don't fit the venture
- Selling stock to an investor who has inadequate capability to help further
- Asking for money without adequate advance preparation
- Selling equity when debt will do

- Taking on too much debt
- Agreeing to a misunderstood deal
- Losing credibility by failing to meet commitments
- Paying too much for capital
- Getting too many shareholders too soon
- Misapplying the capital

Application: *How would you rank the likelihood of the above pitfalls happening to the assigned case venture and why?*

The importance of watching cash was emphasized by Harvey Quadracci, who created a printing company with 1990 sales of $375 million.

> *Nobody understands what cash flow is unless they've lived by it. The experience changes you permanently. I have a telephone in planes, trains, cars and bedrooms because I have a phobia. I break out into a cold sweat if I'm away from a phone. It goes back to those days when I was always calling to ask, "Did the check come in the morning? OK, release those other checks."*[3]

The discipline of handling money with maximal efficiency is one many entrepreneurs learn out of necessity and one which can give their ventures an advantage over older competitors long beyond start-up.

Minimizing Needs

For each of the above pitfalls it is fairly easy to think of one or more preventative actions. The starting point is to prepare financial forecasts which show how much cash will be needed when, and where it should come from. Both the cash needs of the founders personally and those of the venture should be forecasted. Each of these forecasts will be based upon assumptions which could be incorrect in various ways. Consequently for every likely variation in the assumptions, the impact upon cash needs should be explored. Most optimistic, most pessimistic and most likely forecasts would be three in particular to explore.

The first step in developing these forecasts is to make lists of things on which money will have to be spent. Naturally, some cash will be needed for the entrepreneur to live on while starting the venture. Some items for the venture activities include:

- travel, meals and correspondence with helpful contacts
- lawyer fees
- construction of a prototype
- design of a logo

- costs of preparing advertisements
- costs of running advertisements
- fabrication of tooling
- rental deposits
- initial inventory
- office equipment
- production equipment
- license fees
- phone, fax and mail expenses

Application: *What items should the above expense list include for the assigned case venture, and how would the items rank order in terms of amount?*

This list must be developed as fully as possible, and it might be helpful to rank order the items according to total expenditure for the first year. Despite an entrepreneur's conscientious effort to be complete, there will almost certainly be omissions. How will taxes be handled? What if a supplier wants payment in advance or a customer wants (or simply takes) extended credit? What if a supplier raises a price or tacks on some charge for service, COD, or late payment? Was insurance included? What if something breaks or is stolen? What will be done while waiting to replace it? What if there is a lawsuit over something? What if a personal emergency requiring cash arises for the entrepreneur at home? It is altogether too easy to see the need for start-up cash and at the same time to underestimate how great it will be.

Spreading these expenditures out month by month and adding them up will forecast the cash flowing out, which can be cumulated month by month to show a worst case of how much money must be raised in one way or another by the venture. This amount may come from investors, lenders or customers. Assumptions about which of those people will provide how much cash to the company at what points in time must be made with care. What alternative actions can be taken if one or another of them either reneges or simply delays payment?

Pitfalls in forecasting the cash needs are easy to imagine, and some are suggested above. They can also include:

- Failing to list something for which cash will be needed.
- Underestimating how much something will cost.
- Falsely assuming suppliers will extend credit.
- Underestimating how much inventory will accumulate.
- Assuming customers will pay sooner than they will.
- Assuming nobody will make an error handling cash.

- Expecting loans will be processed quickly.
- Expecting investors will pay in promptly.

Application: *How would you rank order the likelihood of the above possible pitfalls happening to the assigned case venture, and upon what factors would the ranking depend?*

The amount of cash needed to start a business obviously will range widely from one venture to another. Amdahl Computer started with $17 million. Apple Computer started with less than $1,000. Some indication of the spread among other fast-growth start-ups appears in a survey of the 500 fastest growing small companies listed by *Inc.* magazine as its "*Inc.* 500." Results of this survey are listed in Table 5-1 below:[4]

Table 5-1 Levels of Start-Up Capital in *Inc. 500* Firms

Start-Up Capital Needed	Percent of Firms
less than $10,000	34%
$10,000 - $49,000	35
$50,000 - $99,000	12
$100,000 - $249,999	10
$250,000 or more	9
Total	100%

The National Federation of Independent Business (NFIB) firms surveyed by Cooper et al. are probably more representative than the "*Inc.* 500" of the overall business population, yet they yielded a comparable pattern, as shown in Table 5-2:[5]

Table 5-2 Levels of Start-up Capital Among NFIB Firms

Start-Up Capital Needed	Percent of Firms
less than $10,000	32%
$10,000 - $50,000	41
$50,000 - $100,000	15
$100,000 - $250,000	8
$250,000 or more	4
Total	100%

The similarity of these patterns seems remarkable considering the difference in longer term performance. The *Inc.* sample of the 500 firms out of all

U.S. industry that have grown the most over the past five years, is a very thin layer of top performers. These data seem to indicate that in terms of start-up capital most top performers begin with much the same level of resources as "typical" start-ups.

Application: Which of the financing amount categories above would the assigned case venture fit into, and how did you arrive at that estimation?

Ways to reduce the amount of cash needed for start-up are virtually endless. Actions an entrepreneur can choose for doing so include:

- Make do without (dining room table for desk?)
- Buy, don't make (use subcontractors)
- Make, don't buy (homemade production equipment?)
- Barter, don't pay cash (free samples for help?)
- Buy used, not new (any auctions of other firms?)
- Buy cheap (hire students, GIs off hours, homemakers)
- Lease, don't buy (copy machine, computer, space, etc.)
- Lease, don't hire (temporary help)

The catch with such approaches is that they usually extract tradeoffs in terms of quality, dependability, speed or the entrepreneur's time. Sometimes less immediate cash outlay requires paying a higher total price, as in the case of leasing equipment. Thus, cash conservation may impose profit sacrifices, while raising cash may require sacrificing ownership, control or both.

Application: Which of the above cash-saving measures should the entrepreneur in the assigned case adopt and what tradeoffs would be required to do so?

Compromise is not always costly. Harvey Quadracci, quoted above, recalled how in earlier days his company enhanced sales by giving customers the impression that it was financially better off than it was.

> *The client would come in and see rolls of paper stacked up but not know that in the middle they were hollow. Or we would have the press printing this one magazine, which had a run of maybe 15,000. The press would print 25,000 an hour. Here comes the client, and we'd start the press up and get him to move very quickly because the paper was going through. Then we'd get him out into the office, and suddenly the whole plant would shut down. "What was that?" he would say. "Oh, it must be everybody breaking for lunch." It's perception.*[6]

Ken Hendricks, a roofing distributor with sales of $250 million in 1990, described how start-up economies continued even after his company had grown large.

We still buy used, but nice, furniture. My desk came from somebody that had gone bankrupt. I've thought about the tears that had to fall on that desk, and it's something that reminds me every day that I'm not going to let this happen to me.[7]

First Cash Sources

Personal Resources

Savings of the founder, as noted above, are the main source of start-up cash for most ventures. Among *Inc.* 500 companies, for instance, the most important cash source for the entrepreneurs themselves and their families to live on during start-up was personal savings in 43 percent of the companies, support from spouse and other relatives in 12 percent, salary from another job in 17 percent and salary from the start-up in only 20 percent of the cases.[8]

When respondents were asked which sources were most relied upon for capital to start the company, the fraction who nominated each category (some nominated more than one) was as shown in Table 5-3:

Table 5-3 Start-Up Capital Sources of *Inc.* 500 Firms[9]

Sources of Capital Used	Percent
Own resources	75%
Mortgage of own assets	35
Corporate loan from bank	33
Partner's assets	29
Personal loan from bank	23
Parents or other relative	20

Curiously missing from this list are sources such as informal outside investors, venture capital investors, corporations and public offerings. These sources too are sometimes used in start-ups, although relatively rarely. A later report on the *Inc.* 500 stated that for 56 percent the main source of seed money was personal savings, 40 percent received loans by mortgaging personal assets. Venture capital was used by less than 2 percent of the companies polled. Corporate loans in this later report showed a 41 percent response, compared to the earlier 33 percent above.[10]

The Cooper et al. study of 2,994 firms brought still more sources into the picture, including outside individuals, venture capital firms and suppliers, as can be seen in Table 5-4.

Table 5-4 Start-up Capital Sources of NFIB Firms

Sources of Capital Used	Percent
Personal Savings	74.6%
Banks	45.8
Friends/Relatives	28.7
Other Individuals	7.8
Suppliers/Trade Credit	6.3
Government Guaranteed Loans	3.2
Venture Capital Firms	1.3
Former Owners (Acquisitions)	8.9

Customer Advances

In some circumstances, customers will advance part of the capital needed to start a business. For research and development work in selected areas, agencies of the federal government will provide grants under its Small Business Innovation Research (SBIR) program.[11] Under this program, federal agencies with research budgets must set aside 1.25 percent of the money in them for grants to companies with under 500 employees.

Grants are given under two phases. The first phase provides up to $50,000 over six months for feasibility analysis of a proposed innovation of interest to one of the 11 federal agencies that are by law required to give such grants. The second phase, contingent on performance under the first, provides up to $500,000 additionally. However, less than 15 percent of first-phase and 40 percent of second-phase proposals were being accepted as of 1989, and the trend was toward the number of proposals growing faster than the available funding.

Contractors frequently receive progress payments on construction projects. Both software and hardware makers in the microcomputer industry have been known to accept orders and advance payments for products to be made in the future. Two contrasting examples of capital coming from customers are the following:

> Pat Sayers founded Nursing Systems International with cash advances from hospitals more than a year before her product, a computerized expert reference system for nurses, existed. She had previously tried selling, as a consultant, a textbook and a slide series, from which she recalled "how tough it really is to reach the market until people are out there saying 'we want it.'" Consequently, when a hospital suggested she develop a system, she asked for payments up front, and received them. In return, she promised the contributors significant discounts on the product. The advances gave her credibility as well as cash that in turn helped her raise the remaining capital needed from other sources.[12]

❖ ❖ ❖

Bob McCray raised half the $500,000 needed to start manufacturing electrical valve equipment from manufacturer's representatives who wanted to carry the product. Each representative was asked for a loan of $5,000 for every 1 percent of national market territory. In return, McCray promised to give the representative repayment on a short schedule, with interest at 1 percent over prime, plus exclusive territory rights and a discount of 50 percent off list in contrast to the customary 33 percent. McCray observed that "They look at us as more of a partner, which is good. We didn't want to be thought of as just another vendor. I certainly have no trouble getting them on the phone."[13]

Application: *What line of persuasion could be tried by the entrepreneur in the assigned case to obtain customer help in financing, and to what degree would that be worth trying? Please explain.*

A study of 132 firms in Iowa by Carter and Van Auken[14] showed that on average more start-up capital had come from debt (52.9 percent) than from equity (46.7 percent) and that most of the debt had come from institutions, not individuals (see Table 5-5). Of further interest was that a statistically significant inverse correlation existed between owners' personal equity and first-year financial difficulties experienced by the firms. The reasons for this are not reported. Possibly, as the authors suggest, the entrepreneurs were deterred from investing heavily in riskier situations by having private information. Alternatively, greater equity investment may have reflected either that the firms were better financed and did not need more capital or that their owners found it easier to raise more cash when needed because of the greater capital base.

Outside Investors

It has been estimated by Gaston[15] that there are around a half-million informal investors or "angels" who help finance new ventures in the United States, but this is hard to verify. Definition is one problem. One person may invest only once, while others make multiple investments. Often the money is advanced as a loan rather than a permanent investment, but later it may be converted to ownership. Someone who invested years earlier, but not recently, may or may not still be considered an investor. People may invest their own money or they may invest for others, and they may invest directly or through another company. The latter have been referred to as "quasi-angels." Attempts to learn through surveys about these various types and how they operate have been frustrated by low response rates, averaging around 5 percent.[16]

Respondents in the Cooper study reported that 7.2 percent began with outside individual investors and 5.6 percent said they received 40 percent or more of their funding from outside individuals.[17] There may be overlap here between "other individuals" and "former owners," and from inclusion of the latter it appears that both start-ups and acquisitions were lumped together. This may also be true for the *Inc.* sample. And it is possible that the outside investors included some who bought into a public offering.

Table 5-5 Sources of Capital as a Percent of Start-up Total

Sources	Mean Percent*
Equity:	
Personal funds	35.6
Partnerships	5.2
Stock to others	3.2
Other	2.7
Total	46.7
Debt:	
Institutional loans	43.8
Loans from individuals	5.3
Sale of bonds	1.1
Other	2.7
Total	52.9

The variety of people who become informal investors in ventures was shown by Aram from a study of 55 eastern Great Lakes region informal investors.[18] These investors were mostly business owners and managers with a mean age between 40 and 50 who made an average of two risk capital investments every three years. The average investment was just under $50,000. A third of the investments were made within 10 miles of home and three-fourths were within 50 miles. Over 90 percent co-invested with typically four other people. Half of the investments were in start-up firms. Typical target returns on investment were over 35 percent for high technology firms and about 25 percent for others. Those are averages, however, from which individuals may deviate widely. Some entrepreneurs have been lent capital at no interest, for instance, with comments such as, "Somebody helped me when I was starting my business; now I figure it's my turn to put something back."

Foreign investors are a rare source of capital for U.S. ventures so far, but may grow in importance in the future. One three-year-old venture reported to have tapped such sources was headed by a former U.S. assistant secretary for international trade. Likely his government work had conferred special know-how, connections and credentials.[19] Theoretically, foreign sources could also be approached for start-up financing by more "ordinary" entrepreneurs. This has probably happened, but to date little, if any of it, seems to have been reported.

---

*   Totals, according to the authors, do not add to 100 percent because of rounding. Why there was no double counting due to combinations of sources, which would cause the total to be greater than 100 percent, was not explained.

The way to find informal investors is to "ask around" selectively, as there are no published lists. There is a computer matching system at the University of New Hampshire and some other universities. But these keep the names confidential. Some likely people to ask for leads include other entrepreneurs, bankers, stock brokers, real estate brokers, accountants, and attorneys. Each contact can lead to others. The search becomes one of exploring a web of contacts to find the rare one who may happen to fit needs of the venture. Some contacts, such as stock brokers and real estate agents, expect commissions on deals that come from leads they provide. Others, such as bankers, do not. Looking for ways to return favors of anyone in the search can help the process.

The most likely sources of capital for a given enterprise may be those who are in the best position to understand and help the business in other ways besides financing, as illustrated by the experience of Jeffrey and Carolyne Greene.

Greene had, in 1979, designed a humorous doll ("FROYD"), which she attempted to sell to toy makers. They complimented the toy, but declined to invest. At the same time, it seemed to her that toy stores needed new products, but toy makers were too conservative to introduce them. After several years of searching she met Jeffrey, then a venture capitalist, who decided to hire the same market researchers who had tested Cabbage Patch dolls and to have them perform the same tests. The results were strongly positive, but toy makers still would not buy.

So the pair decided to start a business and market the product themselves. They began talking with contract manufacturers and retailers as they developed a business plan to raise capital. They sent out 100 copies of the plan and made presentations to ten investment groups, without success. This first round of rejections was followed by a second. Venture capitalists, it seemed, did not take much interest in toys, particularly since some prominent toy companies, Wonder and Coleco, had just failed.

Next, the two tried cutting the project down and seeking as private investors some of the experts and business people they had encountered in researching and designing the venture. Many of these had complimented the product. Now, when asked to invest in it, they did. Sixteen of them put up the $600,000 being sought, and other investors had to be turned away. "The key," according to author Ellyn E. Spragins, "was approaching individuals whose business expertise give them a special appreciation for marketing or the character-development business. Thus, the company's backers include senior executives in an advertising agency, a consumer products company, and a direct-mail business."[20]

Understanding on the part of potential investors can be enhanced by effective presentation, including data, prototypes, demonstrations, expert testimony, a well-written business plan and a carefully rehearsed presentation, ingredients that appear to have been present in the Greenes' venture.

Private Placement

In selling shares of a venture, caution is required. Two general types of stock sales are public offerings, in which the shares are made available to the general public, and private offerings, in which sales of the shares are solicited from a smaller group. Public offerings generally take place only when a company is already running, and are usually the more ambitious of the two types, although there are exceptions. Unless they meet certain exemption requirements, they must be approved by at least one government agency. They will be discussed in the next subchapter.

Private placements do not require government approval, provided they fulfill certain requirements. These are not rigidly defined, but, rather, are subject to flexible interpretations by the government agencies that apply them. The federal agency concerned is the Securities and Exchange Commission. The state agencies go under various names, and each state has one. If the securities are going to be sold only within the state (an intrastate offering), no federal permission is required, but state approval may be.

One requirement for a private offering is that the number of people who are approached to buy shares not be large, roughly no more than 35. Another is that each purchaser of the shares be "sophisticated," capable of understanding the deal clearly; have enough bargaining power to obtain full disclosure of all pertinent factors, especially any risk elements; and sign a statement to the effect that his or her intent in buying the shares is to keep them for investment, not to turn around and resell them in the near term. In the interpretation of these rules, help should be sought from a lawyer who specializes in securities law and actively practices it. It is advisable to get referrals from those who have used such lawyers in order to find one who is highly competent.

Application: *From the viewpoint of a private investor, what kind of a deal for financing the assigned case venture might make sense and why? To what extent should such a deal be acceptable to the entrepreneur and why?*

Early Debt Sources

Early investors may choose to buy shares, loan the company money, or guarantee a loan in return for some incentive. Other sources of debt initially can be finance companies (to support the purchase of resellable equipment) and special interest organizations, such as community groups that may want to help formation of local companies in order to provide jobs.

Supplementary Reading

New Venture Strategies Chapter 4. (Vesper, K.H., Prentice-Hall, 1990)
New Venture Mechanics Chapter 5. (Vesper, K. H., Prentice-Hall, 1993)

Exercises

1. Extend or elaborate the lists of expenses above by examining in detail either what costs were involved in starting an actual business or by planning in detail the needs for starting a specific new business.

2. Ask the owner how the start-up of his or her company was financed and what the problems were.

Venture History

1. What were the resource needs of the company for each of the first 12 months, each of the next four quarters and years after that, however long it has gone?

2. How did the founders go about meeting those resource needs?

Venture Planning Guide

1. Assess the fit of the most promising three alternative sources of capital for your most promising venture idea.

2. Assume the position of each of the three above sources, and formulate terms for extending capital to the venture that would be appropriate from the viewpoint of that source.

Notes

[1] Arnold C. Cooper and others, *New Business In America* (Washington, D.C.: The NFIB Foundation, 1990), p. 16.

[2] George Gilder, *The Spirit Of Enterprise* (New York: Simon and Schuster, 1984).

[3] "Going For Broke," *Inc.*, September 1990, p. 35.

[4] John Case, "The Origins of Entrepreneurship," *Inc.*, June 1989, p. 62.

[5] Cooper and others, *New Business in America*, p. 28.

[6] "Going For Broke," p. 36.

[7] Ibid.

[8] Case, "The Origins of Entrepreneurship," p. 62.

[9] Ibid., p. 58.

[10] "The Year In Startups," *Inc.*, November 1989, p. 66.

[11] Mangelsdorf, Martha E., "*Inc.*'s Guide To 'Smart' Money," *Inc.*, August 1989, p. 51. Also, a useful contact is the Small Business Administration's Office of Innovation, (202) 653 6458.

[12] "The Year In Startups," p. 75.

[13] Ibid., p. 71.

[14] Richard B. Carter and Howard E. Van Auken, "Personal Equity Investment and Small Business Financial Difficulties," *ET&P*, 15, no. 2, Winter 1990, p. 51.

[15] R. J. Gaston, *Finding Private Venture Capital for Your Firm* (New York: John Wiley and Sons, 1989).

[16] Barry Singer, "Contours of Development," *Journal of Business Venturing*, 10, no. 4, July 1995, p. 310.

[17] Cooper and others, *New Business in America*, p. 29.

[18]John D. Aram, "Attitudes and Behaviors of Informal Investors Toward Early-Stage Investments," *Journal of Business Venturing*, 4, no. 5, September 1989, p. 333.

[19]Ellyn E. Spragins, "Globetrotting For Dollars," *Inc.*, August 1990, p. 116.

[20]Ellyn E. Spragins, "Intelligent Money," *Inc.*, June 1990, p. 106.

❏ SUBCHAPTER 5B - Growth Cash

Early Debt

The attractive thing to an entrepreneur about borrowing money, assets, and other people's efforts in creating a business is that it allows retention of ownership. From the lender's viewpoint, however, such financing offers only risk and upside potential limited to the rate of interest. Hence, borrowed money is often hard to get, particularly if the entrepreneur's own resources, as back-up for the loan, or track record, as an assurance of ability to perform the venture, are limited.

Bank Loans

From both the Cooper et al. and *Inc.* survey results described in the preceding chapter, it appears that banks typically play a strong role in the initial financing of companies, as 33 percent and 45 percent, respectively, of entrepreneurs responding to those surveys indicated. Yet often entrepreneurs say they could get no funding from banks in the early stages of start-up. The cliché is that "a bank will loan you money only if you don't need it." Banks don't have loan departments for start-up ventures. However, banks sometimes do make loans to ventures, and they also help ventures with information and other contacts.

Certainly, there is reason for banks to be cautious. First, the money they hold is not their own. It belongs to depositors, who expect to be able to withdraw any or all of it whenever they please. For the bank to have it loaned out to ventures that cannot repay immediately or perhaps at all cannot be allowed. Secondly, banks are severely limited in what they can charge as interest. Thus, while they can lose all, they can't win much. It does not make sense for them to give risky loans.

So why do banks seem to participate in financing so many ventures, according to the surveys? One explanation probably is that a fairly large fraction of the ventures surveyed were not actually start-ups but rather acquisitions that had assets to pledge. A second is that even among start-ups the banks may have lent money not at inception but only after the start-up was running and showing promise of strong solvency. Moreover, some of the entrepreneurs may have had sufficient personal assets to provide guarantees on the loans.

Guarantees can come either from private individuals who have resources to back them up or from the Small Business Administration (SBA) of the federal government. The SBA will guarantee 90 percent of a loan if a bank is willing to risk the other 10 percent. The contact for pursuing this course of action is the bank willing to take that risk. However, even a 10 percent loss is very significant to a bank.

Despite the risks, there are also positive reasons for banks to make loans to start-ups. Banks are in business to "rent" money, and doing so is therefore competitive. Every good customer helps, and founders who are aided by banks in the early days of their ventures often stay loyal to those banks after the ventures have grown and become attractive and profitable borrowers. Banks know this and therefore sometimes will even loan money unsecured to start-up companies. To encourage a banker to help with financing a venture an entrepreneur can:

- Prepare a well-written business plan that makes clear just how much money will be needed (cumulative cash flow forecast with explanatory footnotes), what it will be used for and when and how it will be paid back with interest.

- Seek out an individual bank lending officer who has the authority to make loan decisions, is experienced in loans of the type needed and has a good "personal chemistry" with the type of venture and the founder(s).

The latter task is one that may take some searching. Many entrepreneurs report having been turned down by several banks before finding one that would grant credit. The following entrepreneur recalled the necessity of searching in the right locality to find a bank for financing the purchase of a small business. He had worked out his deal with the seller, and now all that was needed was cash from the bank for a down payment.

> *I made a major error at this point that almost killed the deal. I assumed that my best chance for financing the acquisition was to approach the larger banks in Laurel, the town where the business was located. As a result I didn't go to any local Annapolis banks where friends could get me in the door at the right levels. The banks in and around Laurel wanted nothing to do with me or my deal. I was incredulous. I had assumed that putting the financing together would be a matter of a couple of weeks, at the most.*
>
> *It took six....I was extremely embarrassed to tell people the banks were stringing me along. What was I, some kind of deadbeat?*
>
> *In desperation, I called several friends for help. They got me in to see Annapolis bankers (I didn't know anyone from the local banks because, although I lived in Annapolis, I had worked in Washington since moving to town). They listened. They checked me out. Then I got a yes. Then another yes. Then another, and another. All but one were from strictly local banks. I wasn't a deadbeat after all. In fact, I was able to get pretty good terms.[1]*

These bankers wanted to be sure of the person they were dealing with, which is always an important factor. Other elements that can be influential in getting a bank loan include:

- How debt-heavy the venture will be if it gets the loan.

- What collateral the venture can provide, and how readily cash could be extracted by selling it.

- How solid the customers of the venture are and how certain they are to buy. Having a government or big company contract can make a big difference.

- How fully "loaned-up" versus hungry for loans the bank is.

- How good the bank's recent experience has been with loans like this.

- The extent to which this loan might help relations with other customers, such as perhaps suppliers to the venture.

Application: *What is the best line of persuasion the entrepreneur in the assigned case could attempt to use with a bank to get a loan in light of the above types of considerations that are important to bankers?*

Finding an effective combination of such elements can take considerable homework and searching. The entrepreneur can get a jump on this process by both venture planning and becoming acquainted with prospective bankers in advance of seeking a loan.

Supplier Credit

As noted above in the Cooper et al. data, about 6.3 percent of the time suppliers appear to play an important role in capitalizing start-ups. Like customers, they have a vested interest in what the venture will produce. What they are most likely to extend, however, is credit rather than cash. But most will not do even that for a start-up with no evidence of past performance in paying bills. This can become easy to understand by reading through published lists of bankruptcies. The lists are long, and each represents an individual or company from whom suppliers are unable to recover what they have lent. Consequently, many require COD or even payment in advance by start-up entrepreneurs.

Application: *From which of the suppliers it will need might the assigned case venture most likely get credit soonest, from which latest, and why? How much help, dollar-wise, should that be at which points in time?*

Other Debt Sources

After the company is going, still other debt sources may come into play, such as factoring companies, which buy accounts receivable at a discount for immediate cash. However, such financing is expensive.

Fast Growth Capital

For start-ups that can show convincingly that they are headed for very rapid growth and high profits, there are additional sources of capital. Principally, these are formal venture capital firms, private placements with larger institutions and public stock offerings. None of these would be interested in financing typical small businesses.

Capitalization Stages

Some ventures have sufficiently high margins and low capital intensity to start and sustain high growth without outside capital. Venture capitalists love to invest in those, but may not get the chance since such ventures don't need outside money. Next best are ventures that have profits that are high but not quite high enough to support all their growth. To expand, such ventures must continually "return to the well" for capital. If their growth and profits are strong, there is a high incentive for venture capitalists to invest, because such ventures offer both high rates of return and opportunity to make large enough investments at those high rates to justify substantial effort in checking the ventures out initially, arranging their successive financings and helping their managements as they grow.

Because of this need for repeated successive cash inputs, the financing of high-growth ventures is sometimes described in terms of stages. Pratt's *Guide to Venture Capital Sources* suggests three categories: (1) Early Stage, (2) Expansion Stage, and (3) Acquisition/Buyout financing.[2] Each of these categories in turn can be broken down as follows:

(1) Early Stage

- **Seed capital** is for product development, market research, team formation and planning.

- **Research and development capital** is for similar purposes but set up as a limited partnership permitting tax write-offs against personal income to limited partners.

- **Start-up capital** carries the venture up to but not through first sales.

- **First-stage capital** is for ventures moving into full-scale manufacturing and sales.

(2) Expansion Stage

- **Second-stage capital** is to cope with expansion of receivables and inventory during early growth.

- **Third-stage** or **"mezzanine" capital** is for major expansion and product development in profitable firms.

- **"Bridge" financing** is short in timing, and applies to companies in transition and possible reorganization for going public.

Application: *Which of the above financing stages might the assigned case venture reasonably hope to reach and by what dates?*

(3) Acquisition/Buyout Financing

- Money may go to a *going firm* for buyout of another

- Money may be provided for *individuals* to undertake a leveraged buyout. In this arrangement, the buyer uses the capital for a down payment and for working capital and then pays off the remainder of the purchase price to the seller out of earnings from the business.

Orders of magnitude for different stages were reported on 25 leading venture capital firms in 1989 by *Venture* as displayed in Table 5-6 below:[3]

Table 5-6 Venture Capital Firm Investments

Type	Deals	Price (millions)
Seed & Start-up	20	$12.6
First Stage	66	27.5
Later Stages	4	12.0
Acquisitions	4	17.5

A more recent study of 149 venture capitalists by Elango, et al., found that the extent to which venture-capital firms devoted their money to seed stage ranged by region from an average minimum 7.6 percent in Texas to 25.7 percent in Massachusetts and a high of 33.9 percent in the Palo Alto area of California.[4]

One implication of these stages is that different sources of money and investors with different types of objectives apply to each of them. A study by Freear and Wetzel[5] sampled 236 firms that had raised outside equity capital at some stage from venture capital firms. Among this group 46 percent had raised capital from other individual non-management investors ("informal investors"), most often before the venture capital firms contributed. Their suggestion as to a typically most appropriate sequence for raising capital was that first should come personal savings, then informal investors, then formal venture capital and finally public offerings.

Such staging concepts do not apply to most ventures, which typically start small with insider money, grow somewhat using debt and retained earnings but never advance through stages that use outsider equity capital. As could be seen in Table 5-4 presented earlier, Cooper et al. found that less than 8 percent of ventures drew upon outside individual investors, and less than 2 percent used venture capital firms.

Venture Capital Organizations

Formal venture capital organizations are companies set up to manage pools of investment money by investing it in start-ups and small growth-oriented firms. As of 1992, there were approximately 700 formal venture-capital firms in the U.S., according to Bygrave and Timmons.[6]

They can be grouped into four categories, knowledge of which can be helpful to an entrepreneur seeking to identify as many as possible of the capital sources potentially appropriate for a particular venture, in order to find the best one. These four categories are:

- **Private Venture Capital Firms** Full-time professionals manage pools of money put up by individuals. Most venture capital firms are private. A few are publicly held. Deals are often structured as limited partnerships in which the firm is a general partner.

- **Small Business Investment Companies (SBICs)** By agreeing to observe certain federal guidelines restricting investments, these firms become qualified to borrow federal money at attractive rates and thereby leverage their investment capital.

- **Corporate Venture Divisions** Similar to the above, but the money comes from a corporation, usually seeking "windows on technology" through investment in smaller firms. Operators of these firms are usually employees of the corporation.

- **Amateur Venture Capital Firms** Sometimes a small group of individuals will pool savings to become venture capitalists as a sideline, hobby, recreational, or social activity.

Lines between these types of firms are not always clear, but distinctions can help highlight some important considerations about where to look for capital. All these investor firms seek exceptionally high rates of return, on the order of 30 percent or more per year average, because they are undertaking high-risk deals. All will also want to become involved in the venture beyond simply putting up the money and walking away with some ownership. Typically, they want one or two seats on the board of directors. Some ask for interest on the money they put in by extending it as interest-bearing debt convertible into stock at their option. Others ask consulting fees and become more actively involved in the venture.

Experienced venture capitalists are typically found in those venture capital organizations that have been in business for several years or that are starting out with large sums of money to invest. In looking at potential investments they usually want a clear idea from the outset about when and how they should be able to cash in on their investment, either by selling the venture off to another firm or taking it public. This may conflict with goals of an entrepreneur who would rather stay with a venture and keep it closely held. Of course, cashing in may also be to the advantage of the entrepreneur, and professional venture capitalists will probably be more competent at accomplishing it.

Corporate venture capital investors often have a goal of drawing upon the venture for technical information to serve R&D goals of the corporation. One way this may come about is through interaction between technical people of the corporation and those of the venture as it develops. Another is through merger of the venture into the corporation at a later point in time. Each of these possibilities can have major implications for those running the venture.

Amateur investors raise another set of implications. For them, involvement with a venture is more likely to be a learning experience. This means they will more often than professionals make mistakes such as interfering too much or too little in the venture, arranging deals with counterproductive terms or giving the venturer inappropriate advice. Their funds are also more likely to be limited, so that when the entrepreneur needs further capitalization they will not be able to help. Worse, they may become fearful and defensive, blame the entrepreneur for creating a predicament and thereby generate more problems for the venture.

It can be awkward to get started with one set of investors and want to change to others. Even within types of venture capital firms there are contrasts in goals. Venture capital professionals sometimes specialize in certain types of industries or investments. Because of such contrasts of goals between investors it can be hard or impossible to get a second firm or group to buy into the deal structure a prior group has established. Thus, the choice of which source to begin with can be crucial to determining longer-term support for the venture.

Seeking the Money

Finding venture capital firms is not nearly as difficult as finding informal investors. Such firms are in business solely to pursue venture investments and are generally known among banks and local stock brokerage firms. SBIC type venture capital firms can be identified by calling the Small Business Administration and asking for a list. Publications, such as Pratt's *Guide To Venture Capital Sources* mentioned above, not only list venture capital firms but also give their addresses, phone numbers and investment preferences.

Venture capital firms typically receive hundreds of proposals each year and fund only 1 or 2 percent of them. Thus, much of what they do is screen proposals out, looking for the very small fraction of ventures capable of earning returns high enough (1) to pay for the time to find and work out terms with them, (2) to cover losses on those that don't work out and (3) to provide a return on the capital. Roughly 10 percent of those selected turn out to satisfy their hopes. Much as they would wish otherwise, another 10 percent are complete losers and those in between prove somewhat disappointing. For example, even Sevin Rosen Management, a venture capital firm with $1.7 billion in successful public offerings of its investees' stock, including such companies as Lotus and Compaq, found that 10 out of the 45 start-ups it backed failed.[7]

In approaching such firms it can be helpful, if possible, to obtain introductions by recognized sources, such as others who have dealt with those firms or are known to them. References familiar with prior accomplishments of those applying for capital have proven to be an especially effective part of the screening process to find the few winners. It has become a cliché in the industry that "it is better to bet on a grade A team with a grade B proposal than a grade B team with a grade A proposal." Experience has taught venture capitalists that problems with the idea are bound to arise, and a grade A team is more likely to recognize them early and find effective ways to succeed in spite of them.

The venture itself, of course, must also appear highly promising. Ideally, it should:

- be able to employ enough money to make the investigation and investment effort worthwhile. Deals under $500,000 probably aren't worth their consideration, although there can be exceptions. Elango, et al., mentioned above, found that investment limits ranged according to the size of the funds.[8] At the small end were funds whose limits ranged from a minimum of $300,000 to a maximum of $1.4 million, while in the larger funds the limits were over $1.1 million minimum to almost $10 million maximum per investment.

- be able to earn a high rate of return on that capital, on the order of 30 percent per year and higher. In the sample of Elango, et al, hurdle rates ranged 33.5 percent to 42.2 percent, with a slight indication that the earlier the stage of investment, the higher the rate imposed.[9]

- appear likely to be salable, either to another company or to the public within approximately five years so the investors can cash in.

- be compatible with the kinds of investment interest, expertise and personalities of the venture capitalists.

Guidelines Robert J. Kunze[10] used for developing a venture investment portfolio ranked number one by Venture Economics, a company that tracks venture capital firms, generally included investing only if careful investigation indicated that the venture

- could reach revenues of $100 million within five to ten years,

- could break even in three to five years or,

- could demonstrate the importance of its technology for less than $3 million,

- would be differentiated from its competition by something unique,

- would need less than $20 million in total equity capital to break even, and

- had original employee founders who were high achievers and experts in their fields and had proven functional skills such as engineering, marketing, or research.

Venture capitalists usually expect to see a well-thought-out venture plan that was written personally by the founders. If they get past the executive summary, read the rest of the plan and still have interest in the venture they will typically send the plan for selective review to one or more consultants expert in the venture's proposed line of work.

Application: *Describe a path of development for the assigned case venture that could conceivably make it eligible for professional venture capital.*

The deal, if they make one, will be formulated by the investors, not the entrepreneur, and may include several main provisions, such as:

- debt conditions convertible into equity or debt with warrants,

- a conversion rate that may depend upon performance; better performance by the venture, less equity for the investors,

- interest or consulting fees,

- purchase of "key person" insurance by the venture on certain founders,

- a nominee from the venture capital firm on the venture's board of directors,

- controls on spending or specification of ratio limits, violations of which will allow investors to take charge to ameliorate potential downside investment loss.

An important factor with many venture capitalists is the extent to which founders of the venture have committed their personal assets to it. Founders' motivation can be enhanced both by their committing personal assets and by the consequently larger share of ownership and control they receive for doing so. Venture capitalists want their investees to be as highly motivated toward success of the venture as possible.

How much ownership and control venture capitalists will want is often a concern of entrepreneurs who are seeking capital. In fact, as noted in the last chapter, the capitalists don't want either. What they most care about is the return they get on capital, not who owns how much of the venture. Average rates of return on 131 venture funds, according to a study by Bygrave, et al, ranged from 32 percent in 1980 to less than 10 percent in 1985. This varied greatly, however, according to the age and founding date of the fund, some reaching between 40 percent and 50 percent in peak years and others going negative.[11]

Institutional Private Placements

Other institutions with money that sometimes invest in ventures include insurance companies, pension funds, university endowments, community development funds, family trusts, credit unions, foundations and other variations. Some are profit-oriented, while others have other goals, such as social causes, education and economic development. There is no directory for these, so they must be found simply by asking around and general reading.

Locating a private placement through an investment banker may cost around 5 percent for the broker, another 1 percent to 2 percent as a commitment fee to the institution making the loan, and anywhere from $20,000 to $100,000 in legal fees.[12] Because of these high costs, private placements usually tend not to be for small start-ups, but rather for larger ventures probably farther along. Institutional investors judge their credit ranking by such things as:

- industry rankings of market share, growth rate and profitability compared to competitors
- formulas such as those of Standard and Poors or Moody's
- expected profit multiples of interest coverage
- debt-to-equity ratios and evidence of repayment capacity
- credibility evidence such as use of distinguished accounting and law firms.

Public Offerings

Finally, although it rarely happens, there is the alternative of mounting a public offering to raise venture capital. There are two main parts to this approach. The first is to arrange the offering in such a way that it will be legal. Government regulations have been set up at both national and state levels to protect the public from fraudulent securities sales. The second, and often hardest part, is the task of persuading people to buy the offering.

Offering Types

By far the most expensive and time consuming type of stock offering is the regular full, or **S-1**, offering. This requires application forms that are several inches thick, formal offering circulars, audited financial statements, much help from lawyers specializing in securities regulation, and months of time. State approval is usually also required.

For **smaller offerings**, it is usually possible to get by with exemptions from full registration under one or more provisions of **Regulation D**, although the paperwork is still substantial and the company is responsible for completing it. This simplified form of public offering requires filing Form D with the Securities and Exchange Commission within 15 days after the first sale, every six months after that until the offering is sold, and 15 days after the final sale. Records on the qualifications of each person approached for sale of the securities must be kept in a permanent file at the company. Each offering memorandum must be numbered and discussions with each investor must be noted and dated. Other provisions of Regulation D provide for exemption of a public offering from full registration under the following conditions:

> **Rule 504** permits the venture to sell up to $1 million in securities without registration, subject to the above requirements.

> **Rule 505** permits selling up to $5 million in securities to any number of accredited investors and up to 35 others in a 12-month period. If there are unaccredited investors, a disclosure statement must be prepared containing the information that would be provided in a full registration statement. Accredited investors include (1) institutions like banks, insurance companies, and pension funds with assets over $5 million; (2) individual investors who put in over $150,000, have over $1 million in assets, or earned over $200,000 in each of the past two years; and (3) directors, officers, and general partners of the venture.

> **Rule 506** permits the sale of any amount to any number of accredited investors and up to 35 others. No public advertisement of the offering is allowed. Non-accredited investors must be sophisti-

cated enough to understand the risks and merits of the investment. If there are unaccredited investors, a disclosure statement must be prepared containing the information that would be provided in a full registration statement.

Intrastate offerings are exempt from federal registration, but most states have registration requirements parallel to those of Regulation D on public offerings. Intrastate offering permission is for ventures that do business only locally, and where the offering itself is limited to that state.

On simple offerings there is the alternative of hiring a lawyer for help or of performing the work personally by imitating the paperwork of prior applicants. The main tradeoff is between the time a lawyer would take, much less but at a high cost, versus time the entrepreneur would take to complete the process.

One further option may be merger of the venture with the corporate shell of a company that has already gone public, and therefore has the permission, but is no longer in operation. If shares of the shell already have warrants for shareholders to buy more shares attached, these can be used to raise capital after the merger.[13] If the shell already contains capital, that too helps. Beyond that, the shell may do an additional offering, but permission will again be required. The approach can be legally complicated and is not much used by start-ups.

Getting the Money

Persuading people to buy the public offering is the most uncertain part of raising capital by this route. The entrepreneur may attempt to do it personally[14] or may engage a professional broker to do the selling. The broker may operate on a "best efforts" or "firm underwriting" basis. The hard part of the latter route is to persuade a brokerage firm to accept responsibility for guaranteeing the sale. Going through a broker can cost 10 percent or more of the offering. The smaller the offering, the larger the share of it that will have to be paid to accountants, attorneys and brokers.

Application: Formulate a line of argument to persuade an investor to put up money for the assigned case venture.

Pros and Cons of Going Public

Arguments in favor of public offerings as a way of raising capital for a venture are the following:

- There are a large number of potential investors to go after, and a large amount can be raised without any of them having to invest a great amount.

- The investor pool may become a helpful set of connections for the company.

- It is easier for investors to get their money back out of a publicly-held company, and this may make them more willing to invest.

- Public ownership may make the company more impressive to others with whom it wants to deal.

The following are disadvantages of public offerings for raising venture capitalization:

- Going public can cost a substantial amount of time and/or money.

- The offering may only partly sell, leaving the venture in a lurch.

- More owners gives management more constituents and potential litigants to contend with.

- More owners can make it difficult or impossible for the company to raise equity capital from other sources such as venture capital firms.

- Affairs of the company must be made public, which is a bothersome task and can divulge information helpful to competitors.

Application: *Describe the conditions under which it could conceivably make sense for the assigned case venture eventually to go public, and explain what it would take to reach those conditions.*

Supplementary Reading

New Venture Mechanics Chapter 6. (Vesper, K. H., Prentice Hall, 1993)

Exercises

1. Interview a banker and ask what he or she has learned from experience about lending to entrepreneurs.

2. Locate and plot on a map the venture capital firms most likely to fund ventures in your area.

3. Find and interview a small business investor about his or her experiences investing in ventures.

4. Obtain an offering circular, and describe what should be included in each section for a prospective new venture based upon one of the cases studied so far this term. Also comment on what sections might not apply to the new venture and what others should be added.

Venture History

1. Describe the actual (of those that exist) and projected (for those not reached yet) funding stages and sources of the venture being examined.

2. By what reasoning were alternative sources of funding rejected?

Venture Planning Guide

1. Assess fit for the most promising three alternative sources of capital for your most promising venture idea.

2. Assume the position of each of the three above sources, and formulate terms for extending capital to the venture that would be appropriate from the viewpoint of that source.

3. Prepare a "pitch" to present your venture orally to the most likely source of outside capital for it.

Notes

[1] Hendrix F.C. Niemann, "Buying a Business," *Inc.*, February 1990, p. 38.

[2] Jane K. Morris, and Susan Isenstein, *Pratt's Guide to Venture Capital Sources* (Wellesley, Mass.: Venture Economics, 1989), p. 2.

[3] "Financing," *Venture*, September 1989, p. 19.

[4] B. Elango, Vance H. Fried, Robert D. Hisrich and Amy Polonchek, "How Venture Capital Firms Differ," *Journal of Business Venturing*, 10, no. 2, March 1995, p. 166.

[5] John Freear and William E. Wetzel, Jr., "Equity Capital For Entrepreneurs," in *Frontiers of Entrepreneurship Research, 1988*, eds. Robert H.Brockhaus, Sr. and others (Wellesley, Mass.: Babson Center for Entrepreneurial Studies, 1989), p. 230.

[6] William D. Bygrave and Jeffry A. Timmons, *Venture Capital at the Crossroads*, (Boston: Harvard Business School Press, 1992), p. 72.

[7] "Risky Business," *Inc.* March 1990, p. 31.

[8] B. Elango, Vance H. Fried, Robert D. Hisrich and Amy Polonchek, "How Venture Capital Firms Differ," *Journal of Business Venturing*, 10, no. 2, March 1995, p. 166.

[9] B. Elango, Vance H. Fried, Robert D. Hisrich and Amy Polonchek, "How Venture Capital Firms Differ", *Journal of Business Venturing*, 10, no. 2, March 1995, p. 165.

[10] Robert J. Kunze, *Nothing Ventured* (New York: Harper, 1990), p. 26.

[11] William Bygrave and others, "Rates of Return of Venture Capital Investing," in *Frontiers of Entrepreneurship Research, 1988*, eds. Bruce A. Kirchhoff and others (Wellesley, Mass.: Babson Center for Entrepreneurial Studies, 1988), p. 275.

[12] Ellyn E. Spragins, "The New Quiet Money," *Inc.*, June 1989, p. 125.

[13] Ellyn E. Spragins, "Back-Door IPOs," *Inc.*, September 1989, p. 121.

[14] Ellyn E. Spragins, "Who Needs Wall Street?" *Inc.*, October 1990, p. 159.

Case Questions

General Questions

1. What would be your assessment of this business from an investor's point of view?

2. What price and terms would you reach for on the venture if you were (1) a founder of it and (2) a prospective investor? Please explain your reasoning.

Case 12 - Chem Synthesis Inc. (B)   p. 329

1. How should Jim price shares of CSI for the next round of financing and why?

2. In what order should he approach potential buyers of additional shares and why? What should be his "pitch" to them?

3. What other financial propositions, if any, should he be prepared to consider, under what conditions and why?

4. How, as best you can tell, does it matter whether shares are sold in Canada or the U.S.?

Case 13 - Ampersand (A)   p. 336

1. How should cash needs of the venture project, including contingencies, be dealt with at this point?

2. Whose company is Ampersand? What should the team propose to the Ewings regarding ownership? What should the Ewings ask for?

3. What, if anything, should be written and signed by whom at this point? What, specifically, should be stated?

Case 14 - Bill Foster (B)   p. 341

1. What do you see as Bill's main alternatives for financing, and what plan of action would you recommend he follow for them?

2. What is your assessment of the steps Bill has followed thus far in his search for venture capital ?

Case 15 - Paul van Hague p. 346

1. Describe three possible source(s) of funding that could be approached for this venture, and be prepared to explain your choices.

2. Describe the method of approach you would recommend for each of the above three possible sources.

3   Prescribe the terms each of those sources should impose if it did decide to provide the funding for Mr. Van Hague.

Chem Synthesis, Inc. (B)*
Pricing Shares

How to go about pricing the next issue of stock for raising money to keep Chem Synthesis, Inc. going was uppermost in the mind of Jim Tolivre, the company's chief financial officer and chairman, in early February 1995. Based on past experience, he expected he might be able to sell it to a number of parties, and one question would be which would be best to approach. Another question concerned how to price it. Aiming too low could cause too much dilution for too little money to the company. Aiming too high could fail to produce a buyer. Or, if buyers accepted a price that future performance showed was unwarranted, they could become resentful, making it all the harder to raise still more capital later on.

Sales Projections

Despite its progress year after year in finding new customers and generating new products, CSI had not yet become steadily profitable. While sales had grown from 1990 through 1994, so had losses, as can be seen from the tabulation in Figure 1 below. Prior history of the company and financial statements for the most recent year can be found in the earlier case on the venture, CSI (A). The balance sheets of Ex-

hibit 1 in that case tabulate the number of shares issued and outstanding by year.

Figure 1 - Historical Sales and Profit (loss) Figures *

Year	Sales	Profit (Loss)
1990	$0	$(24,277)
1991	306,289	(191,077)
1992	382,724	(189,512)
1993	467,723	(183,444)
1994	700,862	(295,871)

Projections prepared by Tolivre for 1995 were for sales of $4,000,000 with a loss carry-forward tax shield of $1,000,000. (Exhibits 1 and 2 present his current pro-forma financial projections.) The forecasted sales were based upon customer by customer projections, and were expected to come from, in order of importance, grain bin coating, roofing (expectations for roofing sales had recently increased to around $800,000), paper adhesives, and epoxy sales. There were 11 identified customers, each of which Tolivre expected would purchase over $100,000 of product, totaling $3,500,000. An additional $500,000 of revenue was to come mostly from new customers. He saw these projections as

---

* Written in collaboration with Dr. W. Ed McMullan of the University of Calgary as a basis for class discussion. Names have been disguised.
** All dollar amounts in this case are in Canadian currency.

encouraging, although he noted that they had always been encouraging but later proved to be overly optimistic. He recalled:

> On the first forecast, I got help from a former student who did it as a favor. He specialized in forecasting models at a local accounting firm. He managed to create a complete integrated model with five years of proformas and cash flows. Thinking just of the roofing industry, I tried to work out details month by month, based on bits and pieces of information from here and there. It was elaborate but pure fantasy.
>
> Now that we're farther along, I can base the forecasts on more specific information—customer by customer—plus the cost information we have accumulated from prior months. We still have to guess, of course. One customer is bidding on a job for Bangkok airport and another on a big building in London, Ontario, which they may or may not get. We also still look at industry data from secondary sources too. For instance, the grain bin business is entirely new to us, so we had to look through data from Canadian government statistics to estimate market potential. Altogether, I would estimate that the reasonably-possible worst case sales level for this year will total $2 million; the most likely level will be $4 million, and the reasonably-possible best case will be $6 million. So there is still a lot of uncertainty.

Previous Efforts at Raising Capital

Over the five years, about $1.5 million of the independent investment raised had come from 75 different investors, five of whom worked for the company. All of CSI's employees were shareholders or had share options. Tolivre and Ulrich together controlled about 44 percent of the 19,283,065 outstanding shares before dilution from employee share options. Collectively, insiders had a majority position of approximately 65 percent.

CSI had 70 outside shareholders, each of whom had invested between $5,000 to $100,000 (in one case). The investors were typically well-educated professionals. Although many understood business in general, few understood the complexities of the specialty chemicals industry or of CSI's potential as a manufacturer and marketer of such products.

Jim had raised money for the company through a variety of mechanisms.

- Since the other three founders claimed to have no personal money to invest (it later turned out that one actually did, but hid the fact), Jim borrowed $25,000 from the bank personally and advanced it as a zero-interest loan to the company for initial working capital. Ownership of the company was divided equally, and the other three shareholders agreed to guarantee $6,250 each that the company would repay Jim's loan.

- The first five external shareholders made $10,000 zero-interest loans and paid $1 each for just over 100,000 shares each, starting at 106,000 shares for the first person and decreasing 1,000 shares per person after that down to 101,000 shares for the fifth person.

- Most of the investment came through the sale of one class of voting shares.

- Two people put in a total of $105,000 for convertible debentures which allowed the choice of 10 percent interest, or future conversion to common shares at the most recent arms-length share transaction price at either the time of the note or the end of the year, whichever was lower.

It seemed to Jim that most had invested at least partially out of their faith in his integrity and in his background as a professor of entrepreneurship. The first investors had been insiders, but soon other sources outside were needed. Some leads had come from the company's banker and its accountant, but most had come through referrals by Jim's personal acquaintances—other professors, students, and business people whom he met through his academic work.

Provincial law, he said, provided that a company could remain private by selling stock at any time only to friends, relatives, business associates and sophisticated investors. The latter meant people with $97,000 or more to invest. Jim explained that the company had sold stock outside these categories with an approved offering memorandum. After each 12-month lapse it was permissible to solicit investment for a four-month period from the general public through an offering memorandum. But thus going public imposed other legal responsibilities on the company, such as having audited statements, holding annual share-holder meetings and retaining at least two outsiders on the board of directors. Technically, this meant that CSI was a public company. But its stock was not traded on any market, and it retained certain tax advantages of a private company.

The six largest investors so far had been the following:

- The largest investor had been introduced by a CSI director after the company had been operating for three years. He had been looking for a job as well as investment, but initially he considered the company too small and financially unstable for either. Finally after a year's observation of the company's progress he invested $250,000. About two months later, he put in another $100,000.

- The second largest investor Jim met through the manager of the bank where Jim kept his personal account. Jim had let the banker know about his company and its capital needs. The banker mentioned that he had another customer who might be interested in investing in such a company. Jim asked the banker to suggest that the customer give Jim a call. When the customer did so, Jim arranged to meet with him. Two months later the customer invested $75,000 and then still later another $105,000.

- Third was a graduate student who found out about the business through class. She had been a top undergraduate student in engineering, and her husband shared her enthusiasm for the investment. She had put in $100,000, although her father, an entrepreneur in the construction business with a sizable company, had advised against it. He said he would only invest in a company whose product was the cheapest in the market because that is what his company used.

- Jim was the fourth largest at $93,000 invested within the first 16 months of start-up.

- Fifth was a man who had known Jim when both were students. He now lived in a distant small town. He had seen Jim's picture in the town's newspaper when Jim was coming there to give a lecture and had come to renew the acquaintance. He also happened to be looking for something to invest in. About a month later, he put up $70,000.

- Sixth was a man who invested $50,000. Jim had known him casually. Jim asked a professor at the university who had invested in the company whether he knew of other people who might be interested in investing. The professor spoke to Jim's casual acquaintance and influenced him to invest.

Jim commented on his experience in trying to raise financing for the enterprise:

Raising money was hardest the first year when we only managed to get $50,000 from external sources. Last year we raised $687,621, and that cash inflow, even though it was much bigger, came a lot easier. But I've never pushed people hard. Usually I begin the conversation by qualifying them. I tell about the level of risk, the fact that they could get nothing back, and what the upside might be if things go as we hope. Of the people I qualify, about half so far ended up investing. Over time, though, we have gone through most of our close contacts; so although the investments have seemed to come easier, we have been left with fewer new investment leads to pursue.

He knew that at least three or four of the shareholders were frustrated with the lack of bottom-line results and didn't really want to hear any more "excuses." They wanted results, pure and simple.

A few of the investors, typically those with more money at stake, would phone from time to time asking for an update. Others would encounter him by chance and get answers to their questions. The inside investors had detailed information about the company as a matter of their normal work. The one larger external shareholder received monthly financials. Most, Jim said, seemed to be taking a long-term view, and were not hanging on any news.

Although there was no formal market price for the shares, Tolivre reasoned that the price he could get by persuading people to buy new shares from the company was the defacto market price. Jim put up the initial financing for the company himself by increasing the size of the mortgage on his house. After that, he first sold shares for approximately six cents in the summer of 1990, then he was able to raise the price in subsequent offerings over time as shown in Figure 2 below.

Jim pointed out that whereas most of the stock sales from summer 1990 through December 1993 had been to outsiders, most of the sales after that had been to people now employed by the company.

During 1994 everyone was sufficiently confident those sales would come to support our increasing overhead markedly. We moved from a 4,000 square foot bay in one building to a stand-alone building of 36,000 square feet and increased our workforce from six to ten people. The stock price went up with people's confidence in forecasted future profits. The later drop in per-share price from its June 1994 high of $0.35 resulted from failure of sales to reach expectations.

Figure 2 - CSI Price Per Share Over Time

Time	Share Price ($)
Summer 1990	0.06
Fall 1990	0.08
1991	0.10
Spring 1992	0.07
Summer 1992	0.10
Fall 1992	0.15
1993	0.15
January 1994	0.20
March 1994	0.30
June 1994	0.35
Fall 1994 to present	0.125

Another part of the reason for the most recent price, he said, had been that the company had been introduced by one of its present investors to a man who, on a 10-percent finder's fee (in shares) basis, was seeking investments in the range of $500,000 each for a group of investors. This man offered 12.5 cents per share and Jim consequently offered the same deal to existing shareholders. Some internal (employee) shareholders bought more shares at that price, but they voted down accepting the $500,000 deal. Jim commented:

> *When you are up against it financially over a long period of time as we have been, you tend to follow a principle that says if the money is available, take it. But this time we didn't, at least not yet.*

But Jim knew the company would need more money soon from somewhere. He thought the man who was seeking investments for a finder's fee was still interested in a $500,000 placement, but he was not certain. He also expected that CSI would shortly receive the first of three $70,000 payments for sale of a subsidiary it had created to carry out a project in Kuwait. But that had not yet come. In addition, there were stock options outstanding to employees and a former director at 10 cents per share for 965,000, 600,000, 365,000 and 200,000 shares in 1996 through 1999, respectively, and options to an employee

at 35 cents each for another 667,206 shares exercisable in approximately equal increments over the years 2000 through 2009. The number of shares issued and outstanding to date can be seen in the balance sheet of Exhibit 1 in the first chapter of this case series, Chem Synthesis, Inc. (A).

It seemed to Jim that there was need for an immediate decision about how much additional stock to try to sell now and what people to approach, old shareholders or potential sources of new ones, and if the latter, what types.

Some people had told Jim that he was crazy not to go public and others had said that going public would be crazy. He had been approached by several stock brokers and by an accounting firm specializing in companies going public. An ex-student who was president of a leading brokerage firm had told him to wait, if possible, until he had three years of growing profitability before offering public shares.

Jim presumed that three years were needed to produce three data points for a trend line and told all prospective shareholders that the firm would not be going public until it had three years of rising profits. Then, he told them, he would take the matter up with them and heavily weight the preferences of minority shareholders in the decision. Meanwhile, he promised to pay out 50 percent of net profits above $100,000 after repayment of shareholder loans and a zero interest $250,000 government loan.

EXHIBIT 1 - Pro forma Income Statement, February 1995 ($000's Canadian)

	Jan	Feb	Mar	Apr	May	Jun	Jul	Aug	Sep	Oct	Nov	Dec	Total
Projected Revenues													
Large Alberta Company	0.0	0.0	0.0	93.0	93.0	93.0	186.0	145.0	60.0	0.0	0.0	0.0	670.0
Large Sask Company	0.0	0.0	0.0	0.0	160.0	0.0	160.0	0.0	160.0	0.0	0.0	0.0	480.0
Small Czech Republic Co.	0.0	0.0	40.0	190.0	0.0	40.0	70.0	60.0	0.0	0.0	0.0	0.0	400.0
Large Alberta Company	0.0	0.0	0.0	0.0	0.0	0.0	60.0	60.0	60.0	60.0	60.0	60.0	360.0
Small Kuwaiti Company	32.0	0.0	30.0	70.0	0.0	0.0	70.0	0.0	0.0	70.0	0.0	70.0	342.0
Large Sask Company	0.0	0.0	0.0	20.0	30.0	40.0	60.0	80.0	22.0	0.0	0.0	0.0	252.0
Small Ontario Start-up	0.0	0.0	0.0	30.0	30.0	30.0	30.0	30.0	30.0	30.0	0.0	0.0	210.0
Mid-sized Alberta Firm	0.0	0.0	0.0	35.0	35.0	35.0	35.0	35.0	35.0	0.0	0.0	0.0	210.0
Small Alberta Company	0.0	0.0	15.0	20.0	20.0	25.0	25.0	25.0	20.0	10.0	5.0	5.0	175.0
Mid-sized Sask company	0.0	5.0	0.0	0.0	10.0	10.0	10.0	10.0	15.0	15.0	15.0	15.0	100.0
Mid-sized Thai Co.	0.0	0.0	25.0	0.0	0.0	0.0	25.0	0.0	0.0	50.0	0.0	0.0	100.0
Other	0.0	0.0	10.0	10.0	25.0	25.0	50.0	50.0	75.0	75.0	100.0	100.0	520.0
Total Product Revenues	32.0	5.0	120.0	468.0	403.0	298.0	781.0	495.0	477.0	310.0	180.0	250.0	3,819.0
Sale of PSC Kuwati Group	0.0	70.0	0.0	0.0	0.0	0.0	0.0	70.0	0.0	0.0	0.0	70.0	210.0
Total PSC Revenues	32.0	75.0	120.0	468.0	403.0	298.0	781.0	565.0	477.0	310.0	180.0	320.0	4,029.0
Direct Costs	19.0	3.0	73.0	274.0	220.0	170.0	436.0	279.0	267.0	188.0	108.0	150.0	2,187.0
Gross Profit	13.0	72.0	47.0	194.0	183.0	128.0	345.0	286.0	210.0	122.0	72.0	170.0	1,842.0
Total Administrative Costs	21.1	21.1	22.7	31.0	30.9	31.8	31.7	31.8	33.3	33.4	33.4	33.4	355.6
Sales & Marketing	7.3	13.6	11.7	25.1	29.4	34.8	40.1	40.2	39.1	40.4	40.4	40.3	362.4
R&D Expenses	-3.7	4.7	5.1	9.7	12.2	16.2	17.0	17.0	15.7	15.9	15.9	15.9	141.6
Depreciation	0.0	0.0	0.0	0.0	0.0	0.0	0.0	0.0	0.0	0.0	0.0	0.0	0.0
Total Overhead	24.7	39.4	39.5	65.8	72.5	82.8	88.8	89.0	88.1	89.7	89.7	89.6	859.6
Net Before Taxes	-11.7	32.6	7.5	128.2	110.5	45.2	256.2	197.0	121.9	32.3	-17.7	80.4	982.4
Profit Sharing, Bonus, etc. (7.5%)													-73.6
Investment Tax Credit													60.0
Tax		0.0	0.0	0.0	0.0	0.0	0.0	0.0	0.0	0.0	0.0	0.0	0.0
Net After Taxes	-11.7	32.6	7.5	128.2	110.5	45.2	256.2	197.0	121.9	32.3	-17.7	80.4	968.8

EXHIBIT 2 - Cash Flow Forecast, February 1995 ($000's Canadian)

	Jan	Feb	Mar	Apr	May	Jul	Jul	Aug	Sep	Oct	Nov	Dec	Total
Cash Inflow													
Inflow (Op's)	32	5	120	468	403	298	781	495	477	310	180	250	3,819
Sale of PSC Group	0	70	0	0	0	0	0	70	0	0	0	70	210
Total Inflow (Op's)	32	75	120	468	403	298	781	565	477	310	180	320	4,029
												0	0
Cash Outflow (Op's)												0	0
Material/labour	19	3	73	274	219	170	436	279	267	188	108	150	2,186
Overhead	31	40	61	72	74	74	75	70	70	75	75	75	792
Total Outflow (Op's)	50	43	134	346	293	244	511	349	337	263	183	225	2,978
Financial Transactions													
Opening Cash Bal.	35	34	79	64	155	210	218	479	661	794	834	774	35
Cash flow (Op's)	-18	32	-14	122	110	54	270	216	140	47	-3	95	1,051
Investment Income	10	15	0	0	0	0	0	0	0	0	0	0	25
Grant Income	10	1	2	2	3	3	3	3	3	3	3	3	39
Capital Purchase	0	0	0	-30	-30	-40	-10	-10	-10	-10	-10	-10	-160
Share Repurch. & Loan Pymnt	-3	-3	-3	-3	-28	-9	-2	-27	0	0	-50	0	-128
Closing Cash Balance	34	79	64	155	210	218	479	661	794	834	774	862	862

Ampersand (A)

January 1993 - Initial Capitalization

As the March 15, 1993 beginning of spring break approached, the founding team of Ampersand was optimistic, based upon conversations with Pearl Paint in New York, that they would soon be receiving a $5,300 order for 2,000 Claybords. For prior history of this venture, please refer to the case entitled "Elaine Salazar and Kathy Henderson." Kathy recalled:

> When Elaine came home from New York, we drafted up a one-and-one-half -page letter proposing a test market order for 2,000 boards. We figured the customer, Pearl Paint, would buy on some sort of consignment where they could return the product if it didn't sell, and then if that happened, we could find out why and use the information to shape our marketing strategy. We offered to be at the store for a week and demonstrate the product for their sales staff and customers. Now it sounds from phone conversations as though they will be giving us an order for 2,000 Claybords without any contingencies except that we will have to deliver them by the end of May.

At this news, the team promptly called Charles Ewing, and asked how fast he could make Claybords. He said he could produce at most 300 per week, and that much not for long because it interfered too much with his work in art. About the same time, the team was selected as one of the five teams to compete in San Diego State's North American Venture Plan Competi-

tion in April. Since they were also taking classes full time, they figured there would be much to work on over the one-week spring break.

Anticipating Production

In anticipation of sales they had regarded arranging for production as an important task. With David Shackleton's help the team had searched for ways to accomplish production on a larger scale. Paint shops, they found, were not equipped either to handle their thick mineral coating or to dry these panels once they came off their coating lines. The closest shop interested and willing to coat the panels was nearly 200 miles away in Tyler, Texas. Elaine Salazar and Charles Ewing had visited the shop, persuaded the owner to sign a non-disclosure agreement, and discussed with him the process of putting the mineral coating on the Masonite. The owner had said the team could come and experiment with coating a small batch.

After being coated the 4x8 foot Masonite sheets would need to be cut into smaller standard sizes of 8x10, 11x14, 16x20 and 20x24 inches. The edges of these smaller panels then had to be routed to round their corners and sanded to make the coated surface smooth. This was the most labor-consuming part of the task, which Charles Ewing had accomplished with a hand-held orbital sander. He had expended considerable time and effort learning what grade of sandpaper to use on the sander and how to get the surface smooth.

But he could not do it speedily. The materials for Claybord were relatively cheap. Masonite sheets cost about $15 each and could be cut into several smaller boards. The coating consisted of limited amounts of relatively inexpensive materials. Labor in cutting, routing to round the edges and sanding, on the other hand, could take as much as five minutes per board. By performing this work himself and selling direct to end users, Charles had saved the labor cost and had also been able to escape the high discounts to retail stores. But it consumed more of his time than he wanted to spend.

Changes in the Team

When David and Drew decided not to continue with the venture in the second term beginning January 1993 Elaine and Kathy recruited two new team members. One was Robert Tavarez, who had declined to join their team earlier. He commented:

> I wondered, why did my venture lose and theirs win. I realized that they had a great team and had spent 90 percent of their time on market research. My team had spent 10 percent on that.
>
> At the beginning of the next term I was passing down the hall, and Elaine said, "We need a CFO, because Drew dropped out. How would you like to do that?" I said, "Well, it sounds like a commitment; let me talk to my wife."

A copy of Robert's vita appears in Exhibit 1. The other new member was Scott Bryant, whose vita appears in Exhibit 2. Scott recalled:

> My training had been in mechanical engineering and I had some experience with manufacturing through work with a consulting firm. I had not come to business school with a goal of having my own business, but rather just to learn more about business. At the end of the first term I went to see the venture plan presentations because I had heard that there were great professors in the entrepreneurial area and the program was interesting.
>
> The presentation by Elaine's team really impressed me because the venture they were planning looked so straightforward and feasible. Other ones that had to do with robots and high tech didn't look like the students could really pull them off. But this team's product just seemed to be mud on a board that should be easy to make, and the team had really checked it out with artists. They had strong evidence that the market was really there. I told Elaine, "Hey, if any of the other people don't stay on, be sure to contact me."
>
> In the middle of January, I was signing up for job interviews in the career center where I bumped into David, who had been on the team. It surprised me because I thought he was going to do the venture. I asked him what he was doing there and he told me he had dropped out of the venture. I went right to Elaine. I repeated to her that I would like to join the team, and she asked me to meet with her and Kathy.
>
> One thing she specifically asked about was whether I was capable of fixing machinery. She had lived on a farm. Machinery on farms frequently breaks down, and farmers get good at fixing it. I had studied mechanical engineering, so I knew the theory and something about the reality of machines. But I had never run a production line.

The new team of four decided to meet in a local bar, Scholz's, and plan their activities for the coming term. Robert and Scott both committed to joining the team at least for the term and possibly for longer.

All four team members were also interviewing for jobs at the university's career center.

Anticipating Cash Needs

Following through on the Pearl order was clearly going to require capital. The four guessed that they might need around $10,000. Members of the team would be able to come up with some. There was some debate about how much money would be absolutely necessary to tide the venture over at least until it could win the $5,000 prize in San Diego. The team began to talk about each member about contributing $1,250 for starters to carry the project forward. But how should it be handled? Was this an investment in a business or simply expenses for carrying through a class project? It seemed desirable to aim for as much equality as possible in order to have all team members feel fairly treated and motivate them on the venture.

Also, what sort of formal arrangement, if any, should be established with the Ewings. They too had not only created the product, but had been working for about two years on trying to make a business out of it and had invested an estimated $40,000 to bring that about, including legal expenses for a patent application which was still being worked on.

EXHIBIT 1

Robert Anthony Tavarez

1824 South IH-35 #158
Austin, TX 78704
(512) 448-0635

Education

University of Texas at Austin, Austin, TX
Master of Business Administration, May 1993

San Jose State University, San Jose, CA
Bachelor of Science, December 1988
Major: Business Administration - Information Resource Management
Minor: Cybernetics Systems

Experience
1988

Silicon Graphics Incorporate, Mountain View, CA
Business Systems Intern
- Assisting with the merger with MIPS Computers in Corporate Finance.
- Transferring and reconciling financial data to the ASK MAXCIM system.
- Fiscal month-end and year-end related activities.
- DEC VAX and Personal IRIS operations.

1989 to
1991

Hewlett Packard, Palo Alto, CA
Software Applications Specialist
Development and support for worldwide field accounting systems.
- Programming in COBOL, JCL, and other fourth-generation languages.
- HP3000 mini-computer operations.
- PC and LAN training and troubleshooting.

Accounts Payable Clerk

1988

Lockheed Missiles and Space Co., Sunnyvale, CA
Systems Analyst
- Payroll Accounting implementation team for Tesseract Human Resource Management System.
- Emphasis in user transition and functional operation conversion.

Accounts Clerk

Activities

- Delta Sigma Pi, A Professional Business Fraternity, Regional Director (1991-1993), District Director (1989-1991), Alumni President (1989-1991), Undergraduate President (1988)
- University of Texas Married Student Network (1992)
- University of Texas International MBA Student Association (1991-1992)
- University of Texas Graduate Consulting Group (1991-1992)
- University of Texas/Silicon Graphics Toastmasters (1991-1992)
- University of Texas Hispanic Graduate Business Association (1991-1992)
- San Jose State Executive Council of Business Students Chairperson (two terms, 1988)
- San Jose State University Business Alumni Association Director (1990-1991)

Honors

- 1991 Consortium for Graduate Study in Management Fellowship
- 1989 Western Region Collegian of the Year - Delta Sigma Pi
- 1988 Most Valuable Active - Delta Sigma Pi
- 1988 SJSU Business Alumni Service Award

EXHIBIT 2

Scott A. Bryant

1307-A East 28th Street
Austin, Texas 78722
(512) 472-0806

Education	The University of Texas, Austin, TX, May 1993 • Candidate for the Master of Business Administration • Participant in EuroTrack '92 program held at ESADE (Barcelona, Spain) Texas A&M University College Station, TX, May 1987 Bachelor of Science in Mechanical Engineering
Experience **Summer** 1993	Tenicas Reunidas, S.A. Madrid, Spain • Created initial plan for a system of financial control. Conducted meetings, interviews and documented results, developing my overall Spanish proficiency.
1987 to 1991	Andersen Consulting, AA&Co., S.C., Houston, TX *Senior Analyst - Operations Management:* • Supervised and coordinated the development of a supplier partnership program at a major heating and air conditioning manufacturer, including an in-depth purchasing review. • Directed the creation of a new performance measurement system. • Developed a strategic plan to simplify product flow and improve productivity at a major textile company. Addressed issues/functions of sales, purchasing, organization structure, quality, and alternative pay structures. • Participated in the development of a custom education and cross-training program, focusing on quality and teamwork principles. • Assisted in the development of a Computer Integrated Manufacturing (CIM) Plan at an industrial valve company. *Staff Consultant - Information Systems:* • Designed and coded on-line and batch programs on various hardware platforms for a variety of industries (oil and gas, defense, and distribution companies). • Instructed month-long schools in computer fundamentals to new employees at internal training centers in St. Charles, IL and Manila, The Philippines. • Completed over 800 hours of continuing technical and functional training.
Activities	• Graduate Business Council - Chair of Academic Affairs: coordinated student and faculty involvement in design of new Texas MBA program and curriculum. • Texas Business Weekly - News Editor and frequent writer • Marketing Network - member and participant in Marketing Challenge • Dean's Task Force (MBA program strategy) - selected member • International MBA Student Association - Executive Vice President • Toastmasters (public speaking organization) - member and active speaker
Art Background	Three years of formal art training primarily in fine art drawing. Worked in pen & ink, pastels, charcoal and pencil media. Created sketches and formal works on surfaces ranging from newsprint to fine illustration board.

Bill Foster (B)

By the end of January 1980 Bill Foster was shifting his attention from working out the details of his venture plan to seeking a commitment for start-up capital. He knew that striking a deal with a venture capital group for financing would involve continued negotiations until both sides were willing to accept the terms presented. There were no assurances that the process would be completed within a week, a month or even later. Only one of his four partners had been associated with a start-up; none had been involved with venture capital financing.

Needs, he expected, would be for $6.2 million to cover a three-year development and market introduction effort. He would need about $2 million the first year to develop a working prototype and establish credibility of the team and concept. The founders themselves would personally be able to put in about $75,000 cash at most.

Possible Capital Sources

While recruiting his founding team and working out details of a business plan, Bill had also been gathering information about alternative potential financing sources.

> My philosophy has always been "It doesn't hurt to talk to anybody. You might learn something." So I followed up every lead I got, whether it had to do with raising money, finding people or anything. You may run up a phone bill, but people are generally very helpful. I got leads from headhunters and investors, lawyers and friends. I talked to other people who had started companies.

> They were probably the most helpful of all—those who had recently experienced what I was going through. They would reminisce about those exciting times. Of course, if they were successful and got their operations off the ground, they always liked to talk about it.

> I got many of the new company leads by reading magazines. Some of them have articles about companies that have just started up. I'd just call some of the presidents of the companies that had been interviewed out of the blue, tell them what I was doing, and ask their advice. I met several of the people out in California through those articles.

Bill had found three major options: venture capital firms, private individuals, and other operating corporations. There appeared to be significant differences in the way each of these groups made investments and in the types of deals that might be struck.

Venture Capital Firms

The venture capital firms were the most obvious possibilities. There were a large number of venture firms actively seeking investments. In addition to the best known and perhaps most prestigious firms, there were a wide range of other, less well-known, firms he considered worth contacting. Most were smaller, more recently started, or simply chose to keep low profiles. Contacts with two of these latter firms who expressed interest in Alta had come through one of Bill's partners, Gardner Hendrie. When Gardner was considering joining the team, he had called an old friend, Charles Meyers, for advice. Charles had worked with Gardner 15 years earlier in an engineering company, then gone to California to become involved in venture capital, and through it became very successful. When Gardner explained why he was interested in learning the climate for venture capital, Charles said his company, Pacific Ventures, might be interested. Bill recalled:

> Before I know it, Charles hops an airplane to come and talk with us. Right away he's very interested, partly on the strength of the business plan and partly because of his personal association with Gardner. But he felt we should have an East Coast firm in the lead. He'd be very happy with the New York firms we knew, but also suggested we contact Davidson-Mills, a lesser known Boston company they'd done some business with before. (It seemed that the best known Boston firms generally preferred second-round financings.) I had heard of Davidson-Mills, but had never bothered to call them. I didn't think they did start-ups, and I didn't think they were big enough. But Charles said they'd be good, and they'd feel good about our idea. One of the their partners had prior experience in the timesharing business and knew something about computers himself.

During his early discussions with the venture firms and in talking to the other recently started companies, Bill discovered some apparent ground rules in the venture capital community:

> One rule is that you're not going to raise $7 million on day one. No one has put in that much money. The going first round for my kind of deal is around a million and a half. Maybe you can get close to $2 million, but probably not more than $2 million for a team of untried people. That much would get us just past a working prototype.
>
> Number two is that they are going to have control—at least 51 percent. They're going to do it—there's no way you can get around it. At the same time, they won't commit to anything on round two. They'll talk about what they'll do if you do a good job, but if they don't like what you've done, you may not get that second-round money.
>
> None of it is cast in concrete. You can talk and you can go through scenarios. They'd sit me down and tell me what other companies did. "In 1974 Tandem gave up 74 percent of their company for $1 million. The investor got 72 percent of Prime Computer for $600,000 in 1972." The new start-ups did a little better—the going rate seemed to be giving up about 60 percent.
>
> I also found that many of the venture capital firms without technical backgrounds used outside consultants to help them evaluate high-technology ventures. The people they relied on were heavily booked and might take weeks to schedule.

Private Individuals

Another possible source of financing was from wealthy individuals. Certain tax provisions could make investments in firms such as Alta appealing; most of Alta's early expenses would be for research and development. If the funds for the R&D were provided by a limited partnership most of the expenditures could be deducted by the individuals against other sources of ordinary income. This would effectively lessen the actual after-tax amount at risk for those individuals. If the research proved successful, the investors would typically receive a royalty (normally 7 to 10 percent) on resulting sales. Such royalties would be taxed at long-term capital-gain rates.

Bill had been put in contact with a young individual who had taken an idea from an MBA thesis and built it into a very successful company, which he had recently sold for about $6 million. Now, to invest some of the proceeds he offered to lead a private placement with about 10 individuals each putting up $300,000 to $400,000. Because of potential tax benefits of such a placement and because some of the individuals in it did not get to see as many deals as venture capital firms did, Bill hoped his team would not have to give up so much ownership, maybe only 40-45 percent, if money could be raised this way. However, he expected this route would be more complicated and might require preparation of a private placement memorandum nearly as complex as a full-blown prospectus under SEC Rule 242. This might also require review by the state "Blue Sky" commission. "The SEC might not consider that even a wealthy lawyer is necessarily a 'sophisticated investor' when it comes to a computer start-up," he said.

Other Non-Venture Corporations

Once again, Bill found that people recommended to him as advisers for dealing with venture capital became capital sources themselves, as he began discussions with another company that soon expressed interest in financing the entire Alta start-up. Bill's contact, Gary Jameson, had formerly worked for a venture capital firm. Now he was vice president of administration in a company offering a product that depended on reliable computer systems. This company bought computers from major suppliers, then incorporated them in systems it sold to telecommunications firms. These systems required continuous absolutely reliable operation. Bill commented:

Gary's employer said they were very interested, and even though they were not in the venture capital business, they might fund us to the tune of $7 million. Again, this would be set up as partnership so that this company could get the more immediate tax benefits of expensing the R & D.

Gary said it might be impossible for me to raise money through venture capital sources—and I could be wasting my time talking to venture capital firms. Even though I had run R & D teams, I had never been the chief executive officer of a company, had never run the whole show. He said that venture capitalists were really conservative investors, and it was unlikely that any venture group would invest millions of dollars in a company in which the chief executive officer didn't have a proven track record.

This was the only non-venture capital company Bill had contacted for financing. After seeing the interest it expressed, however, he thought perhaps some other non-capital companies might have similar interests. He had heard that some major industrial corporations, such as General Electric, had in-house venture groups, but he wasn't sure how their investment strategies might differ from those of traditional venture capital companies.

Other Considerations

Striking a deal with any of the financing sources would, Bill expected, require detailed negotiations of unpredictable length with no assurance that a deal would ever be reached. The risks seemed heightened by the fact that the Alta team was untried in launching a company. One factor in their favor was that there had been a number of recent success stories of computer firms starting up and becoming industry leaders. Those deals also served as a growing data base to determine the increased values of the company for each round of financing.

Recent increases in the availability of venture capital also worked to Alta's advantage. Bill pointed out that more money now chased roughly the same number of high-quality investments, so his founding group should have good leverage in negotiating a deal. This could enhance terms for Alta on a whole range of issues, including relative percentages of ownership between investors and venture, relative privileges shareholders might seek through different types of common stock, preferred stock, or debt instruments with convertible provisions or warrants. The extent of voting privileges and membership on the board of directors would likely also be areas for negotiation.

Valuation of the company had to be considered somewhere in the process. With on-going companies, investors could look at the asset-bases and price/earnings ratios. With a start-up, the investor had to consider the concept, the projections, and the team, then decide on the venture's likely future value. Bill expected that more than one round of financing would probably be needed. How the first round of capital was priced and structured would, he supposed, influence the terms of later investment rounds.

Bill commented that an investor's main concern would be the likelihood of the venture's achieving a specified level of profitability in a given period of time. The track records with new products of his founding team could, he said, be a big plus. It had been in the start-up by Gene Amdahl whose record in the computer industry from his prior accomplishments at IBM had allowed him to marshall $17 million in start-up capital. Also in Alta's favor, Bill believed, was the fact that there had been a number of recent success stories of computer firms starting up and becoming industry leaders. Such venture precedents helped determine how stock prices and splits were negotiated between investors and founders at each round of funding.

Working Out Terms

All Bill's team members said they would agree to take smaller salaries than they had earned before. His own would, he expected, be less than half of this former salary and the others would be about 80 percent. The four founding members of the company would split whatever equity they could retain by dividing the number of shares by 4.2. Each of them would receive a 1/4.2 part except Bill. He would receive 1.2/4.2 or a "120 percent" share for putting the team together. Employee stock ownership and shares for other key employees also had to be considered.

Cash equity available among the team totaled between $50,000 and $75,000. Thus, to raise the necessary funds, a differential for stock paid by the venture capitalists and the founders would by required. No formula existed for setting a ratio differential. In some cases, the venture group might pay 10 times the rate of the founders; other times the ratio might go as high as 30 or 40. The figure was partly a function of initial funding required, available equity, willingness by the founders to give up a substantial or even controlling interest in the firm, and expectations on the time frame for future funding or start of shipments to generate revenues. Bill commented:

> Let's say there are 3,000,000 shares in the company and that if the stock was being publicly traded, the current selling price was $10 a share. That would indicate that the value of the firm is $30,000,000. But what would it have to earn to produce that result? If current earnings are $1,000,000 for example, then the price/earnings ratio would have to be 30. Investors would have to be willing to pay 30 times present earnings for access to future earning streams in the company.
>
> For a start-up like ours, you can look

at what our profits are projected to be in the future, adjust that by some perception of risk, and see what similar companies on the stock exchange are selling for in terms of their price-earnings ratios. Or, you could look at the historical pricing of other private placements in start-ups.

Another factor Bill thought important to consider was that more than one round of financing would most likely be needed. If progress as measured against the plan went as scheduled, he expected a better stock price and /or differential could be negotiated in the second round. On the other hand, if delays occurred, he and the three partners would be in a weaker bargaining position and, at worst, might find themselves unable to raise any additional capital at all.

Paul van Hague

Need for a Venture Plan

In April 1980, Paul van Hague, a mechanical engineer, was looking for help to create a business around a new type of saw to be used in sawmills for cutting lumber. It differed dramatically from the standard type of circular saw presently in use. The new saw gripped the circular blade on opposing circumferential edges with chain links (like holding a phonograph record by the edges) rather than having it mounted on a shaft through the disk's center as existing saws did. A photograph of the saw appears in Exhibit 1.

In performance, it differed from conventional rotary saws by making a thinner cut (kerf), thereby producing less sawdust and hence less waste from the lumber. Several years of development effort had been applied to the saw, and considerable progress had been made. However, still more work was needed to complete final development and introduce production machines. To do this, Paul expected a substantial amount of capital and creation of a company would be needed. He was looking for help in developing a plan to bring this about.

He had already gathered information, made performance analysis calculations for the saw, and formulated parts of a business plan to introduce it commercially. He commented:

> What we have at this point is still in the development stage. We've made a prototype and we think it demonstrates that the principle works. But the prototype is not a production machine, and we are a distance away from a commercial model. There are still some unknowns.

In a letter requesting assistance from a professor at a nearby university he wrote as follows:

> Enclosed find the Preliminary Organizational Setup for incorporation of my company. It is an attempt to "design" an organization which:
>
> 1) Allows me to keep control by owning 51 percent of the voting stock.
> 2) Gives four or five people who help me set up this business an opportunity to earn up to five percent of voting stock each.
> 3) Gives investors maximum assurance of a good return on their investment (and avoids double taxation at the same time) by having most investment in the form of subordinated debentures with a reasonable interest rate.
>
> I would very much appreciate your comments on this preliminary setup. Thank you in advance for your help.

Excerpts from Paul's preliminary planning notes are attached as Exhibit 2.

Present Status

Four people had participated in development of the new saw: Paul, his two brothers living in Holland, and his father, who had originated the concept in Holland but was no longer living. A prototype of the saw had been designed, built and tested in Holland, where it was presently housed in a fabrication shop but not used.

Patents on the saw had been obtained in the United States as well as several other countries. An abstract of the U.S. patent description read as follows:

Abstract

A circular sawing machine having one or multiple circular sawing blades driven at their outside periphery by one or more single or multiple strand chains of the type having inside and outside links connected by pins, the saw blades having for this purpose teeth, the teeth which go in between the inside links of the chain doing this with little clearance, and the teeth going in between the outside links of the chain carrying cutting elements wider than the saw blade, but still capable of passing with ample clearance between the outside links.

The saw blade or blades are not supported by a shaft, but shaped annular or flat. The annular saw blades can be supported by circumferentially grooved rollers located at the inside periphery of the saw blades with the blades fitting in the grooves and in addition indirectly by rollers on extensions of the chain pins rolling on a hollow cylindrical member attached to the frame of the machine just outside of the periphery of the saw blades.

The latter rollers can roll in grooves in these hollow cylindrical members, thus not only supporting the saw blades radially, but also axially.

If the chain and cylindrical hollow member enclose sufficiently more than 180 degrees of the circumference of the saw blades, or if there are two or more chains on sufficiently opposed sides of the saw blades, the rollers on the internal periphery of the annular saw blades can be omitted and the saw blades can be flat circular plates instead of annular plates.

Initially, the van Hagues intended to introduce the saw in the European sawmill industry. Work had been done with one European company that had expressed strong interest. However, after the van Hagues had developed a prototype and were about to proceed with a production model, the company changed its mind and canceled the order. Paul recalled that this was quite discouraging to his brothers and him. Other European mills had been watching to see how things went with the first customer. When that one canceled, he said, the feeling was that other European mills, which he characterized as very conservative, would consequently be unlikely to try the saw. Therefore, his brothers had backed away from working on the machine and suggested that Paul, since he had emigrated to the American Pacific Northwest, might pursue the development there instead. Paul commented:

It's kind of slow going. The lumber industry isn't doing well right now, and that makes it hard to find people who are interested. My feeling is that the industry will come back, though. When it does I'd like to have a company and machine in place ready to take advantage of the rebound, which will likely include expansion and modernization of existing sawmills, as well as construction of new ones.

Personal Background

Paul van Hague had been trained through a five-year course of study in Holland as a mechanical engineer, followed by an additional year of training in research and development. After graduating in 1965 he worked for 15 years for both European and U.S. companies mainly in machine design. After emigrating to the United States, he passed the professional engineers' examination and became qualified as a registered mechanical engineer. This field was, he said, "not all that easy." He continued:

> There are a lot of companies that have lost money on new mechanical equipment because they did not design and test with sufficient care to avoid the many things that can go wrong with new machinery.
>
> Quite a bit of my work was in heavy machines. But there were other types as well. Machine design is basically similar in different fields, although the emphasis varies. I worked for Ingersoll-Rand for several years on underground mining machinery, for instance, and there the emphasis is on compact design.
>
> I also worked in the lumber industry. I designed a chipper that worked very well, and some other things. In lumber it's important to maintain very small deflections, as opposed to compactness. Once you catch on to that, the machine design is very similar to that in mining.
>
> More recently I started doing consulting work for a company that makes fiberglass parts, gratings mostly. They needed a machine to sand their product. They tried one that was built for sanding plywood. Prices on it start at $25,000 and go to $700,000. It is very expensive and way too costly for such an application. It doesn't impose such high loads or need such high accuracy in plywood processing. So worrying about keeping deflections small is not so important as in wood machinery.
>
> At first it was hard for me to catch on to these different requirements. But now I am succeeding quite well. This customer needs lighter weight and lower costs. You can get that if you realize how little the loads are and the fact that deflections are not very important.

Origin of the CPC Saw

Inception of the novel saw idea had occurred about 12 years earlier to Paul van Hague's father, who had been engaged as an engineer by a company in the stone cutting business. It was having problems with a large reciprocating saw used to slice boulders into slabs. Paul recalled:

> My dad fixed that saw for them. There were some basic design errors in it. While he was doing that, he decided that the basic concept was not very good. So he started thinking about a better one and came up with this circular saw idea.
>
> He approached the owner of the stone company, which was relatively small, about possibly developing the idea. But the owner said, "we really don't need it. You fixed the old machine so well." Then that little company was bought out by a big company. My dad tried to interest them in the project too, but they had other contracts, and were just not doing any machine development, period. Meantime my dad had talked to some of the people who sintered small pieces of diamond into copper alloy for cutting the stone, and they offered to provide him with a blade free of charge for the new type of saw. So he kept pushing ahead with the idea.
>
> But it was hard to find a machine builder. Stone cutting saws are big, and there isn't that much market for them, especially in Holland which has to import the stones. There is more stone industry in Italy, and dad went there and talked to some people. But it would still require a big machine. That's where the stone saw project stopped. Building a prototype stone saw would just be too much. So he decided to see what the potential would be in the lumber industry. That seemed like a bigger market with different requirements, such as more

emphasis on speed, which began to interest my younger brother.

The younger van Hague, who held a Ph.D. in physics and worked as a specialist in optics for a Dutch university, offered to finance development of a wood-cutting prototype. His job afforded him access to shops where some of the parts could be made experimentally. Some help came also from Paul's older brother, who was head of a research institute space system group. Together, the three carried on the work as something of a hobby after their father died.

Performance Aspects

The principal advantage of the saw, the three believed, was that it wasted less lumber. Because it was held at top and bottom, as depicted in Exhibit 1, the blade was more firmly supported and, therefore, could be thinner. Consequently, it made a thinner cut in the wood and transformed less wood into sawdust. Paul estimated that as much as 5 to 8 percent more usable lumber could result from a log.

At the same time, he said, the saw took less energy to push through the wood. Partly this was because it did not chew as much wood into sawdust. And partly it was because the log passed through the center section of the blade rather than just past the bottom of the blade which in conventional machines pushed against the log's advance. Instead, the log encountered the blade where the blade was moving more vertically and less against the advance of the log. The amount of this energy saving, however, he said was not very important.

He had discussions with people in the wood products industry and the sawmill machinery industry as well as business contacts, bankers and prospective investors whom he sought out for help in moving the venture forward. Using this information he had prepared planning notes, excerpts from which appear in Exhibit 2. Views he encountered sometimes agreed and sometimes conflicted with each other. For instance, three different employees in one very large wood products company, estimated the value of sawdust and scrap variously as $2, $15, and $30-$40 per thousand board feet. Distinction between sawdust and chips was not always clear when people talked about scrap, he noted, although chips were considered much more valuable for use in paper making. Sometimes, however, the scrap was simply burned for fuel, regardless of its composition. "I don't think the wood lost to sawdust is worth more than about $10 to $15 a thousand board feet," Paul said, "but first I was told it was $2, so some of my estimates used that."

Machinery life was another area of question. Without extensive and expensive testing it was difficult to determine just how long a new machine would last. Not only was construction of a prototype expensive, but then it had to be proven by processing a lot of logs. "Even the big machinery makers usually can't afford that," Paul observed. "They often have to collaborate with a lumber manufacturer."

He had followed the customary engineering practice of making estimates during design of machine life based on theoretical computations. However, these were never certain until actual application over years had verified them. Paul judged that technological obsolescence made 20 years a logical life target. He noted that one northwest plant recently torn down had been running its original equipment since 1912. He had also been told that the majority of equipment currently used in the sawmill industry was 40 years old or more. One experienced member of the industry commented:

In spite of old age, that machinery is still running great. The industry is ridiculously conservative. We just don't make major changes in equipment. Sawmills have been being built the way they are now for 40 years and more.

One aspect of the new "CPC" (Circumferential Power Chain) saw design that Paul van Hague thought fit well with present trends was the movement of mills into processing smaller logs. The original old growth timber was being used up, and younger trees that had been planted to replace them were harvested when smaller in diameter. The new machine allowed use of a smaller blade for any log, since without a shaft in the middle more of the blade could pass through the wood. Paul explained:

> *The market in saws can be rather extensively segmented. Not only are there different sizes of logs, but there are hardwoods, softwoods, seasonal differences in cutting, and different types of sawing for different stages in cutting up a log. We are now thinking through design of a resaw for use at the tail end of a mill, in addition to one for the front end. There are a lot of possible choices. It isn't just the lumber industry. There are a lot of other applications too. I think my calculations show that the potential is there.*
>
> *I looked at application in the do-it-yourself market and in equipment for small cabinet shops, furniture shops, and so forth. I talked to Omark Corporation in Portland, Oregon. They're the world's leading maker of chain saw blades, but they recently bought a factory that makes small circular saw blades for table saws and the like. They were very interested in making saw blades for an application of this to any market that company could serve. But they only want to make the blades, because otherwise they start competing with their own customers.*

> *I also know a company in California that can help with the blades, but not the machine. Their man in charge of long-range research said he would talk to some of their customers about it. We have some features that might particularly fit that application. For instance, we have small feed forces because the circular cuts perpendicular to the feed action, whereas in a conventional circular saw the saw either pulls the material in or tries to push it out. That gives our design some advantages, in terms of both accuracy and safety.*

Contacts

Paul had discussed use of the new machine with some large forest products companies. They seemed, he said, to be interested but moving very slowly. Moreover, different ones seemed to be interested in different applications calling for different saw designs, none of which would work for a whole sawmill. Paul commented:

> *The sawmills seem to be coming under a cost squeeze with the foreign countries leaning more toward buying raw logs. Also, the mills are having to adapt more to smaller logs. All this may make them more interested in new types of machinery.*
>
> *There are a few mills willing to invest in new machinery, but only after it is on the market. Once you have a production machine, there are people willing to put it into a plant and try it out. The big mills have manufacturing laboratories for trying new ideas. A large part of what they are doing is trying out the different machines that are on the market. So once you have something that is marketable, it's easier to find people who are willing to buy through the regular route of capital investment. Then it's just a matter of the financial*

people feeling it's worthwhile to risk buying that piece of equipment. The gap between having a prototype and having a production machine for a mill to try, though, seems tough to get across.

I've talked to a number of people I thought might be interested in helping refine and produce our machine. There are two other machine designers I met who have very strong backgrounds in this field and might be interested in joining me, but they don't have money to invest.

Looking for potential manufacturers, I got in touch with a small machine building company in Vancouver, Canada, through a venture capital firm up there. To them our machine looks very big, maybe too big for them. If I spent more time with them maybe they would pick up on it. But they don't seem to have much money. It often seems that the people who understand technical subjects either don't have any money, or if they do, they also have so many good technical ideas of their own that there isn't any left over.

Two other people I approached in Oregon are an electrical engineer and another man who considers himself more of a management expert...I must say he is a very good talker. I did find two smaller mills down there who seem interested in working with us if we can bring them a machine to try.

Seeking Capital

In search of capital, Paul van Hague had talked to other people in business, including bankers and venture capitalists. None, he said, had been very helpful as yet.

Bankers I have talked to all seemed very friendly, and expressed a lot of interest in the company and me. But when it comes to the money, they turn me down. I couldn't even get a second

mortgage on my house.

It's much the same with venture capital firms, only worse. People had told me they were greedy. There seem to be quite a few examples around town where venture capitalists—not just their firms, but the individuals—have taken advantage of entrepreneurs. I think one of their problems is that they want very large profits very fast. They don't understand products that don't become obsolete fast and that take a long time to wear out. They may also shoot you down because of a bad investment they made in some other company they see as similar, even if it isn't. This was one of my painful experiences.

I called the head of a well-known venture capital firm down south and made an appointment to meet with him. When I arrived at the agreed-upon time, he wasn't even there. His assistant had never heard of me but was very nice and offered to hear my story. My impression of the head of the firm may be wrong, but I can't help thinking that he sees himself as sitting in the driver's seat with all the money, so he doesn't have to care. Why else wouldn't he show up, or at least send a apology later if he had to miss the meeting without giving notification?

Anyway, I talked to his assistant for two hours or so. He was very pleasant. He was even interested and wanted some references, which I gave him and he checked. And then after that it suddenly stopped. He sort of gave me a preliminary turn down, and I had a feeling that there was something I didn't know.

When I checked further, I found out they had invested in a California company that makes scanners and computer programs for the lumber industry. This investment didn't grow as fast as they had expected. I think that may have biased them against me.

I followed up the California company further by getting some brochures. They were fairly ordinary. Someone who had bought from them said they were one of the first pioneers with a new technology, but they had lost their lead and were now in the middle of the pack of about 10 other companies. It seems they definitely had a good application, and as soon as that was recognized a lot of other companies jumped in and gave them competition. The opportunity that company was capitalizing on was reduction of labor costs in the lumber industry, which is definitely a promising direction. It occurred to me that we could combine technology like that with our new saw and make it more attractive. But, of course, that would require still more capital.

I'm still willing to talk to venture capitalists, although from what I've seen and heard they don't seem to be too venturesome. I just don't know if the right amount of capital for us to attempt to employ is large enough to interest them, or if the payback will be fast enough and high enough. I have heard from others that too often they want to move too fast. Going into the sell stage too fast has produced some very unnecessary failures.

Looking Ahead

You can't tackle the whole job of getting a machine like this on the market all at one time. I feel there is a lot of potential. I have discussed it with so many knowledgeable people. I feel I have a pretty good idea. I don't think I have overlooked any major technical things. But there is still work to do. I can feel

very confident about it, but development takes time. It doesn't take all that much money if investors are willing to be patient.

I think the first step now would be more development. Maybe it would not require much money. But it is development, and there are not many people willing to invest in just development. Of course, many don't understand it.

As I mentioned, it's very difficult to work up good data on machine life. We have some from the prototype, but probably not enough. One finding from the testing we did was that we must make changes, particularly in the drive, which will be different on the next machine. The chain has a bad reputation at high speed. With a double belt drive it looks like we will be able to go faster and with little or no wear.

I would really like to meet someone who understands this financial stuff and knows how to put a financing proposal together. Instead, I am doing it more or less by myself. It is a struggle because I'm not a financial person. I know something about it from taking accounting courses and so on, which leaves me not completely ignorant. But it's not my field.

My most immediate job is to keep day-to-day things going and feed my family. My brothers and I still do a little work on the machine, but we are also doing other things. A little while ago I hired a young engineer to work with me. But a customer hired him away. It seemed to make both of them happy, so that's okay, I guess. But it didn't help me move toward what I'd really like, which would be to build a business around a proprietary product like this saw.

EXHIBIT 1   The CPC Saw Prototype

CPC saw with removed protective covers.

Patents granted :
   USA   3,799,021   Germany 2121200   Italy 960882
   Canada 148,037   Austria 316848   Belgium 782.295
   Great Britain 1393563   France 72.14553

For further information contact :
        Ir. G. Hammerschlag
        Gezichtslaan 82
        Bilthoven – the Netherlands
        Tel. (030)-782889

EXHIBIT 2   Excerpts from Paul van Hague's Planning Notes

PAUL VAN HAGUE, P.E.
Machine Design - Research and Development - Metric Conversion

THE CPC SAWING PROCESS AND ITS ADVANTAGES

The Sawing Process Generally

Sawing can be defined as cutting a piece of material by moving a thin blade with teeth across it, causing each tooth to remove a small chip of material.

This method of cutting has the following advantages:

1) Compared with shearing and punching it does not significantly deform the material next to the cut, nor does it induce stresses or hair cracks into the adjacent material.

2) Compared with flame cutting, due to the absence of a significant heat input, it does not affect the quality of the material next to the cut and does not cause distortion of the material.

3) Compared with milling, turning and other machining operations, to which it is of course related, it wastes less material due to the narrow cut (or "kerf" as the saw cut width is often called).

4) Compared with more exotic cutting methods, like electric discharge, electro-chemical, ultrasonic, water jet, abrasive jet, laser beam and electron beam cutting, its major advantage is its low cost.

Thus we see that sawing is the major method of cutting material in lumber manufacturing, woodworking and natural stone processing, while it is used extensively in cutting of metal and plastic raw materials produced in bar and extrusion form.

However, sawing has a problem of its own, as everybody who ever used a hacksaw or other hand saw knows. The thin blade gets easily deflected from its nominal position, causing the saw cut to deviate from its intended path and causing inaccuracy in the pieces made.

Every saw has this problem, whether it be one of the many kinds of reciprocating hand saws, the powered reciprocating frame saws, bandsaws or circular saws. Circular saws and bandsaws are often used with so called "saw-guides," pads of babbitt, Teflon or other material having low coefficient of friction. These pads are held against the saw blade and give additional support beyond what shaft (circular saw) or wheels (band saw) can give. Circular saws can be made thicker. However, this solution causes, besides of course a more expensive blade,

EXHIBIT 2 (continued)

more waste of material, since the saw cut will be wider. In fact, it will be a gradual change from saw blade to milling cutter if the blade is made thicker and thicker.

The CPC Principle

The CPC (Central Passage Circular) saw is a circular saw driven not by a central shaft, but by peripheral special chains, guided radially by rollers on the chain pins and axially by saw guides, eliminating the need for a central shaft.

The major advantage of this system is that it allows support of the saw blade for a given saw blade thickness and height-of-cut superior to conventional circular saws, both single arbor and double arbor types, while keeping the advantages of conventional circular saws over band and reciprocating saws.

Our mathematical calculations show that the CPC saw blade support is also much stiffer than that of double arbor circular saws, allowing a kerf for the CPC saw of only one-half to four-tenths that of a double arbor saw.(Of course again, not all of this increase in stiffness has to be used to reduce kerf; some of it could be used to increase accuracy.) In addition the CPC saw has the advantage that even if the saw blade is deflected, it will make a continuous cut, whereas the double arbor saw, if its two saws are deflected differently, will make an ugly ridge in the center of the sawn product.

It must also be mentioned that the CPC sawing principle has another advantage over both single and double arbor circular saws in that it cuts over the full height of the cut more or less perpendicular to the grain (like a band saw). This means that feed forces are very small, the resulting deflections of the machine and the material to be cut will be small, and the accuracy of the cut will be high. Also, when cutting wood, the cuttings will be short and crumbly (not like planer shavings), will easily fill up the gullet spaces in the blade and be easily sucked out of the gullets by a vacuum sawdust removal system, allowing very clean cutting.

Description of the Saw

A CPC sawing machine (Central Passage Circular saw) lets logs and beams pass across the central part of the circular saw. This is not possible with any other circular sawing machine due to the center shaft and its bearings, which block the passage of the central part. A conventional circular saw has a penetration limited to one third of its diameter. A CPC saw has a capacity of more than half of its diameter.

EXHIBIT 2 (continued)

Direct drive and guidance at the outside periphery, sawing teeth of hard metal (carbide) and large gullets for the sawdust between the sawing teeth guarantee a quiet and precise operation of the CPC saw and consequently straight pieces of timber.

Conventional circular sawing machines have a strongly varying direction of the motion of the sawing teeth with respect to the fiber direction of the wood. The cutting direction of the teeth of a CPC saw is always perpendicular to the fiber direction of the wood. Consequently, the sawdust is of a granular nature and can be easily removed.

A CPC sawing machine can be moved easily by truck to a working site, if it appears to be more economical to saw the trees on the spot and to transport the sawn timber afterwards.

Comparison with Band Saws

Band saws do not have a stiff support of the saw blade, mainly because the blade must be thin to bend over the wheels. As a result, band saws are the least accurate of the major saw types. They are popular in the lumber saw mills, because they can saw thick logs, cants, or lumber with narrower kerf than shaft-driven single or double arbor circular saws. Of course some of the advantage of the thin kerf is lost again due to their inaccuracy, requiring substantial removal of material in finishing. The CPC principle also allows thin kerf, but without the inaccuracy inherent in the band saw process and without the need for the large machine frame with the big wheels, the pit in the floor, the expensive and difficult-to-handle blades, and the larger filing room.

Comparison with Frame Saws

With a CPC saw, trees can be sawn into beams or boards and thus it can do work that used to be done with reciprocating saws. Reciprocating saws are big, expensive machines, and reciprocation of their heavy saw frame causes large acceleration and deceleration forces, resulting in wear of the bearings and guides. CPC sawing machines have no dynamic forces and are small compared to reciprocating sawing machines of comparable capacity. The attainable cutting speed of the CPC saws is twice that of reciprocating saws. Moreover, the sawing process is a continuous one, whereas the backward motion of reciprocation saws is idle.

Reciprocating frame saws, like band saws, can saw thick material with relatively thin kerf. However, the reciprocating motion means that in their extreme positions the saw blades do not move, while the feed of the material continues, causing momentarily very large bites per tooth, resulting in rough and inaccurate cutting and requiring large finish allowances. Also, the reciprocating movement does not allow high saw speeds, not even close to those of circular and band saws.

EXHIBIT 2 (continued)

Finally, the continuous acceleration and deceleration of the saw frame requires a large fly-wheel (if at least a somewhat reasonable saw speed is required) and a machine frame that can take the substantial acceleration and deceleration forces, leading to a rather large and heavy machine.

Estimated Savings with CPC Rotary Gang Saw

The savings from using a CPC Rotary Gang instead of a conventional rotary gang result from the thinner kerf and higher accuracy inherent in this new design. Feed speeds will be comparable to those of conventional rotary gangs. See the following table of saw characteristics.

Saw Characteristics	CPC Rotary Gang	Conventional Rotary Gang
Kerf	0.120"	0.160"
To be removed by planing per cut	0.030"	0.050"
Feed speed - max. practical	100 ft/min	100 ft/min

To determine yearly savings, the volume of wood that is converted into lumber instead of sawdust and planer shavings will be calculated for the following "typical" sawmill operation.

- Depth of cut: 4"–12", 7" average
- Feed speeds: 50–100 ft/min, 70 ft/min average
- Average number of cuts per pass: 5
- 2-shift operation, 250 days/year/4 hours of actual sawing per shift (2000 hrs. of sawing/year)

Length of cut sawed in one year:
2000 (hrs/yr.) x 60 (min/hr) x 70 (ft/min) x 3 (cuts/pass) = 42,000,000 ft/year

Volume in cubic feet of timber turned into sawdust and planer shavings with conventional rotary gang saw:
42,000,000 x 7/12 (height of cut, in ft) x (0.160 + 0.050)/12 (thickness of wood removed, in feet) = 428,750 cubic feet/yr. (= 5,145,000 bd. ft./yr.)

Same for CPC rotary gang saw:
42,000,000 x 7/12 x (.120 + .03)/12 = 306,250 cubic feet/yr. (= 3,675,000 bd.ft./yr.)

EXHIBIT 2 (continued)

Savings with CPC rotary gang per year:
428,750 - 306,250 = 122,500 cubic feet/yr. = 1,470,000 bd.ft./yr.

Assume value of lumber = $200 per 1,000 bd. ft.
Assume value of sawdust and planer shavings = $2 per 1,000 bd.ft
Value of savings is then:
(1,470,000/1,000) x ($200. - $2.) = $291,060

Savings with CPC Rotary Gang Saw

Estimated cost of conventional rotary gang: $200,000.
Estimated cost of CPC rotary gang: $300,000.
Assume interest on invested capital is 10%.
Higher interest cost CPC gang: 10% of $100,000. = $10,000/yr.
Higher depreciation cost CPC gang (assuming depreciation in 10 years): 1/10 x $100,000. = $10,000./yr.
Total increase of operation costs: $20,000./yr.
Net savings with CPC rotary gang:
$291,060 - $20,000 = $271,060/yr.

Assuming that the average thickness of the lumber produced with this rotary gang operation is 1.25 inches, the yearly production will be approximately: 42,000,000 (length of cut, ft/yr.) x 7/12 (depth of cut, ft) x 1.25 (thickness of lumber, inch) = 30,625,000 bd.ft./yr.

Note: Power consumption, number and skill of operators required, and maintenance cost for a CPC rotary gang are expected to be about the same as for a well-designed conventional rotary gang.

Summary

The CPC saw has superior stiffness of support of the saw blade over conventional shaft-driven single and double arbor circular saws, allowing approximately one-half the kerf of double arbor saws and one-third to one-quarter the kerf of single arbor saws for the same depth of cut. Also it does not have the problem of a possible mismatch of the two saw cuts, as double arbor circular saws have.

Further, its cutting more or less perpendicular to the grain leads to small feed forces contributing to accurate cut and crumbly cuttings that can be easily removed with a suction system.

Main advantages of the CPC saw over band saws are its more accurate cut, the less massive machine and the smaller, easier-to-handle-and-sharpen saw blades.

Main advantages of the CPC saw over frame saws are its higher speed, neater and more accurate cut and generally less massive machine.

EXHIBIT 2 (continued)

Estimated North American Market for CPC Rotary Gang Saw for Lumber Manufacture

I.   Softwoods
       Production of one CPC rotary gang saw in two-shift operation will be approximately 30,000,000 bd.ft./yr.

       Assume that lumber production from side boards will be approximately the same in magnitude. This means that there is a need for one rotary gang for approximately every 60,000,000 bd.ft. of lumber produced.

       Yearly softwood production in North America (U.S.A. and Canada) is approximately 40,000,000,000 bd.ft.

       Potential market for rotary gangs in softwood production: 40 billion/60 million = 666 machines

       Assume life of a machine approximately 20 years. Thus market would be: 666/20 = 33.3 machines/year   At $300,000 per machine this would be $10,000,000 per year.

       Accessory, spare parts and saw blade business would boost this to approximately $20,000,000 per year.

II.   Hardwoods

       Harder wood and thinner boards would reduce production of rotary gang to approximately 15,000,000 bd.ft./yr. Assume again approximately the same amount of lumber from sideboards, thus one rotary gang per 30,000,000 bd.ft./yr.

       Yearly hardwood production in North America is approximately 7,500,000,000 bd.ft./yr.

       Potential market for rotary gangs is: 7.5 billion/30 million = 250 machines

       Assume life of a machine approximately 20 years. Market would be then: 250/20 = 12 machines/year   At $300,000 per machine this would be $3,600,000 per year.

       Accessory, spare parts and saw blade business would boost this to approximately $7,000,000 per year.

III.   Total Rotary Gang Business in North American Wood Sawing Industry

               $20,000,000 + $7,000,000 = $27,000,000 per year.

EXHIBIT 2 (continued)

Estimate of Capital Needs for Business Development

Four phases can be distinguished in this business development:

1) Preparation
2) First Production Machine
3) Growth
4) Stabilization when limit of market potential is reached

As no capital is needed in the final stabilization stage, this phase is not considered here.

Growth is considered only up to a yearly sales volume of $30,000,000 even though market investigation showed that total business potential, including spare parts, repair work and accessory equipment is in the $50,000,000 to $100,000,000 a year range for North America alone. The first three phases will not be discussed in more detail.

Phase 1 - Preparation

This period prior to design and manufacturing of the first production machine, estimated at approximately six months, is needed for the following activities:

1) Preparation of organization, including incorporation.
2) Negotiations with potential customers.
3) Completion of tests on prototype and demonstration of prototype to potential
        customers.

Expenses for this period will be:

Labor: 1 man 6 months, at $3,333 per month	$20,000
Materials for tests	10,000
Travel, office expenses and other overhead	20,000
Initial cash payment for license agreement	50,000
	Total $100,000

Income: none
Investment Requirement: $100,000.

EXHIBIT 2 (continued)

Phase 2 - First Production Machine

Assume that the first order consists of a rather large $300,000 machine (a conservative approach for calculating capital needs), that the customer wants delivery 18 months after placement of order, and is willing to pay 25 percent of price at placement of order, 25 percent of price six months and 12 months after placement of the order, and the final 25 percent at delivery of machine.

Expenses and income are calculated for this period on a monthly basis (See Table 1 below.) Personnel expenses are based on the assumption that during this period manpower will be on a constant level, a highly desirable situation in a high-technology business. Personnel listed in Table 1 are needed with approximately the salaries and overhead shown.

Table 1: Personnel Requirements of Phase 2

Skill	No.	Avg. Monthly Salary	Total Monthly Expense
Genl Mgr/Engr/Salesman	1	$3500	$3500
Design Engineer	2	2100	4200
Draftsman	1	1500	1500
Assembly Man	2	1500	3000
Secretary	1	800	800
Total direct salary expense			$13,000
Overhead (80%)			$10,400
Total monthly personnel expense			$23,400

Cost estimating, buying, production control and quality control functions will be performed mostly by engineering personnel (who always do this to a certain extent, even in large organizations). Quality control and production control functions will be performed by assembly people, also.

Parts manufacturing will be subcontracted and is estimated at 45 percent of the $135,000 sales price. Payments for parts are assumed to be distributed as follows: $3,000 per month the first six months after receipt of order, $15,000 per month the next six months and $4,500 per month the last six months.

Table 2 shows the personnel and parts expenses on a month-by-month basis. It also shows a 5 percent license fee payable at delivery of the machine, the progress payments for the machine by the customer and the investment capital required on a month-by-month basis. It is assumed that accounts receivable are equal to accounts payable, which eliminates the need to consider them in these calculations. The total amount to be invested will be $303,500. Note, if the first machine turns out to be less expensive, the capital required will be proportionately less.

EXHIBIT 2 (continued)

If sufficient preparatory work with the customer can be done during the six-month, Phase 1 period, final design and manufacturing of this machine will be possible in nine to 12 months, leaving six to 10 months of the 18-month, Phase 2 period for endurance testing of this machine and a strong sales effort helped by being able to show the machine to potential customers.

This would not have significant influence on the amount of capital required.

Table 2: Cash Flow and Capital Required in Phase 2
on a Month-by-Month Basis (Expenses in $)

Month	Payroll+ Overhead	Parts	Licenses	Total	Income	Invest. Req'd
1	23,400	3,000		26,400	75,000	—
2	23,400	3,000		26,400		—
3	23,400	3,000		26,400		4,200
4	23,400	3,000		26,400		26,400
5	23,400	3,000		26,400		26,400
6	23,400	3,000		26,400		26,400
7	23,400	15,000		38,400	75,000	—
8	23,400	15,000		38,400		1,800
9	23,400	15,000		38,400		38,400
10	23,400	15,000		38,400		38,400
11	23,400	15,000		38,400		38,400
12	23,400	15,000		38,400		38,400
13	23,400	4,500		27,900	75,000	—
14	23,400	4,500		27,900		—
15	23,400	4,500		27,900		8,700
16	23,400	4,500		27,900		27,900
17	23,400	4,500		27,900		27,900
18	23,400	4,500	15,000	42,900	75,000	—
Total	$421,200	$135,000	$15,000	$571,200	$300,000	$303,300

Note: Cash on hand at end of period: $32,100.

EXHIBIT 2 (continued)

Phase 3 - Growth

Assumptions for the ensuing four years would include the following:

The first year (third year from startup of venture), one rather large $300,000 machine per quarter is sold; the second year three such machines per quarter; the third year 10 machines; and the fourth year 25 machines per quarter. Not all machines will cost $300,000. Quantities will be different and jumps in sales will not occur exactly at the first of each year. However, these assumptions should allow estimation of the order of magnitude of capital requirements.

It is assumed that all machines will be delivered nine months after receipt of order, and that customers will make progress payments of 25 percent at placement of order, 25 percent three months and six months after placement of order, and the final 25 percent after delivery of machine. Personnel increases are assumed to take place at the same time sales jump, thus the first of each year. Personnel costs assume an average direct salary of $1,700 per month plus 80 percent ($1,360 per month) overhead.

Parts manufacturing will be subcontracted at cost 45 percent of sales price of $135,000 per machine. Parts will cost $6000 per month during the first three months and $9000 per month during the last three months of the period between placement of order and delivery of the machine.

Table 3 summarizes expenses (including a 5 percent license fee payable at delivery of the machines), income and capital needed. It assumes again accounts payable equal accounts receivable, and therefore do not need consideration. Note that the third year still requires a significant investment, but the following years show an increasing profit.

EXHIBIT 2 (continued)

Table 3: Cash Flow and Capital Required in Phase 3 on a Quarterly Basis

| Year | Quarter | Expenses in $ | | | | Income in $ | Investment Capital Required in $ | Profit/Loss |
		Payroll + Overhead	Parts	Licenses	Total			
	1	128,520	18,000	—	146,520	75,000	*39,420	—
	2	128,520	108,000	—	236,520	150,000	86,520	—
3	3	128,520	135,000	—	263,520	225,000	38,520	—
	4	128,520	135,000	15,000	278,520	300,000	—	21,480
	Total	514,080	396,000	15,000	925,080	750,000	164,460	21,480
	1	275,400	171,000	15,000	461,400	450,000	—	(11,400)
	2	275,400	351,000	15,000	641,400	600,000	8,520	(32,880)
4	3	275,400	405,000	15,000	695,400	750,000	—	54,600
	4	275,400	405,000	45,000	725,400	900,000	—	174,600
	Total	1,101,600	1,332,000	90,000	2,523,600	2,700,000	8,520	184,920
	1	697,680	531,000	45,000	1,273,680	1,425,000	—	151,320
	2	697,680	1,161,000	45,000	1,903,680	1,950,000	—	46,320
5	3	697,680	1,350,000	45,000	2,092,680	2,475,000	—	382,320
	4	697,680	1,350,000	150,000	2,197,680	3,000,000	—	802,320
	Total	2,790,720	4,392,000	285,000	7,467,720	8,850,000	—	1,382,280
	1	1,606,500	1,620,000	150,000	3,376,500	4,125,000	—	748,500
	2	1,606,500	2,970,000	150,000	4,726,500	5,250,000	—	523,500
6	3	1,606,500	3,375,000	150,000	5,131,500	6,375,000	—	1,243,500
	4	1,606,500	3,375,000	375,000	5,356,500	7,500,000	—	2,143,500
	Total	6,426,000	11,340,000	825,000	18,591,000	23,250,000	—	4,659,000

*$32,100 was left from Phase 2

Preliminary Organizational Setup of Efficient Machinery Company

At present, Efficient Machinery Company is a sole proprietorship owned by Principal Founder. As soon as a significant business volume has been developed and/or other circumstances make this desirable, the company will be incorporated and 20,000 shares of common stock at a value of $1 each will be authorized for issue. The following types of stockholders will be distinguished:

EXHIBIT 2 (continued)

1) Principal Founder
2) Working Co-Founders (can work for company in their spare time or as employees)
3) Investors
4) Vendor Investors
5) Customer Investors

Founders

Upon incorporation, the principal founder will receive 10,200 shares in return for contributing his sole proprietorship to the incorporated business. Working co-founders will receive, for every "unit" of work performed for the company, either $50 in cash and a common stock share of $1 or a subordinated debenture of $50 and a common stock share of $1. A unit of work will consist of three and one-half hours of work, regardless of the kind of activities the co-founders perform.

After March 31, 1981, a unit of work will consist of three hours of work. The subordinated debentures will be payable within 10 years from date of issue with 12-percent interest, compounded daily, payable periodically or when debenture is paid back at the option of the company. Each working co-founder can earn his way up to 1000 shares of the company. After the company has been incorporated, key-employees, not co-founders, may get co-founder status, allowing them to earn shares as outlined above, upon invitation by the company.

Investors

Investors will receive for every $51 invested in the company a subordinated debenture of $50 and a common stock share of $1. Vendor investors are vendors who accept payment for articles, services, etc. supplied by them in the form of subordinated debentures. For each $50 in such subordinated debentures, they can buy a share of stock for $1.

A customer willing to buy a first machine, a model that has been upgraded but not yet proven, or a machine that is in any other way a risk to him, may be offered opportunity to buy a certain number of shares at par value ($1), but not more than one share for every $100 of equipment purchased. Such a customer will be considered a customer-investor.

Investor subordinated debentures will yield 12 percent interest and be payable within 10 years of issue, like co-founder subordinated debentures. Interest again can be paid either periodically or when the debenture is paid back, at the option of the company.

Further Methods of Investment

When 5000 of the 20,000 shares authorized have been issued to investors, the stockholders can decide by majority vote to authorize issue of more shares of common stock in batches of 20,000 shares with a par value of $1 each. Principal founder and co-founders, if employees of the company when stock issue is allowed, as well as key employees of the company having

EXHIBIT 2 (concluded)

co-founder status, will receive a percentage of new stock equal to the percentage of existing stock they own, at par value ($1 for each share).

Existing investors will have the option to buy a percentage of new stock equal to the percentage of existing stock they own at par value ($1 for each share) provided they invest at the same time in a certain amount of subordinated debentures. This amount, as well as the interest rate and pay-back conditions, will be set by the company. If existing investors do not exercise this option within one month from date of authorization of stock issue, the company may sell the stock to other investors on the same conditions offered to investors holding old stock. When new stock is issued, existing investors will receive for every share of par value $1 they own, X non-voting shares of par value $1 per the following formula:

X = (total no. of new shares) / (total no. of old shares)

Non-voting stocks, if corporation is liquidated or sold, will participate in dividends and in distribution of available funds as if they are common stocks.

Management

The company will be managed by a president assisted by a management committee consisting of himself and up to six vice-presidents. Major decisions, to be defined in more detail at incorporation, will have to be approved by the board of directors.

Changes

Changes in this preliminary organizational setup will not be made until all prospective founders and investors have been notified of the intended changes and had a chance to give the management of the company their opinion about them. Until the company is incorporated, contributions made by prospective co-founders and investors will be loans to principal founder under conditions negotiated individually with him. He will inform prospective co-founders and investors of all such arrangements made.

Effectiveness

This preliminary organizational setup will go into effect when signed by principal founder and one or more co-founders and/or investors.

Chapter 6

Setup

❏ *SUBCHAPTER 6A - Protecting Ideas*

Activities during the time between discovering a business idea, planning its exploitation and having a business up and running are required in all functional areas of the business including finance, marketing, accounting, personnel, R&D and operations. This chapter will take up in its subchapters three topics which cut across these conventional business disciplines.

First will be ways of protecting ideas from competitors. Trademarks, copyrights and patents are legalistic devices for protecting intellectual property such as inventions and designs. Other protection devices include secrecy and innovating fast enough to stay ahead. This Subchapter, 6A, will consider each of these approaches in turn.

Second will be choice of a business legal form, whether proprietorship, partnership or corporation, and things to consider in designing the details of that form. A related topic is that of governmental requirements for establishment of the business. These topics will be taken up in Subchapter 6B following this one.

Third come tasks of setting up shop for operations, which include refining the product or service to ready it for production, choosing a site, arranging to use it, possibly modifying it to fit needs of the business, plus obtaining and installing equipment. Subchapter 6C of this chapter will focus on setting up shop.

Intellectual Property Legal Protection

Most ideas are easy to come by and are therefore cheap. Excellent ideas are rare and can be extremely valuable. Most of Microsoft's profits, which in the 1990s made William Gates the richest man in the world, came from the DOS (Disk Operating System) software package to which Microsoft bought exclusive rights, protected by copyright. Without the copyright protection anyone could have taken it for nothing. Thus protection for an idea can have extremely high importance.

Because the federal government wants to encourage people to develop new ideas it has provided legal ways for those who do so to enjoy monopolies on them. Copyrights, patents and trademarks are those legal mechanisms, and each applies to certain categories of ideas. These legal monopolies can be tremendously powerful for creating and sustaining a business in some cases, although in others they are worthless. Hence, an entrepreneur should have some understanding of them. It is also useful to know that they are not the only ways of protecting ideas or gaining monopoly power.

Copyrights

Written materials and works of art can be protected by copyrights, which are issued by the Library of Congress. Under international agreement, moreover, the U.S. protection is automatic in more than 80 other countries as well. The procedure for securing a copyright begins with writing on the "work of art" a "c" with a circle around it (©), followed by the name of the idea's creator and the year in which it is created. If the work is produced and distributed with that mark, it is automatically entitled to the legal protection.

Taking the further step of contacting the Library of Congress and registering it, there is a way to assure that the creator of the work has laid claim to copyright protection on that date, in case anyone else should attempt to claim the work as theirs. The procedure for copyright registration consists of filing an application and including with it two copies of the work (or a photo if it is art), and a check for $20 with the Copyright Office, Library of Congress, Washington, D.C., 20559. For information call (202) 287 9100. Registering a copyright may be done at any time, but there are advantages to registering it sooner rather than later:

- Registration permits the holder to sue any infringers immediately.

- Registration allows collection of damages from the time of registration.

- Registration within five years establishes validity even if the work is published without a copyright notice.

- Registration at least three months before any infringement allows imposition of attorneys' fees and statutory damages in addition to actual damages and profits in successful infringement suits.

The life of a copyright equals the life of the author plus 50 years. There is a statute of limitations on infringement. Suit must be brought within three years of infringement. Copyright infringement requires that the infringer have had access to the work infringed upon. If the work is proved to have been created independently, there is no copyright infringement. But it is not necessary, and registration can be applied for any time.

There can, however, be significant disadvantages in waiting. Delay in filing precludes recovery of statutory damages, which can range up to $100,000, and attorney's fees for infringements that occurred prior to registration. The copyright holder can recover only actual damages. Some courts have even barred recovery of statutory damages for infringements that occurred after registration when they judged such infringements to be of the same character as those that occurred prior to registration. Although most copyrights apply to written works, there are some other creations to which they have importantly been applied in recent times.

Semiconductor Chip Designs

The Semiconductor Chip Protection Act of 1984 provides that the Copyright Office can issue protection for the design of an integrated circuit chip for a period of 10 years. During that time it is illegal to reproduce, import, or distribute chips that were made using the mask for that chip without permission. The circuit package must bear the mark "mask work" or *M* or an "M" with a circle around it to signify that it is thus protected. Unlike copyright protection on other works, which may be filed for any time after creation, mask-work protection must be filed for within two years of commercial introduction. Innocent purchasers of pirated mask works are not liable.

Software Protection

Copyrighting is the form of legal protection that applies to software unless the software is part of the design of a machine, in which case it may be possible to patent the software/machine combination. In addition to filing for copyright protection, it may be possible to keep some aspects of the software secret.

Music Protection

Music can be protected by copyright, and the composer is entitled to royalties from anyone who makes money by playing it. The American Society of Composers, Authors and Publishers (ASCAP) is an organization dedicated to enforcing this protection. Radio stations are obliged to pay royalties for playing music over the air, and business establishments that play radio music are also obliged to pay. ASCAP employs roving observers to enforce these rules.

As with virtually anything legal, copyrights have their gray areas where disputes are always going on and never fully settled. Currently, computer software copyrighting is a hot legal battleground. In 1992, for instance, a decision was rendered in favor of a company that had been sued for disassembling copyrighted software for purposes of "reverse-engineering."[1] Another decision was rendered in favor of a company that duplicated a copyrighted piece of software in order to understand it.[2] Navigation in such shifting seas calls for attorneys who specialize in that particular gray area. Nevertheless, copyrighting still begins with the simple imprinting step that does not have to wait for an attorney's help.

Defending such a legal monopoly when someone else infringes on it is where attorneys are most needed and also are most expensive. The copyright itself does not prevent anyone from imitating the original work. Only the action of a court can do that. For the court to act a lawsuit must be filed, a verdict must be rendered and action must be taken to get it implemented. Such a process takes time, work and money. Decisions could go either for or against protection on that particular creation. How much legal expense is justified must continually be decided by whoever is paying for it as the litigation moves forward.

Patents

There are three different types of patents. **Utility** patents are used to protect ideas for machines, processes, and chemical compounds. **Design** patents pertain to the shape and design of useful objects. **Plant** patents apply to living organisms and, in recent years other life forms such as DNA. Most patenting efforts are directed at the first of these three types, which will be discussed here first. Only features of products and processes that are new, different, and not an obvious discovery to someone "skilled in the art" are protectable. Expert patent examiners employed by the U.S. Patent and Trademark Office (Washington, D.C., 20231) decide which claims in a patent application qualify for that distinction.

Claims stated in the patent describe specific individual attributes of the invention which the inventor wants to protect. The inventor would like to obtain protection on claims that are as broad as possible and that preclude imitation of any aspect of the invention. But the Patent Office generally requires that they be narrow and specific, and usually when a patent is issued it grants only some of the claims—maybe very few. Possibly the claims granted will be valuable. But if the claims granted pertain only to inconsequential details, the patent containing those claims may offer little protection and be essentially worthless. Hence, it is important, if a patent is to be applied for, that the application process, including claim formulation, be done carefully.

Steps for getting a patent are different from and more complicated than those for copyrighting. The first step is to start as soon as possible keeping and dating records (including sketches) that describe the idea and how it works. As these are extended over time, the various changes and experiments should also be dated and recorded in a page-numbered notebook. These records should be periodically witnessed, dated, and signed in ink with a phrase like "read in confidence and understood" by a couple of other people who are capable of understanding them. This will help prove that the inventor kept working on the idea to improve and "reduce it to practice."

Instructions for setting up and keeping a notebook to seek patent protection are described in material available from the U.S. Government Printing Office and in commercially published works.[3] Among the rules are that the notebook not have removable pages, that each page be dated and signed by the inventor, that the book be witnessed and signed by others, and that pursuit of the idea's development be continuous and diligent. The purpose is to demonstrate that nobody else developed the idea sooner.

Since the date of conception of an idea is especially important, the inventor should consider filing a Disclosure Document with the Patent Office as soon as possible. This can be done for only $6. It is not the same as applying for a patent, and application for the patent should still be made when ready. If the patent application is not filed within two years, the Patent Office will discard the disclosure document.

Apart from the witnessed notes, patenting requires proof that the conception can physically work. It also involves complicated and lengthy activities of application to the U.S. Patent Office and a two- or three-year wait to learn the verdict. If issued, a patent gives its owner a right to sue anyone who violates it. The suit may prevail, in which case the violator will be ordered by the court to stop the violation, and damages will be awarded. Or the suit may not prevail, and the patent may be declared invalid by the court. Even if it is valid, the court may decide that the alleged violator is not violating it. If a judgment is rendered in favor of the patent holder, the damages awarded may justify the time, expense, and trouble of the lawsuit—or they may not. The concept of a patent right is simple, but defending it can be costly, complex, and chancy.

There are two reasons for studying earlier patents that may have been issued in connection with an idea. The first is to make sure that using the idea will not violate a patent someone else holds on it, which can result in costly litigation. The second is that to apply for a patent requires listing prior related patents. Anyone may undertake the search to find them at a patent library, but a professional is likely to do it better and faster. Such professionals may be found in the Yellow Pages of any large city under "Patent Searchers." The way to pick a good searcher is to get help from a respected patent attorney. Typically, a search costs upwards of $200. Copies of issued patents are available from the U.S. Patent and Trademark Office for $3 each. Summary descriptions of new patents appear in the *Patent Gazette*, a 6-by-9 inch paperback of around 400 pages that comes out every week.

Utility patents historically were good for 17 years from the date of issuance. Beginning June 8, 1995, however, the law was changed so that on applications filed after that date the patent rights begin when the patent is granted and continue until 20 years from the day that the inventor filed the patent application. On a patent issued on an application filed before June 8, 1995, the patent term will expire after either 20 years from the earliest U.S. filing date or 17 years from the date the patent is issued, whichever is longer. On patents already in force on June 8, 1995, the new patent laws specify that, again, the term will be the greater of either 20 years from the earliest U.S. filing date or 17 years from the patent grant.

To facilitate obtaining an early filing date, the new law also allows for filing a provisional application with fewer formalities and lower cost. No patent is issued based upon the provisional application, but once that application is filed the inventor has 12 months to file a regular patent application and claim the provisional application filing date. Filing a provisional application requires the following:

- A clearly written description of the invention.

- Any drawings needed to understand the invention.

- A filing fee of $75 if the applicant is an individual inventor or $150 if the applicant is a "larger entity."

- A cover sheet identifying the application as being provisional and including the inventor (s) name (s), residence (s), invention title, name and registration of attorney/agent, correspondence address, and any U.S. Government agency that has a property interest in the application.

Patents cannot be renewed. After a patent lapses the patented design or process enters the public domain. Exceptions occur in the case of drug patents, which may be extended if sales have been significantly delayed by the Federal Drug Administration. Patent application in foreign countries must be made separately, and before issuance of the U.S. patent, for the foreign patents to be valid. Whether to apply in foreign countries depends on the potential markets in those countries. Action against copying in the foreign country cannot be taken until a patent is issued there. But action may be taken to prevent foreign-made copies from being imported or sold in the United States.

Utility patent application costs $690, plus $72 for each claim beyond three, and $20 for each claim over 20. The issuance fee is $1,130. These fees may be halved if the applicant is declared a "small entity," which includes independent inventors. Maintenance fees must be paid at years four, eight and 12; otherwise the patent will lapse. It is advisable to pay these fees several months in advance to be safe.

A larger expense will be involved in hiring a patent attorney and preparing the application. It is necessary to show that the idea can be made to work. If chemicals are involved, they must be specified and the process for using them must be detailed. If machinery is involved, it must be drawn and verbally described in sufficient detail for someone of ordinary skill to be able to make and operate it without a lot of experimentation. Developing this degree of detail to prove workability may cost considerable time and money in addition to the legal fees.

Once a patent application has been filed, it cannot be amended to make changes or improvements in the invention. Instead, a new application that incorporates those changes must be filed. Until the patent is issued there is no legal protection from copiers, so it may be best to keep the product or process secret. Writing "patent pending" on a product during this time may discourage copiers because they may fear that issuance of the patent will make them abandon their attempt to profit from it. However, there is no legal protection from copiers under the term "patent pending."

Whether the expense of searching and—assuming the search indicates patenting is likely—filing for a patent is justified is one of the judgments that may be called for in pursuing a venture. Costs can run into thousands of dollars, and the costs of defending the patent against infringers can cost tens of thousands or even millions more. This may seem discouraging, but possession of a strong patent can be powerful in recruiting capital to develop a venture, or in licensing the idea to another company in return for cash and/or a royalty. It can also pay off by protecting the venture's market. Tony Maglica, for example, concluded that it had been worthwhile to spend $16 million in lawyers' fees over six years to protect features of a flashlight around which his company was built.[4]

As with copyrights, patents grant rights only to sue imitators. Sometimes imitators are able to "design around" the claims of issued patents, and thereby in effect nullify them. Some companies never file for patents, figuring that the technology will be obsolete too soon to benefit from patenting, that courts will not back them up, or that the ideas they protect are not sufficiently valuable. Others obtain dozens of patents on ideas that are not profitable, sometimes just for the sake of having them. They are a form of property, after all, and they do demonstrate genuine invention. Occasionally patents prove to be incredibly powerful, as did those that protected Polaroid's camera from competition by Kodak.

The experience of Exac, a start-up with a better flow meter, illustrates how patent contention can have an enormous effect on the fortunes of a start-up—and can also sneak up as a surprise.

> Exac was founded by an inventor who had developed a flow meter capable of higher accuracy than any others available. Another company, Micro Motion, had also developed a meter that utilized a similar principle. Micro Motion was bought by a large company, Emerson Electric. When Emerson learned, after the purchase, that Exac was introducing a flow meter that would outperform that of the company Emerson had bought, Emerson filed a lawsuit accusing Exac of patent infringement.

Robert J. Kunze, a venture capitalist who had put up the money for Exac, observed that "It's tough to get clear answers from patent attorneys. Exac's patent lawyer assured me we had nothing to worry about, but he was equally quick to point out that it was impossible to predict what might happen in court. He then told me that the Polaroid/Eastman patent suit on instant cameras illustrated that the courts had become very sympathetic to patent holders and very harsh on infringers. For a man who was telling me not to worry, he gave me a lot to worry about."

Seeing that millions of dollars might be needed for defense, since Emerson refused to settle and insisted on going to court, Kunze decided that Exac would have no hope of obtaining further venture capital ("A cardinal rule of venture investing is the money must go for building a company, not to a bunch of lawyers"), and decided to seek a buyer. He arranged a deal whereby another large company, Monsanto, agreed to shoulder the patent litigation costs, which eventually reached $5 million, in return for an option to buy Exac.

In court the jury unanimously found in favor of Exac. Monsanto exercised its takeover option. The investors in Exac reaped three times their money, but the litigation had been debilitating to Exac, with the uncertainty, disruption of work by the employees being interviewed, and legal expenses.[5]

Since the life of a utility patent is limited, and there is no option of renewal, it is necessary to keep exploiting and improving what it protects with additional patentable features that render the original design obsolete and extend the protection time further. Foreseeing how others might foil or supersede a patent was outstandingly exemplified by John Ryan.

The co-founder of Macrovision, a Cupertino, California company, Ryan developed and patented an anti-copying system to protect videotapes. Then to foil those who would make devices to circumvent his system he also developed and patented the technology required for circumvention. With this second patent, his company filed 21 infringement suits against would-be makers and sellers of circumvention "black boxes." Four manufacturers of the boxes settled with his company before the suits, three more settled as a result of them and all 12 distributors agreed to stop selling the boxes.[6]

A catch with any patent is that, when issued, it must make public the technology it embodies. The Patent Office will keep the application secret, and if no patent is issued, the information will be left secret. But issuance of the patent itself will reveal the secret information. Moreover, patent law requires that the patent application disclose the best ways of practicing the invention. If the applicant reveals only inferior ways that are not the best and keeps one or more better ways secret, that may invalidate the patent. Hence, publication of the patent gives competitors an opportunity to learn what is protected and what is not. They can then try to get around the patent. Moreover, if a foreign patent is applied for, the information in that application may, by that country's rules, be made public even though no patent is issued.

Design, as opposed to utility, patents cost $220 to file and $400 for issuance. They are issued for 14 years. Someone may infringe on a design patent without having seen the original; such infringement is illegal, even though it might be inadvertent. This is different than with copyrights. Since design patents are based on shapes, not mechanisms, they can often be easy to design around through simple alterations in configuration, and therefore are generally considered less protective than utility patents.

Secrets

Instead of filing for patent protection, it may sometimes be better to keep the technology of a product or process secret. The formula for Coca Cola is not patented, but is secret (although Mark Pendergrast, who wrote *For God, Country, and Coca Cola* [New York: Charles Scribner's Sons, 1993], claims that he came across the recipe in company archives). Many manufacturing processes that perhaps could be patented are kept secret. How colored adhesive plastic tapes used in graphics are sliced to very thin widths has been kept secret for decades. This has both avoided competitor imitation and saved the substantial costs of searching, filing, and defending patents.

Secrets still involve taking precautions, however. Employees should be asked to sign secrecy agreements. Measures should be taken to prevent outsiders from seeing how production is accomplished. If secrets are stolen, legal action will be needed in addition to proof that such precautions have been taken, in order to collect damages from any secrets that may have been divulged.

The legal rules of trade secrecy are far less codified than those for copyrights and patents. In part they derive from common law, which is to say precedent decisions of the courts. Over the years, judges have made reasoned decisions aimed at fairness, and in time those become general guidelines. In part the rules derive from contract law, wherein there is an agreement between people working together. Thus employees are asked to sign secrecy agreements, contracts under which they promise not to tell others what their employers' secrets are or to use those secrets themselves to compete with their employers. Finally, tort law forms part of the basis for judging disputes over trade secrets. It concentrates on whether one person is wronged by another, and, if so, what compensation the wronged person deserves from the wrongdoer—in this case, through unfair handling of a secret given in confidence. There are no legal time limits to trade secrets.

Court decisions balance these different ways of looking at secrecy disputes and therefore tend to be on a case-by-case basis. Key questions concern whether a secret really existed, whether someone breached a contract or duty and what should be done to remedy the situation.

Reverse engineering to discover a secret is legal, but taking customer lists or formulas from an employer and revealing or using them in competition is not. In one case it was judged illegal to fly over a plant under construction and take pictures of it before the roof was on to discover how it would operate. Falsely posing as a customer or negotiating a contract in bad faith just to learn a company's secrets, taking an insider job to learn these secrets, or bribing employees to disclose company secrets is illegal.

At the same time, an employee's general experience in working for a company would not prevent him or her from using that experience in a job elsewhere. Independent discovery of a way of doing something that another company regards as secret does not prohibit the independent discoverer from using that method. Discovery of a "secret" by reading public literature or visiting public areas of a company is also legal.

Courts have mixed feelings about supporting secrecy rights. They like to encourage development of improvements, and by supporting secrecy rights they give businesses incentive to do so. But at the same time, courts also like to encourage competition and curb monopoly power, which is what secrets give their owners. Courts also lean in favor of an individual's right to earn a living, although at times that may be at the expense of another's right to maintain a secret.

Trademarks

In addition to copyrights and patents, a third type of government-granted monopoly is a trademark. Like patents, a trademark is issued by the U.S. Patent Office, but, like a copyright, the trademark of a product (or, in the case of services, a service mark) applies to a visual design or emblem. A key consideration is that to be registered the purpose served by the mark must be to distinguish the product of the applicant from that produced by others. But the trademark must not otherwise be functional for the product. Even a color may be protectable for the right product. Owens-Corning managed to trademark pink to identify its product, because pink is not a particularly natural color for Fiberglas. But Pepto-Bismol could not register pink because the Patent and Trademark Office construed it to be a soothing color, and therefor functional for the product. Even the sound of a product has been the basis for a trademark application.[7] In 1995 the Patent and Trademark Office announced that Harley-Davidson had filed for a trademark on "the sound of applicant's motorcycles, produced by V-Twin common crankpin motorcycle engines when the goods are in use."[8]

An ordinary word, like water, cannot be trademarked, but a non-word, like "Kodak" when it was first used, can. If a word becomes ordinary through use, as "Zipper" did, then it cannot have trademark protection. The decision rendered on "Zipper" (is it really an ordinary word?) illustrates how, as usual, a gray area surrounds what qualifies for protection. Some trademarks that have been declared generic include Nylon, Cellophane, Thermos, Aspirin, Linoleum, Shredded Wheat, Yo-Yo and Monopoly.

Goods bearing the trademark must be "sold or transported in commerce" interstate to qualify for federal protection of the mark or, under an important 1989 change in the law, the applicant must be able to show a good-faith intention to so use the goods. State governments also register trademarks without this interstate requirement.

For trademarks issued after 1989, the life of a trademark is 10 years. It may be renewed each additional 10 years. Trademark application costs $200 and renewal $300. There are no price breaks for "small entity" applicants as there are with patents.

Before registration, the letters TM or SM (for "service mark" if it pertains to a service) may be used after the name, provided the mark has not been ruled invalid. After the trade or service mark is registered with the Patent and Trademark Office, it may carry the mark ® or the words "Registered Trademark" to so indicate. It is important not to use this indication of registration until the mark has been certified; otherwise, registration may be denied. The name of a company, as opposed to the trademark of a product, may be registered at the state, but not the federal, level.

Tactics used in protecting trademarks include the following:

- Seek nondescriptive words. The purpose of the mark is to distinguish between products, not to describe them. "Celestial Seasonings" is all right, but "Tasty Seasonings" would be hard to protect.

- Search for any other users, both before applying for registration and after registering. After registration, go after any imitators promptly.

- Register the mark at the state level and, when it is clear that it will be used interstate, at the federal level. Renew it six months before it lapses. (Registration is not required to prove ownership of a mark, but it gives better protection.)

- Use the mark as registered. Do not alter it. If change is needed, register a new one.

- Refer to the trade name as a brand. Examples are "Scotch Brand" and "Kleenex Brand," which are terms used by the owners of those names.

- Avoid using the name as a verb. Xerox is careful not to use the term "Xeroxing," which could make the term generic.

- Be cautious in licensing anyone else to use the mark. If others fail to maintain the quality the mark represents, it may be deemed to have lost its identity.

- Flaunt the mark. Otherwise it may be deemed to have been abandoned. Put it on the product, advertisements, displays, tags, and manuals.

Trademarks may be extended from an established product to a new product that conveys the same benefits to a new market (Neutrogena soap to Neutrogena shampoo) or to a new product that conveys new benefits to the same market (Tom's of Maine toothpaste to baking powder).[9] Detailed information about how to apply for trademarks and to renew them is available from the U.S. Government Printing Office and from the Patent Office.

Since international agreements cover trademarks, in applying for them it is advisable to consider filing applications in other countries as well. Trademarking in the United States does not automatically protect the mark elsewhere. Prior registration in the United States can be of help in applying for trademarks in other countries.

Application: *What forms of legal protection should be sought by the entrepreneur in the assigned case for which specific aspects of the product or service?*

Out-Competing

Most companies are not able to gain protection of much power from patents, copyrights or secrecy. Trademarks are only as good as what people believe them to represent in terms of product or service quality and value. Consequently, the main mode of protection used has to be competitive performance in producing, pricing, selling and delivering a product or service.

Donald Beaver invented a better way to soak up industrial fluid leaks. Rather than the current practice of spreading kitty litter on the floor, he proposed using sausage-shaped socks full of absorbent matter which could be laid as more effective barriers and more easily picked up afterward. Calling it a PIG ("Partners In Grime") he patented the product and in 1986 put it on the market. Within three years he gained over 8,000 customers and annual sales of $10 million.

The sales also attracted over 60 imitators. Rather than suing them for their attempts to design around his patent, Beaver adopted improvement tactics, principally in service, to stay ahead. These included:

- Catalog plus telephone plus computer linkup to four warehouses to allow next-morning shipment and three-day or faster delivery on all orders.
- Twenty-day free trial with invoicing only after a company representative has called and found the customer satisfied. (Result: 95 percent pay up)

- In case of product failure, replacement of the product within hours, no charge on that purchase and 10 percent off on the next one.
- Working with customers to make sure the company's products are used as effectively and efficiently as possible.
- Creation of new products through careful attention to customer problems or requests that existing products don't satisfy.
- Including in the annual catalog articles on industrial cleanup to help customers learn better ways to accomplish it.
- Calling each customer twice per year to make sure names are updated and correctly spelled.[10]

Out-competing may begin with a "better" idea or may not. It should aim to include better refinement and execution of the idea. Keeping track of what competitors are up to may also help. Information about them can be obtained legally through a number of means, including talking with suppliers, customers and former employees of the competitors. Their products and services can be bought and examined. Advertising they buy can also be studied with the aid of clipping services ("Clipping Bureaus" in the Yellow Pages) and, if they are public, through their securities disclosures and reports. A yearly list of 1,500 sources of information about companies is also available from Washington Researchers Publishing, 2612 P Street N.W., Washington, D.C. 20007.

Application: *What activities should the entrepreneur in the assigned case set in motion to assure that the venture will be competitive in the more distant future and how?*

Supplementary Reading

New Venture Mechanics Chapter 3. (Vesper, K. H., Prentice-Hall, 1993)

Exercises

1. Interview a local firm capable of helping develop a prototype. Learn what operating policies it has about working with new ventures, and what have been some experiences from which those policies emerged.

2. Generate a scenario for a beta test of some new product idea.

3. Contact at least two patent lawyers, either locally or long distance. Develop a description of how each specializes within patent law, and what, historically, have been the approximate costs of getting patents through them.

4. Learn the location of the patent library nearest you and how far back its patents go. Who mostly uses it and for what?

5. Obtain a copy of the *Patent Gazette*. Note its date, how many of what types of patents it contains (using whatever classification scheme and sampling procedure you choose), and how long, typically, it took to get them issued. How may claims does a typical patent have?

Venture History

1. How long did it take to go from idea to beginning operations in the venture? Make a time line of events with approximate dates.

2. How did the founders test and refine the venture concept? How much did it cost to do so?

3. What thought was given to protecting the venture concept, and what action was taken on it? How much did that cost?

Venture Planning Guide

1. Sketch a proposed trademark and any other protection methods that might apply to one of your ventures and list in detail the steps and likely timing and costs that would be involved in setting them up. List individuals you contacted for information in carrying out this process. Research what is needed to get a patent.

2. Sketch out designs to allow physical demonstration of your product or service idea in three contrasting forms and/or levels of elaboration. Develop cost projections for each of the three.

3. For each of the alternative ways of protecting business ideas (1) describe the steps required to apply it to your venture, (2) list the pros and cons of doing so, and (3) explain the best approach to follow.

4. Impanel a focus group and search for ways of (1) competing with your planned product or service and (2) improving it to stay ahead of competitors.

Notes

[1] *Seega Enterprises, Ltd v. Accolade, Inc.*, 977 F.2nd 1510 (9th Cir. 1992).

[2] *Atari Games Corp v. Nintendo of America, Inc.* , 975 F.2d 832 (Fed. Cir. 1992).

[3] Gary S. Lynn, *From Concept to Market* (New York: Wiley, 1989).

[4] Paul B. Brown, "Magnificent Obsession," *Inc.*, August 1989, p. 89.

[5] Robert J. Kunze, *Nothing Ventured* (New York: Harper, 1990), p. 161.

[6] "Defending Anti-copy Rights," *Venture*, September 1989, p. 72.

[7] Frank H. Foster and Robert L. Shook, *Patents, Copyrights and Trademarks*, (New York. Wiley, 1993), p. 165.

[8] David Edwards, "Letter to Willie G., No. 2," *Cycle World*, July 1995, p. 10.

[9] "Will It Travel?" *Inc.*, April 1990, p. 116.

[10] Rachel Meltzer, "Fending Off The Copycats," *Venture*, February 1989, p. 62.

❏ SUBCHAPTER 6B - Legal Formation of the Company

The existence of a business, like that of an individual, takes a variety of forms. Name, reputation, habits, equipment, logo, location and output are all part of it. Several of these forms comprise elements of its existence on paper, which will be the focus of this chapter.

Government Requirements

A simple one-person business may be able to get away without registering with any government agencies, although it will have to report income to federal and possibly state agencies. The federal form is a "Schedule C" which becomes part of the owner's personal income tax filing. Technically, a city business license may be required, but it is simple and inexpensive to obtain, and failure to get it may not be noticed if the business stays small, as in the case of a couple of college students cutting lawns or painting houses on the side.

If the business becomes more visible, however, it will have to observe more registration and reporting requirements at all three levels of government: local, state and federal. Requirements may vary with geographical locale. In Washington State, for example, they can include the following:

Local

- City Business License - Easily obtained at City Hall for a nominal fee. Forms will automatically come to the venture for paying a Business and Occupations tax based upon sales.

- County Licenses - For businesses that deal with tobacco, juke boxes, shuffleboard games, etc. additional licenses must be obtained from the county clerk. Forms will then come in the mail for county property and inventory taxes.

- Certificate of Firm Name - Filed with the county clerk.

State

- Certificate of Registration - Filed with the State Department of Revenue. Tax forms will be sent automatically.

- State Licenses - Must be obtained for many specialized activities such as contracting, barbering, practicing law or medicine, operating beauty shops or employment agencies. The State Department of Commerce or Department of Licensing can be contacted for a list.

- Corporate Name Reservations - Obtained and annually renewable from the Secretary of State.

- Employer's Requirements - Needed if the firm is going to employ people other than the owner. These requirements include:

    - Registration and Industrial Rating Number from the State Department of Labor.

    - Employer's Identification Number for Employment Security from the State Employment Security Department.

Federal

- Income Tax Forms for the owner and the business, available from the Internal Revenue Service.

- Employees' Income Tax Withholding, also arranged with Internal Revenue. Banks can help with this. It is an important area where mistakes are easy to make and costly.

- Employees' Social Security requirements, verified by the Social Security Administration.

- Application for federal employer identification number (IRS Form SS-4)

For particular lines of work other forms of regulation may apply. Mail order is regulated by the Federal Trade Commission, franchising by state agencies, airlines by the Department of Transportation, trucking by the Interstate Commerce Commission, radio and TV broadcasting by the Federal Communications Commission, importing and exporting by the Federal Trade Commission, and so forth. Some agencies, such as the Occupational Health and Safety Administration and the Environmental Protection Agency cut across many lines of work.

Regulations can change any time, and so must always be checked on a current basis. One source of information to begin with is the U.S. Small Business Administration, which can suggest other points of contact. Another is the State Department of Commerce. Best, however, may be to contact other businesses in similar lines of work and ask what government agencies they must deal with. Cross checking with more than one source may also be advisable.

Need for regulatory approval can sometimes completely stymie a company even though it may have a product that would ultimately be approved. How this could happen is illustrated by the reaction of a solid waste manager, John Conaway, to a new foam product developed by a start-up company, Rusmar, for reducing the costs and extending the life of a landfill.

> *Rusmar looks to have a good product, but here in California the permit pro-
> cess will be a big pitfall. I'd be using Rusmar's foam right now if it weren't for
> the regulatory nightmare. We have a severe capacity crunch. But any time you
> file for a major operational change here—and foam would fit into that category—
> you need new permits from three separate agencies.*
>
> *It would cost us more then $1 million just to apply for them, given all the
> monitoring and documentation they require. I can easily see being required to do
> a very complicated and expensive series of ground water tests and surface/air
> emission tests. Some of these are fly-emergence tests, where you have to get people
> to come out and actually count the number of flies that emerge prior to using the
> foam and then after using it. And even then there's no guarantee we'd get ap-
> proval.*[1]

Still, notwithstanding such barriers, new companies do get started by introducing products that must hurdle them. But often they must bring to bear
more effort and ingenuity, spend more money and take more time to accomplish start-up than they expected.

Application: *In what sequence should steps be taken to assure compliance with any government requirements you
can think of by the assigned case venture?*

Company Name

With millions of companies in business and the U. S. Patent Office registering approximately 25,000 new trademarks per year, it can be a challenge to
find an effective name for a new venture. The choice is important because, like
picking a location, it can stand in lieu of great expenditures in advertising if
done well. Compared to a location choice, it will probably remain with the
company longer. Should it indicate what the company does (e.g. Software
Arts) or not (e.g. Eveready)? Should it be a word with intrinsic meaning (e.g.
Apple) or not (e.g. Kodak)?

There is plenty of room for disagreement. The November 1972 name
change from Standard Oil to Exxon was based upon review of 10,000 com-
puter-generated names which were narrowed to 234, then 16. Finally, eight
were selected for linguistic studies to establish that they had no meaning. In
addition, 15,000 telephone directories were checked for prior use and 10,000
people were interviewed. After Exxon was chosen, another $100 million was
spent to change the names on stations, pumps, trucks, maps, billboards and
224 million shares of stock held by 780,000 people.[2]

With some companies there may be risk of losing identity if the name is
changed. Exxon is big enough to impart meaning to any word. Univac was a
familiar name, as was Honeywell. But did the money spent on creating the
name Unisys to replace them both add to familiarity or image? Who can remember what familiar company names were abandoned to form it?

If a company becomes large it will ultimately make its name familiar. Ford and Hershey were not particularly evocative words by themselves. On the other hand, some names probably do help. Santa Monica, California in the mid-1950s saw the opening of a new soda fountain somewhat off the main thoroughfare, on sixteenth street. The name, Sweet Sixteen, quickly became familiar and is still known to a vast majority of old time and former residents who long since forgot other stores' names, although the enterprise itself is no longer there.

However, the name will not make the company. For years, the name Astrodynamics was owned by an electrician on Hollywood Boulevard who did nothing with it except keep the registration current because he thought it had promise. It was not the name of his electrical contracting company. No great company grew out of it. But it could probably have been a good name than most for the right enterprise.

It is important to choose a name that is not already owned by another firm for the territory where the new venture will operate. Once chosen, the name should be registered with the state department of commerce where the company will be operating and possibly with the U.S. Patent Office to tie up national rights. If international rights may one day have value, then ways of registering in foreign countries as well should be sought.

There are consultants who specialize in company names and there are also references on the subject. *Brand Names: Who Owns What* (Facts on File, Inc., 460 Park Avenue South, New York, 10016) lists 15,000 brand names of 750 firms. *The Trademark Register of the United States* (Trademark Register, 300 Washington Square, Washington, D.C. 20036) lists over 600,000 names on file with the U.S. Patent Office. There are also attorneys who specialize in determining the registerability of company names. And there are services which maintain databases on names that an entrepreneur can use to do his or her own searching.

Application: *What would be two likely alternative names for the assigned case venture, and what are the pros and cons of choosing each?*

Legal Entity

Either by initiative or default, some legal form must be chosen for the business. Three choices include proprietorship, partnership and corporation. Within each of these, particularly the latter two, are other choices to be made. Reasons for choosing one business form over another are easy to identify.

Proprietorship is what the business will be if no action is taken to make it something else. It is part of the owner. If the business is sued, the owner is sued. If the owner dies, the assets of the business individually are part of the owner's estate and debts of the business are owed by the owner's estate. In paying federal income taxes the owner uses a "Schedule C - Income From Business or Profession" as part of the 1040 form and any corresponding state income tax form.

If the proprietorship operates under some name other than the owner's it may be referred to as a DBA (doing business as) enterprise. Most states require that such an enterprise be registered with the county government with some sort of certificate of doing business under an assumed name. Federal taxes are paid through use of a "Schedule C" form.

Partnership is what the business becomes if more than one person owns it, but no action is taken to separate it legally from its owners. There need not be any paperwork to have a partnership, just ownership by more than one person. Such an arrangement can be created by such things as more than one person contributing assets, doing the work of the business or withdrawing profits from it. Actions like these may even create a partnership inadvertently.

Unless there is paperwork to the contrary, the state will assume ownership is equal among the partners. Also, any partner in such a case can commit the business to obligations or be sued for debts of the business. These can be reasons for arranging the legal form and ownership of the business in a formal manner using legal help. To formalize a partnership some sort of certificate of partnership may have to be filed with the county clerk.

If a partner dies a partnership automatically terminates. Hence part of the legal task of creating a partnership is to consider what disposition of the business should be made in such event.

Partnership Agreements can specify that partners are not equal and can spell out such things as duration, conditions for partner withdrawal, division of responsibilities, assets, income and so forth. These agreements should be written, signed, notarized and filed with a county or state agency to maximize their enforceability.

Limited partnership (Ltd) is a variation in which liability for obligations of the company are limited for some partners. There must still be a "general partner" whose liability is not limited. The partnership agreement can specify any arrangements about relationships between partners as above. Venture capitalists sometimes set up investment pools as limited partnerships. The capitalists run the partnerships, and get paid, while the limited partners put up most of the money and have certain rights to participate in winnings of the investments but no say so in operations. After a time specified in the paperwork, the partnership is liquidated and investors receive their specified share. They are owed whatever the partnership says they are.

As with a proprietorship, income taxes of the partnership arise as part of each partner's personal income picture.

Corporate form is the path chosen by most companies that grow beyond the one- or two-owner stage. Setting up the business as a corporation theoretically separates it from the owners in terms of liabilities and taxation. Technically, owners are no longer liable for debts of the business, although lenders may refuse credit unless the owners agree to waive this feature. If the corporation is really set up as a way of getting around the law, the government can easily prosecute the owners. If, for instance, it is set up with insufficient capitalization for debt it takes on, or if the owners use its accounts for their personal affairs, the corporate shell will not protect them. Some other features of a corporation are:

- If owners die or give up their shares in a corporation, it continues. If any partner withdraws ownership from a partnership, the partnership does not automatically continue but rather must be reformulated.

- It is easier to issue, sell and exchange corporate shares than partnership shares. For these conveniences and the liability protection, owners often set up businesses as corporations, despite such disadvantages as requirements for meetings and more paperwork.

- If the corporation is very simple, an owner can set it up personally by purchasing the forms and filing them with the appropriate state agency. Usually, however, there are enough complications to warrant engaging a lawyer who is experienced in the task for help in making sure it is done properly. Hiring a lawyer is similarly advisable in terminating a corporation.

The corporation files its own tax forms, separate from those of its owners. A choice must be made as to whether it will be taxed at the personal rate as an S corporation or at the corporate rate of 34 percent. The subchapter S form is usually preferable if the corporation is paying out its earnings, since they are taxed only once. In contrast, in a regular C corporation, earnings are taxed at the corporate level and then a second time at the personal level. Moreover, S corporation losses can be deducted against personal income of the owners, thereby giving them a tax break if the venture loses money, which often occurs in early stages. However, an S corporation also imposes qualifying requirements:

- It can have no more than 35 shareholders and none can be nonresident aliens;

- It can have only one class of stock, although there can be differences in voting rights;

- It cannot have active subsidiaries;

- It must derive at least 20 percent of its revenues from U.S. sources;

- It must derive at least 75 percent of its revenues from "active" sources (i.e., not dividends, rents, or royalties).

A regular C corporation may be converted to an S corporation and vice versa, but there are restrictions. Legal help in assessing them is advisable.

A consideration sometimes important in forming a corporation is that its stock be issued under provisions of **Section 1244** of the Internal Revenue Code. Essentially, these permit initial investors to charge any loss up to $50,000 from disposition of their stock as a loss against their ordinary income, rather than only against capital gains that they may or may not have. Among the requirements for this declaration are that the stock has been issued to individuals; that it has been issued in return for cash, not other securities; and that the company be a domestic corporation with less than $1 million in capitalization.

Application: Which legal form should the assigned case venture have and why?

The procedure for creating a corporation involves (1) filing articles of incorporation with the appropriate state agency, and (2) depositing at least the minimum paid-in capital amount required by the state. The state issues a certificate of incorporation, which means that the corporation now exists. Beyond that are tasks of issuing shares, appointing directors, electing officers, setting up bylaws and commencing business.

The main items of paperwork in this process are (1) the articles of incorporation and (2) the corporate bylaws. What the articles must contain is specified by the state. In Washington State, for instance, the following must be specified:

- The company name and address
- How long the company is to last (e.g. "in perpetuity")
- What its purpose is (e.g. "any legal business")
- What kinds of shares and how many are to be issued
- How many directors it will have
- Names and addresses of the incorporators

Answers to these questions may be simple or complex. For instance, stock issued may be common. Or it may be preferred, voting, or nonvoting, carry all sorts of different rights, and so forth. Simple answers an entrepreneur may be able to provide without help. More complex questions probably require assistance from a suitably specialized lawyer.

Generally, it is desirable to keep the articles of incorporation as simple and open-ended as possible, to maximize flexibility that the corporation can exercise without changing them. Further structure can be added, to the extent desired, in the corporate bylaws, which need not be filed with any government agency. They remain private and can be changed as the directors wish. Bylaws are enacted by the directors at their first meeting. Typically, bylaws include the following:

- Where and when directors meetings will be held
- What constitutes a quorum
- Who can vote
- How proxies work
- What powers directors will have
- Directors' tenure terms and replacement
- What officers' jobs there will be
- Who the officers will be
- How corporate records will be handled
- Who can sign checks and contracts
- Issuance and replacement of stock certificates
- How bylaws can be amended
- Shareholder rights, such as inspection of records and receipt of financial reports
- Any restrictions on transfer of shares

Standard forms for bylaws, as with articles of incorporation, partnership agreements, and business licenses, can be obtained from legal supplies stores and possibly from other entrepreneurs. The entrepreneurs, however, may have to do some hunting for them because once issued they are rarely looked at again during operation of the company.

Application: *What should be the most important provisions in the paperwork setting up the assigned case venture? Formulate some hypothetical examples to illustrate.*

Preliminary Steps

At the outset, it may not be clear which legal form will be best, and when. There are other things to do—gathering market information, working on prototype design, checking out the competition, locating needed contacts, looking for alternative capital sources, and so forth. If the entrepreneur is working alone, a proprietorship is the natural default for the company's legal form. Later, a decision can be made about whether to incorporate and in what form.

If the entrepreneur is not working alone, however, but is developing partnership-like arrangements with one or more other persons, it may be helpful to develop a written statement of the proposed arrangement. David Packard recalled the first written formalities of planning a company with his college friend, William Hewlett[3]:

During my visit to Palo Alto I got together with Bill Hewlett, and at that

> *time we had our first "official" business meeting. The minutes of the meeting, dated August 23, 1937, are headed "tentative organization plans and a tentative work program for a proposed business venture." The product ideas we discussed included high-frequency receivers and medical equipment, and it was noted that "we should make every attempt to keep up on (the newly announced technology of) television." Our proposed name for the new company: The Engineering Service Company.*

Packard was still an employee of the General Electric Company in New York at the time, and his main reason for going to Palo Alto was to visit his future wife, not to form a company. He returned to New York and stayed with General Electric until June 1939, almost two years after the "business meeting" with Hewlett. The shift from partnership to corporate form did not take place until eight years later, as Packard wrote[4]:

> *In 1947 we incorporated Hewlett-Packard. This allowed for some tax advantages and also provided more continuity to the business than a partnership could. By that time we had also put in place a good part of the top-management team that was to guide the company over the next thirty years.*

A partnership can also come into being by default as co-founders begin working together and representing themselves as being in business together. To guard against the unlimited liability that can arise for a partner through the action of any other partner, White has suggested a form, such as the following, which should be signed by each partner and also be signed and dated by two or more witnesses[5]:

> I, _____ as a co-founder and co-owner of _____ (venture name), realize that we must operate as a partnership in the public's eyes until we are ready to incorporate. I realize that my co-founders and co-owners are placed in jeopardy by my actions and by my commitments on behalf of the venture. Therefore, I agree not to spend over $ _____ in cash purchases or to commit my company to over $ _____ in any agreement without the prior approval of the other partners.

Other statements to consider formalizing at this time include a non-disclosure agreement to be signed by any participant to whom secrets of the venture are revealed and in which the participant promises not to divulge confidential information about the venture to anyone outside without permission, and a non-compete agreement in which a co-founder promises not to enter competition with the venture. The non-compete agreement must specify precisely what lines of business would constitute competition, in what geographic areas, and for what period of time. It is important to remember that courts are generally loath to prevent people from working for a living, even if it involves competing with former employers or partners, and the terms therefore should not be too broad.

Formulating these documents, although they are generally quite simple, may point up the desirability of getting help from a lawyer. However, many people manage without such help at this stage. Those who do get legal help sometimes run into expensive lawsuits later if the cooperative spirit between partners breaks down. Harmony is probably more important to seek than legal shielding.

Supplementary Reading

New Venture Mechanics Chapter 4. (Vesper, K. H., Prentice-Hall, 1993)

Exercises

1. Interview operators of two or three contrasting businesses. For each, make a list of the governmental requirements for permissions and for reporting. Which has it worst and why? Which enjoys more protection from competitors due to governmental entry barriers? How have requirements changed over time?

2. Contact government offices and learn what is involved in setting up foreign trade ventures.

Venture History

1. What paperwork was involved in establishing the enterprise? How much did it cost? Did it provide any instructive experiences?

2. What legal form was adopted for the enterprise, how much did it cost to set up, and how have its provisions mattered?

Venture Planning Guide

1. Compile a list of the licenses, permissions, inspections, taxes and any other government requirements that apply to your venture.

2. Choose a company name and perform a quick preliminary check of its legality.

3. Choose a legal form of organization for your venture idea, and explain why it is appropriate. Describe the document on which that legal form should be recorded, and explain the provisions it should include. Tabulate the steps and estimated costs of executing this document.

Notes

[1] Jay Finegan, "Down In The Dump," *Inc.*, September 1990, p. 98.

[2] Frank H. Foster and Robert L. Shook, *Patents, Copyrights and Trademarks*, (New York: Wiley, 1993), p. 183.

[3] David Packard, *The H P.Way* (New York: Harper Business, 1995), p.32.

[4] Ibid, p.64.

[5] Richard M. White, Jr., *The Entrepreneur's Manual*, (Radnor, PA: Chilton Publishing, 1971), p. 79.

❏ SUBCHAPTER 6C - Setting Up Shop

Time Before Start-up

A 1989 survey by *Inc.* magazine of its *Inc.* 500 fastest growing small firms revealed that 26 percent of the companies had, during start-up, taken only "a matter of weeks" to go from idea to beginning operations. For 37 percent the time lapse was "a few months," for 28 percent it was between six months and a year, and for 9 percent it was more than a year.[1] Cooper et al. reported from their contrasting sample of 2,994 start-ups that, "Although the majority went through a relatively lengthy planning period prior to business entry, 87 percent reported that the time between their first business expenditure of $500 or more and their first cash receipt (sale) was three months or less. Just 3 percent reported the time to be seven months or more."[2]

Myriad tasks must be performed in starting up even seemingly simple businesses. Although some can be done quickly, others may take considerable time and effort. Collectively, for a founder who may have to give top priority to finishing development of a product, raising capital or generating sales, the other things to be done can make the total activity load almost overwhelming. They may include:

Pick a name
Pick a law firm and work with attorneys on idea protection
Obtain a city business license
Obtain a federal employer identification number
Obtain a state business license and tax ID number
Put up a sign
Open a company bank account (require two signatures on checks?)
Set up an expandable accounting software system
Find space, check zoning, apply for permits
Work out lease terms and sign
Make rental deposits
Copy and distribute keys
Have phone and communication lines installed
Get listed in the Yellow Pages, if appropriate
Obtain office furniture and equipment
Get help on graphics, logos and advertising
Obtain business cards
Seek needed cash sources
Refine written plan
Set up correspondence software with letterheads and forms
Buy envelopes

Order rubber stamps
Create payroll system
Set up employee and casualty insurance
Formulate employment policies
Seek out and interview potential helpers
Check references
Recruit needed helpers, arrange terms and tracking systems
Design, prepare and sign confidentiality and non-compete agreements
Set up cash tracking system
Identify suppliers
Work out supplier agreements
Codify returns policies and warranties
Prepare sales literature
Contact distribution channels
Set up servicing arrangements
Formulate pricing and discount schedules
Buy inventory
Prepare tax returns
Revise and refine plan

Application: *Develop an explicit list of main tasks to be performed in the next 90 days of the assigned case venture. Rank them as to your estimate of (1) the personal hours they will require from the founder(s) and (2) the number of calendar days that will elapse between when work on them begins and when it will essentially end.*

Beyond Prototypes

How hard it is to finish a product design, test and refine it adequately shows up frequently in the massively expensive recalls issued by auto manufacturers. Problems beyond the prototyping state also crop up in new ventures, as illustrated by the following examples.

A team of moonlighting Boeing engineers began in September 1970 an on-board weighing system more accurate than those currently on the market for trucks. Twelve months later they had orders for 18 units at $1,250 each and commenced production. A couple of months later rains began, and the product proved vulnerable to them. Complete redesign had to be undertaken and followed-up with reinstallations that nearly broke the venture. As it turned out, the company's response earned it a reputation for servicing that helped sales later. But management observed that it need not have been nearly so costly had testing been better in the first place.

❖ ❖ ❖

A Canadian micro brewery, needing a package for its product and recognizing the very high cost of packaging machinery, seized the opportunity to rent an unused wrapping machine offered by a kraft paper supplier. Some difficulty was encountered in attempting to print the brewery logo on the kraft paper, but production proceeded anyway. When sales began, a more serious problem arose. The package tore too easily, allowing bottles to drop and smash. It took six months to negotiate withdrawal from lease of the machine, locate another to process heavier material, have a designer create a new package and set up to produce it. The entrepreneur commented, "Beware of the easy solution."

❖ ❖ ❖

An enterprise set up to produce an instrument for guiding road graders accurately found, after selling a number of units, that a key component bought from an outside supplier to conserve capital, contained an inherent design deficiency not anticipated in the purchase contract which caused it to malfunction in hot climates. At great expense, the supplier contract was re-negotiated to terminate, another supplier was recruited, and with that supplier a complete redesign of the component was undertaken. The venture survived, but at a cost in dollars, customers and reputation, all of which took years to rebuild.

❖ ❖ ❖

In 1974 a design engineer teamed up with a wealthy investor to create and produce a new hand-held electronic tallying device for the wood products industry. Market studies revealed no competitive products but a sales potential in the range of $17.5 million per year. In early 1973 a prototype was demonstrated at a forest products show. No orders resulted, but visitors to the booth showed such enthusiasm that the investor insisted on going ahead with production and sales. The engineer argued that more field testing was needed, and when the two could not agree suggested that the investor set up a separate company for sales and give the original venture a purchase order. This the investor did, which left him with a large inventory he was not able to sell.

Laboratory testing, field testing, "beta" testing with customers, focus group evaluations and limited trial marketing are all techniques that may help shake out bugs before investing in full-scale production.

Application: *Describe the sequence that might be used for effectively testing and refining the product or service in the assigned case.*

Packaging

The importance packaging can have for a new venture was illustrated by Sophia Collier, whose venture began with a new soft drink, SoHo soda. She recalled:

> *What really made SoHo succeed was when we changed our packaging in 1982. When you're selling a product, the little, tiny billboard that you have is your label, and people are going to see your product and be aware of its label when they're using your product.*[3]

In a broad sense whatever physical way the product or service is presented can be regarded as its package. Fast foods have containers. Table-served food has many physical elements to its presentation, including plates, silverware, napkins, table arrangement and so forth. Oil changes include presentation of a checklist of what was done. How these physical elements used in transmitting services to customers are handled can help or detract from selling and should therefore be evaluated relative to competitors and given careful thought, perhaps with professional help.

For a product there are not only questions of eye appeal and convenience. Such questions as how units can be efficiently combined for shipment, how well they will protect the product in shipment, how hard or easy they will be to display, to open and possibly to steal must be considered. Is disposability important? Can the same package easily be modified or adapted to other uses? How much space will it take, and how much will it weigh? How much will it cost? How should it feel? What should the printing look like? Should there be a stand, backboard or other point-of-purchase display to go with it?

An extensive reference on packaging is the *Packaging Supplier Source Guide* published each March by Cahners, 1350 East Touhy Avenue, Des Plaines, Illinois 60018. A reference on point-of-purchase displays is the annual *Illustrated Guide to P.O.P. and Promotion published by* Creative Magazines, Inc., 37 W. 39th St., New York 10018.

Arranging for Production

Setting up to produce what the venture will sell, whether it is a product or a service, can usually be approached in many ways. Examples of cheap facilities include the fabled dining-room tables and backyard garages that countless entrepreneurs have used for their initial working areas. More elaborate and costly facilities may be required for some types of ventures, such as development and production of a new drug or supercomputer. Between these extremes lie limitless intermediate choices, many of which are feasible for almost any product or service. Their adoption will turn on such factors as what resources are conveniently available, how much capital is required, and, most importantly, what the venture will seek to produce in order to please its customers.

Dimensions of the product or service that may determine whether people will buy it, and that can have significant implications for how a shop should be set up to produce it, include:

1. *Functions the product or service performs.* Making a drawbridge requires some types of equipment. Making flow meters or apple pies requires other types. Providing consulting services on EEOC (Equal Employment

Opportunity Commission) regulations requires little in the way of equipment. Providing analytic chemistry services requires more equipment, special facilities, and different employee know-how, as does aerial photography.

2. *Quality as perceived by the customer.* Colored announcements can be made on copy machines, which may be quite adequate. Alternatively, they can incorporate glossy prints of much higher fidelity, showing truer colors and more detail, but making such prints requires entirely different equipment.

3. *Convenience.* Customers may care about how close the venture's plant is to their own location and how much parking is available. Alternatively, it may be important for the venture to be close to a work force of suitable skills, which may be far from customers. Attributes of the surrounding area, such as noise, safety, and beauty may or may not matter to customers. Level of rent and zoning may be crucial.

4. *Cost.* Starting an airline to fly out of Denver's new airport may provide service that is more convenient for customers. But flying out of Colorado Springs, 70 miles away, may be enough cheaper for some people from Denver to drive the distance and fly from there, particularly if several are traveling together.

5. *Speed of delivery.* This usually requires a larger production capacity. If customers are willing to wait, a smaller capacity may satisfy the same needs by producing more steadily (the tortoise competing with the hare) and perhaps more cheaply.

6. *Dependability of delivery timing.* More reliable production equipment and/or workers may be needed for dependable timing, since shutdowns cannot be tolerated. Flexible delivery timing may allow the use of production facilities rented from others, when available, probably with a savings in investment capital but at higher cost.

7. *Flexibility.* Special-purpose equipment and standardized products and services can lead to a streamlining of operations that enhances quality and dependability in the venture's output. Flexible output often requires more general-purpose production equipment that operates slower, while requiring greater set-up efforts and employee learning to accommodate the changes.

8. *Follow-up service.* If field service is needed, customers can either buy it from someone else, or the venture can provide it. The skilled workers, facilities, tools, and communication equipment needed will depend on the service offered and whether the venture survives to a point where follow-up on its products is necessary.

9. *Rate of modification.* Some products and services become obsolete fast because they are fads, while others must be updated to keep pace with changes in technology and/or how customers' preferences shift and competitors act. This may require flexibility in the venture's production and/or service. It may also require special equipment for engineering design and prototyping to create upgrades.

How these elements are balanced to win and keep customers is central to the venture's competitive strategy and to setting up shop. Choices about them will affect how great a profit the venture can gain, which in turn will affect the venture's ability to attract the necessary resources for financing the shop and start-up.

Make or Buy?

Whether to make or buy what the company will sell can be a major issue in setting up shop. How long it will take and how much it will cost to accomplish delivery, as well as how much investment will be required are all questions that should be answered to weigh the alternatives. Other questions include how well quality can be controlled, how much flexibility there will be to change production levels, and possibly to what extent confidential aspects of the operation must be divulged.

Having someone else make the product or service while the venture does designing and selling only may allow lower initial investment, since then entrepreneur(s) will not have to buy as much in the way of equipment, rent as much space, pay the costs of installing machinery, and recruit or train people as much. It may also be faster and reduce the number of tasks that the founders must perform.

But buying from outside also means that the founders will have less control over the method of production. Effort will be required to find the best suppliers and to work out contracts describing exactly how much product should be delivered, by when, and to what specifications. Some payment is likely to be required in advance, possibly the whole amount of the production order. If the founders discover that changes in the product specifications are needed, these will have to be renegotiated, which will not only take time, but will probably increase costs and delay delivery. Working with the supplier may require the venture to divulge information it would prefer to keep secret. Moreover, the supplier will build into its charges a profit that will thereby be lost to the venture itself. The supplier may even become a competitor.

Seeking suppliers overseas where wage rates are lower may be a way to compensate for some of these disadvantages, but it can aggravate others, as the following example illustrates.

In mid-1985 two Canadians decided to collaborate on a product one had developed, a belt-like device with fabric pouches for carrying audio tape cassettes. How fast to move on it was a question. They wondered whether they should seek sales in the forthcoming Christmas season even though most stores had already done their advance ordering. Based on informal research the two saw the product as a gift that would likely be a hit with teenagers. They had heard, however, that competitors were developing similar products. Maybe the pair could slip in ahead of them by acting fast and taking advantage of the fact that stores usually keep a small amount of slack in their Christmas buying schedules for last-minute additions.

Another question was how to accomplish production. The pair lacked both the resources and know-how to set up a production line, which they expected would take too much time to accomplish anyway. The options seemed to be either to drop the Christmas target or seek out a supplier willing to perform a rush order. Among suppliers, the alternatives were either domestic or foreign. Through personal contacts one partner found a supplier in Hong Kong not only willing to do the work, but to do so at a fraction of the cost compared to domestic producers. A deal was struck.

Some Christmas sales were made, but not as many as hoped. The company survived, but not very profitably. The main benefit of this fast action appeared to be education. Lessons the entrepreneurs said they learned from this experience were that:

- Overseas cost savings are eroded by (1) travel costs to arrange the deal, (2) long distance phone costs to keep things moving, (3) air shipping costs to cope with late deliveries, and (4) correction costs of inability to oversee quality.
- Having to spend extra time on production subtracts time from marketing and reduces sales.
- Even with good contacts, effective control of production and quality at producers who are located far away is difficult and sometimes impossible.
- When a distant producer promises delivery immediately it may mean two weeks, and a promise of one month may mean six to seven weeks.
- Plants in the Orient take Christmas orders in February and gear up their plants to deliver by August. Persuading them to reschedule for rush orders, even though they are willing to do small ones, costs extra.

These entrepreneurs concluded that this adventure, despite its problems and disappointments, had been worthwhile because now they had a business going, knew more about the market, were working on new ideas for expanding their product line and had improved both contacts and know-how for doing better next time. Giving more advance thought to possible problems and ways of mitigating them were precautions they would add.

Laying out a value chain which describes each stage in the process of creating and delivering something to the customer, then considering the costs and benefits to the venture of performing versus purchasing the work of each of those stages can be a useful form of analysis. Also laying out a PERT chart depicting steps and their timing for setting up operations of the various stages in production can be helpful. Beyond their usefulness in making decisions about creation of the venture, these two analyses can add to the strength of a written plan describing the venture for other people, such as potential investors.

Application: *What aspects of the assigned case venture's product or service could be produced through purchase from outsiders? Which ones should and which should not?*

Supplies

Ordering supplies may take some careful estimating and decision-making. Larger purchase orders usually yield price breaks from suppliers as well as possibly better service and delivery from them. However, trade credit needed to obtain supplies, which often is at best hard to get on small orders, will probably be even harder to get on larger ones. Hence bigger orders require more start-up capital. They also raise the risk of loss if what is ordered turns out not exactly to fit the venture's need. If the initial inventory is too small, however, and the lead time for ordering is long, there may not be time to restock before what is on hand runs out. Thus forecasting in this area can be an important part of setup decision making. Gaining the cooperation and help of suppliers will be further discussed in a later chapter.

Application: *What should the schedule of purchases by the assigned case venture be, and how should that contrast with its schedule of deliveries?*

Premises

It may be simplest to take the first location found vacant. It may be attractive to choose a location close to home so as to reduce commuting time. There may be appeal in picking whatever site offers the lowest rent or best purchase terms. But these may be the wrong reasons for selecting a particular site for the business.

The law firms retained by major corporations are typically ensconced in high-priced downtown suites with expensive furnishings, spacious conference rooms and up-to-date office equipment. Job machine shops may contain high-technology numerically-controlled machine tools, but most are located in grimy industrial districts with old and/or cheap furniture in the entry office, giveaway calendars on the wall and no furnished waiting room. Both types of premises probably fit equally well the firms they serve. More economy in the law firm office would lose it the kind of customers it wants, and more elegance in the job shop would simply increase expenses without expanding sales, and therefore hurt profits.

Appearance can be crucial to some businesses. To a retail store, display windows, types of neighboring firms, lighting, fixtures, wall textures, and cleanliness matter. In food service, the style of decoration may need to fit the menu, whether elegant, thematic, or designed to encourage quick eating and departure. Such choices as furniture, floor covering and background music (including type and volume) can affect how much money goes into the cash register.

Location

For retail stores, eating places and some kinds of services, such as shoe repair, location is a crucial variable. To make intelligent guesses about whether sales volume will cover costs and generate a profit, the following must be weighed against the rent level per frontage foot or per internal square foot:

- target customer profiles
- number of certain customer types within a certain radius
- availability of parking
- level of foot traffic
- kinds of other stores in the vicinity
- regulations about permissible signs

Most of these considerations lend themselves to objective analysis; weighing their importance requires subjective judgment. Advice from other people experienced in similar lines of business may be helpful in making such choices, but only if it is heeded.

When Donald Hauck decided to open a small department store in Montevideo, Minnesota, the first site he chose, which was in the middle of the business district, was "too expensive, we thought." He ignored another retailer who said "Don't be afraid of the rent. If you find the right spot, the rent will take care of itself."

Instead, Hauck took the recommendation of a banker who offered enough credit to open the new store in a building Montgomery Ward had vacated. "That alone should have told us something." Hauck recalled. It was located not centrally but rather "about 40 feet too far north" and had no similar stores near it. But the rent was cheap.

A variety of attempts to attract customers with advertising, promotions, sales, changes in decor and even changes in line failed, and Hauck eventually closed the store. But he drew upon this experience in setting up his next store, a bridal shop. This time he chose a site directly across from a major shopping center with a huge lighted sign. "Almost half our customers find us because of that sign," Hauck observed. "I'll never again make the mistake of being 40 feet too far north."[4]

For another type of business the 40 feet might not have mattered as much as the rent. In the next example, for instance, it was more the nature of the building than where it was located that became decisive.

> When a frozen food distributor vacated a cold storage building and moved to a larger one in another part of town, a young man who had been renting a small space in the building to store tree seeds, which he harvested as a part-time job, thought he saw a good opportunity to set up his own cold storage business. The plant was over 50 years old but in good working order, and the rent seemed to him very low. Without much thought he signed a lease.
>
> He then went looking for clients to fill the space but learned that many wanted not just storage space but also services such as processing and packaging in addition to receiving, storage and shipping. He found himself short on both experience and equipment for these. There was no "sharp freeze" capability. The layout included four floors, a very slow elevator, small rooms with many corridors and doors to be navigated, all of which made work slow. The elevator capacity was so limited that each floor needed its own forklift. Low ceilings, small rooms, wooden floors and limited ventilation made the building unsuited to processing lines. Both the loading dock and the approach alley were inadequate to the traffic.
>
> Negative cash flows resulted and prompted him to seek partners. Eventually, he persuaded one to join him in financing legal action to break the lease, move to another plant and begin the business over again, "right" this time, but no longer as sole owner.

The second time around, this entrepreneur knew what to look for from experience he had bought at a high price. Had he done more investigation into what factors were important for a cold storage location to work well he might have done better the first time. Part of such investigation should include not just whether the location is suitable at present, but whether it is likely to remain so. For instance, zoning restrictions could be all right today, but then change. If they did change perhaps a business not within those new rules would be given an exemption to continue under some sort of "grandfather" provision. But if later it needed to expand, the exemption might not apply and the firm might be forced to move.

In a manufacturing business, location requirements would be different from those for a consumer-oriented retail or service establishment. Considerations of importance for manufacturing might include:

- Safety
- Appropriate zoning for the work to be performed
- Availability of a suitable workforce
- Availability of needed suppliers and ancillary services
- Availability of transportation, both in and out
- Utilities, including waste disposal

- Cost
- Community support, including possible financial assistance
- Room to grow

Application: *What should be the criteria for selection of a location for the assigned case venture and what should their rank order of importance be?*

Layout and Flow of Work

Several documents should be drawn up if the venture is to process goods. These may belong in the venture plan, possibly as appendices.

- A picture of the shop floor plan should be made to scale, with a map showing where equipment will be placed.

- With it should be a diagram showing which operations will be performed where, and in what typical sequence(s). These should be described in writing.

- Accompanying these should be a chart showing where materials will be stored and how they will flow from one point to the next.

The timing of operations in these diagrams should also be indicated, and what may go wrong with them should be considered. What if a supplier delivers too much, or too late? How will a rush order be handled? How will rework be handled if mistakes appear in the output? What will be done with the flow of production if a customer suddenly increases the size of an order or cancels one? Who will make these decisions?

When operations are beginning, production runs may be quite small, but thought should be given as to how they will be expanded so that the whole shop does not have to be reworked prematurely. The initial order of inventory may be small, but the company may later have opportunities to buy at volume discounts. What will be the procedures for anticipating needed supplies, how much space will be reserved for larger orders, and how will the reordering of inventory be handled to make sure it gets done in time?

Leases

In addition to any government zoning restrictions, an entrepreneur who chooses to economize capital by renting rather than owning premises must also give forethought to the impact that lease terms can have on a venture. This is illustrated by the following experience.

Having obtained a $10,000 line of credit to set up an imported smoked meat sandwich booth in a mall, an entrepreneur signed a "standard" lease for the site and built a booth himself with the help of his brother and his wife.

When it opened, business started slowly, but then gradually grew. As a complementary activity, the owner started wholesaling meat to a local supermarket chain. Attempts to sell to other markets, however, failed.

Noticing the growth in business at the booth, the building owner allowed three other fast food stores with similar products to start selling, notwithstanding a clause in the lease that the first entrepreneur had understood would forbid such competition. He considered suing but decided that the time and money costs would be too high. Sales growth slowed, but still continued, and net cash flow became strong enough, when coupled with the supermarket wholesaling, to pay an adequate living income plus some accumulation of capital.

Then the building owner closed a deal to put up a new building on the same site and exercised a demolition clause in the lease, which put the sandwich stand out of business. Not seeing a site he considered suitable for another such stand, the sandwich shop owner started looking for partners to raise enough cash to begin a restaurant, even though he realized it would require different practices and skills than did the sandwich stand.

Customarily a "standard" lease has a lot of fine print in addition to "custom" terms of rental amount, timing and conditions for renewal that will be negotiated and written in. It should all be read and considered with care, possibly with the help of a broker friend, an attorney or another entrepreneur. Contingencies to consider may include such things as whether it is possible to sublease; conditions under which the lease can be renewed or broken; what the landlord will provide in the way of security or parking; whether competing enterprises can obtain leases in the same building; what happens if the nature of surrounding businesses changes or too many of them move out; and how flexible the landlord has been in dealing with the leases of other tenants.

Application: *If the assigned case venture were to lease premises, what conditions in the lease should be considered most versus least important?*

Facilities

It was earlier suggested that to minimize start-up cash needs it might be well to lease, not buy; build, not buy; or buy used, not new, in order to save money on equipment. There is no general choice, but at least the alternatives can be considered before making commitments.

On installing equipment there may be choices between doing it personally or hiring professionals. The latter cost more but save time and may do the job better. The following experience of a day care center illustrates how problems can cascade if power wiring is not done correctly:

A short in the wiring started a fire which ruined $54,000 worth of the day care center's equipment, including refrigerators, microwave ovens, television, video recorder, toys, furniture, books and rugs. Fortunately, nobody was hurt and insurance covered replacement of these items. But business had to stop immediately and customers took their children elsewhere. Until the insurance could be collected there was no income, and rent payments drained the owners' capital.

In this case the owners first persuaded the landlord to let them delay, although not discontinue, rent payments. Local community service agencies were implored for donations to help recovery. Customers were asked to return when rebuilding was accomplished, and enough of them did to allow restart of the business.

In addition to power wiring, some businesses require anticipation of present and future computers and other office equipment. It may be cheaper in the long run simply to set up for all reasonable possibilities by installing several types of wiring, including some for unforeseeable future needs. For example, video requires coaxial cable, whereas telephone, fax, and computers presently use ordinary wires. Data can be sent over regular power lines by use of special adapters[5], but fiber optic cables carry more information and will likely be used more in the future.

Projective thinking—creating scenarios and imagining what might benefit from advance remedies—can be a very useful exercise in making facilities and equipment decisions. How will the shop be laid out? Where are bottlenecks most likely to arise? If the company grows, where will the bind first be felt? What chain of calamities could follow from a breakdown? At what points along a growth curve should the next expansion problem be foreseen and from what clues? How far ahead should action be taken to forestall such problems?

Application: *Draw a layout map of the shop in which the assigned case venture should be operating six months after the end of the assigned case.*

Insurance

Anticipating what can go wrong should inevitably be combined with thinking about not only how to prevent problems but also how to insure for those that occur anyway. Some types of coverage to be considered include:

- Fire
- Theft
- Key employee's life
- Liability - Product, Directors', Property
- Health
- Disability
- Vehicles - Company's and/or employees'

- Workmen's compensation
- Business interruption
- Accounts receivable

There are ways to save money. Carefully list and review the things that could go wrong, produce accidents and attract lawsuits. Then apply imagination to the task of reducing the risks of each of those things happening. Design of the product, production, warning labels, layout of the plant, instructions to employees, types of equipment used, application of safety guards and warnings, maintenance of the equipment and plant, storage and handling of hazardous materials, alarm systems, fire extinguishing and escape systems, education of salespeople and customers, and plant security are all areas where precautions can be considered.

There are ways to get help on the task. Employees can help reduce accident possibilities. They can also be motivated to take more care of their own health by being required to share costs of health care. Government literature and inspectors can provide useful suggestions. Insurance consultants and company representatives have experience they can share about how to lower risks and costs of coverage. The state workers' compensation bureau can provide information about how to qualify for discounts based on favorable safety experience ratings.

Some ways to reduce costs of the insurance directly are to (1) consider higher deductibles on policies, (2) consider introducing hold-harmless agreements to get around needs for some kinds of liability coverage, and (3) obtain premium quotations from several competing insurance carriers. A way to check on the financial soundness of the carriers themselves is to look at their ratings in *Best's Insurance Reports* at the library.

Application: *What forms of insurance should the assigned case venture buy, and what is the most it should be willing to pay for each?*

Implementing Plans

By the time these actions to start a business are being taken much of the plan writing, if any, may have faded into memory. The start-up process will take on a life of its own, and most decisions will usually follow automatically from obvious choices. It may help occasionally to refer back to plans for assessment of how things are going. It may be necessary to update plans as a way of thinking through major decisions or to apply for further financing. But the main guide to start-up action in entrepreneurship must be action itself.

Application: *Develop a Gantt and/or PERT chart for steps in setting up the assigned case venture. Preferably, use an overhead transparency.*

Supplementary Reading

New Venture Strategies Chapter 4. (Vesper, K.H., Prentice-Hall, 1990)

Exercises

1.   Interview a local commercial real estate agent. Learn of two contrasting properties for sale or rent. List in rank order of appropriateness some types of firms that could start in each. Explain your rankings.

2.   By phone or personal visit talk to three or four firms from which a start-up might buy supplies. Ask what lessons each has learned from selling to start-ups. What are consequent lessons for entrepreneurs?

Venture History

1.   Sketch a value chain depicting where the venture fits in at two different time points in its history. Insofar as possible, quantify stages of the chain.

2.   On what payment terms were the first supplies delivered to the venture? At what points over the first year did how much credit become available?

3.   Describe how location and facilities decisions were initially made. What would have been either better or next-best choices? Which of those were considered?

4.   What forms of insurance were taken out when, and at what costs?

Venture Planning Guide

1.   Discuss the extent to which the company will make versus buy what it sells, what the pros and cons of different levels of outsourcing would be, and how the choice was made.

2.   Design an ideal location for your business idea. (Alternative tasks may include performing a community analysis, comparing alternative sites, and interviewing a location consultant.)

3.   Look at a standard lease form in a stationery store, and list the main terms that would be acceptable to the company in a lease of premises.

4.   Find a specific, real location for your venture. Obtain details of the lease and setup requirements. Also learn the cost to buy and to build a suitable shop. Project costs over time, anticipating expansion.

5.   Draw a layout of the facility in which your venture will operate, noting the locations and costs of the most important and most expensive assets the facility will house. Explain the rationale behind it.

6.   Describe the procedures to be used for security in the business to protect vital records against any dangers and to forestall robbery or vandalism.

7.   Based on discussions with an insurance broker, list the forms, amounts and estimated costs of insurance and fringe benefit policies that should be used by your

venture. Explain how the choices were made and how the dollar figures were obtained.

8. Find another entrepreneur who should have experience with the above in his or her venture. Ask for comments about the specifics you have developed.

Notes

[1] Donald Hauck, "Location, Location, Location!" *Venture*, April 1987, p. 100.
[2] Cary Lu, "The Wired Office," *Inc.*, August 1989, p. 129.
[3] John Case, "The Origins of Entrepreneurship," *Inc.*, June 1989, p. 54.
[4] Arnold C. Cooper and others, *New Business In America* (Washington, D.C.: The NFIB Foundation, 1990), p. 5.
[5] J. Donald Weinrauch and Nancy Croft Baker, *The Frugal Marketer* (New York: AMACOM, 1989).

Case Questions

General Questions

1. What alternative strategic forms could the venture take that is being contemplated by this entrepreneur? By what sequence of analysis can the best choice be made?

2. Prepare (1) a time line, (2) a Gantt chart, (3) a PERT diagram and (4) a guess at an expense budget for performing setup actions mentioned in this chapter on the venture described in the assigned case.

3. Envisage a hypothetical competitor for this venture. Formulate a plan of action, based upon what you know about this venture, to wipe it out. Describe possible actions that the entrepreneur could take to cope with such an attack.

4. What other issues do you see in the assigned case, how should they be handled and why?

Case 16 - Ampersand (B) p. 409

1. What legal issues does Ampersand face at this point?

2. What should Robert Tavarez do about them?

3. Whose company is Ampersand? What should the team propose to the Ewings regarding ownership? What should the Ewings ask for?

Case 17 - Deaver Brown   p. 411

1. How could the physical facilities needed to start a company such as Deaver and Alex are considering best be determined, and how could the advisability of obtaining those by different methods be cross-checked?

2. If Deaver and Alex did get set up to make strollers and for some reason the strollers did not sell well enough, what else could the two possibly do with the productive capacity they would have established?

Case 18 - Windsurfer (A) p. 428

1. What issues are raised in the court decisions of this case?

2. What else, if anything, might Hoyle Schweitzer have done to maximize the protection of his business idea(s)?

3. What requirements for effective patenting are illustrated by the court decisions in this case?

Case 19 - Windsurfer (B)   p. 438

1. What procedures for trademarking are illustrated by this case?

2. What vulnerabilities of trademarking are illustrated by the court decisions in this case?

3. What "lessons" for a prospective entrepreneur are suggested by the Windsurfer (A) and Windsurfer (B) cases?

4. What requirements for effective trademarking are illustrated by the court decisions in this case?

Case 20 - Ampersand (C) p. 446

1. Assess the team's progress so far. What, with the benefit of hindsight, could they have done any differently?

2. How should the team allocate its efforts now between San Diego, Moot Corp[SM], the boards in the cabinet shop, searching for capital and anything else you think they should consider?

3. To what extent should they pursue the idea of setting up a manufacturing plant and how? How would you answer the questions raised at the end of the case?

Ampersand (B)

February 1993 - Incorporation Decisions

In late February 1993, the founders of Ampersand were reviewing provisions to be included in the legal formation of their company. For prior history of the venture, please refer to the Ampersand (A) case. Up to this point they had done essentially nothing about company legal structure.

The company was going to need a commercial bank account. So far, the founders had been paying company expenses out of their personal checking accounts while keeping careful records of the expenditures, which Robert Tavarez was recording with the help of a $100 accounting software package. Expenditures to date had been quickly consuming the original $1,250 each that the founders had agreed to contribute.

To fill the order from Pearl Paint there would have to be substantially greater expenditures which would be awkward to handle from separate personal accounts. Substantial additional cash, whether obtained from winning at San Diego, as the team planned, or from other sources, would have to be deposited somewhere.

To set up a commercial checking account for the venture they would have to obtain business licenses from the state and the city. They would also need a state sales tax license. Robert observed:

It's a strange situation. You need the licenses to get a checking account, but you have to write checks to get the licenses.

The business had to have some legal form, and it seemed to the team that a cor-

poration was likely the best to adopt. A partnership would probably require more custom legal work and be harder to use for raising money. Elaine called a lawyer she knew back home in Colorado who offered to work on it at no cost. He, in turn, could pass it along to another lawyer whom he knew in Texas to make sure the requirements of that state were met if the team wanted it to be a Texas corporation.

The Colorado attorney raised a number of points that should be considered. It would be simplest, he said, if the shares were all issued to one person, such as Elaine. Later, shares could be issued to others, if need be, through changes in the corporate bylaws. Another decision called for was whether to provide in the articles of incorporation for preemptive rights for existing shareholders. That would mean that if further shares were sold to outside shareholders the existing shareholders, would have the right to buy more shares at the same price per share on a prorata basis. If, Robert observed, there were many shareholders, this could become a complicated procedure.

How many shares to authorize and issue initially was another question the founders would have to decide. These shares would be declared at some par value that would represent the company's initial shareholder's equity, which the team assumed would consist of the $5,000 they had put in so far. How should this be handled if one or more members decided to withdraw from the team?

Another question was whether to choose an S corporation form or a C corporation form. With an S corporation, Robert explained, any losses up to the company's equity basis, $5,000 at this point, and any profits would pass through to shareholders at the personal income tax rate and would not be subject to any separate corporate income tax. A C corporation form, however, would require the company to pay income taxes at the corporate rate, and then if any profits were passed along to shareholders in the form of dividends, those would be taxed again at the personal income tax rate. At the same time, however, a C corporation would allow carry forward of any losses in the corporation without limit.

Moreover, with a C corporation the company could issue other types of stock such as preferred stock or non-voting shares, and stock shares could be held by either individuals or corporations, none of which could be done with shares of an S corporation. Still, an S corporation could be converted over to a C corporation if the shareholders wanted to do so. The reverse was not allowed for five years after conversion. To make this conversion would entail more paperwork and presumably legal fees.

There was also the question of what property the corporation should have at this point. There was as yet no formal written agreement with Charles Ewing concerning his relationship with the venture. He and his wife had been making some sales of Claybord, but they were small and the team had not been following them. He had also spent about $5,000 so far to make application for a patent. But it was still pending and there would likely be more expenses to come, perhaps as much as had been spent so far, before it would be issued. The name Claybord had not yet been registered as a trademark.

As the team member who had been handling most of Ampersand's accounting and paperwork functions, Robert Tavarez felt he should take initiative to make sure its legal choices were handled appropriately.

Deaver Brown

In October 1970 Deaver Brown faced what he regarded as a major decision. He and his partner, Alex Goodwin, could either go ahead in an attempt to start a business producing collapsible baby strollers or they could continue looking for better opportunities. A sketch of a European stroller design that had given them the idea appears in Exhibit 1.

Deaver said that pressing ahead with the stroller idea would be risky. First, the two would be giving up very promising positions in their respective professions. Deaver was earning $25,000 a year as a product manager for General Foods, and Alex was making $14,000 as a lawyer in the U.S. Justice Department's Antitrust Division. Second, conversations with persons who made and sold strollers led the two to regard the product as part of a "dead-end" industry, whose buyers were suspicious of anything "new or different." Since their idea was based on a stroller that would fold up, much like an umbrella, Deaver suspected that potential buyers might be reluctant to purchase such a novelty. Moreover, if there really were a market for such a device, quite possibly some other company established in the baby products, carts, or tubing products business was already moving ahead with development of it. Finally, there was always the possibility that other more profitable ideas for a business awaited discovery by the two.

Countering the risks were a number of considerations which Deaver listed: the prototype had been well received by people on the street who were shown the product. Annual sales of strollers in the United States totaled an estimated $30 mil-

lion which, it seemed to him, should make the market small enough for a start-up to enter. Since he thought the industry was mature and not prone to new products, perhaps an innovation such as theirs could provide the competitive edge they needed to succeed in a start-up. Deaver commented:

> If you're going to be in a horse race, be in one with slow horses so that you stand a chance of winning.

The two had spent over 200 hours researching various industries that they thought might be appealing for a business venture. The stroller had received most of their attention during the last few months, and they had talked with people in their spare time about market potential. To test their ability to sell the product to retail stores, Deaver and Alex rented a booth at a juvenile furniture products trade show—where manufacturers, suppliers and retailers got together to line up their business for the peak consumer season in the spring. After the first day of the show Deaver observed:

> We've spent the past year looking for a way to start a business. We've talked to department store buyers, people on the street who were pushing strollers, suppliers, and just about everyone else we can think of that might have an interest in our product. What we've found is that this is a very stodgy market, from the manufacturer down to the retail outlet. Distribution would really be tough, and we'd need to contract out produc-

tion and work with dozens of suppliers.

At the same time, I think the collapsible stroller idea is a good one, and the consumers we've shown it to think that the lighter weight and convenience of being able to fold it is great. Now that we've tried participating in a trade show with it, I think it's time we made a "go/no-go" decision. Sooner or later, you need to quit agonizing and testing and put your chips on that table, or else pull out of the game so you can play something else.

Personal Background

Alex Goodwin and Deaver Brown had known each other since high school in Rochester, New York. When reminiscing in 1969 about the "good times" they used to have together, they decided to see if they could develop an idea for a business into a full-time pursuit. Alex had worked in Washington, D.C., since graduating from law school at Columbia University in 1968. Deaver attended Harvard, majoring in American History and Literature as an undergraduate, and receiving his MBA from the Harvard Business School the same year Alex graduated from Columbia. Deaver said they both had good jobs, yet neither was comfortable working for a large organization where they couldn't readily see the impact of their efforts.

Deaver recalled that he had pursued a number of sideline ventures while growing up, including a profitable stint as a Fuller Brush salesman. His interest in entrepreneurship led him to enroll in a new ventures course while at Harvard. He talked about what happened:

The course had nothing to do with the little ventures that I had tried before then. So I decided that they must be right, and I must be wrong. I did badly in the course, which was largely just about finance; always had the wrong answers. The experience convinced me I wasn't cut out to run my own business, so I'd better get a job with a large corporation if I wanted to gain some practical skills. General Foods offered me a position where I would be able to have some profit-and-loss responsibility, which I felt would be healthy. So I packed my bags and went to White Plains, New York.

He spent three months in sales training, going from store to store and showing buyers a variety of products offered by General Foods. His sales results led to rapid promotions, first to district manager calling on retail chains, and then to product manager. Deaver recalled that he liked the selling part of the job, a task considered "the dregs" by many of his business school classmates. He added that as he continued to be promoted, his job became less of a "street salesman" and more like a staff assistant reporting to middle and upper management.

Deaver said that his temperament wasn't like that of his management peers at General Foods who seemed to enjoy the glamour of being considered a manager and involved with a Fortune 500 firm:

As a student of American History, management's attitude seems to me like the old British problem of having a prejudice against trade and great respect for lawyers, doctors and the professions. Sometimes I felt like I was dying a slow death by job boredom.

Searching for an Entry Point in the Market

During 1969 and 1970 Alex and Deaver spent part of their time researching markets that might suit them as fledgling entrepreneurs. Deaver described their search as one of conceptualizing. Typically, they would be sitting in a room, staring at the walls and ceiling, and talking about what trends or needs seemed apparent in the market. When they came across a seemingly promising business idea they would go talk with someone in a related line of business and also look up government statistics on the particular industry. Deaver recalled one such search:

One area we were interested in was the fireplace market. Our feeling was that the country was entering the 1970s as a period of consolidation and nostalgia under the Nixon Administration. Nostalgia brought to mind fireplaces and New England. We figured there would be growth in the fireplace market and also some opportunities for innovation. So, I went to a store, found out what was new in the market and got a feel for consumer buying habits by talking to the salesmen.

Alex worked in Washington, D.C., so it was easy for him to look up patents and see what was being developed in the industry. We put the information together and tracked down a couple of owners of patents that looked particularly interesting to us. You've got to realize that a lot of patents never turn into a salable product, so there was some interest by the patent owners about producing the product. We never came to any agreement on the worth of the patents and have put the idea on the back burner for now.

Another market the two had examined was what Deaver termed the "re-education" of business professionals. He speculated that business men and women needed to review the basic skills of selling, production, marketing, and writing from time to time, and that translated into a need for a service. After looking under "education services" in the Yellow Pages, he called up a few people in the trade to seek their advice. It seemed to him, he

said, that continuing education received a lot of lip service but not much action.

For the education scheme to work, some third party would be needed to pay the tuition costs. Corporations that might sponsor the fees, the two entrepreneurs found, either wanted to see immediate results or were already conducting their own in-house training programs. Deaver added that existing services were too technical and tended to over-promise results to students and businesses alike. The trick, he pointed out, would be to get sponsorship from enough medium-sized organizations to justify development of solid curricula and hire qualified instructors.

In addition to talking with persons in the industries they thought promising, Deaver and Alex looked up statistical data to get an idea of market size and potential growth trends. For instance, the U.S. Census of Manufacturing provided details on heating stoves for the home and for juvenile products such as strollers. Excerpts of typical data they found appear in Exhibits 2 and 3.

While the two men used a deliberate approach to focus on services or products, they also sometimes "tripped onto products," like the stroller, as Deaver described it.

Last Spring, Alex was visiting London with his family. They were walking through Picadilly Circus and didn't know what to do with the baby, so Alex went into a department store and bought a stroller. It folded up like an umbrella and people would try to buy the stroller from him everywhere they traveled in Europe; some offered him as much as $200. So when he came back home, he said, "You're not going to believe this. We've been looking around for a product, and I've finally found this juvenile vehicle market—we can make a stroller that works like this one."

Alex explained that there were patents on the design and folding concepts of the British-made stroller. He added that a successful patent defense would likely extend only to the design, since the concept of folding a product had been widely used in many types of products. No product like the European stroller, depicted in Exhibit 1, was currently available in the U.S., so far as Deaver and Alex had been able to learn.

Structure of the Juvenile Vehicle Products Industry

Contemplating the stroller as a possible entry wedge for a venture, the two proceeded to explore what type of industry the stroller was in and who the major "actors" were. First, they talked with manufacturers or suppliers of available strollers and visited department stores to look at displays. Deaver explained that most of the firms had started shortly after World War II, when many men returning from the service found it difficult to get work and viewed the "baby boom" as a growth industry to get involved in. Presently, the largest manufacturer did eight million dollars in sales each year. While statistical data placed strollers in the toys and sporting goods industry, whose statistics appear in Exhibit 2, Deaver said he thought competition would likely come from manufacturers of juvenile furniture.

Both of those industries were populated, it seemed to Deaver, by small, fragmented competitors whose rates of both growth and new product introduction were low. Total shipments for furniture were estimated at $200 million, with the vehicle industry (excluding bicycles) at close to $80 million. Similar figures for strollers were estimated at $16.3 million based on wholesale shipments, F.O.B., during 1967. Of the 45 firms producing children's vehicles, 22 employed less than 10 workers. Eighty percent of stroller shipments were from companies that relied on

that product as their major product. By comparison with similar industries aimed at children, the value added and market potential was considerably less for strollers (see Exhibit 3). Deaver commented:

> *The competition seems to be a hodge-podge of small sleepy companies who haven't offered anything new to the market since they first started business. And since both the primary and secondary markets are present, it's not a matter of building a market for strollers and then convincing people that they should buy from us. The market for strollers is there and people on the street have told us they like our product. On the other hand, it looks like we're in a very stodgy market, from the manufacturer down to the retail outlet. So introducing something new might be hard.*

Deaver expected the fact that another manufacturer in Great Britain was making a similar type of stroller meant that competition could exist almost from the start. The opportunity to become a low-cost producer would depend partly on the response of existing stroller companies to their new product line and partly the extent with which cost savings could be significant for this type of production. He said companies in the juvenile furniture industry were also threats, since they had established lines of distribution. Deaver noted that relatively low technology and lack of patent protection facilitated competitive entry.

Both of the partners felt that the collapsible stroller's convenience should fit well with increased mobility and use of space which young adults enjoyed. With the leading edge of the baby boom from World War II now 23 years old, and the number of births in the United States expected to increase in the coming decade or two, the stroller market might be perceived by some firms as a growth opportunity, which could encourage other companies to enter competition. Deaver said that any such conclusions drawn by a large corporation could spell trouble for their venture, since economies of scale tended to favor large firms over smaller ones:

> I was at General Foods long enough to learn that a little company doesn't stand a chance if they are trying to compete directly with a giant. They simply don't have the resources to draw upon, the cash flow, talent, and ability to weather short-term losses that big companies get from support by other product lines.

One option that the two had considered was to have another product in addition to the stroller. Deaver explained that they had thought of a backpack that would be used to carry children and have an added feature of doubling as a stand-alone chair. This would be accomplished by use of a "U" shaped aluminum support that would keep the pack upright and make it easier to load and unload the child. However he noted that only 150,000 baby packs were sold each year, which might be too small a market to help much. Moreover by starting a company that offered two products instead of one, they would be spreading themselves thinner.

Attracting Interest to the Collapsible Stroller

For guidance regarding design and production, Deaver had turned to an engineering friend, Jim Sloan, who agreed to accept a 10 percent interest in the venture as compensation. Deaver had also started calling machine shops around the country trying to find one able both to make a prototype and to deliver high volume production runs. He said that after talking to "zillions" of people and investigating 200 to 300 companies, the search was nar-rowed to two machine shops: one in Alabama and one in Rochester, New York. His experience with General Foods convinced him that upstate New York was a good test market, since the demographics were similar to the national average. A second advantage he pointed to was that the location was near his present home in New York City and, having grown up in Rochester, he knew that the area had excellent tool making capabilities. The shop owner agreed to produce the prototype, which was completed during the summer of 1970.

Deaver and Alex then took the prototype and went to various stores to solicit interest from buyers—however, the stores showed disappointingly little interest. However, when the partners would stop people on the street to demonstrate how light the stroller was and how it folded, it seemed to Deaver that nearly everyone thought it was a good product. He explained how product quality was important to any business venture the two might attempt:

> There are three categories of products: Those that will never work, those that are great, and those in the middle. Firms like General Foods will have people try a product and they'll say "...it's OK, pretty good," and that will be sufficient. Most products that come to the market are marginal; they're neither good nor bad.
>
> When a really good product is tested, like General Foods did with Cool Whip, people respond enthusiastically: "Yea! It's super!" You can tell pretty early if you've got a good or marginal product.
>
> Consumers we've shown the strollers to seem to indicate it is really a good product. But unfortunately trade buyers and retail customers are two different things. Most of the trade buyers have been telling us that our product stinks.

The buyers, he said, had rejected the

stroller "out of hand" claiming that strength and durability were the primary selling features for strollers, with price close behind. They told the two that lighter weight and the collapsible feature were not enough to offset the higher price ($24.97 retail versus $20.00 for conventional strollers on the market) or the fact that they were an unknown entity in a well established industry; Deaver and Alex hadn't even settled on a name for the company yet. People in the industry had told Deaver that retailers typically received 40 percent off of list price and manufacturers representatives typically received a commission of around 5 to 7 percent of the wholesale price.

Production

From experience in creating a dozen prototypes, Deaver said it could be foreseen that tasks needed to produce strollers would fall into three main areas: materials and equipment, cost control, and people. Making the stroller would require that some parts be made by specialty companies, examples being injection molded plastic parts, and plating work. Items like wheels might be bought standard or fabricated from custom parts. Much of the work would involve simply assembling parts, with the frame, wheels and seat being three main components.

He explained that he had recently taken a mechanical engineering course on line balancing at Columbia University, which gave him some practical skills he felt could be applied to optimizing output. His engineering friend, Jim Sloan, told Deaver that he would be willing to help out in a start-up "crunch" period, but couldn't devote too much time due to his regular work as a research specialist for a local electronics firm. Deaver noted tasks that would be required to transform the raw materials listed in Exhibit 4 into a completed product:

Frame Assembly

1. Cut, bend and drill holes in the aluminum tube.
2. Cut, drill holes and hinge the rear metal support.
3. Cut the front support and bend to attach.
4. Assemble the aluminum frame through inserting v-nuts, bolts, rivets, and plastic fittings.
5. Finish the open ends of the aluminum and cover with plastic plugs.
6. Cut, bend and attach the plastic handles to the frame.

Wheel Assembly

1. Assemble each front and rear wheel, using the hub and axle, hubcap, rubber tire, and vertical attachment to fit with the aluminum frame.
2. Cut, bend, and insert the metal rod braking device in the rear wheel.

Seat Assembly

1. Cut, sew, and laminate the fabric to make the seat.
2. Cut, sew, and attach the fabric seat belt to the seat.
3. Attach the plastic rings to the seat belt as a buckling device.
4. Attach the seat to the aluminum frame of the stroller.

Packaging

1. Fold the stroller to fit within a packing case.
2. Include the instructional literature and replacement parts, if any, with the stroller(s) in the packing case.
3. Seal the case shut with tape and/or staples. (Assumes packing case is

complete, having been cut, assembled and screened to include any artwork promoting the stroller.)

He pointed out that each of these tasks could probably be broken down into more detailed sub-tasks. Whether a group of people would be responsible for part or all of the assembly for a single stroller was a question he had not yet answered. He expected the various parts would have to be arranged along the production line to keep the process moving. Space would have to be provided for inventory and to make sure that a particular order didn't get mixed up with another one. Deaver also listed areas of concern and issues in production that he supposed would arise if he and Alex decided to try making strollers on their own. This list appears in Exhibit 5.

Performing the manufacturing after purchasing parts and subassemblies was only one option Deaver and Alex had looked into. Another would be to purchase and provide all materials and then have an outside manufacturer transform them into strollers. They found that to obtain some of the materials, such as rivets produced to the specific size required, they would have to order amounts sufficient to produce a large number of units. On other materials they would have to order large amounts to obtain substantial quantity discounts to keep costs down. They estimated they would need around $100,000 worth of materials to commence production, plus another $25,000 worth of custom tooling to fabricate the parts.

The best price they had been able to obtain on assembly work was $3.51 per unit from a local manufacturer. Another manufacturer located in Alabama would do the work for a few cents less, but it seemed to them preferable to keep the work near home if possible. The local manufacturer had engaged his lawyer to write up a contract for producing the units at $3.51 each,

and Deaver noted that it did not require purchase of any minimum number of units, which he expected would be to his advantage. The contract also provided that the manufacturer could experience as much as 1 percent scrap wastage of the material. Deaver wondered whether that might not be a bit low.

> *I figure it is to our advantage to have the lawyer for the other side draw up the contract,"* Deaver commented. *"Some people say you should always have your own do it, since your own lawyer is more likely to look out for your interests. But I also understand that if the contract is ever taken to litigation, the court will take note of which side wrote it up.*

He guessed that legal fees to pursue a patent, plus accounting fees might cost around $2,000 per month for the first year or two.

In addition to the assembly work an additional cost per unit of $4.49 was expected for the raw materials and parts which would be purchased from other suppliers and subcontractors for delivery to the manufacturer performing the assembly work. Deaver estimated that returns, allowances and freight might add up to perhaps another dollar per unit, although it was difficult to be sure he had thought of everything and estimated it correctly.

Deaver and Alex had personal savings plus friends and relatives from whom they expected they might be able to obtain personal loans to muster up to around $50,000 cash for start-up. Beyond that they expected they might need trade credit and bank loans against such collateral as their company might have. To curb capital needs, Deaver had weighed the possibility of operating out of his home as against renting an office. He calculated that the former would be cheaper (Exhibit 6), but he expected that prospective creditors or investors might be more favorably impressed by the more businesslike appearance of the later. (Some industry financial ratios appear in Exhibit 7.)

Although they thought it might be preferable to use an outside manufacturer for assembly work, Deaver and Alex were not fully convinced. Deaver said that a major concern for him was how fast the contractor could make strollers, even under the best of conditions. He had only been in the man's plant once and didn't know if the current employees would be sufficient to turn out as many as 100 strollers each day. If more workers, space, or equipment were required, the $8.00 cost might have to be renegotiated lest the contractor be forced to work on a thinner margin or perhaps at break-even. Deaver went on to state that any time that he and Jim Sloan spent at the production facility would be time lost for purposes of other activities important to the venture. Deaver commented on his visit to the proposed manufacturer's plant.

> *The place is an absolute zoo—packing cases at the front of the assembly line, things like that. It's not so easy to take the work to another contractor. I've talked with nearly all of them already and none would give us the time or price we need to be competitive. To think that someone else will do a better job might be wishful thinking. So if we get into production problems with the guy, then will we be worse off than doing it ourselves? Should we have a contingency plan, at what point should it activate, and what should it be?*

Trade Show Selling Attempt

In fall 1970 Deaver and Alex took some prototypes of the stroller to a juvenile furniture industry trade show in New York City, where Deaver had arranged to share another company's booth for $100. This show was expected to be the last trade event before the peak selling season, and major retailers and wholesalers were in attendance. Also, the two expected there would be many manufacturers representatives present seeking new lines to carry in the various parts of the country from which they came.

During the first day of the trade show, Deaver and Alex demonstrated their product for people who passed by the booth and received essentially the same types of responses they had encountered earlier when going from store to store. As a result, they decided that they needed to try some harder selling tactics or the show would also turn out to be a failure for them. The second day they deliberately became more aggressive in "buttonholing" people who were passing by the booth. They also got hold of some friends and had them push strollers around outside the building posing as satisfied customers. Whenever things would grow quiet at the booth, Deaver or Alex or both would push prototypes around inside the building, going to other booths and display areas to attract attention to their product. Deaver commented that this unorthodox approach drew some wrath from other companies at the show. He described his "pitch" as follows:

> *We've shamed people into agreeing they would order from us by saying that if they don't give us an order, they're going to put us out of business. We don't have anything to lose, and we've got some prospective orders dribbling in —ten or so at a time.*
>
> *I tell them that this is the only chance that they'll get to be able to give their customers something new over last year—they owe the consumer a choice. Their reply? 'It's lousy, it isn't strong enough, it's too expensive.' So I say, "You're probably right. But what if you're wrong? Can you afford to be wrong?"*

By the end of the second day, notwithstanding the unpopularity they had earned among some of the other companies displaying at the show, Deaver and Alex had managed to persuade prospective customers to accept some 200 strollers if they were to start producing them. They had also met several manufacturers representatives who said they would be interested in carrying the product in various territories of the country. All the prospective orders they received were in small lots, however, and none had come from any major department store chains. This was an important concern in Deaver's view, because such chains had the capability of moving large numbers of products. They could provide the kind of volume Deaver considered essential to economical operation.

Deaver remarked that the biases of buyers he met at the show regarding consumer preferences in a stroller were much harder to change than he had expected. He added that overcoming this bias would probably be critical if they decided to go ahead with the venture. Otherwise, they would never reach the volume of sales needed to recover their costs or hold any prospects for growth.

A potential selling approach that Deaver and Alex were designing, but had not yet tried, was to display strollers by hanging them folded on a metal rack, much like clothes hanging in a rectangular display rack. Deaver said that eight strollers could be packed in two square feet of selling space. He didn't know how responsive buyers would be to this merchandising approach; the annual reports he had read boasted of "quality displays." But financial data were shown only for the corporation as a whole, not specific product lines. Exhibit 8 presents information Deaver had gathered on major retail chains.

Advertising was another front on which Deaver expected they would need to move. An advertisement in *American*

Baby, a magazine distributed to approximately 1 million homes each month would cost around $800 per month, while advertisements in a couple of relevant trade magazines might cost around $250 per month each. "These would be small ads," Deaver observed, "but that is all anybody uses. It seems to be basically a rather chintzy industry."

At the New York trade show Deaver had been able to arrange to display prototypes at low cost by sharing the booth of another company. Later shows might, he expected, cost substantially more, possibly 10 or more times as much, especially if they had to travel to Chicago or Los Angeles to attend them. Preparation and mailing of brochures to potentially interested stores he guessed might cost another $500 to $2,000, depending upon quality of the brochures and the extent of the mailing.

Choosing the Next Step

As he contemplated the complexities and hurdles facing the venture, Deaver wondered whether its basic strategy was viable at all. The number of orders they could gather from the show seemed likely to be far below what break-even would require. Even if they were able to enter the market, there would be little to prevent others with more resources from following suit. It seemed quite possible that there might be litigation from the British stroller manufacturer. It might very well, he thought, decide to test its patent claims and sell extensively in the United States. Deaver reflected on their current situation in trying to get production issues settled and determine if they, or competitors, stood the best chance of successfully marketing this stroller. He commented:

What are the implications of starting a business in a dead-end industry? What does it take to make it work? Can we erect a sufficient competitive barrier to withstand competition in the future? And if we can, does that come from having the product, control over production, or establishing superior channels of distribution? Is the nature of the juvenile products industry one that will change from dormant and mature to a growth industry again and if so, how could we tell when that will that occur?

Maybe there are other companies that are better suited to breaking the retail bias and fragmentation that now exists. But if we're as close as anybody else, we just might be on the verge of having a very successful business.

If they decided to "go" with the venture, Deaver explained that he and Alex would quit their jobs for a time to work on the business. He admitted that they had invested a lot of thought and time in this industry, but cautioned that the investment

was a sunk cost. He summed up their position in deciding whether to proceed or abandon the idea for the collapsible stroller:

Both the primary and secondary markets are present. So it's not a matter of building a market for strollers before we can try to convince people that they should buy from us.

If we're going to make this business work, I suppose we need to tailor our sales pitch to the store buyers and not worry about the consumer. Consumers will benefit from the fact that the stroller works.

I don't know what the secret is of selling to the retailers . . . maybe that can't even be done. If not, I suppose we had better drop this idea right now and look for another industry to get into. Like I told some buyers today: "Being wrong is unaffordable."

EXHIBIT 1   Sketch of British-made Stroller

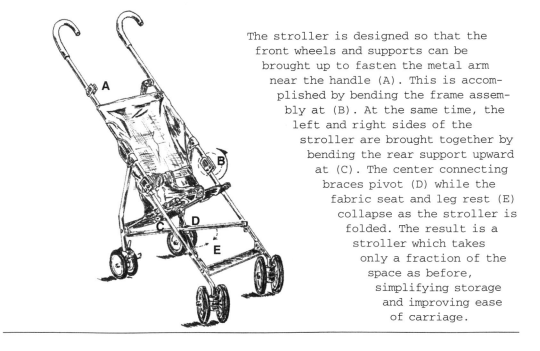

The stroller is designed so that the front wheels and supports can be brought up to fasten the metal arm near the handle (A). This is accomplished by bending the frame assembly at (B). At the same time, the left and right sides of the stroller are brought together by bending the rear support upward at (C). The center connecting braces pivot (D) while the fabric seat and leg rest (E) collapse as the stroller is folded. The result is a stroller which takes only a fraction of the space as before, simplifying storage and improving ease of carriage.

EXHIBIT 2   Sales of Possibly Related Products

INSTRUMENTS AND PARTS: TOYS AND SPORTING GOODS
Quantity and Value of Shipments by All Producers

Product Code	Product	Quantity (million units)	Value ($1,000)	Quantity (million $)	Value (million $)
943 —	Children's vehicles, except bicycles, Total	(X)	99.6	(X)	82.7
943 11	Baby Carriages, including combination carriage-strollers	320	8.2	329	7.4
943 15	Strollers	1,454	16.3	1,023	12.8
943 21	Baby walkers	978	3.3	612	4.4
943 33	Children's pedal driven automobiles & tractors	1,019	9.7	1,055	9.8
943 43	Velocipedes (3-wheeled) and tricycles; including chain-driven tricycles	3,271	23.7	3,113	20.8
943 61	Children's wagons (coaster express, and others)	(X)	(X)	2,562	8.6
943 71	Sleds	1,186	4.9	1,271	5.3
943 81	Parts for children's vehicles sold separately	(X)	1.6	(X)	2.2
943 98	Other children's vehicles, including scooters, sidewalk cycles, 3-wheel play cars, etc.	(X)	28.5	(X)	9.9
944 —	Children's vehicles, except bicycles	(X)	2.8	(X)	(X)
944 02	Children's vehicles, except bicycles (For companies with less than 10 employees)	(X)	0.6	(X)	1.9

EXHIBIT 3 Ratios on Possibly Related Companies

ITEM	Games & Toys (SIC 3941)	Dolls (SIC 5942)	Children's Vehicles, except bicycles (SIC 3941)
Primary Product Specialization Ratio	.88	.90	.81
Coverage Ratio	.96	.70	.61
Establishments' Total...............................	684	340	45
with 1 to 19 employees	354	202	22
with 20 to 99 employees	221	112	11
with 100 employees or more	109	26	12
All employees, average for years	55.1	11.9	3.7
Payroll for year, all employees million $264.9	40.4	19.4	
Production workers:			
Average for year 1,000	46.1	10.7	3.1
March..."	36.3	8.3	3.0
May ...."	43.1	10.3	3.2
August ...."	51.4	12.1	3.1
November ...."	53.6	11.8	3.0
Man-hours ....millions	86.6	10.0	6.4
January-March ...."	16.9	3.5	1.6
April-June ...."	20.5	4.5	1.7
July-September ...."	23.9	5.2	1.6
October-December ...."	25.4	5.1	1.6
Wages ....millions	178.0	34.3	13.9
Cost of materials, etc., Total..................."	490.6	80.0	40.9
Materials, parts, containers ...."			
etc., consumed ...."	427.9	69.9	35.9
Cost of resales................................."	39.3	6.0	2.9
Fuels consumed ...."	2.0	.2	.2
Purchased electricity ...."	5.8	-	.4
Contract work ...."	15.7	5.8	1.5
Value of shipments, including ..			
resale ...."	1113.5	362.0	78.7
Value of resales ...."	27.2	7.2	3.5
Value added by manufacturer ...."	614.3	62.6	38.7
Manufacturer's Inventories ...."			
Beginning of year, total ...."	169.4	17.2	12.5
Finished product..........................."	78.5	7.7	4.0
Work in process ...."	29.0	2.8	3.0
Materials, supplies, fuel, etc., ..."	61.9	3.7	5.6
End of year, total............................."	159.4	16.4	15.9
Finished product..........................."	69.9	8.3	4.1
Work in process ...."	29.0	2.8	3.8
Materials, supplies, fuel, etc., ..."	60.5	5.8	6.0
Expenditures for Plant and Equipment,			
total ...."	35.5	2.6	3.6
New Plant and Equipment, total .."	39.9	2.4	3.5
New Structure and Additions			
to plant ...."	12.5	.3	1.7
New Machinery and Equipment "	21.4	2.7	1.9
Used Plant and Equipment ...."	1.7	.2	(2)

EXHIBIT 4   List of Supplies Needed for the Stroller

Aluminum tubing
Fabric for the seat
  Denim
  Nylons
Plastic handle grips
Fabric strip
Wheels (straight and swivel)
Rubber for the wheels
Plastic plug ends
Plastic fastener
Plastic joints
Wheel axles
Fastening bolts
Thread
Braking device
Front foot rest
Screws
Rivets

Back aluminum hinge piece
Front wheel enclosures
Plastic loops for seat belt
Washers
Plastic covers for wheels
Glue
Wheel lubricant
Fabric laminate
L shaped fasteners
Packing box
Staples

Printing
Instruction sheet
Packing material
Stationery
Sewing needles
Invoice forms

Note: In some cases, Deaver expected to develop second source of materials so as not to be in a production delay situation. Depending on a final agreement to be worked out with the contracting manufacturer, other hand tools relating to the production of the stroller might be required.

EXHIBIT 5 Anticipated Production Issues if Brought In House

I.   AREAS OF CONCERN

   A.   <u>Materials and Equipment</u>
         - Order entry
         - Production planning
         - Product specification
                   1. Performance
                   2. Dimensions
                   3. Style
                   4. Delivery dates
         - Purchasing
         - Inventory control
         - Factory layout and location
         - Make or buy decisions
         - Fixed assets
         - Quality control
         - Retail applications

   B.   <u>Cost Control</u>

   C.   <u>People</u>
         - Plant Mmnager
         - Supervisors
         - Factory and clerical workers

II.   ISSUES TO BE DECIDED

   A.   Method for quality control
   B.   Set-up for production line
   C.   Space set aside and positioning for parts and inventory
   D.   Definition of tasks and sub-tasks
   E.   Record keeping system to monitor production times
   F.   Decisions on second sourcing
   G.   Decisions on cross training of workers
   H.   Methods of shipment
   I.   Packaging and display models for retail outlets
   J.   Invoicing for payment and tie-in completion of order
   K.   Assignment and number of people for each task, group of tasks
   L.   Seasonal and shift scheduling
   M.   Level of inventory to be maintained
   N.   Planning for production capacity expansion
   O.   Assignment of costs
   P.   Pricing changes from productivity improvements

EXHIBIT 6 Projected Offices Expense: Home vs. Traditional

Comparative Monthly Costs

Expense	Office at Home	Traditional Office
Rent	$0	$400
Part-Time Helper	50	500
Phone	2,000	2,200
Office Equipment	0	100
Miscellaneous	50	200
Total	$2,100	$3,400

Exhibit 7 Excerpt from Troy's Manual of Ratios, 1966

Toys, Amusement, Sporting and Athletic Goods (SIC 394)

Sales Volume Record of Total Industry	Year Sales ($Billion)	1958 1.0	1963 1.6	1964 1.8

	Asset Size Ratios, 1964	Under 500	500 to 2,499	2,500 to 9,999	10,000 to 49,999	50,000 and over	Total Industry
	% of Sales						
1	Cost of Sales	74.6	74.5	71.7	70.8	64.8	71.8
2	Executive Salaries	4.9	2.6	1.8	1.0	0.4	2.2
3	Rent	1.7	1.3	0.7	1.0	1.3	1.2
4	Repairs	0.3	0.6	0.6	0.9	0.7	0.6
5	Bad Debts	0.6	0.5	0.5	0.5	9.3	1.6
6	Interest	0.7	0.9	0.8	1.4	9.9	2.1
7	Taxes	2.7	2.4	2.6	2.5	4.5	2.8
8	Contributions	na	na	0.1	0.2	0.2	0.1
9	Depreciation	1.6	1.3	2.2	1.6	1.8	1.7
10	Advertising	1.4	2.2	2.9	5.2	2.0	3.0
11	Benefits	0.5	0.4	1.1	0.7	1.0	0.7
12	P.A.T.	1.9	2.1	3.8	5.2	3.2	
	Ratios						
13	Current	1.5	1.8	2.2	2.1	1.6	1.8
14	Quick	0.8	0.9	1.1	1.0	1.5	1.2
15	Sales/W.C.	8.5	6.0	4.0	4.7	1.2	3.7
16	Sales/Net Worth	6.5	4.4	2.6	3.4	1.2	3.0
17	Inv. Turns	na	na	na	na	na	3.4
18	Liab/Net Worth	2.1	1.1	0.8	1.0	2.3	1.5
	Factors						
19	C.L./Net Worth	152.3	91.0	56.0	65.6	160.1	105.5
20	Inv/C.L.	50.0	49.6	49.0	53.8	10.0	32.7
21	Income/Net Worth	12.6	9.3	9.9	12.8	6.2	9.6
22	Ernings/Income	94.0	91.1	80.5	85.0	54.8	79.9

EXHIBIT 8   Selected Information from Major Retail Chains

Sears

Net Sales	$9,251,000,000
Net Income	$ 470,000,000
Total Number of stores	827
Total Amount of gross floor space (s.f.)	89,600,000

Credit sales comprised one-half of total sales, with 20 million credit customers at year end. Revenues from catalogue orders, direct mail, finance charges, and repair services accounted for 25 percent of net sales. Over 10,000 domestic suppliers are used by 48 buying departments, divided into 805 product groupings (the largest grouping accounts for less than five percent of net sales).

Woolworth's (1970)

Net Sales	$2,507,375,000
Net Income	$76,000,000
Total Number of Stores	3,656
Total Amount of Gross floor space (s.f.)	59,000,000

(over 95% are Woolworth or Woolco Department Stores)

Macy's (1970)

Net Sales	$ 955,976,000
Net Income	$ 20,660,000
Total Number of Stores	61
Total Amount of Gross floor space (s.f.)	14,740,000

Dayton Hudson (1970)

Net Sales	$ 965,400,000
Net Income	$ 19,000,000
Total Number of Stores	see below
Total Amount of Gross floor space (s.f.)	see below

	No. of Stores	Total s.f. of space
Full Line Department Stores	17	7,875,000
Low Margin Discount Stores	25	3,417,000
Specialty Stores	291	not available
Jewelry Stores	204	not available

EXHIBIT 8 (concluded)

FIVE YEAR OPERATIONS SUMMARY

	1970	1969	1968	1967	1966
Penney stores - full line					
Number of stores	240	208	176	141	108
Net selling space (mill. sq. ft.)	19.4	16.5	13.7	10.4	7.4
Sales ($ millions)	1,628.1	1,327.0	1,002.0	661.2	477.7
Sales per square foot ($)	92.97	90.76	85.53	79.13	78.86
Penney stores - soft line					
Number of stores	1,407	1,438	1,476	1,517	1,548
Net selling space (mill. sq. ft.)	18.1	18.4	19.0	19.4	19.5
Sales (millions)	2,119.3	2,156.1	2,105.7	2,105.7	2,042.4
Sales per square foot ($)	115.75	115.22	110.10	105.51	105.03
Catalog					
Number of sales centers	1,019	944	660	637	565
Number of distribution centers	2	2	1	1	1
Distribution space (mill. sq. ft.)	4.1	4.1	2.0	2.0	2.0
Sales-mail order ($ millions)	70.0	61.9	57.7	52.5	40.8
The Treasury stores					
Number of stores	13	10	10	6	5
Net selling space (mill. sq. ft.)	1.5	1.2	1.2	0.7	0.5
Sales ($ millions)	146.2	127.5	85.3	54.1	48.9
Sales per square foot ($)	113.15	107.96	96.83	97.53	92.27
Drug stores					
Number of stores	189	171	157	148	138
Net selling space (mill. sq. ft.)	1.0	.9	.8	.7	.7
Sales ($ millions)	98.0	83.5	71.9	62.8	86.39
Supermarkets					
Number of supermarkets	23	20	17	16	13
Net selling space (mill. sq. ft.)	.3	.3	.2	.2	.2
Sales ($ millions)	88.4	72.4	56.6	45.7	37.8
Sales per square foot ($)	294.98	298.68	259.70	255.27	261.24
European operations					
Number of stores	92	95			
Net selling space (mill. sq. ft.)	1.2	1.2			
Sales ($ millions)	203.8	84.2*	NA	NA	NA
Sales per square foot ($)	119.11	49.26			

Catalog merchandise sold through stores is included in the sales of those stores. Drug and supermarket sales through Penney and Treasury stores are included in the sales of the latter divisions. Food sales by European operations are included in that division's sales. The statistics shown above for drug stores and supermarkets are exclusive of their operations in Penney and Treasury stores.

Reclassification of several stores in 1973 resulted in a net increase of two full line stores and a net decline of two soft line stores. Sales per square foot includes only those stores in operation for the full year.

ᵃ Reflects sales of Sarma, S.A. from July 31, 1969, date of purchase.

Case 18

Windsurfer (A)

The Start-up

Hoyle Schweitzer's inspiration to start a company to manufacture sailboards came from a 1965 conversation with an acquaintance, Jim Drake. The two were comparing two sports they enjoyed, surfboarding and sailing when it occurred to them that it might be possible to combine the two by mounting a sail on a surfboard to propel it.[1]

They began constructing prototypes in quest of a design that could be steered without a rudder, as a surfboard was, but with power coming from the sail rather than a wave. When they achieved a design that worked they applied for a patent for a "wind-propelled apparatus in which a mast is universally mounted on a craft and supports a boom or sail." Twenty two months later, in January 1970, the patent was issued as number 3,487,800. An excerpt from the *Patent Gazette* containing the announcement of this patent appears as Exhibit 1.

Schweitzer, his wife and Drake formed a company, Windsurfing International, to make and sell their invention. The novelty of it attracted attention and even practical jokes: When they displayed it at a boat show, someone modified the sailboard by adding a large helm and portable toilet. But it began to catch on. The Schweitzers bought out Drake in 1973.

Success of the product, however, inspired imitators, and to protect it Schweitzer filed suit for infringement of his patent. In the legal combat that followed, it was discovered that another man, S. Newman Darby, had created a similar device which looked like a door with an upside-down kite stuck into the socket in the center. The rider stood in front of the kite and leaned back against it as the wind blew it forward and propelled the flat door-like board across the water. Darby made no attempt to patent his invention, but a description and photograph showing it in operation appeared in a 1965 issue of *Popular Science*. Thus Schweitzer's patent became threatened.

Schweitzer claimed that his design represented a significant innovation beyond Darby's "prior art," as required to keep his patent valid, because of differences in design of his windsurfer's triangular sail and boom in contrast to Darby's kite-like arrangement. This novelty, Schweitzer asserted, gave much more control to the operator.

Would-be competitors disputed Schweitzer's claim of advance beyond prior art and sold imitations as the sport caught on and the market for sailboards rapidly grew. Schweitzer sued one imitator after another, resulting in a series of court decisions. By 1981 he had spent over a half million dollars on lawsuits and won 40 of them. But there were by then over 100 imitators still doing business. The U.S. Patent Board of Appeals decreed in favor of Schweitzer that his "hand-held wishbone rigging combined with the vehicle swivel mast attachment produces, in our opinion, a unique sailing apparatus which functions with the user in a manner that is completely unrecognized in any art before us." But subsequently the Patent Office rejected

---

[1]Mamis, Robert A., "Hoyle Schweitzer's Decade of Discontent", Inc, February, 1982, p. 54.

that decision, which in turn led to another appeal.

The litigation continued, leading to still further decisions. One from the U.S. Court of Appeals which was rendered in early 1986 appears in Exhibit 2.

EXHIBIT 1   Excerpt from Patent Gazette, January 6, 1970

3,487,798
SEWING MACHINE FOR PRODUCING BELT LOOPS AND THE LIKE
Nerino Marforio, Milan, Italy, assignor to S.p.A. Virginio Rimoldi & C., Milan, Italy
Filed Aug. 28, 1968, Ser. No. 755,932
Claims priority, application Italy, Sept. 7, 1967, 20,221/67
Int. Cl. D05b 23/00, 37/04
U.S. Cl. 112—121.27   11 Claims

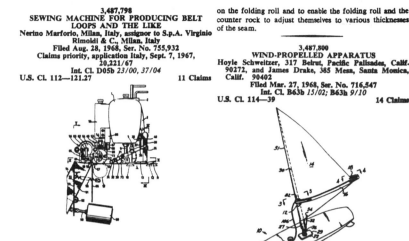

A sewing machine for producing belt loops and the like from off-cuts of random length which are sewn end-to-end to form a continuous lengthwise strip, including means for preventing the cutting knife from cutting said strip along any portion thereof which is of a thickness other than the uniform thickness required for the loops, and also including means for automatically sorting reject loops from satisfactory ones, as well as a counter means adapted to count only the satisfactory loops.

3,487,799
ROOF SEAMING MACHINE
Sven Olof Grönlund, Marumsgatan 16, Skara, Sweden
Filed Apr. 12, 1968, Ser. No. 721,024
Int. Cl. B21d 39/02, 19/04
U.S. Cl. 113—55   2 Claims

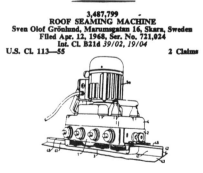

The present invention relates to roof seaming machines for forming standing seams to interconnect adjacent roofing sheets and is of the kind comprising a carriage with pair-wise arranged rolls which successively perform the seaming operation when the carriage is moved along the upstanding sheet flanges. One of the rolls of each pair, hereinbelow termed the folding roll, is adapted to be displaced outward relative to the other roll, herein termed the counter roll, and is acted upon by a compression spring such as to be biased toward the counter roll and to assist in folding the upstanding sheet flange or sheet flanges for producing a single or double seam. Accordingly, one of the rolls must be movable towards and away from the other roll in order to enable the spring to act

on the folding roll and to enable the folding roll and the counter rock to adjust themselves to various thicknesses of the seam.

3,487,800
WIND-PROPELLED APPARATUS
Hoyle Schweitzer, 317 Beirut, Pacific Palisades, Calif. 90272, and James Drake, 385 Mesa, Santa Monica, Calif. 90402
Filed Mar. 27, 1968, Ser. No. 716,547
Int. Cl. B63b 15/02; B63h 9/10
U.S. Cl. 114—39   14 Claims

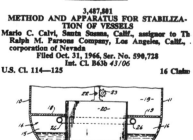

Wind-propelled apparatus in which a mast is universally mounted on a craft and supports a boom and sail. Specifically a pair of curved booms are arcuately connected athwart the mast and secure the sail therebetween, the position of the mast and sail being controllable by the user but being substantially free from pivotal restraint in the absence of such control.

ERRATUM

For Class 114—77 see:
Patent No. 3,487,807

3,487,801
METHOD AND APPARATUS FOR STABILIZATION OF VESSELS
Mario C. Calvi, Santa Susana, Calif., assignor to The Ralph M. Parsons Company, Los Angeles, Calif., a corporation of Nevada
Filed Oct. 31, 1966, Ser. No. 590,728
Int. Cl. B63b 43/06
U.S. Cl. 114—125   16 Claims

A ship stabilization system having passive tanks opposite sides of the ship with an interconnecting passage for the flow of liquid between the tanks. The effective cross-sectional area of the interconnecting passage varied to maintain the natural period of flow of the liquid in excess of the period of roll of the vessel. The cross sectional area is varied in one embodiment by shifting transversely one of the walls defining the passage, and

EXHIBIT 2   U.S. Court of Appeals Decision, January 28, 1986[2]

Background

(1) Proceedings in District Court

Windsurfing International (WSI) sued AMF, BIC and Downwind, alleging infringement of its '167 patent. AMF then sought a declaratory judgment that the patent is invalid for obviousness, unenforceable because of patent misuse, and not infringed. Also, AMF sought the cancellation of WSI's registrations of "WINDSURFER" and related trademarks[3] on grounds that the marks had become generic. BIC sued WSI, seeking a declaration that the '167 patent is invalid for obviousness, unenforceable, and not infringed.

Consolidating the three actions, the district court held a non-jury trial on 13 dates between November 19 and December 11, 1984, filed an opinion July 15, 1985 and entered judgments on September 11, 1985. AMF, BIC, and Downwind appeal from the judgments holding the '167 patent valid and infringed. AMF and BIC appeal from the grant of injunctions.[4] WSI cross-appeals from the judgments holding it misused its patent and refusing to enjoin Downwind.

(2) The '167 Patent

The patent in suit relates to the sport of "sailboarding,"[5] in which participants ride boards propelled by wind striking sails attached to the boards.

A preferred embodiment of the claimed invention is shown in Figure 1 of the '167 patent:

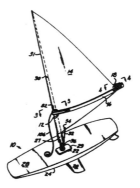

---

[2]282 F. 2nd 995 (Fed. Cir. 1986)

[3]U.S. Trademark Registration No. 962.616. 997.974 1.180.024. and 1.195.641. The district court held that WSI's trademarks have become generic. The district court has not yet entered judgement to that effect and the trademark issue of genericness is not part of this appeal.

[4]The district court permanently enjoined AMF, but "preliminarily" enjoined BIC pending termination of a related action by Intervener James R. Drake claiming an ownership interest in the '167 patent.

[5]We refer to the patented structure as a "sailboard" and not as a "windsurfer" because whether the latter term has become generic is not yet final.

EXHIBIT 2 (continued)

A participant stands on the top surface of surfboard 10 behind universal joint 36, grasps boom 16 or boom 18 (depending on wind direction), and controls the speed and direction of the board by maneuvering the boom to which sail 14 is attached. If a participant begins to lose control in a sudden wind surge, he or she merely releases the boom and the universal joint allows the sail to fall freely into the water.

Claim 15 from the patent is representative:

Wind-propelled apparatus comprising body means adapted to support a user and wind-propulsion means pivotally associated with said body means and adapted to receive wind for motive power for said apparatus, said propulsion means comprising a mast, a joint for mounting said mast on said body means, a sail and means for extending said sail laterally from said mast *comprising two opposed booms secured to said mast for guiding said sail therebetween and adapted to provide a hand-hold for said user on either side of said sail while sailing*, the position of said propulsion means being controllable by said user, said propulsion means being substantially free from pivotal restraint in the absence of said user, said joint having a plurality of axes of rotation whereby said sail free falls along any of a plurality of vertical planes upon release by said user.

The understood limitation sets forth the boom and was added when WSI's U.S. Patent No. 3,487,800 was reissued as the '167 patent.

Issues

Did the district court err in: (1) holding the claimed invention nonobvious[6] (2) finding infringement; (3) holding patent misuse; (4) enjoining AMF and BIC; and (5) refusing to enjoin Downwind.

Opinion

(1) Non-obviousness

On appeal, AMF[7] argues that the district court erred in upholding the '167 patent because it: (a) improperly deferred to decisions by the U.S. Patent and Trademark Office Board of Appeals (Board); (b) compared preferred and commercial embodiments with the prior art; and (c) considered commercial success having no nexus with the claimed invention.

---

[6]35 U.S.C. § 103 provides:

A patent may not be obtained...if the differences between the subject matter sought to be patented and the prior art are such that the subject matter as a whole would have been obvious at the time the invention was made to a person having ordinary skills in the art to which said subject matter pertains.

[7]Because BIC raises many of the same arguments, and Downwind relies principally on the arguments raised by BIC and AMF, this opinion hereinafter refers to the three parties collectively as AMF, unless otherwise indicated.

EXHIBIT 2   (continued)

(a) Deference

[1] In deferring to the Board's decisions concerning the allowance of the claims in the reissued patent, the district court was recognizing the statutory mandate that all patents are presumed valid. The district court carefully considered whether the evidence not presented in the "fiercely contested adversarial proceeding" before the Board would ease AMF's burden of proving facts compelling a conclusion of invalidity.[8] Concluding that the evidence at trial was merely cumulative of that before the Board, the court correctly held that evidence did not enable AMF to carry the burden.

AMF contends that, because the Board did not mention the obviousness of replacing the rig, shown in a publication referred to as the "Darby reference," with the boom disclosed in the '167 patent, no deference is due the Board decisions. The district court carefully reviewed the administrative record and stated that such argument "oversimplifies the depth of the Board's review and assumes the Board ignored other issues raised in the parties' extensive briefs." We agree. Merely because a decision does not mention a particular point "forms no basis for an assumption that it did not consider those elements." Moreover, the district court correctly noted that "the Board . . . reaffirmed its original holding that combination of the hand-held wishbone rigging [boom] with the vehicle swivel mast attachment produces . . . a unique sailing apparatus....'" We are satisfied that the district court did not err in this case in giving "deference that is due to a qualified government agency presumed to have properly done its job."

(b) Comparison

[2] The district court conducted a thorough *Graham*[9] analysis before concluding that the claimed invention at the time it was made would not have been obvious to one of ordinary skill in the art. AMF attacks the district court's findings as clearly erroneous, asserting it compared to the prior art not the claimed invention but commercial and preferred embodiments as representative of the claimed invention (claims, not embodiments, are focus of obviousness inquiry). Those embodiments include a "scoop" on a slimmer hull-shaped board, a skeg (or fin on the bottom at the back), and footstraps. Thus, they argue that the advantages found by the court are attributable to a combination of those design improvements and not to the claimed invention.

The district court did determine that it would have been obvious to replace a kite sail

---

[8]The "proceeding" referred to comprised the initial application for reissue, a protest, an appeal to the Board, a remand to the examiner, a second appeal to the Board, and an appeal to the Court of Customs and Patent Appeals. The district court described these events in its opinion. 613 F. Supp. at 942-44, 227 USPQ at 934-35.
[9]Graham v. John Deere, 383 U.S. 1, 17-18, 86 S.Ct. 684, 693-94, 15 L.Ed. 2d 545, 148 USPQ 459, 467 (1966).
[10]Contrary to BIC and Downwind's contentions, a conclusion that it would have been obvious to replace the sails and add a boom does not require a conclusion that the claimed invention considered as a whole would have been obvious. The claims include more, e.g., a universal joint and its relationship to board, mast, boom and sail.

EXHIBIT 2   (continued)

with a force and aft sail, and to add a second opposed boom.[10] Properly looking to the claimed invention at the time it was made as a whole, the district court correctly concluded that "the combination of the hand-held wishbone rigging with the universal joint produced a vehicle that performs in a manner previously undisclosed by any of the prior art references before us and, indeed, a vehicle with a performance potential that is even now not yet fully realized."

WSI's expert, Dr. Bradfield, conceded that certain advantages were due to particular added improvements, but he consistently maintained that the overall performance capabilities of the claimed invention were mainly due to the combination of the universal joint and the wishbone rigging. The district court found that testimony credible and AMF has shown no basis on which this court could engage in the normally inappropriate process of substituting a contrary credibility determination for that of the district court.

(c) Nexus

Before concluding that the combination of the universal joint with the wishbone rigging would not have been obvious, the district court reviewed the objective evidence, and correctly sought a nexus between WSI's commercial success and the merits of the claimed invention.

In essence, AMF says that the commercial success found by the district court was due in large part to "other economic and commercial factors unrelated to the technical quality of the patented subject matter." Particularly, AMF argues that the great commercial success found by the district court was due to (1) sales of accessories amounting to 10-15 percent of the gross receipts; (2) an extensive advertising campaign and European promotional effort; and (3) more efficient manufacturing and design changes. They argue that WSI's commercial success is of little probative value because it occurred so many years after the date of invention and was not the result of providing any solution to some existing problem or long-felt want.

[3] Having carefully reviewed the record before use, we conclude that the district court did not impermissibly credit the evidence of commercial success. It specifically found that SWI's commercial success should not be "significantly diminished" by testimony that 10-15 percent of gross receipts are from paraphernalia. The court accorded some weight to motivational factors leading to German licenses, but concluded that "widespread recognition and use of the invention" indicated that it would not have been obvious. The commercial success of the invention was found to have been "well beyond the effect" of WSI's promotional efforts.

Absent some intervening event to which success must be attributed, the delay in achieving the great commercial success of the claimed invention in this case does not detract from the probative value of the evidence of that success. Similarly, AMF's suggestion that objective evidence of non-obviousness can be considered only when the invention solves a long-existing problem is unwarranted. Providing a solution to a long existing problem is but one type of objective evidence useful in making obviousness/non-obviousness determinations. Further, the district court correctly noted that copying the claimed invention, rather than one within the public domain, is indicative of non-obviousness.

[4] Having carefully considered AMF's arguments and the evidence relied upon by the district court, we conclude that AMF has not discharged its burden on appeal, i.e., of per-

---

EXHIBIT 2   (continued)

suading us that the district court committed reversible legal error in its determination that the invention would not have been obvious, or that the court's probative findings underlying that determination were clearly erroneous. Accordingly, the presumptive validity of the '167 patent remains unscathed and the judgment upholding claims 15-21 of the '167 patent is affirmed.

(2) Infringement

Downwind alone appeals from the judgment of infringement, urging that its structure does not have a "joint having a plurality of axes of rotation." Downwind employs a flexible rubber tube or rod connecting the mast and the board.

[5] Claim interpretation is a question of law, but we have been shown no basis for upsetting the district court's interpretation of the claims as covering a structure that permits the mast to pivot with respect to and about a number of axes. Downwind's contention that a flexible rubber tube is not "mechanical," and does not rotate, and thus is not a "joint" within the meaning of the claims, is without merit. The word "mechanical" does not appear in the claims, the twisting of the flexible tube is about an axis of rotation, and the tube forms a joint between the mast and board.

[6, 7] Whether Downwind's accused device infringes the claims as interpreted is a fact question, and a finding on that question will not be upset unless clearly erroneous. None of the accused infringers has attempted to rebut the testimony on which the district court relied in finding infringement. Downwind has not shown that the claims must be given its own unduly narrow interpretation or that the district court's finding of infringement was clearly erroneous. Accordingly, the judgment of infringement is affirmed.

(3) Patent Misuse

AMF's allegation of patent misuse is based on this paragraph included in license agreements between WSI and 11 licensees:

Trademarks

LICENSEE hereby acknowledges that the terms "WINDSURFER," "WINDSURFING," and "WINDSURF" and the company logo are all valid trademarks. LICENSEE hereby agrees not to use any of the trademarks identified in this paragraph 10 in any form or fashion in its company name or any of its literature or advertising or promotional material or on any products whatsoever.

The district court said that whether that provision gives rise to a patent misuse defense depends on whether the registered trademarks are generic. Having found the marks generic, the court concluded "that Paragraph 10 has an intrinsically inhibiting effect on competition beyond the scope of the patent...."

The court went on to determine that the "level of misuse" did not warrant rendering the patent entirely unenforceable because the court found the "record insufficient to determine

EXHIBIT 2 (continued)

fairly the extent to which WSI sought to enforce the provision and the extent of any monetary gain to it" and also found the record insufficient to support a finding that "WSI necessarily would or should have known that its mark had become a common descriptive name for the product."

The court set the damages issue for determination at a later time, deferred until that time "the resolution as to what relief, if any, WSI's misuse of its patent privilege warrants," and decided to enforce the '167 patent.

In its cross-appeals, WSI contends that a mere inclusion in a patent license agreement of a promise not to infringe a licensor's trademark does not constitute patent misuse. Acts constituting misuse, says WSI, must be "coercive" toward an improper advantage. WSI argues that it was merely asserting rights it possessed under the trademark laws and, thus, the patent misuse defense should fall.

[8] The doctrine of patent misuse is an affirmative defense to a suit for patent infringement, and requires that the alleged infringer show that the patentee has impermissibly broadened the "physical or temporal scope" of the patent grant with anticompetitive effect. We have seen cited to no authority, and are aware of none, for the proposition that patent misuse may be found on the basis of a patent license agreement provision recognizing and forbidding use of the licensor's validly registered trademarks.

[9, 10] To sustain a misuse defense involving a licensing arrangement not held to have been per se anticompetitive by the Supreme Court,[11] a factual determination must reveal that the overall effect of the license tends to restrain competition unlawfully in an appropriately defined relevant market. A provision in a patent license agreement requiring the licensee to acknowledge the validity of registered trademarks, and to avoid their use, cannot possibly restrain competition unlawfully in an appropriately defined relevant market. The license agreement provision merely asserted and recognized WSI's rights derived from the trademark laws. The assertion of trademark rights can have procompetitive effects, and thus under only the most rare of circumstances could such assertion, separately or as a provision in a patent license agreement, form in itself the basis for a holding of inequitable conduct such as that labeled "patent misuse." It is not an uncommon precaution when licensing a product sold by the licensor under a trademark to prohibit the licensee from using the licensor's trademark on the licensee's product. That is but a matter of business prudence and in no manner misuses the patent right.

That the marks were found generic after trial and long after execution of the license cannot of itself prevent a full enforcement of the '167 patent. Trademark registrations enjoy a statutory presumption of validity. As the district court found, AMF failed to show that WSI granted the licenses or enforced its rights in the marks with knowledge that they were or had become a common descriptive name, and AMF failed to show that WSI should have had that knowledge. On the present record, the district court was improperly persuaded to rest its holding of misuse entirely on an after-the-fact determination that the marks are generic. Be-

---

[11]Recent economic analysis questions the rationale behind holding any licensing practice per se anticompetitive.

[12]We need not, in view of our determination, discuss the parties' contentions respecting the purging of misuse.

EXHIBIT 2   (continued)

cause that was error, the holding that the facts of record established a misuse of the patent right must be reversed.[12]

(4) Injunctions

[11] The law empowers district courts to "grant injunctions in accordance with the principles of equity to prevent the violation of any right secured by patent, on such terms as the court deems reasonable." The statute makes clear that the district court's grant or denial of an injunction is within its discretion depending on the facts of each case. Hence, the district court's grant or denial of an injunction is reviewed under an abuse of discretion standard.

The holding of misuse having been reversed, we need not address AMF's contention that the district court should not have enjoined further infringement of the '167 patent in light of that holding.

AMF argues that the district court improperly ignored its intervening rights, a defense it contends was raised in the pleadings and at the injunction hearing, citing *Seattle Box Co. v. Industrial Carting & Packing, Inc.*, made no mention of its intervening rights defense at the trial.

[12] Nothing in *Seattle Box* addresses the point at which the intervening rights defense must be raised to preserve it. Intervening rights, however, is "an affirmative defense . . . that must be raised at trial." That it failed to make any attempt to prove the defense at trial is in this case fatal. AMF cannot be held to have resuscitated the defense by the mere submission of affidavits at a post-trial hearing. To so hold would run counter to the finality attaching to trials. District courts are under no obligation to consider a defense abandoned at trial. Accordingly, no abuse of discretion having been shown, we affirm the district court's grant of injunctive relief against AMF and BIC.

On its cross-appeal, WSI urges that the district court abused its discretion in refusing to enjoin Downwind. In denying injunction relief against Downwind, the district court stated from the bench:

I am prepared to say at the present time that I do not believe that an injunction against Downwind is appropriate. As bad as Windsurfing's problems I am prepared to believe may be, I do not believe that enjoining Downwind, which is such a small operation, would solve their problems, not that I think an injunction's purpose is simply to solve its problems; and so I mention that because I don't think you need to argue further on that.

The relative size of multiple infringers should not alone serve as a basis for enjoining

---

[13]Downwind said its infringing sales were between 1,000 and 2,000 sailboards a year since it began operations in 1981. AMF was selling about 1,800 sailboards a year during the same four-year period. That sailboards are Downwind's primary product, and that an injunction might therefore put Downwind out of business, cannot justify denial of that injunction. One who elects to build a business on a product found to infringe cannot be heard to complain if an injunction against continuing infringement destroys the business so elected. The district court, recognizing the absence of bad faith on the part of all parties, weighed the effect of its orders on each. In so doing it indicated that WSI's entire business was built on sailboards and accessories, and thus that Downwind and WSI were in the same boat. Under those circumstances, no warrant appears on this record for denying the requested injunction against continued infringement by Downwind.

EXHIBIT 2 (concluded)

continued infringement by some and not by others.[13] The district court articulated no other basis for denying injunction relief against Downwind. On the present record, therefore, we must conclude that the district court abused its discretion in refusing to enjoin Downwind. Accordingly, we remand the case to the district court to reconsider WSI's request for an appropriate injunction against Downwind.

CONCLUSION

The judgment of the district court upholding the validity of claims 15-21 of the '167 patent and finding them infringed, and the grant of injunctions against AMF and BIC are affirmed. The judgment that WSI is guilty of patent misuse is reversed. The case is remanded with instructions to vacate the order denying an injunction against Downwind and to reconsider WSI's request for that injunction.

The appeal is affirmed in part, reversed in part, vacated in part, and remanded.

Windsurfer (B)

Trademarking

In addition to patenting physical features of utility in his sailboard design, Hoyle Schweitzer also applied for trademarks on the name "Windsurfer" and on logos with that name used by his company, Windsurfing International. As the market for his product grew, his trademark as well as his patent came under attack from imitators, and Schweitzer sued in response. Excerpts from the *Trademark Gazette* depicting logos which he registered appear in Exhibits 1 through 3. A description of litigation which ensued appears in Exhibit 4.

EXHIBIT 1 Initial Trademark Registration, 1973

Exhibit 1 - Initial Trademark Registration, 1973

TM 182   OFFICIAL GAZETTE   APRIL 17, 1973

SN 432,256. Mattel, Inc., Hawthorne, Calif. Filed Aug. 9, 1972.

SAND WITCH

Owner of Reg. No. 887,081.
For Toy Model Automobile (Int. Cl. 28).
First use July 24, 1972.

SN 432,257. Mattel, Inc., Hawthorne, Calif. Filed Aug. 9, 1972.

THUNDER BOLT

For Toy Model Automobile (Int. Cl. 28).
First use July 24, 1972.

SN 432,258. Mattel, Inc., Hawthorne, Calif. Filed Aug. 9, 1972.

TOAST-A-TUNE

Owner of Reg. No. 691,606.
For Musical Toy (Int. Cl. 28).
First use July 24, 1972.

SN 432,260. Mattel, Inc., Hawthorne, Calif. Filed Aug. 9, 1972.

ALIVE '55

For Toy Model Automobile (Int. Cl. 28).
First use July 24, 1972.

SN 432,415. Eldora A. Hurley, d.b.a. Earl H. Hurley Associates, Corry, Pa. Filed Aug. 10, 1972.

EXERGLIDE

For Play Swings and Exercise Apparatus for Children and Adults (Int. Cl. 28).
First use June 7, 1949.

SN 432,423. Gayla Industries, Inc., Houston, Tex. Filed Aug. 10, 1972.

SKY-SPY

For Toys—Namely, Kites (Int. Cl. 28).
First use Aug. 11, 1970.

SN 432,424. Gayla Industries, Inc., Houston, Tex. Filed Aug. 10, 1972.

DYNASOAR

For Toys—Namely, Kites (Int. Cl. 28).
First use July 29, 1968.

SN 432,646. Western Publishing Company, Inc., Racine, Wis. Filed Aug. 14, 1972.

Owner of Reg. Nos. 885,922, 931,702, and others.
For Playing Cards (Int. Cl. 16).
First use Aug. 1, 1972.

SN 432,649. Western Publishing Company, Inc., Racine, Wis. Filed Aug. 14, 1972.

Owner of Reg. Nos. 900,803 and 909,516.
For Children's Educational Playing Cards (Int. Cl. 16).
First use Apr. 3, 1970.

SN 433,078. S. S. Kresge Company, Troy, Mich. Filed Aug. 17, 1972.

LI'L MISS KAY SMART

For Children's Toy Jewelry and Children's Toy Cosmetics (Int. Cl. 28).
First use on or before June 18, 1972.

SN 433,097. X-Potential Enterprises, Fountain Valley, Calif. Filed Aug. 18, 1972.

SUPER STIX

For Construction Toy (Int. Cl. 28).
First use June 12, 1972.

SN 433,188. Western Publishing Company, Inc., Racine, Wis. Filed Aug. 18, 1972.

GOLDEN

Owner of Reg. Nos. 896,937, 899,690, and 931,795.
For Jigsaw Puzzles (Int. Cl. 28).
First use July 5, 1972.

SN 433,306. Windsurfing International, Inc., Santa Monica, Calif. Filed Aug. 21, 1972.

WINDSURFER

For Surfboards (Int. Cl. 28).
First use Aug. 15, 1969.

SN 433,342. Montgomery Ward & Co., Chicago, Ill. Filed Aug. 21, 1972.

MY TOWN

For Children's Toys (Int. Cl. 28).
First use June 8, 1972.

SN 433,517. Raider Tackle Manufacturing Co., Chicago, Ill. Filed Aug. 23, 1972.

GATORCRAWLER

For Fishing Lures (Int. Cl. 28).
First use January 1969.

EXHIBIT 2   Trademark Registration from 1974

TM 166   OFFICIAL GAZETTE   AUGUST 20, 1974

SN 7,271. Fantasy Boats, Costa Mesa, Calif. Filed Nov. 26, 1973.

FANTASY

For Boats and Structural Parts Therefor (U.S. Cl. 19).
First use on or before May 15, 1959.

SN 8,013. Windsurfing International, Inc., Santa Monica, Calif. Filed Dec. 3, 1973.

Owner of Reg. Nos. 909,519 and 962,616.
For Sailboats Comprising a Surf Board Type Hull and a Sail (U.S. Cl. 19).
First use on or about Aug. 15, 1969.

Class 14 — Jewelry

SN 3,092. Urschel Tool Co., Cranston, R.I. Filed Oct. 9, 1973.

kenwood

For Jewelry for Personal Wear and Adornment (U.S. Cl. 28).
First use Mar. 19, 1973.

SN 4,511. Bulova Watch Company, Inc., Flushing, N.Y. Filed Oct. 25, 1973.

LONGCHAMP

For Clocks, Watches and Parts Thereof (U.S. Cl. 27).
First use Oct. 15, 1973.

SN 4,595. Empress Pearls, Inc., Los Angeles, Calif. Filed Nov. 21, 1973.

DRIFTWOOD

For Pearl Jewelry Sold Only Through At-Home Parties (U.S. Cl. 28).
First use July 2, 1973.

SN 4,596. Empress Pearls, Inc., Los Angeles, Calif. Filed Nov. 21, 1973.

IMAGINATION

For Pearl Jewelry Sold Only Through At-Home Parties (U.S. Cl. 28).
First use July 2, 1973.

Class 16 — Paper Goods and Printed Matter

SN 877. KCL Corporation, Shelbyville, Ind. Filed Sept. 13, 1973.

AMBER-ZIP

For Reclosable Bags for Hospital Use (U.S. Cl. 2).
First use at least as early as May 19, 1972.

SN 2,751. Farm Journal, Inc., Philadelphia, Pa. Filed Oct. 4, 1973.

COUNTRYSIDE LIVING

Owner of Reg. Nos. 775,394 and 920,415.
For Magazine Published From Time to Time (U.S. Cl. 38).
First use at least as early as Sept. 20, 1973.

SN 7,943. Dayco Corporation, Dayton, Ohio. Filed Dec. 3, 1973.

401

For Printing Blankets (U.S. Cl. 50).
First use on or about July 28, 1972.

SN 7,944. Dayco Corporation, Dayton, Ohio. Filed Dec. 3, 1973.

501

For Printing Blankets (U.S. Cl. 50).
First use on or about July 28, 1972.

SN 7,945. Dayco Corporation, Dayton, Ohio. Filed Dec. 3, 1973.

600

For Printing Blankets (U.S. Cl. 50).
First use on or about July 28, 1972.

SN 7,948. Dayco Corporation, Dayton, Ohio. Filed Dec. 3, 1973.

427

For Printing Blankets (U.S. Cl. 50).
First use on or about July 28, 1972.

SN 7,949. Dayco Corporation, Dayton, Ohio. Filed Dec. 3, 1973.

606

For Printing Blankets (U.S. Cl. 50).
First use on or about July 28, 1972.

SN 8,370. The Saml Dodsworth Company, d.b.a. Dodsworth Co., Kansas City, Kans. Filed Dec. 10, 1973.

UNI-SUN

For Bank Checks (U.S. Cl. 37).
First use on or about Nov. 1, 1973.

SN 8,409. Texaco Corporation, San Antonio, Tex. Filed Dec. 10, 1973.

CAPALOG

For Periodicals—Namely, Product Catalogues (U.S. Cl. 38).
First use as early as 1946.

SN 12,869. E. R. Squibb & Sons, Inc., Princeton, N.J. Filed Feb. 7, 1974.

RYTHRO-LOG

For Diagnostic Worksheets for Laboratory Use (U.S. Cl. 37).
First use Sept. 6, 1973.

EXHIBIT 3 Trademark Registration from 1978

JUNE 27, 1978   U. S. PATENT AND TRADEMARK OFFICE   TM 289

SN 133,616. Bunny Osbrink, Inc., Doraville, Ga. Filed July 11, 1977.

For Tennis Skirts, Golf Shirts, Hats, Visors, and Halters (U.S. Cl. 39).
First use October 1976.

SN 134,078. The United States Shoe Corporation, Cincinnati, Ohio. Filed July 15, 1977.

For Shoes (U.S. Cl. 39).
First use at least as early as May 17, 1977.

SN 134,079. The United States Shoe Corporation, Cincinnati, Ohio. Filed July 15, 1977.

For Shoes (U.S. Cl. 39).
First use at least as early as May 4, 1977.

SN 134,080. The United States Shoe Corporation, Cincinnati, Ohio. Filed July 15, 1977.

FREEMOC

For Footwear (U.S. Cl. 39).
First use at least as early as Aug. 1, 1921.

SN 134,343. Uniform Guild, Inc., New York, N.Y. Filed July 18, 1977.

Owner of Reg. No. 788,771.
For Uniforms for Nurses, Nurses Aides, Medical Receptionists, Waitresses and Beauticians, and Coats or Aprons Worn by Bakery Sales Personnel, Laboratory Technicians and Factory Personnel (U.S. Cl. 39).
First use at least as early as June 1, 1977 ; July 1936, in a different form.

TM 971 O.G.—20

SN 138,095. William W. Artzt, Palm Beach, Fla. Filed Aug. 19, 1977.

BEND 'N STRETCH

Applicant disclaims the word "Stretch" apart from the mark as shown, without waiving any common law rights thereto. Owner of Reg. No. 948,595.
For Children's and Infants' Wearing Apparel—Namely, Pajamas, Sleeping Garments, Overalls, Shirts, Undershirts and Underwear (U.S. Cl. 39).
First use on or before June 28, 1969.

SN 138,550. Windsurfing International, Inc., Marina Del Rey, Calif. Filed Aug. 22, 1977.

WINDSURFING

For T-Shirts, Jackets and Wet Suits for Waterskiing (U.S. Cl. 39).
First use at least as early as February 1970.

SN 139,674. Chief Apparel, Inc., New York, N.Y. Filed Sept. 1, 1977.

LE DISQUE

The mark "Le Disque" translated into English means "the record" (i.e., disc).
For Men's and Boys' Tailored and Pre-Cut Clothing—Namely, Coats, Jeans, Slacks and Tops (U.S. Cl. 39).
First use June 30, 1977.

SN 139,974. L & K Co., Inc., Shelby, N.C. Filed Sept. 6, 1977.

SHELBY STATION

Applicant disclaims the word "Shelby" apart from the mark as shown, but without waiving any of its common law rights to the mark shown in the drawing or any feature thereof
For Ladies' Jackets, Tops and Dresses (U.S. Cl. 39).
First use as early as March 1977.

SN 141,910. The Enro Shirt Company, Inc., Louisville, Ky. Filed Sept. 20, 1977.

CLUBHOUSE

For Men's Dress Shirts and Sport Shirts (U.S. Cl. 39).
First use Aug. 15, 1977.

SN 142,293. Karman, Inc., Denver, Colo. Filed Sept. 23, 1977.

CHUTE #1

For Western Clothing—Namely, Shirts (U.S. Cl. 39).
First use Sept. 5, 1977.

EXHIBIT 4

WINDSURFING INTERNATIONAL[1]
INC., Plaintiff-Appellant.
v.
AMF INCORPORATED.
Defendant-Appellee.
United States Court of Appeals.
Federal Circuit.
Sept. 9, 1987.

Three actions relating to validity, infringement and enforceability of reissue patent for sailing surfboard were consolidated. Appeal was taken. The Court of Appeals held that the district court lacked jurisdiction over action.

MARKEY, Chief Judge.

Appeal from a judgment of the United States District Court for the Southern District of New York holding that Windsurfing International's (WSI's) "WINDSURFER" trademark has become generic and ordering (1) cancellation of its U.S. Trademark Registration Nos. 962, 616 and 1,195,-641 on that mark, and (2) rectification of U.S. Trademark Registration Nos. 997,974 and 1,180,024 by addition of a disclaimer. 613 F. Supp. 933, 227 USPQ 927 (S.D.N.Y. 1985). Because the district court lacked jurisdiction to entertain AMF's claim for cancellation, the judgment appealed from must be vacated.

BACKGROUND

United States Patent No. 3,487,800 for a "Wind-Propelled Apparatus" issued in January 1970. WSI, the assignee, has manufactured and sold the patented "sailboard" since 1969. WSI filed an application for reissue in 1978, and U.S. Patent Re. 31,167 ('167 patent) issued on March 8, 1983.

In 1981, after other manufacturers had entered the "sailboard" market, WSI sued AMF Incorporated (AMF) and others for patent infringement. The district court stayed the action pending the outcome of reissue proceedings. When the '167 patent issued in March 1983, AMF filed a complaint in the same court seeking a declaratory judgment, *inter alia*, that the '167 patent was unenforceable because WSI had misused it.

WSI had since 1977 been sending letters demanding the cessation of all use of "WINDSURFER" except in reference to WSI's products. On August 16, 1983, after an AMF dealer ran a newspaper advertisement using "Windsurfer" to refer to one of AMF's products, attorneys for WSI wrote to the dealer demanding that it cease using "WINDSURFER" and requested a prompt reply "to preclude the necessity of instituting more formal proceedings to protect [WSI's] trademark rights." AMF advised the dealer to stop running the advertisement, and the dealer did so.

In November 1983, AMF filed its answer to WSI's a infringement complaint, amended its complaint for a declaratory judgment, and filed a counterclaim, seeking in both latter instances

---

[1] 828 F.2d 755 (Fed. Cir. 1987)

EXHIBIT 4 (continued)

cancellation of WSI's registrations. AMF did not designate its counterclaim as one for declaratory judgment, though, like its amended complaint, it was clearly such. In its amendment and counterclaim, AMF alleged that "windsurfer" did not function as a trademark because it had become generic. The district court consolidated the actions.

In November 1984, shortly before trial, WSI moved to dismiss AMF's trademark claims for lack of subject matter jurisdiction, arguing that AMF had alleged insufficient facts to create a "case or controversy" under Article III of the Constitution. The district court denied the motion.

The district court held a nonjury trial in November and December 1984 and issued an opinion on July 15, 1985. About WSI's no-case-or controversy argument, that opinion said:

On the eve of trial WSI moved to dismiss the trademark issues on the grounds of lack of case or controversy. The motion was denied. WSI again raises the issue in its post-trial brief. The fact that WSI has sent correspondence threatening to sue at least one of AMF's dealers, along with the fact that the trademark issue is intimately connected with AMF's misuse defense (which AMF clearly has a right to assert), is sufficient in this action to create a "case or controversy" and we decline to overturn our earlier ruling.

The foregoing quote is the entirety of the district court's opinion relating to whether a "case or controversy" exists on the trademark issue. On the merits, the opinion said "windsurfer" had become generic. No judgment was entered at the time the July 15, 1985 opinion was issued.

On September 11, 1985, the district court entered judgment on the patent issues and an injunction. AMF appealed. This court affirmed the judgment that the '167 patent was valid and infringed, reversed the holding that the '167 patent was unenforceable because of patent misuse, and remanded for the district court to reconsider the scope of its injunction.

On January 6, 1987, the district court entered judgment on AMF's complaint and counterclaim, having determined that "'windsurfer' has become and is generic," and ordered the cancellation of two of WSI's trademark registrations and the addition of a disclaimer to two others. No reference to the presence or absence of a case or controversy was made in connection with that judgment. WSI appealed.

ISSUE

Whether the district court had subject matter jurisdiction to entertain AMF's challenge to WSI's trademark registrations.

OPINION

As in any federal case, an action under the Declaratory Judgment Act must present a "case or controversy" within the meaning of Article III of the Constitution. Because this court has jurisdiction to decide the question only because the district court's jurisdiction was based in part on 28 U.S.C. § 1330(a), we look to the discernible law of the regional circuit where the district court sits, here the Second Circuit, in deciding whether AMF's trademark claims presented a "case or controversy" to the district court. We may also look when necessary to guidance from other circuits. Because declaratory judgment actions involving trademarks are analogous to those involving patents, we may also, when necessary, find guidance in the precedents of this court.

EXHIBIT 4 (continued)

[1] The test of determining whether an actual case or controversy exists in a declaratory judgment action involving trademarks is two-pronged. First, the declaratory plaintiff must have a real and reasonable apprehension of litigation. Second, the declaratory plaintiff must have engaged in a course of conduct which brought it into adversarial conflict with the declaratory defendant. Both prongs of the test must be satisfied.

[2] Assuming without deciding that, as the district court's opinion suggests, AMF reasonably feared litigation *if* it began using "windsurfer" in connection with its products, the record contains no evidence that AMF has engaged in any course of conduct, or indeed, any conduct at all, that has brought it into adversarial conflict with WSI respecting WSI's trademarks. AMF acknowledges that it has avoided using "windsurfer" and has so instructed its dealers. Thus AMF fails to satisfy the second prong of the test.

In its complaint and counterclaim, AMF alleged merely that "AMF is interested in using the mark descriptively in connection with its products." AMF cites testimony that AMF has a "desire" to use "windsurfer" in its advertising and promotion, and that other members of the trade have the same "desire." Rather than use the mark, get sued, and fight it out in court, AMF was saying, "We would like to use the mark, but before we do, we want a court to say we may do so safely." Thus AMF's complaint and counterclaim sought an advisory opinion, something a federal court may not give.

A justiciable controversy is one that touches the legal relations of parties having adverse *legal* interests. AMF's "desire" to use "windsurfer" and "windsurfing" descriptively may render its commercial interests adverse to those of WSI, but absent a combination of AMF's use of the mark and threats or suits by WSI, the legal interests of AMF and WSI are not adverse. ("A vague and unspecific 'desire' to practice an invention if a patent should turn out to be invalid smacks too much of the hypothetical and contingent.")

AMF argues that, under section 14(c) of the Lanham Act, its status as a competitor of WSI gives it standing to seek cancellation of WSI's trademark registrations. AMF cites a number of cases from the Court of Customs and Patent Appeals, but those cases involved appeals from the Trademark Trial and Appeal Board, not from district courts. Section 14(c) of the Lanham Act does authorize persons interested in using marks that have become the common descriptive names of articles to petition the Patent and Trademark Office to cancel registration of those marks. It does not, however, authorize suits for cancellation in district courts.

Under the Lanham Act, district courts have the power to cancel registrations, but only in an "action involving a registered mark." "Involving" cannot mean the mere presence of a registered trademark, but must be read as involving the right to use the mark and thus the right to maintain the registration. (In a dispute over a franchise agreement licensing a trade name, "the mere existence of the protected trade name and attendant symbol herein does not provide a basis for federal jurisdiction."); (antitrust defendant's defense of trademark registration made the case one "involving a registered mark" giving the court jurisdiction to order cancellation of that registration). There must, therefore, be something beyond the mere competitor status of the parties to serve as a basis for the court's jurisdiction. Such a basis may, for example, be a suit for trademark infringement (counterclaim of trademark genericness entertained in suit for trademark infringement), or a "case of actual controversy" referred to in the Declaratory Judgment Act, 28 U.S.C. § 2201. As discussed above, AMF's status as a competi-

EXHIBIT 4 (concluded)

tor of WSI does not create such an "actual controversy" effective to create jurisdiction in the district court.

[3] AMF argues that the district court had "pendent jurisdiction" because AMF's allegations of patent misuse concerned trademark provisions in WSI's patent license agreements. Pendent jurisdiction allows federal courts to consider state claims with federal claims when they "derive from a common nucleus of operative fact." It is inapplicable here. Moreover, if AMF's patent misuse theory created a "case or controversy" respecting WSI's patent rights, it did not do so respecting WSI's registered trademarks. The parties here have incorrectly assumed a nonexistent identity of the trademark and the patented invention. WSI, for example, argues that AMF had no standing to challenge the trademarks because it was enjoined from infringing the patent, and AMF argues that it could have used the mark on products made under its pre-reissue "intervening rights." Neither party recognizes that the mark is registered for various classes of goods and services, and that nothing limits its use to the patented structure.

CONCLUSION

AMF's mere desire to use "windsurfer" and "windsurfing" in connection with its products does not constitute a course of conduct placing AMF in legally adversarial conflict with WSI respecting WSI's trademark registrations. AMF, in its complaint and counterclaim, did not present a justiciable controversy. On the contrary, it impermissibly asked the district court for an advisory opinion. The district court therefore lacked subject matter jurisdiction to entertain AMF's claim for cancellation of WSI's registrations, on the ground that "windsurfer" had become a generic term or otherwise. The district court must therefore vacate the judgment appealed from. The case is remanded for that purpose.

Case 20

Ampersand (C)

March 1993 - Starting the First Production Run

Spring break, which ran from March 15, 1993 to March 20, 1993, had been eventful for the Ampersand team. To meet a scheduled delivery of 2,000 Claybords by the end of May for the order they had received from Pearl Paint in New York, they had managed to get Masonite sheets coated with their mineral coating. But they had not yet sanded them smooth as required. The shop in Tyler, Texas where the coating was applied, however, had essentially told the team not to come back because of difficulties with the coating process.

Then at the next stage in the process, a cabinet shop in Austin had cut the boards and routed the edges as it promised, but then refused to follow through with sanding required to make the boards smooth. After trying one or two, the shop owner had concluded that he would lose money on the sanding work. He also indicated that he was not anxious to have any more of the cutting and sanding work either.

So now the coated, cut and routed but unsanded boards rested in the cabinet shop, with the permission of its owner, as the spring school term resumed and the team was obliged to return to class. All members of the team were carrying full course loads, and the problem of sanding the boards awaited resolution. Other present commitments included competition in two more venture plan contests. The first was a contest at San Diego State University on the last day of April. If the team won first place there it would receive $5,000 in prize money that could support the completion of the Pearl Paint test mar-

ket effort in June. Then on May 5 there would be another competition, the International Moot Corp^{SM}, at the University of Texas. Finally, there was the end of May delivery date for finished boards.

Searching for Production Alternatives

When the four team members of Ampersand met to divide up tasks, Scott Bryant drew that of vice president of operations responsible for production. Although he had not previously worked in production, his background was in mechanical engineering. He had been attracted to the Ampersand venture in large part because the product had seemed like a simple one that students without extensive experience in the art materials industry could produce. This was a contrast to other student-proposed ventures which were to make high-technology products where students would be up against tough competition from industry experts. Moreover, the Ampersand team was planning to outsource manufacturing to subcontractors initially, so all that should be needed would be to select competent suppliers, seek out favorable bids, apply adequate pressure to meet the delivery time schedule and check quality.

This, he and his teammates found, was easier imagined than done. One early clue was the fact that David, a member of the team during the preceding school term who had taken responsibility for finding suppliers, had experienced difficulty in doing so. He had, however, found one shop, in Tyler, Texas 150 miles from Austin, that might be able to do the job. Much of its customary work was in painting panels and pegboard for store displays. It had a conveyor line that included coating equipment and saws. But the painting it did was mainly layers of lacquer much thinner than the mineral surface Ampersand needed.

A Pilot Run

Scott arranged to follow through on the small experimental coating run that the Tyler plant's owner had previously agreed to. He ordered some materials and had them sent to the plant. From Charles Ewing, he obtained the new and improved recipe for what he called the "secret sauce" Charles Ewing had developed for coating. Then, traveling to Tyler, he mixed up a batch and applied it. After watching the process, the plant's owner indicated that he was not strongly interested in performing the work. It required a much thicker coating than the painting work he was familiar with and required air drying, which he was not equipped to perform. It appeared to him likely to be unprofitable work.

Other searching by the team through calling around had located a cabinet shop in Austin that might be able to cut and sand the boards. The owner had seemed impressed by the potential quantity of the order, 2,000 units and quoted a price of $500 to process the order. However, he could not perform any of the coating work.

Efforts to find one shop equipped to perform all the manufacturing tasks had so far been completely fruitless. Scott explained:

The way we found people to help us has been to start with the phone and then follow up with a personal visit. I'd call one shop and they would tell me that they can't do the job. So I asked if

they had any idea who else might be able to do it. That usually led to more names, which in turn led to others, and so forth. How many calls to keep making, how many of them to follow-up with visits, how far away geographically to reach were all choices that carved up the time.

Some shops might have been steering away from the work because they were already busy with profitable work and this new job presented uncertainty that they'd rather not deal with. Maybe with personal visits we could turn that around. I'm not sure how much that was the case. But to find out would take more time and travel expenditures.

Weekend Coating at Tyler

During the week of spring break from March 15 to March 20 Charles Ewing traveled from Colorado to Austin to go over plans with the team and plan for the coating run that Scott had arranged with the shop in Tyler to be carried out over the coming weekend. Renting a truck at a cost of approximately $200, they picked up 100 sheets of Masonite and hauled them 200 miles east to Tyler.

They arranged with the owner of the Tyler painting shop to rent his facility over the ensuing weekend for $500 and began arranging racks to set out the Claybord sheets for air drying after they had been coated. Initially, they had planned to buy fence posts to build the racks, but the shop owner happened to have a stack of two by fours that he let them use for that purpose instead.

As the team completed the coating that evening around 6 p.m., tired and worn, they set up fans throughout the 8,000-square-foot facility to try to get the coated 4x8 foot Masonite sheets to dry by morning. It was questionable whether the thick coating would be dry in time for them to load up early to head back to Austin. They had spent 12 hours coating with five people (Charles, Scott, Elaine, Robert, Kathy). But they were elated by the belief that they now had product to send to Pearl. At this point they had no idea of problems they would encounter shortly at the cabinet shop with the sanding process.

An issue they had become concerned about, however, was that the coating shop owner had basically just told the team that he could not and would not do any more board production for them in the future. He, in fact, encouraged the team to set up their own operation. He gave them names of publications where they could look for used equipment and told them that a minimal investment of $15,000 might be sufficient to buy the equipment. He even offered to help the team set up the shop. The team wondered how they would take their next step as they thought about the next time they would have to produce to fill an order when and if Pearl ran out or when the product was launched nationally. None of this had been anticipated.

After a day on the drying racks, the boards were re-loaded on the truck and driven 225 miles southwest back to Austin where arrangements had been made to have them cut to standard sizes, routed to give them smooth round edges and then sanded on top to make them uniformly smooth by grinding away the "orange peel" or slightly rippled finish that resulted from the coating process. The shop owner had quoted a price of $500 for preparing the 2,000 Claybords in this fashion.

The shop owner became uneasy during the first of these tasks, sawing the boards to size, because it took longer than he had expected. After routing the edges and attempting to sand a few boards it became clear to him that he was going to lose a substantial amount of money if he continued. Consequently, he refused to do so and also said he was not much interested in doing the cutting and routing either because he lost money on that too. He told the team they would have to find another

way to accomplish the sanding. He would not do it, but he would let them store the boards in his shop without charge for a few weeks while they sought a solution to the sanding problem.

The procedure used by Charles Ewing seemed safest to the team members because they knew it produced satisfactory Claybords. It consisted of going over each board with an electrically-powered hand-held orbital sander bought at the hardware store. This took approximately two to four minutes to accomplish, depending on the size of the Claybord.

It was now March 21, the first day of classes following spring break. The San Diego competition would begin on April 30. The team would be gone for three days. Then the International Moot Corp℠ contest would follow on May 6. Graduation day would be May 22. The 2,000 Claybords had to be shipped May 21 to arrive in New York by the first week in June, ready with appropriate packaging and display materials.

San Diego might net the team the $5,000 prize they had already factored into the financial statements of their venture plan. But why, one team member asked, should the team spend time on the Moot Corp℠ contest which carried no such cash award? Didn't the team need every minute it could get to finish and ship that first order, rather than participating in academic sport?

From other members of the team came some agreement and some reasons for competing. Competing had spurred them on and caused them to aim for high performance. They also felt some sense of obligation to follow through, since they had made application to compete and had been accepted. The school had, after all, given them opportunity as well as much encouragement and support. Moreover, their first win, in addition to the $500 and office space, had given them favorable visibility, press write-ups they could show business contacts to indicate that their venture had strong merit. It had also led them to at least one potential investor, the competition judge who had approached the team earlier about financing.

Meanwhile, the team had, because of the experience at Tyler, begun thinking more seriously about the possibility of setting up their own manufacturing operation. They decided to estimate what production costs might be on that basis and came up with the figures shown below in Figure 1.

These estimates, they expected, would bear refining. How validly did they reflect the experience at Tyler? To what extent would that be indicative of having a plant of their own? If so, what sequence of steps, and with what timing, should they plan to follow, first for checking out that idea, and second, for carrying it out? What else might they learn by sanding and packaging the rest of the current production batch? Should they even be thinking about that at this point, or were there more important issues? As these questions awaited answers, the team had to return to full-time classwork.

Figure 1 - Estimated Manufacturing Costs Per Square Foot of Claybord

Direct material	$0.31	32%
Direct labor		
Mixing	0.02	2
Coating	0.04	4
Cut/finishing	0.29	30
Packaging	0.10	10
Mfg. overhead	0.22	22
Total	$0.98	100%

Help

❏ SUBCHAPTER 7A - Insiders

Cooperation is at the heart of entrepreneurship, much as entrepreneurs value independence and use it to competitive advantage. Serving customers is cooperation to satisfy their needs and preferences. Obtaining permissions, supplies and the efforts of others to make the venture go requires cooperation. Obtaining information to figure out, step by step, the actions required to start and move the venture forward requires cooperative interaction with others who know bits and parts of what an entrepreneur must learn. Earlier chapters explored to some degree how entrepreneurs get help from financing sources, customers and suppliers. This chapter will consider those somewhat further and look also at other help sources such as partners, employees, various types of advisers and institutions. They will be grouped into two categories. Insiders, those who are relatively permanent owners or employees of the business will be the focus of the first subchapter of this chapter. Outsiders, those who may deal with and help the venture, but are primarily employed elsewhere, will be the subject of the second subchapter.

A company that is up-and-running can be viewed as a puzzle that is already put together. One piece could be the production operation, another the bank account, others the accounting books, the customer orders, the suppliers doing their part, things coming and going through the mail and over the wires and cables hooked to phones, faxes, and computers. Without much imagination, it is easy to see that the puzzle is complex, dynamic, and changing.

The activity that designs the puzzle and puts it together can be defined as entrepreneurship in which more than one person is engaged—not only in the action, but in the design as well. A machine-shop operator may suggest improvements for the venture's prototype, perhaps even risking capital in the form of trade credit to help the venture get started. A venture capitalist may help design the company in addition to advancing cash for it to start, and may become active in staffing—firing the inventor who created the product idea and recruiting someone with more managerial experience to hold pieces of the venture together as it readies its product or service for market and gets sales started.

Although business success stories might suggest that ventures are created by one entrepreneur, it is apparent that many minds have helped design the venture puzzle that turned out to be the company, many hands have slid the pieces around until they fitted together to form a going concern. In a sense, there can be both full and fractional entrepreneurs in the creation process. If it is argued that at any point there is one lead entrepreneur who is the prime mover, it must also be recognized that which person is leader may change over time so that several are in effect "serial entrepreneurs," as when the inventor is replaced by a team builder who is then replaced by a managerial leader. Not only can entrepreneurs be full or fractional, they can also be sequential prime movers in a serial entrepreneurial sequence.

Thus, for the person contemplating entrepreneurship, a fair question might be, "What kind of entrepreneur do you want to be, full or fractional, and, if fractional, for what bit part, and in what act of the serial?" For the person who would like to be the prime mover for some part(s) of the serial, a dozen other questions arise about who the other players should be and how they should be motivated and guided into cooperating in the venture puzzle.

This subchapter will consider aspects of selecting, recruiting, and uniting inside players such as partners. The next subchapter will consider outside players such as professionals who can help in venture creation. It should be remembered, however, that these are not all the players involved. Others have been mentioned in previous chapters, and still others will come up in later chapters of the book.

Cooper et al.[1] found among 2,994 National Federation of Independent Business (NFIB) entrepreneurs that those whose ventures were more likely to be surviving than not surviving after three years:

- Were more likely than not to have had full-time partners (30 percent in surviving firms vs. 25 percent in non-surviving firms)

- Started with more employees

- More often said they obtained important help from accountants (47 percent vs. 41 percent), bankers (35 percent vs. 32 percent) and lawyers (20 percent vs. 17 percent)

For founders of the *Inc.* 500 fastest-growing small firms, help on development of business ideas came from the sources listed in Table 7-1.[2]

Need for Complements

Areas where entrepreneurs need help from other people can broadly be grouped into four categories: (1) information, (2) production, (3) resources and (4) sales. Helpers who can contribute in these four areas can be grouped into seven categories: financers, partners, employees, suppliers, advisers, institutions, and channels. There can be overlap among these seven. For instance, partners may also be financers, and employees may help as advisers. Each of the seven categories can also be subdivided. For instance, there are many types of advisers, including professionals such as accountants and lawyers plus informal advisers, such as other entrepreneurs, to whom a founder might turn for advice.

Table 7-1 Sources of Help on Business Ideas for *Inc.* 500 Founders

Source	Percent of firms
Potential customers	52%
Spouse	51
Partners	50
Colleagues in the same industry	44
Suppliers	29
Professionals such as lawyers, consultants, etc.	26
Potential backers	19

Each category of helper will tend to contribute mainly to one area of need for the venture and will possibly contribute to others secondarily. Table 7-2 illustrates what the patterns might be. Advisers contribute mainly information and financers mainly resources, for instance. Using this table, an entrepreneur might rank either categories of help by type of helper who might be most useful (rank the rows in each column), or type of helper by areas of capability to serve (rank the columns for each row). The point of doing so is to clarify mentally just what help is needed by the venture and who might be able to provide it. Getting the wrong person for a particular need can be expensive, as some entrepreneurs who felt disappointed by partners, for instance, have attested.

Table 7-2 Help Types and Sources

What the Person Can Help with

	Information	Production	Resources	Sales
Financers				
Partners				
Employees				
Advisers				
Institutions				
Channels				

Application: List for the assigned case venture the types of help the entrepreneur will likely need and where it should come from by filling in the grid in Table 7-2 above.

Although the help needs of no two ventures are exactly alike, it may be useful to review the history of one start-up and identify the entrance of help at certain important points during its development. The following sequence occurred during the early days of cable television.

In 1962 a to-be entrepreneur began working for his brother helping install TV cable in a major city. The following year, while he was visiting in a suburb of the city which did not yet have cable, he noticed on a friend's set that the reception was poor. Knowing he could help and that money could be made with a cable system, he knocked on the doors of several households in the neighborhood and asked if they might be interested to see whether a cable could improve their reception. The replies encouraged him.

Using his car as collateral, he borrowed $1,000 from a bank, bought some used equipment from a dealer and started, as a sideline to his regular job, setting up a system. Over the next year he installed a cable system for 17 charter subscribers, and brought in enough cash to pay off the bank.

Six months later, in mid-1965, he got a call from city hall in the suburb telling him he needed a city franchise for his cable system. He duly submitted an application and received the franchise without problem. This sequence raised concern in his mind, however, that perhaps he should tell the phone company that he was using its poles. In response, the phone company demanded he obtain a $5,000 bond to cover any possible damages as well as a lease fee.

Concerned about the implications of liability that had been raised, the entrepreneur decided he should reform his cable company as a corporation. He was not sure how to do this, but had noticed the nameplate of an accountant in one building where he had worked. Now he approached this man for assistance. The accountant said he would help in return for some stock and a small salary. He introduced the entrepreneur to a friend of his who was an attorney. For a customary fee he helped with incorporation, registration of a company name, obtaining a bond and setting up a contract with the telephone company in late 1966.

While these arrangements were being made the entrepreneur had heard about another nearby suburban area where some homes had poor reception. He knocked on some doors in the local area to verify this and noted a nearby hill where a reception antenna to serve the area might work. He applied for a franchise at the end of 1967 and a year later had an approval for it.

During the wait for approval, he began seeking sources of cash to build the next system. By now he had concluded that he had picked the wrong accountant, paid more than he should have for help in setting up the company, and made a mistake in sharing stock. Determined not to share more of it, he tried to borrow for the company expansion from several potential financers whom he approached, but they all wanted stock.

He decided to scale back initial capacity in the new antenna system, seek another bank loan and develop the system incrementally. Pledging his personal assets he borrowed $5,000 and began construction. Costs grew faster than revenues, however, payments to suppliers began to slip, and one supplier brought suit in an effort to take over the company. The entrepreneur hired another lawyer to defend him, who discovered that the supplier had not properly registered his own firm with the state and therefore could not demand payment.

By letting this account payable continue to run and issuing more stock shares with which to pay friends and relatives to help him, the entrepreneur completed setup of the new system in early 1968. Revenues now grew, bills were paid, the number of subscribers continued to expand, and the entrepreneur asked a real estate agent to help him find permanent quarters for the company. The company also hired its first full-time employee in addition to the entrepreneur.

Answers to several questions about what an entrepreneur needs to implement a business idea successfully can be explored in this example. What personal characteristics most affected the successfulness of this entrepreneur? What capabilities did this particular entrepreneur possess that another might not for accomplishing this venture? Whom did he talk to when he first discerned his venture idea? To what extent does it appear that he knew "the right people" in advance? What did he not know that others had to guide him on? How did he find them? Why did they render the help? How could he go wrong in getting the help? How could he go wrong in not getting the help? What should he have learned from this experience about acquiring partners?

What could he have studied in advance of encountering his opportunity that might have made him more effective? Would it have made him more likely to prevail if a competitor discovered the same opportunity at the same time? How might the help that another entrepreneur might need with another venture differ from the experience of this man? Information in the next few sections should help broaden the picture.

Partners

Most entrepreneurs (69 percent), according to the findings of Cooper et al.,[3] began their companies without partners. Twenty percent started with one partner, 7 percent with two and the remainder with more. (Apparently some had outside investors whom they do not consider partners, since only 63 percent said they owned 100 percent of the equity.) In subsequent years the fraction with partners increased, but only by a few percentage points.

In the contrasting sample of *Inc.* 500 firms which quickly grew large it appears that owners much more often ended up sharing ownership. A survey of *Inc.* 500 founders revealed in 1989 that the amounts of equity still held by founders and their families by the time their firms reached "500" status was as follows:[4]

39% still held 100%
18% still held 75%-99%
22% still held 50%-75%
21% still held less than 50%

The general theory advanced for sharing ownership is sometimes cast as a claim that "50 percent of a $100 pie is worth more than 100 percent of a $25 pie." From this *Inc.* 500 sample, however, it appears that a fair percentage of entrepreneurs, almost 40 percent, manage to retain 100 percent of some very valuable "pies."

However, a majority did share ownership. Although their reasons for doing so were not reported, they probably included: to raise capital, to recruit a team to give the enterprise special competence enabling extraordinary growth, or as part of a "strategic alliance" with some other company. A study of electronics companies with sales under $100 million reported in the June 1990 issue of *Inc.* found that 71 percent had some sort of strategic alliance, most often for market channels.[5]

The basic reason for sharing ownership should be to provide extraordinary incentive, and the founder(s) must decide to whom the incentives should be given and for what. McMullan, Lischeron and Cunningham have reported[6] that there seems to be a relationship between sharing of ownership and company performance which follows a "J-Curve" pattern, with specific figures as shown in Table 7-3 below. At the left tip of the J, with fairly high performance in terms of sales and employment growth, are companies where all ownership is retained by founders and investors. In the bottom of the J, with lower performance, are companies in which founders and investors shared ownership with key managers and technical people only. At the high end of the J are companies with shared ownership throughout their employee populations. Not reported were either the stage at which ownership sharing expanded or the extent to which sharing was a cause versus an effect of the company growth.

Table 7-3 Company Growth, 1978-83 vs. Ownership Distribution

Ownership	Average Sales Growth	Average Employment Growth
Founders and Financers Only	156.6%	75.8%
Above plus Managers	64.6	20.4
All Above plus Professional/Technical	91.0	125.3
All Above plus Prod'n/Clerical/Other	597.0	312.1

Notwithstanding this apparent endorsement for sharing ownership, there is a view among many entrepreneurs that it is better to go without partners and retain 100 percent of ownership if possible, even if it means that the company will not grow as safely or as large. Although no systematic study has reported on the hindsight judgment of entrepreneurs who had partners, as contrasted with those who did not, it appears anecdotally that it is easier to find entrepreneurs who succeeded but had trouble with partners and who would not want to have them again, than it is to find entrepreneurs who succeeded without partners but wish they had had them.

Sometimes, however, there is no other workable choice but to share ownership, and then the goal must be to find the right partner(s), make the right deal and develop an effective working relationship as the enterprise progresses. A starting point is self-assessment by the entrepreneur coupled with estimation of what the enterprise needs. Questions in this assessment include:

- What tasks must be performed to make this company go? (The answer can be cross-checked by asking founders of similar businesses to review it.)

- What tasks does the founder know how to perform at various levels compared to those with more experience in them? (Both how well the founders can perform them and how long it will take compared to having "pros" carry them out should be considered.)

- On what tasks can the founder recruit help, and at what cost? (Some "asking around" will probably be needed to ferret out answers to this question.)

Application: *What are the best estimates you can give for the assigned case venture to the three questions above?*

Unfortunately, it often turns out that finding answers to these questions does not ensure success for the venture. The venture idea may not be sufficiently worthy. The founder may not "bring to the party" enough that others will want to join in. Or it may not be possible within the time and resources available to locate a good enough combination of co-conspirators to justify proceeding. Still, the attempt to recruit the needed help may be worthwhile either for its educational value and/or because it can lead to discovery of other worthwhile opportunities and contacts.

Selection

Partners may contribute in any of the four areas: information, production, resources and sales. Within each of these, what can the entrepreneur provide at a competitive level and where is help needed? Is the competition weak enough, or the venture simple enough to provide adequate time for acquiring what is needed along the way, or must it be available from the outset? When needed, can it be hired, or must it be bought with ownership?

The following ambitious start-up was undertaken by an entrepreneur who lacked important prior experience, and therefore needed considerable help to get it going.

Greg Braendel, who was introduced earlier in Chapter 2, was described by *Inc.* as "a 44-year old itinerant Hollywood actor."[7] A cousin who worked in England for Thrislingon, a company that made unusually decorative bathroom partitions, visited and persuaded Braendel to help sell them in the U.S. "My idea," Braendel said, "was to find a manufacturer and then sit back and collect my royalties for 10 years or so. Then I could pursue my acting career."

A U.S. partitionmaker whom he approached declined the job but suggested a distributor, who liked the product and in turn introduced Braendel to a manufacturer's representative. A representative of the British producer came to help Braendel find a U.S. manufacturer, but even together the two were unsuccessful in finding one. Then the Briton suggested that Braendel make them himself. Braendel obtained rights from the British maker in return for a royalty on sales and set about forming a company. *Inc.* summed it up as follows.

"Add it up. He was setting out to build a company—something he had never done successfully—in an industry he knew next to nothing about. He would be making a low-tech product that, while distinctive, could easily be copied. To succeed he'd have to line up reps and distributors all over the country, set up and operate at least one factory and ultimately several more, persuade architects and interior designers to gamble on a new and still-untested manufacturer—and do all this before competitors moved in on his turf. Braendel figured that he could count on his parents back in Pennsylvania for some seed capital, but he had little money of his own and little notion of how to raise more.

"As for the start-up team he assembled, well, an optimist would say that they made up in enthusiasm what they lacked in relevant experience. Braendel's friend, Jack Dunsmoor, 42, gave up a marketing job at Republic Pictures to become Thrislington's vice president. Dunsmoor's half-brother, Tim Haase, only 26, became manager of production, and a young actor named Bo Rostrom, 27, became marketing coordinator. Jo Strate, 63, a friend who was training director for General Nutrition Center, managed the office and kept track of the cash."

Braendel chose well-known professional firms for help. A prestigious Los Angeles law firm, White and Case, helped with trademark and logo protection plus preparation of a private placement memorandum. Peat Marwick helped with preparation of a business plan, for $14,000, and was expected to help further with setup of a computerized accounting system and possibly executive search. Suppliers also helped. DuPont and Formica both sold materials needed in the partitions and offered to help with cooperative advertising and distribution of literature.

Disappointments also followed. A company engaged to perform assembly let the venture down and Braendel and his partners ended up doing the work themselves. One bank agreed to make a loan, but only against Braendel's personal collateral. Later when his venture was going and sought more working capital it was turned down at that same bank and elsewhere. A venture review panel at an "Entrepreneurial Forum" sponsored by Stanford alumni criticized Braendel and his group for undertaking a line of work in which they had no experience. One venture capitalist commented that "We took a vote of five or six people after the meeting and it was unanimous. They wouldn't get the money they needed, and they wouldn't succeed if they did." Two years into the business, however, sales had risen to $2.7 million annually and the company was still going, with plans for continued expansion.

Whether this venture succeeds in the long run or not, it shows how entrepreneurs find help. They start with whatever acquaintances they have and work through them, and they make "cold calls" on professionals such as lawyers, accountants, bankers and suppliers to find people who can provide the needed help.

Recognizing what to look for and what to avoid in partners and other potential helpers calls for both hard-headed assessment—what have they done before, what do they know, what reputation do they have among those with whom they worked, how much compensation do they want?—and subjective appraisal—is this person enjoyable to work with, does he or she seem enthusiastic and reliable, are we getting along well, do motivations match? If there can be an opportunity to work together before cementing the relationship, that may provide even more helpful information.

Application: *Formulate criteria for seeking and selecting one or more partners to complement the entrepreneur(s) in the assigned case.*

Terms

Striking a deal with a prospective helper or partner has two sides: who should add what, and who should get what? Each of these two sides has its objective and subjective aspects. What should be added can be sorted out in terms of the four categories mentioned above: information, production, resources and sales. These four can be aligned with capabilities of the potential helper to see how good the fit should be. Usually, information is the easiest to come by, while the other three, production, resources and sales, may be both harder to get and more important because they require more serious commitment.

Who should get what can be examined through developing answers in specific terms, quantitatively insofar as possible, to such questions as:

- How much would it cost elsewhere to obtain the same thing?

- How much might the venture be worth if it works out, and what is the probability of its doing that well?

- What is the discounted expected present value of the venture's future cash flow, and hence how much would a specific fraction to be shared with a partner be worth?

- Will the partner get a special tax break, such as being able to deduct expenses of the business from personal income?

- Will the partner enjoy insulation from some problems of the business by having part of it set up separately in such a way that the partner shares only some particularly appealing aspect, such as a tax break? Sometimes, for further illustration, a separate partnership will be set up for sales or for ownership of certain facilities. These may be unencumbered, while another part of the business copes with past losses or other risks.

Thinking about what can go wrong should be part of setting up a deal, not because things necessarily will go wrong, but because they might, and thinking ahead may mitigate or head off problems. Examples of potential difficulties include the following:

Two men formed a machining company. At year-end the wife of one of them took a look at the books to prepare taxes and found that the partner had been making unauthorized withdrawals from the company bank account and attempting to disguise them as supply purchases. The partnership was dissolved.

❖ ❖ ❖

One man had a small manufacturing company. He was approached by a second man who offered to help with sales. As proof of his sales ability, the second man obtained from a potential buyer a letter of intent to buy enough to increase the company's volume five-fold for the year. The two formed a corporation, divided the stock 50/50 and both cosigned a note at the bank to obtain working capital. Sales, however, turned out to be far slower than forecast, and with a large inventory the company began to have trouble paying its bills. Creditors, including the bank, pressed for payment.

The original founder became increasingly unhappy with his sales partner who had not met his promises. When, in addition, the founder learned from the bank that the salesman had sold the company truck to help raise more cash for selling expenses, he was furious. He approached the bank and offered to pay off his half of the bank obligation personally with cash. The banker agreed. Then the founder approached the salesman, said what he had done and offered to pay off all the company's suppliers personally if he could have the inventory. The salesman said it would be a mistake, that things would pick up soon. The founder replied that the only mistake had been their becoming partners. He wrote the salesman's lawyer saying his name could no longer be used in connection with the business. Thereafter, the founder operated as a sole proprietor, sold off the inventory and started expanding the business. His conclusion was that the $15,000 he had lost in this process had been tuition for an educational process about caution in taking on partners.

❖ ❖ ❖

Three partners in a fish farm negotiated with some potential "silent partners" to obtain capital. The understanding of the three partners was that the investors would pay the company in a lump sum to be used for expenses during start-up, and they attempted to include this provision in the investment agreement, which they wrote themselves. Shares were duly issued to the investors, but the latter chose to mete out the cash slowly, which frustrated the founders. The investors claimed that costs of start-up were becoming higher than promised and therefore they were entitled to more ownership. The founders sought legal counsel, and were disappointed to learn that the agreement they had drafted left loopholes which gave the investors the upper hand.

❖ ❖ ❖

Bob Ohlson, one of four partners in a computer cable company, saw the other partners as both lacking in vision as to what their company could become and not pulling their weight. He tried persuading first one partner and later a different one to join with him to take over from the other two. Eventually, however, the other three all aligned against him and offered to buy him out. Ohlson rejected the deal, claiming that both the price and the condition that he sign a promise not to compete were unacceptable. Instead he quietly set about organizing a new company in the same line of business. He recruited key employees to come with him, offering shares of ownership in his new company as part of the inducement. Suddenly one day his partners were surprised to find that he and 18 of their 80 employees had left, including three-fourths of the salespeople. They struggled to recover, however, and by a year and a half later the company had grown to 95 employees. The partner in charge, John Berst, however, felt he had nevertheless lost something. "With Bob Ohlson I bared my soul," he said. "Now, I'm reluctant to totally confide in anyone."

Ohlson's new company had also managed to survive and was now up to 36 employees. Reflecting on his departure from the partnership, he commented, "If I had had enough money, I probably could have cleaned the whole organization out. This was a super move on our part. Obviously, I'm more cynical about personal relationships. At one time I would have considered John Berst my best friend in the whole world. And then he went and stuck a knife in my back." [8]

❖ ❖ ❖

Two doctors formed a clinic. One started feeling progressively more overloaded and wanted to hire a third doctor to get some relief. His partner, however, resisted because he knew doing so would cut into profits. After considerable debate, the two agreed that the new doctor would be hired, but the doctor interested in maintaining profits would take no cut in his draw. The other did take a cut in draw, but only for a while, because with the new doctor business and profits soon increased enough to provide the same draw for both.

The variety of things that can go wrong is endless. Not all problems can be anticipated in setting up a partnership, but some of the possibilities can, including provision for dissolution. One "shoot-out" clause sometimes used to provide for possible breakup says that either partner can buy out the other on the terms he or she offers provided the other has the right first to buy on the same terms and declines to exercise it. Thinking through this possibility and other "what if's" can be helped by talking with others who have gone through the process, such as other entrepreneurs and attorneys with new company formation experience. Also helpful, particularly in negotiating arrangements, is to consider the "what if's" alternatively from each party's point of view before taking a position.

Application: *Formulate terms that the entrepreneur in the assigned case should "shoot for" in taking on a partner. Be prepared to explain how the prospective partner should respond to those terms.*

Employees

One way around partner problems, if the founder(s) can raise enough capital, is to hire the help needed with cash. Flexibility is high in hiring and firing when a company is very small. If it grows and adds more employees beyond three or four, things become more complex in terms of governmental restrictions and requirements. At a still larger size, unionization can add further complications. Such consequences of growth are why some entrepreneurs permanently keep their enterprises small.

That is not to say there are no complications. Occupational health and safety (OSHA) rules, both federal and state, still apply. Payroll deductions for taxes and social security must still be made. Premiums for industrial insurance and unemployment compensation must still be paid. And, of course, employees can still sue if they think they have cause and might be able to collect from the venture.

Hiring

One way to avoid such complications can be to hire "temporaries." Rather than paying them directly, the venture can hire their services from other firms that employ them, pay them, take care of their payroll deductions and governmentally-required paperwork. The venture instead simply pays their employer and thereby escapes the complications of putting them on a payroll. Another possibility is to buy services from people who operate as independent contractors, and leave it to them to take care of their own payroll deductions and insurance. Consultants, for example, are hired in this way. Caution is required, however, to remain within the bounds of legality. If the government gets the idea that these people are really employees of the venture who are just masquerading as independent contractors, it will move in to stop the practice and likely impose penalties.

In attempting to attract and recruit desired employees, start-up firms have some obvious handicaps and advantages. Handicaps include:

- relative financial insecurity
- relatively low pay
- limited, if any, fringe benefits
- lack of opportunity to move around within the company
- little or no formal training opportunities
- no association with a "name brand"

To be weighed against these are such advantages as the following:

- a more personal environment
- capability of the company to grow and change faster
- more responsibility and breadth of coverage in work
- opportunity to make a visible difference personally in the fortunes of the company
- opportunity to rise faster as the company expands and perhaps to share a significant part of the ownership which could become very valuable. A very high percentage of Apple's early workforce became very wealthy, for instance. Microsoft's workforce is said to include upwards of a thousand millionaires.

It is up to the founders to "pitch" these potential advantages effectively, and often their own enthusiasm and excitement during start-up helps them do that. Consequently, start-ups, in spite of their handicaps, sometimes manage to recruit some excellent employees. Another advantage they have is that being small and consequently flexible, they can accommodate unusual people who do not fit well in established firms or simply don't like the regimentation such firms impose in pursuit of efficiency. Homemakers, part-timers, members of the family, military people in off-hours, school teachers during summers, handicapped and retired people can be more readily accommodated by start-ups than by companies whose routines have grown more firmly fixed.

Classified advertisements in the local paper are the customary way to locate recruits. Start-ups sometimes find employees in other ways as well, such as through personal contacts, family and friends. Customary checkout procedures, such as contacting former employers and looking into past performance records, are as appropriate for start-ups as for other employers, even though the time required for those procedures may be harder for founders to come up with due to the many other time demands they face.

Application: Formulate a staffing plan for the assigned case venture over the next two years, indicating criteria for selection, specifications for training, projected organization charts and estimated costs.

Pitfalls

Start-ups run into all sorts of problems with employees, just as do other firms. Some examples include the following:

The founder and 65 percent shareholder of a security systems company was out of town inspecting work on a new job when the operations manager, controller and marketing manager, concerned about loose management of the company, approached the company's bank and suggested that the bank tell the founder either to resign or have his loan called. Upon learning of this, the founder contacted his lawyer and the two visited the banker, whom they informed firmly that all relations between the bank and founder were to be kept confidential. They vowed to file suit against the bank for conspiracy if any damage to the company resulted from the bank's meetings with the employees. The employees were given the choice of resigning or being fired and chose the former.

❖ ❖ ❖

The factory of a jacket enterprise burned down. Arson appeared to be the cause, but when the owner appealed to the insurance company for compensation both it and the local fire department indicated they believed management had been behind the fire for the sake of the insurance money. The owner hired a former FBI agent to investigate. This man found, in the fire department records, the notes from a interview with a woman who had been eating in a restaurant near the plant when the fire broke out and had reported seeing a young man enter the restaurant muttering somewhat incoherently about the blaze. An amateur artist, she had also submitted a sketch of him to the fire department. The FBI man showed this sketch to the owner of the jacket enterprise and learned it depicted a former employee. Investigation of the employee's background turned up earlier troubles with the law. Eventually, the employee confessed to setting the fire, the insurance firm paid off and the jacket enterprise continued.

❖ ❖ ❖

The founder of a restaurant said employee stealing was a never-ending problem. Tablecloths, silverware, pots and pans, food and other supplies continually disappeared. He recalled firing one cook who had taken large quantities of food, including whole beef roasts, by putting it in plastic bags, throwing it into the garbage and later retrieving it from the dumpster after hours. The only solution the owner could think of was to be eternally vigilant and accept the fact that some things were bound to go wrong.

These examples illustrate only the tiniest fraction of problems that arise with employees. A new venture at least offers opportunity to start out right with careful employee selection coupled with clear formulation and enforcement of rules. Starting a pattern of careful attention to employee needs and problems can set a positive trend from the beginning, and head off later need to fix dysfunctional habits.

Application: *List, in order of probability, the problems most likely to arise with insiders over the next two years of the assigned case venture and what should be done to forestall or cope with them.*

Supplementary Reading
New Venture Mechanics Chapter 4. (Vesper, K. H., Prentice-Hall, 1993)

Exercises

1. Obtain the views of three entrepreneurs on the subject of partners. Upon whose experience, those of the entrepreneurs or those of others, are they based? How consistent are they with each other, and what do you conclude?

2. Same as above, but for employees.

3. Assess as potential partners some people you met while sizing up the competition or potential vendors in connection with development of a business plan.

4. Based upon examples you have seen in the readings, class and any field searches thus far, how would you answer the following questions:

    *   What kinds of help do entrepreneurs need?
    *   Do creative people need partners because they lack business sense?
    *   How does an entrepreneur tell if contacts or partners are needed?
    *   How does an entrepreneur decide what to do personally versus hire others to do?
    *   How does an entrepreneur choose among potential partners?
    *   What types of people should be avoided for a venture team?
    *   How does an entrepreneur get others to help in starting a business?

Venture History

1. List the cast of characters and where they came into play in getting the venture started.

    *   If it involved partners or investors, what were the deal terms that brought them in?
    *   What does a look at the written agreement reveal?
    *   Which contacts were first delivered when, and how?

2. How did the entrepreneur:

    *   Find, select and recruit employees?
    *   Learn about and arrange for legal requirements?
    *   Learn about and arrange for fringe benefits?

3. Approximately how much time did this require?

Venture Planning guide

1. Assess your strengths and task-relevant experience for carrying through your venture idea. List the areas where complementary talents and capabilities of others might be most helpful.

2. Ask someone else to review and comment on the above assessment. Write a summary of what that person said.

3. Formulate the composition of the best team you think you might be able to recruit to help you start your venture. Describe the incentives you could provide for them to do so and how you would attempt to persuade them to join.

4. Test the incentive system above by writing out a description of it and asking someone else to comment on it.

5. Describe how incentive systems in the company will differ for (1) directors, if any, (2) founders, (3) other managers, (4) key employees, (5) non-key full-time employees, and (6) non-key part-time or temporary employees.

5. List your prior work and/or hobby experience, and note the functional areas (accounting, production, marketing, etc.) in which you would be best-equipped to contribute during start-up of the venture you are developing a plan for.

6. List the capabilities in co-founders that would be most useful to you for accomplishing such a start-up.

7. List the provisions you think would be most important to include in a partnership agreement or corporate bylaws for your venture.

8. Compile biographies of key people for your venture as they should appear in a venture plan. Be prepared to explain what you chose to include and why.

9. Draw organization charts for three different points in time during development of the venture over the first five years.

Notes

[1] Arnold C. Cooper, William C. Dunkelberg, and Carolyn Y. Woo, "Survival and Failure: A Longitudinal Study," in *Frontiers of Entrepreneurship Research, 1988*, eds. Bruce H, Kirchhoff and others (Wellesley, Mass.: Babson Center for Entrepreneurial Studies, 1988), p. 224.

[2] John Case, "The Origins of Entrepreneurship," *Inc.*, June 1989, p. 54.

[3] Arnold C. Cooper and others, *New Business In America* (Washington, D.C.: The NFIB Foundation, 1990), p. 5.

[4] John Case, "The Origins of Entrepreneurship," *Inc.*, June 1989, p. 58.

[5] "Hotline," *Inc.*, June 1990, p. 33.

[6] W. Ed McMullan, J. Lischeron, and B. Cunningham, "Building Entrepreneurial Teams: Some Options, Rewards and Barriers," (Working Paper #88-13, presented TIMS/ORSA, Denver, October 1988).

[7] John Case, "With A Little Help From His Friends," *Inc.*, April 1989, p. 132.

[8] Edward O. Welles, "Blowup," *Inc.*, May 1989, p. 63.

❏ *SUBCHAPTER 7B - Outsiders*

Every business, including a start-up, needs help from outsiders, people who have neither ownership nor employment in the company. An entrepreneur can benefit by becoming acquainted with a number of outside help sources and their costs. Government agencies and libraries provide information without fees. Some types of professionals charge directly for their services, lawyers, for instance. Others, such as bankers and insurance agents, provide counsel without charge and get paid for the other services they offer. Still others offer free counsel on a volunteer basis; for instance, retired executives who work with the Small Business Administration and other business people who serve as advisers "pro bono" to small firms.

Whether free or not, all of these help sources cost time to use, and an entrepreneur must weigh the benefits of outside help against both the time and money costs of obtaining them. Most specialists cost money but save time because they know what they are doing and don't have to stop and learn as a newcomer does.

More important than the cost in either money or time is often the quality of contribution that the venture receives. People who have the strongest proof that they can deliver high-quality performance often tend to charge the highest prices. Is the venture really worth enough to justify such an investment? High-priced help may easily be justified if its benefits can be spread across a large operation. But how can a small one justify such costs? And if it can't, what is an entrepreneur to do? Juggling these dilemmas is not impossible. Entrepreneurs do it all the time. It calls for imaginative and energetic management.

Suppliers

Suppliers were discussed in Subchapter 6C of Chapter 6 in connection with setup of the company shop, and will be considered again in Subchapter 8B. They have a vested interest in seeing a new venture, that might be a future customer, succeed. Consequently, they are predisposed to help if they can and if it will not cost them too much. Large corporations with well-known names may have both talents and connections of value to the venture. They may be able, for instance, to use the venture in their advertisements to capture favorable interest for themselves, while the venture itself gets free advertising. Useful advice in product development, contacts for other help, provision of samples and extension of credit all may come from suppliers.

Against potential gains from giving help to the venture, suppliers must weigh three possibilities: first, that the venture either will not succeed and therefore not be able to pay the suppliers back at all, second, that it will survive but remain very small and therefore not return the investment made to help it, and third, that after it gets going the venture will shift to other suppliers. It is natural for suppliers to favor their most important customers and to avoid those who lack a proven track record of paying bills. Even with such precautions, suppliers continually absorb bad debts. Bankruptcy filings typically report liabilities in excess of assets, which is an indication of bills that suppliers are unable to collect.

The way to find suppliers is by asking around from one referral to the next until the ones needed turn up. Some places to start in this search process include:

- The Yellow Pages of the phone book
- A manufacturers' directory for the city or state
- *Thomas Register* in the library
- Firms that might use the same type of supplier.

Once a suitable supplier is located, a selling job by the customer (entrepreneur) begins. Quality, delivery time, price and credit terms, if any, must be arranged, and usually the start-up founder is at a disadvantage. Some suppliers are sympathetic to entrepreneurs, but most are not so generous that they will jeopardize either money or other customers to help out. They may require payment COD. or even in advance. They may put other orders ahead and deliver later than promised. They may compromise any prior arrangements, and for that reason the entrepreneur must stay in close touch. This may be difficult with all the other demands to be met during start-up, but it may be necessary to get the needed help.

Application: *List the types of suppliers that will likely be needed by the assigned case venture, indicating which five will likely be the most difficult to deal with and why.*

Professionals

Many different types of specialists are available to help ventures. Most provide information, as opposed to production, resource or sales help. Many also provide introductions to other useful business contacts. Generally the more successful the professional, the better the contacts he or she can provide.

Legal Advice

Conventional wisdom advises entrepreneurs always to put important agreements in writing, read and understand the fine print and hire the most competent lawyers they can find to help with these tasks and keep them out of legal trouble. The law never requires that lawyers be hired, and many entrepreneurs have successfully accomplished their own legal work ranging from filing for incorporation to drawing up contracts, conducting their own trials, handling their own public offering applications and writing their own wills. But the conventional wisdom to hire good legal help persists, with the support of virtually all who have done so. A lawyer costs more money than handling legal work personally, but there is usually a more than offsetting saving in time expenditure and mistake reduction.

What an entrepreneur needs to know about the law is (1) where it generally comes into play, (2) how to go about becoming better-informed in those areas where it is likely to become especially important for the particular business, (3) how to find an appropriate lawyer, and (4) how to use legal services effectively and efficiently.

Lawyers help with:

- legal formation (Should the venture be incorporated, and if so, with what provisions?)

- relationships between owners, employees and others (Will the venture need non-disclosure agreements, union contracts or non-compete agreements? Should it have pension or profit-sharing plans?)

- legal protection of intellectual property (Should the entrepreneur file for a trademark or patent? Should the venture sue for theft of trade secrets?)

- contracts (What should be the wording with suppliers, customers, landlords?)

- lawsuits (Where are the litigation risks greatest and how can they be mitigated?)

- taxes (What are the allowable deductions, what must be paid when and what must be reported when?)

- government permissions and requirements (What records must be kept? What applications and reports must be filed and in what form?)

- issuing securities (What advance preparation is advisable? What can and cannot legally be done, and how are approvals obtained?)

- personal property issues (What estate planning should the founders do? Should they be leasing assets to the company?)

An entrepreneur should attain some knowledge of the meaning of each of these categories and the kinds of issues that might arise within them. Some issues are suggested above in the parentheses, but each issue is complex, and the list is by no means exhaustive. Moreover, the ways of dealing with these issues depend on the individual circumstances. Incorporating as a sole owner can be simple, but with partners it tends to become complicated. Government permission for selling stationery is simple. Opening a foundry is complex in some situations and virtually impossible in others. Some start-ups will never sell shares publicly and need not worry about rules governing that. Others that eventually will should explore whether they need to get started right away with certified accounting audits in order to qualify later, and so forth.

Information about each of these topics is available in libraries, particularly law libraries, which are operated both by law schools and by governmental agencies. The standard reference on law firms is Martindale and Hubbell.[1] Talking with other entrepreneurs in related lines of work or who have faced similar situations, and reading up are two "free" ways to become prepared to answer such questions as:

- Is something legalistic called for?
- Should a lawyer be engaged to help with it?
- Should the lawyer be a generalist or specialist?
- Should a large or small firm be engaged?
- Which firm should be hired?
- What should be bought from it?

Application: *Make a schedule of legal tasks to be done during the next two years of the assigned case venture and, insofar as possible, answer the above questions and formulate a legal expenses budget.*

Answers will vary with the source of the opinion as well as the kind of business situation the entrepreneur faces. For instance, many if not most lawyers will advise engaging them early to help with the decision of how and when they should be used. A lawyer from a large firm will point out that large firms have the advantage of employing many specialists to provide most efficient, informed and up-to-date information on whatever legal assistance the entrepreneur needs.

A lawyer from a smaller firm will counter that the large firm will typically assign top partners to the major accounts and use the small firm as a training ground for younger and less-experienced members of the firm. In contrast the small firm may assign a top (or maybe the only) partner, and where specialists are needed it will refer the entrepreneur to whomever is the best specialist in the business rather than simply to one whom the firm already employs and therefore must utilize.

The big firm may respond that it has more numerous and powerful contacts (but why should it draw upon them for a small venture?) and a better-known name to enhance the venture's image (but it will likely charge more. Will the extra money be better spent on that or on advertising, quality improvement, employee training or R&D?). Investigation and application of judgment by the entrepreneur are required.

Some feeling for a law firm can be obtained by briefly discussing with it such matters as these before deciding whether to hire it. It is always appropriate for the customer to ask whether the firm thinks it should be hired, how much it will charge and when the "meter" will start running.

According to a study by the Technology Executives Roundtable, 45 percent of high technology entrepreneurs found their lawyers through business acquaintances, and another 15 percent found them through accountants and bankers. Large law firms were the choice of 41 percent and sole practitioners of only 11 percent.[2]

Picking a Bank

Bankers help with:

- raising money
- obtaining credit reports on other companies
- anticipating financial binds
- numerous other services such as payroll processing, foreign exchange, trust management, business contacts as well as services familiar to individual customers

Critical elements in a banking relationship, aside from whether it has expressed willingness to lend money to the venture and on what terms, are which bank officer will handle the venture's account, how much interest that person takes in the venture, how comfortable the entrepreneur is with that particular person and how much weight that person carries within the bank. When a banker says "I'll have to take that up with the loan committee" it is usually not a particularly auspicious sign. When the banker who is dealing with the entrepreneur moves to some other activity in the bank and is replaced by someone else as the venture's contact, it is sometimes the worst possible sign.

Application: *Assume the role of a banker, and comment on the attractiveness of the assigned case venture as a client.*

Accounting Help

Accountants work on

- setting up financial reporting and control systems
- evaluating financial performance
- anticipating financial needs
- tax computations and auditing

Cooper et al. found in their survey of National Federation of Independent Business firms that initially bookkeepers were most often considered important sources of counsel (46 percent), followed by bankers (32 percent), other business owners (28 percent) and suppliers (28 percent). Later in the venture's development the accountants were still regarded as high in importance, while bankers were regarded as less so.[3] Bankers are chosen, according to a survey by the Technical Entrepreneurs Roundtable, much the same way as are lawyers, at least by technology entrepreneurs. Most frequently business acquaintances are the source of referral (44 percent), while bankers and lawyers are the source only 18 percent of the time.[4]

Application: *Prepare a forecast of the CPA time needed by the assigned case venture over the next two years, and explain the tasks it presumes.*

Selecting Insurance

Insurance brokers help with:

- many forms of insurance, including fire, theft, liability, directors' liability, auto, key person life coverage, health and accident, and pension plans

- ways of reducing risks (e.g. fire, security and safety systems)

One choice to be made is between an agent who represents a single insurance company and a broker who represents many different ones. Convenience favors the latter when there are different types of insurance to be bought, which is the case in starting a new company. But it is crucial to find a broker who is fully competent. Insurance policies contain many fine points. For instance, suppose the venture has a contract with a customer guaranteeing delivery of products. The plant burns down, and fire insurance covers the loss. But the customer sues for damages due to non-delivery of what was promised. Will the insurance cover those too?

Shopping around among several insurance companies by talking to their agents is a way of cross-checking on both coverage and rates. Another way is to hire an insurance consultant who is paid by the hour rather than through a percentage commission, as are agents and brokers. Yet another is to check with other entrepreneurs whose businesses, although not directly competitive with the new venture, are similar enough to require comparable insurance coverage.

Advertising

Advertising agencies help with

- design of brochures, displays, packages, advertisements
- placement of advertisements

- placement of public relations messages

The *Standard Directory of Advertising Agencies* lists all but the smallest. For a start-up company with drastically limited cash, however, the smallest may be preferable, and that must be found locally by "asking around."

Application: *Describe specifically the help an advertising agency might provide for the assigned case venture, and explain whether it should.*

Designing Facilities and Products

Industrial designers help with

- graphics, plus styling of products and packages
- human factors such as ease of use, foolproofness, comfort, safety, and so forth in design

Sophia Collier, who found package design to be so important to her SoHo soda pop start-up, as was mentioned earlier in the first subchapter(6a) of Chapter 6 in connection with product development, tackled the design task first by reading extensively at the library about printing and packaging and then seeking out a professional for help.

> She chose a general style, "art deco-ish," then sought out names of designers specializing in that style. One of them, Doug Johnson, expressed interest in the project until she told him she had no money. Then he told her to forget it.
> But she persisted, and eventually persuaded him to accept a royalty for his help. "The fact that I kept coming back suggested that I would be as tenacious with other things," she said. "It gave him more faith in me."[5]

Other elements of her advice in addition to persistence included taking the time to learn about printing, the effects it can produce and how to get them most economically, then making the designer a working partner by selecting one who is personally compatible, providing information as completely and early as possible, staying in close touch as the job progresses and paying on time.

All these types of advisers may be able to help in finding other useful contacts. The way to evaluate such advisers is to learn about what they have done before and to talk with other people who have worked with them. This leads naturally to further contacts. As a general rule, smaller companies do better working with smaller professional firms and agencies. That way they represent a relatively larger share of the professionals' business and are more likely to get the attention of top members in the professional firms rather than being relegated to apprentices.

Application: *List the tasks for which professional designing and graphics help will be needed by the assigned case venture over its next year, and estimate the workhours those tasks may require.*

Engaging Consultants

Consultants can be found on virtually any topic. Unfortunately, some will claim expertise on almost any issue, even though they may not have that expertise. Making inquiries with other business people who have bought a particular consulting service is probably the best way to check it out. Some specialize in helping prepare business plans, but those who read the plans usually prefer that they be written by the entrepreneurs who will carry them out.

Other Advisers

In addition to professionals there are numerous other types of ad hoc advisers, including the following:

Networks

The crucial role of business contacts in assisting start-up has long been known, but relatively few systematic studies of it have been undertaken. Part of the difficulty is that the contacts are so varied, and which are most useful is both unpredictable and idiosyncratic. Many times the most useful contacts are those that were acquired before it could be foreseen either that they would be helpful or how they might help. Hence, business contact building is something worth starting at any time, the earlier the better. Moreover, according to a study by Butler and Hansen, breadth in social networks appeared to expand the set of options open to entrepreneurs for start-ups.[6]

Application: *Describe the kind of contacts' network the entrepreneur in the assigned case should seek to develop, and suggest how it might be done.*

Directors

Every corporation must have directors, and this necessity provides a platform for recruiting advisers in that capacity. But a director's motivation is always a key question. Providing help usually requires effort and effort usually calls for compensation. There may be some people who will provide effort gratis to a start-up. Here and there an entrepreneur who has prospered and wants "to give something back" or a retired executive who is more concerned with being active than with compensation may be willing to contribute to the venture without compensation. Most others will require it, either in the form of pay, ownership or possibly expenses to meet at a vacation spot. How to provide enough compensation with meager resources can be a major problem for a start-up wanting help from directors. There may be the alternative of an exchange of free help in return from the entrepreneur, but the entrepreneur may not be able to afford the time.

A second problem concerns directors' legal liability. Insurance can be bought to protect directors against lawsuits in performance of their work. But it is usually expensive, reflecting the fact that the risks are significant. These in turn impose a disincentive for people to become directors.

If a company has great ambitions of growing and perhaps one day going public and can back those ambitions up with a convincing plan, it may be able both to attract prominent directors and use them to bolster its image. However, that rarely seems to happen. Even among the *Inc.* 500 companies, which were selected for their high growth rates, 43 percent were found to have no outside directors.[7] At start-up and among more "ordinary" small firms this percentage would likely be as great or greater.[8] It appears that those companies that add such directors most often seem to do it out of needs that arise downstream from start-up when they and directors can both offer more to each other.[9]

Application: *List the kind of people the assigned case entrepreneur should recruit as directors or an advisory board. Explain what would be in it for them, and lay out an agenda for their next meeting.*

Shareholders

The founding shareholders may include both working and silent (investing or lending only) partners. Silent partners may or may not live up to that name. Those who are not silent may or may not be helpful in their counsel. If they have put their savings into a start-up and it is struggling, they may become anxious about the risk they have bought and consequently plague the entrepreneur with questions and worries about how the business is coming along, when they will be able to get their money out, and so forth. Seasoned entrepreneurs may be helpful advisers as shareholders in start-ups (as Ross Perot may have been to Steve Jobs at Next), but newcomers are less likely to be. Even the value of professional venture capitalists as advisers is the subject of debate as research on it continues. The general answer seems to be that it depends.[10]

Venture Capitalists

If the start-up is one of the very few that draws cash from venture capitalists, it is likely to get helpful contacts from them as well, and the venture capitalists will probably interact with management on both strategic and operating problems. Typically, venture-capital firms require seats on the board of directors, and inevitably work and plan with management during the funding process, not only when it begins but repeatedly after that as more capital infusions are needed. In their study of 149 venture-capital firms, Elango, et al. found that the amount of time venture-capital firms spent on working with their investees typically ranged from around seven hours per month to more than 35 hours per month.[11]

Institutional Help

Recognition that new ventures create jobs and add useful new products and services has inspired institutions of various types to help them.

Associations

Trade Associations can be very helpful providers of information on specific industries. Sources of information about them include The *Encyclopedia of Associations* and the *Directory of the National Trade and Professional Associations of the United States.* These will likely be available at the downtown library if not the local business school library. The associations themselves gather and share information, providing contacts, newsletters and meetings where members can exchange helpful suggestions and moral support.

Application: *In the library, look at a list of associations and state which one(s) the entrepreneur in the assigned case should consider joining and why.*

Government

Federal Government agencies attempt to favor small firms in making purchases and issuing R&D contracts. The Small Business Administration in particular helps by guaranteeing bank loans to start-ups and small firms. It also offers free consultation services, seminars and literature on many aspects of starting and running small businesses. A telephone call to the nearest SBA office can provide an inventory of services available from the agency. A library source of information is *The Monthly Catalog of U.S. Government Publications.* These can be bought from the Superintendent of Documents, U.S. Government Printing Office, Washington, D.C. 20402.

Three government programs under the Small Business Administration that provide direct assistance to smaller firms are the Small Business Institute Program, in which participating universities assign student consulting teams to work with the company, the Service Corps of Retired Executives (SCORE), in which retired executives donate their services and the Active Corps of Executives (ACE), in which currently active executives do so. None of these programs costs money to the company.

State Governments usually seek to help start-up and small firms through publication of booklets on requirements for setting up a business in the state, and sometimes other services. City governments also try to help in various ways. Both the local chamber of commerce and the state department of commerce are places to call for finding out what help is available. A 401-page overall directory published by the U.S. Small Business Administration is *The States and Small Business: A Directory of Programs and Activities*. Another of 170 pages is the *Directory of Federal and State Business Assistance* which is available from the National Technical Information Service (catalog number PB88-101977).

The pros and cons of drawing upon government programs vary from case to case. Some impose strings, while others do not. Some cost money and others are free. The effectiveness of a given program depends upon the particular government people running it, what their prior experience is, how heavily they are scheduled at the moment, and so forth. So it can pay to investigate, provided not too much time is spent on that task.

Universities

Universities provide extension courses on starting and running businesses. Participating in such a seminar can be a way to meet other entrepreneurs who can help. Some universities also operate Small Business Institute programs in which students provide consulting services to entrepreneurs, as mentioned above, for course credit. Some universities also operate Small Business Development Centers in which professionals are employed to provide free consulting services to small firms.

Places to contact at the university are its office of extension programs and its business school. If the entrepreneur has a particular type of help in mind, such as market research or setting up an accounting system, then contact with the chairperson of the department teaching that subject may also be a good place to start.

Application: *Formulate a consulting assignment that might be suitable for a team of students seeking to help the entrepreneur in the assigned case.*

Incubators

Incubators have been set up in some communities to help companies get started. Some provide cheap rent for a year or two. Many provide ancillary services such as Xerox, phone answering, secretarial and possibly accounting and legal help. If the incubator is affiliated with a university, it may also provide access to use of laboratory facilities and to help from faculty and students.

Association with other entrepreneurs using the incubator may help provide useful contacts as well as moral support and mutual problem solving.

The number of incubators, according to the National Business Incubation Association, grew from 55 in 1984 to nearly 400 by 1990,[12] more than 100 of which were linked by electronic mail.[13] The largest fraction of incubators (39 percent) are those affiliated with local government agencies and development agencies. Next (17 percent) are those of universities, followed by centers run for profit (14 percent), according to the above association.[14]

As an indication of performance, one incubator in Chicago, begun with a $1.7 million federal grant, was able to report after nine years of operation that it had served 142 companies with such things as cheap rent, shared services and space, business plan help, group consulting and eventually low-cost loans. Sixteen percent of the clients had failed, and one who had grown to 17 employees commented that "It's a shame not all start-ups have this kind of assistance."[15]

Supplementary Reading

New Venture Strategies Chapter 2. (Vesper, K.H., Prentice-Hall, 1990)
New Venture Mechanics Chapter 4. (Vesper, K. H., Prentice-Hall, 1993)

Exercises

1. Make a list of as many as possible different types of professionals a start-up might obtain help from. For each, note how the amount of payment is determined. Describe the pros and cons, from the venture's viewpoint, of these incentives and what cautions are consequently advisable.

2. Interview an entrepreneur and find out how he or she took care of each of the tasks listed above under professionals. Which tasks turned out to be most critical, and which did professionals give the most help with and/or cost the most for help on?

3. Find out the cost of directors' liability insurance. Discuss alternative answers to the question of who should want to serve as director in a new venture and why. Discuss implications of your answer from an entrepreneur's perspective.

4. Interview one or more of the following to learn what experiences they have had in working with start-up companies as well as what they have concluded from those experiences. Describe your findings and the implications they should have from an entrepreneur's viewpoint.

   a. Lawyer
   b. Accountant
   c. Insurance broker
   d. Advertising agent
   e. Banker

5. For three of the above professionals, make a list of things that can go wrong if he or she does not do a good job for the venture. Be prepared to comment on how the entrepreneur could detect such problems in time to avoid serious trouble.

6. Locate a venture incubator. Describe what it offers, what it charges and how it compares to conventional commercial real estate as a location for three contrasting types of start-ups.

7. Develop an inventory of the governmental assistance programs for entrepreneurs in your local community. Sort them into those aimed at ongoing small firms versus those that help entrepreneurs during start-up.

Venture History

1. On a list of all the help sources noted in this chapter:

   - Which came into play when?
   - How would each rate in helpfulness?
   - How much did each cost?

2. For those of the above that had the most positive or negative impact, what was the chain of events?

Venture Planning Guide

1. List the professional services that would be needed to implement your plan. Prepare an itemized list, with dates, of the costs of those services and the firms that could be expected to provide them at those costs.

2. Pick a banker, lawyer, accountant and any other professionals to be engaged by the venture you are planning. Explain the rationale of your choice.

Notes

[1] *Martindale-Hubbell Law Digest* (New Providence, N.J.: Martindale-Hubbell).

[2] "Hands On," *Inc.*, July 1989, p. 99.

[3] Arnold C. Cooper and others, *New Business In America* (Washington, D.C.: The NFIB Foundation, 1990), p. 7.

[4] "Hands On," p. 114.

[5] J. Donald Weinrauch and Nancy Croft Baker, *The Frugal Marketer* (New York: AMACOM, 1989).

[6] John E. Butler and Gary S. Hansen, "Managing Social Network Evolution and Entrepreneurial Benefits," in *Frontiers of Entrepreneurship Research, 1988*, eds. Bruce Kirchhoff, Bruce H. and others (Wellesley, Mass.: Babson Center for Entrepreneurial Studies, 1988), p. 430.

[7] "Hands On," *Inc.*, October 1990, p. 151.

[8] Flynn Bucy and Sam Seaman "Relationship Between Role, Composition and Perceived Benefits of Boards of Directors for Privately Owned Firms," in *Frontiers of Entrepreneurship Research, 1988*, eds. Bruce Kirchhoff, Bruce H. and others (Wellesley, Mass.: Babson Center for Entrepreneurial Studies, 1988), p. 499.

[9] Elizabeth Conlin, "Unlimited Partners," *Inc.*, April 1990, p. 71.

[10] Joseph Rosenstein and others, "Do Venture Capitalists on Boards of Portfolio Companies Add Value Besides Money?" and Harry J. Sapienza and Jeffry A. Timmons, "Launching and Build-

ing Entrepreneurial Companies: Do The Venture Capitalists Add Value?" in *Frontiers of Entrepreneurship Research, 1989*, eds. Brockhaus, Robert H., Sr. and others (Wellesley, Mass.: Babson Center for Entrepreneurial Studies), 1989, pp. 216 and 245, respectively.

[11]B. Elango, Vance H. Fried, Robert D. Hisrich and Amy Polonchek, "How Venture Capital Firms Differ", *Journal of Business Venturing*, 10, no. 2, March 1995, p. 168.

[12]Leslie Brokaw, "New Businesses," *Inc.*, May 1990, p. 25.

[13]Martha E. Mangelsdorf, "Hotline," *Inc.*, July 1990, p. 27.

[14]Leslie Brokaw, "New Businesses," *Inc.*, August 1990, p. 21.

[15]Martha E. Mangelsdorf, "*Inc.*'s Guide to 'Smart' Government Money," *Inc.* August 1990, p. 60.

Case Questions

General Questions

1. How well do capabilities of the entrepreneur in the assigned case align with tasks that must be performed to make the venture a success? What complementary talents should he or she seek and through what specific sequence of actions?

2. Envisage some suitable individuals, in terms of their experience and capabilities, whom the entrepreneur(s) might reasonably be able to attract to this venture situation. Briefly describe each of them. Describe what the principal founder should be willing to give up in order to recruit them. Should they accept such terms?

3. Formulate a set of guidelines for the entrepreneur(s) in the assigned case to follow in hiring (if any) such professionals as you think should be hired to help start the venture.

Case 21 - Bruce Milne (A)   p. 482

1. Develop a grid which lays out on one side the names of people in the case who should receive ownership in the venture. Along the other side list what different people can best contribute to the venture.

2. State how ownership and responsibilities should be divided in the venture and explain why.

Case 22 - Dick Redman   p. 487

1. What ethical issues do you see in this case, and how should they be treated?

2. If the prospective entrepreneurs in this case decide to start a firm of their own, how should the responsibilities and ownership be divided and why?

Case 23 - Andrew Hammoude (B) *p. 493*

1. What sorts of contingencies concerning ownership should be provided for in the bylaws of a company like Imagesystems? What would be the best procedure for working them out among the founders?

2. What advice from the MIT Forum should the company's founders follow and why? What advice should it reject and why?

3. Which of the MIT Forum commenters would be the best one to add to the company, if possible; which would be the poorest, and why?

Case 24 - Chem Synthesis Inc. (C) *p. 499*

1. What is your assessment of Jim's letter and how it should be changed, if at all?

2. Comment on how your answer to the above question might be different depending upon whether you were (1) Jim, (2) any other employee of CSI, (3) an outside CSI shareholder, or (4) a CSI competitor.

3. Should this letter be sent before, concurrently, or after Jim pursues the next round of financing for the company, as described in CSI (B)?

Bruce Milne (A)

As 1979 ended, Bruce Milne, the sales manager of a minicomputer sales company office in Seattle, was considering how to structure ownership in a new company he planned to start with two of his co-employees. The company they worked for sold DEC minicomputers to accountants for the combined functions of accounting and word processing. Bruce had watched with increasing interest as microcomputers had expanded in capabilities and he expected that it was only a matter of time before they too would find application in both accounting and word processing. Because they were much cheaper than minicomputers he expected that once they entered the market for those functions they would spread rapidly. His idea for the new company was to capitalize on that opportunity. To get started he wanted Brian Duthie and Lauri Chandler to join him as partners.

Antecedents of the Idea

Bruce Milne had been engaged in ventures of one kind or another since childhood. He recalled:

> When I was 8, I was already trudging around selling Christmas cards. I liked to buy the stock, go around presenting it to people, make the sales and collect the money. To me it was fun.

Later, as a business major at the University of Washington, he "always had two or three businesses going at once," he recalled. "It was to prevent starvation, because nobody was paying my way."

For instance while working as a lifeguard, he met parents who wanted swimming lessons for their children. Consequently, he rented time at a local pool and set up a swimming school which employed up to four instructors. He continued:

> I'd been a swim instructor and a coach. Then I became a lifeguard for the city. Parents were always asking if there were someplace they could send their kids for lessons. I saw that there were a lot of private pools, and a lot of people in one housing complex wanted lessons. I went to a private pool there, and they let me use the pool until two o'clock on my own. For instructors I hired some fraternity members at the University. I had all the paper boys in the north end put flyers out, and I had a little pyramid scheme where for every customer you bring in, you get a dollar off on your own child. We had a babysitting service where if you bring them for a half-hour they could have a babysitter for two or three hours, so you could go shopping at the Northgate shopping center. We were deluged because we had the cheapest babysitting service in town, plus swim lessons.

He also bought, repaired and sold used Volkswagens, ran a barber service, sold cookware, imported and sold Swiss watches and renovated houses.

After graduation in 1970, Bruce spent the remainder of his savings on a trip to Europe, after which he returned to Seattle and looked for a job. He made application to the University of Washington Business School. He was accepted, but decided not to go. He worked for a company called Canadian American Security Holders (CASH), which was a collection agency. "I thought you'd make money quick at that," he said. "But it was a fly-by -night operation." He soon looked for another job.

In the newspaper classified section, he noticed two jobs of possible interest, one selling office copiers and the other selling computers. "My dad always told me to go to work for a big company," he recalled. After interviewing both he chose the latter and in 1971 went to work for Burroughs Corporation, "It was lucky I made that choice," he said, "because the other job would have been a dead end."

He went through Burroughs' training program and became a sales representative. "The job started at only about $600 to $700 a month," he said. "It took me about five years working full time to get up to the level of income I'd had working part time for myself." He once again went to the University, where he took a couple of night courses toward an MBA, but then dropped out.

In 1973 he encountered a new opportunity in the company.

I had gone to school in Mexico during my sophomore year and always thought it would be interesting to get into international business in some way. There was a guy from Burroughs who was flying through on his way to Japan. My boss said, "I'll see if he can interview you between planes." So I went and said I wanted a job internationally. I was cocky at 24. I said, "I can outsell anybody you have." He said "OK." So I went sight unseen to Puerto Rico. I took a pay cut. I guess a lot of people didn't like that job. It was funny. My three worst subjects in school were Spanish, accounting and computer programming. And so now I was selling

computers for accounting applications in Puerto Rico.

By age 24 he became the youngest sales zone manager in the company. He also got married to a co-worker from Burroughs in Seattle with whom he had stayed in touch.

She had been in real estate sales, and got her job as a Burroughs sales representative after she sold the local sales manager his house—a big 12,000 square foot place in West Seattle that had been a girls' school.

Beginnings of a Business Idea

Software for computer accounting systems at the time was almost entirely a custom activity in the mid-1970s, he recalled.

At one point my wife and I set up another business on the side called Systems Analyst Programmers, because Burroughs would not let us hire any programmers, and we needed them to sell and service the systems for Puerto Rican customers. At Burroughs you had to do your own programming, so we did this other business on the side to try to save some of the installations we had. At one point we had guys from about 10 different companies working for us.

I also picked up software on trips to the United States. Wherever I went around the country, to Chicago or Los Angeles, I'd head straight for the software backroom, rip off a copy of everything they had and take it on the plane with me back to Puerto Rico. So I built a library, even though I wasn't a technical guy, because the software they had in South America was garbage.

Then in 1974, Bruce again decided to apply to business school.

Everything seemed to go in two-year

cycles. After about 18 months in one spot I'd start to get the feeling it was time to move on. I applied to Harvard, IMEDE and Wharton. Then to my pleasant surprise on three successive Saturdays I got acceptances from each one. I felt great. My grades had been passable, but not so good as to give me confidence I'd be accepted.

He started at the Harvard Business School in 1975, majored in finance and spent the following summer working as an intern at nearby Digital Equipment Corporation (DEC).

The question I worked on was basically how do we train the original equipment makers (OEM's) who resold and installed DEC's computers, something DEC itself didn't do. That gave me a great exposure to their OEM channels who developed and sold systems and helped develop the custom software that always had to be part of the package.

During my second year I developed a thesis on "The role of the distributor in a computer environment." It was one of these two-credit courses you could devote your life to. My wife and I sold the report to a number of big companies, including IBM, and made several thousand dollars on it that helped pay tuition. It was the most comprehensive report on that topic available at the time.

It looked at the time like software was going to be a marketing bottleneck. Prices of computers were coming down. People were projecting that computer prices were going to come down by 75 percent, while costs of marketing would triple. Companies like IBM, Burroughs and NCR only sold direct. DEC did almost all its selling through the OEM systems houses. The question was how would you extend the channels around

them? How would you manage those channels? How would you recruit? What should be the credit policies, and so forth? Stores selling software were unheard of.

Following graduation in 1977, Bruce and his wife sought a way to return to the West Coast. Bruce took a job with a Portland, Oregon DEC distributor, Alpine Corporation, to help develop a sales office in Seattle. There his belief that better ways of standardizing and distributing minicomputer software were bound to come continued to grow. He recalled:

I said to Alpine management, "you guys already have a lot of software. Why don't you get a guy in Boston, a guy in Philadelphia, and one in Baltimore and make them dealers to resell your stuff so people won't always be reinventing the wheel. You can get leverage and build a big company." There were no big companies selling minicomputers at that time. The biggest we had at DEC was about $3 million a year, and every year the biggest would go out of business, because they would grow, and they would have all this custom software, they'd overextend themselves . . . and we'd be eating their receivables. They were always trying to supply the stuff with lots of custom applications. DEC would help put them out of business because it would take four months to make shipment, and meanwhile the distributors would run out of cash.

His interest in microcomputers also continued to grow as their capabilities increased. In his travels Bruce became acquainted with John Torode, who studied computer science at the University of Washington, then went to Berkeley to teach, while on the side developing a company to make microcomputers. He was the first, according to Bruce, to develop a machine with two floppy disk drives. It seemed to Bruce that it was only a matter of time before machines like that began to benefit from development of standardized software and find application in offices such as those of the accountants to whom he was selling minicomputers.

Teaming

One of the people he began discussing these ideas with was a co-worker, Brian Duthie. Brian had studied industrial engineering and business at Berkeley, then joined Western Electric in 1969, where he worked in product testing. After hours he studied computers at a nearby technical school. Jobs with other companies followed, selling minicomputers for a sales firm, developing software for an insurance company, then working for a computer consulting firm, mainly installing a purchase order system for Boeing. Seeing insufficient growth in that job, he joined Alpine, where he found himself working for Bruce. Together, the two were responsible for over 40 percent of sales in the 40-person company.

When Bruce, frustrated by Alpine's rejection of his business development ideas, first began talking with Brian about creating a new company, the idea was that they might begin developing microcomputer systems on the side. Bruce developed a connection with Altos Computer in California and suggested that Brian might develop software to go with Altos hardware to make a complete system they could sell to accountants.

But attendance at a night course gave Bruce a different perspective. One of the speakers who had developed several successful companies stressed the idea that he had never been able to do it part time. It was necessary, he said, to take the full plunge if the company were going to be ambitiously growth-oriented. Brian, however, was cautious. Neither he nor Bruce had much savings, and Brian's wife was expecting their first child.

Hoping to persuade Brian, Bruce suggested they visit John Torode in California to see his dual floppy microcomputer. On the trip they could also visit the only company Bruce knew of that offered a standard general ledger software package for minicomputers. Bruce commented:

> Brian, like a true techie, was glad for the chance to get inside a computer "factory" and meet the machine's designer. Then we went over to the software company, told them we might be interested in distributing their product, and asked for a demonstration. We had a yellow pad with us that we took notes on. The demonstration was supposed to last 45 minutes. But after 20 minutes we said we had seen enough. The notes we took on the yellow pad were deficiencies and we already had four pages of them. Like any good programmer, Brian always knew he could make something better. And if this was the leader of the industry, they were in for real trouble.

Now Brian was ready to go with the new venture. The idea would be to sell DEC minicomputer systems with existing software for the short term to derive income, which would support development of better software by Brian for the longer term. The software would be for microcomputers, and when it was ready, the new company would sell systems combining it with Altos computers to accountants.

Bruce had also persuaded his secretary, Lauri Chandler, to join the team. Lauri had become skilled at word processing on the minicomputer systems Alpine sold.

Designing the Ownership Structure

As Bruce saw it, each of the three would bring different ingredients to the new venture. Brian would be crucial as the "resident genius" software developer. He would also be important in helping sell and install minicomputer systems for income while the company was getting started.

Lauri would help with two functions. One would be to run the office of the new venture itself. The other would be to serve as a consultant on the word processing aspects of the minicomputer installations sold during the company's first phase of existence.

Bruce would take primary responsibility for selling minicomputer systems during the first stage. He expected one major problem would be to obtain the computers to sell, since the company, because of its smallness, would not initially qualify as an OEM for DEC. "It's ironic," he observed. "One of the very systems I helped set up at DEC would now prevent us from becoming an OEM for them."

However, Bruce had become well-acquainted with DEC's channels and believed he would be able to buy through contacts he had in a consortium headquartered in North Dakota. This would reduce the discount they would receive on equipment from 30 percent down to perhaps 25 percent, but he expected it would enhance speed of delivery, since the buying consortium always had more units on order than a typical systems house handling DEC products, and therefore could provide faster and more dependable delivery.

Bruce would also be responsible for raising capital. Each of the three, it appeared, would be able to muster $10,000. To do so, the three would have to commit all their personal savings and, in some cases, borrow from relatives. Bruce would be able to go without salary in the near term, thanks to his wife's income, but the other two would need to be paid. So it seemed clear to all three that more capital would have to be raised. Bruce knew of three individuals he might be able to raise another $10,000 each from within a couple of months if they could get the company set up and operating. One was an entrepreneur with a cheesecake manufacturing company to whom Bruce had sold a minicomputer. The second was a lawyer whom Bruce had tried to sell without success, but had nevertheless become a good friend. The third was a former competitor who had recently made large profits from shares he held when his employer went public.

If the new firm were able to raise another $30,000 from these individuals, Bruce expected that it might last only a few months, after which, if Brian were successful in developing the microcomputer software, they would need another infusion two or three times that large to move ahead with its distribution. How he would accomplish that, he was not sure. He supposed it would necessitate recruiting more shareholders from somewhere.

Bruce also knew some sales prospects to whom he thought the new company would be able to sell minicomputer systems in the near term. But as in the case of the potential sources of capital, that possibility remained to be tested.

His immediate problem was how to structure ownership between himself and his two initial colleagues, both to get the company started and to establish a base for further development in the future.

Dick Redman

In the fall of 1990 Dick Redman and two associates working with him at Pacific Mogul Tours in Portland, Oregon, were considering which of several alternative career directions to take. One would be simply to stay with Pacific Mogul in their present jobs. A second would be to attempt a buy-out of their employer. A third would be to undertake a start-up of their own, by one of several possible routes. They had been trying to explore each of these options discreetly without compromising their jobs, but this was becoming increasingly difficult. Consequently, all were feeling pressure to make clear decisions promptly and take decisive actions one way or the other.

The Tour Business

Travel tours produced by Pacific Mogul could be bought from any travel agent. Someone wanting to take a trip through the Canadian Rockies, for example, could arrange the trip without buying such a tour, either by arranging tickets with airlines and accommodations directly or by doing so through a travel agent who would make them directly. There might be a flight to Vancouver, followed by a train ride to Banff, then a hotel stay in Banff, where the person might arrange to take a sightseeing bus, and so forth. The individual, with or without an agent, would plan these details directly and personally cope with any problems they produced on the trip.

Alternatively, the person might purchase from a company like Pacific Mogul a pre-packaged tour in which all of these tickets and accommodations were already set up for pre-established itinerary. Then the traveler would write out one check for the whole package. The tour might again begin with a plane ride to Vancouver, and perhaps there the traveler would be met by a tour guide who would lead all those who had bought that particular itinerary through the travels it entailed. Advantages for the traveler of this arrangement would be that the same trip, when bought as a package would be cheaper than buying the individual components of the trip separately. Additionally, it would be more convenient to have all the arrangements worked out in advance rather than having to take chances and piecing them together. Having a tour guide to solve any problems that arose enroute could further enhance convenience.

The function of Pacific Mogul in this process was to design and arrange the different components of the tour, airline reservations, hotel reservations, tour guide and so forth. The company would set it up for some anticipated number of travelers, perhaps 30. Travel agents then would make commissions on sales they made to travelers. The advantage to the travel agent or retailer who sold the tours to consumers was the ability to offer individual customers the rate and convenience advantages of group travel without having to organize a group. For its part, Pacific Mogul would, in effect, collect groups of travelers by selling through all interested travel agents, and would make its profit through buying the tickets and accommodations at quantity discounts.

To make this work, Mogul had to be

able to do several things. One was to design attractive trips. The itinerary, accommodations, sightseeing excursions, and timing of events had to be such that people would like to experience them. It would be a mistake, for instance, to combine too many days of traveling without an appropriate number of days of layover and relaxation. But too many of the latter in series might let travelers get bored. Accommodations had to be suitably matched in quality to tour price, and the total price had to fit pocketbooks of people likely to want to do the things the tour involved. Any misalignments might not sell, or worse, would produce unhappy customers, who in turn would spoil the tour company's reputation with travel agents.

Selection and training of tour guides was also important to the process. Mogul normally hired college students in summer. They did not receive much in the way of cash, but had all their expenses paid to accompany tours. At the conclusion of a tour each customer was asked to rate the quality of all elements of the tour, including the guide. Those guides who received lowest ratings were promptly dropped from Mogul's roster.

To maintain tour components, Mogul's president, Walter Langdon, and his son, who was vice-president of the company, continually traveled to various hotels, arranging for blocks of rooms at needed dates, and negotiating prices and terms. Hotels customarily allowed cancellation of reservations only up to a certain date before use, after which Mogul would have to pay.

To market tour packages, the two also visited key agents in selected parts of the country, according to the particular tours and markets for which they were aimed. The company spent approximately $40,000 per year on elaborate colored brochures with photographs and written information describing the tours. These were given away at trade shows and mailed to agents around the country. Typically, trade shows were sponsored by major airlines. At those shows wholesalers who made substantial use of the particular lines in their tours were given free booths for displaying tours and distributing literature. Travel agents were given free travel to attend these shows, where they would circulate among the booths, picking up information on tours they felt their clientele might find of interest. In its Portland office Pacific Mogul maintained several WATS lines, so travel agents could make collect telephone calls to obtain information about its tours.

The Three Associates

Dick Redman began his MBA studies at Portland State in 1986 and graduated in 1988. For three summers during school, he worked as a tour escort for Pacific Mogul. He recalled:

> I would welcome 40 people from all over the USA, when they arrived in Portland to begin the tour. Then for the next 14 days I would accompany them around, making sure everything worked as advertised on the itinerary they had bought and doing my best to solve any problems that arose in such a way as to keep every customer as happy as possible.

Upon graduation, Dick was invited by Walter Langdon, Mogul's president, to join the company full time as vice-president for operations. This, in effect, meant he was in charge of all the tour escorts and responsible for seeing that things went smoothly during the tours. In negotiating to accept this job, Dick told Mr. Langdon that the salary was less than he could earn elsewhere with his MBA. Mr. Langdon, he said, replied that if Dick did his job well and got along in the company, there would be opportunity in the near future to obtain a share of ownership in the company as well as profit sharing as additional incentive.

Jack Miller, like Dick Redman, was in his late 20s when he, too, joined Mogul Tours in 1988. Prior to that, he had graduated from college in liberal arts, spent two years in the military and then joined the sales office of a major hotel chain, where he rapidly rose to national sales manager. He then briefly worked for another Pacific Northwest tour wholesaling company before joining Pacific Mogul as vice president for marketing. He was now responsible for opening facilities negotiations, which were then followed through by Dick Redman, and for carrying out sales campaigns directed by the president. Jack said he chafed somewhat at this direction and wanted to make more of the marketing decisions himself.

Ellen Wilson was in her late 30s. She had worked as a stenographer before getting married and then had quit her job to raise a family. When her children were grown, she began to look for another job and happened, in 1981, to meet the son of Walter Langdon, who at that time was just beginning to set up Pacific Mogul. She recalled:

> *I came in on the ground floor when the company was just starting and worked on a lot of different aspects of getting it going. Essentially, I handled all of the internal operations of the office except bookkeeping, while Walter designed the tours, set them up and sold them to the agents.*

As of late 1990, Ellen was in charge of office operations, responsible for seeing that paperwork, including correspondence, ticket processing, reservation confirmation and other records—as well as phone communications—were handled effectively. She said, however, that she would prefer to have more influence on policy decisions

of the internal operations, not just responsibility for seeing that they were implemented.

Like both Dick and Jack, Ellen said she was dissatisfied with her pay. The three of them, although they had never seen financial statements of the company, believed that Walter Langdon and his son were taking home substantial bonuses. The company was prospering, as judged by the number of tour sales it was closing compared to competitors. Both Langdons were exhibiting signs of prosperity and both had withdrawn substantially from operations, leaving it to employees to carry on the work all day while the two owners put in only brief appearances at the office each morning. Essentially, the trio felt that they were doing most of the management work for low pay while the Langdons were reaping the rewards of leisure and high pay.

Buy-Out Negotiations

The ownership sharing opportunities, which Dick Redman had discussed earlier with Walter Langdon, had to Dick's disappointment, never materialized. Whenever he attempted to bring the subject up, Mr. Langdon indicated that the right time had not yet arrived, and Dick had begun to wonder if it ever would. Then, to his surprise, he learned that the Langdons had been discussing with outside parties the possibility of selling the company. Jack Miller was surprised at this news also. He and Dick approached Walter Langdon and suggested that rather than selling the company to outsiders it might make sense to sell to employees instead. Mr. Langdon, Jack recalled, said, "All right, why don't you see what you can do about making me an offer?" Jack continued.

> *That was all I needed. Through some people I had met who knew about the financial community, I got in touch with a local stock brokerage house. I didn't*

know exactly how much we needed, but the business appeared to be very profitable, and it didn't need a lot of capital for fixed assets. The brokerage house said that some of their clients liked to get involved in private placement deals, so they should have no trouble raising as much as a million dollars.

But when we went back to Walter with that, he really blew up. He said he would want at least a million and a half, and that we had no business going around talking about the company being for sale. Through his attorney, he sent a letter to the broker saying something to the effect that any representation by us was without the knowledge or authority of the owners of the company, and any actions the broker would take based upon these representations would be at the broker's own risk. The broker called us to apologize and gave us his sympathy.

Neither Dick, Jack nor Ellen had any substantial savings with which to buy the company, or alternatively, to start one. Consequently, Dick and Jack began searching for contacts who might be able to help, and found two additional alternatives. Details of the terms could not be worked out because the exact amount needed had not been established. However, the first source, a venture capital group with enormous financial resources, indicated willingness to consider providing all the capital needed in return for 60 percent of the stock. Terms would include continuing the three associates at pay approximately 30 percent above their current rates and giving them a free hand in running the business; nobody in the venture capital group had any experience in the travel business, nor did they want to acquire any.

A second potential source was a travel agency, which said it might be willing to share ownership on an equal basis, 50 percent for it and 50 percent for the three associates. Salary conditions would be similar to those suggested by the venture capital group. The agency had, to a limited extent, developed some tours of its own, which it would turn over to the three as part of the deal. Financial resources of the agency were somewhat limited, however, and its main customer was one airline which had been considering some schedule changes. If it eliminated certain flights in which the agency specialized, the agency would have serious problems and could possibly fail. Financing from the agency would be provided on an installment basis to ease the drain.

Strategic Options

It seemed to the three that there were several directions they might choose to pursue. One would be to continue trying to buy out the Langdons, either wholly or partially. Perhaps they could satisfy the Langdons and achieve their own desires through a buy-out that worked in stages or based upon some sort of contingencies. However, they did not know what the Langdons might find acceptable in that regard, or how to find out, since prior attempts to explore the subject had failed.

A second option would be to set up a new tour wholesaling company. This would require substantial expenditures. Dick expected the biggest expense would be salaries for setting up an office, working up tour packages, preparing advertising materials, arranging reservations and selling to travel agents. This could take several months, during which income would start and rise slowly as tours were sold. Preparation of advertising brochures would probably cost about $60,000, he said. Printing he expected would cost another $20,000, and other advertising from $40,000 to $60,000. All these estimates had to be rough, Dick said, because the only people privy to financial information at Mogul had been the two owners.

Other major items he estimated were mailing expenses for the brochures, as much as $30,000, attending trade shows, possibly $20,000 to $30,000, and other company travel, at least $2,000 per month. Taking incoming phone calls collect and making outgoing sales calls might cost around $2,000 per month. Office space should be available for $1,000 to $1,500 per month. Office supplies, utilities and other expense items might add another several thousand, but he was not sure. There would be expenses for minor supplies in connection with tours for things such as bag tags, but these should not be much, perhaps $6 per customer. Dick's feeling was that if the company managed to sign up between 1,500 and 1,800 customers during the year, mostly in the summer, it would be doing fairly well.

Once they decided what to include in the tour, they could estimate selling prices and variable costs for tours in a relatively straightforward matter. Typical markups of the industry could be computed by working back from their prices and a knowledge of variable costs. The three associates worked up a half dozen tour designs based upon what they knew to be selling well for other firms, and Dick computed likely sale prices and variable costs for those tours, as shown in Exhibit 1. How sales might vary from one tour to another, he was not sure. He noted, however, that gross margin did not vary too greatly among them anyway. On the average, he expected each tour might run 10 times with around 30 travelers.

A third option would be to keep their jobs with Mogul and continue as before. The company was growing, and the three were advancing, both in responsibility as the number of people subordinate to them expanded, and financially through salary raises and bonuses. Since they were largely running the company while the Langdons were not around, it seemed to them their bargaining positions might be

good for attempting to obtain more substantial raises and perhaps a share of company profits. Should this fail, they all believed they would have no trouble obtaining other similar jobs, since they felt they had built good reputations based upon the work they had performed for Mogul.

Issues of Concern

How to work things out with the owner was something all three associates had been considering. Dick commented:

> One matter that concerns us is loyalty. How much do we owe our employer? How far should we go in any of these strategic directions based on that loyalty? All three of us have learned a lot working here, and we are grateful for that. But we are somewhat dissatisfied, and we have been frustrated in trying to work things out with the company so far. Our employer is probably pulling somewhere on the order of $200,000 to $400,000 of profit out of this company, based upon mostly our work, as we see it. For that we don't seem to be getting paid very much, and we would like to see that change.
>
> The company is healthy and growing, but the owner's price seems awfully high, since people in the financial community have told us a P/E ratio of around two or three is more typical for a company like this.

An additional concern was division of ownership and responsibilities. Discussions among the three associates had tentatively concluded that Jack Miller would most likely become president, since he had the most experience as a travel business executive. But Jack's feeling was that the office or president should carry with it a substantially higher salary than those of vice presidents, which the other two would then hold. The other two disagreed with this and felt that since they were basically partners and peers, they should share equally in ownership and salaries.

Starting a new company would raise some of the same concerns. The three believed it would be crucial to obtain accommodation commitments from certain popular hotels that could pick and choose among tours because they tended to fill in advance. Also crucial would be to recruit enough of the 30,000 travel agents around the country to sell the tours actively in competition with the other 400-odd tour wholesalers currently in operation. For this reason, the three expected that raising capital for selling expenditures would be needed. Whether these kinds of commitments could be obtained, the three did not know. But they agreed it would be unethical to contact prospective accommodation operators and travel agents for a company of their own as long as they were employed by Pacific Mogul. They believed word of such attempts would get around and would both end their jobs and make it difficult for them to obtain similar jobs elsewhere.

EXHIBIT 1   Estimated Tour Pricing

Tour	Per Traveler Selling Price*	Per Traveler Variable Costs**
A	$1,110	$852
B	$1,190	$844
C	$1,250	$914
D	$1,490	$1,186
E	$1,750	$1,396
F	$1,090	$824

---

*   Assumes an average of 30 travelers per tour.

**   Includes expenses and salary of tour guide or escort.

Andrew Hammoude (B)

The M.I.T. Forum

Dr. Andrew Hammoude and his partners had applied to the Seattle chapter of the M.I.T. Forum to have their business plan reviewed and to receive expert advice for their venture. (Please see the Andrew Hammoude case for further background.) The M.I.T. Forum was an activity organized by the Alumni Office of the Massachusetts Institute of Technology. Entrepreneurs could submit their plans to a local chapter of the Forum, which would then select one for review by a volunteer expert panel. The panelists would be chosen based on relevance of their expertise to the particular venture. They would review the plan, meet with the entrepreneur, examine the product or service and develop appropriate advice.

This advice would be presented at a public, two-hour meeting in the evening. The meeting would begin with dinner. By the time dessert was being served, the presentation would begin. The entrepreneur and his or her colleagues would stand before the assembly and describe their enterprise. Then each member of the expert panel would present his or her observations and advice. After that, members of the audience would be invited to ask questions and make comments, which would conclude the evening.

IMAGEsystems was the subject of an M.I.T. Forum meeting in Seattle on November 14, 1988. The panelists included two founders of profitable and rapidly growing small firms in microcomputer applications, a sales executive from a major microcomputer manufacturer, and an ana-lyst from a venture capital firm. The following is a digest of their comments and those of others in the audience after the entrepreneurs' presentation.

Panelists' Comments
Entrepreneur #1

I came out of a very technical background myself and went through much the same thing as you. When we first started our company and were talking to the banks, looking for cash flow commitments to fund our operations and our receivables. The banks were not ready to put more at risk than we were. So you should quit your jobs when you are ready to become a company. Until that, you have not made a commitment that you are a company.

Divide responsibility now. Write it down. Have succinct job descriptions of what each of you is going to do. There is an instinct for all of you to want to be involved in all aspects of the company. The result is that you will all be juggling parallel work, which will lower your efficiency tremendously. Communication is an n-factorial process. When there are four of you, that's not much of an overhead. But when you grow to eight, 16 or 32 people n factorial becomes a very large number. You need to establish clearly defined channels of communication and responsibility. With the latter must go ownership. You must own responsibility. If you have that early on, then you won't be in each other's way, and you will be effective. Decide what it is now and get it done.

You have spent 30 years obtaining technical skills that will give you an unfair advantage in the marketplace. It is important that you obtain similar levels of business skills. You must draw on those to be successful. You must find assistance for those: financial, legal, sales and marketing.

The model we followed was a good one. You don't need a CPA, but you do need a part-time bookkeeper. You need to get off on the right foot. Get in touch with one of the significant accounting firms, have somebody help you set up the books correctly and get you going. Have them recommend someone who can help you on a part-time basis. But get your books set up correctly first. The accounting firm also will know the banking community and can help by making introductions for you there, which can go a long way in helping you get your line of credit.

You don't need a lawyer in house, but you need one to get set up correctly. There are certain issues that we struggled with early on that paid dividends later. Think about your current team. You're all best of friends now. So were the five of us when we started our company. But as our organization matured, our personal goals changed and some of us parted ways. You need to think now, while you're all still good friends, what will you do, how will you divide the stock, what are the rights of people that leave the company with their stock? Should there be buy-back options? Will the company self-destruct if one of you decides to change lifestyle?

The company will live or die based on its ability to sell products in the marketplace. This is not the time to give somebody in the company on-the-job training in sales. You need to find somebody who has been there before and who has taken a company through the stages

you are struggling with. You should consider a staged approach. Somebody who has taken a company to thirty or forty million in sales is not what you need at first. Such a person would be very expensive. But you do need somebody who has taken a company out a few years to around three to five million in revenues. You want that person to have ownership in the company, to own stock, to lust after making it succeed and seeing that stock mature into something of value.

Can you bootstrap the company and grow internally, or do you need outside capital to grow and fund the company? We cannot answer that for you. It is a question you have to answer yourself. But here are some questions to consider.

You are looking at what is claimed to be a fast-growing market with a limited window of opportunity for introducing this product and achieving market penetration. So there are certain boundary conditions that will control whether you can grow from inside or need outside capital.

What is a significant window of opportunity? If you are going after less than 30 percent of the market, you ought to get out right now. How long can you afford not to be a significant player and still be able to capture 30 percent of the market? What do you expect the life of your sales cycle to be? Does it take two weeks or six months from first contact to closing a sale? Each has different implications for recovering return on investment.

How long a production run can you afford? How long will it take to do a run? What are the cash requirements to initiate that production run? When must you pay for all the costs? Basically, the question is what volume of inventory can you support today to support the sales and cash flow? An-

swers to these questions will reveal whether you can bootstrap your company or will need outside capital to enter the market through the window of opportunity you have.

Be extremely conservative with your costs and sales estimates. A company that fails in this area will not be a candidate for additional venture financing. It's far better to start with more cash than to run out and find you need more and are at the mercy of the venture capitalists.

Judging from your plan, you are positioning your product as basically the "high-priced spread," versus something cheap and ubiquitous. That may be appropriate, but I'm concerned that the company may be driven by academic rather than market goals. What is the real market opportunity for entry? Almost every other word you speak should be "customer." You must be customer driven, market driven. Maybe the high-priced spread is the right approach, but you really need to understand who the clients are and how you can meet their needs.

So in summary, you have a tremendous challenge and exciting time ahead of you. I wouldn't exchange running a company for anything. Yours is an exciting business, and it is admirable that you are asking the questions you are. I wish we had done that at your stage of growth.

Entrepreneur #2

From my experience since starting our company just two years ago, I'd say you have to hock everything you have, take out a personal loan, open a garage someplace and get started. You need that level of commitment before anyone will be willing to buy your products. They won't buy if they think you are hedging.

If you want to become known as the lead company in the industry, with 30 percent of the market or more, you will have to buy market share out of profits. You must set a goal of reminding yourself every morning to become a customer-driven company. To do that you must get early sales revenues from somewhere. For a venture capitalist to be interested, you must ask who is the end-user and why will he buy? Are the unfair advantages I have worthy of the price?

I would go out in brute force; buy a list of all the system integrators in the United States. Get on the phone and start calling, working down from the top. You need to wrap something more around the technology that you have for a specific purpose and niche. Look for a niche in which somebody is selling hundred-thousand-dollar-plus workstations, because there you can sell for a higher price. That will let you show some profit, which is the only way you will motivate investors.

The big players are coming into this industry. There are no entry barriers. You have an opportunity to enter with low investment, seed capital and guerrilla tactics, personal loans, licensing of the technology, selling one-offs here and there to individual R&D groups. This can give you a toehold. But in about two years these opportunities will not exist. The market you're addressing seems to be a large number of vertical segments— people building products for specific end-user, vertical applications in fairly narrow markets number from 25 to maybe several hundred, if you are lucky.

In a couple of years it's not going to be much of a hardware game anymore. The big computer makers will be bringing in products and pulling the distribution channels together for more effective distribution. That will bring down margins and raise barriers to entry.

Microcomputer Company Sales Executive

You have to be the best in some area and get some wins soon. We are looking hard at the possibilities of this market. We use market consulting firms quite often. Second and third opinions can really help. You have to consider what segments you want to work, how big they are and how fast they are growing.

There are three major areas of distribution we consider: (1) direct sales with your own sales force—loyal but costly, and it has to be large for mass market, (2) distributors—they are order-takers; you must advertise and generate sales for them. (Plusses are that they will hold inventory), (3) value added resellers—people providing solutions to a problem, who take pieces of hardware and software and provide a total solution to their customers; they really know their market. They are people you could really get on the bandwagon with, but only after you decide on what market you are really going after.

Venture Capital Analyst

What are your goals? To develop a nice little company and maybe sell it off or continue running it? Or to go public? Some entrepreneurs prefer the former, but we are only interested in the latter.

You must understand and properly project your cash requirements. Venture capitalists don't like to be surprised by urgent calls for more cash. How much you aim to raise should be tied to a set of milestones or goals closely aligned with product development and with some sort of customer satisfaction or adoption rate.

If you write a plan and decide you will need $5 million to become self-sustaining, don't try to raise it all at once—that would sell you short. If you can take a smaller amount first and use it to reach a greater valuation for your company, then you can charge a higher price for ownership.

Banks are an unlikely source for you. I am on the board of two companies with sales of around $30 million. Neither of them got bank money until they had three quarters of profitability. Venture capital is next least likely, because it wants hotter deals than yours is at this point. Our deal structure depends on the business, its plan, prospects, etc. But the typical deal is 60 percent going to the investors and 40 to management, with half of that set aside to cut in other key people the company will need to recruit in the future. There are pros and cons to that, and some other venture capital firms do it differently, but that's the way we typically work.

Individual investors would be a better bet for you. Accountants, consultants and lawyers can lead you to them. Your most likely source, though, is suppliers and customers. See if you can't figure a way to get a customer sold to the point of putting up $200,000 to get you started.

You should go out and hire a big-six accountant. A lot of companies have developed accounting software packages. Each accounting firm has its favorite. Get the right package the first time, because correcting it later can be a disaster. One company I knew had its MRP supplier go into Chapter 11. The company was shipping about $8 million in hardware revenues. The hardware price was over $55,000, there were a lot of parts in it, and we had no idea where they were. We couldn't get the source code, because the company was in Chapter 11.

Part-time bookkeepers can be very helpful in accounting and even beyond that. Having the proper controls set up within the company, so one partner can't take money without the other one knowing it, is very important.

A company we were involved in down in Dallas had two very good people running it. The president was 65. The other was a very bright 35-year-old marketing woman with an MBA from Northwestern, who was one of the sharpest marketing people I ever met. I got a call from her on a Thursday asking me to please come down.

She had done some snooping and found out that the president's wife had terminal cancer. His company had been in trouble since it started, so we had been putting money in every three weeks. That president had been embezzling to pay medical bills, because he wasn't taking any salary, and he had no insurance coverage on his wife. He never told anyone in the company or any of the directors. So you have to set up controls in the company to make sure money doesn't disappear.

Comments from Members of the Audience
(Each paragraph denotes the start of a different person's comment.)

An engineer is always in the final stages of development. Don't make that mistake.

Could you sell your product to GE or Phillips rather than the user? Their expertise is not image processing but rather in manipulation of the signals coming back. Your opportunity is to sell the OEM a better tool set.

Those big companies are looking for strategic partners because they know they cannot do things fast internally.

To enter the radiologist market you might try selling to medical schools.

There is a company called Strider Technology that does imaging for radiological applications.

(Dr. Hammoude) *We will have to look into that.*

You and your partners should use a Saturday to develop matching lists of goals.

(Response from Dr. Hammoude) *We do have different temperaments. I am glad my partners heard you say this. I think we should have more bull sessions, but have encountered resistance from some of my partners. It's hard to justify a bull session when we have got to get software out.*

How many people in this room have seen a market research projection from Dataquest, or from Frost and Sullivan or anyone else that was right for three years ahead? You will learn far more from just meeting with several of your clients.

(Computer Sales Executive) *The first thing you need to do is identify what market you are really after. We use focus groups of a dozen or so behind a videotaping mirror. It is frustrating the way our message does not get across.*

You should visit computer hardware companies in Seattle and Portland to describe your product and get ideas.

If you can get a strategic partner you may be able to use market research they have done.

Four sources of market information are (1) customers, (2) competitors, (3) potential competitors, and (4) market research firms. To get information from that fourth one free, call another company that has bought it and borrow the report from them.

Be careful not to waste your time on people who don't know the market. Identify several thought leaders around the country and go see them.

You could pick one industry, like real estate, and lash together a demonstration of your product, something zippy, then rent a small booth in a show and take orders.

That suggestion is dangerous. If you can't deliver, it can ruin your company.

(Entrepreneur #1) We find that general market data are not very helpful. But specific questions such as "What are the advantages of this competitor" can be very powerful. You can task somebody to go learn that.

(Venture Capital Analyst) Investors may find the "top down" market information of interest because it gives clues about total potential for growth.

It is very hard to get market data from a company like Dataquest about a market that has not developed yet.

(Venture Capital Analyst) You will need some of those reported market numbers to use as references in developing your business plan. You can't pull them out of thin air for that purpose. But since you have not identified a need for what you are developing, I don't see how you could possibly generate any numbers and I can't imagine any source you could go to for numbers. Don't quit your jobs until you know what the need is for your product. Who needs it?

You should get the market reports simply to verify the numbers you have come up with and possibly to identify surprises that you have not thought about.

I used to be a venture analyst, and I remember looking at marvelous numbers in business plans. They never came true.

Don't keep working for perfection. Pick a niche and get started. You can move to other niches later.

I'm not sure you need a niche. Can you make it cheap enough to go after larger markets?

You have no market, no user, no sales experience, no manufacturing experience. You have a product that is difficult to sell because you have to educate. You have no money, consensus or plan. Why don't you sell your technology as soon as possible for whatever you can get for it and do something else.

(Entrepreneur #1) I think there is a lot of merit to that comment. But I think our country would lose a lot of its special value if all the founders of small companies understood the odds that they are up against. They would not do startups. I think it is important that sometimes there is a little naiveté, there is bravery and things are born. I think you are asking the right questions. I think you're going in the right direction. The odds are overwhelmingly against you. But a lot of people have made it.

(Moderator) I think from the M.I.T. Forum's standpoint, we'll close on that comment rather than the previous one. Thank you.

Chem Synthesis, Inc. (C) *

Communicating With Co-Owners

In February 1995 Jim Tolivre, chief financial officer and chairman of the board of Chem Synthesis, Inc. (CSI), sat in his office pondering the draft of a letter he had recently written to his shareholders. A copy of this draft appears in Exhibit 1. He wondered whether it should read differently and, if so, how. For further background on the company, please refer to two prior case chapters, CSI (A) and CSI (B).

At the last annual shareholder's meeting in late spring 1994, Jim had promised reluctantly to write a quarterly letter to shareholders updating them on the company's progress. As the months passed he waited for the good news that always seemed to be just out of reach. Even the other members of the management team had supported his delay in writing; however, he thought the time had come to act. The question, as he saw it, was how to tell shareholders that the only good news was the company's potential, a story he had told many times before. The plain fact was, however, that CSI had sustained its fifth straight year of losses.**

Although he didn't yet know whether CSI would survive its current cash crisis, he thought it would. There seemed to be enough money available or obtainable to make it through to April when substantial orders were predicted. The prospects for raising more cash, he said, were good. But he couldn't be sure. He shuddered at the idea of writing a letter to the shareholders that reflected only optimism and then have the company fold for lack of cash. However, he said, now was not the time to lose faith. Losing faith could be catching.

---

* Written in collaboration with Dr. W. Ed McMullan of the University of Calgary as a basis for class discussion. Names have been disguised.
** All dollar amounts in this case are in Canadian currency.

EXHIBIT 1: Draft of Letter to Shareholders

CHEM SYNTHESIS, INC.

A Story of Struggle and Survival

January 6, 1995

Dear

We begin this story in January 1994 with prospects and promise for growth with a lack of results and end this story in January 1995 with more prospects and promise for growth and a persistent lack of acceptable results. The short version of the story is your investment is alive and that based on current events, we feel that the future will be prosperous. However, the past is loaded with learning experiences (a euphemism for losses which the optimist would call loss carried forward). On March 21, 1995 Chem Synthesis, Inc. (CSI) will be five years old as a corporation, an average time period some research shows that it takes manufacturing enterprises to become profitable. There is still time for us yet.

The promise and prospects at the beginning of 1994 centered on the Czech Republic and our ambitious agents for that country. They promised $4,000,000 in sales contracted and in place with a variety of government departments and businesses. They had details in abundance and were willing to reduce their projections to writing. We believed them. I'm sure they believed themselves. We moved to a 36,000 square foot facility first on the basis of this promise and the necessity of being prepared. The financing was all to be in place with Czech banks based on the strength of government contracts. The second support for the move came from the fact that our R&D people had succeeded in meeting a difficult combination of desirable features for a repulpable paper coating for a $200,000,000 company on the Toronto Stock Exchange. The product was urgently required to their specifications and at their bidding. The sales volumes involved would have largely covered the overhead according to the figures they provided.

When we moved, we were covered twice over and given the confidence of the parties, the good times were set to roll around the summer of 1994, and believe you-me, we were ready for good times after four years of struggle and two previous failed launches (the first with a strategic alliance partner, Highdry, and second with a low-cost direct-sales strategy into the U.S.). It seemed that we never had adequate funds to spend on sales and marketing, but then again our marketing strategy failed to provide clear signals of which patterns of expenditures would be worthwhile. In retrospect it would have been easy to have spent a lot of money (had it been available) on shot-in-the-dark projects. Our collective ignorance showed more than once.

EXHIBIT 1: (Continued)

Spring was promise delayed. First the discovery by our customer for repulpable paper coating that they had provided one criterion too few. They had not adequately thought through the application issues and when the pilot test came, the product failed for its inability to withstand shear force. Back to the lab. When you change one small criterion for a chemical formulation you are forced a long ways back towards square one with no clear picture of how long it will take, or even if it is possible to create a new and more complete formulation. I remember asking Ted in June how he would determine when we should stop chasing a formula for an, as of yet, non-existent product. He said by way of answer, "When I run out of good ideas." As it turned out, it was the end of the following month when we produced our first feasible formula for the generation-two product. I have since asked myself on more than one occasion, how do you know whether you are whipping a dead horse or not by pursuing a company from one year of losses to the next year of losses. My answer at the current time is "when your opportunities are persistently waning more than they are waxing." As I said before, we are still getting deeper into the wax.

By April we had been madly manufacturing and shipping product to the Czechs and were awaiting the first round of sales and thus payments, and a second, even larger round of shipments. Meanwhile, in the Czech Republic it rained and we waited. We waited through April, as it rained through May and June we waited, and waited even more. They hit a 40-year record for rainfall in that time period. Anything they tried to put on a roof was washed off. Once again we learned the agony of waiting and faced the prospects of diminishing sales and fading hopes. Then to make matters worse, our roofing system proved inadequate without fabric over one of three substrates, raising questions of the credibility of our products. The bank financing had never been large enough to get the level of inventory over there that our agents were sure was needed. Their biggest applicator folded. The agent decided our roofing fabric was too expensive so they substituted a Czech-made fabric. But when the applicators found out that the fabric was made in the Czech Republic they refused to use the system. They feared that Czech-made products were inferior; as it turned out they were right—it was inferior. We tried substituting the fabric with a cheap American made fabric. It was of a decent quality, but it was almost unworkable. The summer was a disaster of shattered dreams. Not only was our plan unraveling in front of our eyes, we had little idea of where to go from there. By mid-July, our prospects had waned massively. In retrospect, new ideas were percolating through August, but I was still in shock all the way through to September 1.

There were three new prospects replacing the old ones in the summer. Two of our people identified a niche market for an acrylic-based coating (similar to the roofing product) for use in coating the base of grain bins. As events have had it:

EXHIBIT 1: (Continued)

- the market was local (hurrah).

- the market was a true niche market.

- the competition was either of poor quality or three times the price.

- the product could be trialed cheaply.

- the distribution channels were large, accessible and cooperative.

- the margins were good.

- the need was strongly felt and the cost low per grain bin protected (e.g. $20 for a 14 foot bin).

- the farmers had money.

- the trade fairs for getting word out were established.

These things we discovered through time as we quickly moved the product from one to 26 stores in just over a month, the last month in which the product can be used before winter. United Farmers of Ontario, a $350-million business, is working with us not only to market the product in Ontario and possibly Saskatchewan and Manitoba. Also, they have committed to help us with contacts into the U.S. Our projections of sales of this product into Ontario alone is $600,000 plus for next year.

Meanwhile, a relationship we began in February with a Kuwaiti agent was maturing. He advised us to bid on a turnkey operation to coat the third largest communications tower in the world. This actually came to full awareness as the grain bin coating was still evolving. We put together a bid through the summer and into the fall. The contract was to be let in September, then October, then November. Right now I think that the negotiations may be complete in January. We should make some money on this but for a variety of reasons we are shifting to a consultant role from that of a subcontractor. Our Kuwaiti agent is also buying StoneSet epoxy and roofing product from us. He continues to bid on projects and has always paid the full price on purchase order even though his terms are 50 percent on order and 50 percent prior to shipment. The Kuwaiti agent continues to provide us with more prospects.

EXHIBIT 1: (Continued)

Then there is our repulpable paper coating for Bindo Packaging. It has been tested in a U.S. production setting and passed. The next step is a local pilot test in Niagara Falls. This time, they have been much slower and painstakingly more careful in their introduction. They don't want to blow it this time. In reality we get closer and closer to yet one more goal line.

In the early fall, we also produced a low-cost fire retarding primer for yet another agent with would-be clients lined up and ready to purchase. First they were to purchase in October, then November and then . . . The first order is/was to be for approximately $310,000. Could it be just around the corner? We heard the other day that it was coming again.

And then there are the current advances in epoxies: a new system for agricultural usage, a better (in fact world-class) StoneSet and an industrial flooring product with good chemical resistance targeted at a market currently emerging by government fiat. One point that you should be getting by now is that through all the mayhem of our sales and marketing efforts, our R&D team has kept a steady stream of world-class products at world-competitive prices coming our way. The opportunities abound. In reality the game is one of prioritizing. Our first priority is the agricultural distribution channels and markets, in part because we have the right lead products and for all the reasons previously given. Next year roofing is expected to provide 5 percent or less of the gross margin contribution, indicating that we are currently much more than a roofing products company. Our roofing products hold promise for large sales over time but they are currently not a priority because the roofing market for liquid applied acrylics is more expensive to penetrate than are some of the other markets we are addressing.

Over the time frame discussed, there have been a number of personnel changes, in particular the additions of Les Banner (agricultural sales), Bill Harman (production management), Tom Smitz (sales support), and Don Jensen (sales and general management). Ron Standal (sales) has left us. Chuck Matchet (product engineering) was with us March through August and plans to be with us again by May 1995. It is also significant to note that a sizable financial investment to the continuing development of the firm was collectively made by four of the five new people. The continuing work force includes Ted Ulrich (R&D), George Hammond (R&D), Jan Kahn (administration), Ralph Gill (production) and me (administration and finance).

EXHIBIT 1: (Concluded)

In summary, the development of this company has been more slow and more difficult than I would have ever imagined. The vision of an R&D-based, specialty chemical company marketing world-class products into international markets is alive and well. It is an industry which has been successful in some of the most expensive countries on the earth such as Switzerland and Germany. In our region, however, we are one of only a few companies formulating and producing polymers and polymer-based products—another being Nentech. Nentech specializes in bulk commodity feed stocks. CSI is somewhat downstream in final product formulation. The other players in the polymer game are extruders of plastic products—a somewhat less scientifically demanding activity. From our relatively unique vantage point we should start to accrue benefits over time. These specialty chemical businesses may be difficult to get started, but once established, they can grow very big and become very profitable.

Jim Tolivre

Chapter 8

Start-Up

❑ *SUBCHAPTER 8A - Selling*

Crucial action steps in getting a venture started are to obtain customer orders, deliver on them, collect payment, and keep repeating that cycle, which may require additional financing if the enterprise grows. In each of these areas—selling, delivery and collecting—problems can lie ahead that are worth worrying about at start-up to ward them off or at least be able to respond effectively when they crop up. The problems may occur immediately, later or both.

Based on information from 120 of the 500 fastest-growing firms identified by *Inc.* magazine in 1987, by far the most frequent problems Terpstra and Olson[1] encountered during start-up were in sales and marketing (see Table 8-1).

Table 8-1 Frequency of Problems During Start-up

Problem Areas During First Year	Frequency %
Sales and marketing	38
Obtaining external financing	17
Internal financial management	16
General management	11
Product development	5
Human-resource management	5
Production and operations management	4
Economic environment	3
Regulatory environment	1
Total	100%

Five Pathways to New Venture Sales

The different ways to get sales in an enterprise can be grouped into five categories: (1) responding to customer requests, (2) advertising, (3) opening a store, (4) selling by personally "hitting the road," and (5) paying others to do the selling.

Responding

The first of these, responding to some customer's request, is a way many ventures have begun. The entrepreneur was approached by someone either asking how to obtain something or asking the entrepreneur if he or she could provide it.

> ASK Computer was started by Sandra Kurtzig when, as a sales representative for General Electric's computer operation, she was asked by a potential customer for something her employer did not offer. When she informed the customer of this, the customer asked why she did not start a company of her own and provide it. She did.

Sometimes, customer requests are more formally publicized. The *Commerce Business Daily*, for instance, prints notices of things the U.S. government would like to buy. It awards contracts totaling $200 billion per year, and its agencies are encouraged by federal policy to buy from small firms when they can. The Small Business Administration helps police these rules and is a good contact to make for information. Other helpful documents are *The U. S. Government Purchasing and Sales Directory*, and *Doing Business With The Government*. State governments also post notices of things they would like to buy and provide information for those interested in bidding on them.

"Catches" in serving as a government contractor include the possibility that some other contractors may have established relationships with agencies that give them advantages in "competitive" proposals. Other drawbacks include drawn-out approvals, slow payment, and programs coming and going capriciously at the whim of Congress and red tape. The following company apparently encountered grief from a combination of governmental factors.

> Comcraft, an independent young phone installation company, noticed a request for quote in the *Commerce Business Daily* in 1987 for installation of a phone system in an Army Corps of Engineers office. Terms of the government request said the system could be either a "key" system or a more complex "PBX" system. For the latter system, however, approval of the General Services Administration would be needed because a PBX would duplicate to some degree a system already used by the GSA, which owned the building used by the Army.
>
> The company's founder, Dominick Macaluso, Jr., discovered that the Army would save over 75 percent of the charges it was paying for use of GSA lines if he installed a PBX system. He said, "We were told that the Army would get anything it wanted, that it would march four-star generals down if it had to." Concluding that he could give the Army a bargain, a PBX system capability for a key system price, he proposed a PBX. Two Army technical evaluators visited the company, examined its equipment and were "enthralled." Comcraft received official notice that it was the most technically-qualified, lowest-cost vendor.

Before it could celebrate, however, the company received another notice, this time from the GSA, that it had disapproved the proposal. Comcraft began a series of appeals. But the end of the government's fiscal year was approaching, motivating government agencies to spend up their budgets. Hence before the appeal process was complete, another company had been given the contract. Instead of the Army getting its savings, the GSA kept its rental income. The GSA telecommunications chief said, "We had already paid for those lines." Comcraft had no contract and was out approximately $25,000 it had spent pursuing it.[2]

For some markets and lines of business a practical device to facilitate response to customers is use of an 800 telephone number and possibly an answering service. Costs include installation plus any directory listing costs and a rate per call depending on where it comes from. A Boston company selling live lobsters, for instance, found it cost them $200 for installation, $1,500 per year for directory listing and roughly $2,000 per month for calls, as compared to twice that amount previously spent on responding to collect calls.

Advertising

A second way to get sales is to advertise. The most obvious starting point for many firms is to buy an advertisement in directories such as the Yellow Pages. Thumbing through a phone book makes it quickly apparent that the advertisements vary in size and content. Each advertiser has made independent decisions about which design will be most effective for what purposes. There are choices to be made about which directories, for which geographical areas, what sizes of advertisements, how many should be listed, under what names and with what contents and graphics. The phone company itself may be of some help, and beyond that an advertising agency may have good advice. Visiting some advertisers and asking what their advertising experiments have taught them can also be informative.

Paid advertisements in newspapers, magazines, radio and television are other avenues of advertising. Yet another is to write articles which papers and magazines will print free as information. Posting notices, passing around flyers, sending sales letters, literature, newsletters, staging free lectures, public relations events or stunts and sending samples through the mail are ways of putting out news of what the venture has to offer. Either starting a catalog or seeking space in another company's catalog is also an option.

- In the heyday of hi-fi, many companies started by advertising do-it-yourself kits for building amplifiers, tuners and such in magazines.

- In the early days of the microcomputer, companies such as MITS, IMSAI and Osborne rapidly generated large sales through advertisements in magazines.

- Flyers stuck under auto windshield wipers or under the door at home are familiar advertising to most consumers.

- Coupon books can be handed out free to students starting the school year and to homeowners.

Another variation on advertising is the use of public relations techniques to get word out about the venture's product or service. Approaches for doing this include the following:

- Writing technical articles for magazines or journals where the publicity can help, or where the publication can be held up to substantiate the technical validity of what the venture sells. Testing the articles by asking other authorities in the field for critiques can help shape them into forms more likely to be accepted.

- Sending press releases to newspapers, magazines or other media announcing what is new about what the venture is up to. These have to contain elements that would be considered news. Testing and comparing ideas for their content against other published news items can be a way of assessing their likely publication. Brainstorming with sympathizers can help generate ideas for making the releases more catchy or newsworthy.

- Seeking interviews with radio or TV to demonstrate what the venture will offer. Practice on audio or videotape and possibly sending copies of the final tapes to stations may help with invitations. These too should be catchy, with visual displays, specimens, props, demonstrations and possibly participation by the interviewer or audience in order to retain interest.

- Becoming involved in publicity causes, public events and/or stunts to draw attention to the company. Corporate contributions to Public Broadcasting System and National Public Radio programs, local arts and music programs, student contest prizes and charities are one form. The founders of Fratelli's Ice Cream, for instance, chose to cosponsor Fourth-of-July fireworks for local visibility in Seattle.

How much to spend on advertising and publicity is a special problem for a new venture. For advertising expenditures in established companies, there are often rules of thumb, such as 1 to 5 percent of gross sales . In a new venture there may be no sales yet and possibly no appreciable amount of available cash, so the percentage could range from an infinite percent of (no) sales to zero. Yet a new company is usually unknown and therefore may have especially great need for advertising. Since its resources are typically very limited, it needs to find ways of getting the most advertising for the least money. To do that, in addition to seeking free publicity, here are some possibilities:

- Business cards and flyers are inexpensive.
- Homemade newsletters can be more effective than slick advertisements for some markets.
- Many small, inexpensive ads can add up to major impact over time.
- Classified ads are much cheaper than display ads.
- Piggybacking on ads of others can allow cost sharing.
- Suppliers often share advertising costs.
- Off-hours on radio, back corners in trade shows, poor locations for signs and last minute fill-ins are often available at low rates and sometimes work.
- Advertising departments of papers, magazines and radio stations will provide free help in ad design.
- Advance payment may yield discounts.
- It may be possible to pay by bartering rather than with cash.
- Frequent checking to see whom the ads are affecting and how can help cut costs.

Information about advertising costs can be found in publications of the Standard Rate and Data Service, available in many libraries as well as from the service itself, whose address is 3004 Glenview Road, Wilmette, Illinois 60691. It lists, for instance, thousands of cooperative advertising programs available from manufacturers throughout the country. The "bad news" about advertising is that the average American is hit with an estimated 500 advertising messages per day but remembers only 12 of them. How to be remembered on an extremely small advertising budget calls for careful thought and very sharp focus of the message.

"Specialty advertising" involves imprinting a company name on innumerable gift items such as calendars, mugs, clocks, rulers, pencils, pens, knives, paperweights, jewelry, bumper stickers, decals, combs and so forth. Although expensive on a per person basis, such advertising is usually sharply-focused so that the total cost is not so great and the impact is high. One company that gave empty flower pots and followed up with flowers to put in them estimated that its campaign was more effective and cost around $5,000 in contrast to an estimated cost of $20,000 for print advertising or $200,000 for a magazine campaign. An important question to consider, aside from cost, is whether the gift will be more effective as a door opener, a reminder or a memento of thanks after a sale.

Application: *What alternative advertising approaches might most likely help the assigned case venture get its first sales? Illustrate on one or more transparencies. How would their costs probably compare? Which should be used and why?*

Storefront

Easiest to see are ventures that got sales through the third approach, which is to open a store. Important variations on this approach are to set up a display at shows, fairs, malls, and auctioning. Choice of location, methods of display and advertising, selection of inventory, pricing, credit policies and methods of dealing with customers are variables that crucially influence results. For some "name brand" chains there are elements of science in controlling these variables. But the science is never perfect, and for new ventures there is inevitably considerable suspense in first opening the store. For some new stores the customers show up soon. For others it takes time to build up a clientele. The fact that many storefronts change tenants from lease to lease demonstrates that for many stores the clientele never becomes adequate to continue the business.

Aspects to consider with a storefront include not only location and cost, as discussed earlier, but also decor, use of signs and point-of-purchase displays, how much inventory to carry, how best to display it and how to arrange the store layout.

Storefronts can be either stationary or mobile, permanent or temporary. One variation, often used by start-ups to make their existence known, test customer responses to what they offer, study what competitors offer, and recruit sales agents, is to open a booth or rent part of the space in someone else's booth at a fair or a trade show. The cost per lead at a trade show has been estimated at around $100 and the added cost of follow-up to close the sale at roughly another $100, though clearly this would vary depending upon a host of variables (selling handicrafts at a fair certainly costs nothing like that), so that the total cost per sale through that avenue would be roughly $200.[3] A guide to show costs is published annually by the International Exhibitors Association of Annandale, Virginia. These costs include those of the exhibit itself, plus the entry fee, travel, transportation, setup, samples and literature expenses. Other helpful information about shows and their costs is published in *Trade Show Week* (2,000 shows) and *Exhibit Schedule* (10,000 shows).

Things to be mapped out clearly in advance include who will be coming to the show(s) selected,what information will be sent in advance, given out at the show or sent later as followup to show attendees, what information will the venture seek to obtain from attendees, what sales results will the venture seek to accomplish through the show, who will help out (sometimes suppliers and/or local governments will), and how the activity itself will be managed. Innumerable "tips" on making the most of trade shows are available in books and magazines that can be located through such sources as those above or the National Association of Exposition Managers. Another way to learn is simply to attend some shows locally. The State Department of Commerce, Chamber of Commerce or local Convention Bureau can provide information about shows coming up.

Designing a layout and display, whether for a store or a show, is an art form that can be very helpful to sales, if well done. Someone with visual talent and originality may have inspiring ideas for how to do it. Those without such gifts can either study the displays of others and copy what works or ask for help from those with the talent.

Application: *What types of storefronts might be most useful for the assigned case venture and how?*

Personal Selling

"Hitting the road," calling on customers and selling personally is a fourth approach to create sales in a new venture. The first sale in a venture is often made by the entrepreneur personally. After that, if the venture survives and grows, subsequent sales are usually made by others. In personal selling, a particularly important quality is credibility as perceived by the potential buyer, as illustrated by the following example.

> In 1974 a young man from the Pacific Northwest with an interest in photography learned of the success that a cousin in Southern California was having in producing and selling wall-sized photographic murals. He decided to set up a firm like his cousin's and installed the necessary photographic equipment in a darkroom to do it. Then he began calling on potential customers, telling them what he could do and asking whether they had favorite photos they would like to have made into decorative murals. Unfortunately, his verbal descriptions were not adequate to obtain orders. Consequently, he prevailed upon his cousin to lend him page-sized photographs illustrating different applications the cousin had made in California. When accompanied by these examples, his sales pitch was successful, orders began to come, and before long he was able to replace his cousin's examples with those of his own.

Developing new contacts in personal selling is hard, but can be very rewarding and may be essential. It calls for self-discipline and initiative. Because time is such a scarce resource for a founder, it is vital to define with care whom to go after, what to seek from them, how much effort to apply in each attempt and how to assess the results in planning each next action. Contact building constantly calls for judgment. Insufficient persistence can render efforts futile. However, too much of it applied on the wrong tack can be even more wasteful.

If there is a "technology" side to what the venture will offer, then one way to explain that technology to prospective customers may be to invite them to seminars where it will be explained. These may be given at trade shows, trade association meetings or advertised directly. It is easy to rent a meeting room in a hotel to present the seminar and to advertise it to prospects through direct mail or newspaper advertisements. The seminar can be without charge or for a fee, depending upon what it offers and how prospects are likely to feel about it. Familiar examples are "personal finance" and "real estate" seminars occasionally advertised in local papers. Usually the person attending such seminars first receives information free and is invited to buy literature, tapes and additional seminars for a price. Seminars for industrial customers are usually less carnival-like.

When Bruce Milne and his partners developed a new software package for accountants he organized a seminar presentation to which he personally invited a small number of professionals. There they were able to learn just how the program worked and what it did for them, as well as to exchange information with each other about their needs, problems and possible solutions. Milne put his message across and received feedback that was helpful both in refining his package and securing customers for it.

❖ ❖ ❖

William Delphos became an expert in low-cost government resources for smaller firms to develop overseas sales when he worked for four years as a White House appointee in foreign investment. To find customers as a consultant on the subject, he spent $1,000 putting together a humorous cartoon slide show, then persuaded an electronics trade association to include it among the programs available to their 21 councils across the country which continually offer various programs to their members. This exposure, he said, gave him both credibility and opportunity to display his expertise to prospective customers for his consulting services. He found it best not to attempt any selling at his seminar but to follow up afterwards with a letter to each participant.[4]

Some other ways of personal selling that particularly lend themselves to sharp focus on selected audiences include the following:

- Sales Letters. Mailing lists can be purchased which include only people who fit particular parameters. Companies with such lists will do the addressing, mailing, more if desired. They can be found in the Yellow Pages. Tips on sales letters can be found in books on business communications and magazines such as *Direct Marketing*. Probably several rounds of letters will be needed to "get through."

- Telephone Selling. Although it is sharply focused market-wise, this approach is expensive in time and money compared to sales letters. Advantages, however, are that it allows progressive interrogation of the people called, and can yield much better information. Information about this approach is available from the American Telemarketing Association, 104 Wilmot Road, Deerfield,

Illinois 60015. However, the best way to find what works is to write out a script, follow it and modify it with each call until it "peaks out" in effectiveness. The final version is almost certain to be greatly changed in both contents and performance.

Application: *What types of personal selling should be needed at different stages as the assigned case venture develops?*

Paying Others

The fifth approach to selling is to pay others for handling it. Alternatives include hiring salespeople as employees, engaging independent representatives, or selling to "middlemen" such as brokers, wholesalers, catalog houses or retailers. Each of these costs money. *Sales and Marketing Management* estimated the cost of an average sales call at $118 in consumer markets, $162 in service markets and $179 in industrial markets. McGraw-Hill estimated the average overall cost as $230 and added that it takes on the average 5.5 calls to get an order. Costs differ depending not only on what is being sold, but also the type of representative used, what the representative does and, of course, how well the selling effort is managed.

Application: *Prepare for presentation in class a personal selling "pitch" for the product or service of the assigned case venture.*

With each mode of selling there are tradeoffs to consider. For example, independent representatives must be paid only if they accomplish sales, which eliminates the risk of paying for no performance. Commissions, which are paid as a percentage of sales, range considerably as shown in figures of Table 8-2 below, which were taken from *Sales and Marketing Management* magazine's annual "Survey of Selling Costs."

Table 8-2   Sales Commissions in Different Lines of Business

	Percent of Commission Paid		
Line of Business	**High**	**Average**	**Low**
Advertising	24.2%	16.2%	8.1%
Toys, Novelties	12.8	9.3	5.9
Robotics	12.4	10.3	8.2
Building Supplies	10.7	7.7	4.6
Electronics	10.4	8.5	6.5
Consumer Electrical	6.7	5.6	4.6
Lumber	6.4	5.1	3.7

Application: *If the assigned case venture were to pay others to sell for it on commission, what should the commission percentage be and why?*

In addition to the commission, however, there are costs of samples, literature, communications and training that the venture must pay. Moreover, independent agents typically concentrate on only those sales that are largest or come easiest, which is likely to leave out the product of a new company. Selling through brokers and wholesalers lowers the risk of collection problems, but such middlemen have to be convinced that retailers will buy from them, or they will not carry the line. Similarly, retailers must be convinced that consumers will buy, which may require the venture to spend money on advertising and promotions, and those, if not successful, can cost enough to break the venture. Failure can also occur if the venture is successful in persuading consumers, but the wholesalers and retailers do not stock up fast enough to capitalize while the demand exists.

It is not unusual to sell through a combination of the above approaches. For instance, advertising in the Yellow Pages at least and by other means as well, is widely used in combination with a storefront for retailing. Also common is to start with one means of selling and shift to others over time. Some examples include:

An electronics company sold its first few products personally, then rented a booth at a trade show where it distributed advertising brochures and recruited manufacturers' representatives. Technical articles were written for magazines to get word of the products out further. Ultimately, sales grew to a point where the company began adding its own sales employees in place of the manufacturers' representatives.

❖ ❖ ❖

An olive oil company began packaging and shipping in a garage and selling to wholesalers. Due to zoning restrictions the founders moved their operations to an empty storefront. Passersby started asking to buy directly and the founders changed the storefront to a retail operation and moved packaging and shipping to another rented plant.

❖ ❖ ❖

A bakery producing muffins started by selling retail out the front door but found it could make more by selling wholesale out the back door to restaurants.

❖ ❖ ❖

An ice cream company set out to introduce another brand of premium ice cream, only to conclude that it was too late. Other companies had grown too dominant in that market. Consequently, the company dropped its own brand and shifted its sales efforts to persuade stores to buy its premium product under their brands instead.[5]

❖ ❖ ❖

A food packaging company, rather than develop its own brand, leased the brands of other well-known companies for royalties ranging from 3 percent to 5 percent of its gross sales and did the selling itself.[6]

Another variation worth considering, particularly after the venture has developed some "marketing muscle" of its own, is to exchange that capability with another company that is strong in a different marketing territory through joint distribution. Each can be a commissioned agent of the other, sales leads can be exchanged, costs can be shared on advertising, trade shows and incoming phone calls. Each can help the other with information about competitors and ideas for sales campaigns. However, as with any partnership, the load and benefits can get out of balance and lead to breakup, so attention must be given to fairness to keep such a relationship working.

Companies that provide good results to their first customers tend to find other customers coming to buy because they have learned through word of mouth that the companies are good suppliers. A common factor among ventures that succeed in building sales and having them expand through word-of-mouth seems to be effective concentration on maintaining what customers perceive as a high and consistent level of quality.

Application: *If the venture were to engage others to sell for it, how should they be recruited and what training and support should they have?*

Pricing

Setting prices in a new venture poses the same questions, options and dilemmas as in established firms. Some to consider are the following:

- Are there competitive prices to be met?

- What price will cover incremental costs?

- How fast will a "cream skimming" (high initial) price attract competitors?

- Will a lower price convey an image of cheapness and make it impossible to price higher?

- What will the price/sales volume curve probably look like?

Although scientific methods can help explore some aspects of pricing, there is no science for determining prices themselves. Some ways of obtaining information that may be helpful in an inevitably judgmental pricing process include:

- Gather information on competitors' prices and how they have changed relative to each other and over time.

- Compute carefully what it will cost the venture to produce and sell what it produces.

- Ask selected people in a focus group and/or survey what they think would be appropriate prices, how much they would pay and what quality image different prices might convey.

- Ask suppliers, agents, wholesalers, trade associations and other members of the industry for their opinions on appropriate pricing.

- Plan to experiment with different levels of price to determine what will work best, remembering that it will probably be easier to lower prices than to raise them, and that sooner or later competition will arise.

Conventional business wisdom, which has been corroborated by studies of the Strategic Planning Institute (PIMS) and others, is that the highest ROI correlates positively with selling high-quality offerings and pricing them correspondingly high. Trying to enter as a low-cost competitor by offering lower quality or even comparable quality has statistically been a losing strategy.

Application: *How should the venture price what it offers, and how should that change over time? What is a first guess as to what the price should be initially?*

Supplementary Reading

New Venture Mechanics Chapter 7. (Vesper, K. H., Prentice-Hall, 1993)

Exercises

1. Obtain or devise something to be sold and ask for an order to buy it through personal "cold calling." Describe the criteria you used for selecting your prospect(s), how you located them, made contact and attempted to close. State also what the results were and how you would alter any of the above elements in a next effort.

2. Obtain through phone or personal interviews some cost information on three of the five general sales approaches described in this chapter. Comment on which approaches are suited best for obtaining sales in new ventures with contrasting types of products or services.

3. Interview two or more:

    a. Independent sales reps and/or
    b. Wholesalers

    Ask what experiences each has had in dealing with start-ups. Describe the implications for entrepreneurs.

4. Determine the cost per audience member for five of the alternative mechanisms mentioned in the section on advertising above. Assess the differences in cost and why they might be justified.

5. Learn what services an advertising agency can provide for a start-up, how long it takes to deliver them and how much it charges for those services. Analyze the alternative of using one versus performing its tasks personally when founding a venture.

6. Select five different business signs and describe what you believe to be the purposes of each, in rank order. Discuss how the signs differ from one another and why. Assess what you believe would be their relative effectiveness if they were all being used for start-up firms.

7. Learn what the restrictions are on (1) billboards in selected areas of your city and (2) signs posted on motor vehicles in your state. Assess the relative effectiveness of these two types of signs for a specific hypothetical start-up firm.

8. Examine and compare the window displays (or alternatively the interior layouts and decors) of five stores. Prepare a grid with dimensions which in your view make differences in effectiveness along one axis and names of the stores along the other. Assess how visual techniques used by the stores compare to one another.

Venture History

1. Which channels were chosen for the venture's sales out of what (maybe not considered) alternatives and how? How did they (or will they probably) change later and why?

2. What does selling through those channels cost?

3. How do customers learn about the venture's product or service?

4. How were prices first set and later changed (if they were)?

5. How and when were the first three sales of the venture made and by whom?

Venture Planning Guide

1. In 750 words describe a hypothetical scenario for the first two or three sales your venture will make. Include descriptions of the customers and scripts of the sales transactions.

2. Brainstorm a promotion plan and cost it out.

3. Prepare a detailed expense budget monthly for the first year for each of two alternative contrasting sales programs in your venture. Compare the projected costs of the two in dollars and founder hours.

4. Explain the rationale by which prices were assumed for financial forecasts of the venture.

5. Describe the procedures that will be followed for creating the next round of sales forecasts and how the forecasting methods of the venture will change as it develops.

6. Describe the policies and procedures that will be used for updating the venture's product or service as the venture moves forward, including how that activity will be staffed, how decisions will be made, and how the activity will be budgeted.

7. Describe the system to be used for tracking competition and forecasting competitors' moves.

Notes

[1] David E. Terpstra and Philip D. Olson, "Entrepreneurial Start-up and Growth: A Classification of Problems," *ET&P*, 17, no. 3, Spring 1993, p. 5.

[2] Ellen Forman, "Deal Carefully with Uncle Sam," *Venture*, September 1989, p. 14.

[3] J. Donald Weinrauch and Nancy Croft Baker, *The Frugal Marketer* (New York: AMACOM, 1989).

[4] Ibid.

[5] Paul B. Brown, "When Quality Isn't Everything," *Inc.*, June 1989, p. 119.

[6] Tom Richman, "A New Lease on Growth," *Inc.*, July 1990, p. 107.

❏ SUBCHAPTER 8B - Producing

Some aspects of getting production underway were considered in earlier chapters. Chapter 5 on finance raised the question of what to make versus what to buy in connection with minimizing cash needs. In Chapter 6 the subchapter (6c) on setup discussed this further and provided illustrations. Selecting a location and obtaining needed equipment and facilities were also considered in Chapter 6, and hiring employees for production was treated in Chapter 7. What remains is to integrate the management of these aspects, head off problems insofar as possible and cope with those problems that can't be headed off.

Application: Prepare a PERT chart of the actions needed to start up production in the assigned case venture.

Things that Can Go Wrong

The aim in producing is to deliver the right amount on time with appropriate quality at a cost at or below target. Two categories of problems that can prevent such an accomplishment are (1) difficulties that are beyond management's control and (2) adversities that management should be able to anticipate and cope with. Among the former are such events as:

- Natural disasters, such as fires, floods, and earthquakes.
- Man-made problems such as robbery, arson, and riots.
- Customers changing their minds about what they want without warning.

Problems that management should be able to head off include:

- Failure to anticipate supply needs.
- Inadequate or inappropriate workforce.
- Insufficient or incorrect instructions to employees.
- Equipment failure due to improper maintenance.
- Lateness due to lack of planning.
- Flaws due to slack quality control.

Application: List the 10 most likely things that could go wrong in producing the product or service of the assigned case venture during start-up.

Supply Problems

Problems with suppliers are common among start-ups. The relationship is new, the order is probably small and the start-up may not be around long.

Slow delivery, high prices, poor quality and demand for payment in advance may all arise. There may not be much a start-up can do about these things. By anticipating such possibilities, it can seek to bolster its image, possibly by obtaining introductions or putting up a good "front." It can seek out alternative suppliers and request bids to stimulate competition among them. It can decide which elements of performance on the supplier's part are most important and seek to obtain written guarantees on those by trading off other elements of less importance. For instance, it might offer a premium price or payment in advance for a guarantee of quality or delivery.

In the following example, more drastic action seemed to be called for and was taken.

> In 1985 Hollis Savin started the Yuppie Gourmet, Inc. to produce "upscale snacks." In October 1986 the candy company she had contracted with to manufacture her product suddenly confronted her with a demand for cash payment and as an alternative offered to buy her out for a low price. "He had us backed against a wall," she recalled. "He had our inventory locked up in his warehouse. I was resigned to selling it. I was going to hand over $400,000 in unfulfilled orders.
>
> "But my mother convinced me not to give up." Instead, Savin rented a lock cutter plus three trucks and talked her way past the security guards. "We got the boxes packed up when no one was paying attention and were off to southern Illinois, where my husband had found another candy company with the facilities we needed. They produced thousands of pounds of product and shipped it out. We met all our Christmas orders. By early 1989 the company had sales of $1.7 million.[1]

Application: *Describe the three most important actions to be taken in the assigned case venture to prevent disappointing performance by suppliers during start-up.*

The start-up may initially be at the mercy of suppliers, unable to obtain much (if any) trade credit, priority on delivery timing, or careful attention to preferences. By paying cash and working at personal communication, the entrepreneur should be able to get adequate supplier service. As the start-up begins to survive and grow, it should be able to pick and choose among suppliers, in part based upon which of them have given it the best service initially. Feelings of gratitude may appropriately play a part in building good supplier relationships for the longer run, but developing a rationalized rating system for choosing suppliers can also help. Eight criteria suggested by two small-business scholars based upon a survey of 449 firms in six industries include those shown in Table 8-3 below.[2]

The authors suggest that such criteria be weighted, and that each supplier be given a numerical score such as from one to five on each criterion, which is then multiplied times the weighting of that criterion, after which the weighted scores are added to give an overall score to each supplier. This information can provide a rational basis for choosing suppliers and can also give feedback to suppliers. Diplomatically handled, this can help suppliers improve and earn their gratitude, to the advantage of the start-up.

Table 8-3 Supplier Criteria

		Weight	Points	Score
				(= Weight x Points)
a.	Consistent quality	_____	_____	_____
b.	Dependable delivery	_____	_____	_____
c.	Net price	_____	_____	_____
d.	Attitude of supplier	_____	_____	_____
e.	Reputation of supplier	_____	_____	_____
f.	Production capacity	_____	_____	_____
g.	Technical assistance	_____	_____	_____
h.	Financial stability	_____	_____	_____

Production Problems

Another way to avoid supplier problems is for the venture to do its own production. However, that can lead to other difficulties. To be able to produce at a competitive level of excellence usually requires practice and possibly training. Even with those things there can be problems if the plant and equipment are new and somewhat unfamiliar, as occurred in the following venture.

In March 1973, three people, an experienced potter, an architect and an investor, founded a company to make "stoneware" dinner plates. Equity of $42,000 plus loans of $16,000 from the founders was supplemented by an SBA guaranteed loan of $40,000. The founders signed a lease for plant space and ordered production equipment. The needed "pug mill" to prepare clay, RAM press to form it, and kiln to fire it arrived during July and August. Setup and debugging of the equipment continued through the summer, and the first firing occurred in October. It produced samples for test marketing in local specialty shops, but not a production run.

Only 10 percent of the output was of adequate quality, and the remainder had flaws, which the company continued to struggle with month after month. Enough "firsts" were produced by December to exhibit at the Los Angeles gift show in January, where responses to the line seemed favorable and $15,000 worth of orders were received. However, the company's "pug mill" seemed to be producing inadequate clay, and flaws were also showing up in the glazing process.

By March the company was almost finished. It had not been able to deliver on orders, its capital was used up, the bank was demanding payment, and one of the founders wanted out. The many months of struggle with production problems finally began to produce better results, however, and failure was narrowly averted. By late 1975 the company was operating at a profit, though not a large one. Subsequently, however, it lost out to competitors and disappeared from the scene.

This great a delay in accomplishing high-quality production is hard to excuse when the technology is so well established. The company's failing seems to have been not obtaining adequate expertise, which it could certainly have bought with less cash than it took to grope through a self-education experience. While the problems are going on, however, that can be harder to see. Every day there is hope that the solution will soon be found. The last experiment worked almost right, and the next one may be the answer.

When the technology is new, rather than old as in this example, the convenient solution of hiring appropriate expertise may not be available, and the entrepreneur may have no choice except to experiment. But even then there may be expertise in closely related fields that can be hired to help. Hence, it is still wise to budget for such help, as well as for experimentation in planning. An advantage for the start-up with new technology should be that it will also be new for potential competitors, and they too will have to spend the time and money to learn.

At the earliest stage, an entrepreneur may need to handle many or virtually all of the operations tasks personally. Venture capitalist Robert J. Kunze described the contrast between early operations in a new venture and those to be found in established companies through the example of a venture in which he considered investing:[3]

> *Dr. Black was an accomplished researcher on paper, but he had only managed a few laboratory technicians and a secretary. He had been a product manager and twice successfully transformed technical theories into successful commercial products. All his work had been done with RCA's checkbook and infrastructure, however. The availability of a corporate infrastructure meant that if Black needed special equipment, someone researched the problem and bought it for him; if a fixture needed to be machined, the head of the machine shop took care of it; if he needed a micrograph, the analytical laboratory made one; if his telephone broke, someone fixed it.*
>
> *TM (the new venture) would have no infrastructure. Dr. Black would have to take care of almost everything himself, from getting the permits to work in the building to locking up at night.*

These were limitations that Black apparently initially learned to live with. Hiring only a secretary, a maintenance man, and an engineering graduate, he set about designing, building, and delivering machines. However, sales were minimal and some customers were sending their machines back. For operations to progress beyond the barest inception point, more qualified people were needed, but Black was not getting them. Kunze continued:

> *When I asked him about his people and dealing with the tasks at hand, and plans to sell milling machines while rapidly developing the deposition machine, Black dismissed my concerns with a wave of his hand. He had done this type of work before, he said. He had created an electron milling machine that worked, and*

left alone, he would build a deposition machine in six months. No, thank you, he didn't need to hire any hotshot engineers (or marketing people). He needed people who would do what he wanted when he wanted it, nothing more, nothing less.

In this case the venture capitalist turned down the venture and Black raised money from other investors, who demoted him to director of engineering. Some time later the company went bankrupt, after which Black was convicted of selling technology secrets to the Russians.

The sequence that leads to orderly operation may be relatively smooth if the company develops slowly, building on the competence of a founder with a talent for managing and leading as well as producing. However, in start-ups involving the development of new technology, the pressure to beat competitors to market can be, at best, harrowing or, at worst, fatal. Robert J. Kunze observed that initially things may work fairly well while the team is small, everyone knows each other, communication lines are short, goals are clear and shared, and everyone pitches in whenever something needs to be done. But then, he says, comes the hard part:[4]

> *Within months of the start-up anguish usually sets in. Though everyone has worked hard, no important goals have been met, at least not those that would reduce the fragility of the business. During this time new people have been hired and no one has had time to integrate them into the company's work plan. The boss has continually set unrealistic and unachievable goals and everyone has bought into them. The employees have done their best, but after a while they start to grumble. Prototypes don't work and need to be re engineered quickly. If anything, there seems to be more, not less, risk, more questions, fewer answers. The 60- to 80-hour workweek takes a physical and mental toll. Life outside work takes a real licking. Some companies never escape this hellhole. After six years of hanging away, they run out of money and go south.*

The folklore of new projects, including entrepreneurial ventures, has absorbed an awareness that accomplishments tend to take longer than expected and cost more than predicted, there tend to be more ways that things can go wrong than right and no matter how many things are done right, only one thing done wrong can undo the whole effort. A whimsical codification of such observations has taken a form referred to as "Murphy's Laws," which include the following:

1. Anything that can go wrong will.
2. Of the things that can't go wrong, some can.
3. The thing that will go wrong is the one that will do the most damage.
4. If it can be done wrong, it will.
5. Nature always finds the weak spots.

6. Bread always lands butter-side down.

7. Things always go from bad to worse.

8. If everything seems to be going well, look again.

9. If the prototype works perfectly, the production units will fail.

10. It is impossible to make things foolproof—fools are too ingenious.

11. No matter what goes wrong someone will have known it would but not have said so.

However, many ventures find a way out, survive, and prosper. Kunze described the instance of a biomedical start-up by a researcher whose plans neglected consideration of how to mass-produce the new vaccines it created. Eventually, the founder was fired by the investors as the company struggled to solve technical problems, missed its forecasts, and overspent. Kunze described how, under new management, operations were straightened out as follows:[5]

> *Gradually, piece by piece, we began to solve the manufacturing problems, cost problems and quality problems. The entire staff attacked the problems in parallel. The financial people developed, revised and finally installed a cost accounting system that worked. This required immediate price increases in products we had thought profitable but that turned out to be big losers. We didn't lose a single customer.*
>
> *Research and development people worked in the factory, teaching the new production workers how to work consistently, to control all the variables such as temperature and ingredients, and to measure precisely the passage of time. This research and development exposure to the factory had an additional benefit. Our scientists learned firsthand about production problems and were able to go back to their laboratories and improve the processes.*
>
> *The biggest help in operating the business came from stabilizing or fixing the sales-forecasting technique. Because the manufacturing cycle took two months from start to finish, the vaccine-in-process could not be increased, decreased, or changed without discarding the entire batch. The salespeople, trying to expand their territories and eager to please, had influenced the manufacturing people to change direction every week. The management stopped what should have been an obviously misguided operating mode, developed a two-month forecast system, and stuck to it.*

Quality

Studies by the Boston Consulting Group and others have shown that typically higher profitability is associated with higher share of a served market. The Strategic Planning Institute has found similar results and also that market share tends to be driven by higher quality.[6] Moreover, higher quality allows both higher prices and higher margins. Thus, aiming for high quality is often a logical way to seek high profits.

In a start-up firm, there are two more reasons for emphasis on top quality. First, as an unknown the firm may have a hard time attaining credibility. If it can demonstrate exceptional quality, this may help with that problem. Second, by selecting a segment of the market that desires exceptional quality, the venture may narrow the front on which it must compete. The narrower the segment, the less it may be of interest to larger competitors and the more the venture can concentrate its limited selling resources.

Just how quality should be defined deserves careful attention. Sometimes a quality problem—that is, a gap between the actual and the appropriate quality—is obvious, as may be seen in this experience described by the venture capitalist Robert J. Kunze:[7]

> *One meter failed our quality control pressure test by exploding. Since our meters were hooked up "in line" by customers, an exploding meter could cause a flood of potentially dangerous materials. We had to shut down production, find the cause of the failure, and fix the problem.*
>
> *After a week of nail biting, we discovered the welding on the flange of the meter was defective because of contamination. This was a break for us because we could inspect all weldings by X-ray to determine which ones were bad. We screened out a few dozen bad flanges, repaired the defect, and were shipping safe meters within two weeks. That episode cost Exac about $300,000 in lost sales and unabsorbed overhead. A bigger problem would have destroyed the company.*

The important definition of quality is the one implicit in the customer's buying decision, not necessarily what the entrepreneur thinks is high-quality or even what the customer says it is. Ferreting out this "real" definition can begin with careful thought and "armchair" analysis, but may also require customer interviews, analysis of past customer buying decisions, focus group comparisons against competitors' offerings, systematic quantitative analysis of product or service features and, finally, experimentation.

Sales follow-up leading to word-of-mouth advertising can be viewed as both a part of the sales function and part of the production function. That is, the two should ideally work together so that the result is more customers asking to buy what the company has to sell. If this does not happen it can be regarded as a reflection on the quality of what the venture is delivering.

Application: *Describe the five most important actions to be taken in the assigned case venture to maintain appropriate quality of output during start-up.*

Setting Output Levels

With either a new product or a new service, another challenge will be to set output levels appropriately. Too high an initial output and there may be too much inventory expense or worse yet, the second generation may have to be introduced before the first one is sold out. Too low an output will likely mean higher unit costs due to setup expense and may mean risk of running short on supply and thereby leaving an opening for competitors. In an established company guidance in setting output levels can come from trends that are apparent in hindsight, and from familiarity with customers and their needs. In a new company, the guessing may have less historical information as a basis.

> A hobbyist who made model rockets decided to start producing them for others. The rocket would be 14 inches long, consisting of an aluminum tube capped by a Styrofoam nose cone. For sales the founders planned to advertise in hobby magazines and sell direct by mail for $10.95. This was about 10 percent to 20 percent more than products of competitors. But whereas competitors' rockets used flammable fuel, this one would be powered by freon from cans usually sold to power horns.
>
> Costs of the product were estimated to be $3 each, and the founders figured that if they built an inventory of 300 and spent $200 on the first advertisement, it would leave just enough of the capital to cover operating expenses. The question of what volume to produce was thereby automatically limited. They chose to manufacture in batches of 100 to simplify scheduling, accounting and analysis. Actual order volume turned out, conveniently, to average about 300 rockets per month.

Application: *Make a schedule as best you can of output volume for the assigned case venture during start-up.*

Pitfalls of Expansion

It would seem as though management of production should be relatively easy if the venture begins with low initial sales followed by a slow, stable growth trajectory thereafter. The venture might develop routines that work smoothly with expansion. The founder could either relax and follow those routines or hire someone else to tend the business, leaving the founder free to pursue something else.

However, many seemingly simple start-ups, even if they grow only slowly, are in fact not all that simple. One thing that keeps them on the run is the threat of competitors trying harder or coming in with better approaches. Another may be expansion of the business, made necessary by growth in the number of customers coupled with the threat that competitors will arise to serve them if the venture does not.

> Tim Phillips, a young man from Calgary honeymooning in Montreal, noticed a store which seemed to be prospering from sale of croissants. Reflecting on the fact that he had never seen such a store in Calgary, he persuaded his bride that they should try starting one when they returned home. Thanks to

economic recession in Calgary they were able to lease a prominently located storefront downtown at low rent. They signed a lease, bought kitchen equipment and began many long weeks of experimentation to teach themselves the art of making croissants.

When they felt they had the product right they opened the doors to public sale and began calling on other stores and restaurants to offer their product wholesale. Sales began and grew strongly. Within a few months as many as 70 calls per day fed in wholesale orders. For each an invoice was written, then combined with others to determine batch sizes of different flavors for the night shift to bake and to prepare a schedule for the delivery driver to use at 4 AM the next morning. Any excesses in the batches were offered at the retail counter.

As volume grew, the scheduling became more hectic. When customers ordered late in the day, the batches and delivery schedule had to be redone. More and more often, Tim found himself rushing out early in the morning to fill special orders that had come in at the last minute.

Eventually, Tim applied three solutions. The first was to hire a second delivery driver to start three hours after the first. The second solution was to become less flexible about accommodating customers with special orders. Third was to use a microcomputer for programming the batches and delivery schedules. In hindsight he felt the problem could have been solved earlier and saved him considerable strain and discomfort. He also concluded that he should have bought expert help in learning to make croissants, rather than resorting to experimental self-teaching.

❖ ❖ ❖

While in the Army, Bob Carver had designed in his mind a revolutionary new circuitry for high-fidelity amplifiers. Upon discharge he made some and sold them to stores for which he had repaired television sets prior to his Army induction while working his way through a master's degree in physics. Two stereo magazines tested his product, and subsequently published "rave reviews" on it. Thereupon his business, Phase Linear, took off.

He hired friends to help with assembly in the rented basement of a supermarket. Two additional new amplifiers with different power levels were added to the line, and they too were embraced by the market, causing sales to shoot up even faster. The workforce went from less than a dozen friends who worked closely and well together without supervision to over 50, including many teenagers fresh out of high school. Now the lack of supervision and loose, friendly atmosphere was accompanied by progressively more problems as loud music boomed through the shop. Some workers were getting drunk at lunch time, others were taking dope. Those who asked for raises got them while those who did not ask got none. Facilities became sloppy and overcrowded. Costs were rising faster than income, and quality was suffering.

Carver concluded that he was not the person to deal with these problems. Instead, he advertised for a general manager and from among the applicants selected one freshly graduated MBA to become general manager and another to become controller. These two young men instituted conventional formal management systems. Computer systems were installed for accounting, inventory and asset control. Production systems were installed to manage flow and control quality. Personnel procedures were formalized and an employee manual was written. Benefit and profit-sharing plans were introduced, as well as training programs for employees. The company turned around, prospered and eventually was sold to a large Japanese firm.

"Theory Y," which assumes that people are naturally oriented toward company goals, may apply marvelously at the earliest stages of a company when the goals are clear and working relationships of founders and employees are close. But there seems to come a point where the tools of regimentation, such as formal assignments, incentive pay, clear job definitions and a chain of command are necessary. By anticipating this eventuality and planning for it in advance it may be possible to head off some costly mistakes and panic.

Application: *List the main problems and action to prevent them as production expands in the assigned case venture.*

Supplementary Reading

New Venture Mechanics Chapter 8. (Vesper, K. H., Prentice-Hall, 1993)

Exercises

1. Develop a PERT chart for opening a business based on one of your venture ideas other than that of your venture plan. Contrast it with the PERT of your venture plan.

2. Choose a simple product such as a toy or kitchen utensil, new or existing. Determine what processes should be used for manufacturing it out of two alternative materials. Make a sketch of it with representative dimensions and specifications for making it out of those materials. Estimate the production costs at three contrasting order quantities.

3. For a product such as the one above, choose two competing brands. List the dimensions on which quality can be measured. Rank these dimensions in what you consider to be their relative importance. Rate the two products on these dimensions, weight the ratings according to rank and add up the totals to see how they compare. Divide the totals by price and assess again. (Additional Option: Follow by asking two other people to perform the ratings and rankings. Discuss how their views differ and what significance the results should have for the producers if those results turned out to be typical.)

4. Call the U.S. foreign trade office (by long distance if not in your city) of some foreign country. Learn and list as many steps as possible involved in making overseas and importing some simple new or existing product. Include on your list the names, numbers, dates and addresses of contacts you made.

5. Make a list of contrasting alternatives for storing inventory, noting the costs, advantages and disadvantages of each for one or more hypothetical ventures.

Venture History

1. Develop, in hindsight, a PERT diagram with dates indicating the sequence of actions to produce/deliver/service on the company's first few orders.

2. Describe the production skills and procedures needed for the venture to perform competitively. How did the founders acquire them?

3. What opportunities to head off production problems were there in the venture, and what was done about them?

Venture Planning Guide

1. Describe the policies that will be used for managing quality, including how standards will be set, what economic tradeoffs will be made, and who will make the decisions.

2. List the main "make or buy" decisions that the venture will face initially and during its first two years.

3. Prepare a supplier rating sheet to be used as your venture develops purchasing experience and clout.

4. Describe the systems that will be used to manage inventory levels initially, and as the venture develops over the first two years.

5. Explain how the objectives of reliability and quality will enter into the early stages of new product or service development.

6. Describe the steps through which new products or services will be transferred from development to operations.

7. Indicate how follow-up servicing will be performed to cultivate customer loyalty.

8. List the main areas in which employee policies will have to be developed. Indicate which ones will be easy to formulate and which will be trickier. Explain how the trickier ones will be resolved.

9. Project a sequence of start-up actions for your venture, and prepare a Gantt chart of the main steps.

10. Prepare a PERT diagram of the steps for starting your venture.

11. Make a list of things that could go wrong during start-up of your venture. Indicate rank order of the items in three different ways: (1) likelihood of occurrence, (2) cost of occurrence, and (3) difficulty or cost of prevention.

Notes

[1] Jeannie Ralston, "Specialty Food With All the Trimmings," *Venture*, February 1981, p. 43.

[2] C. David Wieters and Lonnie L. Ostrom, "Maintaining Effective Suppliers: A Small Business Approach," *Journal of Small Business Management*, 1, no. 2, Spring 1986, p. 149.

[3] Robert J. Kunze, *Nothing Ventured* (New York: Harper, 1990), p. 105.

[4] Ibid., p. 212.

[5] Ibid., p. 128.

[6] Robert D. Buzzell and Bradley T. Gale, *The PIMS Principles* (New York: Free Press), 1987.

[7] Robert J. Kunze, *Nothing Ventured*, p. 162.

❏ SUBCHAPTER 8C - Controlling

Arranging for Needed Numbers

Operating under the pressure of a cash squeeze is a common necessity in start-up ventures, and for many it leads to shutdown. Three means of dealing with this squeeze are to maximize collections, to minimize expenditures, and to recruit more capital infusions as the venture continues. Essential to all three is possession of accounting information that is current, accurate, understood and utilized.

Need for Records

A catch in setting up records for a start-up is that the need for them may not be apparent until the company has been in business a while and something goes wrong. Examples include the following.

- A company was prosecuted by state tax collectors for not collecting state sales tax from customers who might have used the products they bought from the company themselves rather than reselling them.
- An attorney who had not kept adequate time records for billing clients found himself losing money because he was undercharging in an attempt to avoid overcharging.
- An office machine repair company found itself running out of some types of parts, which delayed work, while having excess inventory of other parts. Employees' time on jobs was not fully accounted for in billings.
- An architecture firm found itself having to substantiate for a lawsuit the work it had done on a building where the contractor had stopped work because the customer contested some of the work and refused to pay.

In each of these cases the best time to set up good records was at the start of business, while the easiest thing to do, and in the short run the cheapest as well, was not to.

Application: *List the records and files the assigned case venture is likely to need in chronological order of when they will probably first be needed.*

Developing a Records System

Whatever records and accounting system is set up at the start will likely change considerably over time, and this can be another lure into the pitfall of not setting up something adequate. What makes sense for most start-ups is to begin with a very simple system and reshape it over time fast enough to stay ahead of problems or at least keep up with them so they don't become too severe. Some of the variety in sequences is illustrated by the listing in Table 8-4 below, though it was selected by convenience and may not be generally representative.

Table 8-4 Accounting Systems Evolution: Sequence through which Venture Went to Different Accounting Systems

Venture	Accounting System				
	Check Register	Simple Books	Pegboard System	Computer System	Book-keeper
Auto Dealer			1		2
Bakery		1		2	
Bldg. Mat'ls.		1			2
Carwash		1		2	
Costume Maker	1				2
Daycare Center		1			2
Restaurant					1
Personnel Agency	1				2
Retail Store		2			1
Sheet Metal Co.	1		3	4	2

Sometimes accountants help the processes of transition between these stages. They also help with tax preparation at year end and with auditing.

An engineering professor who committed his entire savings to buy a manufacturing company found that it was losing cash, but he could not figure out why. There was no way of tracking materials in and out of inventory, no check on what was on hand, and no clear record of how old accounts receivable were. Labor costs were not charged to anything in particular, and the only record of expenses was the company checkbook. He had no knowledge of accounting and with cash so short was loathe to hire an accountant. His response was to learn personally where every bit of money was, how much was there, what came, what went and when so he could, in effect, have the control system in his head. After a year or so he had brought expenses under control and raised profits enough to hire an accountant.

The next entrepreneur also hired an accountant, but apparently got the wrong one and regretted it.

A locksmith decided to branch off from his employer and open his own shop. Initially, he kept track of inventory by observation; income, receivables and cost of goods sold by saving copies of invoices; and other expenses by the check register. As business grew, however, these procedures became cumbersome and he hired an accountant, who set up books, periodically up-dated them and produced income statements which at year end were used for tax preparation. The locksmith did not understand how the books worked but judged from the income statements that the business was doing well.

Based on apparent prosperity, he hired more locksmithing staff. By his third year of operation the company was losing money and almost out of cash. Trying to figure out how that could be, the locksmith discovered that many of his accounts receivables had become severely aged and inventory had been depleted. The company had actually been losing money though it showed a profit.

His response was to fire the accountant, install a computerized account-ing system and learn how to operate it himself. By following up accounts overdue he improved his cash position. He was also able to analyze job costs to revise prices and improve profitability. However, now he found himself bur-dened with accounting which did not interest him and was unable to work on locksmithing, which he enjoyed.

Just which numbers are the best early warning indicators of the need for action varies from one company to another. For one company it may be hours billed, for another collections and cash balance, or billings, bookings and back-log. For retail stores, a particularly important number, often representing as much as 70 percent of assets, is the inventory. If it is short in items of impor-tance to customers or if much of it is "dead" and not moving, performance of the store can be drastically diminished.

Thus, choosing the most important numbers to track most closely can be very important. One parts distributor said his key numbers to monitor were sales, gross margins, out-of-stock levels, personnel counts and overtime hours.[1] Based on the wrong numbers one wood products company was advised by its accountants to liquidate. Another accounting firm was hired and showed with simpler reports that the company was basically solid. Those reports also showed how to strengthen it further, and the company went on to greater pros-perity.[2]

The individualism of needs in setting up books for a venture is under-scored by a survey of Certified Public Accountants that found that 81 percent of those specializing in small companies had clients that did not use generally accepted accounting principles.[3] Many used only tax accounting or a cash ba-sis, according to their individual requirements.

Selecting software also is an individual matter. Checking with a variety of sources before choosing is a likely starting point. Such sources include opera-tors of similar firms, a trade association for the company's line of work, accountants serving similar firms, software retail stores and trade magazines of the firm's industry.[4]

Application: *Develop a chart of accounts for the assigned case venture, and indicate the date when each is first likely to be needed up through year two.*

Maintaining Liquidity

There are two parts to maintaining liquidity: keeping cash outflows down and keeping cash inflows up. The former includes both controlling costs and controlling disbursements related to both costs and accruals. The latter includes collecting from customers, pursuing trade credit and possibly raising additional outside capital.

Danger of Running out of Cash

Three elements that determine the need for cash in a company are its margin, its growth rate and its capital intensity. If the margin is too slim the venture can lose money and cash. If its growth rate is high, there will be need to support more receivables, inventory and possibly plant and equipment. A high enough margin may be able to cover these with retained earnings, but not if capital intensity is high. Consequently it is very easy for a venture to fall into a need for more cash. If it cannot be obtained, then the founders will at best have to cut back on expenditures, give up more equity or possibly see the venture fail.

> In 1974 a Seattle man undertook to start an indoor tennis club. He sold 150 memberships, obtained a bank loan, built a facility that could accommodate 600 members and opened the doors in September. He found that to break even he would need at least 250 members. Month by month the club lost money while he sought to recruit more members. This depleted his cash and soon creditors were pressing for payment. As the deficit grew he was compelled to shift his efforts to recruiting investors rather than members. Eventually he was able to put together a consortium of Canadian and American investors to take over the business and its $50,000 loss. He was left with no business and no job, but relieved that he had not let down the members whom he had initially recruited.

In hindsight this entrepreneur might have seen that there were at least three things he could have done better. The first would have been to forecast cash flows with more care, which would have revealed sooner the crunch that was inevitable. The second would have been to line up more adequate financing in advance, rather than having to seek it when things were desperate. Third, he could have controlled operating costs more carefully and thereby reduced cash drain.

Minimizing Non-Cash Assets

Seeking to minimize cash needs, discussed in Chapter 5 (subchapter 5a) in connection with initial financing, is worthy of continued attention and effort as the venture begins to take hold. There may be natural inclinations to add expensive but non-essential things: new facilities and equipment, bigger inventory, refurnished offices, and maybe company cars. As the venture becomes visible, it will also become a target for others who have things to sell, such as computer systems, accounting services, advertising ideas, security systems, and charitable causes. These may play on a founder's ambition to build a bigger and more successful company by implying that such accomplishment can be bought and erected like a stage prop or a window display.

Desire to increase sales and please customers can allow accounts receivable to string out. Why antagonize people by pressing for payment if it might cause them not to buy as much? Sales are needed to break even and earn profits. There is plenty else to do without worrying about how fast customers are paying. It's easy to be comforted by the fact that receivables are a symbol of successful sales, the more the better. Besides, the receivables can always be used for borrowing at the bank if more cash is needed. It's also easy to forget that the bank will loan at most only a percentage of the receivables, not the face value, and maybe nothing at all. Moreover, the borrowed money will cost interest and probably other charges which constitute further cash drain.

> Donald Weck and Harvey Levine started Love At First Bite in 1981 to make pate's and quiches. In the second year they started borrowing money to add staff and equipment. Weck recalled, "We spent way too much money on things we had no business spending money on. We took out a $15,000 loan for a computer that we didn't need. We hired a controller for $30,000 when we were only grossing $400,000 a year." By 1985 the company, $200,000 in debt, was advised to declare bankruptcy. Instead Weck fired the controller and the bookkeeper, reorganized the production staff, persuaded the bank to restructure its loan and managed to restore profitability. By 1988 the company was debt-free with sales of $1.2 million per year.[5]

Constant vigilance is needed to minimize cash drain, and staying constantly informed of any cash commitments is something a founder must do. Signing all the checks is one action that may help. Others are to keep a running file on receivables aging and to discuss any major financial commitments with a banker or someone likely to hold conservative views on spending. Maintaining a cash flow forecast and paying careful attention to it particularly before making any commitments for expansion should be another rule.

Holding Down Expenses

Although incurring expenses and having cash outflow don't necessarily coincide, minimizing expenses is a natural companion to minimizing non-cash assets to conserve cash. The value of vigilance appears in the following case.

A machine shop owner noticed that his total materials costs were running far in excess of the amount he was estimating on jobs. Seeking the reason, he also noticed that scrap from the shop seemed somewhat too abundant. Figuring that excessive material waste might be occurring because workers had free access to the shop's materials inventory, he decided to hire a stock clerk who would check both incoming freight and shipments against invoices, have workers sign for materials checked out against jobs and maintain a running inventory of not only raw materials but also work in process and finished goods. Materials costs shortly came into line with expectations.

Application: *Develop a projected cash flow statement for the assigned case venture, and indicate for each expense item the range of flexibility through which it may be reduced by economizing.*

Strategic Tuning

A logical approach to controlling costs might seem to be going line by line through the income statement and looking for ways to cut. But that is not the way CEOs of high-performing small companies do it, according to the editors of *Inc.* who interviewed them. Instead, they reported that "the motivation to cut costs becomes a departure point for something much more far-reaching. It forces a CEO to reexamine the entire company, to rethink its structure, what it does, even his or her role in it."[6] Examples the article cited to illustrate this point included the following.

A construction company operator knew there was waste, but not where. The first task, rather than seeking cost cuts, was to make financial information on jobs uniform so they could be compared. This revealed that big jobs were more profitable than small ones and gave better ideas about what types of business to seek.

❖ ❖ ❖

A quick oil change operator who emphasized having a qualified staff and providing exceptional service, found his margins slipping. Looking for places to cut costs he decided the only option was to reduce advertising. However, upon further analyzing ways to increase profits rather than cut costs he decided it would be better to leave advertising alone and expand capacity.

❖ ❖ ❖

The CEO of a company selling computer printing equipment, supplies and services analyzed how the people in his company spent their time and concluded that too much of it went to less profitable activities. Rather than cutting costs, he changed the composition of his workforce, adding some people with new expertise and laying off others whose specialties were less profitable.

❖ ❖ ❖

The owners of a security systems company found that installation costs were exceeding estimates they used in bidding. A new incentive system that paid installers by satisfactory job completion rather than hours brought costs down.

Cost control can begin much earlier than these examples display. Dan Bricklin, one of the founders of Software Arts, which introduced the first microcomputer spreadsheet program, Visicalc, but subsequently failed to distinguish itself successfully, recalled missteps reaching back to company conception.

> We had no models for a software company, so we operated on the book-publishing model, which turned out to be wrong. We thought we could just develop neat products and sell them—without realizing that different organizations were needed for different types of products. We didn't appreciate that the overhead appropriate for one product might be totally inappropriate for another. So there was a lot of waste. I could see it in my company, and I saw it even more when I did consulting for Lotus. It wasn't purposeful. People just didn't understand what was necessary and what wasn't.[7]

Figuring out which costs are necessary is something the initial business planning process can help with. But it is likely to require some trial and analysis, as well. Venturing is largely a process of experimentation. Although the entrepreneur may have a clear vision of what the venture is to be and perhaps even plans that have been carefully thought out, reviewed by other knowledgeable people and refined based on their feedback, there will still be continual adjustment of important dimensions and possibly major changes in the venture's strategy as it moves forward.

Foreseeing Greater Systematization

As a venture's inception advances through clock and calendar, its competition will naturally tend to increase. The market opportunity the venture has seized will, if worth pursuing, become increasingly visible to others, and—if its pursuit is effective—so will its ways of going after the market. In short, the new venture will have to work hard if it is not to be surpassed and eclipsed by its competitors.

It is not simply a matter of the founders' thinking, planning and acting. Top performance requires the participation of all the company's members constantly working toward smarter procedures, in a coordinated way. The degrees of success of such procedures have been described by Boag[8] based on a sample of high-technology Canadian start-ups. His sample was relatively small—only 20 companies—but this enabled the companies to be studied in greater depth than would have been possible with a larger number. Boag found that the ventures' success varied according to thoroughness of their marketing control systems. Briefly, the pattern was as follows, from least successful to most successful companies:

Least successful - Lowest growth rate (four companies)
- Engineering culture
- No rationalization of marketing focus, co-founders and others seeking sales part time
- No strategic planning or task planning
- Ad hoc meetings
- No systematic sales performance measurement
- No rationalized motivation or reward system linked to desired performance

Better but below par (ten companies)
- Sales culture
- Formalized sales department, but still some shared functions
- No strategic planning, but some task assignment to cope with delivery problems
- Some systems for tracking sales development and budget
- Monthly committee meetings with varying participants
- No profit-tracking systems on sales
- Price-cutting responses to competitor threats
- No rationalized motivation or reward system linked to desired performance

Above par (four companies)
- Goals down from the top, plans up from the bottom
- Frequent scheduled meetings, coordination of plans into combined documents
- Real-time tracking of sales performance and costs by segment
- Analysis of reasons for departures from plans
- Emphasis on cost control in both manufacturing and marketing
- No strategic planning
- Rewards linked to desired performance

Highest performance and growth rate (two companies)
- Technology niche emphasis
- Frequent scheduled meetings, more emphasis on coordination, task specialties
- Emphasis on strategic forecasting and planning to direct the company
- Working through coordinated control systems that measure performance
- Responding to performance feedback with corrective actions

Boag noted that it is not possible to separate cause and effect. Greater control of system rationalization may be the result, not the cause—or at least, not the only cause—of better performance. Even so, it is something the entrepreneur should probably contemplate early on. Failure for it to occur will be something to worry about, whether as a cause or an effect.

One co-founder who considers it a cause is Randy Fields of Mrs. Fields' Cookies. In that company, computers are used for real-time managing of inventory control at geographically scattered stores. For managers of the stores, as much as possible is pre-programmed to automate production decision making. Fields commented on the importance of this automation as follows:[9]

> *The three biggest differences between us and our competitors are quality, our control systems and Debbi's focus on service. The (computer) technology empowers the people by freeing their time to spend more time on the quality of the product and the service to the customer, which is the driver. The real role of management is to get people to do what they wouldn't do without you there.*

Seeking Additional Cash

Chapter 5 on finance described alternative sources of outside capital and discussed how they may be tapped at the outset. As the venture progresses through start-up it will likely be necessary to move from one source to another and continue seeking more cash. If the venture reaches a stage where it is showing some success, it should find raising capital easier than it would be at inception. Suppliers, once they see that the venture can pay bills and is likely to continue in that capability, will begin to extend trade credit to it. Banks will usually loan something against accounts receivable. Potential investors should become easier to recruit, either as working partners or, if a way can be shown in which they are likely to recover their cash with a healthy profit, as silent partners.

Application: *Based on a cash flow projection for the assigned case venture, indicate the amounts of cash to be obtained from outside and the three most likely sources, in rank order, for obtaining that case infusion.*

Supplementary Reading

New Venture Mechanics Chapter 9. (Vesper, K. H., Prentice-Hall, 1993)

Exercises

1. Contact a franchisor, learn what systems it provides for management and size up what you could use from such a firm for starting a new venture. Describe how you might satisfy those needs on your own without buying a franchise.

2. Contact three CPA firms and ask what they recommend in the way of accounting services for a start-up. How do their answers differ depending on whether the start-up is in services or manufacturing? How do the CPA firms compare? Which would you more likely pick for which kind of start-up and why?

3. Interview two entrepreneurs, and ask how each controlled cash flow during start-up versus how they control it now. What did they learn from their experience and how?

4. List the kinds of records problems that can crop up as a company develops from start-up, and describe systems to cope with those problems.

5. Contact several firms founded in the past 10 years and check against Table 8-3 the sequences through which their accounting systems evolved. Identify the events which triggered changes in them over time. Assess the timeliness of the changes.

Venture History

1. What did the accounting system consist of when the first check to pay for some aspect of it was written? How did it evolve from there?

2. How did the chart of accounts change over time?

3. What non-accounting records are kept, and how did the system for keeping them evolve?

4. How did solvency of the venture shift over time and why?

Venture Planning guide

1. Design a filing system for information on customers, competitors, media and suppliers. Design a vendor application.

2. Design the initial chart of accounts for your new venture. Estimate how it may change with time both in the accounts listed and the relative priorities of their importance. Explain why. Indicate also where a microcomputer and different forms of help from outside might best fit in.

3. List what you expect will be the most critical numbers to monitor in your venture. Rank order them in importance and explain why you chose that order.

4. List the sequence of conversations with specific other people that would be required to implement a venture plan. Insofar as possible identify who the individuals would be, where they are located, what action by them would be desired and what should be said to them to gain that response. Include whether the contact would be by phone or in person, how long it should take and in what sequence it should occur, giving calendar dates and days of the week.

5. Describe the systems that will be used to monitor purchasing, check writing, petty cash reserves, expense reporting, and employee honesty.

6. Indicate how profit centers will be established, both initially and over time, as the venture develops. Include a description of how costs and revenues will be allocated to assess profits by different centers.

7. Describe budgeting procedures and how these will change during the venture's first three years. Indicate how they will be used for controlling costs.

8. Schedule the expected times at which the venture plan will be updated, how that will be done, and who will be responsible for what tasks to get it done.

9. Project the expected future times at which outside sources of cash and alternative fall-back sources will be approached for financing, indicating the alternative sources and order in which they will be tried. Explain the rationale.

10. Explain the venture's policy toward use of financial leverage and how it may be expected to change over time.

11. Tell how management by (1) objectives, (2) exceptions, and (3) motivations will operate both initially and two or three years downstream in the venture.

Notes

[1] Charles J. Bodenstab, "Keeping Tabs on Your Company," *Inc.*, August 1989, p. 131.
[2] Jill Andresky Fraser, "Straight Talk," *Inc.*, March 1990, p. 97.
[3] "Hotline," *Inc.*, September 1990, p. 31.
[4] "Network," *Inc.*, May 1990, p. 21.
[5] Jeannie Ralston, "Specialty Food With All the Trimmings," *Venture*, February 1981, p. 43.
[6] Bruce G. Posner, "Squeeze Play," *Inc.*, July 1990, p. 68.
[7] "My Company, My Self," *Inc.*, July 1989, p. 35.
[8] David A. Boag, "Marketing Control and Performance in Early-Growth Companies," *Journal of Small Business Management*, 2, no. 4, Fall 1987, p. 365.
[9] *Anatomy of A Start-Up*, (Boston: *Inc.* Publishing 1991), p. xix.

Case Questions

General Questions

1. Project a plan for development of sales, production and control in the assigned case venture.

2. State key assumptions underlying the plan and contingency plans to be adopted if they prove invalid.

3. Which functional areas are easiest to plan for and which are hardest?

4. Which are most important to plan for, the harder or easier ones?

Case 25 - Bruce Milne (B) p. 543

1. Devise a plan for overcoming the obstacles to sales in this venture.

2. Describe and weigh the pros and cons of the seminar selling Bruce is using. For what products and services is it best suited?

Case 26 - Vic O'Brien p. 545

1. Develop profiles of three contrasting potential customers for Vic's store, and design a means of focusing on each in particular in order to get each one to buy something from the store.

2. Formulate three contrasting future portraits of success that could be developed from the venture Vic has started, and describe what it would take to achieve each of them.

Case 27 - Ampersand (D) p. 556

1. What other course of action could the team reasonably have followed over term break? How does it compare to the one they did follow?

2. What are the main choices they face now, what are the pros and cons of each, and which should they pursue?

3. Prepare an estimated balance sheet for the company as of June 1993 and an estimated income statement for the venture to date.

4. Suppose you were a member of the Ampersand team as of the time of this case. How would you weigh staying with the venture versus accepting a $60,000 per year job offer with a major corporation?

Case 28 - Ampersand (E) p. 559

1. What is your assessment of the financing offer being extended to Ampersand? If you had the money, what would you offer them?

2. What "rights" should a team member have if he or she left the team at this point?

3. What should the team include on its list of "positive covenants" to be a good model for other start-ups as the prospective investor is proposing?

4. If the team gets the investment and moves ahead, what should the salaries of the team members be and why?

Case 29 - Ampersand (F) p. 561

1.   Why didn't the distributors pick up the product?

2.   What options do Elaine and Kathy have for generating sales, given the reactions of distributors?

3.   Should the product rollout and advertising program be modified?

4.   Will the team have to set up its own manufacturing facility? How should it proceed to fulfill the orders that Kathy and Elaine have promised retailers for shipment in September?

5.   Should the venture continue?

Case 30 - Chem Synthesis, Inc. (D) p. 564

1.   How should Jim respond to the fax from abroad?

2.   Are there any guidelines CSI should adopt for anticipating issues like this in the future on international business sales?

Case 31 - Matthew Clark and Steve Wilson p. 567

1.   Devise as best you can a forecast of the production facilities and talents this company will need quarterly over the next three years. Indicate the main options and which you would choose for satisfying those needs.

2.   Develop a list of the capabilities currently possessed by DAS, and contrast it with those of "pros" that might be operating in the same industry. Discuss ways that DAS can best seek to capitalize on its strengths and compensate for its relative weaknesses.

Bruce Milne (B)

In January 1980 Bruce Milne and Lauri Chandler gave notice to their employer, Alpine Data Systems, that they were resigning. Working initially from the den in Bruce's house, they incorporated their venture as Dataword, Inc. on February 22. A third partner, Brian Duthie, joined in the formation, but still remained on the job at Alpine, reluctant to leave because of concern about risks in the new enterprise coupled with the prospect that his family responsibilities would shortly increase with arrival of a new child.

The business plan was not formally reduced to writing at this point, but Bruce was working on it in anticipation that they would need to raise cash beyond the initial $27,000 they could muster from savings and family members. They reasoned that to generate short-term sustaining income the three would continue selling minicomputers with third party software while working on the side to develop a new software product, which they would bundle with Altos microcomputers to sell as accounting systems for accountants. Bruce would work on lining up suppliers and customers. Brian would develop the new software, and Lauri would run the office. All three would also work on selling the existing minicomputer systems and on consulting, Bruce in accounting systems, Lauri in word processing and Brian on programming.

Because they aimed eventually to provide systems for both accounting and word processing, they chose the name Dataword for their company. In fact, however, they knew they would have to choose initially between the two software

packages, accounting versus word processing, for development. Lauri favored word processing because that was her field of familiarity. The other two partners favored accounting, because they had seen what they believed were weaknesses in the market leader of that field, which would give them particularly strong competitive advantages. Accounting was chosen for the initial thrust.

The income-generating strategy did not work as well as they had hoped. They did manage to sell some minicomputer systems as planned, deriving momentum from some leads that came their way as they left Alpine and from their ability to point out that they had proven track records with these established systems. However, a problem all along had been that such major systems invariably required extensive installation and service follow-up work as customers learned to operate them. This took a great deal of the founders' time, and although Brian finally was persuaded in March 1980 to leave Alpine and join the venture full-time, it was still difficult to work on the new software, perform enough consulting and selling to pay the bills and try to line up suppliers and customers for the new microcomputer system all at the same time.

Bruce was able to operate with no salary because of his wife's job, but the other two could not, and there were other expenses of operating the office. It was necessary to add other employees, a part-time secretary and a part-time programmer. Two offices were rented, one in which Brian could concentrate on programming and the other for Bruce's and Lauri's selling and consulting work.

To cope with these expenses as their initial capital dwindled, Bruce undertook to raise more seed capital. From three individuals he raised $10,000 each. One was the proprietor of a cheesecake manufacturing company, a former customer of Bruce's at Alpine who had become a personal friend. The second was an attorney whom Bruce had long tried without success to sell Alpine products, who had also become a friend. The third was a former competitor who had reaped substantial financial gains when his employer, in which he held a share of ownership, had gone public. He too had become a personal friend of Bruce's. The contributions of these investors brought the total capitalization of Dataword to $57,000.

With expenses exceeding revenues by about $10,000 per month Bruce could foresee that something would have to be done soon as fall approached. Although it was not clear that the new software would be ready, he began making arrangements to hold a seminar for accounting firms at which the new system would be displayed and sales orders to buy it would be solicited. This, Bruce observed, would be the first time, so far as he knew, that seminar selling had been applied to microcomputer systems.

The new software was, in fact, not fully complete as the day of the seminar arrived. But there would be enough to display what its capabilities would be. Bruce decided to keep the seminar on schedule. There would, he figured, be a month or two of leeway after taking orders, during which the Altos computers would have to be obtained and delivered to customers, and during that time Brian could put on the finishing touches.

At least, that is what the Dataword founders hoped. Bruce knew they would have reached the limits of their solvency by the time of the seminar. There would still be about $27,000 cash in the bank, but the company would have unpaid bills of approximately the same amount. Brian and Lauri were aware of the cash balance, but not the accounts payable amount. Bruce did not think it would help to have them worrying about financial problems in addition to their other job responsibilities.

But it seemed clear to Bruce that they absolutely had to get orders at that seminar. He had been working on terms of a limited partnership offering which he believed might bring in another $50,000 if they could get orders on books to substantiate that the company had a future. If they could not get the orders, however, it looked to him like they would not be able to raise more capital. In that case he expected they would have to use their cash to pay existing bills and Dataword would be finished.

The seminar was held as scheduled, presenting the new microcomputer accounting system with Brian's developing software package, "Datawrite," and went off as planned. Several accounting companies showed up, asked questions and seemed satisfied that the new system offered a much more economical system, around $25,000 compared to over three times that for other systems, to meet their needs.

The only problem seemed to be that they would not be willing to place orders unless Bruce could answer one more question for them. "We have bought new systems before only to end up with a mess of new problems in getting them to work," they said. "How do we know we will be able to rely on the performance of this new system you want us to order from you?"

Vic O'Brien

In December 1971 Vic O'Brien, an electrical engineer at Colossal Technology Corporation in Seattle, faced a decision of whether to give up on his attempt to set up a hi-fi speaker manufacturing and retail business, or to press on with it, and if so, how. He had opened the store as a part-time activity run by other employees during his working hours. Since opening the store in July, his sales totaled $2,850, contrasted with rent of $1,450 and employee salaries of $4,360.

Vic had not paid himself any salary to date and the savings he had used for start-up were eroding faster than he could replenish them from his job as an engineer. He commented that he wanted the new business to succeed, but if there was no way to do so, he didn't want to "throw good money after bad."

Personal History

Born in Tacoma, Washington, the son of a newspaper circulation manager, Vic O'Brien graduated from high school in 1960 and attended Gonzaga University for two years, majoring in liberal arts. He then married, moved to Seattle and took a job with the phone company to support his family, which soon included a new baby. By working full time for the phone company he was able to qualify for tuition support from the company to attend the University of Washington, where he shifted his major to physics but took as many electives in electrical engineering as possible. By carrying a full course load, he was able to qualify for university housing at low rent.

His interest in electronics developed in high school, where he built an ultrasound modulator as a hobby project. In college he put together a hi-fi system. Components such as tuners and amplifiers he found were cheapest if made from kits. For a speaker he decided to follow do-it-yourself instructions he found in *Popular Electronics* magazine. He bought the basic speaker, which then needed mounting in some sort of box, through the mail from Lafayette Radio. Then he built a cabinet for it in the dirt-floored garage behind his house. Instructions for building the box called for arranging holes and baffles with measurements to be made using other electronic instruments. To buy these and the other electronics parts he needed at wholesale, Vic obtained a state resale tax number and city business license and called himself a business, O'Brien Research Associates. When the speakers were finished, their sound pleased him. He recalled:

> The guy who wrote the article really didn't know what he was talking about technically, but the speaker sounded great anyway. What impressed me even more, though, was how much less the unit cost than buying something with comparable performance at a retail store.

As another hobby project, Vic decided to install an intercom in his house. To maximize discounts he could get on parts and also to earn money to pay for them, he decided to set himself up as a business installing intercoms for other people as well. He placed a classified advertisement in the local paper, which brought him his first customer. He met his next customer in the parking lot of an electronics supply store. Vic described what followed.

> *He turned out to be a builder. So I asked him if he would like some intercoms installed in the house he was building, and he said he would. Out of that I was able to pay for wiring my own house.*

Vic's interest in business continued to grow as he started reading books about it. One told about James Ling, an entrepreneur who was becoming spectacularly successful in the '60s after starting as an electrical contractor, particularly impressed Vic. He began thinking how he might be able to emulate Ling.

Following his graduation in physics from the University of Washington in 1964, Vic quit the phone company and went to work as an electronics engineer for the standards laboratory of a large Seattle company, Colossal Manufacturing. His interest in entrepreneurship, however, continued. He found many at Colossal, he said, who felt confined and restricted by their jobs, and consequently formed outside businesses, both as creative outlets and as potential career-escape vehicles.

One of these entrepreneurs was another engineer in the standards laboratory with whom Vic became friends. Vic recalled:

> *Management drove him into his own business with the kind of stupid policies big companies are so good at coming up with. The standards lab was set up just to serve Colossal divisions, but they all had this beautiful expensive equipment for measurement work. So some outside companies started buying service from the lab, and it started making money on that too, which was fine.*
>
> *But then a new manager came into the lab. He was the bullslinger type who gets along great with management but is not strong technically. Good technical types often deprecate their work when you ask about it, but if you let them show it to you they get all enthused. Bullslingers, on the other hand, will tell you how great it is but won't have anything to show you. When a bullslinger moves around in the organization, he tends to attract others like him. They all keep looking up at higher management to see how they are doing, instead of down where the action is. It's like a basketball team with its players all watching the clock, and pretty soon they lose the game.*
>
> *In the standards lab they decided to make more money off outside customers by raising prices. And at the same time they decided to make the other Colossal division managers happy by giving them higher priority in the lab. This meant the other divisions didn't have to plan and schedule their work as carefully. It also meant that the outside customers got poorer service for the higher prices.*
>
> *My friend saw this as handwriting on the wall and set up his own lab outside to catch customers as they dropped away from Colossal. Then as the workload in Colossal's lab began to decline, management started surplusing some of its test equipment. This meant they were selling off very expensive equipment for as little as 10 cents on the dollar. My friend would buy it, which strengthened his own lab and gave him the capability to take more work away from Colossal, causing it to surplus still more equipment, which he would buy, and so forth. Before long our management was laying people off right and left. I got my termination notice but was picked up by another department.*

A Speaker Manufacturing Venture

Vic continued his outside interest in hi-fi speakers, spurred on by concerns about his job at Colossal. He and his brother pooled $500 of savings, bought a table saw, other tools, plywood, speaker cones, wire and other materials and began fabricating speakers in his basement. As with the intercoms, he ran classified advertisements in the local papers, this time offering "engineering prototype speakers for sale, half price." To their disappointment, very few sales resulted.

They did receive a phone call from another man who was selling stereo hi-fi systems door-to-door. He asked the two what they would charge to make speakers for him. They responded with a price of 25 percent above raw materials cost. He immediately placed an order and, because the brothers were short of working capital, also provided them with an inventory of speaker cones he had already bought for another local man to use in building speakers for him. Production began in batches of 12. To carry plywood, Vic bought an old Volkswagon van. Finding the rear doors too narrow to accept 4-by-8-foot sheets, he cut slots at the door edges to widen the entry. Vic commented:

> We were working hard, building speakers, spending money, and buying materials and tools, but for some reason we weren't getting anywhere. We began selling some of the speakers direct ourselves, but when the man we had been building for found out we were doing that, he became very unhappy, especially since we were selling inventory of speaker cones he was providing for us free. It also turned out that when he visited our shop, he had been taking note of just what tools we had and exactly how we were building things. He was setting up his own shop to copy our designs. So to some extent we were both cheating on

each other. I decided that if I was going to be successful in business, I needed to learn more about how it was supposed to work by going back to school.

Business Education

Vic and his brother liquidated their business in 1967 by transforming the remaining raw materials into speakers and selling them. With tuition provided by his continuing Colossal job, Pat enrolled in the University of Washington Graduate School. Vic said:

> They wouldn't admit me to the Business School. I don't know why. So I got in as an unmatriculated graduate student and every quarter with a lot of effort persuaded professors in the business school individually to admit me to their courses on an overload basis. After I had taken a bunch of courses successfully in that way, I went back to the admissions office and showed them I was earning good grades and was headed toward graduation anyway, so they might as well admit me. They did.

At the suggestion of the friend who started his own standards laboratory, Vic also took a night course at the University on small business management. Sponsored by the Small Business Administration, but taught by a series of professors, the course especially influenced Vic's thinking about how a company might be managed more effectively than he believed Colossal was. He recalled how the instructor had divided the class into two competing teams.

> My friend who had the laboratory was made leader of one, and I was leader of the other. We were given some Tinkertoys, and each team was supposed to build as high a tower as it could in a given period of time. One team was hierarchically organized with a leader at

the top directing it, and the other was egalitarian and non-directive, with each person adding to the effort as he saw fit.

My team was the non-directive one, and we built a tower that was vastly higher than the directive team did. Most of us also rated the project as more enjoyable than most of the people on the directive team did, although there were a few people who dissented with the majority in both groups. The instructor told us that it always turns out that way. The non-directive team always builds a higher tower and likes the job but there are a few people on it who don't like the non-directive way of working. I decided that the next time I had a business it would be egalitarian and give maximum freedom to the individuals working in it so we could outperform our competitors the way my team had in building the Tinkertoy tower.

Vic's Work at Colossal

In 1969, Colossal's industry underwent a substantial downturn and Vic's discomfort with his job at Colossal increased. Vic continued:

People were getting laid off all around me. One day in 1969 my boss called me into his office, where his desk was all covered with pink layoff notices for different people. My wife had just had a new baby. I looked at those notices and asked what he wanted to see me about. He told me we should go to his boss's office, which we did. His boss said we should go down to the cafeteria where we could talk. The look on his face didn't make me feel easier. I figured this was it for me. Then they handed me my five-year pin, congratulated me on receiving it, and had a big laugh about how they had scared me. To them it was all a big joke. But it really made me mad.

Vic also felt he and others were often not recognized for their contributions to the company. He described an episode in which another employee had been responsible for developing a piece of electronic equipment. After working several months, the man had been unable to make it work. With a contract deadline near, Vic had taken over the job, and by dint of great effort and many overtime hours had "pulled off a miracle and got the thing working." No congratulations had followed, he said, simply other tough cases of a similar nature as recognition of his exceptional troubleshooting performance. Later he noted that one of his superiors presented a paper on Vic's technical accomplishments. "He did the paper better than I could have," Vic said. "So that may have been best for the corporation. But after all, it was my work. How could I get ahead in this kind of a system?"

Vic enjoyed some parts of his work at Colossal, notably the electronics, but other aspects he did not.

The huge parking lots, commuter traffic, numbered badges and hierarchical atmosphere turn me off. The individual often doesn't matter at all in that kind of a system. One day, just as an experiment, I made a conscious effort to do absolutely no work all day. Normally I really put out a lot, but when I cut it down to zero it produced no effect at all. Nobody even noticed, which I guess is why so many people at Colossal devote their efforts to politics, social activities, and other games instead of getting work done. In a small company, things could never be that way for long.

Opening a Store

By early 1971 Vic had completed his MBA studies and, now freed from coursework but still employed by Colossal, he decided to start another business, this time a hi-fi retail store. This, he thought, should be a more effective way to sell his own speakers than the classified advertisements had been, and by selling at retail he expected he could realize a higher profit margin than he had earlier, when manufacturing for the man who sold door to door. He still had the table saw and other tools from his earlier manufacturing adventure. His wife, who had recently inherited property worth approximately $10,000, agreed to invest half that amount if Vic would sell the dune buggy he had built and invest the proceeds from that as evidence of his "moral commitment."

From one of his university courses in taxation he had concluded that a "Subchapter S" corporation combined the desirable feature of permission to write off for tax purposes any company losses against personal income, as in a proprietorship, with the limited liability advantages of a corporation. To form one, he looked up the state statute, which he found gave good instructions, and phoned the office of the Washington Secretary of State to clarify issues as he ran into them. Since he understood three directors were required, he recruited a friend, not associated with the business in any other way, to join himself and his wife on the board. He made application to the U.S. Patent Office to register the company's name, Sound Array, for trademark protection.

An additional reason for forming a corporation, Vic said, was so he could issue stock in lieu of pay until the company built up cash for that purpose.

Only the government can issue dollars. But stock is another form of currency, and anyone can issue as many shares of that as he wants by simply forming a corporation. In a sense, it's a legal way of printing your own money.

Vic authorized his new corporation to issue up to 50,000 shares at a par value of $1 a share. To himself he issued 2,439 shares for investing that number of dollars in terms of equipment, purchased supplies and cash. An opening balance sheet for the store appears as Exhibit 1. He later had the corporation issue debentures, convertible into 5,000 shares of common stock at her option, to his wife for $5,000 she invested.

To find a location, Vic decided to concentrate on the area near his house, since he wanted it to be convenient in his off-work hours. He looked up census data on personal income and learned that the north end where he lived, although it contained many modest homes such as his own, which had been built as part of a military tract in World War II, on the average had fairly high personal income. There were several small business districts near his home, each having one or two blocks of small stores. He drove through all of them, looking for any empty storefronts. One he noticed had recently been vacated by some sort of photographic enterprise. Inside it had been partitioned into many small rooms for sales, picture taking and developing. The room bordering the sidewalk was 12 by 16 feet with a large display window along the walk.

One thing Vic particularly liked about that location was the rent: $225 per month on a two-year lease. In addition to the price, Vic commented on two other reasons favoring this location:

It's about two miles from a major shopping district serving the University of Washington. I figured that by locating near the University, we could sell to the University market and tap a good labor supply at the same time. Hi-fi is still pretty much a hobby-oriented business and the heavy buyers are young men in the 18-35 year age bracket. If you figure that half the 30,000 students at the University are male, that's a pretty good base to draw from.

Vic signed the lease. Then, after work and on weekends, he and his wife went to work on the empty building, cleaning up, constructing shelves and decorating. They moved shop equipment for making speakers from Vic's basement and set it up in one of the back rooms. To ration his modest capital carefully, Vic ordered a small inventory of medium-priced hi-fi equipment, tuners, amplifiers, turntables and other accessories. These he obtained through the former door-to-door salesman, who was now in the manufacturing business himself, having copied Vic's speaker cabinet designs and shop facilities. The man was doing quite well selling his speakers to dealers in Seattle and also western Canada.

Vic spread the products out on the shelves but found the inventory was insufficient to keep the store from looking bare. He decided to fill the shelves by displaying some stuffed toys his wife had designed and been selling on her own. In addition, he visited thrift shops and stores such as the Goodwill and Salvation Army to obtain antique looking electronic goods to cover blank space and to sell if anyone took an interest in them.

Initial Operations

The store opened for business on July 1, 1971. Prices were set substantially below the competition on all items, the lowest being speakers made by the company, depicted in Exhibit 2, which were sold at approximately half the price of competing lines in other stores. Vic did this to compensate for the limited range and selection available in his store, which was less than half that of competitors, the nearest of which was in the University business district, about two miles away.

Other disadvantages he began to notice were that the only parking available at his store was along the curb in front and at the side of the corner on which the store stood. There was no lot. However, he also noted that the severity of this problem was not terribly great, since there was relatively little traffic in the area. Many cars passed in the morning and evening when people were traveling to and from work, but during the day there was very little street traffic, and almost none on the sidewalk. There was no large grocery or other store in the area. On the street running north from Vic's store were half a dozen businesses, such as a beauty salon, an antique store, a dry cleaner and small restaurants on each side of the street. Running south were houses on his side and a graveyard across the street. To the east and northwest were simply houses.

To operate the store and make speakers during the day while he was at Colossal, Vic hired his next door neighbor, an engineer recently laid off by Colossal. This man agreed to work for $4 per hour, half in cash and half in stock. This, Vic figured, would not only save money but also enhance employee dedication to company success. Teaching the new salesman to make speaker cabinets and install the speakers in them was easy, Vic said, not so much because the man was an engineer, but simply because the job was very elementary and uncomplicated. He recalled:

> We decided to start with one model called the Sound Array 3. It's similar to some name brands we sell, but much cheaper. Our speaker is a three-way system with a 1 $\frac{1}{2}$-cubic-foot box housing a 12-inch woofer and a tweeter which we hook together with appropriate crossover circuits. What we're essentially doing is making the box and then putting the speakers and wires in. I guess you could call us a wood-processing operation.

An illustration of the company's initial speaker product appears in Exhibit 2.

Vic's View of the Speaker Industry

Vic regarded speakers as part of a growing market that was changing from being hobby oriented to reaching the general consumer. The industry had seen great changes in the past 10 years as transistors and solid-state circuitry made their way into stereo components. He mentioned five speaker manufacturers that were doing well in the Seattle area: KLH, JBL, EPI, DR and Austin. He commented on how speakers were priced and marketed:

In any given market there are more brands than strong dealers. If a strong dealer pushes your product, then you'll do well. Manufacturers and distributors are willing to haggle over margins and differentials in wholesale and retail price, because there is a lot of margin to work with. They know that if they can get a dealer to push their line, he'll sacrifice margin for extra volume. That's where we have an advantage. We can sell our own products directly to the customer and avoid the mark-ups in between—our price is half that of our competitors, and we still get the same dollar margin from the sale. The only thing we need now is enough volume to put us over break-even.

Another concern Vic expressed about the speaker industry was what he termed "marketing hype." He explained that manufacturers would put out response graphs which indicated how much distortion existed from hearing the music through the speaker as compared with sitting in front of a live band or orchestra. Supposedly, good speakers would show a frequency response graph that was flat for different volumes that a listener might desire. Retailers would then use the graphs that were flattest to push a particular brand, even though a customer might be listening to two similarly priced speakers and prefer the sound of the one which appeared to have worse response.

Vic explained that there were many ways the charts could be rigged and that their apparent flatness was not necessarily a valid measure at all. Much more useful, he said, would be to have a spectrum analyzer, which could be employed both for designing better speakers and for demonstrating their qualities relative to other brands. He noted, however, that the cost of such an instrument was around $4,000.

Speaker parts, on the other hand, were comparatively cheap. Vic said the rule of thumb that speaker manufacturers typically used in designing and pricing their products was that the speakers in a system should be worth one-fifth the price of the system. Thus, a $100 speaker unit, consisting of a finished cabinet with speakers assembled in it would have $20 worth of speaker components in it. The remainder would be spent on assembling and finishing the cabinet, advertising, overhead, dealer margin and profit. By selling Sound Array 3 speaker units at approximately $120 each, Vic explained, he could install higher quality components, such as the woofers (see Exhibit 2), at two to three times normal costs and still earn a tolerable margin.

A bigger cost, he said, was that of the cabinets. The raw cabinet box might not cost much more than it would cost simply to test the components and pack them for shipment in cardboard. But assembly of the cabinet, and especially the application and rubbing of the finish plus stapling on of fabric to cover the front, made it cost more than the components that were inside. Other producers of speaker units, he said, would buy components that were cheaper and lower in quality than his, install them in cabinets that were sealed so that customers could not see what they looked like, and figure that since they could not be seen, customers could not discern the quality difference.

Other hi-fi products, such as tuners, amplifier, tape decks and turntables were typically manufactured by very large overseas companies. Stores like Vic's bought from them at 25 percent to 30 percent off retail price, depending on such things as how much they bought, how far ahead they ordered and whether they were buying on the basis of some "special" the manufacturer was offering. A big store, he said, might sell as much as $30,000 to $100,000 per month of such products.

Selling

Store sales were $300 in July, largely thanks to friends of Vic's who came to see the shop. Sales dropped to $150 in August when Vic's neighbor quit to accept another engineering job and recommended a friend to take over the store's operation during the day. Vic hired the individual and soon hired still another man the neighbor recommended. Both were described by Vic as "hippie types," with long hair and old clothes.

The men would work in one of the back rooms building speaker cabinets, then come forward to the showroom when a customer came in. Vic described the scene as less than conventional:

> When one of these guys sees a customer coming he tends to get excited and run to the door. Then, while he's standing there blocking the doorway before the customer can get in, he does a number about how great the speakers are. Meanwhile, the other employee, who is very shy, usually gets so uncomfortable from this that he goes into the back room to hide.
>
> I'll admit our place doesn't look much like a retail store and there's probably some skepticism on the part of customers when they come in. We're offering them a pretty good deal in terms of a high-quality speaker at a really low price.

Vic's own approach was to invite customers to hear how name brand speakers sounded and then let them listen to the Sound Array speaker for comparison. Vic said his strategy was to let people realize that they could get the same quality sound for half the money they would normally spend.

By September, with two men in the shop, sales rose again to $300, and in October, after a third man had walked in the door, asked for a job and been hired, they rose to $1,000. Vic began to take heart that things were picking up and that the unstructured form of management he found so effective on the Tinkertoy class project was going to work for him in business too. Employees were allowed to work on a flexible hour basis as long as someone was around to run the store. The business, he said, was small enough that a worker could determine when a shelf needed to be adjusted, the floors swept or other work around the store required attention.

Vic admitted they hardly looked like conventional salesmen, with long, sawdust-filled hair and tattered clothing, but he believed them to be intellectually bright, particularly the one he had most recently hired, and his impression was that about one customer out of four who came in the shop bought something, a figure he understood to be comparable to the experience of other hi-fi stores. One customer who came in asked if he could look at what was going on in the shop, and then asked if he could simply buy parts to make a speaker himself. One of Vic's salesman readily obliged. Later, when Vic asked what price the parts had been sold for, he learned that the salesman, not knowing what to charge, had given a figure equal to three times what Sound Array had paid for them. Apparently, the customer happily paid the price and left with the parts.

He noticed as other customers occasionally came in and bought parts, that not only were they willing to wait while employees scurried around the shop gathering them up, but also the customers seemed to be reasonably confident that they would be able to put them together. The thought occurred to him that if customers could make buying and assembly decisions well on their own, perhaps he could sell through mail order. He also surmised that there might be problems in selling beyond the Pacific Northwest region if mail order were attempted:

> *People think that you can operate all over the country with mail order and that since Washington is 3 percent of the population, you can sell 97 percent of your product outside the state. But I have my doubts when it comes to speakers. People like to come into the store and listen to the equipment before they decide to buy it.*

In order to go to a mail-order distribution strategy, Vic expected money would have to be spent on advertising and in development of catalogs and instructions. The most that Vic calculated he could afford in ad space at present would be a single one-inch column in the leading metropolitan newspaper, or presumably a somewhat larger space in a more localized paper, since ad rates scaled up and down with circulation volume. He said he had no idea what preparing a catalog would cost or what other means of advertising might be available to him to help boost sales.

Pressure for Decisions

In November sales turned down again to only $450, and in December, when Vic had hoped they would be buoyed by Christmas buying, the total came to only $550. At this rate there was not enough to pay for the parts, rent and utilities (consisting of a $50 per month phone bill, the rest being included in the rent), let alone three men in the shop plus something for Vic. All four earned $4 an hour, but Vic paid himself in stock, not cash. Vic's savings were low, and he could see that if he were to shut down there would be some time required to accomplish that and to find someone else to take over the remainder of his two-year lease.

It seemed there were many directions the company could take if there were only more time and capital. It might be possible to open other sales channels for the speaker manufacturing operation, as the former door-to-door salesman had done. Or the company might perhaps be able to sell through mail order, if it could work up a suitable catalogue and mailing list. The company had as yet done practically no advertising, as other hi-fi stores were able to do with apparently good results, so there seemed to be potential for improvement there. Vic noted that the main local newspaper, *The Seattle Times*, charged around $10 per column inch per day. The local student tabloid, *The Daily*, charged around $50 for an eighth of a page or ten column inches (5 cm), but had less than a tenth the circulation of the *Times*.

Undoubtedly there were also other options he had not yet thought of. The company's sign said simply, "Soundarray," in big letters, and underneath in smaller letters, "stereo speakers, amplifiers, turntables." But he wondered what he could do about any other marketing alternatives with only about $2,000 of savings left.

Those savings were taking on a new meaning for him as the large company for which he worked, Colossal, was also sinking into trouble. More and more layoff notices were coming around, and Vic feared that although his technical work at the company was progressing well there might be one of those unwelcome pink slips coming his way any day.

EXHIBIT 1 Opening Balance Sheet of Sound Array, Incorporated

Start of Business, July 1, 1971

Cash	216.83		
Accounts Receivable	0		
Inventory	1,457.00		
Prepaid Expenses	324.57		
Current Assets			1,998.40
Leasehold Improvements	76.25		
Less: Depreciation	0		
Net		76.25	
Equipment and Fixtures	961.64		
Less Depreciation	0		
Net		961.64	
Lease Deposits	475.00		
Organization Expense	64.50		
		539.50	
Fixed Assets			1,577.39
Total Assets			3,575.79
Accounts Payable	1,136.79		
Taxes Payable	0		
Accrued Expenses	0		
Unearned Revenue	0		
Notes Payable			
Within One Year	0		
Current Liabilities			1,136.79
Long Term Notes			0
Capital Stock Issued and Paid For			2,439.00
Total Liabilities and Capital			3,575.79

EXHIBIT 2 Speaker Construction

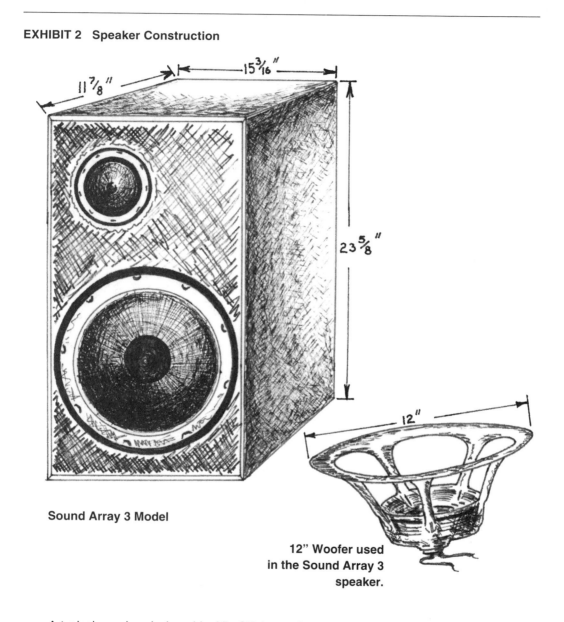

Sound Array 3 Model

**12" Woofer used
in the Sound Array 3
speaker.**

A typical speaker designed by Vic O'Brien and made by Sound Array is shown at left. Wood was cut and assembled to the dimensions shown. Then the speaker components were mounted and wired together within the enclosure.

The tweeter (high pitch sound) is the circle at the top left of the speaker. The woofer (low pitch sound) is at the bottom and also shown below dismounted.

A fabric cover would be mounted in front of the speakers and the wood would be finished, depending on customer preference.

Vic estimated that it took about eight hours of employee time to complete one speaker.

Case 27

Ampersand (D)

May 1993 - Finishing the First Production Run

You know, this just isn't going to work the way we're doing it. We're behind schedule and we're losing money.

Scott Bryant, vice president for operations of the Ampersand venture, was talking to his team members in the Austin, Texas garage of Kathy Henderson, vice president of marketing. Around them were piles of Claybords, some finished, others being sanded and still others awaiting sanding. The premises were dusty and noisy with four hand-sanders being operated by a workforce of students and street people hired as temporary workers to complete the company's first production run for shipment to Pearl Paint, a retail art supply store in New York.

Robert nodded in agreement with Scott's gloomy pronouncement. The venture would lose money by completing the order, but it would also lose more money if it did not and presumably if they did not complete the order, the work they had done to date would be wasted and the possibility of turning the venture into a success would also be gone. In addition to the cost of the shipment, however, would also be that of sending team members to New York so they could spend a week demonstrating the product for sales employees and customers at Pearl. Was this further investment justified, or might it mean throwing good money and time after bad?

Finishing the First Order for Shipment

At least Ampersand had more money available for completing the order in May 1993 as the last term of their MBA program drew to a close. The preceding month they had traveled to San Diego and won first prize, $5,000, in the North American Invitational Business Plan Competition at San Diego State University. When asked how their checks should be made out, other teams that had won cash prizes said to divide the money equally among their members. The Ampersand team asked simply that the check be made out to their corporation. They had also followed through with the International Moot Corp[SM] competition at the University of Texas, in which they had won fourth place.

As final examinations were completed, the team returned to the task of completing the 2,000 Claybords that rested in the cabinet shop in Austin where they had been sawed and routed but not sanded. The team had searched for alternative ways of completing the boards, wrapping them, adding appropriate instructions and labels and shipping them. They had considered the possibility of trying to get the boards sanded by some sort of automatic machine, but that seemed risky. If it did not work and the boards were ruined they would be stuck with no boards to finish, and the Tyler shop where the boards had been coated had already told them not to come back for more. The team concluded that they would have to do the sanding themselves using the technique developed by Charles Ewing for hand-held sanders.

With the permission of Kathy Henderson's landlord, Scott and Elaine made numerous trips hauling the load of boards in their small compact cars from the cabinet shop to the landlord's garage. The team then bought four orbital sanders from a local hardware store for around $100 each, rented a shrink-wrap machine for $100 a week from a packaging company and set up tables for processing Claybords on the landlord's back porch, yard and garage.

For labor, the team recruited friends from school and hired workers from among the day labor pool that showed up downtown each morning looking for jobs. Then the noisy, dusty job of sanding began. With the four team members plus two other hired people working from 7 a.m. until 9 p.m. each day for 10 days, they finally finished the boards. In the course of this effort, neighbors had complained of the dust and noise, and the Austin Police Department had come out to see what was going on.

An added complication was discovery that approximately half the boards had to be discarded due to debris found embedded in the clay as a result of dirt that had been in the air during the coating process in Tyler. Fortunately, there was enough extra coated board to overcome this scrap rate, but to use it the team had to return to the cabinet shop and ask the owner to please saw and route an additional 200 Claybords. Recalling his grief on the first load, the owner at first tried to avoid the job, then accepted it at double the rate of the first job and then said he was still losing money on the work.

This final 200 boards at least gave the team enough to complete the order for 2,000 boards. On graduation day, May 22,

1993, they at last sent the shipment off to Pearl Paint. Scott's question to Robert about whether the venture was really worth continuing, however, was still open. Clearly, they had lost money so far, and no certain way to turn it around was yet in sight.

Whether to Shift From Outsourcing to Manufacturing

Since the most serious problems so far had come from dealing with subcontractors, it seemed that possibly a better approach would be for Ampersand to set up its own manufacturing facility. Scott observed:

> *Looking for suppliers has been a continuous process for me. I'd call one and when it turned out not to fit, I'd ask them for suggestions about others, and that way I'd find lots of possibilities. But all the subcontractors we had used so far told us to please go away and not come back. When I tried to find new ones, I'd throw out numbers of possible volumes of work and they would get interested. Then they would ask about the process and I would describe it. They would tell me, that it sounded interesting, that they would like to think about it, and they would call us back. But then in fact they wouldn't call; and if I called them, they would tell me that they were too backlogged with other jobs to consider our work.*

Prices for machinery, if Ampersand wanted to set up its own plant, ranged into six figures. An automated sander, for instance, they found could cost upwards of $60,000. A paint line might cost an additional $30,000 to $150,000, while a forklift might cost another $5,000—all in used condition. Leasehold improvements, such as shelves, lighting, venting and fans, they estimated, might add $10,000 to the cost of a plant. There would be need for licenses, permits and inspections from various governmental agencies. In all, it appeared that the cost of setting up a shop might range upwards of $150,000, and if things did not work right and had to be modified or replaced, the number would go higher still.

The initial capital had at this point been almost entirely used up. Some founders were at the end of their personal resources. They believed they could finance the product demonstration commitment they had made to Pearl Paint, but not much beyond that. Moreover, the only sale they had definitely lined up so far was that of the demonstration order. Did the company really merit continued effort and substantial further investment?

Against this prospect, team members had received job offers of as much as $60,000 with major successful companies. All had continued interviewing for jobs. Did it make sense for them to continue for little or no pay in trying to start a venture that so far had not collected from a sale and would only have a loss to show when they did collect on the delivery they had made?

Ampersand (E)

June 1993 - Seeking More Cash

In early June of 1993 the Ampersand founders had decided to pursue financing through their mentor, the judge from the first competition who had taken a continuing interest in their adventures, as well as helping them with counsel and contacts. They had each put up $1,250 in January of that year, with the understanding that the company would pay that money back if and when it could. In April they had won the $5,000 first prize in the San Diego State national venture plan contest.

This prize money had carried them through final production and shipment of their first order to the Pearl Paint art supply store in New York City. The test market initiative had been extremely successful. Elaine, Kathy, Charles and Barbara sold well over 600 pieces of Claybord during their one-week demonstration at Pearl Paint in New York City. The store was excited and committed to continue purchasing the product. According to the main buyer, never had a new product been launched so successfully.

Now they felt they were ready to mount a campaign to wholesalers of art supplies across the country and begin full scale production by setting up their own factory. To do that would take much more money, they estimated on the order of $300,000. Their mentor, the December 1992 competition judge, was now firmly offering to lend the company $290,000 in return for 10 percent interest and 30 percent ownership in the company. He suggested that the team "shop the deal" to see if they could find better terms.

Further conditions he desired were that the company would set up manufacturing in Austin, not Colorado, and that it would serve as a model for the Community Investment Corporation, a local enterprise set up to help new ventures and aid economic development of the area. For instance, its legal papers should be brief, clear and usable as "boilerplate." In effect, this would combine the resources of more than one venture and thereby allow ventures to help each other.

He explained that his goal in creating the Community Investment Corporation (CIC) was to cultivate a diverse group of companies with goals focused on the community. Companies funded through CIC should be committed to reinvesting a portion of their profits in the community, specifically in east Austin, an underdeveloped area. He believed that a new model for corporations should be forged.

As a contrary case, he cited a highly successful company that had begun in Austin and been fully supported by the community in its early years. Now that the venture had grown large it was pressuring the community to give it tax breaks with the threat of moving out if it did not get them.

He, a successful entrepreneur himself, had weathered the ups and downs, run companies himself, taken them public and achieved success. Moreover, he had by now served as a mentor for the team, spent considerable time with it and given guidance the team considered very helpful. Consequently, the team said, his views on corporate philosophy deserved careful consideration.

The team had considered similar philosophies in planning their own company. Some had looked into other forms of enterprise where business and community were considered in combination. One program both the investor and the team had been impressed by was an initiative in Bangladesh where the community provided seed capital, guidance and assistance to local entrepreneurs. These entrepreneurs, when they became successful, then reinvested part of their profits back into the community to continue extending help to others.

Jointly, the investor and team agreed that Ampersand should formulate a list of positive covenants under which it would operate to apply this sort of philosophy in Austin.

Ampersand (F)

July 1993 - Sales Up then Down

By July 1, 1993 the Pearl Paint order of 2,000 Claybords had been shipped and billed at $5,300. Thus a major first sale was on the books. Now the team began contacting major art supply distributors in order to reach hundreds of other stores across the country. In addition, the company's advertising campaign was underway as projected in its business plan.

Ampersand had now received a capital infusion of $100,000 as the first installment of $290,000. Scott Bryant and Robert Tavarez were moving ahead with plans to set up production facilities. They were searching the country for needed machinery and locating plant space.

But then Kathy Henderson called from San Francisco with a disturbing message. The art distributor they had been counting on to serve as a sales channel there had declined to give an order for Claybord, because it did not believe that art supply stores it served would buy enough Claybord to justify wholesaling it. By itself, this news would not have been alarming. But coupled with similar responses that had already come from other distributors, it seemed more ominous. Should Ampersand really be mounting a costly marketing campaign as planned? If not, how should the plan be changed?

Further information about the team's intentions can be seen in the Prize-winning Plan case.

Demonstration at Pearl Paint

The team's idea for the test market at Pearl Paint was to simulate in smaller scale a national rollout of the product, including all display items and advertising copy. This would allow each of the advertising and promotional vehicles such, as the direct-mail initiative and in-store demonstration materials, to be tested prior to a national launch. While attending classes, Kathy found a local art student to help her design the direct-mail brochure. She researched mailing lists to identify professional artists nationwide who would be targeted for mailing. To test the list, she purchased names for the New York City area. Working with a local mail house in Austin, Kathy sent a mailing to 2,000 artists in New York City. Over 200 artists replied, requesting samples of Claybord, a response rate that the team considered outstandingly strong.

In early June, Elaine Salazar and Kathy Henderson together with Charles and Barbara Ewing, went to New York for a week to demonstrate Claybord at Pearl Paint. During that week, the team worked together every day from 10 a.m. to 5 p.m. demonstrating Claybord to the artists shopping through Pearl. They set up a display at a different location in the store each day. Charles Ewing would demonstrate use of the board by painting and illustrating different media techniques. Meanwhile, the others talked to artists and sold Claybord. At the same time, they sought to use the experience for learning, as Elaine recalled:

> *Our week in the store we used to gather lots of information about other products and to talk to the Pearl sales staff on the floor. We learned about merchandising ideas, how the staff perceived the product, and the importance of training floor sales staff on the product. We also had a chance to talk to a multitude of different artists, especially artists working in a variety of different media. We were able to see their reactions to the Claybord and to determine how to position and sell the Claybord in the future.*
>
> *Probably one of the most important finds during the Pearl demonstrations is that we began to realize that Claybord was appealing to artists working in all types of media—from inks to oils. Originally, we had positioned the product as a surface for pen and ink artists only.*

The team's demonstration drew many favorable comments from artists, and helped the store sell more than 600 units. At the end of the week the store's buyer expressed amazement that sales had been so high. This encouraged the team to move ahead on a program aimed at selling to 10 top distributors nationwide plus 20 of the largest retail stores. These large stores, they estimated, might sell to around 100 customers per day. They were not sure how many bought from Pearl, which was visited by an estimated 10,000 shoppers per week. The team expected to offer Pearl and the other large stores the same discount of 62.5 percent that it gave to wholesale distributors. Small and medium-sized stores would receive 50 percent off retail from distributors, while distributors kept 12.5 percent of the retail price.

National Product Rollout

Marketing plans called for sending out a direct-mail brochure offering free samples to 50,000 artists, and buying full-page color advertisements in the August issues of two magazines, *Artist* and *American Artist* at $7,000 per placement.

In the Ampersand offices at the Austin Incubator, Kathy and Elaine sat down with a large map of the United States and divided up the country into sales territories and planned sales trips into the ones they assigned themselves. Their goal was to complete their first level of sales calls in all their territories by November. On a limited budget, they planned their trips so that each would be able to take advantage of their acquaintances for free board and room.

They began by telephoning the stores and distributors they planned to visit. A typical response, Elaine recalled, was for the contact to say something like, "We're not interested in ordering at this point, but send us a sample and we'll take a look at it." Ampersand sent the samples, but rather than waiting for further response from the customer, Elaine and Kathy began traveling to make personal sales calls.

Distributors' responses began to fall into a pattern of rejection. Typical comments they made were:

- Leave us a sample and we'll show it to our reps.
- An interesting product, but I'm not sure we'll want to handle it.
- Let us think about it.
- We'll have to see if we get orders from the stores.
- Go out and create a market for it. Then we'll talk.
- We haven't had any requests for it from the stores.

At the large stores contacted, responses seemed to be more favorable, though not nearly as spectacular as the reception Ampersand had received at Pearl Paint. By the end of July, after four weeks of their calling on distributors and stores, no distributors had placed an order. But 1,000 Claybords were ordered in total by 10 stores for delivery by October 1. Typically, a store would order only the $270 introductory package, which included 92 boards of various sizes and a display rack. Each rack displayed the Claybord concept in two slogans. One said to "draw, scratch, wash, ink, erase and paint your heart out." The other said, "Claybord, a better finish to start with."

These slogans had been developed by an advertising agency Ampersand had hired. In addition to the magazine advertisement placement fees, which were paid to the agency to pass along to the magazines, around $15,000 had been paid to the agency for concept development, layout and design.

An estimated 20 stores and five distributors had been contacted thus far, while Elaine and Kathy had spent approximately 15 days on the road and $1,500 on travel expenses. However, the anticipated sales results were not occurring, and they believed that something would have to change.

But what? Should the advertising plan be cut back, postponed, or should it be carried out and let further sales trips come after that, when Ampersand could show distributors that more stores were buying the product? Should the team somehow change what they were offering, or start selling directly to small stores as well as large ones, and if so, at what discount structure? Should they try selling direct to artists? How could the company tell whether its market concepts were appropriate?

Meanwhile, Robert and Scott were also on the road looking for machinery with which to set up a manufacturing plant. To ship product by September 15, they would have to move into an empty shop by August 1, set up production equipment and get it into operation by the end of that month. Prior to that they would have to find empty shop space at a cost that would allow them to make a profit, and also find and order appropriate manufacturing equipment to be delivered at an appropriate time for setting it up. They had heard that real estate costs in Austin were high. But how much could they afford?

As these questions that seemed to call for immediate answers arose, another question also suggested itself. Should they try to delay everything until better information was available? If so, by what steps should they arrange the delay? For how long? What information in particular should they obtain, and how?

Chem Synthesis, Inc. (D)*

Venturing Overseas

The fax machine at Chem Synthesis, Inc. (CSI) had just printed a 10-page message from Korea. As he picked it up, Jim Tolivre was anxious, because he could see it was coming from an intermediary through whom he hoped CSI might be able to find new markets in an important Asian country. CSI, he observed, needed more sales to reach the break-even it had not yet attained. Scanning through the document, he paused at a phrase concerning $10,000** for "unexplainable business costs."

For further background on CSI, please refer to the earlier chapters of this case series: CSI (A), (B), and (C).

The fax was from Dr. Taihee Park who was writing from a port city in southern Asia. Dr. Park, a professor of business at an Asian university, had been introduced to Jim by a mutual friend two years ago. Park had readily accepted an informal arrangement to become CSI's intermediary in his country. Since then Park had introduced CSI's founders—including Ted Ulrich, the CSI chief scientist—to three construction companies, two investors (one being Park himself), and one chemical engineer from that country. All ex-

pressed interest in doing business with the Canadian firm. The strongest interest came from a construction company whose president was a relative of Park's. The company had purchased CSI product samples and had tested them at a construction site in the harbor city. Based on the success of the test, Jim had expected immediate orders. But they did not come. Apparently, the selling process in Park's country wasn't that simple, as Jim gathered from today's fax.

In the fax Park proposed that CSI apply for the "National Quality Standard," (NQS), a mark that would give "a preemptive priority for selection" of CSI products in Park's country, "other things being equal." No company in North America yet had the NQS, Park wrote. He described the steps CSI must take to earn the NQS, summarized below:

- Organize factory processes in line with NQS requirements.

- Finance a one-month visit of an Asian specialist to verify that the CSI factory meets the NQS requirements.

* Written in collaboration with Dr. Joan Vesper of the University of Washington, Dr. Byung Ju Cho of Ajou University in Korea and Dr. W. Ed McMullan of the University of Calgary as a basis for class discussion. Names have been disguised.

** All dollar amounts in this case are in Canadian currency.

- Submit formal application for the NQS to the Ministry of Industrial Promotion.
- Finance a trip to Canada by an official from the Ministry for an on-site check.
- Participate in "a lot of social meetings."
- Participate in a review session with people from interested areas including affected industries in Park's country who would debate the application.

The process would also require cash, Park explained—$10,000 up front for processing and service costs and another approximately $10,000 for "unexplainable business costs to make things happen." Such costs would cover travel, entertaining, gifting, and in some cases, "tollgate money," using Park's term. Park assured Jim that another relative would be able to provide Park the $20,000, at the relative's own risk, to cover these costs. Tolivre said this puzzled him. Park continued:

How can I explain all those complex things in words which are most likely inconceivable in your mind? You will never know how many times I have pondered over the moral or ethical issues I should encounter in the course of building business with you in this chaotic society. Frankly speaking, I wished many times to quit. I am sure that you saw instances when I hid my occupational status as professor in the business meetings when you were in our city. I tend to be very selective in giving out my CSI business cards. I do really hate to use the word "bribery," but without buying people with money, nothing, they say, can be done, particularly in the construction industry.

As Jim pondered the fax, he had mixed feelings. He and his partner had been ac-tively pursuing sales in Park's country for 18 months, including taking three trips there to test products on site. They had been assisted in this by receiving international travel grants which the Provincial Government made available to encourage more economic diversification, and exports. Tangible results had been meager—they had sold only small quantities of product for the tests. Perhaps the mark of the NQS would open the door to large orders. But the means of earning that mark raised questions in Jim's mind. For one, he had no idea what in CSI's small plant could occupy a visiting specialist from Asia for one month. And why should CSI divulge product ingredients and procedures to outsiders when secrecy was the company's only weapon against imitation? Moreover, if no other North American company had the NQS, yet many companies from North America were selling products in Park's country, why should a small, struggling start-up be the first to apply for the mark?

Yet in another part of the fax, Park wrote that if a company, however small, was to operate globally, "it should be prepared for handling the cultural differences in business." He went on:

People in our country are different, behaving very differently. I'd like to encourage you to understand things in our country in its context, not in Canadian context. You came to us to do business with our people in our market. We did not come to you to do business with Canadian people in the Canadian market. So you have to follow our habits and practices. Please don't conceive our country's way of doing business through the mind structure you have been accustomed to. It seems that you expect me to translate or interpret our country's things into things you may feel comfortable to handle. Or, more preferably, you may want me to fix things in our country to fit into the way you may desire in Canada. Do you think I am possible here? No. Rather I may be good in fixing our country's things in our country's way, but not in Canadian way.

Whether or not he should try to sort out the ethics of another country was a question Jim had thought about before in the abstract. But now it seemed to have taken a concrete form. Some Canadian policymakers held the view that Canadian business people should try to operate by the best standards of their own ethics at all times—for example by limiting and fully disclosing the size of gifts to business contacts abroad. How deeply should Jim delve into any suspicions about how another society handled its international business? Should it be left up to the society of any country to sort out its ethics for itself? Did Jim's responsibility end with selecting trustworthy people in the other country to work with? Both he and his partner trusted Park. Conversely, they sensed that it was important to Park to trust and to be trusted by the Canadians. While the partners had expressed their trust in words, perhaps, Jim thought, Park was asking them to demonstrate trust by pursuing the NQS.

The fax in Jim's hand requested a quick reply. He expected that major orders might hang in the balance.

Matthew Clark and Steve Wilson

I guess the essential decision is how fast do we grow? Too fast takes too much money and we may fall on our face. If we grow too slowly, we may lose the market. Our first burst of growth will determine whether we make or break in this venture.

Steve Wilson leaned back on his chair in April 1981 and talked about the electronics venture he and three Harvard College classmates had started 16 months earlier. Their product was a device for analog-to-digital conversion enabling Apple II microcomputers, which ran on the CPM operating system, to process data from laboratory sensors that measured such properties as temperature, light and pressure. A description of its application appears in Exhibit 1.

Steve and his friend Matthew Clark were working full time to fill the 10 orders they had received for their product since placing their first advertisement the previous May. They had borrowed cash from family and friends, rented space in an old warehouse in East Cambridge, and started production while still pursuing their bachelor's degrees in liberal arts. To locate suppliers and subcontractors who could help them get shipments moving, they had started with the advice of friends and frequent use of the Yellow Pages. Financial records consisted of a running list, kept in a ledger, of expenses from the time the business was started in January. A summary of this list appears in Exhibit 2.

Now, Steve remarked, they needed to map out a complete strategy for the venture. He said that writing a business plan might be the best way to sort out many issues facing them. These included financing, marketing, hiring employees to build the instruments, designing an organizational structure that fit with their personal goals for the venture, choosing advisers for legal and accounting assistance, and providing a way to measure their progress for the next 12 to 18 months.

It was hard, they said, to find time for all these tasks. They were behind on filling orders, and constant interruptions prevented the two from production work on a full-time basis. Steve commented:

Maybe it's been a mistake not to explore the administrative and financial aspects more than we have. We need to spend more time on those issues. It's just that we've been trying to get the products done and sent to our customers so we'll have some money flowing into the business.

Origins of the Business Idea

Steve Wilson had been interested in electronics for most of his 21 years. He had learned about it as a teenager by assembling and repairing stereos and other home equipment, as well as from self-study of basic engineering principles. After graduating in 1977 from public high school in Concord, Massachusetts, he enrolled as a science and engineering major at Harvard. Within a few months, however, he withdrew, having discovered that he liked "fiddling around" with hardware better than theoretical study. He recalled:

I was very discouraged after the first

semester and knew by the end of my freshman year that I should switch my major to liberal arts. I was never happier with any decision than I was with that one. But since engineering had always been a passion with me, I wanted to continue dabbling in it. So, I sought jobs that required engineering skills and began working in the school's biology lab to automate an experiment they had been working on. It let me do some engineering design work and served as a balance to my studies in anthropology and sociology.

Steve's job involved an experiment concerning the concept of "biological clocks" in plants and animals. Lab technicians conducted the experiment, which sometimes lasted days or weeks, and resulted in hundreds of thousands of measurements printed on graph paper by a recording machine. Variations in the plotted line on the paper (similar to printouts of earthquake tremors on a seismograph) were then measured by hand and recorded in a journal for later study. The work was tedious, slow, and prone to errors in transcribing the data.

The lab wanted to eliminate manual recording of data and use a microcomputer to collect, store and interpret the information. The trouble was that microcomputers could not translate waved lines on a graph into digital information to process it. A device was needed to change the analog measurements (i.e., a continuous stream of varying voltages or currents from sensors that measured properties such as temperature, pressure, light, or wave frequency) to exact digital signals (i.e., decimal equivalents). This sort of translation was being done for larger minicomputers but required equipment that typically cost $10,000 or more. In addition, the translation required expensive on-line computer time for instantaneous collection and ma-

nipulation of the data. These costs, coupled with advances in technology, now made it attractive for the school to try introducing a peripheral device that might allow a desk-top computer, such as the Apple II, to collect and process experimental data. Not much earlier, Steve said, such a step would have been impossible.

Tackling the job, Steve managed to develop circuitry that worked for one experiment. The lab director then asked him to make additional units for other similar experiments. These, as Steve's paper in Exhibit I pointed out, could save considerable amounts of time and money while improving the accuracy of data. As more units were requested, made, and put to use, he began to think there might be commercial applications for the device, and that he could capitalize on them by starting his own business.

By this time, Steve was in his junior year at Harvard and had just met a classmate who was majoring in psychology, Matthew Clark. The two struck up a friendship and began talking about starting a business to manufacture instruments like those Steve had designed for the biology department. Matthew, who had some experience in commercial art, suggested that Steve work on engineering and product development while he did marketing and administrative tasks. As they chatted about the idea with friends, two others also expressed interest in working on the venture. These were Mike Fridkin, an economics major, who knew how to write microcomputer software, and Steve Brand, who was studying history and sociology.

Steve and Matthew continued to talk about the idea. They listed what it would cost to incorporate, buy stationery and get a minimal supply of parts for developing circuit boards. In early May 1980, they decided to name the business "Data Acquisition Systems," and set up shop in the basement of Matthew's Cambridge home.

Although a commercial prototype wasn't yet developed, they placed a small advertisement in *Microcomputing Magazine* to test for interest in such a product. Steve remarked that the laboratory models had given him confidence that they could complete the necessary design work and drawings by May 28. "Besides," he added, "everyone in the computer business announces their products before they're ready for delivery."

Developing a Prototype

That advertisement, plus another small one in *Byte*, drew more than 2,500 inquiries from across the US and Canada, which the partners considered very encouraging. Steve and Matthew worked on their business between classes and answered calls from scientists inquiring about their product. By the end of May, they had received five orders. Unfortunately, work on the prototypes progressed much more slowly than they anticipated. Not only was the design work complex, but Steve said, a number of other issues relating to the business took their time away from developing the product. Finding suitable office space was one example he cited.

> When the semester was over, we found our present space in this warehouse and spent a lot of time fixing it up. Other people argued with us that this was an odd priority to begin with; that we should just continue to work out of a garage until we had a product finished. But we felt it was important to have a more professional environment to work in and to present the image of an established business. So the first part of the summer was spent getting the office in order.

A typical sequence for developing many new products, Steve had been told, was to build a prototype and then measure its performance to determine the specifications. Then, after some small refinements, the finished product would be advertised in hopes that a waiting market for a device with those specifications would appear. In his own case, however, Steve had developed the specifications first, to fit his laboratory assignment. Then he had modified those specifications based upon telephone conversations with scientists responding to the ad. The modifications turned out to be substantial and required more development work than he had expected.

His design used a modular arrangement that allowed users to "plug in" modules to provide different functions or expand capacity for different data collection efforts. Steve explained that this feature would also allow him to keep up with technological advances in computers by continuously developing upgrade modules that could be shipped to customers to ward off product obsolescence. Thus, while the housing of a unit would not change, users could install new modules to keep the inner workings up to date.

Designing circuitry for the modules also took more time than anticipated. Steve recounted how, with Matthew's assistance, he learned as he went in developing the prototype instrument :

> Laying out all the printed circuit work was something we thought would take about a week. In fact, it took about two months. We knew nothing about how to make printed circuit boards and couldn't find anything written on the subject to help us. It's just sort of a skill that you pick up. We had some materials to work with and a friend of a friend who manufactured prototype boards. We spent days and nights working on the design and it wasn't until August that prototype boards came back based on design work we had done.

While waiting for the circuit boards, the

two talked with friends and called possible suppliers to find other parts needed for the instrument. They would leaf through the Yellow Pages, then telephone machinists and silk-screen printers about prices and willingness to do the work. Four subcontractors were lined up in addition to the person making the circuit boards. First was a machinist to provide the metal cases that housed the electronic parts, second was a company making printed circuit boards; third was a painter to finish the case panels and fourth was a silk-screening company to do lettering for the front of the instrument. Matthew explained how they chose among alternative suppliers.

> *We just went around and talked with a lot of them, got bids in an informal way, and chose in part by how we felt we'd be able to get along with the individual on a continuing basis. We've been pleased with the results for the most part. The only one we're thinking of changing is the machinist, for the sake of lowering our costs.*

When they had received the circuit boards from the subcontractor in August, the two began assembling a prototype. Once complete, it was tested and, to Steve's dismay, didn't work as expected. He explained that the problem "didn't make any sense." He rechecked the connections and reviewed the logic he had used in designing the modules, but test output still showed erroneous data. After a month of troubleshooting, Steve discovered the problem: a short in the cable connecting the instrument with the host Apple II computer. They had tried to build all the cable connections on their own, even though they lacked some tools to do the job properly, and this had been painfully instructive:

> *The lesson was that we should never try to do something we aren't properly equipped to do. You're tempted to try the work as a way to cut costs when, in fact, you end up spending more time and money than if the task had been subcontracted in the first place.*

As the venture entered its sixth month, there still was no finished product to ship to customers. Steve had taken a year off from school to work on the business full time. The other three had continued their final year of undergraduate work, with Matthew juggling both the business and school work on as close to a full-time basis for both as he could.

Cash needs were met through an initial payment of $1,000 each from Steve and Matthew and through loans from family and friends. By the end of October, the two had spent between $10,000 and $15,000 on rent, materials, sub-contracting costs, telephone, advertising and related expenses. No salaries had been paid, and customers had been told that they would receive finished products shortly after the prototype had been fully tested and documented.

By mid-November, a prototype was finally completed and tested successfully against the specifications Steve had written the previous summer. To celebrate, the two invited personal friends and others who had helped on the project to a product introduction party. Local computer distributors were also invited, one of whom turned out to be the area distributor for Apple. Steve and Matthew reached an agreement with him that he would serve as their distributor and would buy at least five instruments each month. He would be entitled to whatever price discount was customary and would help advertise the product in addition to making direct sales efforts. Steve added that there was nothing written in the way of an agreement. "We just shook on it."

A flyer, excerpts from which appear in Exhibit 3, was prepared describing the product for advertising purposes.

From Prototype to Business

When product shipments started in January 1981, Steve said, the venture entered a new phase wherein a number of tasks the two had ignored while developing the prototype would soon have to be faced, despite an intensifying shortage of time. Initial customer reaction to the product seemed favorable, but the two agreed that they would need a much larger customer base before they would be comfortable about long-range prospects for the venture.

They estimated that they currently spent about 40 percent of their business time on product development or assembly, and the other 60 percent talking with customers over the phone, calling suppliers, or listening to sales representatives who came by the office to tell them of computer-related products and advances in the field. Steve explained that they had been able to reduce one source of frustration by working with sales representatives as a way to purchase parts and products components.

> *We never knew this—that it paid just to establish friendly contacts with sales representatives whose task it is to bridge the purchasing gap. They've helped us enormously in the past few months. Another thing we found is that sales reps who aren't with a particular company tend to be less helpful. They're less informed about the product, lack dedication to the company they represent, and, in our opinion, don't speak for the company —just themselves.*

Production

Steve estimated that each instrument took approximately 10 hours to assemble and test. He expected that production time could eventually be reduced to eight hours for each unit. Per-unit costs consisted of the following: $70 for the metal case and painting of the panels; $90 for the printed circuit board; $3 for the silk-screen lettering; and between $500 and $525 for the other components such as wire, cable, switches, buses, and electronic equipment. Labor costs for assembly averaged an estimated $100. Parts costs are listed in Exhibit 4.

Receipt of metal cases was expected to take between four and five weeks. To date, Steve and Matthew had ordered only once with the subcontractor, and delivery had been made approximately one month later. They believed six weeks should be allowed for the printed circuit boards, while silk-screening could be done on very short notice.

Most of the engineering was done by Steve, although Matthew had acquired enough skills by helping with the prototype to assist in assembly of the product. They set a goal for delivery time at between "off the shelf" and three weeks. Current quotes to customers were between six and eight weeks for delivery of an instrument. The two also wanted to build up a stock of replacement components for quick service, but had not yet been able to do so because of a lack of cash and the demand by some suppliers for a certified check or cash upon delivery. Matthew remarked that only a few suppliers allowed them terms of net 30, but he was working to increase their number. "The worst part," he said, "is the time needed to fill out all the forms they send us."

Steve was still doing product development on additional modules that could be plugged into the instrument. He commented on his progress up through March of 1981:

> *We've finished four of the ten modules, which sounds like we're only 40 percent complete. Since the main development was in the prototype and chassis design, I would say that we're closer to 80 percent complete. The drawings*

are nearly finished, so we hope engineering can be wrapped up by the middle of summer.

The standard unit consisted of five modules, each with five channels available for receiving data and two channels for output. Six slots were incorporated to allow a user to plug in additional modules as desired. Matthew pointed out that this feature was the product's primary strength, since the expansion capability provided a wide range of possible applications and made it easy to incorporate state-of-the-art technology.

For adequate production space, the two expected they would require a new location in the next 12 months. They preferred to remain in Boston or Cambridge and not move to suburbs as had many high technology firms. They also discussed a need for appropriate personnel to assist with hardware and software development. Mike Fridkin was writing software part time, while Steve Brand helped on a variety of tasks. Both planned to enter graduate school in the fall, Mike as a law student at Harvard and Steve as an overseas student in the social sciences.

Marketing

Advertising costs had been assumed by the distributor as part of an informal agreement worked out in late 1980. Steve and Matthew expressed some dissatisfaction with the distributor's performance, noting that the one or two advertisements he had placed to date hadn't even mentioned their product except in reference to peripheral products available to augment the Apple line of computers. The distributor frequently referred inquiries directly to them instead of calling up on his own to learn more about the product. As a result, Steve guessed they spent an average of an hour and a half on the telephone for each sale made. This could be in the form of one call or up to six conversations with the same person, answering specific questions about the instrument's performance. Steve added that they hadn't had much success in telling the distributor to respond to customer queries directly. They hoped the owner's manual which was expected back from the printer in the next week or two, would solve the problem and also help the distributor to promote their product and company name.

Steve estimated that 80 percent of those who called about the product had heard of it through the distributor, while 10 percent had seen the instrument in a customer's office or lab and 10 percent had seen the early versions Steve designed for Harvard. Those who learned of the product through the distributor had to be referred back to him if they wanted to purchase a unit. Others could buy direct from Steve and Matthew. Steve said the percentage of people who inquired after seeing the instrument in use by a present customer was increasing, and he expected this trend would continue.

As of March 31, 1981, seven Standard Systems had been sold, at a cost of $1,500 each. The sales had been made in recent months, and 15 orders remained outstanding for similar units. The distributor had yet to purchase any units from the company. Total revenues for the company to date were $10,500.

Current wholesale and retail prices for the instrument were set at $1,300 and $1,650 respectively. The 27-percent discount allowed to the distributor was contingent on provision of advertising support. Steve explained that if they resumed advertising on their own, or worked out a marketing relationship with a manufacturer such as Apple, they would attempt to lower the discount, although he wasn't sure what figure would provide them with sufficient margin and still meet competitor's prices. A tentative price list appears as Exhibit 5.

The competition consisted either of other small manufacturers who relied on printed circuit boards to be inserted into the host computer or, in a couple of situations, a separate peripheral unit. Steve considered these products were inferior, both in performance and ease of use, to those of Data Acquisition Systems. Not only did they lack the feature of modular design, but he questioned whether competitors would be able to provide complete documentation and follow-through support to customers. Service and reliability were becoming two of the most sought-after features for computer-related products, according to Steve, who reasoned that because many people were not used to working with microcomputers, service would be essential in building a customer base and product loyalty.

One problem Matthew said had to be overcome was getting Data Acquisition Systems' name out before the public. He believed the company's size and obscurity were hampering efforts to attract sales, and he doubted that many prospective customers knew their product existed. That was where the instrument's compatibility with the Apple Computer could prove valuable. He commented:

> The people at Apple know that peripheral equipment which is compatible will help increase their sales, and they've taken some small companies "under their wing" in terms of promotion and support. There's one company I know of that was as small as we were six years ago. It got to talking with Apple and the firm has grown incredibly fast since then.

Matthew said that although he and Steve hadn't talked directly with any people at Apple thus far, they hoped to do so in the next six months, to determine whether Apple might be willing to help promote the Data Acquisition Systems' present and future products.

Finance

Through the third quarter ending in January 1981, the venture had spent most of the $10,000 in loans provided by relatives and friends in addition to $2,000 capital paid in by Matthew and Steve. Terms for repayment had been set up on an individual basis spread over the next two years. Interest ranged from zero to 10 percent, and only two of the loans had written repayment schedules—most were verbal assurances to repay. Steve mentioned that he and Matthew wanted to begin as soon as possible repaying those who had helped the venture get started.

To date, no financial statements existed for the company. Neither Steve nor Matthew had spent much time recapping expenditures until the past month (see Exhibit 2). Steve said they were trying to figure out their current monthly overhead rate and how it should affect pricing. Both had limited acquaintance with business administration—Matthew had taken an introductory financial accounting course the previous semester, but found it confusing.

Banking relationships had consisted only of setting up an account at a nearby bank. The partners had avoided talking with loan officers because they figured that a business such as theirs wouldn't be able to get a loan until revenues were coming in regularly. "The only way we could get a bank loan now," Steve suggested, "was if one of our parents co-signed a personal note. That's something we would rather not do, so we simply haven't talked with any bankers so far."

Steve and Matthew had discussed the possibility of raising money through venture capital or private stock offerings, but their need for legal advice and mistrust of venture capitalists had deterred them.

They thought they might explore those directions further, however, some time in the next 12 to 18 months. Steve explained that he and Matthew wanted to retain control over the business as much as possible. He regarded financial negotiations as "painful," and added that he would probably consult a family friend involved in the financial community who had offered his assistance. Several investors had approached the two with offers of financial backing. Steve commented:

We've had venture capitalists come in and we are simply terrified, not knowing what they want out of the deal. About three or four months ago, two very preppy looking types came in. They were in their mid 30s, talked and acted very slick, and started leaving information about themselves and sample prospectuses. They were in the building because some other man was trying to talk them into renovating the place. The landlord had told them about us and when they walked in, they were very interested, seeing that we were working off the coattails of Apple. Through deliberate negligence on our part, we wrote that relationship off; venture capital is something we don't want to get into quite yet.

Administrative Concerns

Steve mentioned personnel as another problem area. Addition of an employee would not only allow the partners more time for paperwork and administrative tasks that had been put off, but would also enable them to build instruments faster. Other demands on their time had slowed production until only one instrument was being produced every two weeks. Steve and Matthew decided to look for students who enjoyed a variety of tasks, had a basic understanding of electronics and were willing to work part time or full time. This would allow the partners to maintain flexibility in scheduling and avoid problems they said might occur if they hired a person much older than themselves Steve commented:

We would look first and foremost for people who are good with their hands and enjoy assembling things. We'd also pay attention to getting people with diverse talents, versatile people who enjoy a variety of tasks. We figure that because there are so many universities around, the resource pool we have to draw on here in the Boston area is immense.

With the expected loss of Steve Brand and Mike by fall, Steve Wilson said engineering talent would be another area of need. He mentioned that he wanted to avoid the controls and hierarchical structure common to most businesses and instead emphasise creativity and independence to attract and keep talented programmers, analysts and engineers. He saw high turnover and lack of company loyalty as the norm for high technology firms. "But whether we will be able to overcome that when other companies haven't," he added, "I'm not sure."

Regular salaries, the partners expected, would be paid to any employees hired full time. They estimated that industry rates for software and hardware development personnel with little or no experience were between $20,000 and $30,000 per year. With benefits and overhead, the cost of hiring an engineer experienced in the electronic industry they thought would be between $50,000 and $75,000 per year. Steve explained that in contrast they had only begun paying themselves any type of salary within the last two months. He recalled how the four divided their first "paycheck" at the end of February:

It's not regular or large enough to

call a salary; "stipend" would be a better word. We divided $300 four ways for about 150 hours of work, so the hourly rate was close to $2. We developed an elaborate system to split the money. Two-thirds was distributed according to the number of hours each put into the business during February. The remaining third we divided equally as compensation for all of the unpaid work and commitment to the venture.

Steve and Matthew talked about other administrative tasks they either handled piecemeal or took care of as best they could. If a legal issue arose and seemed to need attention, one of them might spend most of the day at the Harvard Law Library or talking to a friend to find out what should be done. Matthew recalled, for example, researching import-export regulations to learn what might be involved in trading overseas.

Aside from discounts allowed to the distributors, selling and administrative costs were estimated to be running between $300 and $400 per month. This included rent, utilities, typewriter rental, office supplies, and any ads that the company might place directly. Salary costs were not included. Steve explained that any payment of compensation was a matter of examining expenses at the end of the month and seeing if any money was left for salaries. "It's not a very sophisticated method," he admitted, "but it has worked for us so far."

Whether the product should be patented was another question that concerned the two. Matthew recalled that they had considered filing for a patent, but lacked the $3,000 to $5,000 he estimated an attorney would charge. He had discovered that, under patent law, a company had one year from the time it first advertised a product to file a patent application on it. This meant that he and Steve had one month left in which to find a lawyer and complete the writing and filing of the necessary documents. Otherwise, they would forfeit rights for patent protection of their present design. Matthew went on to explain that to have any lasting value, the patent should be as "global" as possible in terms of protecting the design and possibly even the process, commenting:

It takes some incredibly extensive research of existing patents plus good writing, and that's why you go for the best patent attorney you can find. It also means spending a lot of money which we don't have right now.

Steve and Matthew said that within the coming year, they would like their company to reach a position where it had completed development of the first product, was shipping products regularly, occupied a new office in Boston or Cambridge, and employed around 10 workers full time. Steve added that his plans for completing school were "somewhat hazy, perhaps in the next year, but definitely within the next three." Matthew would be finished by June and able to devote his attention to the business with fewer distractions. They had thought about recruiting advisors, and explained that they would probably rely on personal friends or friends of the family for legal and financial assistance.

Both mentioned name exposure as being very important in "getting the jump" on competition and building a base for steady orders. Steve said that among the many issues and tasks awaiting them in the next 12 months, an overriding concern was to search out and retain qualified personnel.

We've found that a lot of pretending goes on initially in starting a company like this. You have to convince yourself that you are not just students fooling around. It takes a couple of months to stop laughing when you answer the phone with your company name. But if we are going to succeed in the long run, we will have to do a lot more. I think we will have to bring in very talented engineers and build a reputation for techni- *cal excellence. The prospect of hiring people is exciting. But it's also very scary, because we are going to have to come up with enough money on a regular basis to meet a payroll.*

EXHIBIT 1 Excerpt from "Personal Computers in the Scientific Laboratory" by Steven F. Wilson

THE SMALL COMPUTER IN THE RESEARCH LABORATORY

The value of a small computer in the research laboratory has long been appreciated, not solely for computational tasks, but for automated data acquisition and experimental control as well. In such applications, the computer directs the complex experimental procedure, collects scientific data in real-time from all types of transducers and instrumentation, and then reduces, analyzes, and periodically stores this information on magnetic disk. Later, the researcher may review and graphically represent the derived data on an interactive CRT terminal. Sections of special interest can be automatically highlighted and expanded, critical points probed, and parallel sequences contrasted. For a permanent record, these results can be plotted on an X-Y recorder or printed in tabular form, all on command.

But the computer alone is inadequate for such a task. Analog conversion hardware is required for the processor to meet the analog environment on its own terms. Physical parameters are measured with any conventional transducer—thermocouples, strain gauges, photo multiplier tubes, a multiplexed analog-to-digital converter, all under computer control. Tens or even hundreds of thousands of conversions per second at up to 16 bits accuracy can be achieved. Further, with appropriate algorithms and hardware, the computer can generate any type of analog signal—from precision DC reference voltages to complex high-frequency wave forms. The full circle back to the analog environment is achieved.

The versatile minicomputer of the 1960s demonstrated well the merits of such a system, for all the experimental sciences—and medical applications as well—but at a high cost. At $10,000 or more, many laboratories found such instrumentation beyond their means. In addition to the high cost of sophisticated analog conversation circuitry, this expense derives from the unusual demands placed on the CPU by real-time tasks. Significantly, even the least expensive minicomputers proved too costly when dedicated to a single experimental task. Real-time data acquisition is largely incompatible with time-shared systems, as the input/output task cannot be delayed: timing is dictated by external experimental constraints.

The advent of the microcomputer coupled with that of the new integrated analog conversion technology has brought about a drastic reduction in system costs with only minimal loss of capabilities. As a result, the implementation of compact and highly versatile computer-based data acquisition systems is now possible at a cost of under $3,000. The introduction of such systems promises to have a rapid and profound effect on the methods of experimental research in the 1980s.

EXHIBIT 1 (concluded)

LEVELS OF IMPLEMENTATION

We justify such a forecast by pointing to the dramatic effect such equipment will have on the resources of the scientist. Previously, the researcher faced a two-fold limitation. First, technological limitations in analog instrumentation severely curtailed the number of discrete observations retrievable from the study of short-lived phenomena. If, for example, a scientist had only a chart recorder or an oscilloscope at his disposal, its response time would severely limit his ability to closely study the kinetics of a chemical reaction or the characteristics of a single neuronal impulse. Second, long-term experiments were limited by the expense, tedium, and potential for error implicit in the technique of manual data transcription. In either case the paucity of experimental data reduces the strength of theoretical conclusions.

Computerized data acquisition, by contrast, provides an abundance of data—in a short-term experiment perhaps tens or even thousands of observations per second, and in long-term studies an essentially unlimited number of error-free data points. Even more significant, the power of statistical analysis is for the first time fully at the service of the scientist.

A RESEARCH APPLICATION

At the Biological Laboratories at Harvard University, several APPLE II computers and early versions of the DAS-5 have been in use for over a year for biophysical measurements in the laboratory of Professor J.W. Hastings. One application involves the study of organisms omitting light according to a circadian rhythm, a kind of biological clock with an approximate periodicity of 24 hours. This phenomenon is the single-celled equivalent of the phenomenon we experience most notably in the discomfort of "jet-lag," the readjustment of our own biological time-keeping mechanism to an environment that is newly out of sync with our own clock. It appears that virtually all species exhibit this behavior. The aim of the researcher is to investigate the nature of this timekeeper, and to discover means of controlling it. Typical experiments have involved the subjection of the cells to variations in temperature, light exposure, and chemical environment, and the monitoring of the biological clock for several days. Because the week long experiment must be regarded many times under different conditions, the computer proved an invaluable addition.

Before the computer was implemented, measurements were made by placing vials containing the appropriate culture of luminescent cells before a photo tube and recording light emission over long periods on a chart recorder. The analysis of these paper records proved tedious, because the recorded light intensity was found to be composed of two components, a continuous low-level glow, and randomly spaced bright flashes which last 0.1 to 1.0 second each. Quantitative analysis of these flashes was not feasible from chart records, but it was clear that they did not share the periodicity of the glow. Previously, it was necessary to discern the glow level from the sporadic intensity of the flashes by inspection of the chart records with a straight edge. The analysis of the data produced by a single six-day experiment required that someone measure the height of some 8,000 pen deflections, each corresponding to the glow of one vial at a given moment, and then transfer by hand these values to a data table or directly to graph. Fortunately, the computerized data acquisition system permitted this task to be accomplished in a real-time statistical algorithm. This software technique sacrifices information about the kinetics of the individual flashes but efficiently determines the integrated light level from each of the two sources—flash and glow. Thirty or more samples of the organism undergo varied chemical treatment by the researcher and are then placed in a mechanical turntable. A motor driven photo multiplier carriage passes sequentially, under computer control, from one vial to the next. The entire sample-holding structure has provisions for a temperature-controlled circulation water bath.

EXHIBIT 2 Tabulation of Expenditures

	Feb Thru May	June	July	Aug	Sept	Oct	Nov	Dec	Jan	Feb	Total
Office Remodel, Improve	0.00	839.60	41.50	16.53	24.95	10.01	0.00	0.00	16.80	31.91	981.30
Office Supplies, Computer	1.16	8.19	63.74	0.00	0.00	0.00	24.76	7.54	26.88	20.70	152.97
Tools, Equipment	0.00	1,642.25	367.75	28.88	0.00	0.00	0.00	13.99	19.82	0.00	2,072.69
Electronic Parts, Hardware	0.00	0.00	239.24	243.51	116.22	178.43	2,105.09	1,103.08	1,647.87	598.38	6,231.82
Telephone Charges	0.00	82.57	102.68	98.68	0.00	46.88	87.89	82.34	90.64	127.00	718.68
Rent, 3d Street	0.00	150.00	150.00	150.00	150.00	150.00	150.00	150.00	150.00	150.00	1,350.00
Utilities	0.00	0.00	16.86	0.00	0.00	0.00	0.00	0.00	0.00	0.00	16.86
Insurance	0.00	0.00	0.00	0.00	0.00	75.00	0.00	97.00	0.00	0.00	172.00
Legal, Incorporation	144.00	0.00	0.00	0.00	0.00	0.00	0.00	0.00	0.00	0.00	144.00
Post Office, UPS, etc.	53.50	0.00	157.17	52.00	36.24	8.00	18.45	44.57	50.00	28.00	447.93
Copy, Offset	86.58	0.00	123.97	154.47	0.00	215.64	121.99	123.32	0.00	25.61	851.58
Graphic Arts Supplies	33.18	0.00	50.82	19.68	0.00	11.24	38.05	0.00	23.96	20.63	197.56
Selectric Typewriter	50.00	0.00	0.00	0.00	0.00	63.00	0.00	378.00	0.00	0.00	491.00
Advertising	98.50	0.00	0.00	0.00	0.00	0.00	300.00	50.00	0.00	50.00	498.50
Publ, Books	0.00	15.98	23.29	15.11	0.00	0.00	0.00	0.00	0.00	0.00	54.38
Expense Account	0.00	0.00	0.00	0.00	0.00	22.74	490.00	0.00	0.00	15.50	528.24
Wages, Stipends	0.00	0.00	0.00	0.00	0.00	0.00	0.00	300.00	50.00	750.00	1,100.00
Subcontracts	0.00	0.00	0.00	0.00	0.00	0.00	0.00	3,364.90	1,780.61	104.00	5,249.51
Total	466.92	2,738.59	1,337.02	778.86	327.41	780.94	3,336.23	5,714.74	3,856.58	1,921.73	21,259.02

EXHIBIT 3 Excerpts from Advertising Flyer

DATA ACQUISITION SYSTEMS, INC.   CAMBRIDGE, MASSACHUSETTS

DATA ACQUISITION SYSTEMS, INC.

Data Acquisition Systems: A manufacturer of
state-of-the-art   precision analog conversion
instrumentation engineered to meet the exacting
requirements of science, medicine, and industry.
DAS anticipates the rapid implementation of low
cost   conversion   and   control   systems for
distributed processing in diverse applications
around the world.

THE MODEL 5 ANALOG INPUT/OUTPUT SYSTEM

The Model Five Analog I/O System. It's the
extraordinary new analog subsystem from DAS.
For the first time, a microcomputer-based system
can meet your most exacting specifications of
performance and reliability.   The power and
precision of computerized data acquisition were
previously available only to the minority of
specialists who could afford the expensive
minicomputers and their costly data acquisition
peripherals.   With the DAS-5 and the APPLE II
microcomputer, you have a powerful, universal
data   acquisition   package   that   offers the
combination of speed, accuracy, and flexibility
of systems costing five times more.

In the laboratory, the DAS-5 is a remarkable new
research tool for automatic data acquisition,
analysis,   and   display,   as   well   as   for
experimental automation and control.

In industry, the DAS-5 permits cost-effective,
reliable implementation of localized process
control.

CONDITIONING, CONVERSION, AND CONTROL

All in one package. With the DAS-5, you create
a total link to the analog environment. The
system is modular and fully expandable. A full
family of modules for conditioning, conversion,
and control allow you to tailor your system to
the task at hand.   And you pay only for the
capabilities you need. The DAS-5:

*Up to 256 extra single-ended inputs, or 128
differential, all in the same chassis *Up to 8
precision   12   or   16-bit D/A outputs with
switch-selectable voltage and current ranges
*Up to 16 channels of 4-20 milliamp Current Loop
Outputs   *1.5   microsecond   12-bit A/D
*Programmable   Gain   Amplification   *Direct
Memory Access Controller under development

Best of all, the system is ready to go.

EXHIBIT 4 Estimated Parts Costs

das

DATA ACQUISITION SYSTEMS, INC.   (617) 491 5051

March 30, 1981

"Parts" = cost of parts in module described, including subcontracting, but not including labor; "New" = new prices as listed on price list; "Margin-Dir" = the margin of profit on direct sales to customers over the parts cost expressed as a percentage; "Dist-Price" = the price of the same parts when sold to a dealer or representative; "D-Marg" = the margin of the distributor, assuming he or she sells at the same price as our direct sales; expressed as a percentage above 100 percent, the price he or she paid at the Distributor prices; "Marg-Dist" = the margin of profit over the price of parts on sales made at the distributor's discounted prices.

	PART $	NEW $	MARGIN DIR %	DIST-PRICE	D-MARG %	MARG-DIST %
Standard System	700.00	1,650	236	1,300	27	186
Case, Power, w/Front	301.24	450	149	375	20	124
System Controller	28.14	190	675	145	31	515
Analog Input Card	79.72	330	414	250	32	314
ATC (Prot)	91.42	345	377	265	30	
A/D	137.47	400	291	295	36	215
5 A/D	342.48	650	190	525	240	153
Single-Ended	53.55	244	373	150	33	280
Single-Ended (Prot)	65.25	215	330	165	30	253
Differential A	151.62	350	231	275	27	181
Differential A (Prot)	163.32	365	223	290	26	178
Differential B	165.62	370	223	290	28	175
Differential B (Prot)	177.32	385	217	305	26	172
Transducers (4-CH)						
12-Bit D/A	71.46	260	364	190	37	266
16-Bit D/A, 15 LIN						
16-Bit D/A,16 LIN						
4-20 MA	221.83	450	203	375	20	169
GP Dig I/O	38.78	90	232	65	38	168
Univ. Dig. I/O Proc						
Apple Int	22.83	60	263	50	20	219

222 THIRD STREET   CAMBRIDGE, MASSACHUSETTS 02142

EXHIBIT 5 Tentative Price List Effective March 25, 1981

das

DATA ACQUISITION SYSTEMS, INC.   (617) 491 5051

DAS - 5 Analog Input/Output System

Description	DAS Retail	Distrbtr.
Standard System, for the APPLE Computer	1,650.00	1,300.00
System Controller Module	190.00	145.00
Analog Input Module, Standard Inputs	330.00	250.00
Analog Input Module, Protected Inputs	345.00	265.00
Successive Approximations A/D Converter Module	400.00	295.00
Very High Speed A/D Converter Module	650.00	525.00
Input Expansion Module (Single Ended)	200.00	150.00
Input Expansion Module, Protected Inputs	215.00	165.00
Input Expansion Module with Differential Inputs, High Accuracy Standard Inputs	350.00	275.00
Input Expansion Module with Differential Inputs, High Accuracy Protected Inputs	365.00	290.00
Input Expansion Module with Differential Inputs, High Speed Standard Inputs	370.00	290.00
Input Expansion Module with Differential Inputs, High Speed Protected Inputs	385.00	305.00
Low Level Input Module for Transducers	*	*
12 Bit Precision Digital to Analog Converter Module	260.00	190.00
16 Bit Precision D/A Converter Module, 15 Bit Linearity	*	*
16 Bit Precision D/A Converter Module, 16 Bit Linearity	*	*
Dual Channel Current Loop Output Module	450.00	375.00
General Purpose Digital Input/Output Module	90.00	65.00
Universal Digital I/O Processor Module	*	*
Case and Power Supply, Full Front Panel	450.00	375.00
Case and Power Supply, OEM Front Panel	*	*
Apple Computer Interface Card and Cable	60.00	50.00

* Contact Data Acquisition Systems for prices on these parts.

Notes:

1. Software package and complete documentation covering all areas of system operation and implementation are included in all system purchases.

2. The Standard System, described in the Specifications Sheet, includes Modules 1,2,3 and two of #8, standard case with front panel and power supply (DAS-5-CPF), interface card for the APPLE computer (DAS-5-AI), software package, and complete documentation.

3. System configurations other than the Standard System may be constructed to suit your analog requirements by adding more modules at the above prices to the Standard System, or should all the elements contained in the Standard System not be required, by purchasing the DAS-5-CPF chassis and any combination of modules form the list above. Consult the guidelines under "Module Selections" in the Specifications Sheet, page 6. The APPLE interface card is included free of charge in all system purchases.

4. Quantity discount information is available upon request.

5. Consult our distributors or the factory for delivery information.

6. APPLE is a trademark of the APPLE Computer Company.

Chapter 9

Acquisition

❏ *SUBCHAPTER 9A - Prospecting*

Many firms outlast management by their founders. Hence opportunities for new owners to acquire those firms eventually arise. Sometimes the acquirers are other corporations which want to invest spare resources or simply to expand their empires. Sometimes the acquirers are investors who see the potential of higher returns in majority ownership of smaller companies. Recent years have seen many venture capital firms follow this path, for investment purposes.[1] Finally, sometimes the acquirers are entrepreneurs. In fact, it appears that about a third of entrepreneurs enter business through takeover, while two-thirds start businesses from scratch.[2] How takeover by an entrepreneur can come about is the focus of this chapter.

To enter a business usually requires physical resources. They can include such things as a shop, equipment and inventory. Resources can be obtained new or used and can include only selected parts of a business or a whole ongoing business: the name, customer lists, procedures, contracts, trademarks and perhaps consulting help from the former owner. Advantages of buying an ongoing concern include:

- **Time** is saved from start-up activities (which are usually much more consuming than expected).

- **Risk** of the unexpected is reduced by existence of a "track record" upon which to evaluate the business. Cooper et al. found for instance, that firms acquired by entrepreneurs were more likely to be still operating after three years than those started fresh (69 percent vs. 63 percent).[13]

- **Resource requirements** may be reduced if the seller will advance credit and the buyer can borrow additionally from other lenders against company assets.

- **Procedures and habits** of employees, suppliers and customers, which are costly to set up, are already in place.

Such assets are sometimes bought whole and sometimes in part. Franchisors, for example, offer not a going concern, but such elements as an established brand, procedures and equipment which have been developed, tested and proven, training in how to perform functions of the business, guidance in selecting a location and running the business, and possibly help in financing it.

Application: *To what extent does each of the above advantages of buying outweigh start-up as a way of entering the assigned case venture?*

The discussion that follows here will consider, first, the possibility of acquiring an entire going concern and, second, in subchapter (9b), the halfway alternative of buying a franchise instead.

Search

The acquisition process can be divided into three general stages: (1) finding a company to acquire, (2) evaluating it, (3) negotiating the acquisition and (4) managing the acquisition after the deal. The most difficult and crucial of these is usually the first, to find a company that is an attractive acquisition. Less attractive acquisitions, such as small businesses with profit records that are marginal or worse, that require long, tedious hours of work for low pay and that are prone to failure are easy to find through "business opportunities" sections of newspapers and through commercial real estate brokers.

However, businesses that have a significant proprietary advantage in a brand, a product, or a skilled workforce are much sought after by many buyers. Small manufacturing companies with these characteristics are frequently approached by established firms on the prowl for acquisitions. Owners of such firms frequently enjoy owning them and are not anxious to sell. When they do reach a point of wanting to sell they can fairly easily find interested buyers and typically prefer to sell to those buyers with the greatest resources and/or demonstrated business success record as proof that they will carry on the firm successfully. So for a would-be buyer the biggest problem is to find an attractive firm whose owner is inclined to sell to him or her.

One way acquisitions are found is through employment. An aging owner may want to change lifestyle and therefore sell to a younger employee in his or her company. Or in a larger company, top management may decide to sell off a department or division for one or more of the following reasons:

- The division no longer fits well with the corporation's main thrust or goals.

- The division is losing money and is distracting management attention from higher priority concerns.

- The corporation is short on cash and can increase liquidity by selling something off.

- The employees have seen a way to make the division worth more and are consequently offering a price higher than the corporation feels the division is worth as part of the corporation.

An example of employee buyout as a way of entering business is Leslie Otten, whose venture turned out to be a ski resort.

In his mid-20s, Otten was working for a ski resort in Vermont when his employer dispatched him to manage a small resort it had recently acquired in Maine. "He was stuck in the back of nowhere," his wife Chris observed, "and people paid little attention to him....Every spring he'd say, 'We're outta here,' and we'd write up a new resume. But then he'd stay around to paint the chair lift."

It troubled him that the owners showed no inclination to invest and build the enterprise up further, and around 1976, four years after he had joined the company, Chris recalled, he began talking about what he would do "if this were my place."

By 1980 the resort was losing $240,000 per year on revenues of $541,000, and the owners were open to selling it. "I turned 31 years old," Otten said, "and I was ready for something. You could have put me almost anywhere, into almost any venture." He arranged with the owners to take ownership of the business in exchange for an $840,000 note.

He began by cutting costs, then adopted a strategy that contrasted with other ski resorts by emphasizing the quality of the skiing rather than amenities of the lodge. Financial performance turned around. By 1986 the company's profits were over $1.6 million per year and by 1988 they were over $6 million.[4]

Otten encountered the fortunate coincidence that the company he worked for was one he could acquire. In general, however, such an event is unlikely. For the entrepreneur who decides to pursue an acquisition-entry strategy there may be no other choice except to go looking for an available company. Some possible sources of acquisition leads include the following:

- Classified ads in the "business opportunities" sections of both local and national newspapers. In local papers small service firms will predominate, along with "hustles" for making money without knowing much, doing much or investing much, so they will say. Classified advertisements for more substantial types of businesses such as manufacturing companies are more likely to be found in national papers such as the *Wall Street Journal*.

- Business brokers. Usually, these are real estate brokers whose licenses permit them to claim brokerage fees on sales of businesses as well as properties. Typically, however, the business listings are a small or virtually non-existent sideline. Aside from the classified listings, there simply don't tend to be many businesses actively looking for buyers. (If a business for sale was highly attractive, why would the broker not buy instead of sell it?)

- Cold calls. The fact that a business is not looking for a buyer does not mean its owner would not sell it if the price and terms were "right." The owner may be comfortable and not willing to consider anything but an unjustifiably high price. Or possibly the owner will have become unenthused about the business and just not yet reached a point of seeking a buyer. Entrepreneurs have found firms like the latter simply by walking in office doors and asking at one company after another until hitting "pay dirt."

- Other contacts. Besides business brokers, people who might know about firms for sale include:

    - Bank trust officers responsible for custody of companies whose owners have died.
    - Attorneys whose clients want to rearrange their estates.
    - Commercial loan officers who may have loans out to firms in need of new management and funding.
    - Accountants with clients who need management help or want to get out of their firms.
    - Other entrepreneurs who know of colleagues who should want to sell out.

Application: *Which of the above sources should be most likely as a way of finding the assigned case venture as an acquisition for one who had no prior link to it?*

A positive aspect of seeking to buy a business is that the task of finding one lends itself much more to systematic searching than does the opportunity for starting a new one. That is not to say the finding is easy. But the number of possibilities, although large, is at least finite, and they can readily be located, categorized and checked out. The diary of an entrepreneur, Hendrix Niemann, who went searching for an acquisition after losing his job ("If 'resigned' suggests that it was entirely my doing, that's not a fair characterization") included the following comments.[5]

> *I started by wading through the ads slowly, one by one...ANSWERING/ BEEPER SERVICE...ANTIQUE RESTORATION...AUTO BODY/PAINT....I had absolutely no idea what I was looking for—but I'll know it when I see it. Certain names and/or phone numbers kept popping up. These must be the brokers or agents for the owners.*

I had started my first business, a regional magazine, along with my college roommate when I was 24. We ended up being taken over five years later. I started a magazine for someone else....and I had been the CEO of an independent TV news company in Washington.

This time I wanted to do it all myself; no partners, no investors, just me.... I'd contact all the lawyers, accountants and bankers in Annapolis. Surely they would have a client or friend who wanted to retire. I pictured a friendly man of around 65, getting tired, nobody to turn the company over to, wanting to take care of his longtime employees. Not greedy, doesn't want a lot of money down, a nice long-term payout. I'm his salvation, and the company's. A nice little business. Doing a couple million. Doesn't really matter what it is. No retail, of course, but maybe light manufacturing or some kind of distributorship, or a niche service business... How tough can it be to find something like this? I'll probably have several to pick from.

Nothing. A dry hole. Dead ends....The time had come to take on the business brokers....I started with the one offering the hospital transcription service. Like many business brokers, he was a realtor who had kind of backed into selling businesses. He had no formal business or accounting background. He came to our appointment armed with a confidentiality agreement and four typed pages about the transcription company. The first three showed revenues and expenses for 1986, '87 and '88. The fourth sheet was a projection for 1989. There was no balance sheet, no customer list, no promotional literature, no written history of the business. He said none of that existed, that he had spent days just pulling together what I held in my hand....

On to the next....He said, "I need some venture capital. I happen to be a small investor in a company that's going to make a computer screen that will revolutionize the industry." He told me all about it, for an hour and a half. I asked him if he had any companies for sale that I might be interested in. "Not right now. I'll call you." And so it went.

The difficult task of search continued, and eventually Niemann located a lead which worked out through answering a blind classified advertisement in the *Wall Street Journal*, "after 17 business brokers, dozens of blind ads and four months." The advertisement for this company had been placed by a business broker. Other entrepreneurs have found their leads through brokers and methods which failed previously. No systematic study has been made of which search methods work best for what kinds of entrepreneurs and what kinds of ventures.

Checkout

Once contact with a company whose owner is open to selling is made, the task is to check it out for "fit." This process must work from two viewpoints, that of the owner and that of the buyer. From the owner's perspective, why is this the best buyer available? Unless the buyer is going to pay cash, what is the assurance that he or she will be effective enough as a new owner to assure that the business will survive and make its payments on time? The present owner may be emotionally attached to the company and to its employees. Will this buyer be the best person to take care of them, see that the firm continues and prospers? What evidence is there in the buyer's prior experience to support such a hope?

From the buyer's side a different set of questions applies. Some deal with the current balance sheet. What assets and liabilities will the buyer really get with the business? Other questions deal with future cash flow. Can the company cash inflows meet its needs, plus those of the new owner plus whatever payments are required to carry out terms of the takeover? Depending upon the company, here are somewhat more specific questions to consider:

Assets

- Which assets will be bought as part of the deal and which will not? Will the building stay with the owner? If so what will be the terms of the lease? If those had been the terms previously, how would the company's income statement have looked? If there is a present lease, is it transferable, how long will it run, and are there rights to renew, reassign or sublet? Will it constrain the business?

- Company name, patents, trademarks, licenses, customer and mailing lists, credit records, supplier arrangements, know-how for performing the work, ongoing pattern of employee and customer activities. Are they effective? How assuredly will they be retainable by the buyer? How hard would it be to replicate them? Will the seller or competitors have incentive or be able to undercut them? What is the company's reputation? According to whom?

- Tooling, fixtures, equipment and furniture. To what extent are they in good condition and up to date? How much could they be sold for separately? How much would it cost to replace or upgrade them?

- Inventory and receivables. How much must the company be prepared to carry? Which ones will be transferred in the sale and how? How will they be valued, at what time and by whom?

Liabilities

- Accounts payable. What will they consist of at the time of sale, who will pay them when, and what is the assurance that the seller will follow through on any promises?

- Hidden liabilities. What precautions should be taken, both through inspection and in the purchase agreement, to cover any non-apparent liabilities, such as impending lawsuits, customer claims, outstanding warranties or other obligations of the company? Are all obligations such as time payments, back taxes, and accrued employee holiday pay considered and provided for by written promise of the seller?

- Credit. Does the company have any problems with suppliers that may surface later? How good will credit be under the new owner?

Cash Flow

- How much working capital has the company needed in the past, and how will this change under new ownership? How will the timing of payments to suppliers and collections from customers shift after the sale?

- What will the future pattern of sales most likely be, and what capital will be needed to finance that?

- How will the buyer cover living expenses simultaneously with purchase payments to the seller?

- Have all new costs of recruiting, repairs, modernization, redesign or retraining been included?

Application: *How should the above checkout questions be rank ordered for application to the assigned case venture?*

Perhaps more important than any of the above questions is that of whether any other issue of importance has not been considered. Every business is a special case with unique issues of its own. Possibly, the entrepreneur will think of new questions through careful analysis and development of a plan to make the most of the business. It might be advisable to consult an expert on that particular type of business, such as the operator of a similar but not competing firm. Certainly, it will be advisable to bring in one or more experts on such subjects as law, accounting, appraisal and taxes.

The main indicator of whether a company acquired by an entrepreneur will succeed is most often how well the company was doing before takeover. A company with a well-accepted product or service can be hard to kill, while one without that may be hopeless, regardless how dedicated and intelligent the new management. Copies of the income tax reports filed by the business and/or its owner over recent years can be very helpful for gauging past performance. They may be on the conservative side as regards net profit and salaries, since there is incentive for the owner to minimize taxes by expensing as many things against them as possible. However, if cost of goods sold is computed based upon inventory valuations that were already written down in prior years, then that figure may be an understated cost. Another understated cost may be depreciation if equipment was already written off in prior years.

Prior experience in the business or in a similar line of business may help, but is clearly not a prerequisite for success with an acquisition. Many entrepreneurs who took over firms in lines of work where they had no prior experience have succeeded magnificently. Interestingly, it is not so easy to say the same for companies that acquire other companies.

Valuation

Such analysis of financial records is an important part of determining what price and terms should be suitable for buying a business. If the seller has already proposed a price, there is the choice of whether to haggle over it or to accept the price and negotiate on terms instead. For assessing price, a variety of approaches are possible including:

- Seller's offered price
- Present value discounted future cash flow
- Present value with a control premium[6]
- Multiple of earnings of comparable companies
- Balance sheet book value
- Book value corrected to include goodwill
- Market value indicated by other offers
- Price of similar companies sold
- Replacement cost
- Liquidation value

Application: *Insofar as possible, develop a sale price for the assigned case venture using each of the above methods. In light of them all, what would be a fair price?*

An important element to include in assessment of the firm is what salary and other fringe benefits accrue to the buyer. These may, particularly in smaller firms, be much greater than the profits. Whether they or other customary company expenditures have changed recently and thereby affected the apparent profit level can also be important.

In the case of Hendrix Niemann, the business broker, Lauren Finberg, sent him a package of information which included proposed terms of a deal. He recalled:

> *Of greatest importance to me was a two-pager showing how I could purchase the company with 100 percent financing, get the owner his purchase price, service the debt and still take out 75 percent of what I had been earning before.[7]*

Subsequently, however, an item-by-item physical valuation of the assets, coupled with new figures showing decline in earnings lowered the company's estimated worth and cash-generating ability. Niemann continued:

> *When the inventory was complete, it came in at 60 percent of its stated value on the balance sheet and $16,000 less than my accountant's worst-case scenario. We talked about what the company was worth and agreed that with the combination of the ongoing losses for the year, the old receivables and the inventory reductions, it was worth about half the previous year's book value. And that was to be our offer, no more, no less, take it or leave it. Book value. Period. The purchase price had come down a full 50 percent from the amount we had agreed to that July day in the hot, unlit Italian restaurant. The offer was accepted within 24 hours.[8]*

Disappointment in the true value of assets, as opposed to what the seller claims they are worth, is a frequent occurrence among buyers. Another entrepreneur who bought a company which included general-purpose machines recalled a setback even after he had taken the precaution of having a used-equipment dealer give him an appraisal on them.

> *I had bought equipment before based on appraisals. Normally, there would be a statement at the bottom of the dealer's appraisal sheet to the effect that "as of this day we will agree to pay X dollars for this equipment." That lets you know that it is really worth the figure they give. But this time I did not notice that the statement was different, and instead it said something to the effect that "this is our best judgment as to what this equipment is worth." As it turned out, the equipment was actually worth only about 60 percent of the estimate, and I got stuck.*

This company buyer also found other problems with the business. Financial statements prepared by his own accountant turned out to contain substantial errors which lowered the value of what he thought he had bought. The company's job costing system was woefully inadequate and had to be revamped. Finally, the head man in the shop, who knew the most about how to run it and had been considered invaluable to the buyer, turned out to have a serious drinking problem and had to be let go. The buyer ultimately was able to keep operating at a profit, but one substantially lower than he had projected.

One way of viewing a prospective venture which may help in valuation is to consider acquisition versus start-up of the same firm, which could avoid many of these "inherited" problems. Could the prospective entrepreneur accomplish such a start-up? How much would it cost and how much time would be required? Answering these questions should help bracket the high end of what could justifiably be paid for the company.

Accuracy of Appraisal Methods

Based on information from sales of 258 closely held firms in the southwestern and western United States, Harper and Rose found that combination methods of valuation appeared to be the most accurate.[9] They compared the valuation figure obtained by various individual and combination valuation methods with the prices at which the companies were actually sold, and found that the average difference or error was 6.69 percent. All the individual methods, such as book value, discounted cash flow, and so on, yielded substantially higher errors than this, while the two most effective combination methods, on average, were adjusted book value and capitalized earnings, and capitalized earnings and comparable sales, or what similar companies had sold for (see Table 9-1).

Table 9-1   Accuracy of Alternative Valuation Methods

Method		#	Average Error %	Average Absolute Error %
1	Adj. bk. & cap. earnings	61	6.0	9.0
2	Cap. earnings & comp. sales	10	-6.3	8.3
3	Past transactions	7	-7.4	9.8
4	Adjusted book value	9	8.2	12.9
6	Cap. earnings or P/E	31	-9.7	11.4
7	Adj. bk. & comparable sales	9	10.5	11.6
8	Comparable sales	16	14.8	18.1
9	Capitalized dividends	5	-19.8	24.1
10	Discounted cash flow	6	19.9	23.9
11	Replacement cost	5	24.4	24.4
12	Capitalized revenues	7	36.8	36.9
13	Unadjusted book value	7	-35.5	35.5
	Other combinations	81	8.9	11.5
	Other single methods	4	-26.7	26.7
	Total	258		
	Overall Average		6.7	13.9

Some individuals, it appears, tend to be better at forecasting the prices at which closely held companies will sell. From the same study, see Table 9-2 for how various categories of appraisers compared. Most accurate seemed to be consultants and, least so (surprisingly perhaps), venture capitalists.

Table 9-2 Accuracy of Different Appraisers

Appraiser Background	#	Average Error %	Average Absolute Error %
Industry consultant	9	6.0	9.9
General consultant	26	-8.0	10.4
Academic faculty member	34	8.5	8.9
Industry employee	8	13.0	13.0
Buyer's business broker	37	-14.1	15.8
Seller's business broker	27	16.7	17.0
Venture capitalist	38	24.7	25.7
Other, or no response	79	9.2	10.9
Total	258		
Overall Average		6.7	14.8

Credibility

The seller is likely to care greatly about two things: First, that he or she is fully paid in accordance with whatever deal is struck for the business, and second, that the business continue in satisfactory condition, maintaining jobs for its employees and carrying on the entity which the seller grew accustomed to regarding as an original proprietary creation, a personal property or both. To feel assured that these will happen, the seller will want the company sold to someone capable and dedicated to accomplishing them.

A record of integrity should clearly be regarded as necessary for the buyer, since that person will, after takeover, be in a position both to "loot" the business and to let purchase payments lapse. A tight contract may be able to mitigate damage from such acts to some degree, but cannot prevent them entirely. If a buyer with integrity cannot be found, the seller would likely be better off either to keep the business or else to liquidate it.

A young man, here referred to as "H," had passed through a series of ventures, one of which had failed and gone into receivership. Subsequently, however, he accomplished a successful acquisition, which was sold and left him with money to invest. With a partner he began looking for possibilities.

The partner inquired at banks about possible firms to buy and came up with several leads. On the way to one of them with H he was describing it as a small distributorship owned by an elderly man and his wife who seemed to be slipping in their capability to run the business and might do well to sell it before anything went seriously wrong with it. He recalled being surprised when H looked at him with a big smile and said, "Let's see if we can steal it."

Shortly thereafter, the partner received a call from a venture capitalist he knew who said he had heard the partner was looking for deals with H. Did the partner, he asked, know about H's previous business practices? Did he know H had gone through personal bankruptcy for $7,000? No, the partner replied. The capitalist recounted how his firm had invested in a venture run by H, who had bordered on fraud in running it.

"For instance," the capitalist said, "he counted sales early and expenses late. He would have his people put stuff on the loading dock, tally it sold, then take it back into the shop. We lost a couple hundred thousand on our investment in that company, but that isn't what made me angry. It was H's dishonesty.

"I can give you names of other reputable people who will bear me out on this. This guy is a pathological liar. If you get involved with him, you deserve what happens to you and so does whomever you two buy a business from."

After this conversation, the partner quietly stopped looking for acquisitions, made himself hard for H to get hold of and went on to other things, as did H.

Among acceptable potential buyers with unsullied reputations credibility will be determined by further factors such as the following five:

Financial Strength A buyer with savings may be able to make a substantial cash down payment to give substance to the deal. Pledging any personal assets, such as home equity, may help. Even greater help will be co-signature by another individual with substantial assets.

Track Record "What has this person done before that demonstrates he or she can tackle a difficult problem and see it through to a solution despite major obstacles?" This will be a natural question for a seller to ask. Another is "What challenges has this person failed to tackle or tackled and failed to meet?" Asking for references and asking the references for other references are logical ways to seek answers.

Related Experience Having worked in the industry of the acquisition will look especially good, even though acquisitions frequently are made by people without that advantage. More relevant, perhaps, will be prior experience in general management, which demonstrates the buyer's capability to run a business.

Persuasiveness Selling is inescapably an emotional experience, and although it would seem logical to base the deal on more objective factors such as those above, sellers in fact prefer to sell to people they like. Careful study of the business followed by thoughtful planning and forecasting of its future under the prospective buyer, as well as diplomatic handling of the checkout and negotiations, may overcome other weaknesses on the buyer's part.

Seller's Urgency If the seller wants badly to sell and does not have other attractive buyers, that may be the most powerful persuasion of all. Unfortunately for the buyer, such a circumstance is not something the buyer can create.

To the extent it can be controlled, the seller has the choice whether to sell or not. Sometimes, sellers postpone selling too long, then get in a hurry to complete it and aren't able to muster the self discipline required to attack the selling task in a systematic and thorough way, which gives the buyer a strong advantage.

Supplementary Reading

New Venture Strategies Chapter 9. (Vesper, K.H., Prentice-Hall, 1990)

Exercises

1. Interview someone who acquired a firm. Ask how he or she found it and how someone else looking for a firm to buy could best go about finding one.

2. Discuss the appropriateness of a search criterion which says simply, "I'll know it when I see it."

3. Carry out one or more search modes, such as using the "business opportunities" section of the newspaper classified advertisements, contacting a business broker, or cold calling on companies to find a business for sale.

4. Test the theory that "any business is for sale if the price is right" by interviewing the owner(s) of one or more local firms.

5. Draft a list for checking out a prospective acquisition, and apply it as best you can to one or more local firms, whether they are for sale or not.

Venture History

1. What opportunities can be seen in hindsight for the founders of this venture to have bought out an existing company rather than to have started a new one?

2. How could those have been discovered by the founders through a deliberate searching process?

3. How well-qualified as buyers should the founders have seemed from a seller's point of view?

Venture Planning Guide

1. Describe the elements in your proposed venture that could be obtained by acquiring one or more other existing companies, and estimate the cost of obtaining them through acquisition versus fresh start-up.

2. Assess the options of start-up versus acquisition as a way of entering the venture you have been working on.

Notes

[1] Natalie T. Taylor and Frederick A. Hooper, Jr., "Entrepreneurial Buyouts - Developments and Trends 1978-1988," in *Frontiers of Entrepreneurship Research, 1989*, eds. Brockhaus, Robert H., Sr. and others (Wellesley, Mass.: Babson Center for Entrepreneurial Studies), 1989, p. 575.

[2] Arnold C. Cooper and others, *New Business In America* (Washington, D.C.: The NFIB Foundation, 1990), p. 5.

[3] Arnold C. Cooper, William C. Dunkelberg, and Carolyn Y. Woo, "Survival and Failure: A Longitudinal Study," in *Frontiers of Entrepreneurship Research, 1988*, eds. Bruce H. Kirchhoff, and others (Wellesley, Mass.: Babson Center for Entrepreneurial Studies, 1988), p. 234.

[4] Bill McGowan, "The Turnaround Entrepreneur," *Inc.*, January 1990, p. 53.

[5] Hendrix F.C. Niemann, "Buying a Business," *Inc.*, February 1990, p. 28.

[6] Ellyn E. Spragins, , "Locking Up Good Value," *Inc.*, November 1989, p. 157.

[7] Niemann, "Buying a Business," p. 38.

[8] Ibid.

[9] Charles P. Harper and Lawrence C. Rose, "Accuracy of Appraisers and Appraisal Methods of Closely Held Companies," *ET&P*, 17, no. 3, Spring 1993, p. 21.

❏ SUBCHAPTER 9B - *Dealing*

Negotiation

If the buyer is regarded as highly credible by the seller, negotiating the purchase can be a very short and simple process. As a division officer in a privately held aerospace corporation, Daryl Mitton was well-known to the managers above him when his CEO decided the company should rid itself of Mitton's division.

> *No sooner did he announce that my division was to be sold, than he suggested that I buy it. We came to an agreement on terms of the sale in very short order. I would buy the "hard" assets at book value. His firm would loan the total amount for the purchase of these assets, with the loan secured by the assets and repayable over five years. I would purchase the existing inventories for cash, payable in 90 days. His firm would supply headquarters support services for up to 90 days at cost.*[1]

It was to Mitton's advantage in working out his deal that the company knew him, and he was intimately familiar with the division he was buying from having worked in it.

In contrast, Hendrix Niemann had no prior knowledge of his acquisition, and the path to agreement on a deal was correspondingly bumpier. His deal to buy the company had almost foundered repeatedly: on down valuing of assets, finding hidden liabilities, learning that key employees were set to leave, running into trouble with banks trying to obtain financing, and at the last minute further problems with the seller's attorney. The deal had been on the attorney's desk two weeks before closing. But it received no attention, drew no suggestions for changes and provoked no objections until Niemann went to the bank, obtained the down payment check, on which interest immediately began accruing, and arrived at his attorney's office, where Lauren Finberg, the broker, was already waiting to close the deal with the seller, Peter Klosky and Peter's lawyer. As Niemann described it:

> *Peter and his attorney were late. When they did arrive, they wanted to rewrite the whole deal. Better for Peter's taxes this way. We're not changing any amounts, just the way it's paid out. And, by the way, we're not satisfied with the collateral you're using to secure the note to Mr. Klosky. Did we neglect to mention that before? Well, it doesn't really matter if we settle today, does it?*[2]

Niemann and his attorney refused to yield, gambling that the seller would give in. He did, and the deal went through. Had it not, there would likely have been further protracted negotiations, more legal expenses and in the end, perhaps no deal at all, just the search for another job.

Application: *List and rank the strengths and weaknesses in bargaining positions of buyer and seller in the assigned case.*

Deals

There are two principal dimensions to deals, the price and the terms. Usually, a seller will have a price clearly in mind and some ideas about kinds of terms that will be acceptable or desirable. A possibility, for instance, might be:

Price $500,000

For Going concern, name, tooling, equipment, customer list and records, plus inventory valued at $200,000, to be verified by mutual physical count at time of deal; price to be adjusted according to any discrepancy. Seller will keep company bank account and receivables. Seller also agrees to pay all payables outstanding at time of purchase. Buyer assumes the existing lease.

Down Payment 30 percent at time of closing.

Terms Balance to be paid over five years with interest at 2 percent over prime on unpaid balance.

In this deal the buyer must come up with a down payment and working capital except for inventory. Possibly this can be borrowed at the bank, which would make it a completely leveraged buyout. Personal savings may still have to be used by the buyer to live on until the company generates enough cash to meet payroll, plus debt payments plus salary for the buyer. Savings may also be needed for coping with unwanted surprises—a machine breaks down, a theft occurs, some supplier wants advance payment, legal fees of the deal are higher than expected, and so forth.

Variations on such deals are endless. Making part of the purchase price a consulting contract to the seller, for instance, makes that part tax-deductible to the business, although not to the seller. If the seller claims the company has higher earning potential than the buyer believes, then perhaps part of the price should be in the form of a royalty on sales for a specified period of time based upon the seller's claim. Or to lower the price, perhaps the seller may keep some furniture or some general-purpose equipment of the company which is not immediately needed for production. To make the deal more secure to the seller, possibly the buyer will agree not to take any cash out of the company personally, living on income provided by a spouse perhaps, until a certain percentage of the outstanding debt is repaid. Or perhaps the buyer's promise to pay can be backed up by a cosigner, who in turn may take a percentage interest in the company or a royalty on sales.

The shop itself, if the company owns it, may be included in the deal, or the seller may sell all the assets except real estate and lease the shop to the buyer. Leasing can lower the purchase price and let the seller retain an income stream from rent. In such a case, of course, the buyer needs to add to the cash outflow, rental costs which may not have appeared there historically. Many other details must be considered as well, such as:

- What assets of the business guarantee any note the seller may be accepting? Must other loans to the company be subordinated?

- Should the seller sign a non-competition agreement, and if so, for what activities, time and geographical area?

- Is every single asset to be transferred listed in the agreement?

- How about shares of any stock, articles of incorporation and minutes of shareholders' meetings?

- Is there certification that shareholders have duly authorized the sale?

- What does the seller guarantee about outstanding liabilities, claims or lawsuits against the company?

- Does the seller have partners, and if so, are they signing too?

- Exactly when does the buyer take over what? Are there any protections for the seller to cover things the buyer might do after sale?

- What are the buyer's longer-term aims for the firm? Are there any constraints on how the buyer can dispose of assets or the business?

Application: *What would be answers to the above questions insofar as possible for the assigned case venture?*

Signing the deal will complete the third of four big tests involved in business entry via acquisition. The first is to find an acceptable company to buy, as discussed in the preceding subchapter (9A). Second is to demonstrate credibility to the seller, as mentioned earlier in this subchapter. Third is the deal, and fourth the transition to new management. It is at this fourth stage that many acquisition deals, particularly when the acquirer is a larger corporation, falter and ultimately fail. Corporation managements tend to perform heavy-handed acts, such as changing the name of the acquisition, imposing new internal systems and new managers, showing disregard for methods that have traditionally worked well for the acquired company and disrespect for its employees. These kinds of measures add confusion and drive out key employees who have other options so that the acquired company, even though it may be able to draw on greater financial strength from its new parent, becomes weaker and ultimately gets sold again or possibly even closed down.

Application: *What deal terms, in order of importance, should (a) the seller and (b) the buyer seek to obtain in the assigned case?*

Although systematic statistics are limited, entrepreneurs appear to fare much better with their acquisitions than do corporations.[3] They are dependent on existing employees and know it, consequently treating them with care and respect for their views and interests. Because they are typically risking everything they own and will earn for the foreseeable future, they simply must find ways to make their acquisitions work out, and usually they do.

Franchising as a Compromise

An alternative which combines some elements of taking a job, starting a new company and taking over one already going is to buy a franchise. In their study of 2,994 small firms, Cooper et al. reported that this option often played a role.

One quarter (26 percent) began operations with some type of franchise, though just 12 percent reported that at least three-quarters of their sales came from franchised goods or services. The latter 12 percent corresponds to the number who operated under a franchise name (11 percent). No relationship existed between the possession of a franchise or operation under a franchise name and survival. However, a negative relationship existed between the percent of franchised sales and growth.[4]

It was estimated in 1989 that there were over 3,000 franchise chains in the U.S. operating over 500,000 outlets.[5] Restaurants were estimated in 1990 to account for 102,000 outlets, gas stations 112,000 and business aids and services 67,000, with the latter having grown 21 percent since 1988.[6]

Many franchises are simply dealerships (e.g. a Ford dealership). Others are so-called "format franchises" wherein some company with a proven operating formula, such as McDonald's, sells (1) rights for use of that formula, plus (2) training, (3) special equipment, (4) help in choosing a location, (5) periodic review and guidance on performance, plus (6) advertising and (7) use of the brand in return for an up-front franchise fee and/or a royalty on sales.

Claimed advantages of starting with a franchise are that the entrepreneur need not look farther to find a business idea, need not invest time in puzzling out a plan for the business and learning how to pick a location, and may not have to search for financing, which the franchisor company may conveniently provide. There are also claims that odds of failing are lower, since the formula has already been proven to work at other locations. Doubt about the latter claim, at least, has appeared in the study of 2,994 firms by Cooper et al., which found no relationship between possession of a franchise or operation under a franchise name and survival three years after start-up.[7] Undoubtedly, survival of some franchises is much more probable than others.

Of more significant interest to the prospective franchisee should be the level of profitability. Cooper et al. did find that franchise-based start-ups grew faster than independents. However, profitability assessment must take into account (1) the amount invested in shop, equipment and inventory, (2) the cost of the franchise fee, and (3) the impact on profits of any royalty fees. After subtracting those, discounting for a suitable return on the investment in the business, and taking into account the hours worked, the income to the franchisee may not be very attractive. It will probably cost more to start a franchise than to buy or start a comparable business, and the profits, after royalties, may well be less with a franchise. Certainly, the freedom to manage will be less.

Some indication of franchise costs can be seen in the following examples:[8]

- CelluLand (cellular phone stores) - Fee $25,000, royalty 5 percent, plus store cost $80,000 to $250,000

- Papyrus (greeting card stores) - Fee $29,500, royalty 6 percent, plus store cost $70,000 to $150,000

- Valvoline (auto oil change) - Fee $35,000, royalty 6 percent, plus store cost $55,000 to $100,000

Net income is generally not reported, but varies widely with volume and how the owner chooses to allocate expenses. The projected income statement for a new pizza franchise was reported in 1990 by *Inc.*[9] (See Table 9-3.)

Of the $325,000 investment required, it was projected that $75,000 would be for equipment, $13,000 for a point-of-sale system, and $135,000 for the modular building to house the store. Experts in similar industries polled by the magazine were divided about whether the concept, fast window-pickup pizza, would succeed. Most said no.

Very important beyond financial considerations is the extent to which the entrepreneur will find the work of franchisee satisfying. A franchise typically places very significant restrictions on flexibility in managing. What products or services to offer, how to make them, how much to charge, how to advertise, what decor to have in the store and how to run operations may all be tightly controlled by the franchisor, leaving the franchisee feeling more like a middle manager or shop worker than an entrepreneur. Perceptions vary among franchisees, however, and some see their work as more entrepreneurial than others.[10]

Because of abuses in the past, laws have been developed to curb and control franchisors, and these vary from state to state. Consequently, it is advisable to engage a lawyer who specializes in franchises and has extensive experience in the state where the entrepreneur's business is to be located. Checking with other franchisees who have bought from the same franchisor and perhaps with some of their employees is another obvious precaution to take before buying.

The Chamber of Commerce, the Better Business Bureau and banking connections may also be able to add helpful information to that which will be provided by the franchisor.

Table 9-3 Sales and Expense Projections for a Proposed New Pizza Franchise

Sales		$520,000
Expenses		
Food Purchases	140,400	
Other Costs of Goods	36,400	
Labor and Benefits	145,600	
Royalty	20,800	
Advertising	26,000	
Land Rent	25,000	
Utilities	15,000	
Delivery Expenses	6,500	
Miscellaneous	28,900	
Depreciation	43,642	
Total Expenses		488,242
Net Profit Before Tax		$31,758

Some pitfalls that others have run into in dealing with franchisors in the past have included:

- Formats that may sound good but don't really work
- Promises of training that are not fulfilled
- Fees and charges by franchisors that eliminate franchisee profits
- Franchisees becoming stuck with unsalable inventory from the franchisor
- Promises of advertising that are not fulfilled
- High-pressure selling that does not allow the prospective franchisee to evaluate sensibly
- Failure to reveal negative aspects of the franchise firm's past performance
- Failure by the franchisee to appreciate just what it will be like to work "for" the franchisor
- Failure by the franchisee to obtain input from other franchisees and a qualified franchise lawyer before signing the franchisor's contract

Checklists for evaluating franchisors and their franchises are readily available in books about franchising and from governmental agencies such as the

Small Business Administration. Many of the problems that might arise, however, are difficult to anticipate either with or without a list. One entrepreneur, who later became highly successful in building a company, American Photo Group, which he sold to Eastman Kodak for an estimated $45 million, recalled his first business as a franchisee.

> *I had a Burger Chef franchise when I was 21. It was terrible. I was thrown into two weeks of training at a hamburger school, and I didn't understand anything. I worked seven days a week, 12 to 15 hours a day. I took off one afternoon for my wife's uncle's funeral. I didn't know what was going on. I couldn't tell day from night—for seven months. I must have been one of the worst managers Burger Chef ever had. But I had so many things go wrong. We were in a shopping center that was under construction, and there was a big economic crisis. Interest rates shot through the roof. So they stopped building the shopping center and shut down the road in front of us. The whole thing was a disaster. My father-in-law helped finance the deal, and we lost everything he put into it—$70,000.* [11]

Franchises can be acquired second-hand as going concerns, just as can independent businesses. The fact that the franchise may be well-known and that the unit for sale may have records of its past performance does not assure that the buyer is getting full value for the purchase price.

A 41-year-old Seattle man had worked independently in home remodeling and operating his own auto generator repair shop. Through an acquaintance he learned of a transmission repair shop for sale operating under a well-known franchise. Records indicated that the present owner had been able to draw an income from the business which the prospective buyer found attractive.

Several days after taking over, he was told by the employees that they had been promised raises and would quit if they did not receive them. Not knowing how he would replace them, the buyer agreed, and found his labor costs were now 70 percent of revenues instead of 60 percent. Shortly after that he found that many people who needed transmissions repaired were poorly prepared to pay cash for the work, and as a result his cash flow squeezed ever more tightly.

Total sales were also disappointingly below what they had been under the previous owner. Discussing this with workers in the shop, the buyer was told that prior management had seen to it that virtually every car brought into the shop for inspection was found to need expensive repairs urgently, regardless of its condition. Such a procedure had not occurred to the buyer, who prided himself on honest business practices.

Finally, order processing in the shop, he found, was sloppy. Estimates were lost, there was no way to trace labor costs on jobs, transmission parts could not be found, and it was impossible to reconcile the company checkbook. To correct these problems, the buyer started a job-numbering system to trace labor and parts costs, hired a part-time bookkeeper to reconcile accounts, negotiated with a finance company to provide cash with which customers could pay for work, and raised prices to cover his increased labor costs.

Sales, however, continued to lag, and the buyer consequently resold the business at a loss, took a job elsewhere and struggled to collect from the new buyer, who soon had trouble making payments due on the shop.

Thus this entrepreneur shifted from one strategy to a second. The first was to operate as a franchisee. The second was to buy and resell a franchise. The latter strategy, although not profitable for him, is one that can be successful. The other two most likely ways to make substantial profits on franchises are either to find a successful business formula and sell it by becoming a franchisor or to acquire multiples of franchises, if possible in the early days of a to-be-successful franchise, before the price of it has gone up.[12]

Although the average individual franchisee may make a meager income and relatively low return on investment in exchange for long hours of hard work, the top layer of most successful franchisees appear to enjoy sales on the order of 30 percent and more above average and profits still higher. The secrets of such performance appear to lie in straightforward application of good management disciplines, careful attention to many fine details and, above all, finding ways to motivate employees in providing exceptional service to customers.[13]

Application: *What would be the pros and cons of buying whatever franchise might make most sense, as opposed to buying the assigned case venture, for the entrepreneur in the assigned case?*

Supplementary Reading

New Venture Strategies Chapter 10. (Vesper, K.H., Prentice-Hall, 1990)

Exercises

1. Discuss with the owner of a local business what characteristics a "person most logical to buy" that business would have. Rank those characteristics in order of (a) importance to the seller, and (b) likely effect of the bargaining strength of the buyer.

2. Interview someone who bought a business, and learn about how the terms were arrived at. Also learn about competing buyers, either real or potential at the time, and evaluate their relative bargaining strengths and what they could do about those strengths.

3. Study one or more local firms both by observation and by reading whatever you can find about that type of business. Determine an estimated selling price for the business, and explain how you arrived at that price.

4. Draft a list of criteria for checking out a prospective franchise, obtain information about an available franchise by following up a business opportunities advertisement, and apply the checklist to evaluate it.

Venture History

1. What selling price and terms would it be reasonable for the founders to ask for the venture at two contrasting stages in its development?

2. Who would have been a good buyer at each of these stages, and how could a seller have gone about deliberately searching for such a person?

3. In hindsight, what does the founder(s) conclude about the advisability of start-up versus acquisition as a way of entering independent business?

Venture Planning Guide

1. Describe what you expect would be the margin of negotiation for the needed elements of your enterprise through acquisition of one or more existing firms, and describe a strategy you might use for striking the best possible bargain.

2. As an acquisition for some other person whom you specify, assess the value your venture should have at points six months, one year and two years down the path of start-up.

3. Describe your expected bargaining position for selling your venture at three contrasting states projected by the plan of its future.

Notes

[1] Daryl C. Mitton, "The Anatomy of A High Leverage Buyout," in *Frontiers of Entrepreneurship Research, 1984*, eds. John A. Hornaday and others (Wellesley Mass.: Babson Center for Entrepreneurial Studies, 1984), p. 414.

[2] Hendrix F.C. Niemann, "Buying a Business," *Inc.*, February 1990, p. 38.

[3] Robert B. Brown, John E. Butler, and Karl H. Vesper, "Performance After Acquisition: The Role of Entrepreneurs," in *Frontiers of Entrepreneurship Research, 1989*, eds. Brockhaus, Robert H., Sr. and others (Wellesley, Mass.: Babson Center for Entrepreneurial Studies), 1989, p. 575.

[4] Arnold C. Cooper and others, *New Business In America* (Washington, D.C.: The NFIB Foundation, 1990), p. 5.

[5] Carol Steinberg, "The Right Deal," *Venture*, June/July 1989, p. 53.

[6] Leslie Brokaw, "New Businesses," *Inc.*, May 1990, p. 25.

[7] Cooper and others, *New Business In America*, p. 5.

[8] Echo M. Garrett, "Ten Franchises on a Fast Track," *Venture*, March 1989, p. 21.

[9] Joshua Hyatt, "The Next Big Thing," *Inc.*, July 1990, p. 44.

[10] Cecilia M. Falbe, Ajith Kumar and Thomas C. Dandridge, "Industry and Firm Influences on Entrepreneurial Behavior Among Franchisees," in *Frontiers of Entrepreneurship Research, 1989*, eds. Brockhaus, Robert H., Sr. and others (Wellesley, Mass.: Babson Center for Entrepreneurial Studies), 1989, p. 559.

[11] "Thriving On Order," *Inc.*, December 1989, p. 47.

[12] Jeannie Ralston, "Franchisees Who Think Big," *Venture*, March 1989, p. 55.

[13] Curtis Hartman, "The Best-Managed Franchises In America," *Inc.*, October 1989, p. 68.

Case Questions

General Questions

1. As best you can estimate the financial capacity of the entrepreneur involved, what sort of price and terms in a buyout should this person seek?

2. Assess the attractiveness of the entrepreneur in the assigned case as a business buyer from an owner's point of view. Describe the sort of terms you would recommend an owner seek in selling to such a person.

3. Rank the entrepreneurs studied thus far in the assigned cases, including this one, as potential company buyers. Explain the reasons for your ranking.

4. What should the entrepreneur(s) do at the end of the assigned case and why?

Case 32 - Bob Mighell   p. 608

1. What can Bob gain by taking over the product line he is looking at?

2. If he buys it, what should be his plan of action and what should be his contingency plan?

3. What should he be interested in obtaining, what is the most he can justify paying for it, and what might be appropriate terms?

4. How would Bob's capabilities for making a go of the venture he is considering compare to yours and why? What could you do to compensate for what you see as his advantages?

Case 33 - Michael Hoppe   p. 619

1. Is Michael an appropriate person to be seeking a venture to buy? What are the pros and cons, and how do they balance out?

2. Assuming the answer to the first question is "yes," what would be the best way for him to go about finding the "right" company to acquire?

3. What have been the most and the least effective aspects of his approach so far?

Case 34 - Terry Allen   p. 626

1. Who would be the ideal person to buy this business, from the seller's point of view? How could such a person be sought? How does the proposed buyer match that profile? How could the proposed buyer best improve the fit?

2. Formulate, as realistically as you can, a hypothetical competitor grid for the venture described in this case. Discuss actions that could move the venture to a stronger position in the comparison.

3. Assess the alignment between the skills and abilities of these two prospective entrepreneurs and what the venture will require.

4. By what sequence of actions could they maximize their potential win from this venture opportunity?

5. What deal should they offer the prospective seller it they want to give this venture a try?

6. If they do buy the business, in what ways would you expect their work experience to be different than it is now?

Bob Mighell

It was the end of spring quarter 1991 and second year MBA student Bob Mighell was working to make what he considered to be a major decision. Should he purchase the Biopsy product line from his former employer, Branton Instrument Company, and start his own company or should he move ahead with a job search and work for someone else?

The Biopsy Product Line

A biopsy procedure consists of a doctor removing a small piece of tissue from a patient and observing the sample under a microscope. The biopsy equipment sold by Branton Instrument Company* was specifically used to obtain samples from the stomach, the intestine and the small bowel. These instruments were used by gastroenterologists who specialized in digestive diseases.

The original instruments were developed in 1957 by James Branton, founder of Branton Instrument Company, and Russell Robins, a gastroenterologist at the University of Washington's Medical School. The products were never patented, which Russell Robins attributed to a "folly of youth." The product line expanded through the early 1960s to include three different instruments. Those three instruments had, according to Branton, changed little since they were developed. A typical example of these instruments is depicted in Exhibit 1.

Bob Mighell's Background

Bob was born and raised in the Seattle area but decided to move away and attend

* disguised name

Dartmouth College right after graduation from high school. At Dartmouth Bob's interest in both medical products and entrepreneurship was kindled. He spent five years at Dartmouth working as a research assistant while earning degrees in both Liberal Arts and Mechanical Engineering. The research dealt with artificial joints. Bob's job required him to work in a machine shop where he learned to operate end-mills, lathes and other general machine shop equipment. His engineering degree thesis was written on Bob's design of a surgical instrument he developed for installing artificial joints.

During his last year at Dartmouth, Bob took an entrepreneurship course at the Tuck School of Business, which was located right next door to Dartmouth's Engineering School. In the course, Bob prepared a business plan to manufacture and sell snowboards, which at the time were an emerging sport. After graduation he took the business plan back to Seattle, incorporated as Edge Snowboards, and tried to raise the money to get the venture off the ground. Bob could only get $500,000 committed out of the $1,000,000 needed and the project folded.

After the snowboard project, he went to work for Branton Instrument Company as a manufacturing engineer. After two years with Branton, Bob decided he really wasn't interested in being an engineer all his life and would rather run his own small company. His experience with his snowboard venture had left him feeling he needed to know more about business management. With that in mind, he entered the University of Washington's MBA program in the Fall of 1989.

Possibility of a Buyout

The idea for the buyout originated in 1987 when Bob was having lunch with his usual group of manufacturing engineers, and his boss at Branton. They were talking about the different products Branton made and Bob's boss made the comment, "You know, someone could probably buy that biopsy line, set it up in their garage, and make a pretty decent living with it." Although Bob didn't follow up with the idea at the time, he remembered it and had always thought there might be a possibility that he could buy the biopsy line. Even though he worked as a manufacturing engineering and the biopsy line was officially under his control, he never once in the two years he was at Branton had to do anything with that particular product line. Bob thought that this was a good sign since the only things he ever heard about were the problems and if he hadn't heard anything about biopsy department in two years, the process must be well in control.

After Bob had left Branton to pursue his MBA, he had remained close friends with several of his co-workers. Bob called Brad, who had worked with him as a manufacturing engineer and asked what Brad knew about the biopsy line. Brad had been with Branton for several more years than Bob and knew much more about the biopsy line. Brad told Bob that there were only two people who worked in production on the biopsy line and neither of them worked more than half time. The other half of their time was taken up working on other products. The main pieces of equipment Brad knew that were required to produce the biopsy instruments were a couple of small jewelry lathes and an old end mill. Brad didn't know whether the end-mill and the lathes were used for producing other products or not. He also didn't know much about the sales figures but thought that they might be going down. He told Bob that he thought that Branton was planning to phase out the biopsy department over a period of five years. Brad said he thought the chances were pretty good that Branton would want to sell the biopsy line but the person Bob really needed to ask was Mark Rathman, the vice president of operations.

Bob's call, the next day, to Mark was very brief and went like this:

Bob: Hello Mark, this is Bob Mighell. I don't know if you remember me, but I worked there two years ago as a manufacturing engineer.

Mark: Sure, I remember. How's the MBA program?

Bob: It's great! A lot of hard work but I am learning quite a bit.

Mark: So, what can I do for you

Bob: I was interested to know if you would be willing to sell your biopsy line?

Mark: You bet! Do you have a buyer in mind?

Bob: Well, actually I was thinking of buying it myself. Can we get together and talk about it?

Mark: Sure. This week is pretty bad since we are just finishing up the quarter, but how about next Friday at 7:00 AM?

Bob: Sounds great, I'll see you then.

Mark had not hesitated a moment in saying that he would be willing to sell the biopsy line and Bob felt encouraged that he should pursue this opportunity. Before meeting with Mark Rathman, Bob wanted to learn a little more about biopsy equipment in general and Branton's instruments in particular.

Information Gathering

Bob invited another former coworker, Bill, over for dinner and explained that he was interested in buying the biopsy line. Bill had never worked very closely with the biopsy line and said he couldn't offer Bob much help, but he had an extra product catalog and price list that he would be willing to drop by the next day.

The catalog offered Bob his first complete picture of what he would be buying. There were basically three products that were being offered: The Multipurpose Suction biopsy, the Hydraulic biopsy and the Crosby-Krugler biopsy. They were all fairly similar in construction and appearance to the product shown in Exhibit 1.

Bob next spent some time at the University of Washington's Medical School Library researching the topic and found several references to Branton's instruments. The earliest reference, dated July 1959, was an article in *Gastroenterology* which was the official publication of the American Gastroenterological Association. In the article, Russell Robins and James Branton described their Multipurpose Suction biopsy instrument, which was almost identical to the one Branton was offering for sale in 1991. This product had basically not changed for over 30 years and was still selling.

In prepation for the meeting with Mark Rathman, Bob made a list of questions, which he sent in a letter to Mark (see Exhibit 2). He had two aims for the letter. The first was to remind Mark of the meeting and the second was to let Mark know that Bob was serious.

Bob recalled that his meeting with Mark was very informative. Mark explained that Branton wanted to get rid of the biopsy line for several reasons. He said he felt that the sales had been rather flat for a few years at what he estimated to be around $100,000–$120,000 per year. The total company sales were around $70 million and this little department was a "pain in the neck." Other products were expanding and this product line was taking up valuable space in a increasingly cramped building. He said they found it a problem that none of the FDA required procedures had been written on how to assemble the product. When Mark was pressed by Bob on the actual sales figures for the last few years, Mark looked up the last two years and said that 1989 sales were $115,000 and 1990 sales were $97,000. The 1990 sales were split among the biopsy products as follows:

	Total	Foreign
Multipurpose	$27,653	$ 6,000
Crosby-Krugler	$ 7,175	$ 3,000
Hydraulic	$ 5,610	$ 3,000
Repair Work	$56,257	$ 5,700
	$96,695	$17,700

Bob asked Mark if he could have a copy of a tabulation which Mark had been reading. Mark said that would be no problem and called in his secretary to make some copies (see Exhibit 3). The reports also showed a gross margin for the product line of around 40 percent which seemed terrible to Mark and was another reason he was interested in selling. Bob remembered from his time at Branton that other product lines he had worked on had gross margins in the 60 to 70 percent range.

Mark also mentioned in this meeting that the marketing department had just recently sent a letter to their biopsy customers saying that they were planning on discontinuing the product line. He said that they had gotten some response back from doctors who were very disappointed with the news. He seemed to remember that the doctors who were the most disappointed were the pediatric doctors. Mark said that if Bob were to buy the company, he would not have any problem in having Branton's salespeople refer all sales leads to Bob's company.

Bob left the meeting with Mark with the agreement that Mark would talk with Tony Perri, Branton Instrument's president, and see if he would approve the sale of the biopsy line.

At this point Bob recalled thinking that if he bought the biopsy line, he would run the company as a one-man shop. With his manufacturing and machining background, he thought he could easily handle the production. Combining this with his MBA, he felt he could take care of marketing and financing requirements of the company as well. With $100,000 in yearly sales and a 40 percent gross margin, it seemed to him there would be enough money for him to support his wife and two young children.

Before calling Mark back, Bob returned to the Medical School library to do a little more market research. In a reference book entitled the *Medical Device Registry* he found a list of five other manufacturers who made products listed under the subheading "Suction Biopsy Instruments." He called all five but could only get information from two of the companies. One had gone out of business and two would not give out product information to non-doctors. From the information he did receive from the two companies, it did not appear that their products performed the same function as Branton's equipment.

Other information that Bob gathered from the library included information on medical product and supply companies from *Standard & Poors 1990 Handbook* (see Exhibit 4) as well as information on medical manufacturers from *Robert Morris Associates 1990 Annual Statement Studies* (see Exhibit 4).

After several days of trying to get through to Mark, Bob finally reached him on the phone and found out that Tony had given approval to sell the biopsy line.

Mark said that they would be willing to sell the line for what they had in inventory, which he said was $73,000 as of 12/31/90. He also said that for that price he would throw in some of the equipment as well. Bob asked Mark if he had any sales figures prior to 1989 easily available. Mark said he had some for 1987 and 1988. 1987 sales were $153,000 and 1988 sales were $138,000. Mark sounded a little surprised as he read the numbers to Bob and he said, "It looks like sales aren't level after all, it looks like there is a downward trend."

Bob still wanted to speak with two other people in the company. The first was Sarah Morgan who was the marketing manager for medical products and the other was Dennis Olson, who actually produced the product. Mark said that he would speak to Sarah and Dennis and let them know Bob would be calling.

Bob's first call was to Sarah Morgan. She sounded a bit confused at first and thought he was someone else. She said that she had heard that someone was interested in buying the company a couple of months ago, but she didn't know that it was Bob. Bob thought that it couldn't be him that she was thinking of since he had only been talking with Mark for less than three weeks.

Bob was particularly interested in finding out if Sarah could explain the downward trend in sales. She said that she had never really paid much attention to the biopsy line and, in fact, never advertised the product, never went to any medical shows to promote the product nor ever raised the prices in the five years she had been on the job. She felt that the product was mainly sustained by word-of-mouth advertising between doctors. She assumed that the drop in sales was due to the expanding use of endoscopes by gastroenterologists. Endoscopes have fiber optics and allow the doctor to view where he is going in the body.

Bob asked Sarah about the letter she

sent telling the customers that she was going to drop the product line. She said that she had sent the letter in January to about 1500 doctors. The doctor's names had come from a list of doctors who had bought the product over the past several years. She mentioned that she had gotten some letters back from a few doctors saying that they were disappointed with Branton's decision to drop the product line. She talked about the pediatric doctors that Mark had mentioned and felt that there might be a special market niche. She said that she would send Bob some product literature and a list of some of the doctors who wrote back in response to her letter.

Sarah also told Bob that she had just received the first quarter's sales results and that for the first quarter of 1991, biopsy sales had been $50,000. She felt that the high sales for that quarter were due to the letter she had sent out.

The next person Bob spoke with was Dennis Olson who was in charge of making the product. Dennis was a goldmine of information according to Bob. Dennis had been making the product for the last 20 years and knew everything about how to manufacture the whole product line. Bob found out that, although there were current drawings for all products, there were indeed no written procedures on how to make any of it. Dennis proudly showed Bob a part that was about the size of a pinhead that had six holes drilled through it, a slot down the middle and was threaded on the outside. Although Bob had worked in a machine shop for several years, he wasn't sure that he had the skills required to make a part that complicated.

Dennis also showed Bob the equipment that was used in making the biopsy instruments. The main pieces were an end-mill, like Bob thought, and the jewelry lathes but there was also an industrial size lathe that was required as well. Both the end-mill and the large lathe were used exten-

sively to make products other than biopsy equipment. Dennis also mentioned another piece of large equipment that he used for honing certain parts that was located in the basement. Honing is the process of smoothing out a hole made previously with a drill.

Dennis told Bob that he had entertained the thought of buying out the biopsy line and running it himself but was too concerned about the liability issue. Bob told Dennis that he too had worried about the liability issue and had called an insurance firm that had been recommended to him by an owner of a small medical device firm. The insurance agent said he would need to know a bit more about the product's history but estimated that the insurance would probably cost around $12,000 per year.

Bob and Dennis were talking about the letter that Sarah had sent out when Dennis said, "Wait a minute, I think I have a copy of that somewhere." After rummaging through several files he pulled a copy of the letter out and showed it to Bob. The letter was dated January 14th and the letter said that Branton would stop selling the biopsy line on February 1st.

As Bob and Dennis were talking more about how the instruments are assembled, Bob asked Dennis about how much time he spent working on the product. Dennis said that if he were to devote the required time to keep up with the orders, he would work on it about 20 hours a week. He said that he hadn't really been working on the product due to priorities in other areas and he figured that there was at least $20,000 in backorders. Bob was interested in the backorders because Mark had mentioned that Bob could take all the backorders with him if he bought the biopsy line.

After his meeting with Dennis, Bob called Sarah again to verify what he had read in the letter. She confirmed that the letter had said that they would stop taking orders for new products on February 1 but they had actually taken orders until March 1. She also said that they had been telling any customers that called that they had committed themselves to providing repair work for the next five years. The next day Bob received a packet from Sarah that contained product information as well as a short list of doctors who used Branton's biopsy equipment and their phone numbers.

Bob decided that he would call a few of the doctors on the list to get their views of the product and hopefully learn more about the biopsy market. The general consensus he found among the doctors was that Branton produced very good products that "last forever" but they were all beginning to use endoscopes instead of the Branton instruments. One doctor Bob spoke with was Russell Robins who had developed the instruments with James Branton. Dr. Robins himself admitted that he was no longer really using the instruments. Some doctors said that they hadn't used the instruments in three or four years while some of the pediatric physicians said that they used them as much as twice a week. For a certain procedure on infants though, there was no other comparable product on the market.

Bob was interested in this pediatric market but wanted to find out how many pediatric gastroenterologists there were in the United States. Through the American Gastroenterological Association he found out that The American Board of Pediatrics is the association that would board certify this specialty. Bob called the Board and they told him that they had just given their first board for a pediatric gastroenterologist in 1990 and 267 doctors had passed. Bob called one of these pediatric specialists on his list from Sarah and the doctor estimated that there were no more than 500 practicing pediatric gastroenterologists in the United States.

One doctor told Bob that if he really wanted to talk with more gastroenterologists he should attend the big yearly Digestive Disease Week convention being put on by the American Gastroenterological Association at the end of May in New Orleans. This was the year's biggest convention of gastroenterologists and over 7000 were expected to attend.

Decision Time

Bob felt he had gathered quite a bit of information over the past two months but now he had to put it all together and make a decision. Should he continue pursuing this opportunity or should he focus his attention on getting a job with another company. Graduation was less than three weeks away and he wanted to get on with whatever his career was going to be.

EXHIBIT 1   Biopsy Instrument Example

Peroral Hydraulic Suction Biopsy Instrument

EXHIBIT 1   (concluded)

The most advanced biopsy instrument available for obtaining multiple biopsies from any level of the gastrointestinal tract

The Branton Peroral Hydraulic Instrument is an excellent diagnostic aid for obtaining biopsies from the more distal, previously inaccessible areas of the small bowel.

The instrument has the significant advantage of being able to deliver biopsies rapidly to the exterior while the tube itself remains in place. This makes it possible to follow physiological processes as they occur by both morphologic and chemical techniques.

With the Branton Hydraulic Instrument, both normal and pathological physiology can be studied in patients under normal circumstances, without anesthesia, fasting, or other procedures normally required.

Improved technique.

The Branton Hydraulic Instrument was first used for experimental production of the lesions in idiopathic sprue, and has been used for histochemical, electron microscopic and biochemical studies of fat absorption in man. It has been used in many other experimental applications and has also been used in routine diagnostic applications. As an example, biopsies of lesions in the ileum or distal jejunum have shown tuberculous lymphoma and regional enteritis. Prior to the availability of this instrument, such diagnosis would have required laparotomy.

Precision design.

Capsule design and controlled suction limit the size of the biopsy. However, careful patient management should be observed during biopsy procedures to reduce to a minimum the possibility of bleeding.

The fluid delivery system insures consistent and rapid delivery of the biopsy. Improved methods of attaching the tube to the capsule have resulted in better performance with less maintenance than in earlier models.

Each unit complete.

Each hydraulic instrument (Catalog #9127-002) comes as a complete kit including the capsule, radio-opaque double lumen plastic tube, vacuum gauge, sample jars, instructions, carrying case, actuating pump, and CO$_2$ cylinder.

The capsule and knife with spring.

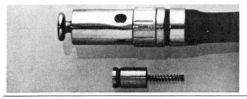

Capsule cross section

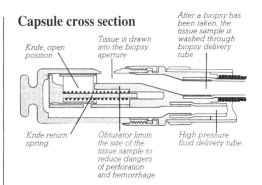

Knife, open position.

Tissue is drawn into the biopsy aperture

After a biopsy has been taken, the tissue sample is washed through biopsy delivery tube

Knife return spring.

Obturator limits the size of the tissue sample to reduce dangers of perforation and hemorrhage.

High pressure fluid delivery tube.

Actuating Pump

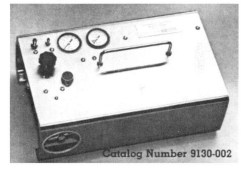

Catalog Number 9130-002

The Branton actuating pump (Catalog #9130-002) is an improved design featuring quiet operation and push-button control. Tyrode's solution can be used safely in the pump and capsule. Carbon dioxide gas is utilized to actuate the pump mechanism which, in turn, delivers solution to the tube at controlled pressure. Carbon dioxide does not enter the patient tube.

Each pump unit consists of a 5 lb CO$_2$ cylinder, pressure multiplier with stainless steel chamber for use with Tyrode's or saline solution, pressure regulating valve and electric control.

Ordering Information.

Description	Catalog Number
Complete unit 115V (including instrument and pump)	9127-002
Complete unit 230V (including instrument and pump)	9127-003
Hydraulic suction instrument (only)	9129-001
Hydraulic actuating pump only 115 V	9130-002
Hydraulic actuating pump only 230 V	9130-003
CO$_2$ cylinder	4026-001
Monofilament plastic mesh for handling specimens. Sufficient for approximately 500 biopsies.	1905-001
Silicone lubricant for knife and capsule (5.3 oz. tube)	1906-002

Note: Since the capsule, knife and tube of the 7mm hydraulic instrument are carefully matched and fitted at the factory, it is essential that all three parts be returned together when service is required.

EXHIBIT 2   Bob's Follow-up Letter

March 30, 1991

Mark Rathman
Vice President, Operations
Branton Instrument Co.

Dear Mark,

I am writing in response to our phone conversation last week about the possible sale of Branton's biopsy department. I look forward to meeting with you at 7:00 on Friday, April 5th, to discuss this possibility further. In preparing for our meeting, I have come up with a list of questions. Not all of them need to be answered right away but I hope they will help in guiding our meeting.

1)   What exactly is involved in the business? What percentage is new product manufacturing and what percentage is service? What are trends in the industry?

2)   What were the sales and earnings for at least the last five years and what are your projections for the next few years?

3)   Where and how are the products sold? Do your current salespeople promote and sell the product?

4)   Do you have any separate financial records for the biopsy department?

5)   What assets would be included in the purchase? Such as: product name, patents, trademarks, customer and mailing lists, credit records, supplier arrangements, know-how for performing the work, documentation, tooling and equipment.

6)   Inventory and receivables: How much do you normally carry? How will it be valued and by whom? How much would be transferred in the sale?

7)   What liabilities would be included in the purchase? What do the accounts payable consist of and who will be responsible for them? Any impending lawsuits, customer claims or other outstanding obligations of the biopsy department?

8)   May I speak with James Branton about biopsy equipment and Sarah Morgan about the market for this product?

Thank you for your time and I look forward to meeting with you on Friday.

Sincerely,

Bob Mighell

EXHIBIT 3   P&L by Product, 1990

	Multipurpose Biopsy	Crosby Kugler	Hydraulic Suction	Ulcer Maker	Parts & Labor
Sales	27,653	7,175	5,610	1,025	57,661
Discounts	0	0	0	0	711
Returns	0	0	0	0	693
Net Sales	27,653	7,175	5,610	1,025	56,257
Material	4,323	1,068	1,178	363	8,956
Labor	3,842	1,279	665	127	9,991
Overhead	6,635	2,010	1,608	303	16,725
Total Costs	14,800	4,357	3,451	793	35,672
Gross Profit	12,853	2,818	2,159	232	20,585

EXHIBIT 4   Selected Stock Data - Medical Products and Supplies (from Standard and Poor's *Analysis Handbook*, 1990)

Year	Profit Margin %	Dividends % of Earnings	Price Earnings High	Price Earnings Low
1965	12.39	29.73	35.70	22.54
1966	13.28	25.53	37.28	27.62
1967	13.10	25.86	53.12	29.83
1968	13.14	26.87	55.78	40.75
1969	13.90	26.92	58.28	41.41
1970	12.63	27.50	58.71	34.66
1971	12.59	26.14	45.83	39.10
1972	12.64	24.27	52.94	38.73
1973	12.71	22.31	46.45	34.49
1974	13.16	20.14	31.12	16.91
1975	13.09	18.02	26.03	19.00
1976	14.00	18.27	21.18	16.82
1977	14.30	20.25	15.15	11.39
1978	13.88	21.83	14.91	11.18
1979	15.60	29.97	13.17	10.62
1980	15.20	30.42	15.46	9.96
1981	16.11	30.79	11.59	8.12
1982	16.23	31.63	17.37	11.69
1983	16.89	34.81	18.23	15.19
1984	16.78	40.63	16.37	11.98
1985	19.36	36.80	17.15	10.93
1986	18.77	45.38	26.73	17.70
1987	17.10	28.65	20.72	14.75
1988	16.87	27.73	15.91	12.08
1989	17.65	28.04	17.10	12.86

EXHIBIT 5   Selected Robert Morris Ratios

Annual Sales	0-1MM	1-3MM	3-5MM	5-10MM	10-25MM	25MM & Up
ASSETS	5.4	10.6	4.7	14.8	7.7	9.6
Cash & Equiv.	34.6	27.2	28.2	26.9	34.4	26.4
Net Receivables	25.7	28.4	36.5	27.5	29.6	28.9
Inventory	4.0	4.2	2.0	2.9	0.8	2.3
Other Current	69.7	70.3	71.4	72.2	67.5	67.2
Fixed Assets	20.5	24.0	25.5	18.6	26.2	23.5
Intangibles	4.4	0.4	0.3	3.3	1.7	4.0
Other	5.3	5.3	2.7	5.8	4.6	5.4
Total	100.0	100.0	100.0	100.0	100.0	100.0
LIABILITIES						
Short Term Notes	11.9	6.2	12.8	7.4	9.3	7.2
Curr. L T Debt	6.0	4.9	2.6	1.9	1.6	1.3
Trade Payables	14.6	11.3	14.8	10.7	12.7	8.3
Taxes Payable	0.5	0.9	0.2	0.7	0.8	1.5
Other Current	17.3	9.0	9.9	9.2	11.5	8.5
Total Current	50.3	32.3	40.3	29.8	38.0	28.8
L T Debt	19.4	13.9	16.0	9.7	8.8	13.4
Deferred Taxes	0.0	1.2	0.2	0.8	0.4	1.8
Other L T	10.3	5.2	1.5	5.0	7.6	3.1
Net Worth	20.0	47.4	42.0	54.5	47.2	54.8
Total	100.0	100.0	100.0	100.0	100.0	100.0
INCOME						
Sales	100.0	100.0	100.0	100.0	100.0	100.0
Gross Profit	49.4	53.5	42.9	47.3	41.8	44.6
Expenses	47.4	45.9	38.9	39.7	35.7	30.8
Operating Profit	2.0	7.6	4.0	7.6	6.0	13.9
Other Exp.	1.0	1.5	1.0	1.0	1.6	2.0
Profit Before Tax	0.9	6.1	3.0	6.6	4.5	11.9
RATIOS						
Current	1.4	2.3	1.9	2.4	1.9	2.3
Quick	0.8	1.5	0.9	1.6	1.1	1.5
Sales/Receivables	7.6	7.0	6.9	6.3	5.8	5.8
COS/Inventory	4.0	2.6	3.2	3.1	3.9	2.9
COS/Payables	15.7	9.5	8.0	8.5	11.6	10.7
Sales/WC	13.8	5.9	6.6	4.6	5.7	3.8
EBIT/Interest	2.2	3.9	1.9	8.7	6.3	4.3
Fixed/Worth	0.8	0.4	0.5	0.3	0.4	0.4
Debt/Worth	5.8	1.2	1.2	0.9	1.2	0.7
Sales/Fixed Assets	12.6	8.3	9.1	9.4	7.4	6.2
Sales/Total Assets	2.3	1.8	2.1	1.6	1.9	1.5

Michael Hoppe

The following is the report of an MBA student at Arizona State University, who in 1989 set out to find a company to buy as a way of entering self employment. Names have been disguised.

Entrepreneurship Paper

This paper will trace the methods and activities that were a part of my search for a business to purchase. The acquisition of a going business concern seemed like the most promising alternative for me to begin my career as a self-employed businessman. I do not have any great ideas for new products or inventing revolutionary new technology. Also, because my capital is very limited, the financing of an existing firm with a track record of established profits is considerably easier.

Before I began my search, I formulated some thoughts about the "ideal" company to purchase. The current owner would be 55-70 years of age and ready to retire. The business should be mature and not have experienced significant growth over the past two years, because the current owner should be content with his current workload and income level. These ingredients usually indicate that a more aggressive owner and management could increase sales and profit levels in a reasonably short period of time. This could permit me to increase the value of the company and sell it at a substantial profit after two or three years.

The business would also need to be "asset heavy," allowing use of the company's own assets for collateral. I felt it was essential that the owner consent to a non-compete contract for a minimum of four years. Since I do not have any highly technical expertise in any one area, I would insist upon a management consulting contract for myself for one year, or for one business cycle. Ideally, the owner would undertake a considerable portion of the financing to reduce the amount of outside financing required and thus eliminate the need to dilute my ownership. I would also want current customer lists, prospective customer lists, as much inside information as possible about selling techniques the owner had used over the years, and a subjective or quantitative evaluation of them, if available.

While my "ideal" owner and company may appear to be cast in a fairly rigid mold, I think there is ample room for flexibility. Not all the above characteristics are essential. The only area that would seem to be missing from this ideal is the *product*.

Because of my limited experience, I deliberately left this area more flexible. I did not want to limit myself to a few product lines. I would prefer a product (or service) that was on the verge of taking off, and would shortly be an item desired in everyone's home. The important factor for my business is that it must make a profit the first year, and that sales can be increased 30 percent or more by the second year. This would give me an income and asset base to expand into areas where a new product or market might be developed, and very large returns could be obtained.

With this ideal owner and company implanted in my mind and my notebook, I began to search for a company. I knew full well that such a search process might take many months or even years.

Initial Search

I began seeking conversations with numerous people to learn how a person can discover which businesses are for sale. I felt there was a "good old boy" network, but was not at all certain about how to get into it. Being a student, I started by talking to professors from both previous and current classes whom I thought might be involved in some consulting work in the business community. I hoped they might direct me to useful contacts and also might provide some inexpensive advice on pitfalls and "cons" to beware of.

This initial search led me to the Business Advisory Services Group at Phoenix Commercial Bank. After several telephones calls and transfers around the department, I obtained an appointment with Dave Brown. He said he could "tell me things I'd never read and might take years to learn."

He also said to be careful of companies whose assets were severely understated and whose owners did not want to increase their book value so as to be liable for increased taxes. After a company has been purchased, the federal tax collectors at the Internal Revenue Service will typically audit that firm in the next tax year, and if the assets were not transferred at a realistic value, I could be held responsible for a large tax liability. He said that since a company of interest to me would probably be some form of corporation, and if I purchased such a firm, only the stock would change hands. It would be entirely too costly to dismantle the existing corporation and form a new one with myself as the stockholder.

He also stressed to me the importance of obtaining good legal and tax advice before signing any documents. He gave me the names of two attorneys and some tax people who were very good and had

handled many acquisitions over the years. Finally, since the department he worked in performed a considerable number of valuation studies, he offered the bank's services to me. His advice was well taken, and he stated that although very few firms that are for sale flow through his department, he would inform me if he found one that fit my criteria. He also gave me the names of two business brokers in Denver: Robert Haller and Dean Valley.

I visited one of the brokers immediately, since his office was near the bank. He asked what my net worth was and told me he did not deal with clients whose net worth was below a million dollars. I left with very little new information except his advice to construct a personal financial statement.

Next, I called Dean Valley and chatted on the phone. I told him what I was looking for and went to visit him. He was more a real estate salesman, selling Mom-and-Pop type operations than a business analyst. For some reason, which I cannot specify, I did not like or trust him and did not analyze any of the businesses he represented. None of them came close to my criteria for the "ideal" acquisition anyway.

A Tavern

By now I was getting anxious to analyze a business, so I started reading the business opportunities section of the local newspapers and the *Wall Street Journal*. Finally, with some apprehension, I began making calls. I inquired about a tavern in the west end and decided that, even though it did not meet my criteria, I would go and take a look. It was for sale by a broker whose name I do not recall. He gave me the address and told me to meet him there.

I was not expecting a plush club, but I also did not expect such a rat hole. The owner wanted $20,000 cash. For this I would receive ownership of the fixtures, furnishings and company name. He offered to sign a non-compete clause for a 15 mile radius, and said he would help me learn the business for three months at the rate of $100 per day. I would also receive $1,000 of inventory which consisted of 10 barrels of beer, some unspecified gallons of wine, and beer and wine glasses.

The rent was $560 per month, with three years left on the lease. Utilities and insurance had averaged $160 per month and were not anticipated to change. The current owner said he was withdrawing $40,000 per year, which was the entire profit. He had owned the tavern for five years and was now retiring.

The furnishings and assorted contents of the tavern appeared to be in rather poor condition. I felt the entire tavern would need complete remodeling and, definitely, new fixtures. I also got the feeling that the owner might decrease the purchase price or extend more favorable terms. But the remodeling might cost something like $5,000 to $20,000, and I was not sure how I could finance that. Also, I was not sure I would want the current customers patronizing the tavern if it were mine. They seemed like a pretty rough bunch.

So that opportunity has left me with some real problems to ponder. But at least by looking at it, I began to get into the water and become motivated to continue my search.

A Store

After a few more days of reading advertisements and making telephone calls, I decided to look at an import shop in the south end of town. I made an appointment and met the broker at his office. There we went over, in moderate detail, the aspects of the business and the terms of sale.

The owners were two gentlemen from India. They imported goods from India to the United States and sold wholesale as well as retail. They said the wholesale business had been keeping them busier than they had anticipated, and they had not been able to devote adequate time to the retail business.

The retail store has no real track record of sales. The owners kept it open only five hours per day, and said they didn't really know what the volume of business was. The store has two-and-one-half years left on its lease in a small shopping center. The center is relatively modern, and even on a Wednesday afternoon appeared to have an adequate volume of traffic. The rent is $882 per month for 1,260 sq. ft., of which 200 sq. ft. is office and bathroom. There is no storage space except in the office.

The owners want $24,000 cash for which I would receive the inventory which they said this is worth $20,000 wholesale or $50,000 retail (wholesale is 40 percent of the retail price). I would also receive the minimal amount of fixtures, which they valued at $2,400, and a machine for imprinting T-shirts. This machine transfers designs, pictures and slogans to T-shirts, which they sell for $9.95 at a cost of $4.00 each. They claimed the machine cost $1,600 six months ago. They said that as wholesalers they would also give me a discount on merchandise I purchase from them for two years. The amount of the discount was unspecified, and so far, I do not have a firm commitment from them on it.

Some of their inventory appeared to be of minimal marketable value. Most of it was made up of carved wooded boxes, tables, plus brass ashtrays and water pipes. There were also 150 Indian print dresses that to me looked hideous. I suspect that, perhaps, it would cost me around $20,000 cash to rent a store and buy inventory with comparable or higher marketable value. Anyway, I don't know if they transferred the goods to the store at an inflated price.

The fixtures were mounted to some cheap carpeting, which was stained. Shelving had been homemade out of 1-by-12-foot boards. I don't think it would cost a great deal to replace something like that if

I tried to set up a new store myself. Finally, the fact that there weren't any profit and loss statements or documentation on the cost of the inventory has left me suspicious. The store is not set up as a separate business entity from the wholesale operation, so I suppose I would have to incur additional expense to form a corporation.

I expect I could lose a maximum of around $20,000 if the inventory proved to be of no value. I felt I could liquidate the inventory for around $10,000 if I had to shut down, but I have no idea of a maximum profit. The profit potential seems entirely dependent upon the volume of business attainable.

The break-even volume per month would seem to be:

Rent	$882
Utilities & Insurance	140
Return on Investment at 20%	4,000
Fixed Costs	$5,022

Break-even Sales = $5,022/(1-0.4) = \$8,370/\text{mo}$

When $2,000/mo. is added for my salary, the break-even sales volume increases to $11,666/mo. or $140,000/year. This equates to $112/sq. ft., or an inventory turnover of almost three times. This appears to be a "double" turnover rate, but much above five times would appear to be high. If the turnover was five times per year (I have assumed that $20,000 is an adequate inventory), the sales volume would increase to $250,000 per year.

Sales	$250,000
COGS (40%)	100,000
Gross Margin	150,000
Fixed Costs	84,264
Profit Before Tax	$65,736

Feeling uneasy about this company too, I began reading the business opportunities sections of newspapers again. One positive result was that I started to feel more adept at screening businesses for sale against my established criteria.

Hospital Equipment

The next company I chose to investigate further was advertised as a hospital equipment firm. From a preliminary screening over the telephone, it seemed to meet most of my criteria, so I made an appointment to meet with the broker.

This business has been in operation for two years. Its owner has three other firms, which he says are more profitable, and since he felt he could not devote an adequate amount of time to this business, he wanted to divest himself of it. It is a wholly owned subsidiary of another firm in which the owner is sole stockholder. Its line of work is supplying hospitals with total nurse-patient communication systems. This firm has an exclusive franchise with Bunting Corporation to sell all of its products in the Rocky Mountain region. Because Bunting manufactures the product and delivers only when ordered, I see no need for warehouse facilities.

The profit margin is claimed to be an incredible 50 percent of sales, something I have not yet verified. All the sales have been to hospitals. The owner feels he has been successful with relatively minimal effort because he provides the installation. This he contracts out to electrical contractors in the area of the job, thereby eliminating the need for any permanent employees.

A balance sheet as of July 31, 1988 is attached as Exhibit 1. The accounts receivable are due from hospitals where work is nearing completion. The owner claims that none of these are in arrears. Construction is said to be in progress at several unspecified jobs that the owner said are continuing on schedule and have no unforeseen cost overruns in them. The inventory consists primarily of several demonstration units for sales presentations. The accounts payable are owed entirely to Bunting Corporation for goods received.

A profit and loss statement for the year ended July 31, 1988 is attached as Exhibit 2. As can be seen, the profit is very high for such a low sales level. The ending inventory figure is very high when compared with the number on the balance sheet. The administrative expenses are only direct expenses. There are no salary payments to the owner.

The company has two salesmen who will leave with the owner. I suppose this business is not large enough at present to warrant more than myself and a secretary. The owner will agree to a consulting contract at $300/day plus expenses. He will also sign a non-compete clause and will turn over all customer and contractor information sheets.

The owner stated that the overriding theme of the sales presentation and of the entire product line is that of efficient patient care. The competitors do not install their equipment unless pressured to do so. This appears to be the firm's competitive advantage.

Now for the deal. The owner wants $100,000 for the company. I buy the assets and the liabilities. He wants $50,000 down and the remaining $50,000 to be paid quarterly over five years at 6-percent interest. He has hinted to me that the terms are flexible.

What do I receive for this? I don't exactly know. The owner is not willing to give me an overabundance of information without some commitment on my part. He mentioned to me that with a binder, he would allow me to go through his accounting books, and we would itemize everything included and not included in the purchase. The broker has said he signed a statement that everything exists as he has presented it in the financial statements.

At this point, I considered letting this business pass. I did not have access to $50,000—even though the owner might lower the down payment to $30,000. In talking with the owner, I discovered that he felt a minimum of $20,000–$30,000 would be needed for working capital with a business volume of $2 million. I did not know where I could raise $60,000–$90,000 that would be necessary for the down payment and working capital requirement. Also, since the business did not meet the criteria of a large hard-asset base, I did not feel I could borrow the money because of the lack of collateral.

Then, out of nowhere, the broker asked me if I would consider taking on partners. He said he and his own partner would be interested in a 50-percent position if it was agreeable to me. Since this took me slightly by surprise, I informed him at the end of our meeting that I would get back to him after I studied the business a bit further. This is where the deal now stands, December 1989.

Future Analysis

To conclude this report, I will detail action and information I think I need to gather before a final discussion can be made on this deal.

An analysis of the specific assets and liabilities that are included in the company must be made. This will not be possible until some earnest money is presented. Also, an analysis of the profit and loss statement items should be made to learn the actual profitability of the company and determine if there are unallocated costs that should have been charged against the business.

Also I want to know exactly the specific products I have a franchise for in the four states and whether there are any restrictions, requirements, etc. included in the franchise agreement. I need to satisfy myself that it is indeed an exclusive franchise, and I need to learn what terms of payment Bunting Corporation requires.

The owner thought I could take over the office next door to him. I need to determine the cost and terms of the lease. He is also in the process of negotiating a contract for a $2 million installation, and I must determine whether I would receive the contract and the profit.

I expect to contact my lawyer before I get to the earnest money stage. He should help me cover all the bases by giving me advice about things to look for and questions to ask of the owner and his partners.

I expect I should visit several of the installations the company has made locally and one or more projects that are still under construction. This should let me get more feel for the dynamics of the business, and obtain an appreciation for problems encountered during construction. I also want to learn how much supervision is re-quired of the contractors. This, I suppose, will entail analysis of past practice and of the type and cost of people who do such work.

Since the owner has been using the salesmen from his other company, I need to learn how much they are compensated and how much time they have devoted in the past year to this company. Finally, I guess I should look for contacts in the hospital business to check on the reputation of this company.

But this is all new to me. How can I tell how well I've been doing and whether I'm on the right track about where to go from here? What else, specifically, should I look for or investigate? If I do decide to try making a deal, how should I begin?

EXHIBIT 1   Balance Sheet   July 31, 1988

CURRENT ASSETS:

CASH	$8,142
ACCOUNTS RECEIVABLE	109,964
CONSTRUCTION IN PROGRESS	52,970
INVENTORY	4,240
OTHER ASSETS	
EQUIPMENT	14,962
TOTAL ASSETS	$190,278
LIABILITIES	
ACCOUNTS PAYABLE	82,942
OWNERSHIP	
RETAINED EARNINGS	107,336
	$190,278

EXHIBIT 2   Profit and Loss Statement   **June 30, 1987–July 31, 1988**

SALES

Columbine Hospital		$496,370
Columbine Hospital other		54,390
Mallett Hospital		53,508
Mallett Hospital other		14,232
Other		83,740
Gross Sales		$702,240
Beginning inventory	$18,350	
Purchases	291,930	
Ending Inventory	71,314	
Cost of Goods Sold		$238,966
Gross Profit		$463,274
Installation Expenses		
Intermountain Business Systems	$32,842	
Mallett Installation	9,580	
Administration Expense	55,290	
Installation material		
(Columbine Hospital)	62,932	
Total Expense		$160,644
Net Profit		$302,630

Case 34

Terry Allen

Terry Allen was being "courted" to take over a failing business. In January 1980 he had approached the Small Business Investment Corporation (SBIC) of Vermont with an idea of starting a publishing and seminar business on marketing. After he had shown the SBIC managers his resume and told them about his entrepreneurial background, they suggested that he consider taking over a game manufacturer in which the SBIC had invested $35,000.

The manufacturer produced a board game called *All About Town*™, which was somewhat like Monopoly™ except that, instead of real-estate properties, the board depicted retail stores and other business enterprises of an actual city. Each player drew game money bearing the name of a local bank and then embarked on shopping trips around the game board with the objective of using less money and returning "home" sooner than the other players. Local merchants of the real city represented by the game paid to have their names on the board as advertising and were invited to sell the game as dealers. The game producer thus obtained revenues from two sources: merchants who advertised on the game board, and customers who bought the game. The idea had been well received by some merchants, chambers of commerce, and shoppers during the Christmas holiday season, but as yet sales had not been sufficient to cover costs, and the game manufacturer had more debts than it could pay.

The Vermont SBIC managers said they believed Terry was the type of person who could turn the company around, and they encouraged him to develop a proposal for doing so. He was intrigued by the idea, but

wondered whether he should take the job. A recent divorce had reduced his personal net worth to near zero. He had subsequently remarried, gaining four children to support in addition to three from his previous marriage. He currently taught marketing at the University of Vermont, and he was working on a doctorate in business at the University of Virginia, which required occasional trips to Charlottesville and a substantial amount of time.

He had also acquired a seat on the Chicago Options Exchange and three days after returning from his honeymoon, he learned that the person representing his seat had lost him $20,000 from speculating. This depleted his cash, but he was still receiving $1,000 per month from a business he'd sold the previous year. He commented on the prospect of taking over the game manufacturer:

> *I could develop a game just like that on my own, but it would probably take me a year. So the value of the company to me is in terms of what one year of my time is now worth. I could either try to sell the game in as many cities as possible or sell a franchise in a limited number of locations for, say, $5,000 each and a percentage of the gross sales.*
>
> *Either way, I would probably farm out the manufacturing and do the selling on my own. It looks like a great opportunity to make money. I just don't know if this is the right time for me to take on another business.*

Personal Background

At age 15 Terry had told his family he

was going to attend Harvard Business School and become a millionaire. His early enterprises included a 170-house paper route, a lawn-mowing service that wore out a rented mower in one summer, and a biweekly backyard carnival featuring his collection of 50 pet snakes, which netted him nearly $50 per show. Later, while attending Wesleyan University in Connecticut, he learned that the school bookstore refused to carry paperbacks. He began selling them himself. He also held two jobs while doing his course work plus engaging in social and athletic activities, and he began selling do-it-yourself kits for making paperback books into hardbacks. For the latter, he traveled to New York and secured the New England-area franchise. He borrowed the $2,000 required for inventory from four people whom he hired to sell the kits. Thinking there might also be a market for the kits nationwide in veterans' hospitals, he mounted a direct mail campaign. Overall, he made around $2,000 on the book venture, more than enough, he said, to offset the $1,000 loss he had incurred on stock investments made with his scholarship funds.

Following graduation from Wesleyan in 1961, Terry entered Harvard's MBA program. By his second year there he had started a roommate-matching service for the Boston area and been elected chairman of the Small Business Club. As graduation approached, he said, he felt an "instinctive urge to live in Vermont," and consequently wrote every company with over 40 employees in that state. Among the four job offers that resulted was one he accepted to become assistant to the president of a Rutland-based manufacturer of plywood reels for wire and cable.

He soon left that job because, he said, "I felt that by nature I was more a promoter than a manufacturer." He obtained an insurance broker's license and took over a general insurance agency, which he continued to operate for the next eight years. He purchased an abandoned schoolhouse and converted it into a 140-bed ski dormitory. His other real estate dealings grew until he averaged $30,000 per year in commissions, owned 21 buildings, and leveraged his cash flow to include $200,000 in personally-signed mortgages. He became a director of the Rutland Cooperative Savings and Loan Association, and after a year on the board was elected president, "in recognition of the fact that I was the only one who bothered to ask questions at board meetings," he recalled.

In 1966 Terry bought a franchised rental store called Taylor Rental Center in Rutland. This acquisition he expanded over a three-year period into a chain of six rental stores in New England and upstate New York, renaming it Green Mountain Rentals. This expansion he began by starting a store from scratch in Glens Falls, then taking over a store through a distress sale in Hamden, Connecticut, and buying a rental business from a retiring proprietor in Manchester, New Hampshire. Finally, he acquired two others, one in West Hartford, Connecticut and one in Barre, Vermont.

Each purchase was structured to fit his financial liquidity at the time of acquisition. Equity investments, secured and unsecured notes, and sale with lease-back of the assets to the company were all part of Terry's financial dealings to build his rental-store business. He worked to smooth out seasonal cycles common to the rental industry by adding snowmobiles and a line of winter party accessories that complemented the peak demand for tools and equipment during summer months. To attract more new homeowners to the stores he used a service called Welcome Wagon, which sent them discount coupons.

However, he soon decided he could perform this advertising service better himself by starting one of his own, which he called Merchant's Welcome Service.

This business sent direct mail to new homeowners, whom he located through local real estate associations and by perusing records in the Registry of Deeds. Terry found that a mailing that cost 9 cents per letter offering a $3 discount coupon averaged a response rate of 10 percent with a typical rental order of $11.25. He then recruited other merchants for inclusion in the mailing, asking a fee of 30 cents per mailed letter and promising that the coupon book would include only products and services that didn't directly compete with each other for a given location.

This business began to grow, but he began to encounter difficulty servicing debt on the rental service and consequently in 1970 he decided to sell it. He managed to find in New York City, a man attracted by the idea of escaping from metropolitan pressures to run a small business in a quieter location who could come up with cash for both the tangible assets and the Green Mountain Rental name.

Terry now concentrated on building up the relatively low-capital-intensity Merchant's Welcome Service. He believed it had greater profit potential and could be expanded geographically. He also developed a derivative venture that used the new homeowners list to produce reports of interest to real estate brokers on property transfers in five different states. By 1976 he had built sales of the Merchant's Welcome Service to 2,000 clients in eleven states, and he decided to sell both it and the real estate report business.

Next, he worked at Harvard Business School for a year as a research associate, writing cases on small business. He decided to pursue a Ph.D. in marketing and enrolled at the University of Virginia at Charlottesville. To supplement his somewhat sporadic income from stock options, he taught business courses at Babson College in Wellesley, about 15 miles from Harvard. He initiated a course in entrepreneurship, which later became a major area of study for the college.

Moving to Virginia to concentrate on his doctoral work, Terry juggled his time between schooling, his commitment at Babson, a consulting contract he obtained in Fort Lauderdale, Florida, his seat on the Chicago Options Exchange and a publishing company he acquired in late 1978. The publishing company produced booklets developed by a university professor on sex education aimed at teenagers from low- and moderate-income households. Terry recalled that he bought the business for the value of its inventory, $17,500, and sold it nine months later in 1979 for $40,000. He observed:

> *I found that in nine months, I had a company that had turned a $30,000 profit and had a lot of momentum for future growth. But then it developed that I was about to lose my key employee. Also I didn't really trust the judgment of the professor who had written most of the material and now wanted me to distribute books that I would just as soon avoid. The woman running daily operations was interested in buying me out, and there were some other opportunities in California and Chicago that looked promising. I could have received more for the company, but the $40,000 was a clean and quick way to sever the business relationship before it could turn sour.*

His main interests became his seat on the Chicago Options Exchange and what he termed some "minor real estate investments." He said that he went into ventures without worrying about the amounts or sources of capital that might be required to start or acquire them:

> *Too many people are preoccupied with raising money. That's the easiest thing to do, in my mind. I've developed what I consider to be a hierarchy of capi-*

tal sources which can work for anyone who is looking to get into business. The trick is to go to the right source and cater to that person's main objective.

For some, it's making more money and for others it's ego. For still others, it's the romance of being connected with entrepreneurship. And finally, some consider financial deals a matter of self-preservation. I like to start at the top of my hierarchy and work down; there are fewer guardian angels than strangers or secured lenders, but also there are generally fewer strings attached with their money.

A sketch and brief description of Terry's hierarchy of venture capital sources is reproduced in Exhibit 1.

History of Aladco Corporation

The company Terry was now being invited to buy, Aladco, Inc., had been started in 1976 by an advertising salesman in his early 20s who got the idea while stalled by traffic in a New England town. As he sat in his car it occurred to him that if he had a local town map perhaps he could find a better way around the jam. Then he thought about how local businesses might be used as landmarks on the map, like the properties on a Monopoly™ game board. Maybe, he thought, those businesses could be charged an advertising rate to be listed on the map. And the map could be sold…perhaps as a game if other Monopoly-type elements were added.

He sketched an example freehand, and with nothing more than that managed to sell one city on the idea. Then he used the game produced for that city as a sample to get orders from other cities. Thus Aladco became a business. Its new game, named *All About Town*, was expected by its inventor to be mainly a gift that would sell during the Christmas shopping season.

Area businesses that agreed to partici-

pate each paid a $400 base fee to be depicted on the board or cards. Play money and coupons advertising other enterprises were also part of the package. Participating stores were given exclusive distribution rights for the game in their respective cities. Local chambers of commerce were encouraged to participate to add a sense of legitimacy and serve as a single point of contact for selling advertising spots on the board.

Depending on the chamber's involvement, the game could also make money for that organization. It seemed to Terry that responses from chambers (illustrated in Exhibit 2) and the general public had been positive in many instances. A promotional brochure included testimonials such as the following from people who had purchased the game or received it as a gift:

I loved it. The action was intriguing. I loved the way it was set up.
—Plymouth, Massachusetts

We received an All About Town Holyoke (Massachusetts) game for Christmas. I was thrilled. As you can see, we live a long way from our home town and this will be a favorite reminder for us. I'm glad you thought of it.
—Caruthersville, Maryland

Through the end of 1979, *All About Town* had been accepted in 19 cities, listed in Exhibit 3, all but two of which were in New England. Participating merchants received a 40-percent discount from the game's retail price of $12.50. They paid for advertising at rates similar to those for small advertisements in the local newspaper, but received visibility in a targeted audience similar to direct mail.

Timing game sales to peak right after the Thanksgiving holiday coincided with a publicity blitz in the local press and other media on an exchange basis. The game would include on its board or pieces television stations, radio stations and newspapers in the city without charge. In exchange, the media organization had to provide an amount of air time or space worth what a retail store would pay for participating in the game.

As further incentive to retail consumers, redeemable coupons were included with each game for such things as discounts on automotive work or free piano lessons. For cities with significant non-English-speaking populations the directions and cards were also printed in other languages. The *All About Town* game as described by Aladco's promotional brochure, excerpts of which appear in Exhibit 4, seemed to offer appeal to any city. Yet the company's cash flow position had been deteriorating. Terry said that by the time the Vermont SBIC discussed it with him the corporation was near bankruptcy.

> *They've just had their phone disconnected, they have no assets to speak of, their inventory is worthless, they've overdrawn their checking account, and they are about $10,000 behind on payroll taxes to the government.*

Financial Information

The distribution of outstanding Aladco stock was as follows:

SBIC of Vermont:	33 1/3%
Single Private Shareholder:	30
Company Management:	25
Other Shareholders:	11 2/3
Total	100%

Terry's impression from talking to the venture capital firm and other shareholders was that they would love to recover the capital they had invested in the firm, and that some of them had hard feelings because things had not worked out as promised. Terry said the founder had told him the initial deal with the SBIC was to have been that the SBIC would put up $30,000 in return for a third of the stock plus $5,000 as debt. On that basis the founder said he had gone out, solicited orders and made commitments with suppliers for large numbers of games. But at closing its deal the SBIC insisted upon applying the $5,000 for stock and the $30,000 as loan money, terms the founder felt compelled to accept because he was already committed to customers and suppliers. Now, the founder retained only a fourth of the outstanding stock, and in addition he was personally liable to the Internal Revenue Service for $9,000 in unpaid withholding taxes, which he could not pay. He had also been obliged to guarantee personally the $30,000 SBIC loan.

The most recent investor in Aladco had agreed to put approximately $40,000 into the business despite its lack of financial records, but had taken the precaution of having his own accountant review such records as were available and prepare a balance sheet, which appears as Exhibit 5. Cash on hand was $4.96, and Terry said he believed the realizable value of the accounts receivable and other assets listed was little at best or zero at worst. He noted that the company had failed on its promise in some cities to get games delivered before Christmas, and this had caused some retailers to cancel their orders and others to become "stuck" with games that wouldn't sell quickly. Of the five cities signed by the corporation for 1979, according to Terry, only two received their shipments in time for the holiday season. In the other cases, the printers had refused to ship the finished product until they were paid for their services.

Terry explained that the accounts payable items reached back to the previous year (1978). A further problem, not reflected in the financial figures, he said, was that the company had developed a bad reputation among some chambers of commerce that had worked with it in the last year or two. He recalled telephone conversations he had conducted with some of them:

> *I've called up the chamber executive in every city that has had a game. The story I keep getting is that the game is a fantastic idea, people love it, but the supplier has not kept his word. Apparently Aladco has repeatedly run into problems of not fulfilling production schedules, while its sales force has been undependable because of personnel leaving shortly after joining the company.*

Terry was unable to obtain any profit and loss statements for the company. Apparently, financing had been obtained "as needed," and neither the founder nor the SBIC operators had substantial experience in accounting or finance. The company had never prepared operating statements for management purposes, and Terry concluded that excessive expenditures draining off company cash had been one result. He noted that the company rented a rather plush office for $400 per month and the founder, drawing a salary around $35,000 per year, had driven an $11,000 company car which was totaled after three weeks with no insurance coverage. Terry interviewed one of the eight artists whom the company employed full time, and was told that they had gone to great lengths to make work last and to look busy, even though not enough new game orders were coming to keep them occupied. Terry deduced that two full-time artists would have been adequate if careful planning and management had been applied.

Production

Aladco's founder had estimated manufacturing costs at just under $5 per game,

based on figures shown in Exhibit 6. Terry said he thought these figures were probably fairly reliable as estimates for contracting the work out because they were based on actual experience of the company. However, he noted that the college community of Burlington, 12 miles from his home in Hinesburg, Vermont, included art students who could work at home on graphics for the game and its cover, which might allow him to produce the games on his own more cheaply. Checking with a printing-equipment supplier, he learned that equipment for doing much of the printing work himself would cost approximately $10,000. Excerpts of summary financial information for printing and publishing companies appear in Exhibit 7 (from Robert Morris Associates) and Exhibit 8 (from Dun and Bradstreet). Making the parts and assembling them into games would require coordinating a number of steps, from artwork through quality-control checks to ensure that all the right items were in each game box. Each game with all its components, as listed in Exhibit 9, weighed approximately two pounds.

Terry expected the majority of shipments should begin around October and run through mid-November for the Christmas season. He had inquired about renting space in a local Grange hall. Terry commented that a number of people in town had said they had wanted to buy the hall since the Grange had gone out of business eleven years earlier, but had been told that it was not for sale. Terry had difficulty learning just who might have the authority to sell it. Each person he talked to referred him to someone else until he had talked to nearly a dozen people. Finally, however, he established contact with appropriate authorities and worked out terms under which he could lease the hall for four months at $250 per month and then pay an additional $25,000 for full ownership. He commented:

I know the man who owns a business next door to the hall tried to buy it recently but gave up when he couldn't find any interest in selling. If I don't sign the deal now, I'll bet he'd be glad to.

For his workforce, Terry expected he could recruit local young people willing to accept minimum-wage employment on a seasonal basis for assembling the games. He had worked out a per-game cost estimate of his own, based on production and color printing of the box and game board by outside contractors, black-and-white printing done either in-house with the used printing equipment or outside, and assembly done in the Grange hall. His cost estimates appear in Exhibit 10. He thought he could oversee production himself part time, since he expected it would be fairly routine, while he took care of sales and other aspects of the business in addition to his schooling and other activities.

Marketing

The company had used a direct-commission force to sell. It recruited salespeopole through classified advertisements. Each was given a territory, samples and literature, but no expense account. Terry commented:

Apparently they hired anyone who walked in responding to the want ads. And these would not tend to be the world's most high-classed salespeople. Often, they would be salesmen nobody else would hire on a salary basis. One of them would sign on, somehow get himself to a town that didn't have a game, and talk one of the local hotels into trading him lodging for a listing on the game board. Then he'd go to a restaurant and swap advertising for meals, and at a car dealer he would swap for a

car rental. He might not worry too much about how the game turned out, how many games were sold, or whether they were delivered on time. There was always another town to start swapping with.

Terry was considering two marketing alternatives. The first would be to sell franchises to individual chambers of commerce in cities that expressed interest in the game. To check the feasibility of this approach, he drew up a pro forma income statement and disclosure information sheet that could be sent to inquiring communities (Exhibits 11 and 12).

A one-time franchise fee of $5,000 would purchase game rights to a city. The franchisee could have Terry manufacture the games or look for another production source on its own. A franchise would extend five years, with an option to renew or amend the agreement. Terry's pro forma income statement (Exhibit 11) assumed an annual 3 percent royalty payable to Terry, averaging $300 per franchise. Thus, by signing up between 30 and 40 cities, he would gain $150,000 to $200,000 annually from franchise fees. Overhead would consist of telephone, legal expenses and office supplies, with any games manufactured at a unit cost of $6. Whether to promote the game more than once during the five-year period would be up to the franchisee.

How often the game could be repeated in a city was, said Terry, an open question. One chamber official had estimated that the game probably couldn't be done more than once every ten years. However, several merchants who had sold out their games had written to ask whether the program could be repeated the following year.

An alternative to franchising would be to sell the program directly to chambers of commerce and individual local merchants in a city, keying on the advertising benefits possible with the game. With this approach, he said, his goal would be to work from a base of 10 or 15 cities per year, up to 50 or more communities. Depending on the success of the program in a given locality, he figured the game might be repeated once every three to five years. He said he hadn't formulated criteria for choosing participants, but would talk with any reputable person or organization that appeared interested in having his or her community involved.

To do the selling Terry figured he could recruit business students during summer and assign them to visit various cities where they would obtain advertising orders form local merchants, including banks, large department stores, smaller retailers and local media, and solicit orders for shipments of games. The students could choose to sell directly or through commissioned sales representatives whom they would hire themselves. Each salesperson's goal would be to gererate orders for at least 4,000 games, packed 12 to a case. In this way Terry thought he could use advertising revenues to pay for his selling expenses and cover production costs with retail sales of games. He had drafted a possible commission schedule (Exhibit 13) and a price list (Exhibit 14).

It seemed to him that the franchising approach would take less of his time and probably be a safer course to follow. On the other hand, the profit potential from directly selling to as many cities as possible and controlling rights to the game at every stage seemed limitless. He had been told that one of the drawbacks in franchising was that franchisees tended to look for a continuing earning stream, not a single revenue source every few years. Regardless what decision he made about the venture, Terry said he didn't have any cash of his own to invest. His options loss had taken care of that.

Terry noted that there was no direct competition because the game was unique. However, if the game began to sell well someone else might invest the time and expense to make something similar. One company that concerned him particularly was located in California and sold advertising products exclusively to chambers of commerce. He observed:

> They spend half a million dollars a year marketing to chambers of commerce, and if and when they decide to focus that kind of money on competing with me, I suppose I'm dead.

Decision Point

> My first inclination is to go ahead anyway because I think it's a good way to make some money. Whether the franchise or direct selling approach would be better, I'm not sure yet. Either way, I'd really like to try a business with a manufactured product. I've never really been involved with production from the standpoint of my own business, and I'd like to prove to myself that I can do it.

> On the other hand, I don't want the business to become a siphon for my time. The whole basis for valuing the company is on the year of my time that it would save me to take over versus trying to replicate the concept.

> My teaching will continue, and I also want to work on a system I've developed over the past three years to recoup my losses in the market. And, oh yes, there's my dissertation, which I have yet to finish. The people at Virginia are anxious for me to show progress on that, so I'll probably tie up a good deal of my time on doctoral studies in the near term.

> Whether this game is the best opportunity for me right now, I'm not sure. On paper, it looks tempting, but . . .

EXHIBIT 1   Terry Allen's Hierarchy of Venture Capital Funding Sources*

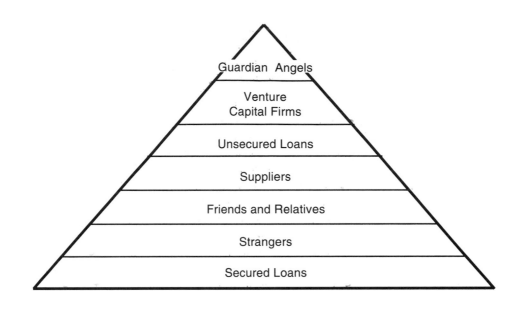

*Terry said that as one progressed from the top of the "pyramid" downward, the frequency of sources in each category increased. At the same time, the number of "strings" attached to the money tends to increase as well. Guardian angels included private individuals willing to finance a venture, based on their confidence in the entrepreneur and business. Venture capital firms offered a ready source of funds, yet were typically geared to business ventures promising high growth rates and rates of return.

Unsecured loans included trade credit or borrowing against personal credit cards, while secured loans were the traditional vehicles used by banks and financial institutions. Terry regarded borrowing money from friends and relatives as "tainted" money, due to the personal relationships involved. Strangers included unexpected sources of capital that might be discovered by the entrepreneur in the course of seeking out financing for his or her business.

EXHIBIT 2 All About Town Comments from Chamber Officials

I checked three chambers before we signed with them. The three chambers all spoke very highly of ALL ABOUT TOWN, and all made from $5,000 to $11,000 for their chamber.

> Executive Director
> Peru Area Chamber of Commerce
> Peru, Indiana

People who see it (the ALL ABOUT TOWN game) love it. The game is very popular. We made about $13,000 on it.

> Executive Vice-President
> Bangor Area Chamber of Commerce
> Bangor, Maine

I have never seen a project approved, by any Board of Directors I ever had, with so much enthusiasm. It's a real winner.

> Executive Vice-President
> Greater Fall River Chamber of Commerce
> Fall River, Mass.

All 4,000 games were sold out in less than two weeks . . .

> President
> Chamber of Commerce of Greater Portland, Portland, Maine

I found it to be one of the most unique promotional tools for any community in which I have been involved.

> Executive Vice-President
> Lake Champlain Regional Chamber of Commerce
> Burlington, Vermont

. . . one of the best combination community-promotion and fund-raising projects I have ever seen in our business.

It is a hot item to sell and promote. A chamber will make at least four figures and could make five. We did extremely well.

EXHIBIT 3 All About Town Editions*

Manchester, New Hampshire (1975, 1977)
Concord, New Hampshire (1975)
Keene, New Hampshire (1975, 1977)

Holyoke, Massachusetts (1976)
Nashua, New Hampshire (1976)
Greenfield, Massachusetts (1976)
Springfield, Massachusetts (1976)
Hartford, Conn. (1976)

Worcester, Massachusetts (1977)
Plymouth, Massachusetts (1977, 1979)
Waterville, Maine (1977)

Bangor, Maine (1978)
Augusta, Maine (1978)
Portland, Maine (1978)

Fall River, Massachusetts (1979)
Burlington, Vermont (1979)

Newport, Rhode Island (1980)
Peru, Indiana (1980)
Anniston, Alabama (1980)

* *Earlier years are approximate.*

EXHIBIT 4 Excerpts from Aladco Advertising Brochure

Aladco manufacturing representatives will accumulate local information and use the following presentation to show local business owners the proven benefits and techniques of participating in *All About Town* as an advertiser and as a retailer.

Aladco was incorporated in March of 1976 to develop and market *All About Town*. *All About Town* is a beneficial community project that enables local business people and their chamber of commerce to promote all the good things their city has to offer.

Aladco's PERSONNEL work with each chamber of commerce to personalize the "game of their city" and make it truly "a special edition."

Prearranged PROCEDURE & POLICY allows each business to participate by working with their chamber of commerce and to benefit by the development of a product that reflects PRIDE in their business and in their community.

All About Town is a very profitable, high-volume, retail merchandise item sold exclusively in participating business locations. The game is a unique product that teaches people how to travel from their house, or any place in their city, directly to a business' front door!

The young people of the area enthusiastically identify familiar locations on the game board and the street where they live. *All About Town* is the first item they bring out to show and play with visiting friends and relatives.

The elder, established residents of the area are very proud of the city where they have lived and raised their families. They purchase copies for themselves and their families and send copies to the folks who have moved away.

All About Town games have been sent to almost every part of the world.

The business, professional, and industrial people in a community become involved in the game through their role as local consumers, and their support makes the game of their city possible.

Newcomers and vacationers find the pictorial map of the game board the easiest way to learn how to get around the town. Because customers were carrying game boards in their cars, we now include an extra game board label in each game, folded as a map, for convenience.

Employees take pride in seeing the place where they work pictured on the game board. Retail establishments make money selling the games. The industrial attractiveness of the area is demonstrated by depiction of existing industry. Civic, historic and cultural points are sponsored by participating business and industry. Rehabilitation centers, schools and their faculties endorse the educational value of *All About Town*. Literally ... "We have something for everyone."

Most people remember details of Monopoly™ over 10 years after they last played it... This shows that "People remember the details of games they've enjoyed for years and years!"

Through the medium of a game, we are teaching people in local communities who the businesses are and what they offer.

EXHIBIT 4   (continued)

And, through the inclusion of valuable, redeemable coupons, *All About Town* will bring identifiable new faces through these businesses' doors, proving the value of participating in the game of their city . . .!

Major chains and independent businesses - banks, realtors, clothiers, jewelers, grocery stores, insurance companies, cleaners, theaters have ALL participated on previous editions of *All About Town*.

All About Town's continuing success is demonstrated by letters and editorials from local consumers, folks who have moved away, past participants and teachers.

Newspaper headlines, radio-talk shows, plus television 6 and 11 O'clock coverage stimulates widespread interest in each edition of the game before it is released. A multimedia promotion introducing the game and its retail outlets is coordinated with a press conference announcing the game's availability.

In Portland, Maine, 6,400 copies were sold out in the first 2 1/2 weeks causing the entire promotional campaign to be held off until the spring reprints were available.

It doesn't actually rain money from the sky when *All About Town* is released, but it does generate multiple thousands of dollars that flow back into the edition's community. The greatest profit is made by the participating businesses that sell *All About Town* to the public and keep 40% of the retail price. In Portland, this product generated in excess of $26,000 in retail profits.

The second largest profit is made by the local chamber of commerce for introducing Aladco and *All About Town* to their community, providing the local information that personalized the "game of their city" and distributing the completed game when released. The chamber can expect to net between $6-12,000 from the first printing of *All About Town* on their city.

Business owners, the chamber of commerce and the community profit in image, recognition and dollars and cents, while everyone involved in this game is a winner!

SUMMARY
1. *All About Town* enhances the image of the chamber and the community on business, industrial and consumer levels.
2. Your role includes: introducing Aladco and *All About Town* to your community and members, making appointment calls for Aladco's representative and providing details that personalize the 'game of your city' to make it truly a special edition.
3. Advertising packages range from $400 to $4,000. A minimum of 40 participants or $16,000 is required.
4. Games wholesale are $7.50, including shipping, and retail at $12.50. Retailers net 40% or $5.00 per game.
5. The program takes 12 weeks from initiation of sales to release of games.
6. While promoting "all the good things your city has to offer," *All About Town* should generate $5-12K for your organization of its first edition.

EXHIBIT 4 (concluded)

AT NO EXTRA CHARGE CHAMBER RECEIVES:

(1) Logo on box cover, (2) Logo on board, (3) Full, basic participation package, (4) Rules - from cover 2-color ad, (5) Up to 6 free locations chosen by you, (6) Control of design and clients to be approached, <u>NO RISK</u>, (7) Potential future membership levers, (8) Community goodwill and exposure, (9) A means to promote "all the good things" your city has to offer.

CHAMBER COMMUNITY PROFITS

40 businesses participating @$400.00(min.)=$16,000.00
  10% profit to chamber $1,600.00
4000 games wholesaled @ 7.50 ea. = $30,000.00
  10% of wholesale as distributor profit   3,000.00
  Add'l retail margin of $5/game x 400 games   <u>2,000.00</u>

  Total of Above $6,600.00

  2% override on gross participation and wholesale   <u>920.00</u>

  Net Profit to Chamber $7,520.00

* * * * * * * * * * * *

50 businesses participating @$600.00(avg.) = $30,000.00
  10% profit to chamber $3,000.00
5000 games wholesaled @ 7.50 ea. = $37,500.00
  10% of wholesale as distributor profit   3,750.00
  Add'l retail margin of $5/game x 500 games   <u>2,500.00</u>

  Total of above $9,250.00

  2% override on gross participation and wholesale   <u>1,350.00</u>

  Net Profit to Chamber $10,600.00

COMMUNITY RETAIL PROFIT ON 5,000 GAMES = $25,000.00

EXHIBIT 5   Aladco Inc. Balance Sheet

BALANCE SHEET
Period ending 12/31/79
Prepared without audit for management use only

ASSETS

Current Assets
Cash—Bank of New Hampshire	(448.35)	
Cash—Depositors Trust	4.96	
Accounts Receivable	46,230.07	
Accounts Receivable—Employees	1,756.57	
Inventories	6,286.84	
Deposit	530.00	
Accounts Receivable —Stockholders	11,170.46	
Total Current Assets		65,530.55

Property and Equipment
Furniture and Fixtures	7,101.21	

Less: Accum. Depreciation
Res. for Dep'n, furn. & fixt	(942.49)	
Net Property & Equipment		6,158.72
TOTAL ASSETS:		71,689.27

EXHIBIT 5   (continued)

BALANCE SHEET
Period ending 12/31/79
Prepared without audit for management use only

Current Liabilities

Notes Payable—Shareholders	6,000.00	
Taxes Payable—FICA & W/H	3,995.82	
Account Payable/Production	131,143.49	
Total Current Liabilities		141,139.31

Long Term Debts

Notes Payable—SBIC	29,630.20	
Notes Payable—Comm. Credit	2,073.86	
Notes Payable—Sales Mgr.	6,157.20	
Accrued Commissions	3,487.65	
State Scale Company	38,761.68	
(Secured by receivables)		
Long Term Debt		80,110.59
Total Liabilities		221,249.90

Equity

Capital Stock	23,000.00	
Retained Earnings	(81,333.06)	
Net (Loss) Income	(91,227.57)	
Total Equity	(149,560.63)	
TOTAL LIABILITY AND EQUITY		71,689.27

Note: Assets—Accounts Receivable, Stockholders is uncollectable but has to be shown bringing the Net Loss to $102,398.03

EXHIBIT 5   **(continued)**

Accounts Receivable

1.	Hesser College	232.00
2.	Toy City	840.00
3.	Treisman's	504.00
4.	Augusta, Maine	2,572.29
5.	Burlington, Vermont	3,847.16
6.	Peru, Indiana	7,804.68
7.	Anniston, Alabama	22,954.34
8.	Plymouth, Massachusetts	7,455.60
	Total Receivables	$ 46,210.04

Inventory

1.	Plymouth, Massachusetts	500 games @ 4.70	$2,350.00
2.	Manchester, New Hampshire	99 games @ 3.50	346.50
3.	Keene, New Hampshire	39 games @ 4.70	183.30
4.	Augusta, Maine	504 games @ 5.97	3,008.88
5.	Anniston, Alabama	504 covers @ .52	262.08
6.	Anniston, Alabama	1,512 boxes @ .09	136.08
	Total Inventory		$6,286.84

Accounts Payable

American Premium	$42,770.88	Llewellyn Co.	$207.86
Baird & Bartlett	1,036.80	Manchester Oil	517.67
Bay State Box Company	6,818.57	Miles Kendex	417.00
Cook Cover, Inc.	434.86	Mills Industry	200.48
Budget Rent-a-Car	633.88	Moore Center	387.18
Concord Answering Serv	100.00	N.E. Telephone	1,451.09
Concord Electric Co	22.92	N.E. Audio Vis	38.75
Cullity & Kelley	690.87	Poore E.W.	244.00
Domesticare	150.00	Procorp	3,156.26
Easobox Company	9.30	Proj Triangle	1,522.30
Easter Seal Society	894.51	Quick Print	55.46
Eckstrom, Harold	164.50	Royal Press	5,374.61
Fall River Inn	82.44	Ryder Truck	80.85
Fish & Richardson	135.00	Safeguard Bus	266.96
Friend Box Company	1,815.77	Soney Co.	125.00
Granite State Ofc Sys	184.42	Stewart Nelson	212.00
I.B.M.	226.75	Tom-Ray Ofc Supp	120.99
Kelley Services	61.05	Szararz, Inc.	704.71

EXHIBIT 5 (concluded)

Kopy Korner	40,079.64	Tyler Press	7,320.17
Label Art	551.61	U-Haul	135.37
Lafayette Press	9,551.40	United Broadcast	327.00
Longevin & Roberge	800.00	Welcome Aboard	895.00
Little M.G. & Son	<u>51.61</u>	W.F.E.A.	<u>136.00</u>
Subtotal:	107,266.78		$23,876.71
Total Accounts Payable	$131,163.49		

EXHIBIT 6 Aladco Inc. Production Cost Analysis

<u>Production Cost Analysis for Fall River, Massachusetts</u>

Number of Games:<u>8,454</u>   Date Completed:<u>10/12/79</u>

	ITEM	AMOUNT	UNIT COST
I.	In-House Art and Production		
	A.Direct Time	$3,694.40	.437
	B.Art Administrative Team	439.61	.052
	C.Art Supplies	997.57	.118
II.	Color Printing (Labels, Maps, Playing Pieces)		
		4,784.96	.566
III.	Small Copy Printing		
	A.Coupons, (Travel Cards, Playing Pieces) 13 sheets		
	B.Money		12 sheets
	C.Rules and Parts List		2 sets
	D.Shopping Lists		2 sets
		13,526.40	1.600
IV.	Small Copy Collating	1,454.09	.172
V.	Boxes (Cover, Laminating, Bottom)	1,935.97	.229
VI.	Mfg Matls/Production	13,526.40	1.600
VII.	Delivery	1,268.10	.150
VIII.	Total	<u>$41,627.50</u>	<u>$4.924</u>

EXHIBIT 7 Selected Averages of Commercial Printing Companies (SIC 2751) (Robert Morris Associates, 1979)

ASSET SIZE	0-250M	250M-1MM	1-10MM	10-50MM	All
ASSETS (%)					
Cash	8.4	7.9	6.3	9.7	7.6
Accts Rec	28.0	30.6	30.1	27.3	29.7
Inventory	13.8	16.2	21.0	19.2	17.3
Other Current	2.7	0.9	1.2	0.3	1.4
Total Current	52.8	55.6	58.6	56.5	56.0
Fixed (net)	39.0	34.8	32.5	36.8	35.3
Intangibles	1.8	2.0	0.2	1.3	1.3
Other Non-Curr	5.5	7.7	8.3	6.5	7.3
Total	100.0	100.0	100.0	100.0	100.0
LIABILITIES					
Notes (Sh Term)	10.3	7.5	7.8	1.5	8.0
Cur Mat LTD	4.3	5.1	3.7	0.8	4.3
Accts Payable	14.1	15.8	15.4	7.3	14.9
Accrued	5.7	7.6	7.6	7.7	7.2
Other Current	3.3	4.1	2.9	2.7	3.4
Total Current	37.6	40.0	37.5	19.9	37.8
LT Debt	24.5	17.6	17.0	14.8	18.9
Other Non Curr.	0.6	1.7	1.8	5.7	1.7
Net Worth	37.3	40.7	43.7	59.5	41.7
Total	100.0	100.0	100.0	100.0	100.0
INCOME DATA					
Net Sales	100.0	100.0	100.0	100.0	100.0
Cost of Sales	59.1	66.6	74.6	67.1	67.6
Gross Profit	40.9	33.4	25.4	32.9	32.4
Operating Exp.	35.2	27.8	18.9	22.3	26.3
Operating Profit	5.8	5.5	6.5	10.6	6.1
Other Exp.	0.8	1.5	0.4	0.3	0.9
Profit Before Tax	5.0	4.1	6.0	10.3	5.2
RATIOS					
Current	1.5	1.5	1.6	2.7	1.6
Quick	1.1	1.1	1.0	1.8	1.1
Sales/Receivables	9.2	7.8	7.1	6.8	7.7
COS/Inventory	13.7	11.0	8.7	6.9	10.3
Sales/WC	14.6	13.0	10.8	5.3	11.6
EBIT/Interest	5.3	5.2	4.4	na	5.2
Fixed/Worth	1.1	0.8	0.7	0.6	0.9
Debt/Worth	1.5	1.5	1.4	0.8	1.5
Sales/Fixed Assets	6.2	7.0	6.3	4.5	6.6
Sales/Total Assets	2.6	2.4	2.0	1.7	2.3
Lease/Sales	2.4	1.8	1.5	na	1.8
Ofcrs Comp/Sales%	6.7	6.4	3.1	na	5.5

EXHIBIT 8   Excerpts From D&B KEY RATIOS, 1979

SALES	SIC 2741 Miscellaneous Publishing				SIC 2751 Commercial Printing, Letterpress				SIC 2752 Commercial Printing, Lithography			
	to 50M	50-2MM	2MM+	Total	to 50M	50-2MM	2MM+	Total	to 50M	50-2MM	2MM+	Total
Curr Assets/Curr Debt	1.60	2.23	3.28	2.27	1.61	2.40	2.34	2.09	1.50	2.22	2.07	1.90
Profit/Sales %	5.76	5.26	5.90	5.65	5.58	5.20	3.94	5.13	5.65	6.35	3.44	4.95
Profit/Net Worth %	28.49	27.26	11.97	31.31	44.08	20.08	15.96	23.16	40.67	23.37	14.70	24.28
Profit/WC %	26.23	48.02	19.63	27.73	45.82	39.37	26.93	36.92	34.71	51.02	27.23	38.74
Sales/Net Worth	5.71	4.81	2.56	3.93	5.47	3.69	3.30	3.92	5.63	4.10	4.16	4.60
Sales/WC	3.66	6.42	4.27	5.73	6.39	6.67	6.11	6.46	6.79	7.82	7.48	7.30
Coll. Period(days)	38	41	54	46	32	41	46	38	32	42	49	39
Sales/Inventory	14.0	25.0	6.5	12.1	26.0	20.8	12.8	20.5	32.6	26.1	14.0	26.9
Fixed Assets/Net W	42.1	39.7	29.3	36.1	93.0	66.3	59.6	72.7	91.0	69.1	69.3	80.1
Current Debt/Net W	65.3	39.3	29.9	35.6	52.2	35.5	40.4	40.4	51.1	40.5	58.1	48.7
Total Debt/Net W	105.8	67.8	37.4	65.6	101.0	55.4	60.2	68.1	93.0	68.3	102.0	82.4
Inventory/WC	21.4	32.8	37.8	32.2	28.9	33.3	46.7	33.6	21.1	28.0	52.9	28.9
Current Debt/Inv.	223.1	209.8	119.2	139.7	225.1	189.3	143.6	196.8	312.7	281.4	177.5	266.0
Funded Debt/WC	31.0	55.1	31.4	42.8	129.2	66.9	40.0	74.4	88.2	69.4	74.3	77.9

EXHIBIT 9   Manufacturing Specifications of All About Town Special Edition

The following materials are included in each game:

Game board label and folded map: (maps optional)	Size: Approx. 536 sq. inches. Material: 70# offset litho coated one side. Printing: 4-color process plus varnish.
Game board:	Size: Same as game board label and map. Material: 90 pt. chipboard, laminated with label and backing paper. Cutting: die cut with 6 interlocking pieces.
Casemade gamebox:	Size: approx. 10 1/2 x 13 1/2 x 1 1/4. Material: 60# chipboard wrapped with 60# offset litho. Printing: 4-color process. Includes tray for pieces.
Travel cards:	Size: 12 to each 8 1/2" x 11" page (number of pages varies according to number of participants) Maximum number of Travel cards: 96. Material: 110# index or equivalent. Printing: 1-color on colored stock.
Hazard cards:	Same specifications as travel cards. Quantity: Three pages per game.
Coupons:	Same specifications as travel cards. Quantity: Determined by client ads. Maximum 96. Acknowledged by label on each game.
Shopping lists:	Size: 6 or 8 per 8 1/2" x 11" page. Quantity: Two pages per game. Material: 90# index or equivalent. Printing: 1-color on whit stock.
Rules:	Size: 11" x 17" folded. Material: 50# litho. Printing: 1-color on white stock.
Money:	Size: Approx. 4" x 2". Quantity: 20 each of 5-8 different denominations determined by client ads.
Dice:	Size: 3/8" cubic. Quantity: 2 per game.
Playing pieces:	Minimum of 6 per game, maximum of 12. Plastic pawns. (Special printed playin pieces are optional.)
Packaging:	Corrugated cardboard cases. Size: Approx. 14" x 11" x 15". Quantity: 1 per each, 12 games. Weight packed: Approx. 38# each. Note: Games individually shrink-wrappe in plastic before packaging.

EXHIBIT 10　Terry Allen's Estimated Manufacturing Costs

(Per Game in 3,000 Unit Quantities)

Fixed Costs:		Costs Per Game
30 line drawings at $10 each = $300		$.100
Cover art = $400		.133
Typesetting, and layout, cards = $600		.200
Game board, layout and paste-up		.200
Color separation - cover = $450		.150
Total Fixed Costs		$.783

Variable Costs:		
Game board (complete diecut) includes printing label		$.880
Gamebox (includes printing label)		.452
Money (5 colors, 20 each)	($.196)	.140
Coupons (3 sheets)	($.113)	.040
Travel cards		
Hazard cards (13 sheets)	($.481)	.242
Shopping lists		
Rules	($.050)	.022
Dice		.036
Plastic stands		.062
Stick-on labels		.030
Printed playing pieces		.100
Packing boxes		.050
Assembly (including double shrink-wrap)		.600
Total Variable	($3.050)	$2.654
Total Cost	($3.833)	$3.437

(Figures in parentheses represent best outside quotation received for printing to be done in-house.)

EXHIBIT 11   Terry Allen's Pro Forma Earnings Statement for Franchisee

Advertising Sales	$30,000
Sales of 4,000 Games @ $7.50	30,000
TOTAL INCOME	$60,000
Cost of Games	$24,000
Initial Franchise Fee	5,000
Continuing Franchise Fee (3% of Advertising Sales)	900
Fee to chamber of commerce (Not mandatory)	3,000
Travel, Office, Postage	1,000
TOTAL EXPENSES	$33,900
NET PROFIT	$26,100

These advertising sales figures are based on the average sales experienced in the last five New England <u>All about Town</u> editions (Augusta, Maine; Bangor, Maine; Portland, Maine; Fall River, Massachusetts; Burlington, Vermont). These figures may be checked by counting the number of advertisers on each game and multiplying by the *All About Town* standard fee schedule of $400 minimum per advertiser.

Sales of 4,000 games at $7.50 each is projected. The actual number of games sold in the above five (5) cities was greater than 6,000 games per city. *All About Town*, Inc is recommending, but not insisting, to franchisees that fewer games be distributed in the future (to help achieve a sold-out situation and build demand for future years).

Cost of games is based on franchisee employing franchisor to manufacture said games. If franchisee elects to have another company manufacture these games, actual costs may be greater or less than $6.00 per game.

<u>CAUTION</u>
These figures are only estimates.

EXHIBIT 12   Disclosure Statement Outline

(Copied from Terry Allen's Worksheet)

<u>Note to Self:</u> The prevailing statute for providing information to prospective franchisees is detailed by FTC regulation, located in 16 CFR 436.1 et. seq., FTC Trade Regulation Rule Concerning Franchising and Business Opportunity Ventures.

General Information

1.	Identifying Information as to Franchisor
2.	Business Experience of Franchisor's Directors and Executive Officers
3.	Business Experience of the Franchisor
4.	Litigation History
5.	Bankruptcy History

Terms of the Franchise

6.	Description of Franchise
7.	Initial Funds Required from a Franchisee
8.	Recurring Funds Required from a Franchisee
9.	Affiliated Persons the Franchisee is Required or Advised to do Business with by the Franchisor
10.	Obligations to Purchase
11.	Revenues Received by the Franchisor in Consideration of Purchases by a Franchisee
12.	Financing Arrangements
13.	Restriction of Sales
14.	Personal Participation Required of the Franchisee in Operation of the Franchise
15.	Termination, Cancellation, and Renewal of the Franchise

Other Conditions Concerning the Franchise Agreement

16.	Statistical Information Concerning the Number of Franchises (and Company-owned Outlets)
17.	Site Selection
18.	Training Programs
19.	Public-Figure Involvement in the Franchise
20.	Financial Information Concerning the Franchisor

EXHIBIT 13   Commission Policy

All sales persons selling *All About Town* shall be on the following commission schedule:

1st $5,000 cash advertising sales:	15% of cash collected
2nd $5,000 cash advertising sales:	20% of cash collected
Over $10,000 advertising sales:	25% of cash collected
Commission on game sales:	10% of cash collected
Commission on media trade outs:	7% *

If a salesperson is to collect the full 10 percent commission on the sale of games, he/she must also be responsible for delivering the games and picking up the money. If it is not possible for the salesperson to be available to perform these tasks in November when the games are delivered, either he/she may arrange for someone else to do it, or all About Town, Inc. will arrange it. In the event that *All About Town* arranges for delivery and collection of money on game sales, a 5 percent commission will be paid to the original salesperson, and 5 percent will be paid to the person who delivers and picks up the money. Our truck will deliver games to all accounts who order at least 12 cases (1 gross), 144 games. The salesperson is not responsible for collecting these sums, and will be paid full commission as long as the merchant pays upon delivery.

Commissions are payable each Monday on sales made through the previous Friday, as long as all of the art work is included with the contract. Commissions will be held up until art work is sent in.

The first $50 of a salesperson's commissions are held in escrow until the salesperson has terminated with *All About Town,* and then it is paid to him/her upon his/her turning over of all sales materials to the appropriate sales manager.

---

*NOTE: Radio stations may be traded one case of games (12 games) at retail for every $1,000 of trade-outs at regular advertising rates (maximum 24 games).

EXHIBIT 14   All About Town Price List

BASIC PACKAGE

$400
1. Shopping List
2. Travel Card
3. Game Board Square (with line drawing or black and white logo)
4. Rules Index Listing
5. Redeemable Coupon (optional)

EACH EXTRA LOCATION INCLUDING ALL ABOVE FEATURES: $350

Billboard: $200
Hazard Card: $100
Outside Rules: $200 (one color in addition to black)*
Inside Rules: $100
Masthead: $300
Denomination of Money: $300
Sponsorship: $200
Additional Travel Card/Shopping List Combo: $200
Additional Color - Travel Card: $200
Additional Color - Game Board Square: $100
Playing Piece: $300

* THE COLOR ON THE ADS WILL BE THE SAME FOR ALL OUTSIDE RULES - THE FIRST ADVERTISER WILL CHOOSE THE COLOR

Chapter 10

Careering

❏ *SUBCHAPTER 10A - New Business Entry*

How to succeed as an entrepreneur is not much a matter of magic. Coincidence sometimes plays an important role, as in other activities. Anyone can choose to start a business, and those who do are apparently much like other people. In hindsight, prior related work experience often seems particularly important. Founders tend to be more highly educated than the average, but the amount of education does not seem to correlate with success. However, many entrepreneurs continue to pursue training, particularly that which is job-specific, rather than concerned with business in general. They draw important assistance from contacts. Personal savings help increase power and choice. Spotting opportunity and performing competently are highly important in entrepreneurship as they are in other occupations. Rendering service at an attractive price to others is here, as elsewhere, the basic justification for being paid.

To the degree that any professional can exercise a monopoly, higher pay can result. But with an independent venture, the entrepreneur may be able to delineate this proprietary edge more sharply than in a job and thereby garner more profit from it. That doesn't necessarily indicate anything special about the person, just the vehicle of employment. Acquiring a professional edge and choosing company creation to capitalize on it have traditionally come largely from unplanned evolution for most entrepreneurs. The extent to which future generations will use information about that evolution to develop entrepreneurial careers more systematically remains to be seen.

Those Who Become Entrepreneurs

Over two-thirds of new ventures are in relatively easy-to-enter lines of business, namely retailing and services. But higher success rates are experienced in other lines such as manufacturing and professions.[1] Prior work experience, including at least some in a supervisory position, provides much of the qualification to perform these start-ups. Over three-fourths of start-ups are done by men. Those whose ventures survive are usually married, and many (40 percent of male founders and 64 percent of female founders) have working spouses.

Founders' Ages

Frequency distributions of the ages at which entrepreneurs start businesses usually find the maximum point somewhere between 30 and 40 years of age, most often about halfway. Cooper et al. found that start-ups most frequently occurred in the five-year interval between ages 30 to 34 (21 percent).[2] Ronstadt found a similar result among Babson College graduates, with 31 percent in this five-year age band.[3] This pattern parallels the age distribution of the general population and so seems unsurprising.

It may also be that at earlier ages the entrepreneur has not yet learned enough about some kind of business to be able to compete against other companies that are already established. Before that age, a would-be entrepreneur may not have enough savings to live on while setting up the business, nor enough contacts or credibility to gain support from others. At ages beyond this 30-to-40-year range, the potential entrepreneur may be less likely to start for other reasons. He or she may have reached a point of income and success in some other occupation that makes it hard for the probable expected payoff of a start-up to measure up. Time commitments and financial responsibilities to family may have become greater. The amount that can be lost in terms of savings will likely be greater. Thus the incentives for venturing will have become lower and the risks higher, making entrepreneurship relatively less attractive.

But these are only generalities. Individual cases range widely. Some entrepreneurs start very young, the founders of Apple and Microsoft being examples. Others start much older than the typical, though it is hard to think of any examples whose success was even remotely as great as those two. How such patterns work has not been much studied.

Kinds of Entrepreneurs to Become

There are many possible schemes for displaying alternative types of entrepreneurial jobs. One is by industry in which the start-up is performed. The sample of 2,994 start-ups studied by Cooper et al.[4] was dominated greatly by retailing and services, as shown in Table 10-1.

Within each of these categories further breakdowns into virtually unlimited subdivisions can be made, as the Yellow Pages and *Thomas Register* or any manufacturers' directory readily illustrate. Thinking about them might stimulate ideas about kinds of acquisitions to consider or jobs to look for, but not likely kinds of start-ups to undertake. In order to glimpse a useable start-up opportunity, however, a would-be entrepreneur will likely need much more close-up vision than such categorization allows.

Table 10-1 Start-ups by Line of Industry

Business	Percent of start-ups
Retailing	46%
Services	19
Manufacturing	8
Construction	7
Professions	5
Finance	5
Wholesale	4
Other	6
Total	100%

Entry strategy can also be used to classify entrepreneurial jobs, according to interviews with 106 entrepreneurs conducted by Gartner et al.[5] The six "archetypes" thus identified were:

Escaping to New Work A secretary and a speech therapist taught themselves something about pet stores by studying some, running one for a couple of days, renting a site, buying stock and opening the doors.

Deal Making The inventor of a novelty product personally developed sales channels, subcontracted manufacturing and created a firm to coordinate these functions.

Providing Expertise A specialist in compensation left his job, incorporated, and recruited clients from his former employer.

Buyout A long-time bicycle enthusiast retired from the military, bought an existing shop and improved its performance.

Aggressive Service An investment banker incorporated, set up his own office to provide an innovative service, recruited the needed contacts and expanded his service to other parts of the country.

Methodical Organizing An MBA frustrated by life as a corporate employee formulated criteria for an industry to start in, assembled customer focus groups to scan that industry, discovered a weak product and set up to introduce an improved design.

Application: *Which of Gartner's archetypes most closely fit the assigned case entrepreneur, and what sort of knowledge and skills in general would those types most require?*

For each of these and other such types it is possible to consider examples and assess just what would be required to compete with such a person. That may help a would-be entrepreneur decide what kinds of start-ups to avoid, which to pursue further and what complements to seek, either through more learning or by recruiting partners.

Success Patterns

Cooper et al. reported from their study of 2,994 NFIB entrepreneurs aver-aged across all types[6] that some controllable characteristics of those whose start-ups were more likely to be surviving after three years than not surviving included that entrepreneurs with surviving ventures:

- Were more likely to be college graduates (27 percent vs. 18 per-cent)
- Were on average slightly older (36.4 vs. 35.4 years) although founder age and firm growth were not correlated
- Had held fewer full-time jobs (4.2 vs. 4.9 average)
- Were less likely to have a goal of organization building (28 per-cent vs. 35 percent)
- Started with more capital
- Were less likely to have continued to hold other jobs
- Were more likely to have started with similar products and ser-vices (32 percent vs. 27 percent), similar customers (31 percent vs. 24 percent) or similar suppliers (31 percent vs. 25 percent) to those of their prior work
- Were more likely not to be in retailing (44 percent vs. 53 percent)
- Were more likely to have a goal of not working for others (19 per-cent vs. 15 percent)
- But were less likely to have left prior jobs out of dissatisfaction (24 percent vs. 29 percent).

Application: *How well does the assigned case entrepreneur align with the statistical success patterns listed above?*

These authors reported the rate of discontinuance overall in new firms was about 11 percent per year, as contrasted with a figure of 10 percent by others (Reynolds and Tauzell) and higher than 11 percent by still others (Shapero). *Not* correlated with success were levels of prior management experience, prior business ownership, sources of initial funding, number of hours worked per week (the average was 56 to 57 hours), having come from a business versus non-business background, having taken business courses, or having parents who owned businesses.

The folklore that successful entrepreneurs tend to come from parents who were self employed does not fit *Inc.* 500 founders, in two-thirds of the cases. The theory that entrepreneurs who become most successful usually had busi-nesses when they were children was also not true almost two-thirds (63 percent) of the time for *Inc.* 500 entrepreneurs. Nearly three-fourths (72 per-cent) said they acquired the main skills they needed as company builders during adulthood, not childhood. Prior employment was where most learned what they needed for start-up. For 59 percent the company that made the *Inc.* list was the first one they had started, while 41 percent had started another company previously.[7]

Founders' Professional Qualifications

A repeating theme in both the *Inc.* and Cooper et al. studies is the importance of prior work experience in preparation for entrepreneurship. When asked to identify the single most important source of ability to build a company, over two-thirds of the *Inc.* 500 founders cited work or professional experience in an industry. Founders, it appears from the Cooper et al., study, not only tend to start companies that are in the same industries as their prior employment, but also tend to have concentrated their work experience on fewer jobs. In contrast to the general 30-to-34 aged population that averages 6.7 jobs, less than 25 percent of founders had over 6 jobs and almost half (46 percent) had held three or less. Moreover, fewer prior jobs for the founder tended to correlate with higher odds of venture survival.[8]

Reasons that related and concentrated work experience helps are not hard to imagine. Work puts the would-be entrepreneur in position to examine the frontier of technology, and/or the market and specific customers where opportunity can best be discerned. Work provides practice against standards required to compete and thereby hones excellence. It helps a would-be entrepreneur judge whether he or she truly could compete with an independent venture and adds to self-confidence in making a venture choice. Through work the would-be entrepreneur can acquire contacts vital to operation within the particular industry, and from work should come savings which can help finance the start-up. More founders preferred doing technical or selling work in their venture to managing it (38 percent versus 28 percent). However, the great majority of founders were sufficiently successful in those jobs to reach supervisory positions, which likely developed skills in managing, not just doing the work of the venture.[9]

Emphasis on technical skills showed up in educational backgrounds of the founders studied by Cooper et al. Founders on average progressed farther in education than the general population. For 40 percent of founders, schooling included at least some courses in business. But more dramatic was the finding that 57 percent had courses in vocational or professional training. Moreover, after founding their firms, owners continued to take courses with a focus on industry-specific rather than general business subjects. Curiously, however, although schooling was correlated with likelihood of start-up, it had no correlation with likelihood of survival or growth of the venture.

The apparently strong role of prior work experience in founding ventures adds interest to the study of exceptions. Vast numbers of them must exist, since the correlation is far from perfect. How could someone without such experience start a successful new enterprise? Clearly one way would be to have had avocational rather than vocational experience with the product or service.

> Debbie Fields had no prior start-up experience and no work experience in the pastry business when she opened her first cookie store in Palo Alto. But she had been making cookies since she was a child and was highly skilled at making cookies that other people liked.[10]

❖ ❖ ❖

> Ted Hatfield had no experience in start-up or manufacturing when he decided to make a replica of his great-great grandfather's long rifle and take it to a shooting contest. But he had grown up with guns and taught himself how to repair and rebuild them. When he received orders at the contest for 20 guns he started making them personally in a rented garage and also learning how to make them more efficiently through use of modern machine tools and subcontractor help. Over the next 10 years sales grew to $2.5 million with a backlog of 2,000 guns on order.[11]

Four other ways to start up in an unfamiliar business with some chance of succeeding are (1) through acquisition of a going concern, (2) by taking on a partner who has the requisite experience, (3) by entering a business that is very simple to operate, such as some forms of retailing (e.g. small shops) and service (e.g. house-painting or housecleaning) or (4) happening to find a new industry where there is not yet any competition and where firms with related skills don't see enough growth to enter (e.g. early days of making surfboards or skateboards).

Application: *How well do the assigned case entrepreneur's professional qualifications fit the assigned case venture and what could best be done to enhance the fit?*

Founders' Personal Attributes

For most, if not all, new business opportunities, it would seem that there must be others whose experience, circumstances and awareness qualify them as well as those entrepreneurs who take advantage of them. Is it simply chance that makes the difference? Or is it the ever so slight distinctions that make no two circumstances identical? Or are there differences in habit, personality or individual motivation that cause some of the qualified candidates and not others to be entrepreneurs?

Studies of psychological attributes have turned out to be inconclusive. Entrepreneurs seem to be much like everyone else after they start companies, and nobody has systematic evidence to show that they were different from others before they started them. Studies to match those who could and did against those who could and did not perform the start-ups have not been conducted.

Even if they were, the history of psychological testing suggests that results would be varied and each individual would be left to wonder whether he or she fit the "typical" entrepreneurial pattern or was an exception to it.

There have been attempts to classify types of entrepreneurs according to psychological tests (e.g. craftsmen versus opportunists, for instance), and statistical correlations of significance were reported. However, the study of 4,814 entrepreneurs by Woo, Cooper and Dunkelberg, for instance, found that although at one level such classification might be possible, significant divergencies could exist under similar labels.[12]

So a practical operating rule for a would-be entrepreneur is probably not to worry about whether he or she fits any supposed psychological profile and concentrate instead on whether a venture is worth doing and whether he or she wants to do it.

Application: How well do the assigned case entrepreneur's personal attributes fit the assigned case venture, and what could best be done to make the most of the fit?

Career Paths

The variety that is characteristic of entrepreneurship in general is also true of the career paths that lead to, through and from it. Notwithstanding the occasional stories of people who "resolved to become an entrepreneur and make a million before age 30" and did it, most entrepreneurial career paths are steered more by unforeseen events than planning and rarely lead to a million. They do include points of decision, where choices can be made that are consequential, however, so there can be reason to learn something about how they work and where the choices may lead.

Predicting how much choice any particular would-be entrepreneur can expect to have is problematic. Anyone can try venturing. Many can venture and survive at it, though the financial compensation, notwithstanding some big winners, is usually low and the hours are long.

Venture Career Starting Points

Most entrepreneurial careers, like most venture ideas, follow from jobs. The entrepreneur gets an idea on the job and pursues it independently. The entrepreneur gets fired from a job and venturing looks better than another job. The entrepreneur quits a job, looks around for something else to do and decides upon venturing. These are particularly common starting points, but they represent only part of the path list, which includes the following:

- Job to venture
- Unemployment to venture

- School to venture
- Retirement to venture
- Homemaking to venture

Examples of each of these can be read elsewhere[13] but are fairly easy to imagine. The most common path, according to the study of Cooper et al. is from either job or unemployment to venture. Most often, the prior job was in a business with 100 or fewer employees, and that job was left either due to its being discontinued, by being fired or by quitting without plans. Locating the start-up within a radius of 150 miles was another frequent pattern.[14]

In addition to starting point, other important variables could include extent and nature of prior education and experience, amount of savings and capital available through contacts, technical or market advantages, personal financial responsibilities, health, alternative job openings and personal aspirations.

Finally, there is simply capacity to perceive opportunity. To illustrate, the emergence of commercial applications for biological science suddenly increased the fraction of biologists who embarked on entrepreneurship. Similarly, the emergence of cheap microchips vastly increased the number and percentage of computer designers who took up entrepreneurship, and in turn the wide availability of cheap computers vastly increased the number of computer programmers who saw entrepreneurship as an attractive career. Less obvious was the effect that discovery of oil on Alaska's North Slope had on entrepreneurship. It seems to be only rarely that public employees drop their civil service jobs to become entrepreneurs, but when the pipeline boom generated lucrative opportunities for those in Alaska with arctic know-how, such as how to keep sewers from freezing in an Eskimo village, federal employees of such agencies as the Public Health Service who had been doing such work suddenly left their jobs to start ventures in the private sector. In 28 percent of the sample reported by Cooper et al., the entrepreneurs said their start-up resulted when "a good opportunity came along and I jumped."[15]

Venture Participation Roles

Although entrepreneurship may commonly be regarded as only one role, that of the person who heads a venture, there are, as seen in Chapter 7 on Help, many different ways to participate in a venture, including the following:

Banker Not many become founders, but some do. Some start banks. At one Seattle bank a management advisory group set up to help entrepreneurs spun off to become an independent enterprise.

Accountant Some branch out to start their own accounting firms. Dave Ederer, a "big six" accountant, was asked by one of his clients, a heat treater, to buy his business so he could retire. Ederer did so, then went on both to buy and start other firms.

Other Professionals Consultants to small firms sometimes become best qualified to take them over and do so. Seattle's Tel-Tone, for instance, was taken over by a consultant who had served the company for several years. Lawyers sometimes take shares of start-up stock in return for services. An advertising agent, asked by an inventor to help market his product, ended up forming a team to buy rights and start a company to make and sell it.

Venture Capitalist Each venture capital firm is itself a start-up. Usually partners and employees of those firms participate on boards of their investments. It is not uncommon for employees of the venture capital firms to slide over into managerial positions with stock options or ownership in ventures.

Informal Investors To qualify, wealth is required. That wealth can be used to participate in start-up however the investor wishes, if not in one venture, then in another.

Founding Team Member Becoming a part-time team member while keeping another job is possible. Such people are usually picked for what they very specifically contribute in skills, contacts or resources.

Venture Employee If the bargain for ownership is not struck at the time of employment, it is usually hard to get it later unless all employees are included. The finding by Cooper et al., that entrepreneurs most often were previously employees of smaller companies does not indicate how recently-started those companies were.

Scholar Some scholars of entrepreneurship start ventures, most often in consulting. Scholars in engineering and sciences more frequently seem to start proprietary product firms and firms that grow larger.

This is obviously only a sampling of roles in which a would-be entrepreneur might interact with ventures. But they illustrate some of the possibilities.

Application: *How well-suited would the entrepreneur in the assigned case be for each of the above eight roles, in rank order, before the venture versus after?*

Role Sequences

Some would-be entrepreneurs undertake other jobs, not necessarily involved directly with ventures, as intentional preparation for entrepreneurship. The most ambitious study of this pattern was undertaken by Ronstadt, who tracked careers of over 200 Babson College business major graduates. He reported that those who chose a prior career to prepare for entrepreneurship tended to start entrepreneurial careers younger and stay with them longer (over 25 years long) than those who had not thus prepared. Within that group, those who started the other preparatory career younger tended to wait longer to take up the entrepreneurial career.[16] This seems to support the impression that time is generally required to prepare for starting a business.

Despite this work by Ronstadt, the career patterns of those who chose jobs deliberately as stepping stones to entrepreneurship have not been much studied. Regrettably, nobody has reported any further follow-up of the early studies by Ronstadt or others like them. It is not known, for instance, how well the various venture participation roles, including that of founder, serve to enhance chances for succeeding as a founder or even which are most likely to lead to becoming a founder.

Start-up Versus a Job

Most people with jobs keep them rather than leave to start their own companies. Much of the reason may be that they are not exposed to entrepreneurial opportunities in their work or don't effectively discern them. Many may not be qualified to compete as entrepreneurs. And for still others the deciding factors may be such advantages of established company employment as:

Higher pay and greater fringe benefits in return for shorter hours and more clearly delimited responsibilities. (The average salary plus bonus of an *Inc.* 500 company CEO in 1989 was only $104,802,[17] not high compared to the top 500 physicians, lawyers and *Fortune* CEO's. Of course, the *Inc.* CEO also likely has ownership value increase as additional compensation.) Ability to move around within the organization if one part of it becomes uncomfortable. Opportunity to learn proven, effective procedures that have been worked out at considerable investment over time. More availability of company training programs. Possible chances to move ahead and be able to apply massive resources to achieve organization goals. Prestige from association with a well-known company name.

Salaries on the average are higher in larger companies, according to U.S. Census Bureau data for 1987. Companies with annual sales over $1 billion paid employees average salaries twice as large ($24,066) as those of companies with sales of less than $1 million per year ($12,870). Interestingly, diversified large companies paid on average 30 percent higher than single-industry companies.

Notwithstanding these advantages in pay and fringe benefits, entrepreneurs leave jobs in established companies, both large and small, because of other characteristics of those jobs such as the following:

Too much regimentation and lack of perspective in the confinement of a narrow specialty. Not enough opportunity to move ahead and make more money. Uncertainty over where management will take the company next. Risk of suffering because of the mistake of a boss or of being swept out in a whole-sale layoff. Possibly having to move home and family at a big company's whim to one unfamiliar and possibly less attractive geographical location after an-other. Lack of freedom and encouragement to generate ideas that have promise or to follow through on new ideas that might have promise. Inability to see the impact of one's own efforts on performance of the organization. Lack of individual recognition for contributions to that performance.

One entrepreneur, Steve Bostic, who had formerly worked in big compa-nies characterized some of the negatives of that experience as follows:

> *You have no control over your own destiny. You can succeed in a big com-pany and still get the axe. That's the ultimate risk. I see it happen all the time with people I know in big corporations. They work their butts off, do a great job and then get thrown out or forced into early retirement. It doesn't matter how high up you go, either. In my own case, the further I moved along in the corpo-rate environment and the higher I got, the more I realized I was not in control. And the situation is even more turbulent now. In the old days, the guard would change and you'd realign yourself with the new guy's thoughts. Today the whole division gets sold out, spun out, divorced.*[18]

For many, the path leads first to employment where necessary learning oc-curs, savings are accrued and contacts are made, and thence to entrepreneurship where those advantages are put to use. Steve Bostic, notwith-standing his criticism of big-company employment, also drew upon it as education for his own start-up.

> *I advise young people to get the corporate education but have a clear plan. Move around. Learn what you need to learn. Then step out of the corporate envi-ronment and get into your own enterprise....*
>
> *I was fortunate that my first job after Burger Chef was at American Hospi-tal Supply Corp., where they really teach you to sell. They teach a systematic approach to selling to an entire hospital. We had a 250-man sales force at Ameri-can. When I left after about five years, I'd moved up to the top 10 or 15, not because I was such a great salesman, but because I had learned the process.*[19]

That it can often be important to know the process is emphasized by the large percentage of entrepreneurs who start only businesses they are experi-enced in. A study by Koller, for instance, reported that 38 percent of the entrepreneurs interviewed said their personal contribution was that of actu-ally producing the product or service of the venture themselves. Only 24 percent had no prior experience in that type of work.[20]

After comparing a sample of 208 practicing entrepreneurs with that of 102 others who seriously considered entrepreneurship but then abandoned the effort, Ronstadt[21] concluded that higher odds of leading a start-up could be achieved by:

- Starting to prepare for venturing sooner in life.

- Being prepared to accept modest, rather than highly ambitious, venture goals initially, or else seeking out major financial backers.

- Seeking partners with suitable industrial experience.

From the findings of a study by Cooper et al., it appears that there is a relationship between at least the last two of these three elements and the size of the start-up. Apparently a larger start size requires better experience and more likely a team.[22]

Application: *List and assess the pros and cons of venturing versus seeking a job at the time of the assigned case for the assigned case entrepreneur.*

Maintaining Mind Set

Navigating alone in the sea of commerce, an entrepreneur may at times find it challenging to maintain the optimism and enthusiasm needed to keep paddling energetically. Books on "positive thought" offer innumerable suggestions for ways to maintain a productive attitude. Established companies provide pep talks, house organ articles, retreats, training programs, picnics and many other mechanisms to maintain morale.

Franchise firms, whose franchisees operate much like lone entrepreneurs in many ways, provide analogous services, with agents who rove the country working with franchisees and providing periodic performance reviews through which franchisees can compare their sales and profits to other periods and industry norms. They also stage annual meetings where vendors display their wares, franchisees meet one another and swap experiences, inspirational speakers lecture to the group, contests are held and prizes are awarded. In local areas, franchisees meet for some of the same activities on a smaller scale.

Analogous services are offered to independent entrepreneurs through all sorts of trade associations. Some specialize by line of business, others by geographical area and others by size of business. The National Federation of Independent Business specializes by type of ownership. Other groups concentrate on "family businesses" or "home-based" businesses.

From these precedents several alternatives for "staying in tune and in touch" can be seen for independent entrepreneurs:

- Join one or more appropriate associations.

- Contact and become acquainted with several other entrepreneurs in similar situations.

- Enroll in local courses that convene groups of similar interests.

- Read and consider the advice of "positive mental outlook" books.

- Subscribe to industry trade magazines.

- Take breaks from the business occasionally to get recharged at association meetings or other "getaway programs" such as are offered by universities and independent consulting firms.

- Hire experts occasionally to review the business. If possible, recruit free advisers, possibly by exchanging a similar service with them.

Application: *How would you rank order the advisability of the above seven alternative actions for the entrepreneur in the assigned case (a) at the time of the assigned case versus (b) one year after the case, as best you can tell?*

The choice of ways to "recharge"is individual. One entrepreneur said that when things got grim in his business, he found he could always cheer himself up by asking himself how the business would look to him if he no longer owned it and somebody offered to let him have it for free.

Supplementary Reading

New Venture Strategies Chapter 3 and Appendices A and B. (Vesper, K.H., Prentice-Hall, 1990)

Exercises

1. List your personal goals, pick an industry, segment it, display the goals, problems of attaining them and possible solutions for those problems in a table or grid. Then describe how the array of alternatives in the grid could be narrowed down to an overall plan of action for achieving the goals.

2. Examine two or more case histories of entrepreneurs. Compare and contrast key elements they drew upon such as know-how, contacts and resources as well as "track records" and "happenstance" for starting new enterprises. Comment on the extent to which (1) either could have started another's venture, (2) either could have deliberately designed a career which would have led to the start-up, or (3) you could plan a career deliberately to culminate in such a start-up.

3. Contacts Network. Map your contact network. Identify gaps. Formulate activity patterns that could be intentionally adopted to render it more likely effective for start-up.

4. Synthesis. Prepare an essay of not more than 1,000 words on how, in general, a person might design a career that will likely lead to successful start-up of a specific type of business.

5. Personal Strategic Plan. Formulate a combined analysis of your preferences, history, present, role requirements, task-relevant prior experience, competencies, and ability to apply each of the entrepreneurial thought modes. Prepare a per-

sonal strategic plan by which you could become founder of an ambitious venture based on this analysis.

6. Feedback. Exchange one of the above with someone else, possibly after you apply the assignment as best you can to them and exchange feedback.

7. Franchising. Contact one or more franchisors, and obtain information about what franchising offers. Formulate a career plan designed either (1) to end up in ownership of such a franchise, or (2) to end up starting a firm which will successfully compete with such a franchise. Include discussion of the pros and cons of both approaches.

Venture History

1. What turned out in hindsight to be the most valuable task-relevant prior experiences of the founders?

   a. When and how were they acquired?
   b. To what extent can they be seen as an intentional self-education experience in preparation for venturing?

2. What personal savings policies and practices did the founders follow prior to start-up? To what extent did or could they have had impact on the start-up?

Venture Planning Guide

1. Describe what you would do next to improve upon your venture plan if there were more time and resources available.

2. Formulate a personal plan by which you could put yourself into a better position than you are now to carry forward the venture described in your venture plan.

Notes

[1] David L. Birch, "The Truth About Startups," *Inc.*, January 1988, p. 14.

[2] Arnold C. Cooper and others, *New Business In America* (Washington, D.C.: The NFIB Foundation, 1990), p. 2.

[3] Robert Ronstadt, "The Decision <u>Not</u> To Become An Entrepreneur," in *Frontiers of Entrepreneurship Research 1983*, Eds. John A. Hornaday, Jeffry A. Timmons, and Karl H. Vesper (Wellesley: Babson Center for Entrepreneurial Studies, 1983), p. 202.

[4] Cooper and others, *New Business In America*, p. 15.

[5] William B. Gartner, Terence R. Mitchell, and Karl H. Vesper, "A Taxonomy of New Business Ventures," *Journal of Business Venturing*, 4, no. 3, May 1989, p. 169.

[6] Arnold C. Cooper, William C. Dunkelberg, and Carolyn Y. Woo, "Survival and Failure: A Longitudinal Study," in *Frontiers of Entrepreneurship Research, 1988*, eds. Bruce H. Kirchhoff, and others (Wellesley, Mass.: Babson Center for Entrepreneurial Studies, 1988), p. 225.

[7] John Case, "The Origins of Entrepreneurship," *Inc.*, June 1989, p. 53.

[8] Cooper and others, *New Business In America*, p. 22.

[9] Ibid., p. 3.

[10] Debbie Fields, and Alan Furst, *One Smart Cookie* (New York: Simon and Shuster, 1987).

[11] Geoffrey W. Norman, "The Real Hatfield," *Inc.*, October 1990, p. 127.

[12]Carolyn Y. Woo, Arnold C. Cooper and William C. Dunkelberg, "Entrepreneurial Typologies: Definitions and Implications," in *Frontiers of Entrepreneurship Research, 1988*, eds. Bruce H. Kirchhoff, and others (Wellesley, Mass.: Babson Center for Entrepreneurial Studies, 1988), p. 173.

[13]Karl H. Vesper, *New Venture Strategies*, Revised Edition (Englewood Cliffs: Prentice-Hall, 1990), Chapter 3.

[14]Cooper and others, *New Business In America*, p. 4.

[15]Ibid.

[16]Robert Ronstadt, "Does Entrepreneurial Career Path Really Matter?" in *Frontiers of Entrepreneurship Research 1982*, Ed. Karl. H. Vesper (Wellesley: Babson Center for Entrepreneurial Studies, 1982), p. 540.

[17]Bruce G. Posner, "Executive Compensation 1989," *Inc.*, September 1989, p. 74.

[18]Steve Bostic, "Thriving On Order," *Inc.*, December 1989, p. 48.

[19]Ibid., p. 51.

[20]Roland H. Koller, "On the Source of Entrepreneurial Ideas," in *Frontiers of Entrepreneurship Research, 1988*, eds. Bruce H. Kirchhoff, and others (Wellesley, Mass.: Babson Center for Entrepreneurial Studies, 1988), p. 200.

[21]Ronstadt, "The Decision Not To Become An Entrepreneur," p. 192.

[22]Arnold C. Cooper, Carolyn Y. Woo, and William C. Dunkelberg, "Entrepreneurship and the Initital Size of Firms," *Journal of Business Venturing*, 4, no. 5, September 1989, p. 317.

❏ SUBCHAPTER 10B - Sequels To Entry

The importance of contemplating during start-up what the later evolution and ultimate disposition of a venture will be varies among participants. For the entrepreneur there is plenty to think about in working through the many immediate tasks of start-up without worrying farther ahead. But others may feel differently. Outsiders who put money into the enterprise will likely want to know just how and when they will get it back. Employees may be interested in longer-term career implications. Customers may want assurance that the venture will be there to back up what it sells them. Suppliers will care about being paid and beyond that whether the venture will afford them opportunity for expanded and continuing business transactions. Thus inevitably, founders have to have some concern with where the venture is likely to lead in the longer term if disputes among such stakeholders are to be avoided.

A Southern California entrepreneur founded a company making high-performance electrical equipment such as motors, fans and pumps. He loved designing and working on the equipment, and the company succeeded in gaining a series of contracts first from the defense department and then from commercial aircraft makers. This built sales rapidly, but because the work did not carry high margins the company needed external capital for expansion. Through private placement it raised the capital, but the founder had to give up voting control to outside shareholders. They were interested in return on their investment, while he liked to work on technical advances. If a motor failed in some distant city he would typically catch a flight to go work on it, learn what was wrong and devise improvements in the design.

While he was working on technical problems, other aspects of the company, such as contract completion, cost control and bidding on new work would tend to slacken or drift off target, and before long profits would diminish and sometimes slide into the red. When this happened the investors would become upset and start badgering the founder about sticking to his job as CEO rather than design engineer. He would "get back to business," and profits would come back into line. But only for a while, because then he would relax, delve back into technology and the loss cycle would begin again.

After several years of discomfort with this pattern the outside investors, unable to find anyone whom they felt could replace the founder, reached an agreement with him to sell the company to a larger corporation in which he would continue to operate as division head of his company. He soon left to form another firm, which he kept small so as to retain complete control.

Venture Types

To this entrepreneur the goal of independence and being able to follow his technical enthusiasms was more important than building a large company or maximizing wealth. Other entrepreneurs have both other goals and other constraints on their ability to choose. Many have to take what they can get in the way of a venture and do what they can with it. Some venture types, which they may or may not be able to choose, include the following.

Job Replacement Ventures Some venture because they lose a job, cannot get a job or cannot stand a job. The venture is an escape from unemployment.

Lifestyle Ventures Some entrepreneurs deliberately leave jobs for ventures that may not pay as much, simply because they prefer the independence and like the work better.

High-Pay, Stably-Small Ventures Lack of competition thanks either to occupation of niches unnoticed or too small to attract others or due to entry barriers such as patents, proprietary assets, secrets or special skills enables some ventures to operate with high margins and yet stay small.

High-Growth Ventures Similar advantages to those above coupled with large or growing markets enable some ventures to expand rapidly. The top layer of this group is represented by the *Inc.* 500. Interestingly, its composition changes considerably every year, both in terms of specific firms on the list and in terms of the industries represented among the leaders. The explanation includes elements of science, art and luck.

The odds are that a given entrepreneur will be headed for one of the first three types of firms or some combination of them not involving high growth. Almost all ventures stay smaller than five or six employees. Cooper et al., found that only 37 percent of start-ups added to initial employment in their first three years, only 11 percent added four or more employees while 11 percent, although they survived, actually shrank.[1]

It is a minority of small ventures that yields high earnings and attractive fringe benefits for owners. Most give low pay and security for long hours of work topped by bookkeeping, tax preparation and red tape compliance that cuts into evenings and weekends. But at least it's an honest and truly productive living, not under the thumb of a boss or confined by the regimentation of someone else's organization. That does not mean that ventures give owners as much control over their lives as they expect. Cooper et al. found that whereas 78 percent of founders saw such control as an important motivation, 61 percent later were disappointed in the extent to which they attained it.[2] At the same time, however, 82 percent of those whose businesses survived three years said they would form them again, even though 32 percent said they were disappointed in how well they had done.[3]

Application: *How would you distribute the probabilities among the above four venture types as what the assigned case venture might become if it succeeds?*

Growth Venture Life Stages

Whether most founders could continue to manage their ventures if economic forces opened greater growth opportunities for them is usually moot, since their ventures don't grow. But high growth can strike where not expected. A poll of the *Inc.* 500 fastest-growing small firms in America revealed that 50 percent began as "regular but small" businesses and 48 percent began as informal operations in a garage or home. Only 2 percent began with all systems in place for fast growth.[4]

Folklore has it that those who start businesses are usually not suited to running them if they grow. Examples sometimes suggested to bear this out are Steve Jobs of Apple, Adam Osborne of Osborne Computer, William Lear, creator of the Lear Jet and other innovations, and earlier "greats" such as Edison, Steinmetz and Durant. But there are also easy-to-find counter-examples, such as William Hewlett and David Packard of Hewlett-Packard, Donald Douglas of Douglas Aircraft, and Edwin Land of Polaroid. So the folklore is sometimes true and sometimes false.

It appears that when ventures do grow many experience similar problem sequences and stages. Several authors have depicted "typical" sequences, beginning with Buchele's "Key Crises"[5]. To this have been added Steinmetz' "Critical Stages"[6] Thain's "Corporate Stages"[7] and Greiner's "Evolution/Revolution Stages."[8] A synthesis of those stages, problems and possible actions called for by the founders, if still in charge, includes the following.

1. **Imbalance** The founder's strengths, if not complemented by a well-rounded team, can produce a start-up strong in some areas, such as technical or marketing expertise, for instance, and weak in others such as production or finance. The result can be failure. The most likely remedy is to recruit complements or subcontract in weak areas. The study of start-ups by Cooper et al., found that at the earliest stages in a venture the typical owner personally participates in production of the venture's product or service.

2. **Cash Crunch** Development or initial sales come slower than expected and the company runs out of money before it really gets going. Solution: Anticipate with cash flow forecasts, maintain effective records monitoring, and line up potential sources ahead of needs.

3. **Delegation** Mistakes occur because the founder is trying to make all the decisions and can't keep up. Solution: Hire, take as partners or, if time allows, train people to take on parts of the leadership task.

4. **Leadership** Even with delegation from the founder, mistakes again arise with further growth if those to whom responsibilities have been given cannot themselves delegate and develop the leadership capabilities of those organizationally under them. More formal organization structure,

control systems, communication channels, training programs, budgeting, work standards and so forth are called for.

5. **Finance** Growth goes beyond what the company can finance internally. Ownership must be shared outside. Privacy must be sacrificed if the company is to grow further.

6. **Prosperity** On one side of the company's growth tightrope lies complacency and on the other lies chaos. This calls for self-criticism, complemented by bottom-up reviews and participation at all organizational levels, help from knowledgeable outside counsel, careful monitoring of performance, forecasting, planning and evaluation.

7. **Bureaucracy** Systems set up to suppress chaos impede flexibility, innovation and eventually productivity. Central authority can't deal well with diversity. The solution is to divisionalize and grant more autonomy to disparate units. Profit centers are created.

8. **Sprawl** The autonomy leads to less coordination among units. Line incompatibilities and uncoordinated resource allocation occur, product lines match less well, and direction becomes unclear. The solution may include some merging of units, more formal planning and review procedures, policy statements from headquarters and coordination sessions between division heads.

9. **Stagnation** The policies, paperwork and meetings created to control sprawl drain off energy and stifle initiative needed to maintain clear thrust. Bureaucracy rises again. Poor financial performance may lead to contention with shareholders as well as infighting that dampens morale and wastes resources.

10. **Vacillation** The cycle of tightening central authority versus decentralizing goes back and forth. Products mature and profits rise, leading to diversification efforts, and perhaps corporate venturing. Those consume capital and the mature products become obsolete, leading to losses, cutting off innovation efforts, retrenching, restructuring, more centralizing, and the cycle begins again.

These stages and solutions are oversimplified characterizations of complex processes. But they give some indication of problems that lie ahead that are worth at least some reflection in advance. For a given entrepreneur they suggest a basis for asking how far down the trail he or she wants to travel, is qualified to be useful or wants to learn "new tricks" in order to become qualified.

Application: *Sketch out a scenario by which the assigned case venture might develop into a large enterprise. At what level of employment might each of the 10 challenges arise? What could the entrepreneur do in advance to prevent or to mitigate it?*

Challenges of Fast Growth

Based on information from 120 of the 500 fastest growing firms identified by *Inc.* magazine in 1987, Terpstra and Olson[9] reported that problems encountered after start-up were most frequently in the area of sales and marketing, as can be seen in the rank ordering of problems by frequency in Table 10-2 below. As mentioned in Subchapter 8A on selling, this was even more often (38 percent versus 22 percent here) the top category mentioned for problems during start-up. Other changes in problems beyond start-up were that external financing dropped to the bottom of the list from second position during start-up and human resource management and organization design became much more significant problem areas.

Table 10-2 Fast Growth Problem Areas Beyond First Year

Problem Areas beyond First Year	Frequency %
Sales and marketing	22
Internal financial management	21
Human resource management	17
General management	14
Production and operations management	8
Regulatory environment	8
Organization structure/design	6
Product development	2
Economic environment	2
Obtaining external financing	1
Total	101%*

*Error due to rounding.

Characteristics of Fast Growers

Comparison of two data bases, one on recent start-ups and the other on more mature firms to see what characterized the fast-growers in each of these groups, was performed by Siegel, et al.[10] They found that extensive prior experience in the relevant industry among the management group was a common characteristic of both smaller and larger high-growth firms.

Exits from Ventures

Whether or not the venture survives and grows there is always the option of withdrawing one way or another. Sooner or later founders and venture must part ways. There are several paths by which this can come about.

Departing from Management

The best way to withdraw from management seems to be to plan for retirement and groom a successor. Founders who have been ousted by investors due to business problems often seem to leave with some bitterness, usually blaming others for the problems. Owners who withdraw for personal reasons without preparing for this in advance typically seem to do so either by selling the company at a lower price than they could have received with more careful transition efforts or else replacing themselves with managers who don't work out well, possibly because the founders keep meddling.

Departing from Ownership

The happy ways to relinquish ownership are either to "go public," to sell to another entrepreneur under non-distress conditions or to sell to another company with which the venture is a good fit. When the acquirer is another company whose markets and technologies do not fit well with the acquisition, the odds are that the acquisition will not work out well. If they do fit well but the new management is not sensitive to pitfalls of takeover, the odds, again, are that it will not work out well and the founders' "baby" will be injured.

How owners of 359 firms, over three-fourths of which had sales of less than $14 million, expected to cash out of their enterprises was reported in 1990 by the American Institute of Certified Public Accountants[11] as can be seen in Table 10-3 below.

In Case of Failure

Entrepreneurship requires optimism and founders are usually optimistic. Over two out of three estimate their chances of success at 80 percent or higher, according to the data of Cooper et al.[12] But it is an awkward fact that start-ups sometimes fail. The rate of failure is not as high as often supposed. On the average roughly 10 percent of firms per year are discontinued, some of them presumably for reasons other than failure, but many of them due to failure.

When that happens, many people may be let down: the founders, suppliers, investors, customers and lenders. The less they are let down, the better, and it therefore makes sense, though it is not enjoyable, to consider in advance such questions as the following:

1. What, in order of likelihood, are the ways things could go wrong and cause this venture to fail?

2. What might be early warning indicators that one or more of those events is coming?

3. What could be done about such events early enough to minimize the chances of failure?

4. What could be done in advance to minimize the costs of failure, both financial and otherwise?

Application: *How would you answer each of the above four questions for the assigned case venture?*

Table 10-3 Expected "Cash-out" Methods

Method	Percent
Sell to a Large Corporation	26%
Sell to Outside Investors	25
Pass Company Along to Family	22
Sell to Insiders	16
Go Public	3
Liquidate	2
Don't Know or Other	6
Total	100%

Application: *Which of the above departures from the assigned case venture should its entrepreneur aim for if the venture develops successfully?*

Termination

Procedures for closing down a company depend on whether it is a proprietorship, partnership, or corporation and whether it is solvent. Cases of insolvency will be discussed later in connection with bankruptcy.

Simplest to close as well as to set up is a proprietorship. Paying all the bills and notifying the state and city to stop the renewal of business licenses are the only legal requirements. There may also be employees to pay, assets to sell, leases to terminate, signs and telephone listings to remove, customers to notify and warranties to honor. If the company has set up retirement plans for employees, these may need attention. Presumably, the reason for closing down will be that not much has been going on with the company. Otherwise, there should be something to pass along for someone else—possibly employees or an outside buyer—to run.

Partnerships are more complicated to shut down or liquidate. A partnership may automatically be terminated by the death of a partner, depending on how the arrangement is legally structured. State laws govern partnerships, and three things are generally required under those laws to terminate them. The first is dissolution, which means that the partnership agreement is ended by the withdrawal or death of a partner, or by other action. The second is winding up, which essentially means stopping operations, fulfilling obligations, paying creditors, collecting receivables, and selling off assets. The third is distribution of assets according to provisions of the partnership agreement.

In addition to the state laws governing the existence of a partnership are federal laws recognizing it for tax purposes. Federal rules as to what constitutes the termination of a partnership are different from state rules. For instance, either the buyout by one partner of another partner's interest or the cessation of operations constitutes federal termination. Since the rules may change at either state or federal level at any time, it is generally advisable to hire a lawyer who specializes appropriately and is up to date on these rules to help with the process.

Corporate termination is similarly complex and governed by state rules as well as federal tax rules. The death of an owner does not affect the life of a corporation as it does a partnership. A corporation has its own life. State laws specify what is required to terminate it; as with partnerships, legal help is advisable.

Bankruptcy

There are three types of bankruptcy. By far the most common is **Chapter 7**, which accounted for over 580,000 filings in 1993. This type may be voluntary, if declared by the owner, or involuntary, if suit is brought by creditors who have not been paid. In either case it essentially involves complete liquidation of the company. A trustee, either elected by creditors or appointed by a court, takes charge of the business's assets so that creditors may be paid off from the assets, although often virtually nothing is left for them after legal and accounting fees are paid.

Second most common are **Chapter 13** bankruptcies, of which there were around 240,000 in 1993. This type applies to individuals and proprietorships only, and must be entered into voluntarily. Provided that unsecured debts are less than $100,000 and secured debts less than $350,000, the individual submits to the court a plan for paying off debts on extended terms for the following, in order of priority:

- Secured creditors
- Administrative expenses
- Operating expenses of the business
- Wage claims up to $2,000 per person
- Employee benefit plan contributions
- Claims of consumer creditors
- Taxes
- Other creditors

If the court agrees to the proposed plan, the entrepreneur may keep operating the business to follow the bankruptcy plan and creditors must go along with it whether they want to or not.

Most often reported in business news stories, although it is the least common type of bankruptcy, is filing for protection from creditors under **Chapter 11**. It is used by corporations to keep going and attempt to recover from the fact that they cannot pay all their bills. There were only 3,043 such filings in 1993, down from a high of 24,740 in 1986. A plan for dealing with creditors must be submitted to the U.S. Bankruptcy Court proposing specifically how claims will be dealt with. The plan may propose to pay only a portion of what the corporation is owed, or to stretch payments out over a longer period of time, or to offer stock to creditors in place of repayment. If the plan is approved, the company must follow it and attempt to fulfill it. Less than a fourth of such firms manage to do so, usually because they waited too long before filing for protection.

How to tell when the venture is not working is a function both of how the venture is supposed to work and where it is along the path of development. If there is a written business plan, then one sign of alarm may be that forecasts in the plan are not being achieved. It may be possible, however, for it to appear that progress is on schedule when it is not. If, for instance, the company has produced its goods, sold them and collected from customers, the financial statements may look all right. But customers may be having trouble with the goods that will lead to large returns and/or to collapse of the market. Possibly the deliveries have even laid a basis for lawsuits which will crush the venture. Or the venture may be on track, customers may be happy, and just ahead are as yet unannounced moves of competitors that will obsolete what the venture offers. Many ventures in the microcomputer industry, for instance, were doing fine until IBM and Microsoft introduced the DOS standard and made it dominant in the marketplace, rendering obsolete the operating systems of those other ventures.

Thus, some signs that the venture isn't working may be obvious, as when it can't raise needed capital, recruit key people, obtain supplies or get customers either to buy or to pay for what they bought. Other signs such as technical obsolescence may be harder to discern. But what to look for should be thought through as part of the planning process, so that if the venture is not going to work out, at least the founders can take action as early as possible to minimize the downside losses.

Application: *If the assigned case venture were to develop along a satisfactory projection over the next 12 months, where would it be and what warning signals should the entrepreneur be on the alert for?*

In Case of Success

The biggest success stories are those few start-ups whose owners manage to sell ownership on the public market. If the company manages to get its shares listed on a public exchange, the owners can choose when and how much of their interests to sell. Such a listing does not occur unless the company has grown fairly large and has even larger growth prospects in the future. So the total valuation of a company that manages to arrive at this stage has usually grown fantastically from its origins, and the founders are correspondingly well off.

Selling shares publicly, however, does not guarantee listing, and there are many companies with shares fairly widely distributed that are not publicly traded, not easy to make money from and not all that successful. They simply have the restrictions of public ownership and the burden of dealing with many owners without the luxury of easy ownership sale.

Selling the venture to a larger company is another way for entrepreneurs to cash out. By this path the entrepreneur may exchange shares in the venture for shares in the larger company and/or cash and/or a continuing consulting contract. Since acquiring companies often pay high prices for what they buy, this can be a lucrative way to depart from venture ownership. The downside is that acquiring companies on average don't do very well at keeping their acquisitions healthy or happy, and that can leave the founder wealthy but disappointed.

Selling to another entrepreneur or team of entrepreneurs is more likely to yield a lower price for the venture but also to have the venture continue to operate more successfully. The selling entrepreneur will probably receive cash, a payout contract, some sort of continuing consulting contract in exchange for ownership of the venture plus an agreement not to start another one that will compete with it.

Supplementary Reading
New Venture Strategies Chapters 1 and 3. (Vesper, K.H., Prentice-Hall, 1990)

Exercises

1. Apply question two below, under venture history, to one or more other ventures besides that of the history.

2. Are there any "most important truths" of entrepreneurship, and if so, what are they?

3. What can be learned about entrepreneurship from studying it versus attempting it?

Venture History

1. How did the founder(s) initially envisage the longer-term pattern of development of the venture, how has this vision changed over time and why?

2. How does the rate of increase in personal net worth of the founder(s) compare to what it would be if they sold the venture, invested the proceeds and took jobs?

Venture Planning Guide

1. Present your venture plan to someone who could be important in helping it succeed, such as a banker, investor, key employee or important customer or supplier. Take note of the feedback they provide and describe how you would improve on your plan for a "next round" effort at carrying it forward.

2. Describe what you have learned from your work on a venture plan, and tell how you would go at such a plan differently if you had it to do over again.

Notes

[1] Arnold C. Cooper and others, *New Business In America* (Washington, D.C.: The NFIB Foundation, 1990), p. 1.

[2] Ibid., p. 12.

[3] Ibid., p. 11.

[4] John Case, "The Origins of Entrepreneurship," *Inc.*, June 1989, p. 54.

[5] Robert B. Buchele, *Business Policy in Small and Growing Firms* (Scranton, Penn.: Chandler Publishing), 1967.

[6] Lawrence L. Steinmetz, "Critical Stages of Small Business Growth," *Business Horizons*, February 1969, p. 29.

[7] Donald H. Thain, "Stages of Corporate Development," *The Business Quarterly*, Winter 1969, p. 33.

[8] Larry E. Greiner, "Evolution and Revolution as Organizations Grow," *Harvard Business Review*, July-August 1972, p. 37.

[9] David E. Terpstra and Philip D. Olson, "Entrepreneurial Start-up and Growth: A Classification of Problems," *ET&P*, 17, no. 3, Spring 1993, p.5.

[10] Robin Siegel, Eric Siegel and Ian C. MacMillan, "Characteristics Distinguishing High-growth Ventures", *Journal of Business Venturing*, 8, no. 2, March 1993, p. 169.

[11] *1990 Small Business Report* (New York: American Institute of Certified Public Accountants, 1990). See also *Inc.*, October 1990, p. 152.

[12] Cooper and others, *New Business In America*, p. 4.

Case Questions:

General Questions

1. Project the reasonably possible highest annual rate of wealth increase this venture could generate for the entrepreneur. State the main assumptions on which this projection is predicated, and comment on the likelihood that they could come true.

2. Assess the qualifications and proclivities of this particular entrepreneur for undertaking the particular type of venture he has in mind.

3. Critique the actual career path to date that the entrepreneur in the assigned case has taken and assess its appropriateness to the particular type of venture he or she is undertaking.

4. Within the realm of what is reasonably likely, design an ideal career path for undertaking the venture this entrepreneur has in mind. To what other types of ventures might such a career path be suited?

5. Develop a projection along which the venture might develop for two or three years. Describe the options for the entrepreneur to get out of it at three points along that path. State which of the options you think would be best and why at each of those three points.

6. Identify the assets, both intangible and tangible, that the entrepreneur has built into the venture as of the time of the assigned case. Specify the dollar value you think each of these two types of assets should have as of the time of the assigned case to:

    a. The entrepreneur.
    b. Two contrasting potential buyers, real or hypothetical.

Cliff Dow and Steve Shaper   p. 681

1. What are the price and terms at which buying the business should be attractive to Cliff?

2. Explain the likelihood that the business should be worth more to someone other than Cliff.

3. Judging from Cliff's experience what could a person do to increase chances of encountering a buyout opportunity like this?

Ampersand (G)   p. 689

1. What should the team do about the coated Masonite purchase opportunity and why?

2. What appear to be the team's best options for making the most of Ampersand as of the end of the case?

3. What is your assessment of the career direction members of the Ampersand team have chosen? Have they reached a "point of no return" on this career path? Where is (or was) that point and why?

4. Now that you have a year of hindsight on the Ampersand business plan, how would you change it if you had known when it was written what you know now?

5. Could more education about entrepreneurship have enabled the Ampersand team members to have done anything better than they did, and if so, how?

Cliff Dow and Steve Shaper

In June 1990, four months after receiving his MBA degree from New Hampshire University, Cliff Dow was contemplating with his wife and with another couple whether to drop his job hunting plans and instead buy a store selling classical guitars in Portland, Maine. He knew he was on the "short list" of a major national consulting firm which had said it would notify him with the next month whether it would hire him. He expected the consulting work would be able to pay him more than working in the store, but the job was not certain to materialize. The store, however, had just been put up for sale by its owner, and both Cliff and his prospective partner, Steve Shaper, expected it might sell soon, as the owner said there were already several buyers who said they were seeking financing and expected to make offers within the next week or two.

The Company

Classicraft Guitars was a 15-year-old store in the old section of Portland, which in recent years had been transformed into a chic shopping and tourist area. The first owners of the store had been practicing musicians who had developed it as a sideline and, according to Cliff, given it a good reputation as a source of high-quality instruments with a non-commercial atmosphere. In the back of the store, they had installed several soundproof rooms where they and others gave lessons in classical guitar playing.

Over time, however, the owners found there were conflicts between their occupation as musicians and the work of tending the store, and three years earlier they had sold it to a second owner. The buyer was a guitar maker, who rearranged part of the store into a work area where he both built and repaired instruments. He too, Cliff said, maintained a reputation for handling high-quality instruments and the store was known to have the largest selection of exclusively classic guitars in New England north of Boston. However, this owner had found himself in conflict between his instrument building work and that of tending store, and after three years decided to sell the store and confine his activities solely to manufacturing.

The store at this time utilized about 1,100 square feet on the ground floor of a four story building. It included an entry area approximately 15 feet wide, which opened off a side street near the main thoroughfare in Old Portland. Guitars were displayed in front windows about four feet wide on either side of the front door. Inside, there were guitars hanging along the wall on one side, and on the other side, a display of sheet music, records and instrument cases. At the back was a mahogany office desk with a computer terminal on top and a doorway leading farther back to a hallway with more guitars on the walls, a locked display case with the most expensive instruments costing up to $3,000 and two soundproofed practice rooms where two experienced teachers, one of whom was an initial founder of the store, gave guitar lessons.

Steve Shaper

Steve and Cliff had been friends since

working together as retail clerks for a sporting goods store. Steve spent some time in the service following high school, then went on to the University of Maine, where he received both his undergraduate degree and a Ph.D. in English. He then took a faculty position and became a professor of English. He had also been a serious student of classical guitar, taking lessons for many years and playing mainly for personal satisfaction. This avocation he shared with Cliff. The two also shared enthusiasm for long-distance running.

Steve's wife, Sharon, had studied business administration at Portland State and then gone on to become a C.P.A. with the Bangor office of a major national accounting firm. The couple did not have any children, but expected they would in the future.

Cliff Dow

Cliff had gone to the University of New Hampshire following high school. Initially he majored in engineering, but after his sophomore year, he transferred to business administration because it appeared to him that engineering offered "too much dull grind and not enough life. My Dad was an engineer," he said, "and frankly, it didn't look like all that much fun as a career."

Following graduation in 1979, Cliff took a series of jobs in retailing. The same year, he married his wife, Chris, whom he had met at the university through a common interest in running. In retailing he also gravitated toward athletics and worked mainly in sporting goods stores. Chris too went into retailing, starting as a clerk in a women's clothing store. By the time Cliff decided to go back to business school for an MBA degree, Chris had risen to upper management in a chain with 200 stores, over which she had responsibility.

Cliff, however, said he had grown tired of retailing and did not see attractive opportunity for further advancement. He de-

cided to major in finance and international business. On the side he had become interested in Japanese. As part of his degree program, he had completed a summer internship with a firm in Japan. He commented:

> As fate would have it, the Japanese company happened to be in retailing. So there I was again, back where I didn't want to be. But it was a good experience anyway.

Cliff also developed an interest in entrepreneurship, and even went so far as to extend his graduation by one quarter in order to take the university's entrepreneurship course. As a project for the course he developed a plan for a venture. He recalled:

> It was—you guessed it—a retail store. My concept was to start a store in sporting goods, which was something I had lots of experience in. It would differ from most sporting goods stores by offering a wider variety of products, lessons, tours and other sports-related services. It would aim to be the sporting goods superstore of them all. But when I tried to analyze it objectively I could not find a competitive advantage that really seemed likely to work against competitors who could readily imitate anything I came up with, and who would have the resources, skills and established position to do it as well or better.
>
> I learned a lot in the course about how businesses get started. I had developed confidence in some aspects of venturing, but not in my ability to spot a truly workable venture idea or to finance one even if I did find it. At the end I felt frustrated that I had not actually been able to extract from it a truly viable competitive entry wedge. I had

wanted the instructor to give me one. But what I found was that by the end of the course, I had developed a plan for a business idea that was not really workable and that I could not finance even if it was.

Worst of all, it seemed that the task of finding an effective entry wedge was still all up to me. It seemed as though all I could do was keep looking and try to be receptive to opportunity if and when it arose without being able to make it happen. So I really didn't see much likelihood of becoming involved with a venture in the foreseeable future, and I put aside the idea of becoming an entrepreneur.

Following graduation Cliff interviewed for jobs in several areas, particularly product management and management consulting. A major national accounting firm had shown serious interest in him as a potential recruit for its consulting activities. Several interviews followed, and the firm had told him that he was likely to receive an offer, but not for a month or two while the firm firmed up its overall staffing plans.

Shop For Sale

It was during this interlude that he noticed in a classical guitar magazine the advertisement for sale of Classicraft. He had started learning to play the guitar since before elementary school, and his interest in playing had continued ever since. Classicraft was a familiar place to him for buying instruments and music, and he shared the opinion of other classical guitarists that the store was tops in its geographical area for high-quality classical instruments.

He mentioned the advertisement to Steve Shaper and asked whether Steve might have any interest in pursuing it. As they talked, the idea seemed unlikely to work out. They estimated that the cost of a store like Classicraft would probably be in the range of $100,000 or so. That would be substantially beyond what they could pay without borrowing, and both doubted they would be able to get a loan to buy a business anyway. Cliff said:

We decided it couldn't hurt to approach the store owner and ask how much he wanted. We were surprised when he gave us a figure right off the bat. Then, when the figure turned out to be $30,000 we were even more surprised, and I had to work hard at suppressing delight. That is the kind of figure we can finance personally from savings.

Records of the store were minimal, consisting of a check ledger for expenses and a general ledger for keeping track of sales. The owner had also made available his tax filings for the preceding two years, copies of which appear in Exhibits 1 and 2. He was proposing to sell all the inventory, fixtures and furniture but retain his guitar building tools. The inventory consisted of finished guitars, sheet music and small items such as strings, picks, stands and cases, which he estimated were worth $19,000. The furniture and fixtures he said were worth approximately $5,000. As a total price, he told Cliff and Steve he wanted $30,000.

Two teachers each paid $150 per month for use of the practice rooms. Lesson charges were typically $25 per hour, of which the store received $2. Steve noted that one had been an initial founder of the store, and was very well known and respected in the local music community. He also taught in the music department of the university as well as at a local school of the arts.

Cliff and Steve had examined the store and made an asset list of their own. Based upon estimated purchase costs of inventory and estimated depreciated value of furniture and fixtures they reached an estimated total for the list of $18,592, as shown in Exhibit 3. Cliff noted that based upon his prior retailing experience, it seemed to him that the inventory turnover rate of some items was low and characteristic, at the values they had given it, of "dead stock." Based on historical figures he had projected turnover rates by category as shown in Exhibit 4. He concluded:

> There should be a turnover rate of at least 2.5 on any category, and on some it looks like the store is doing half that.

Cliff further commented that, although the present owner was a knowledgeable and pleasant person, he did not seem to be operating all that effectively.

> He is very low key and doesn't seem to use suggestion selling at all. At the same time, the store could seem intimidating to visitors. The guitars are not labeled, and they are tied down in a way that makes it hard to take them off the wall so they can be played. The owner doesn't really encourage people to play them, maybe because he's afraid they might get scratched, or because he is preoccupied with making and fixing instruments. Or maybe he just doesn't think people want to play them or would be more likely to buy them if it were easier to do so.
>
> The way he has sheet music and records stacked in milk crates isn't very orderly, and the workshop area creates dust that leaves the overall level of cleanliness lower than you could wish for. The store seems to me to be entirely out of some items that sell best, probably because the owner has had to make hard

choices between taking income and investing in inventory. There aren't any CD's at all in the stock or any electronic instruments or equipment like amplifiers.

Need for a Decision

> The question is whether we should do it and if so what terms and conditions we should propose to the owner. For me, it would mean dropping the possible job opportunity, which I expect might pay somewhere between $40,000 and $60,000 per year. There is no way Steve is going to quit his teaching job and move himself and his wife to Portland to run the store.
>
> He said he and his wife are willing to put up half the money if Chris and I put up the other half. But then, who takes responsibility for the store? Chris and I can get by on her income, but we definitely plan on expanding our family in the near future, and that will both require money and deflect her activities away from earning it. If I take on the store, that will plunk me right back into—there it goes again—retailing, though I must admit I really like the store, the guitars and other people who are interested in them.
>
> Steve and I figure we have enough interest in this possibility that we should figure out what steps would best be involved in going ahead with it before we decide whether to do that or to drop it. He tells me that, after all, I'm the one who studied business and should be able to spell out all the considerations, contingencies, best plan, pros and cons of going ahead. If we don't move on this thing fast and in the right way, it seems to us very likely that someone else will. So there I am. What should I say?

EXHIBIT 1   Classicraft Tax Filing for 1988

| SCHEDULE C
(Form 1040)

Department of the Treasury
Internal Revenue Service (3)
Name of proprietor | **Profit or Loss From Business**
(Sole Proprietorship)
Partnerships, Joint Ventures, Etc., Must File Form 1065.
▶ Attach to Form 1040, Form 1041, or Form 1041S.   ▶ See Instructions for Schedule C (Form 1040). | OMB No. 1545-0074
1988
Attachment
Sequence No. 09 |

Name of proprietor
Randolph Price
Business: Retail Sales - Classical Guitars and Accesories
Principal Business Code: 4333
Business Name and Address: Classicraft Guitars,
*   41 Lundy Lane, Portland, ME 04102*

E Method(s) used to value closing inventory:
  (1) ☒ Cost   (2) ☐ Lower of cost or market   (3) ☐ Other (attach explanation)

F Accounting method: (1) ☐ Cash   (2) ☒ Accrual   (3) ☐ Other (specify) ▶ ....

	Yes	No
G Was there any change in determining quantities, costs, or valuations between opening and closing inventory? (If "Yes," attach explanation.)		x
H Are you deducting expenses for business use of your home? (If "Yes," see Instructions for limitations.)	Y	
I Did you "materially participate" in the operation of this business during 1988? (If "No," see Instructions for limitations on losses.)	x	

J If this schedule includes a loss, credit, deduction, income, or other tax benefit relating to a tax shelter required to be registered, check here . ▶ ☐
If you check this box, you MUST attach Form 8271.

Part I Income

1a Gross receipts or sales	**1a**	90,462 53
b Less: Returns and allowances	**1b**	1,800 00
c Subtract line 1b from line 1a. Enter the result here	**1c**	88,662 53
2 Cost of goods sold and/or operations (from Part III, line 8)	**2**	48,186 54
3 Subtract line 2 from line 1c and enter the gross profit here	**3**	40,475 99
4 Other income (including windfall profit tax credit or refund received in 1988)	**4**	
5 Add lines 3 and 4. This is the gross income ▶	**5**	40,475 99

Part II Deductions

6 Advertising	**6**	650 74	**23** Repairs	**23**		51 22
7 Bad debts from sales or services (see Instructions)	**7**		**24** Supplies (not included in Part III)	**24**		305 50
8 Bank service charges	**8**	591 74	**25** Taxes	**25**		1,398 11
9 Car and truck expenses	**9**		**26** Travel, meals, and entertainment:			
10 Commissions	**10**		**a** Travel	**26a**		
11 Depletion	**11**		**b** Meals and entertainment		88 00	
12 Depreciation and section 179 deduction from Form 4562 (not included in Part III)	**12**	2,694 91	**c** Enter 20% of line 26b subject to limitations (see Instructions)			
13 Dues and publications	**13**	133 90	**d** Subtract line 26c from 26b	**26d**		88 00
14 Employee benefit programs	**14**		**27** Utilities and telephone	**27**		3029 95
15 Freight (not included in Part III)	**15**	522 23	**28a** Wages			
16 Insurance	**16**	647 27	**b** Jobs credit			
17 Interest:			**c** Subtract line 28b from 28a	**28c**		
a Mortgage (paid to banks, etc.)	**17a**		**29** Other expenses (list type and amount):			
b Other	**17b**	3,878 27	*Contributions....10.00*			
18 Laundry and cleaning	**18**		*License/Permits.105.00*			
19 Legal and professional services	**19**	295 00	*Security System.462.00*			
20 Office expense	**20**	271 11	*Training/Education.945.00*			
21 Pension and profit-sharing plans	**21**					
22 Rent on business property	**22**	10,625 00		**29**		1522 00

30 Add amounts in columns for lines 6 through 29. These are the total deductions ▶	**30**	26,704 95
31 Net profit or (loss). Subtract line 30 from line 5. If a profit, enter here and on Form 1040, line 12, and on Schedule SE, line 2. If a loss, you MUST go on to line 32. (Fiduciaries, see instructions.)	**31**	13,371 04

32 If you have a loss, you MUST check the box that describes your investment in this activity (see Instructions) . . . .
  32a ☐ All investment is at risk.
  32b ☐ Some investment is not at risk.
If you checked 32a, enter the loss on Form 1040, line 12, and Schedule SE, line 2. If you checked 32b, you MUST attach Form 6198.

For Paperwork Reduction Act Notice, see Form 1040 Instructions.   Schedule C (Form 1040) 1988

EXHIBIT 2   Classicraft Tax Filing for 1989

.OULE C n 1040) epartment of the Treasury Internal Revenue Service (3)	**Profit or Loss From Business** (Sole Proprietorship) Partnerships, Joint Ventures, Etc., Must File Form 1065. ▶ Attach to Form 1040 or Form 1041. ▶ See Instructions for Schedule C (Form 1040).	OMB No 1545-0074 **1989** Attachment Sequence No. 09

Name of proprietor
Randolph Price
Business: Retail Sales - Classical Guitars and Accesories
Principal Business Code: 4333
Business Name and Address: Classicraft Guitars,
    41 Lundy Lane, Portland, ME 04102

E Method(s) used to value closing inventory.   (1) ☒ Cost   (2) ☐ Lower of cost or market   (3) ☐ Other (attach explanation)   (4) ☐ Does not apply (if checked, skip line G)

F Accounting method: (1) ☐ Cash   (2) ☒ Accrual   (3) ☐ Other (specify) ▶ ....

		Yes	No
G	Was there any change in determining quantities, costs, or valuations between opening and closing inventory? (If "Yes," attach explanation.)		X
H	Are you deducting expenses for business use of your home? (If "Yes," see Instructions for limitations.)		X
I	Did you "materially participate" in the operation of this business during 1989? (If "No," see Instructions for limitations on losses.)	X	

J If this schedule includes a loss, credit, deduction, income, or other tax benefit relating to a tax shelter required to be registered, check here . ▶ ☐
If you checked this box, you MUST attach Form 8271

Part I Income

1	Gross receipts or sales	1	92,046 71
2	Returns and allowances	2	250 00
3	Subtract line 2 from line 1. Enter the result here	3	91,796 71
4	Cost of goods sold and/or operations (from line 39 on page 2)	4	52,686 64
5	Subtract line 4 from line 3 and enter the gross profit here	5	39,110 07
6	Other income, including Federal and state gasoline or fuel tax credit or refund (see Instructions) . . .	6	42 13
7	Add lines 5 and 6. This is your gross income . . . . ▶	7	39,152 20

Part II Expenses

8	Advertising	8	2872 16	22 Repairs	22	18 92
9	Bad debts from sales or services (see Instructions)	9		23 Supplies (not included in Part III) .	23	202 13
10	Car and truck expenses . . .	10		24 Taxes	24	737 69
11	Commissions	11		25 Travel, meals, and entertainment:		
12	Depletion	12		a Travel	25a	
13	Depreciation and section 179 deduction from Form 4562 (not included in Part III) . . .	13	2824 63	b Meals and entertainment .		120 50
				c Enter 20% of line 25b subject to limitations (see Instructions) . . .		24 10
14	Employee benefit programs (other than on line 20)	14		d Subtract line 25c from line 25b	25d	96 40
15	Freight (not included in Part III) .	15	353 09	26 Utilities (see Instructions) . .	26	1547 04
16	Insurance (other than health) . .	16	622 44	27 Wages (less jobs credit) . .	27	
17	Interest:			28 Other expenses (list type and amount):		
a	Mortgage (paid to banks, etc.) .	17a		Security System......462.00		
b	Other	17b	4033 76	Training/Education...500		
18	Legal and professional services .	18	1295 00	....		
19	Office expense	19	1211 56	....		
20	Pension and profit-sharing plans .	20		....		
21	Rent or lease:			....		
a	Machinery and equipment . .	21a		....		
b	Other business property . . .	21b	10,975 00		28	

29	Add amounts in columns for lines 8 through 28. These are your **total expenses** . . . . . . ▶	29	27,256 82
30	**Net profit or (loss).** Subtract line 29 from line 7. If a profit, enter here and on Form 1040, line 12, and on Schedule SE, line 2. If a loss, you MUST go on to line 31. (Fiduciaries, see Instructions.)	30	11,895 38
31	If you have a loss, you MUST check the box that describes your investment in this activity (see Instructions). . . . . If you checked 31a, enter the loss on Form 1040, line 12, and Schedule SE, line 2. If you checked 31b, you MUST attach Form 6198	31a ☐ All investment is at risk. 31b ☐ Some investment is not at risk.	

For Paperwork Reduction Act Notice, see Form 1040 Instructions.   Schedule C (Form 1040) 1989

EXHIBIT 3   **Tally of Classicraft Assets By Cliff & Steve as of October 11, 1990 (dollars)**

Inventory	Value	Furnishings	Value	Fixtures	Value	Depreciables	Value
		Velvet wall	128	Carpet	234	Fixtures	3,232
Guitars		Posters	81	Floor tile	204	Furnishings	3,051
Carlos 080	400	Flwrs & vase	51	Slide window	51	Total	6,283
Granini 1/4	70	Seashell	8	Slide door	127	(Acc depn)	-2,255
Granini 3/4	73	3 humidifiers	170	Track lights	595	Book Value	4,028
Castilla 3/4	40	Desk chair	68	Adj light fixt	18		
4 F Saez 4A	572	Teak desk	213	Wood doors	20		
P Saez 6A	153	Large fan	25	Wood beam	34	**Assets**	
P Saez 8A	168	Small fan	17	Paneling	82	Inventory	14,596
Artensano 20	137	2 metal chairs	34	Plaster board	51	Book F&F	4,028
Tak C1325	255	2 wood chairs	26	Access. shelf	26	New items	328
Dauphin 535	467	Wood stool	21	Record shelf	10	Total	18,952
Hirade 7	620	Bulletin board	13	Bath shelf	13		
Hirade 8	660	Oak displ case	510	Mirror	4		
Hirade 10	1,050	Small oak case	34	Guitar cabinet	213		
Osterby 17	1,800	Oak shelf	191	Alarm system	359		
Total	6,465	Coffee table	17	Storage cab	213		
		Lamp	51	Book display	127		
Cases		Orientl rugs 2	213	Door alarm	17		
7 GC 318	105	Carpet pieces	4	Hanging sign	510		
GC 316	14	Clock radios 2	26	Wall sign	128		
Used	25	Trunk	42	Door handles	106		
SLM	58	Kitch appli.	42	Front window	90		
AT	65	Humidity gage	13	Total	3,232		
2 ATB Blk	138	File boxes	60				
2 ATB Brn	146	Plastic crates	37				
Total	551	Waste baskets	14	**New items (Expensed)**			
Lights & dec.	51	Floor light	15				
Other (est)		Extension cords	13	Large fan	31		
Accessories	830	Display guitar	38	Small fan	16		
Records	450	Interior signs	64	Folding chairs 4	35		
Music, Books	5,400	Sndwch sgns 2	723	Couch	130		
Strings	900	Fire exting.	34	Phone	56		
Total	7,580	Cash box	4	Calculator	45		
Card table	15	Total	3051	Total	328		

EXHIBIT 4   Classicraft Turnover Computed by Cliff

	Guitars	Strings	Access.	Books	Records
1990 Proj. Sales	59,235	5,185	3,886	8286	474
CGS %	56	41	56	68	58
1990 CGS	33,172	2,126	2,176	5,634	275
Inventory @ Book	7,016	900	830	5,400	450
Inv. Turnover	4.73	2.36	2.62	1.04	0.61

Ampersand (G)

December 1993 - Commitment Decisions

Following the successful sales demonstration week at Pearl Paint, the Ampersand team had moved ahead on setting up their own production plant. Plant space at a bargain rate had been located through assistance from contacts of the Austin Technology Incubator. Scott and Robert had flown all over the country locating machinery that would be needed for painting, drying and cutting. They now had their initial capitalization, $100,000 as a first installment with more promised contingent on performance and need. They were encountering a series of decisions about how best to apply it.

They expected to need sharply increased Claybord production the coming months to provide samples and to meet demand as it expanded at Pearl Paint and developed at other stores. The first production run had almost all been shipped, and the team wanted to get more inventory as quickly as possible. But the plant space that had been lined up would not be available until August, and installing machinery seemed likely to take well into September. How could the team get more inventory before that?

The team decided to try repeating the steps they had followed on the first production run. They contacted the shop in Tyler and asked the owner if he would relent on his policy of not taking any more of their work. His answer was a firm, "no". But there was no other choice, they said. They had to have his help for coating the boards. Just this one more time, and then

they should be able to do the work in their own plant. Finally, the shop owner agreed, but just this one more time and that was it!

But then there would be another round of all that tedious hand sanding. Scott looked for other alternatives. Based on many phone calls and visits around Texas there did not seem to be any. Finally, Scott located a company near Dallas with an automated sander and the owner there agreed to let the team use it for $1,300 to process the coated boards. Scott commented:

> It sanded the 2,000 Claybords in just six hours. The only trouble, aside from what seemed like an exorbitant charge for that amount of time, was that the sander didn't get the boards smooth enough. It put on scratches that we had to grind away with our same old hand-held sander process anyway.

Maybe, the team thought, a change in the coating process would help. They decided to try a different primer on the Masonite prior to application of the clay layer. Experimentally, they tried different materials, baking a clay layer on them using the oven in Kathy's kitchen. Finally, they found one that seemed to help. This added some cost for the extra layer. But at the same time, it seemed to reduce the sanding needed, although more experimenting would be needed to ascertain how much.

Checking into the cost of obtaining Masonite coated with this primer, they learned that they could buy a single load of 2,000 4x8 foot Masonite sheets with primer already on them for $19,000. Until now they had been paying $15 each for plain panels. How much might this help the bottom line, they wondered, and should they go for the volume purchase? Estimated financial statements for the period ending December 31, 1993 appear in Exhibits 1 and 2.

One reason to be cautious about the volume purchase, the team could see, was that sales had been considerably below expectation. The team had at first thought they could sell through distributors who would buy in large quantities, around $3,000 on average per order. The distributors would use these quantities to feed smaller amounts to the hundreds of retail art supply stores around the country. In fact, however, no distributors at all had bought the product as of December 1993, mainly because the stores had not asked them for it.

Kathy and Elaine had consequently retargeted their personal selling efforts at the retail stores themselves. They had mounted an advertising campaign through art magazines and developed an introductory package consisting of a display rack and several sizes of Claybord to be put in it. This package was priced to the store at $270. The team's expectation was that smaller stores would buy just this package and that larger stores would order the package plus additional Claybord in quantities similar to the first order for $5,300 that the company had received from Pearl Paint.

All efforts to recruit distributors had been discontinued in July 1993 as Kathy and Elaine began contacting stores. Typically, they would first telephone, inform the store that a new product was available,

briefly mention the advantages of Claybord and ask if they could send a sample. After about one week they would telephone again. They would inform the store that it would receive the same discount structure that normally went only to distributors. Such a discount, the team had learned through its early inquiries in the market, was rarely received by these stores. And they would ask if the store would be willing to place an order.

The typical answer by the store would be to say that they had not really had a chance to try out the product yet and it might be better to call again at some later time. At that point, Kathy or Elaine would inform the store of dates when they were planning to be in the store's area and ask for an appointment or permission to drop by and demonstrate Claybord.

Usually, the store would agree to such a visit. Kathy or Elaine would drop by the store and demonstrate the Claybord. A typical demonstration consisted of marking the board with ink or a marker pen and then rubbing it off. They might also mark on it with colored pencil and suggest to the store owner, "here, you try it." They would point out that the Claybord could be used with all types of media, including inks, oils and watercolors, and show a couple of actual pieces of art on Claybord painted with different media.

They would show the store a picture of the rack that came with all four sizes of Claybord for display and would reiterate the low price to the store that would result from its being given the distributor's discount. With this sales approach, Kathy and Elaine found they were able to obtain orders from about 70 percent of the stores they visited. By December 1993, they had placed Claybord in around 90 stores total.

To their disappointment both the small stores and the large stores were only buying the minimum $270 introductory package. Some chain stores were taking only the minimum order and dividing it among the stores in the chain.

Thus it appeared to the team that they were facing several decisions. Should they seek lower production costs by taking advantage of the volume purchasing opportunity? What should they do about the gap between expected sales they had depicted in their business plan and the actual sales they were getting? They were also aware that their bank balance had been declining.

EXHIBIT 1 - Ampersand Balance Sheet for the Period Ending December 31, 1993

Balance Sheet

Assets

Cash and Equivalents	$4,655
Accounts Receivable	17,051
Inventory	20,644
Prepaid Expenses	1,872
Total Current Assets	44,222
Plant and Equipment	56,362
Furniture and Fixtures	5,409
Accumulated Dep'n., Plant & Equipt.	(6,693)
Accumulated Dep'n., Furn. & Fixtures	(693)
Other Noncurrent Assets	9,287
Total Other Assets	63,673
Total Assets	107,895

Liabilities

Accounts Payable	$13,766
Accrued Expenses Payable	874
Accrued Taxes Payable	3,328
Current Debt Due	13,568
Long Term Debt	291,107
Other Long Term Note	5,000
Total Liabilities	327,643

Equity

Capital Stock	1,000
Paid In Capital	4,555
Retained Earnings	(225,303)
Total Equity	(219,748)
Total Liabilities and Equity	107,895

EXHIBIT 2 - Ampersand Income Statement for 1993

Income Statement

Revenue

Claybord Sales	$35,465
Artist Tool Sales	0
Other Art Boards	0
Royalties/Other Income	0
Total Revenue	35,465

Cost of Goods Sold

Direct Costs	34,962
Mfg. Overhead	23,198
Depreciation	6,786
Other COGS	1,800
Total Cost of Goods Sold	66,746
Gross Profit	(31,281)

Expenses

Administrative	22,733
Marketing	108,697
Salary	48,697
R&D Expenditures	3,242
Other Expenses	6,297
Total Expenses	189,666
Operating Profit	(220,947)
Other Income	6,064
Other Expenses	10,420
Net Profit/(Loss)	(225,303)

Venture Plan Excerpts

This appendix presents excerpts of 18 important elements from a variety of unrelated venture plans. These elements and the pages they appear on are:

These excerpts are intended to illustrate alternative ways to convey information and to serve as a starting point for exploring ways to make plans better. Selected to stimulate ideas more than to serve as models, any of the excerpts can be criticized and improved upon. Questions the reader may wish to consider in examining them include:

- For what types of plans would the type of presentation in this excerpt be most suitable and for what types least suitable?

- What alternative forms of presentation could be used to convey the same information as this excerpt? Which ones would be most appropriate for what circumstances?

- How could this excerpt be improved? Would there be any way to modify the excerpt so that it would be able better to stand on its own and/or tell more about the venture without making it longer?

1 TABLE OF CONTENTS EXAMPLES

2 EXECUTIVE SUMMARY EXAMPLES

A. Passenger Airline

The company plans to offer scheduled jet passenger service in the Seattle-San Francisco, Seattle-Denver and San Francisco-Denver markets. The company expects that its principal competitors will include the following commercial airlines: United, Western, Alaska, Northwest, PSA, Wien and Frontier. All of these competitors are larger, have a history of successful airline operations and have greater financial resources than does Air Washington.

The company intends to compete on the basis of price, flight frequency and passenger service. For example, Air Washington's proposed fare in the Seattle-San Francisco market is $77. This fare represents a savings of 45 percent to 62 percent over current Tourist Class fares in that market. The proposed fare in both the Seattle-Denver market and San Francisco-Denver markets is $109. This fare represents a savings of approximately 57 percent over the current Tourist Class Fares in these markets.

Air Washington plans to provide a total of 11 round trips per day in its system, consisting of 6 round trips per day between Seattle and San Francisco, 2 round trips per day between Seattle and Denver, and 3 round trips per day between San Francisco and Denver.

The company plans to offer a high level of in-flight passenger service, including full meal service appropriate to the time of day, competitively priced liquor, full baggage service, and advance reservations and seat assignments. Few of the carriers currently service the company's proposed markets offer this combination of passenger service.

Most of the company's competitors incur greater costs, primarily due to higher equipment and labor costs. The company plans to operate modern, efficient airplanes with highly motivated and productive employees, thereby achieving cost savings that will allow it to charge lower fares and still generate a profit. For further details and elaboration see Exhibit B.

B. Tunneling Machine

The goal of this business plan is to secure venture capital for financing of the Ramex Corporation. The capital would be applied to the design, development, production and marketing costs of a proprietary tunneling machine. Based on an optimistic forecast, it is estimated that approximately $1.5 million would be required; however a commitment of approximately $2.6 million is requested, which would cover such contingencies as strikes, excessive lead time on critical components, interim financing for production machines, or unanticipated development problems. The design concept of the Ramex machine is based on the use of a massive reciprocating cutter head, which is driven by a 2-stroke, free-piston diesel engine. Energy developed by the reciprocating cutter head is used to fracture the rock at the tunnel face. The cuttings produced are then picked up and conveyed to the rear of the machine for removal from the tunnel. This concept offers several advantages over rotary machines, which are currently the accepted standard in the industry. These advantages include sharply higher penetration rates, greater reliability and reduced manufacturing cost of both cutters and machine. Because of these advantages it is believed that this machine will be capable of dominating the entire industry within a few years.

The development and testing of a full-scale prototype is expected to take two years. During the design and development phase the company would be primarily engineering oriented. As the development progresses, administrative functions would be phased in to produce and market the equipment. The first year of operation would be spent producing design drawings and in supervising the fabrication of the prototype by subcontractors. The second year would be spent in assembling the prototype and testing it in the shop. The last phase of development would be the on-site use of the machine by a prospective buyer. This last phase would provide the first expected source of revenue for the company. At the conclusion of this test period Ramex will begin full-scale marketing and production based on customer orders.

The basic design concept is a significant technological advance, and it is expected that the patents pending will insure that Ramex will retain exclusive rights for its production. The Ramex Corporation also expects that the tunneling machine will have excellent profitability potential both because of its proprietary nature and improved performance characteristics. Preliminary figures estimate that the production costs for a typical machine will be $380,000 and the selling price to be $1.2 million. Based on these estimates for a 10-foot diameter machine, the company can operate profitably with the sale of one machine per year. It is expected that sales volume will exceed $20 million per year within five years. The total potential market exceeds $60 million per year.

3 DESCRIPTIONS OF PRODUCTS AND SERVICES

A. Yacht Exchange

We propose to establish a mechanism by which yacht owners in Hawaii and the Puget Sound region can exchange sailing time on their vessels. We believe a significant market for this service exists, as it will provide the yacht owner with an opportunity to explore new waters at a cost of little more than that of sailing out of his own marina.

CONCEPTUAL PLAN

Pacific Yacht Exchange proposes to act as an intermediary between individuals who wish to trade sailing time on their boats. Traditional impediments to doing this have been problems associated with the mechanics of the exchange and with security. We intend to capitalize on the economies of scale available in both these areas.

Potential customers will be first contacted by advertisements placed in sailing periodicals based in the Northwest and Hawaii. Those who respond will be sent a brochure describing our service and the sailing opportunities in the matched area. An application form will also be sent which will be used as the primary screening device. This form will require both a resume' of sailing experience and a set of personal references. In addition, general facts about both the applicant and his yacht will be requested for matching purposes.

Having carefully examined and checked an applicant's qualifications and background, we will make arrangements to inspect the client's boat. This step is felt to be necessary in order to exclude poorly maintained vessels (and their owners) from consideration and to confirm some of the facts on the application form. A further benefit will be to enhance our credibility and rapport with the client. We also plan to take color photos of each yacht to provide to the client who will be matched with it.

Physical matching of clients will be accomplished with the aid of a microcomputer. Specific matching criteria to be used will be (in order of importance): boat size and equipment, age and family status, and personal factors (i.e., smoker vs. non-smoker). For the initial exchange we anticipate providing a model contract specifying the dates of the exchange and recourse should problems occur. Liability considerations will be clearly spelled out in the contract. The penalty for failure to provide sailing time received will be equal to the cost of a barebones charter rental. Whether P.Y.E. or the client should be responsible for collection is undetermined at this time. Legal advice will be sought in drafting the model contract. Future exchanges between the two parties will be accomplished without our participation.

While P.Y.E. will make every effort to insure that the exchanges go smoothly and will offer personal assistance should problems arise, we expect that the parties involved will take primary responsibility for the successful completion of the exchange.

B. Disk Drive Venture

PRIAM, a California corporation, was founded to develop, manufacture, and market mass storage devices for small business computers, distributed processors, and word processors. The initial product is a low-cost disk drive based on state-of-the-art Winchester technology.

Winchester disk technology was first introduced by IBM for its large systems due to the significantly lower cost, higher reliability, and higher capacity offered by this new technology. IBM shipped the first Winchester disk (IBM 3350) for the large S/370 systems in early 1976. PRIAM intends to rapidly bring this new 3350 technology to the small business computer market, thereby leap-frogging competitors who are using non-Winchester technology or early versions of Winchester (i.e., IBM 3340).

The uniqueness of PRIAM is that this product will be the lowest possible cost 30-40 megabyte Winchester disk drive using a fast-access mechanism.

The market for low-cost Winchester disk drives under 50 megabytes is expected to explode over the next five years. Unit shipments will reach levels experienced by today's floppy disks. This explosion will be driven by small business computing, distributed processing, and word processing demands for reliable, low-cost mass storage. The fastest growth segment within these markets will be multiple-terminal systems, which demand fast disk access capability to satisfy multiple users running multiple programs that share on-line data bases.

Competition also senses this market opportunity, and a variety of entrants are making plans or introducing products. Most entrants will find Winchester technology surprisingly difficult to design and manufacture efficiently. Shugart and CDC will be the toughest competitors. Shugart can be beaten on performance in multiple-terminal applications and matched in cost at the 30-megabyte capacity level. CDC can be beaten on cost. However, both companies have strong, established market positions and product introduction leads that will need to be overcome by PRIAM's superior price-performance product.

The PRIAM strategy is to capitalize on the window that has opened as a result of the expected shift to Winchester disk technology. The high twin barriers to entry of the difficult technology and heavy capital requirements will be overcome with a Winchester-experienced team and institutional-level financial backing. Product development will focus on achieving the low-cost design in a small, reliable package. Later product enhancements and additions will be aimed at building a disk product family. Financial leverage will be used during the launch, since most successful OEM businesses generate cash after momentum has been achieved. Manufacturing rights may be sold in Europe or Japan in order to minimize dilution. PRIAM will sell its product direct to OEM's in the U.S., but will initially use distribution offshore. Selling expense will be minimized by focusing on OEM's rather than end users. Other overheads will also be minimized to allow more effective price competition. PRIAM will target on the multiple-terminal small business computer (SBC), clustered word processing, and distributed processing markets. Initially, one or two large OEM's will be targeted to get the PRIAM disk accepted in the industry. Only one standard product will be offered, and variations/options will be limited. The factory will be focused on that single product, and costs will be driven down to achieve the low-cost position. Strong manufacturing controls will be emphasized to allow rapid but controlled growth. Time-phased investments will be made in automatic production equipment. Class 100 clean room conditions will be established to ensure superior product reliability.

Financing PRIAM will require an equity investment of $4.1 million during the first two years. The first round of financing will be $1.5 million. Other capital will be raised via an equipment lease line, a receivables line, and inventory advances.

C. Mobile Lung Densitometer

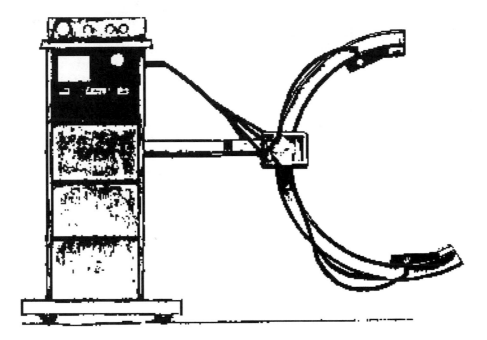

4 NOTATION OF RISK FACTORS

Magazine

Projections. This Prospectus contains certain financial projections. Although no representations can be made that the circulation or advertising levels indicated by the projections will be achieved or that projected costs or cash flow will correspond even approximately to actual costs or cash flow, those projections reflect the current estimates of management of the results that are likely if circulation or advertising can be increased and the costs controlled as reflected herein. These projections are subject to the uncertainties inherent in any attempt to predict the results of operations for the next five years, especially where a new business in involved.

Additional Capital. Assuming the test projections are successful and publication of the magazine is commenced, it is estimated that at least $1 million of new capital will be required before positive cash flow is achieved. There are no commitments for any of these funds, and no assurances can be given that such funds will be available, and if available, no prediction can be made of the terms and conditions of such additional financing. Partners in the Partnership will be given the right to participate in this additional financing. To the extent this right it not exercised, a substantial dilution of the partners' interests will probably result.

Staff. To commence publication of the new magazine, it will be necessary to recruit a new staff. A full staff has not yet been recruited, and no assurance can be given that a qualified staff can be hired on reasonable terms.

Taxation. For the tax treatment of gains or losses to Limited Partners of the Partnership, see "Federal Income Tax Consequences."

General Risk. Starting a new magazine is a highly speculative undertaking and has historically involved a substantial degree of risk. The ultimate profitability of any magazine depends on its appeal to its readers and advertisers in relation to the cost of production, circulation, and distribution. Appeal to readers and advertisers is impossible to predict and depends upon the interaction of many complex factors.

Competition. The magazine business his highly competitive. In promoting the sale of *Venture*, management will be competing with many established companies having substantially greater financial resources.

5 COMPETITOR ANALYSIS DISPLAY

(Disguised due to confidentiality)

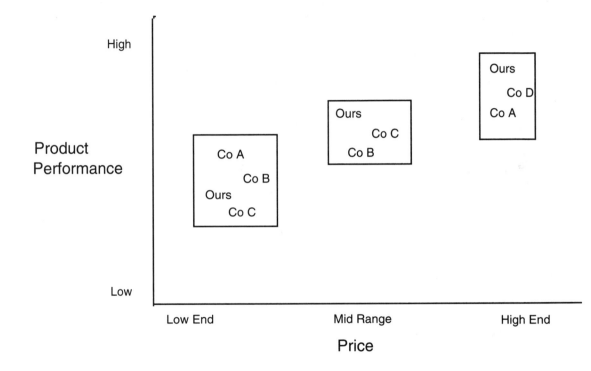

6 MARKET SURVEY RESULTS

A. Electronic Equipment Manufacturers

FIRM	Do own design	Familiar with CAD/CAM	Use CAD/CAM	Can afford own CAD/CAM	Are Interested in our services
Ospcon Ind.	yes	yes	no	no	yes
Eldec Corp.	yes	yes	have one	-	-
Circuits Eng. Inc.	no	-	-	-	-
Avtech Corp.	yes	yes	buying one	-	-
Solid State Syst.	no	-	-	-	-
Weico Corp.	yes	yes	no	no	yes
URS Inc.	yes	yes	have one	-	-
Universal Manuf. Corp.	no	-	-	-	-
Interface Mech.	yes	yes	no	no	no
Huntron Instru.	yes	yes	no	no	no
DDP Systems, Inc.	yes	yes	have one	-	-
Advanced Electronic App.	yes	yes	no	no	yes
Albar	yes	yes	no	no	no
Fluke John Mfg. Co.	yes	yes	yes	-	-
Micro-Mation Inc.	yes	yes	no	no	yes
Pacific Applied Electr.	no	-	-	-	-
APS Electronics Group	yes	yes	no	no	yes
DC Electronics Inc.	no	-	-	-	-

Of the ones who design:

Familiar with CAD/CAM	100.0%
Actual users	38.5%
Cannot afford own CAD/CAM system	61.5%

Of the ones who design and cannot afford a CAD/CAM:

Interested in our services	62.5%

7 MARKETING PLAN ELEMENTS SUMMARY

Plan For Distribution & Promotion of the Sperm Motility Meter

	Distribution	Promotion
Year 1	1) Seminars/Symposiums 2) Personal contacts - Dr. Lee. 3) Mail and telephone orders 4) Central Office Manager for traveling, sales and marketing efforts	1) Publish paper 2) Word of mouth 3) Brochures for seminars, mailings
Year 2	1) Seminars/Symposiums 2) 3-4 Salespeople for traveling sales and marketing efforts 3) Mail and telephone orders	1) Advertising in professional and scientific journals 2) Media 'free' promotion 3) Word of mouth 4) Brochures for seminars and mailings
Year 3	1) 10-12 Salespeople for traveling sales and marketing efforts 2) Mail and telephone orders	1) Advertising in professional & scientific journals 2) Brochures for seminars and mailings

This plan is analyzed quantitatively in the financial projections of Appendix A.

8 PRICING RATIONALE

	Labor Hours	Material	
Fan Rotor		$2,500	
Fan Box	80	200	
Gear Box & Install	20	500	
Test	20		
Box & Ship	8	50	
Misc. Hardware		25	
Balance	2	125	
Other, Outside Service		50	
	130 Hrs.		3,450

Labor Cost	$7/Hr. x 130 Hrs. =	910
Labor O/H		910

Labor & O/H Total   1,820

Total Cost $5,270

Assume 30-percent gross profit
  (This amount to revenue on Operating Income Exhibit)   2,266

Selling Price $7,536

9 SALES PROJECTIONS

A. Target Market Area: Washington State 1981, Year 1

Projected undergraduate degrees conferred in market area: 14,284

Area of Study	Number of Degrees	System Usage Rate (in %) Best /Expect/Worst			Number Using Service Best/ Expect/ Worst		
Business	2100	60	50	30	1260	1050	378
Education	1257	50	20	—	628	251	0
Social Science	1776	45	20	—	799	355	0
Public Affairs	529	45	20	—	238	106	0
Health Professions	914	40	30	10	411	274	91
Fine and Applied Arts	476	30	10	—	143	48	0
Physical Science	311	55	40	20	171	124	62
Biological Science	745	55	40	20	410	298	148
Communications	435	40	20	—	174	87	0
Engineering	714	60	50	30	428	357	214
Agriculture	568	50	15	5	284	85	28
Others	4459	25	10	5	1115	446	223
Total	14281				6061	3481	1144

Target Market Area: Washington, Oregon, Idaho & California 1984, Year 2
Projected undergraduate degrees conferred in market area: 107,582

Area of Study	Number of Degrees	System Usage Rate (in %) Best /Expect/Worst			Number Using Service Best/ Expect/ Worst		
Business	13938	60	52	30	8363	7248	4181
Education	7187	50	25	—	3594	1797	0
Social Science	17912	45	25	—	8060	4478	0
Public Affairs	3527	45	25	—	1587	882	0
Health Professions	4450	40	35	10	1780	1557	445
Fine and Applied Arts	5254	30	15	—	1576	788	0
Physical Science	1483	55	45	20	816	667	296
Biological Science	7300	55	45	20	4015	3285	1460
Communications	1928	40	25	—	771	482	0
Engineering	3618	60	50	30	2171	1809	1085
Agriculture	2859	50	25	5	1430	715	143
Others	38126	25	15	5	9311	5719	1906
Total	107582				43694	28703	9516

10 START-UP MILESTONES

7/82	1/83	7/83	1/84	7/84	1/85	7/85	1/86	7/86	1/87	7/87
Clinical Traits	Publication of results	Begin Production	Delivery of first Lung Densitometer			Sustained Production				
Market Research; Obtain Capital; Pro-totype Development	Marketing; Obtain Kickoff Orders									

Radtech, Inc. Schedule

7/82	1/83	7/83	1/84	7/84	1/85	7/85	1/86	7/86	1/87	7/87
Commitment for Lung Densitometer			Delivery of first Lung Densitometer	Commitment for Second Project		Commitment for Third Project	First Delivery of 2nd Project	Commitment for 4th Project	First Delivery of 3rd Project	Commitment for 4th Project

11 GANTT CHART

	1/1	2/1	3/1	4/1	5/1	6/1	7/1	8/1	9/1	10/1	11/1

Develop venture plan and define concept.

Identify specific equip., personnel, and financial requirements.

Investigate and evaluate available CAD/CAM hardware and software.

Procure market demand information through a local market research company.

Draft job descriptions and initiate personnel search.

With "GO" decisions consult lawyer and accountant.

Hire computer consultant.

Develop standards and operating procedures.

Select and train personnel.

Begin soliciting purchase orders.

Take delivery on system.

Begin operations.

12 PERT CHART

A. Items

For VTC - For The First Year of Operations

Project	Activity	Time Required (months)	Precedence
A.	Preliminary Activities	4	-
1.	Finalize incorporation arrangements		
2.	Investigate sources of loan		
3.	Evaluate text program of product		
4.	Get legal aid - engage a lawyer		
5.	Enquire about tooling equipment		
B.	Establish contacts	3	-
1.	Contact suppliers of raw materials and equipment		
2.	Approach potential customers		
C.	Starting operations	2	A
1.	Incorporate officially		
2.	Secure loan		
3.	Set up office		
	- rent office space		
	- hire secretary		
	- arrange for utilities		
	- business insurance		
	- bank account		
	- set up accounting system		
4.	Buy tooling equipment		
D.	Place first order	1	B,C
E.	Deliver first order	1	D
F.	Aggressive marketing activities	continuous	E
G.	Evaluation of operations	2	E
1.	Product performance		
2.	Customer response		
3.	Competition's response		
4.	Level of sales		
5.	Cost and profitability		
H.	Further evaluation of expansion into manufacturing	3	E
I.	Decide on manufacturing	1	H
J.	Prepare for manufacturing operations	3	I
1.	Purchase necessary equipment		
2.	Additional employees		
3.	Additional space		
K.	Start full manufacturing operations	continuous	J

(See chart next page)

B.   *Chart*

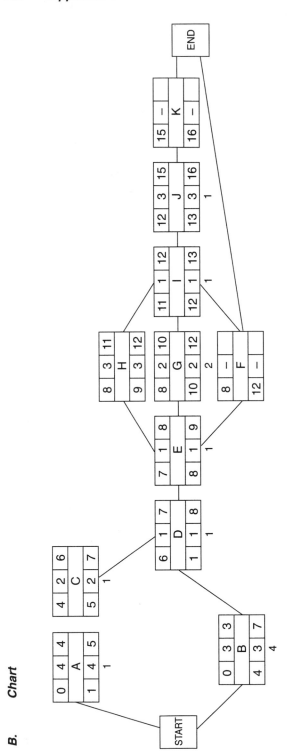

NOTE: Target for starting manufacturing is July 1990.
       Time available - 16 months.
       Time now March 1989 - period 0.
       Figures below the boxes represent the amount
       of float available - duration activity can be
       delayed without affecting operations.

KEY   D: Duration - Months

EST	D	EFT	EST: Earliest Start Time
-----	---	-----	EFT: Earliest Finish Time
Activity Code			LST: Latest Start Time
LST	D	LFT	LFT: Latest Finish Time

13 BREAK-EVEN ANALYSIS

Radio broadcasting is a relatively high fixed-cost business. The only variable cost element that changes month-to-month with sales is commissions. These commissions include payments to agency and internal sales personnel.

Consequently, the basic costs structure of the business is:

Sales	=	100%
Variable Costs	=	27%
Contribution	=	73%

Using a contribution margin of 75 percent, we can calculate a sales (profit) break-even and a cash break-even.

As noted in Exhibit 8, the percentage of agency commissions to total sales is 12 percent. The difference between 12 percent and 27 percent (total variable costs) represents commissions paid to representatives and manager overrides. This 15 percent amounts to $75,000—which is included in operating expenses of Exhibit 8. Once removed, total fixed costs are:

$$\$340,000 = (\$305,000 - 75,000) + 20,000 + 45,000 + 45,000$$

Consequently, "profit" break-even is:

$$\$466,000 = \frac{\$340,000}{.73}$$

By removing non-cash expenses (depreciation and amortization of goodwill), a "cash" break-even can be calculated as:

$$\$377,000 = \frac{\$340,000 - 20,000 - 45,000}{.73}$$

These break-evens represent respectively 93 percent and 75 percent of sales.

14 COST BREAKDOWN

Projected Expenses

Our "Expected" case assumption (see Exhibit 1) includes first-year expenses of $924,500. The larger dollar expenses for the first year are discussed below under separate headings. We assume that during 1983, we will receive cash payment for one-third of the revenue billed, but two-thirds will remain in accounts receivable until the following year. Also, the four officers will be able to contribute approximately $5,000 each for a total of $20,000. Therefore, a total of $619,500 is required from outside sources.

Prototype Development: Based on the success of clinical trials in the fall of 1982, we expect to complete our first production model prototype by January 1983. The costs associated with this specimen are listed below:

Off-shelf equipment:	$35,000	Mobile X-ray operator
	5,000	2 X-ray tubes at $2,500 each
	3,000	X-ray detectors and counting electronics
	5,000	Data acquisition and computer
Custom Machinery and labor:	6,000	C-arm assembly
	3,000	Machinery
	3,000	Engineer assembly
	———	
Total	$60,000	

The amount of $60,000 is the expected production cost of a machine and is used as the cost of sales estimate in pro forma income statements presented in Section IX. In addition to the $60,000, we expect to spend an additional $40,000 developing this prototype.

15 APPLICATION OF FUNDS

The Partnership will be formed for the purpose of developing and conducting a mailing to test the feasibility of founding a business magazine called *"Venture . . .* the magazine for entrepreneurs." A positive response to the test mailing in excess of 2 percent would generally be required before advancing to the next stage of the magazine's development. If the response falls below this, the project will in all probability be abandoned and no salvage value is anticipated.

If the test is successful, the next step will be to prepare for the start of regular publication of the magazine, which will involve recruiting a staff, selling advertising, establishing relations with suppliers, commencing direct mail promotion, and raising a substantial amount of additional capital (see "Prepublication Phase").

It is projected that the proceeds of the sale of interests in the Partnership will be expended approximately in the following manner.

Direct Mail test	
(80,000 pieces)	$24,000
Advertising Agency	4,000
Office and Travel	2,250
Magazine Design	1,750
Legal	3,000
	$35,000

Interests in the Partnership will not be registered with the Securities and Exchange Commission. The Partnership is relying on an exemption from registration for the sale of securities, which do not involve a public offering. Accordingly, each purchaser will be required to agree that his purchase was not made with any present intention to resell, distribute, or in any way transfer or dispose of his interest in the Partnership, except in compliance with applicable securities laws, and that he meets the suitability standards described herein.

No person is authorized to give any information or representation not contained in this memorandum. Any information or representation not contained herein must not be relied upon as having been authorized by the Partnership for the General Partner.

16 PRO FORMA FINANCIAL STATEMENTS

PRO FORMA INCOME STATEMENT
(Best Case Scenario)

	in thousands of dollars				
	1990	1991	1992	1993	1994
Sales Revenue	$2,000	$5,280	$5,980	$6,160	$6,390
Expenses					
Cost of Goods Sold	624	894	1,055	1,108	1,393
Gross Margin	1,376	4,386	4,925	5,052	4,997
Selling & Admin Expense	30	79	90	92	96
Depreciation Expense	1	1	2	2	3
Salaries Expense	40	68	90	100	140
R and D Expense	40	106	239	246	256
Interest Expense	12	0	0	0	0
Utilities Expense	2	3	3	3	4
Insurance Expense	8	33	60	87	114
Total Overhead Expenses	133	290	484	531	613
Net Income Before Taxes	1,243	4,096	4,441	4,521	4,384
Income Tax Expense	497	1,639	1,776	1,808	1,754
Net Income After Taxes	$746	$2,458	$2,665	$2,712	$2,631

PRO FORMA BALANCE SHEET

	in thousands of dollars				
Assets	1990	1991	1992	1993	1994
Current Assets					
Cash	$224	$1,673	$4,278	$6,931	$9,214
Accts. Receivable	250	660	748	770	799
Inventory	50	132	150	154	160
Misc.	20	53	60	62	64
Fixed Assets					
Tooling	240	580	509	641	1,068
Molding Machine	0	140	182	140	98
End Mill	0	44	57	44	31
Oven	0	11	9	7	4
Total Assets	784	3,293	5,992	8,748	11,437
Liabilities					
Current Liabilities	5	13	15	15	16
Other Liabilities	20	53	60	62	64
Total Liabilities	25	66	75	77	80
Owner's Equity					
C/S (1.8MM Shares)	12	12	12	12	12
Retained Earnings	746	3,204	5,868	8,581	11,211
Total Equity & Liabilities	$783	$3,282	$5,955	$8,670	$11,303

17 CASH FLOW PROJECTION

First Year Cash Flow Chart

Month	1	2	3	4	5	6	7	8	9	10	11	12	Yr
Cash at beginning	$0	$153,883	$125,958	$98,033	$70,108	$50,978	$31,848	$12,718	$15,574	$18,430	$21,286	$46,129	
Revenue Receipts		13,192	13,192	13,192	21,987	21,987	21,987	43,973	43,973	43,973	65,960	65,960	369,376
Cash from Outside Src	675,000	0	0	0	0	0	0	0	0	0	0	0	675,000
Tot. Cash Avail.	675,000	167,075	139,150	111,225	92,095	72,965	53,835	56,691	59,547	62,403	87,246	112,089	1,044,378
Operating Expenditures													
Salaries	28,817	28,817	28,817	28,817	28,817	28,817	28,817	28,817	28,817	28,817	28,817	28,817	
Maintenance	4,050	4,050	4,050	4,050	4,050	4,050	4,050	4,050	4,050	4,050	4,050	4,050	
Office Lease	1,250	1,250	1,250	1,250	1,250	1,250	1,250	1,250	1,250	1,250	1,250	1,250	
Tel. & Util.	1,000	1,000	1,000	1,000	1,000	1,000	1,000	1,000	1,000	1,000	1,000	1,000	
Advertising	15,000	3,000	3,000	3,000	3,000	3,000	3,000	3,000	3,000	3,000	3,000	3,000	
R&D	2,000	2,000	2,000	2,000	2,000	2,000	2,000	2,000	2,000	2,000	2,000	2,000	
Misc.	1,000	1,000	1,000	1,000	1,000	1,000	1,000	1,000	1,000	1,000	1,000	1,000	
Tot. Operating	$53,117	$41,117	$41,117	$41,117	$41,117	$41,117	$41,117	$41,117	$41,117	$41,117	$41,117	$41,117	$505,404
Other Cash Expenditures													
CAD/CAM Systm	$450,000												
Off. Site Prep.	10,000												
Furniture	5,000												
Legal & Acct.	3,000												
Total Other	$468,000												$468,000
Fed. Income Tax	0	0	0	0	0	0	0	0	0	0	0	0	0
Tot. Cash Expen.	$521,117	$41,117	$41,117	$41,117	$41,117	$41,117	$41,117	$41,117	$41,117	$41,117	$41,117	$41,117	$973,404
Cash at end	$153,883	$125,958	$98,033	$70,108	$50,978	$31,848	$12,718	$15,574	$18,430	$21,286	$46,129	$70,972	$70,972

18 FOOTNOTES TO FINANCIAL PROJECTIONS

1   Estimated at $48,000 per machine; $38,400 in lots of 10 (20-percent manufacturing discount)

2   Estimated at $12,000 per machine

3   One salesperson at $10,000 base salary plus 5-percent gross sales commission 1/83 to 1/85
    Two salespeople 1985, 1986; 3 for 1987

4   Includes cost of attending annual medical equipment trade show at $8,000

5   Four officers: CEO at $30,000, others at $25,000 for 1983, 1984; CEO at $60,000, others at $50,000 for 1985, 1986, 1987

6   One salesperson 1985, 1986
    Two salespeople 1987

7   One salesperson 1983
    Two salespeople 1984, 1985
    Three salespeople 1986
    Four salespeople 1987

8   Four officers: CEO at $30,000, others at $25,000 for 1983, 1984; CEO at $100,000, others at $85,000 for 1985, 1986, 1987

9   Capital needed:

First-year expenses	($924,500.)
Expect to receive one-third gross sales, two-thirds as accounts receivable	285,000.
Capital needed	639,500.
Contributed by officer	20,000.
Required from outside funding	($619,500.)

Venture Plan Rating Form
San Diego State University

This appendix presents the forms given to judges for evaluating the venture plans of an international venture plan competition conducted annually by the School of Business at San Diego State University. They were adapted by San Diego State from forms prepared and copyrighted by Dr. Alan J. Grant for use in a venture plan contest held annually at Babson College for Babson students and are reproduced here with permission.

SAN DIEGO STATE UNIVERSITY
Entrepreneurial Management Center

NORTH AMERICAN INVITATIONAL BUSINESS PLAN COMPETITION

Spring 1993

EVALUATION CRITERIA

Feasibility of the Business Plan. The winner(s) will be the individual or team whose plan conveys the most promising combination of significant capital gains potential, attractive investment possibilities, and actual implementation; i.e., the more likely the plan is to become a going venture, the better.

Product/Service Description. The business plan should provide a clear description of the proposed product or service offering.

Marketability of the Product or Service. The business plan should be able to demonstrate that there is a viable market for the product or service. It would be helpful to use the results of market surveys and demographic studies to support your argument. Specifically, the plan should focus on size of the market, growth potential of the market, and strategies to enter the market.

Strength of the Management Team. The business plan should profile the key members of the firm's management team. You must demonstrate to the reviewers that the management team possesses the necessary skills, drive, and desire to carry out the plan in an effective and efficient manner.

Description of Operations. The business plan should present a logical approach to resource procurement, product development and distribution. Plans for layout and design of facilities should also be included in this section.

Assessment of Risk. The business plan should recognize the types and nature of risks associated with starting the new venture.

Sales Analysis and Forecasts. The business plan should include sales forecasts for at least the first three years of operation. Heavy emphasis will be placed upon your ability to present a logical argument in support of the projections.

Capital Requirements. The financial projections contained in the business plan should demonstrate that the firm will have sufficient capital to implement the idea.

Return on Investment. The financial projections should be able to demonstrate that equity investors will be receiving a satisfactory return on investment over a three- to five-year period.

Organization of the Business Plan. The final business plan should be put together in a professional and logical fashion. Writing style and overall appearance are important. Each business plan should contain a two-page executive summary that highlights the critical elements of the overall plan.

BUSINESS PLAN OUTLINE

The format of the following guide is intended to help the Business Plan author include responses to the evaluation questions most asked by investors/venture capitalists and others who might be interested in taking a debt or equity position in an enterprise.

The general guidelines provide rules for the organization and cosmetics of the Plan. The balance of the guide suggests that the details of the Plan be best organized into the underlined ten section titles. This is not intended to be a firm rule of Business Plan composition but is so stated for the sake of completeness.

Except for the Executive Summary appearing as the first section, the presentation of the Plan can be made with whatever emphasis the author believes will be of most interest to the prospective investor.

Plans should include, on the cover page, a proprietary caution and a request that the Plan not be reproduced and be returned if there is no interest. Most investors will verbally indicate that they will be careful not to disclose the contents of the Plan to others, but few will sign any confidentiality agreement.

Firms, such as venture capitalists, see many plans that contain overlapping technical and/or marketing strategies. For the most part, they are extremely ethical and, although they will not sign such an agreement, will comply with the author's requests.

GENERAL GUIDELINES

IS there a cover page on which the company is identified by name, address, and telephone number? IS the date and Copy number included?

IS there a concise Table of Contents <u>with</u> page numbers?

IS it less than 40 pages, including Exhibits?

IS it neatly assembled and covered?

ARE <u>all</u> Figures and Exhibits discussed and referenced in the Text?

TYPICAL SECTIONS

<u>EXECUTIVE SUMMARY</u>

CAN it be read in 5 minutes, i.e. IS it no more than 4 pages long?

DOES it share the entrepreneur's dreams?

ARE the objectives stated and qualified?

WHAT are the highlights of the plan?

HOW many $$s will be needed WHEN, and for WHAT use?

WHAT ROI can the investor expect at the time of the exit scenario?

PRODUCT/SERVICE DESCRIPTION

WHAT is it?

WHY would it be desired? by WHOM?

HOW will it benefit customers?

WHAT will it replace?

CAN it be legally protected or defended?

MANAGEMENT & ORGANIZATION

WHO'S running the show? WHAT'S his/her or their background?

WHO will provide professional business guidance to the enterprise, e.g., the Board of Directors, Outside Accountants and Legal Counsel?

WHO will handle the functional specialties of financial communications and controls, marketing, engineering, manufacturing, administration, etc.?

WHAT is the corporate pace, i.e., objectives, milestones, Gantt chart, organization progression?

OPERATIONS (for a product)

HOW is it made? WHERE is it made? WHAT are the key components?

WHAT will be the make/buy components strategy?

HOW much will it cost?

OPERATIONS (for a service)

WHAT value or benefit will be provided?

WHY would the user choose this company?

HOW are the services differentiated from other providers?

IS the cost/benefit economics evident to potential customers?

MARKETING STRATEGIES

WHAT is the size and growth potential of the market sectors <u>available</u> or to be <u>created</u> for the product?

WHO are the potential customers? Have any of them shown initial interest?

WHO are the competitors?

WHAT are their strong and weak suits?

WHAT are the barriers for others to enter?

MARKETING TACTICS

HOW is the product to be differentiated?

HOW is margin to be obtained? Quality / Promotion / Price / Service?

HOW is the product made available to the end user'?

FINANCIAL ASSESSMENTS

WHAT are the key financial parameters that describe the company over the five-year period, e.g. sales, income, break-even, positive cash flow?

WHAT are the premises upon which they are based? ARE they optimistic, most probable, pessimistic? Describe each case!

FINANCING

WHO owns the company? to WHAT extent?

HOW many $$s are needed and

HOW will they be used?

WHAT portion of the company can be shared?

On WHAT terms?

WHAT return can the investor expect? WHAT are the exit scenarios?

RISK EVALUATIONS

WHAT are the economic, competitive, human, and financial resources risks?

WHAT changes might they have on the plan's financial parameters?

HOW many more $$ might be needed if the plan's goals are missed?

HOW will delays in development and manufacturing be made up?

TYPICAL EXHIBITS

Five-year pro forma statements

These must be prepared using GAAP and contain the standard schedules, i.e. Income Statement, Balance Sheet, and Changes in Financial Position. A Cash Balances schedule is mandatory.

Organization Progression

A chart or charts showing first and last year's structure with names, positions, and titles.

Milestones

Gantt- or Pert-type charts depicting the probable start and completion dates for key objectives.

Product Descriptions

Sales literature or clearly legible drawings showing relative size and other designated characteristics.

Resumes

Applicable background data on all officers and directors prefaced by a brief title and position statement.

Market Statistics

Published industry data showing date and source of material.
Market research backup materials.

Venture Plan Rating Form

University Of Texas, Austin

International Moot Corp®

This appendix presents forms used by judges for evaluating the submissions in an invitational collegiate venture plan competition conducted annually by the School of Business at the University of Texas, Austin. They are registered and are reproduced here by permission.

ompany: _____

Please evaluate the <u>business plan</u> on the following aspects:
(Using this rating system: 1=very poor, 2=poor, 3=fair, 4=adequate, 5=good, 6=very good, 7=excellent)

I.   Elements of the Plan (20%)

1.   Executive Summary
(clear, exciting, and effective as
a stand-alone overview of the plan)   1   2   3   4   5   6   7

Comments/Questions: _____
_____
_____
_____

2.   Company Overview
(business purpose, history and
current status, overall strategy
and objectives)   1   2   3   4   5   6   7

Comments/Questions: _____
_____
_____
_____

3.   Products or Services

(description, features and benefits, pricing,
current stage of development,
proprietary position)   1   2   3   4   5   6   7

Comments/Questions: _____
_____
_____
_____

4.   Market and Marketing Strategy
(description of market, competitive
analysis, needs identification, market
acceptance, unique capabilities,
sales promotion)   1   2   3   4   5   6   7

Comments/Questions: _____
_____
_____
_____

5.   Management
(backgrounds of key individuals,
ability to execute strategy,
history of team, personnel needs,
organizational structure)   1   2   3   4   5   6   7

Comments/Questions: _____
_____
_____
_____

In rating each of the above, please consider the following questions:
- Is this area covered in adequate detail?
- Does the plan show a clear understanding of the elements that should be addressed?
- Are the assumptions realistic and reasonable?

Please evaluate the <u>financials</u> of the plan:

These should be presented in summary form in the text of the business plan and follow generally accepted accounting principles.

(Using this rating system: 1=very poor, 2=poor, 3=fair, 4=adequate, 5=good, 6=very good, 7=excellent)

II.   Summary Financials (20%)

1.   Cash Flow Statement
     (effective as record of
     available cash and as planning
     tool: Detailed for first two years,
     quarterly/annually for years 3-5)   1   2   3   4   5   6   7

     Comments/Questions: _____
     _____
     _____
     _____

2.   Income Statement
     (consistent with plan and effective
     in capturing profit performance;
     Quarterly for first two years
     Quarterly/annually for years 3-5)   1   2   3   4   5   6   7

     Comments/Questions: _____
     _____
     _____
     _____

3.   Balance Sheet
     (Effective in presenting assets,
     liabilities and owners' equity)   1   2   3   4   5   6   7

     Comments/Questions: _____
     _____
     _____
     _____

4.   Funds Required/Uses
     (Clear and concise presentation
     of amount, timing, type, and use
     of funds required for venture)   1   2   3   4   5   6   7

     Comments/Questions: _____
     _____
     _____
     _____

5.   Offering
     (Proposal/terms to investors- indicate
     how much you want, the ROI, and
     the structure of the deal;
     possible exit strategies)   1   2   3   4   5   6   7

     Comments/Questions: _____
     _____
     _____
     _____

Please evaluate the <u>presentation</u> on the following aspects:

(Using this rating system: 1=very poor, 2=poor, 3=fair, 4=adequate, 5=good, 6=very good, 7=excellent)

III. Presentation Skills (20%)

1. Overall organization

(Materials presented in clear,
logical and/or sequential form.)   1   2   3   4   5   6   7

2. Ability to relate need for the company

(Meaningful examples, practical applications,
etc.)   1   2   3   4   5   6   7

3. Ability to maintain judge's interest   1   2   3   4   5   6   7

4. Responsiveness to judges

(Answered questions, adapted to judge's
level, needs, etc.)   1   2   3   4   5   6   7

5. Quality of visual aids

(Slides, outlines, handouts, etc.)   1   2   3   4   5   6   7

In rating each of the above, please consider the following:

- Do the presenters demonstrate competence in their presentation skills?
- Are they poised, confident and knowledgeable?
- Do they think effectively on their feet?

Strengths of Presentation

Weaknesses of Presentation

Additional Comments

Please evaluate the <u>viability</u> on the following aspects:

(To be completed after reading the plan and viewing the presentations)
(1 indicates definitely no, while 7 indicates definitely yes.)

IV. Viability of Company (40%)

		Definitely No						Definitely Yes
1.	**Market Opportunity**							
	(There is a clear market need presented as well as a way to take advantage of that need.)	1	2	3	4	5	6	7
2.	**Distinctive Competence**							
	(The company provides something novel/unique/special that gives it a competitive advantage in its market.)	1	2	3	4	5	6	7
3.	**Management Capability**							
	(This team can effectively develop this company and handle the risks associated with the venture.)	1	2	3	4	5	6	7
4.	**Financial understanding**							
	(The team has a solid understanding of the financial requirements of the business.)	1	2	3	4	5	6	7
5.	**Investment Potential**							
	(The business represents a real investment opportunity in which you would consider investing.)	1	2	3	4	5	6	7

Company Strengths

Company Weaknesses

Additional Comments

Case Index

Topic Index